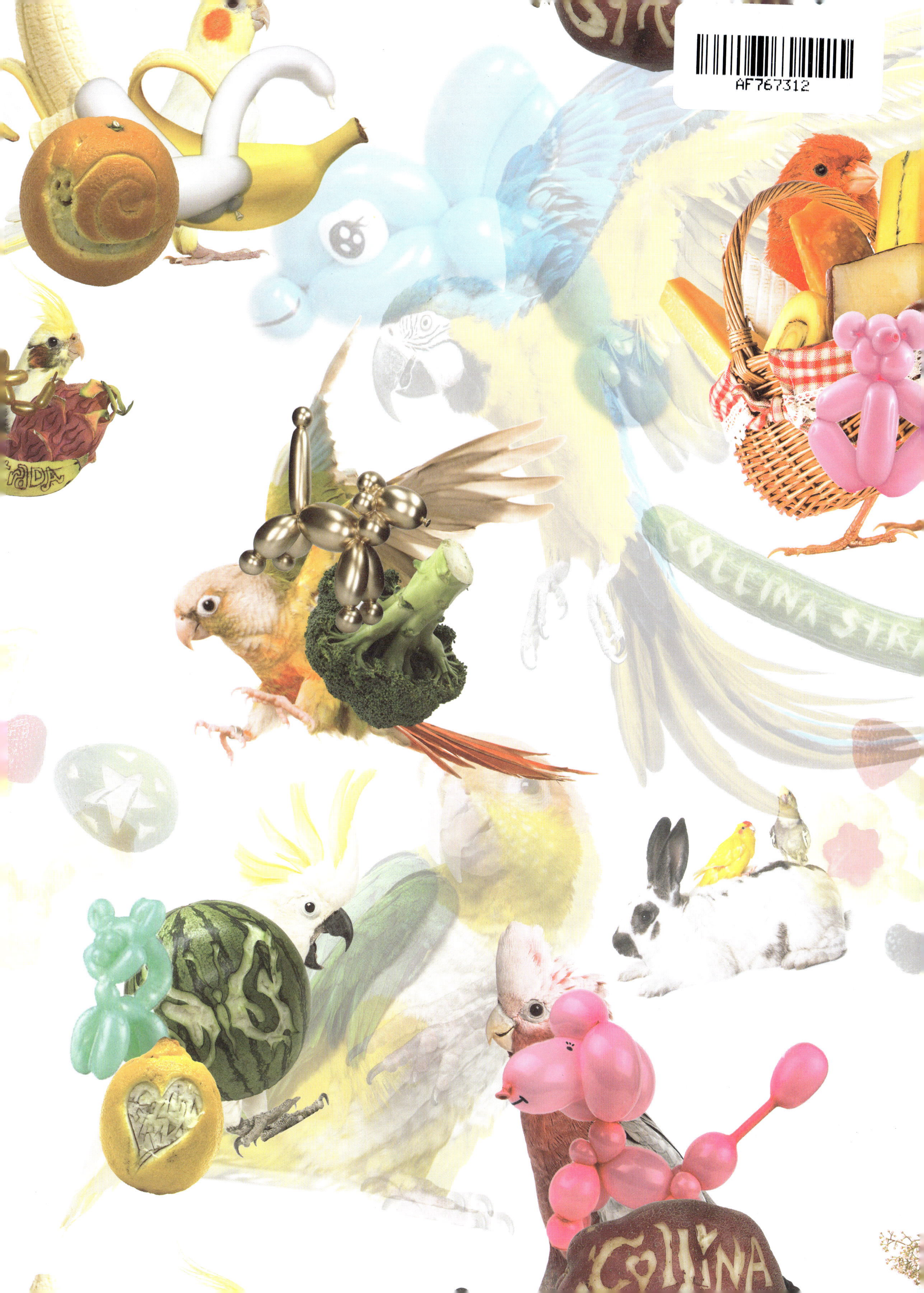
COLLINA
Collina

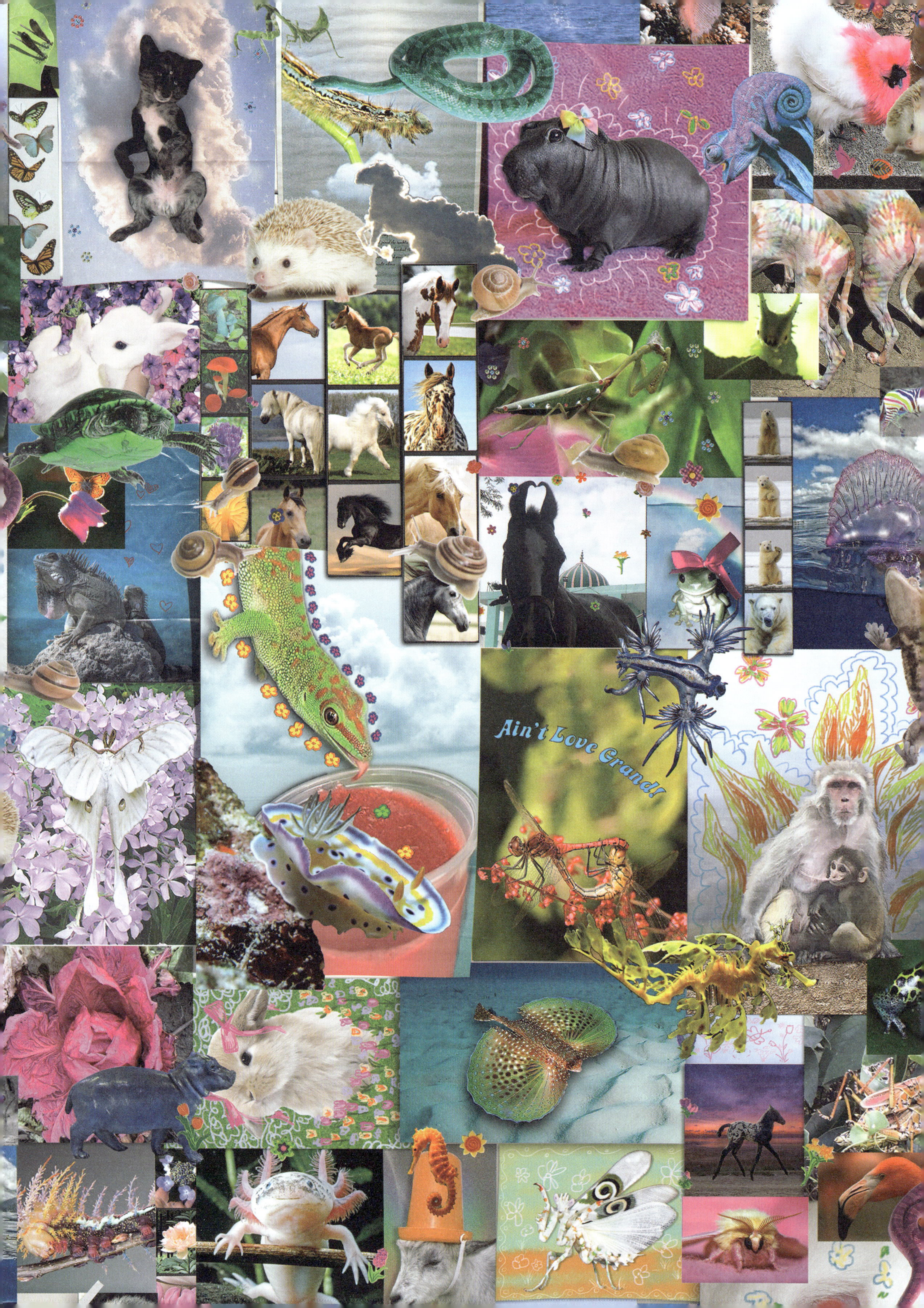
Ain't Love Grand!

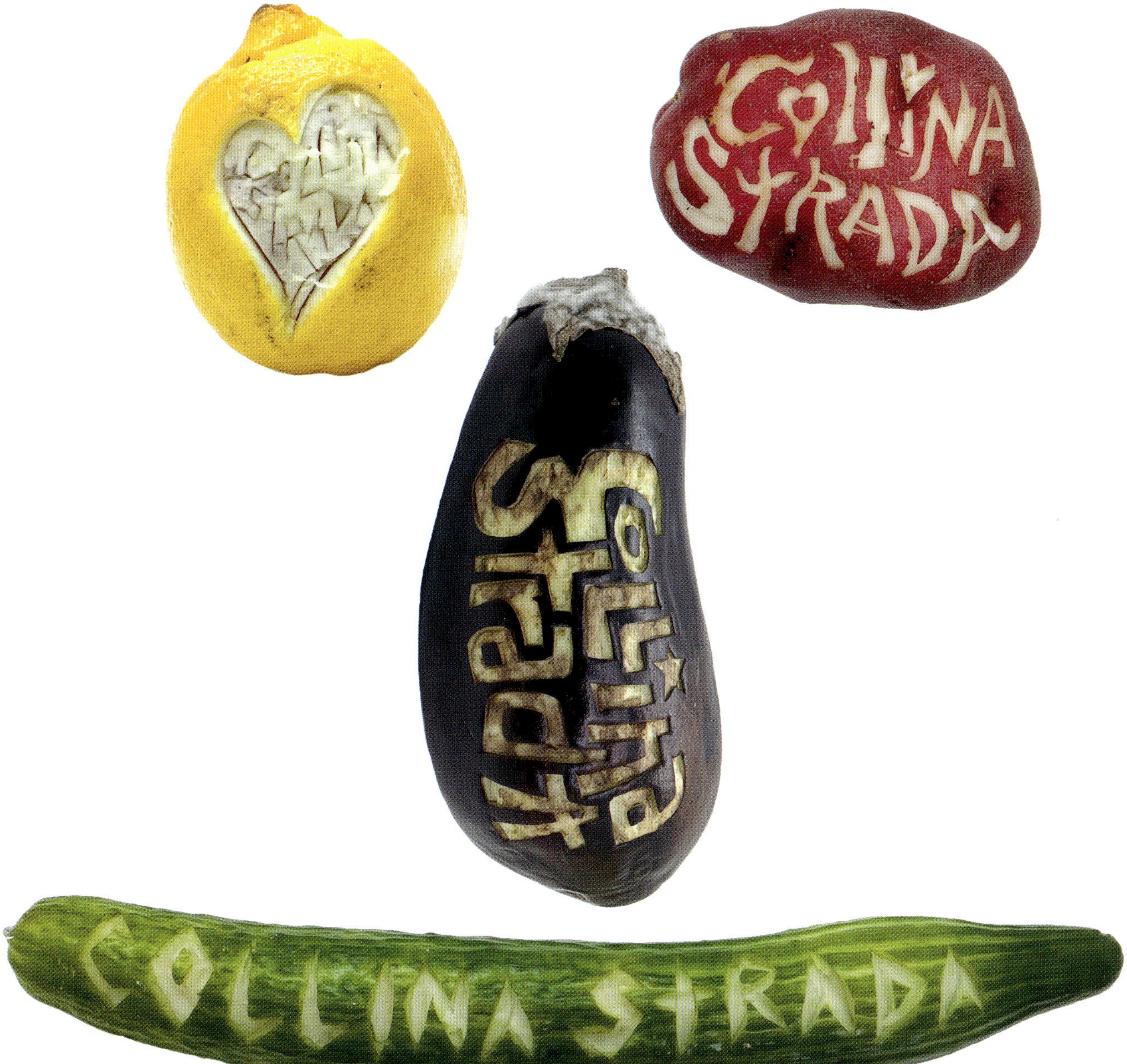

COLLINA STRADA
COLLINA STRADA
COLLINA STRADA

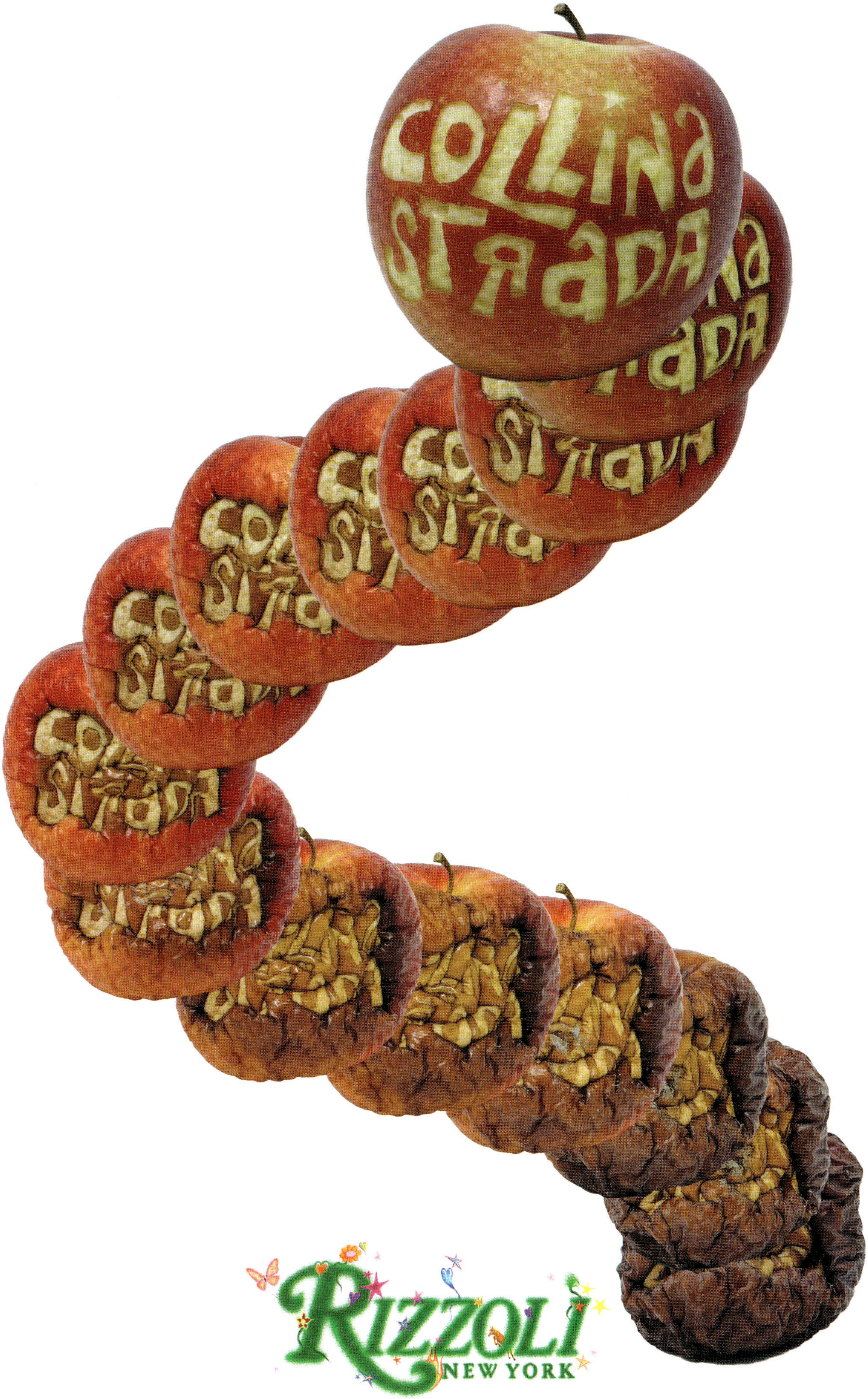

RIZZOLI
NEW YORK

New York · Paris · London · Milan

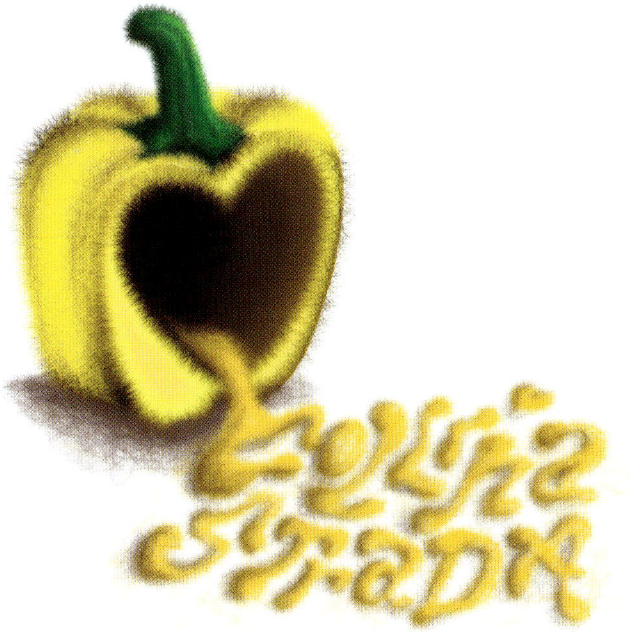

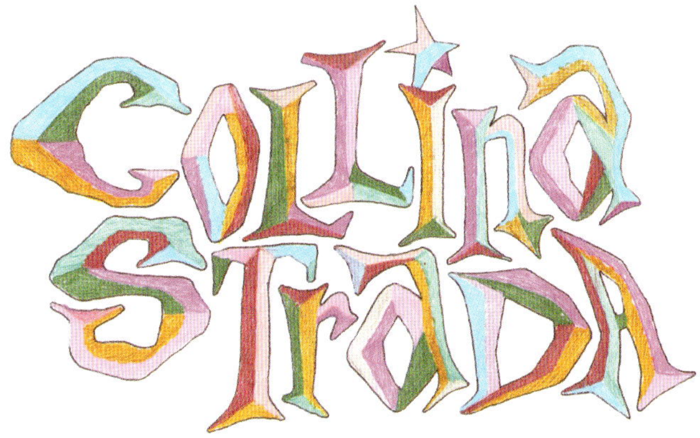

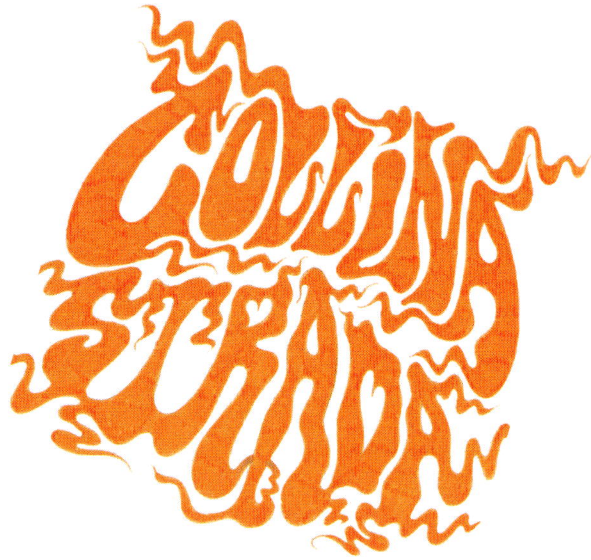

First published in the United States of America
in 2023 by Rizzoli International Publications, Inc.
300 Park Avenue South
New York, NY 10010
www.rizzoliusa.com

For Rizzoli:
Publisher: Charles Miers
Editor: Meaghan McGovern
Editorial Consultant: Ian Luna
Editorial Coordinator: Lauren Gallow
Production Managers: Barbara Sadick and Maria Pia Gramaglia
Production: Olivia Russin
Copy Editor: Angela Taormina
Proofreader: Grace Sparapani

Book Design: Charlie Engman

For Author:
Brand Creative Director: Hillary Taymour
Brand Art Director: Charlie Engman
Illustrations: Justin Hager
Book Text Design: Rachel Quan
www.collinastrada.com
Instagram.com/collinastrada
Youtube.com/@collinastrada

Printed in China

2023 2024 2025 / 10 9 8 7 6 5 4 3 2 1

ISBN: 9780847873357

Visit us online:
Facebook.com/RizzoliNewYork
Twitter: @Rizzoli_Books
Instagram.com/RizzoliBooks
Pinterest.com/RizzoliBooks
Youtube.com/user/RizzoliNY
Issuu.com/Rizzoli

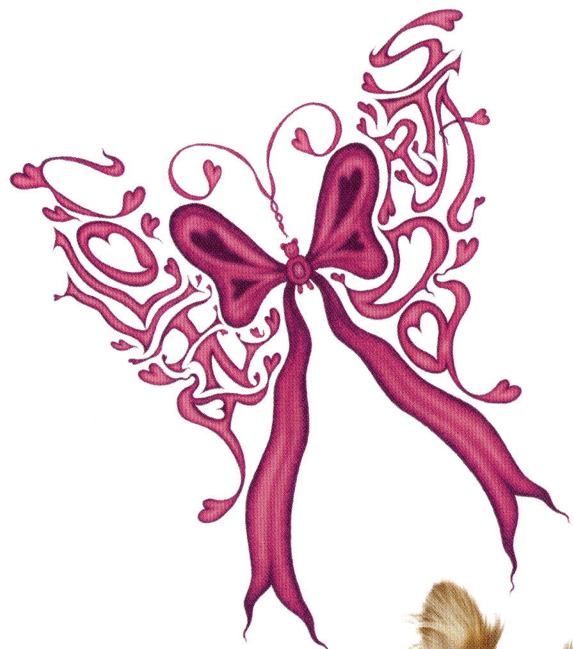

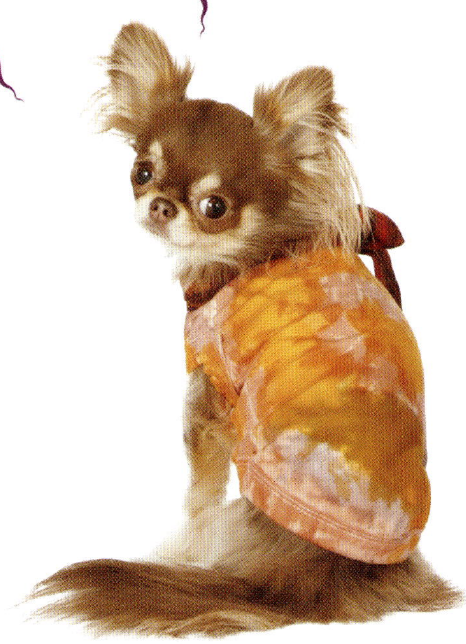

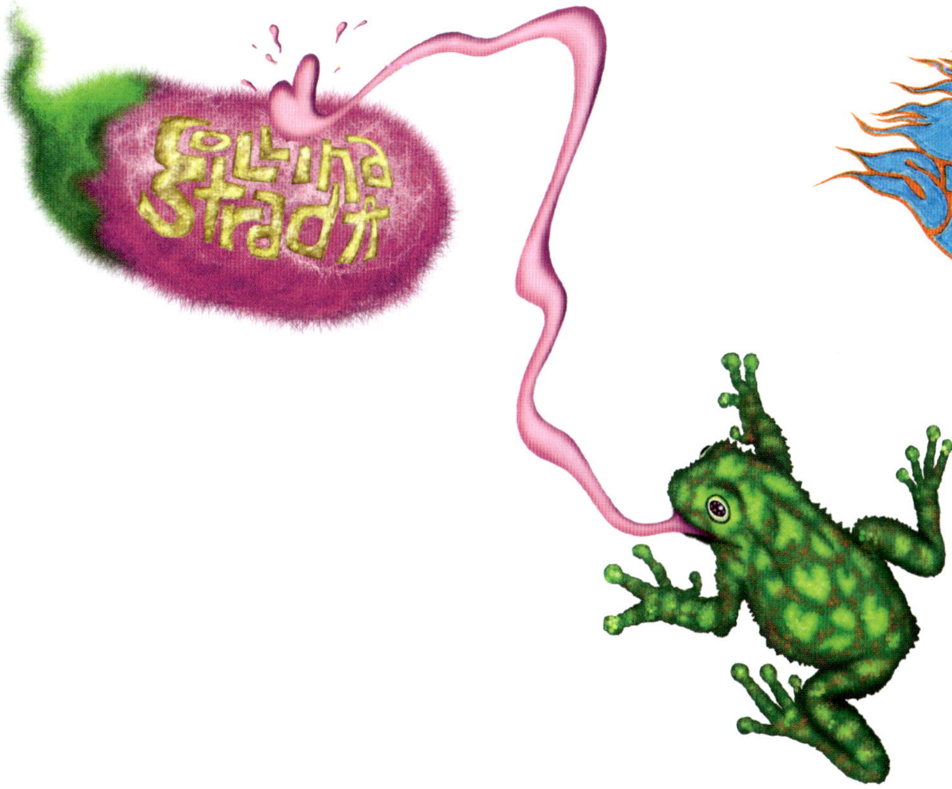

TABLE OF CONTENTS

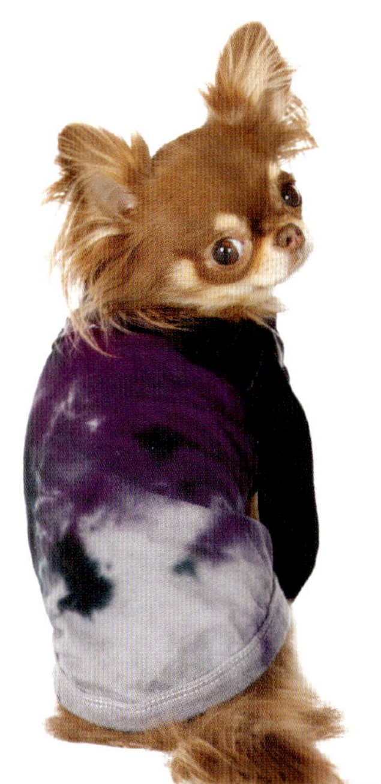

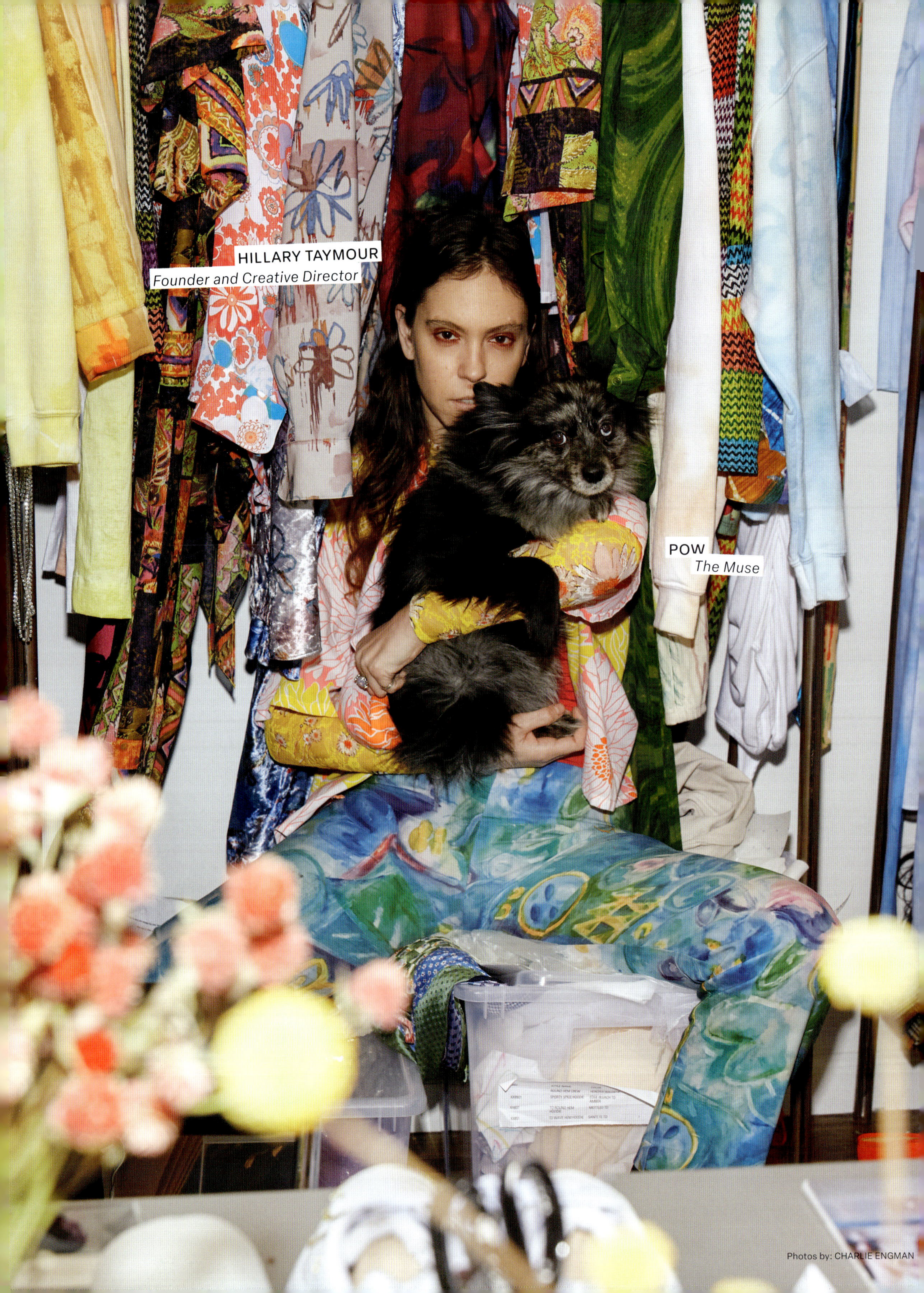

Photos by: CHARLIE ENGMAN

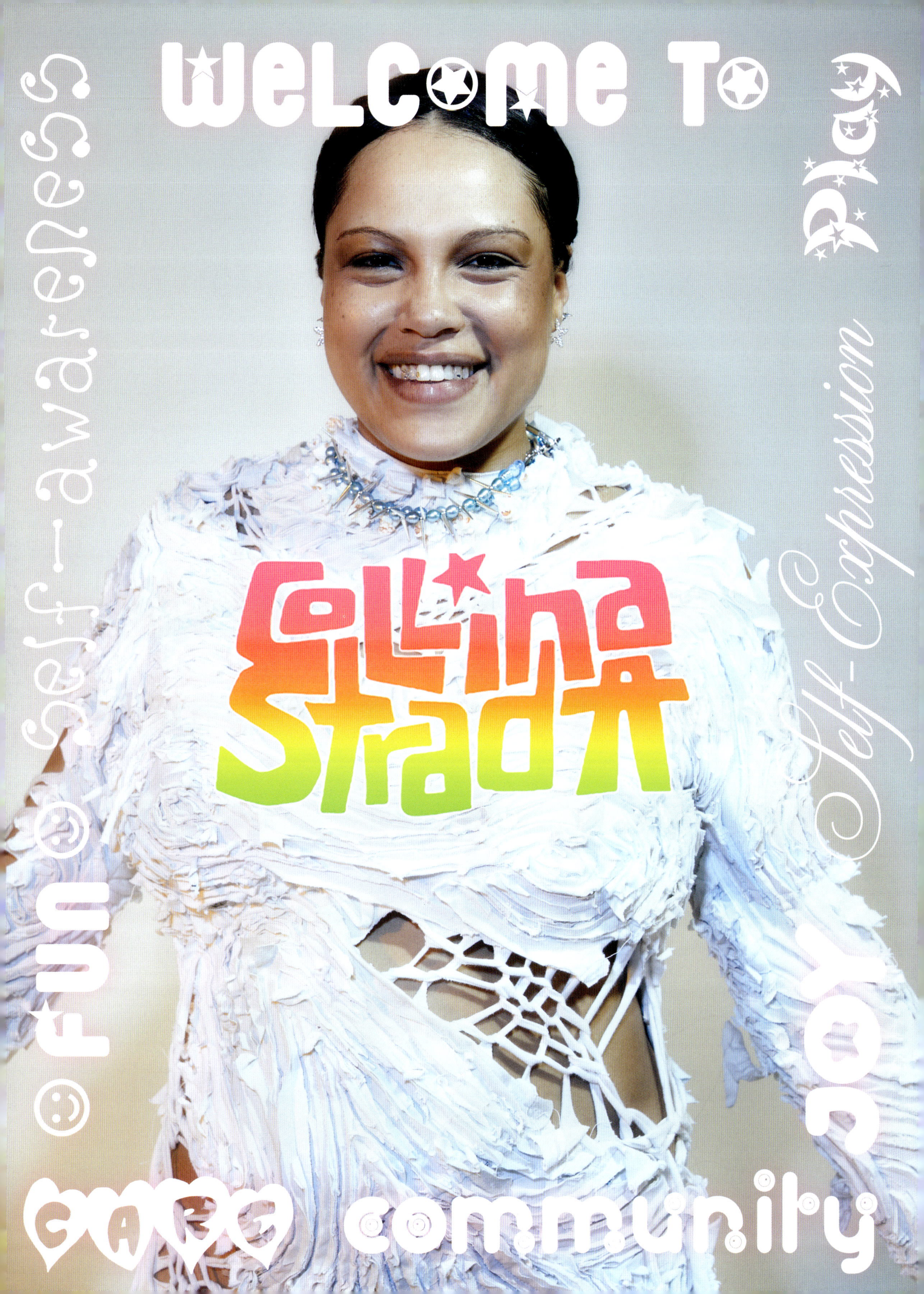
WELCOME TO
Play
Self-Expression
JOY
community
CARE
FUN
Self-awareness
Collina Strada

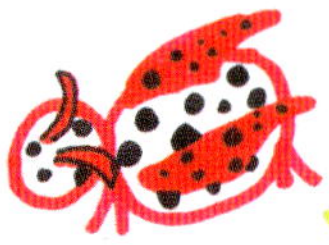

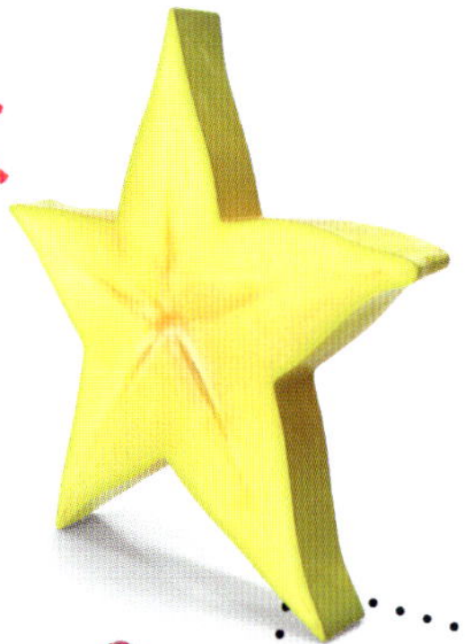

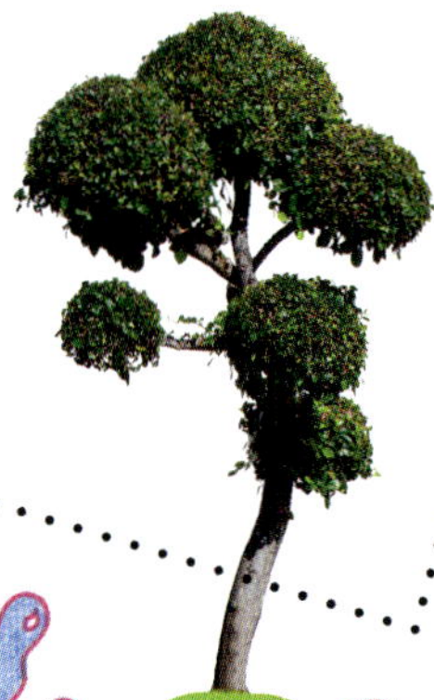

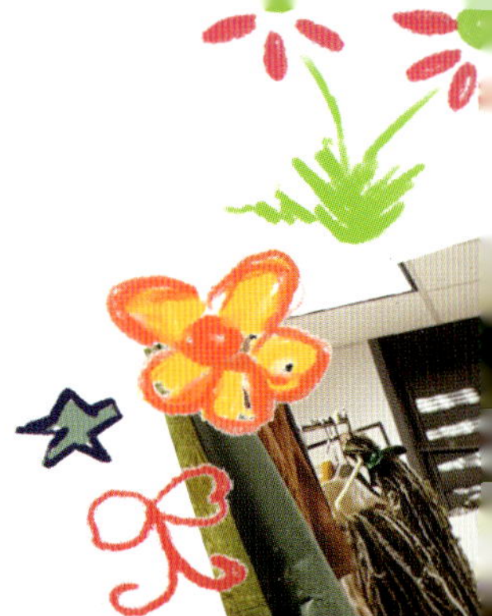

Collina Strada Timeline

2008
In fashion school in LA, Hillary Taymour designs a handbag for herself that gets so much attention she decides to start her own line of handbags. She calls it Collina Strada, after a nickname given to her in school.

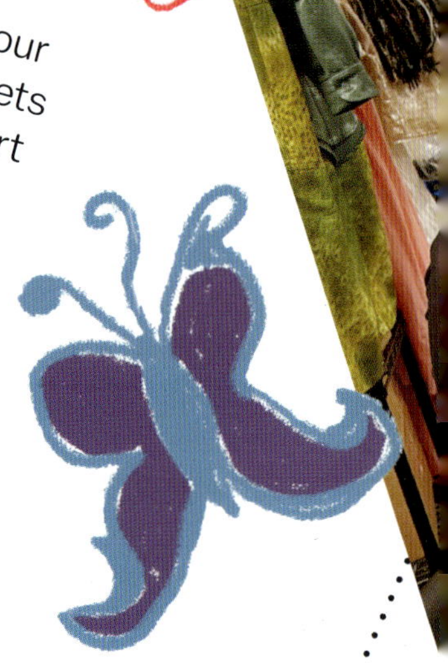

2009
Collina Strada's first collection of handbags launches in stores.

2010
Taymour moves to New York, where Collina Strada is now based. Taymour meets Charlie Engman via a Craiglist ad. He soon begins creating the Collina Strada visuals.

2012
Collina Strada releases its first ready-to-wear collection.

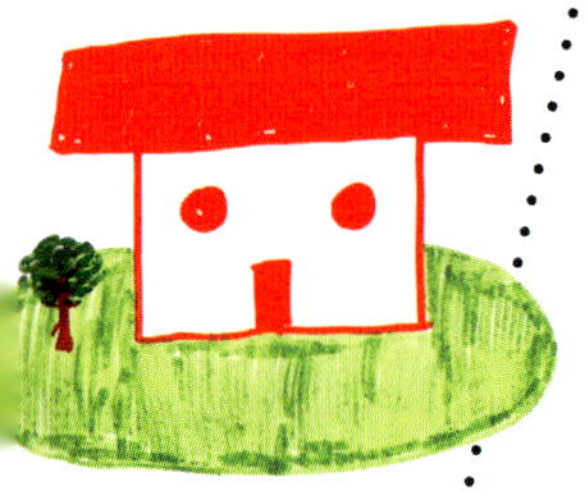

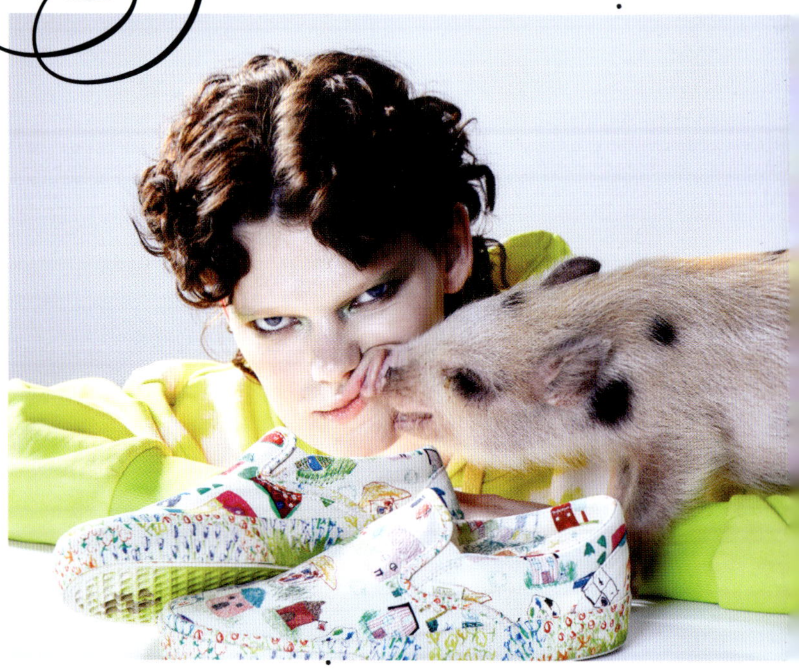

2015
Collina starts presenting with the Milk Made program, shifting the brand's focus to expansive casting.

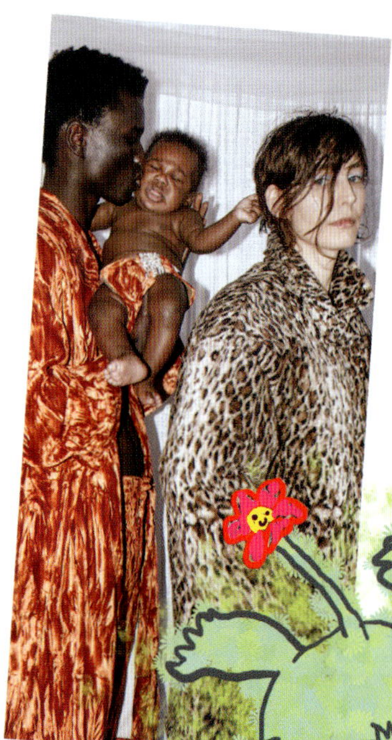

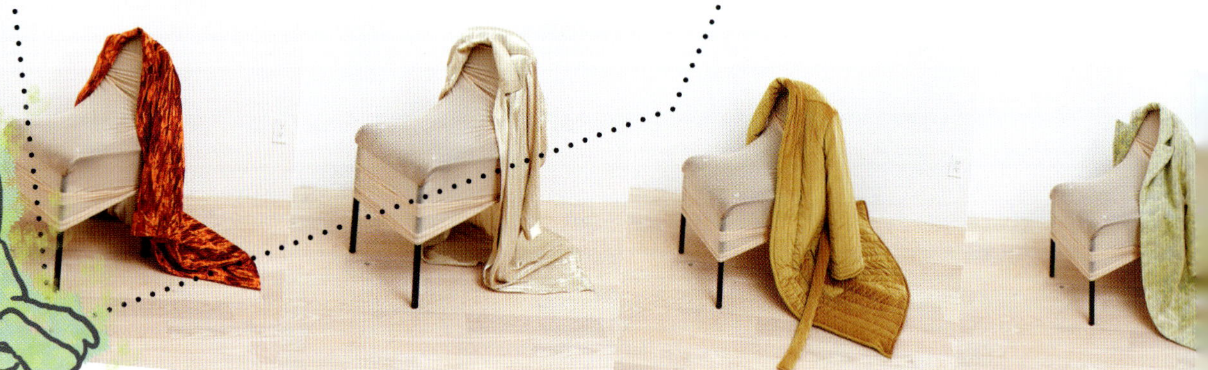

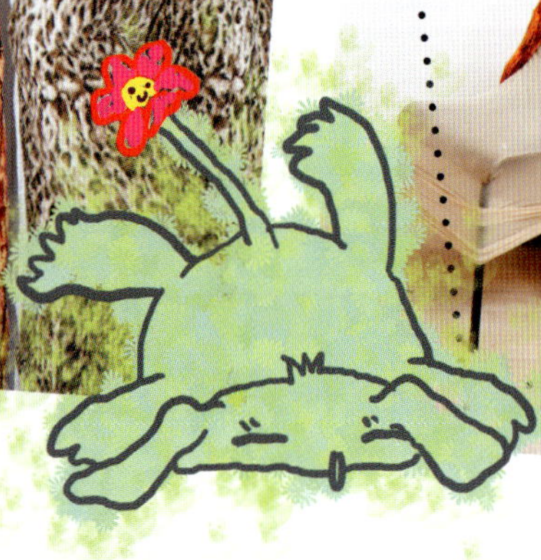

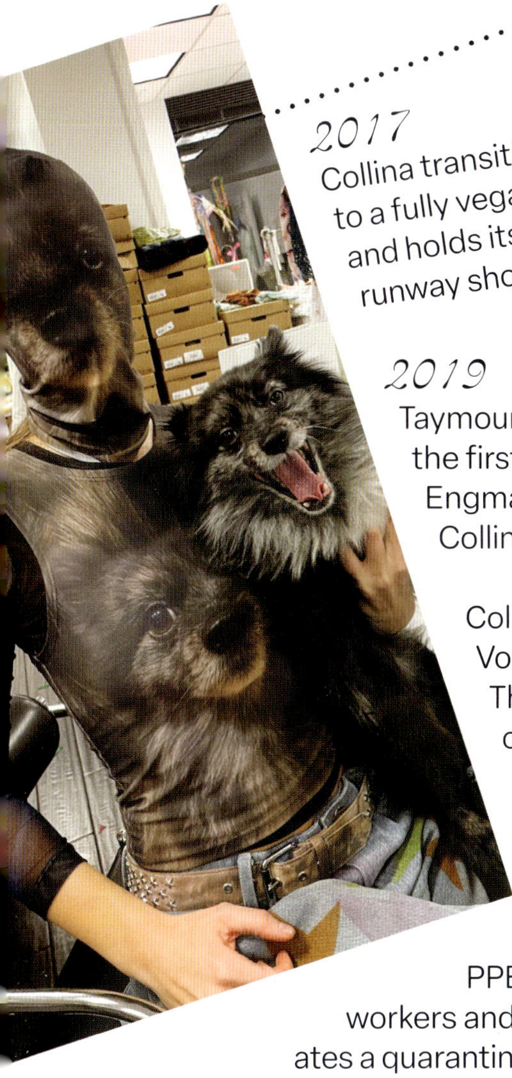

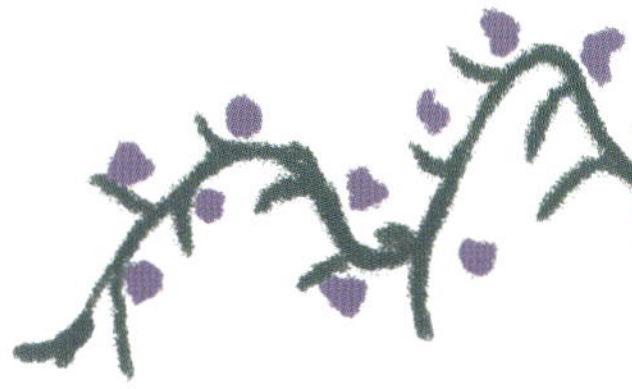

2017
Collina transitions to a fully vegan brand and holds its first runway show.

2019
Taymour and Engman collaborate for the first time on a full collection, and Engman becomes the art director of Collina Strada.

Collina Strada is named a CFDA Vogue Fashion Fund finalist. The brand solidifies its focus on sustainability, making it a permanent pillar of the brand.

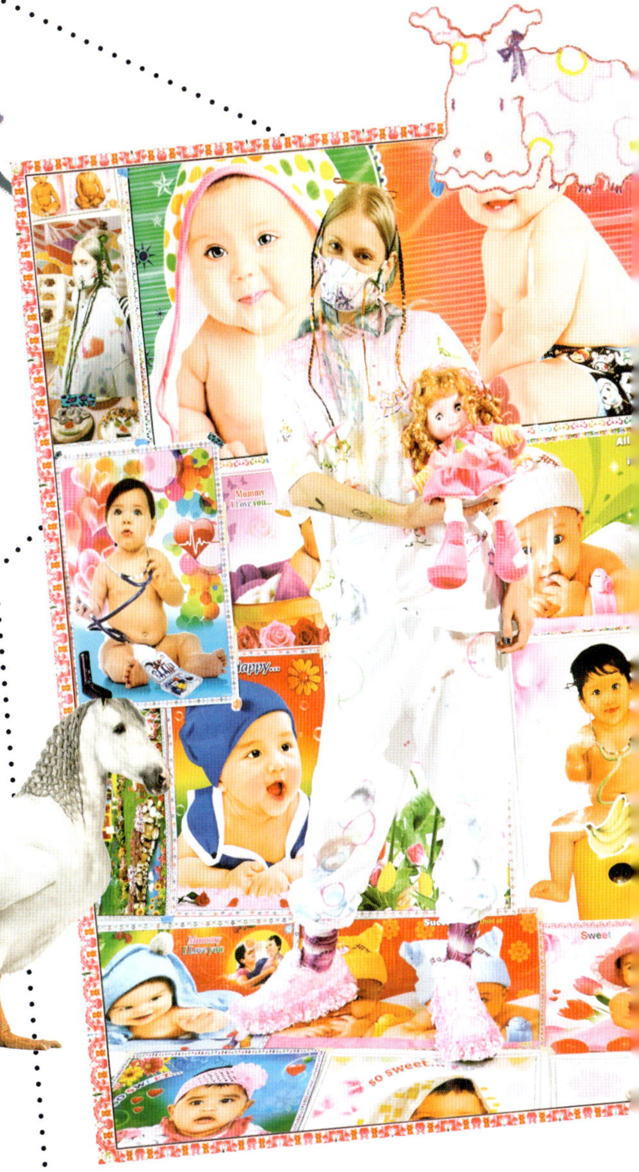

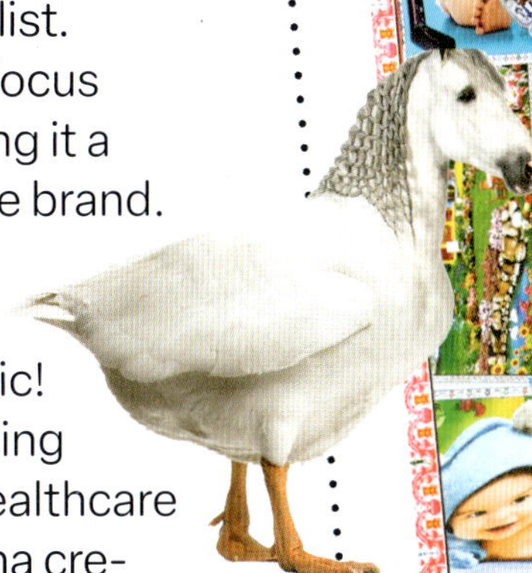

2020
COVID-19 Pandemic! Collina begins making PPE medical masks for healthcare workers and the community. Collina creates a quarantine capsule collection, donating all proceeds to COVID relief aid. Collina begins embracing immersive digital media as a way to share its vision with the world.

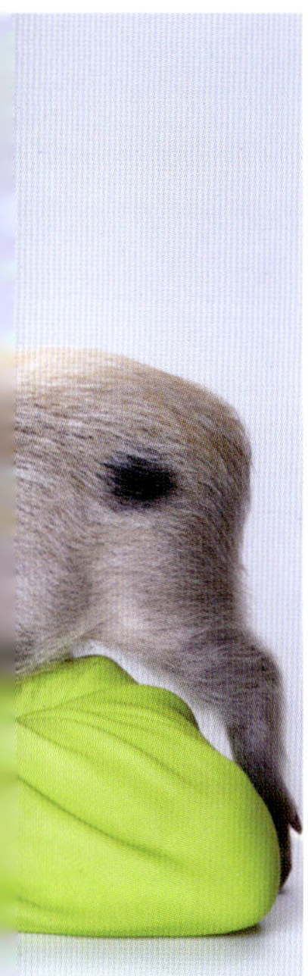

2021
Collina Strada partners with Gucci and creates an original video game called Collina Land.

Collina brings musician and transgender icon Kim Petras to the Met Gala.

Collina Strada opens New York Fashion Week and is the first brand to hold an in-person runway show since the start of the COVID-19 Pandemic.

2022
The brand is featured in the September issue of Vogue as a key player in "Fashion's New World".

2023
Collina continues Collina-ing

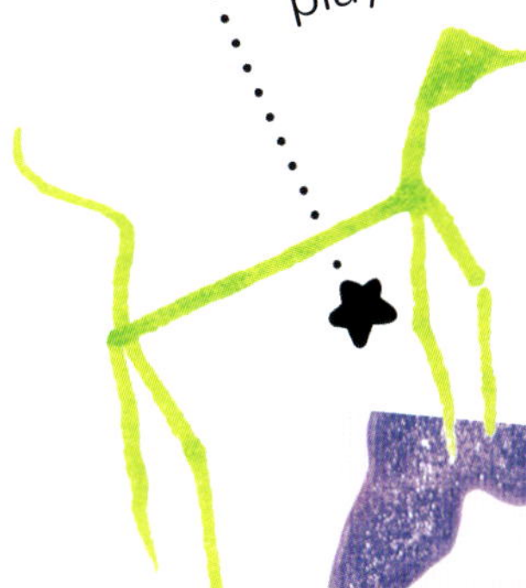

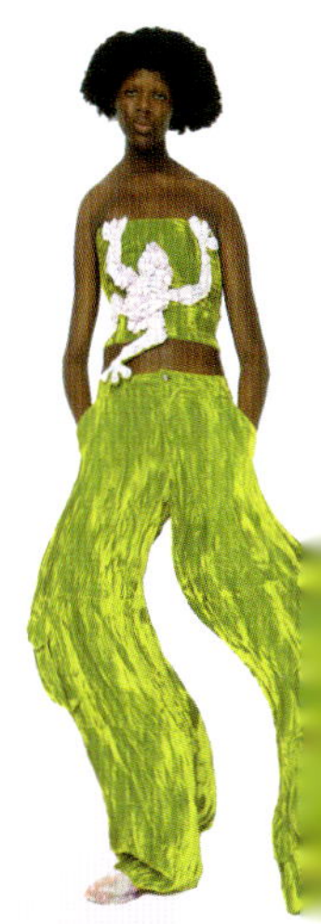

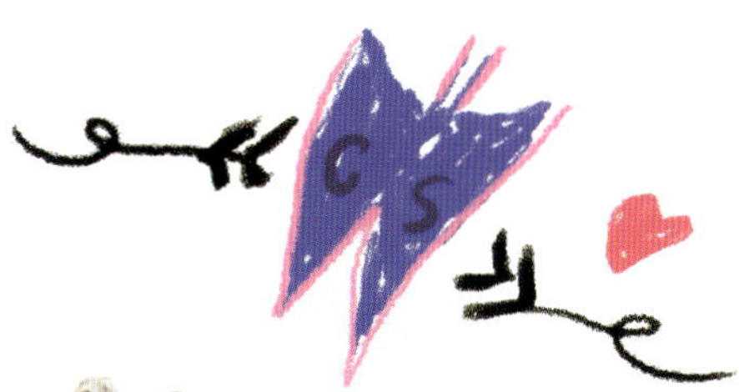

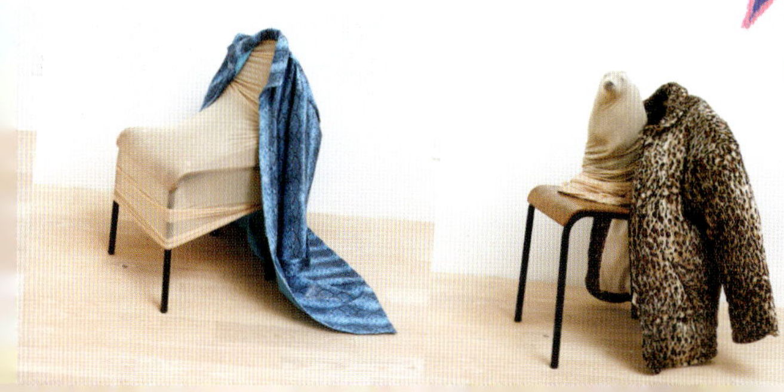

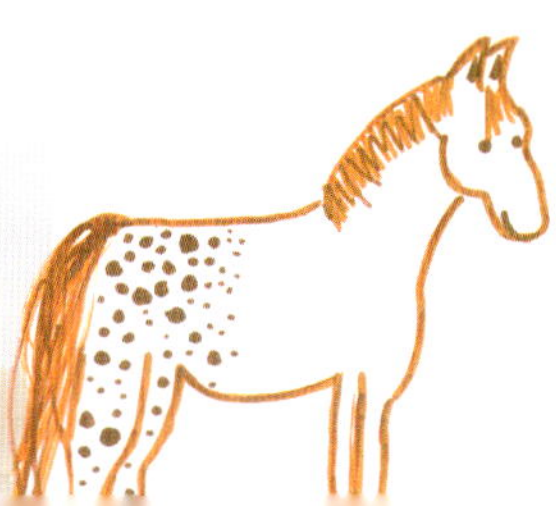

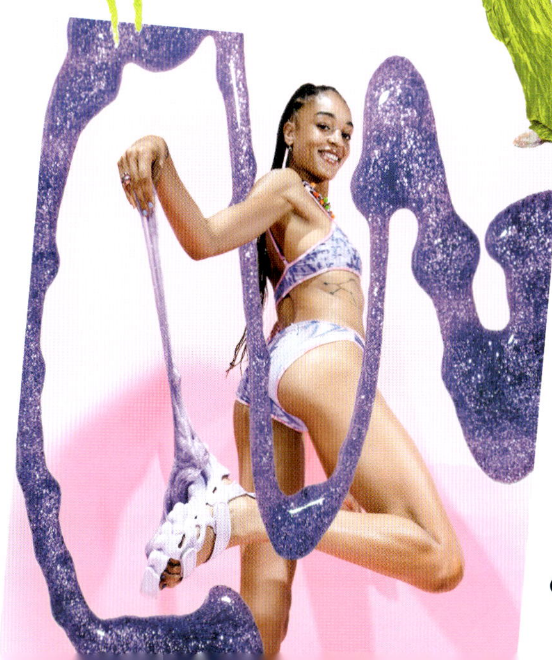

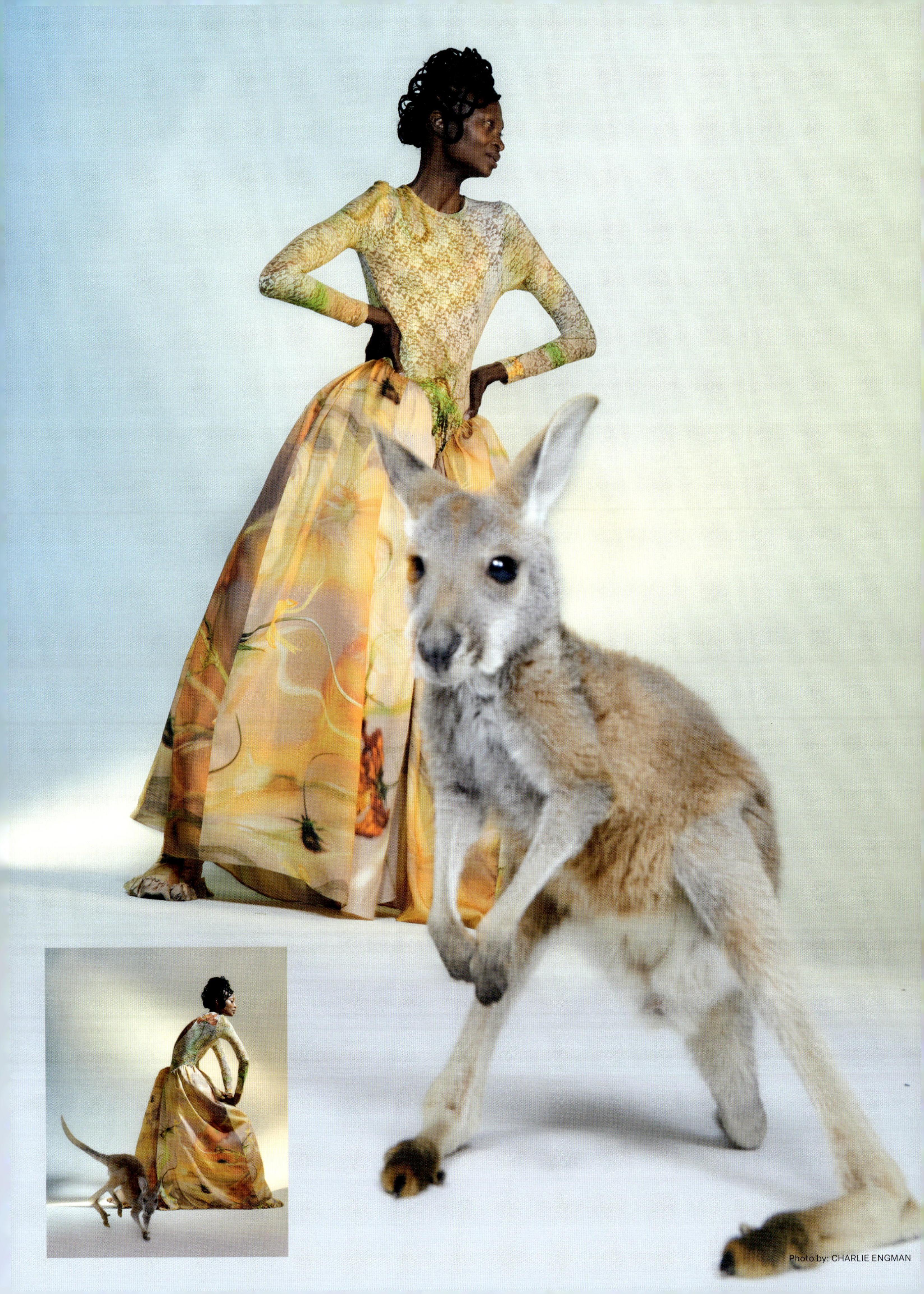

Photo by: CHARLIE ENGMAN

Soft n Sexy

WORDS BY RACHEL TASHJIAN

Most designers, I am sorry to inform you, are not thinking of you. They are thinking of themselves and of making something extraordinary or, at least, interesting; they are thinking of their rivals and how to best them. Often, this is the stuff of great fashion—everything has its place in the world, after all!—but it's not really wearable and that makes it less fun.

Collina Strada, on the other hand, is thinking of you.

A Collina Strada dress is one of the few things that looks good on everyone. It billows in the right places and is tight in the other right places; it shows off your beautiful arms and your lovely shoulders. Your ass looks great striding ahead underneath its rippling silkiness.

Its colors, though they scream like happy banshees, make everyone look warmer, lovelier—in large part because these are clothes that make you feel happy, even serene. And everyone looks hotter when they look serene!

Hillary always tells me she likes to design by thinking about the person, usually the woman, first. How will she live her life in this dress? How will she commute? Go out to dinner? Be at a job? I don't think her consideration ends there. I suspect, because she is a humanist, Hillary thinks: how will she care for her friends in this dress? What will make her smile while wearing this sweatshirt? How will she, wearing this hot pink crushed velvet coat, make herself feel better after a dumb, rotten day?

I have never seen a stupid or offensively designed top or dress or pair of pants by Hillary. I've just never seen a Collina garment that makes me say, "Well… that doesn't make sense." A person can picture nearly everything she makes on their body. That's saying something.

And the clothes go with everything. Most clothes that are about community are really about giving yourself over to the life and look of the clothes. That can be exciting; that is why cults are so appealing to so many. But with Collina, you're invited in. You bring yourself to the clothes and animate them with your own spirit. It's as if the garments are begging you to bring them to life.

Somehow that pragmatism encompasses tie-dyed sweatshirts with rhinestones and painted flowers. The woman who dresses with Park Avenue polish—wearing her doodle pants under a classic coat, let's say—sees herself in these clothes, as does a woman who dresses from a pile of thrifted clothes on her chair everyday. It can be your one beautiful statement piece or your entire wardrobe. These are clothes that work hard for you, because they know how rough it is out there.

I wrote several years ago about Hillary's work being a sustainable pioneer, because she wouldn't call the clothes "sustainable." She's even more right now than she was then. Because what is at the root of buying less, buying better, loving clothes but loving the planet more, is loving your stuff differently—expecting more from it, and finding things that actually rise to the occasion, because they're beautifully made and special and timeless. They invite you into their rhinestoned, well-hydrated, brightly colored world and say, "How can I help you today, even just by being soft and sexy?"

SUSTAINABILITY CHEATSHEET

USE DEADSTOCK

Deadstock is fabric that is left over, unwanted, or not needed by the designer or brand that originally ordered it. Using deadstock extends the lifespan of fabric and reduces resource extraction and waste.

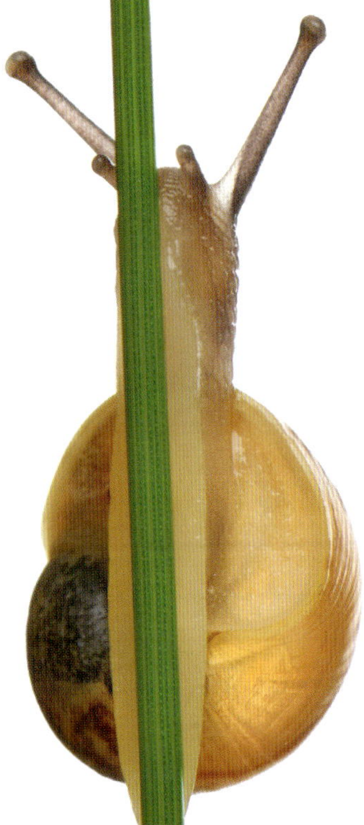

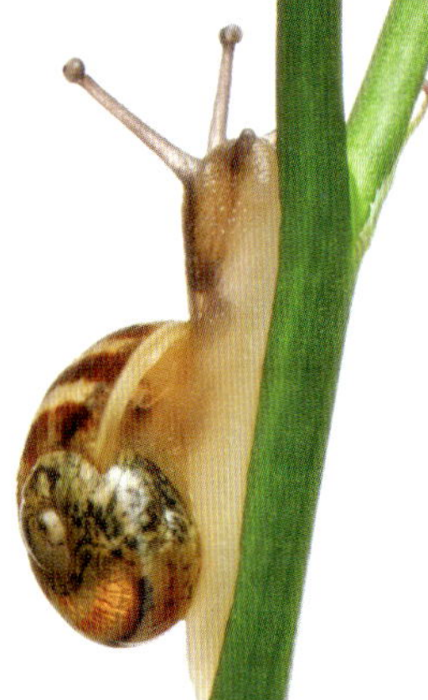

PRODUCE LOCALLY

We have dramatically cut down on shipping emissions by producing our collections primarily in New York City. We work with a few family-owned factories across midtown Manhattan, through which we are able to hand cart fabrics between the cutters and sewers. Wherever possible, we build a relationship with the actual humans who manufacture the majority of our clothes.

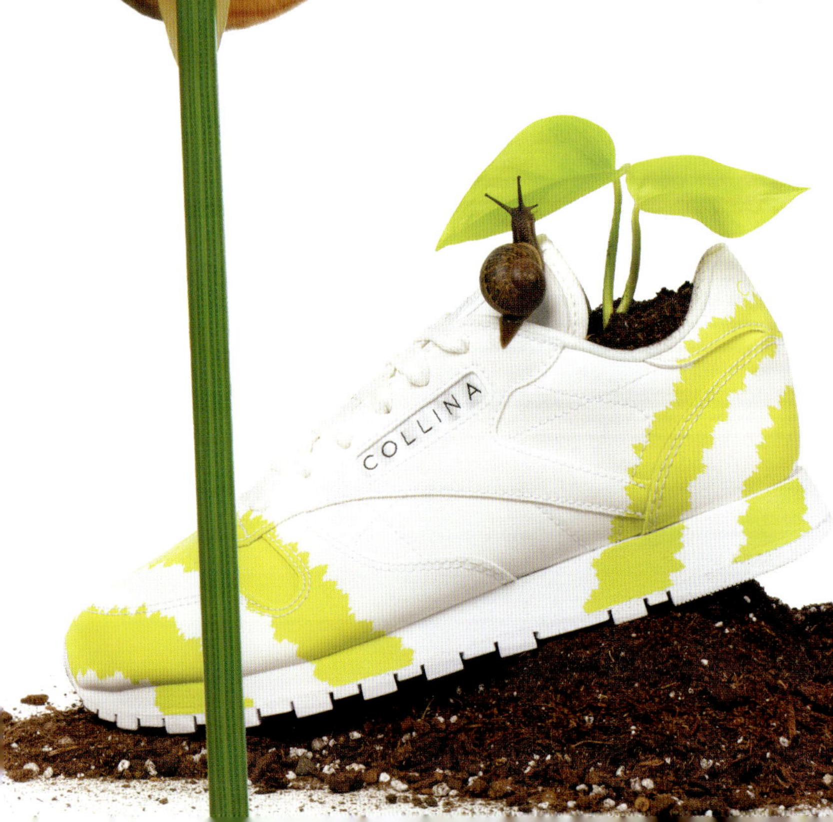

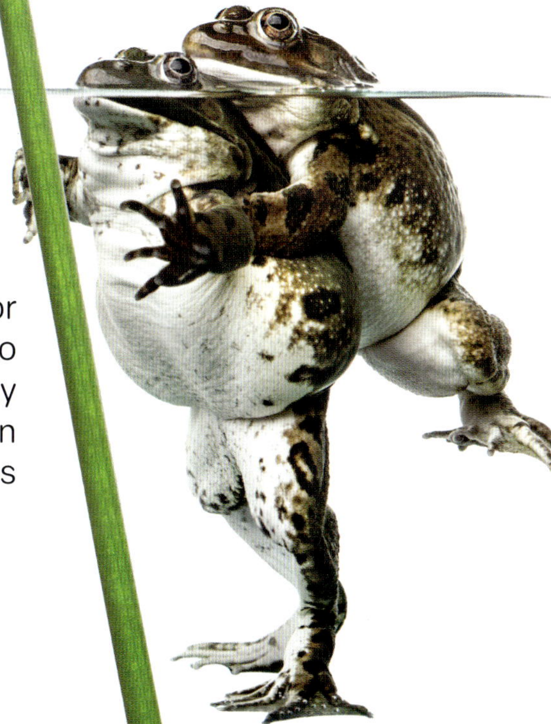

Upcycle

Upcycling is a process of taking an existing item or material and giving it new value by repurposing it into something else, often something of higher quality or utility than the original item. For example, we turn secondhand t-shirts from Ghana into tops and dresses (learn more in the booklet on page 81).

Use Green Materials

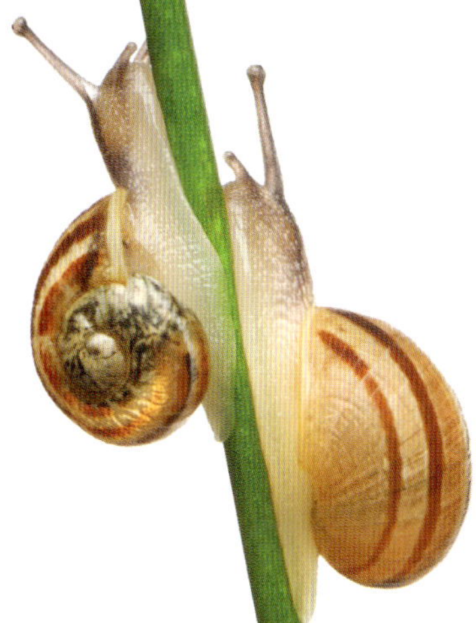

We use a fabric called rose sylk, which is an organic, biodegradable cellulose textile made from fibers extracted from the natural waste of rose bushes and their stems. The fiber is stripped and processed to create a luxurious and soft hand-spun fiber, similar to silk or bamboo. And our knits are made in Portugal, using leftover materials from the production runs of other companies. This means the fabric of our hoodies changes seasonally, but we don't mind. :)

Be Slow

Each season, we have carryover styles to reiterate the slow fashion movement. Not everything has to be new and not everything has to be now.

Perfect Is the Frenemy of Good

It's nearly impossible to be fully sustainable (whatever that means), and individual action is necessary but not sufficient for change. The important things aren't piety and purity but effort, communication, transparency, and knowing what "enough" means to you.

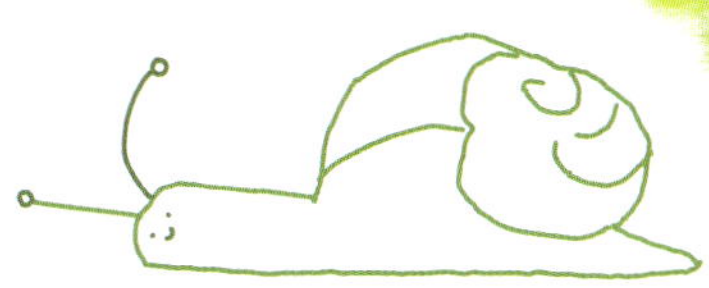

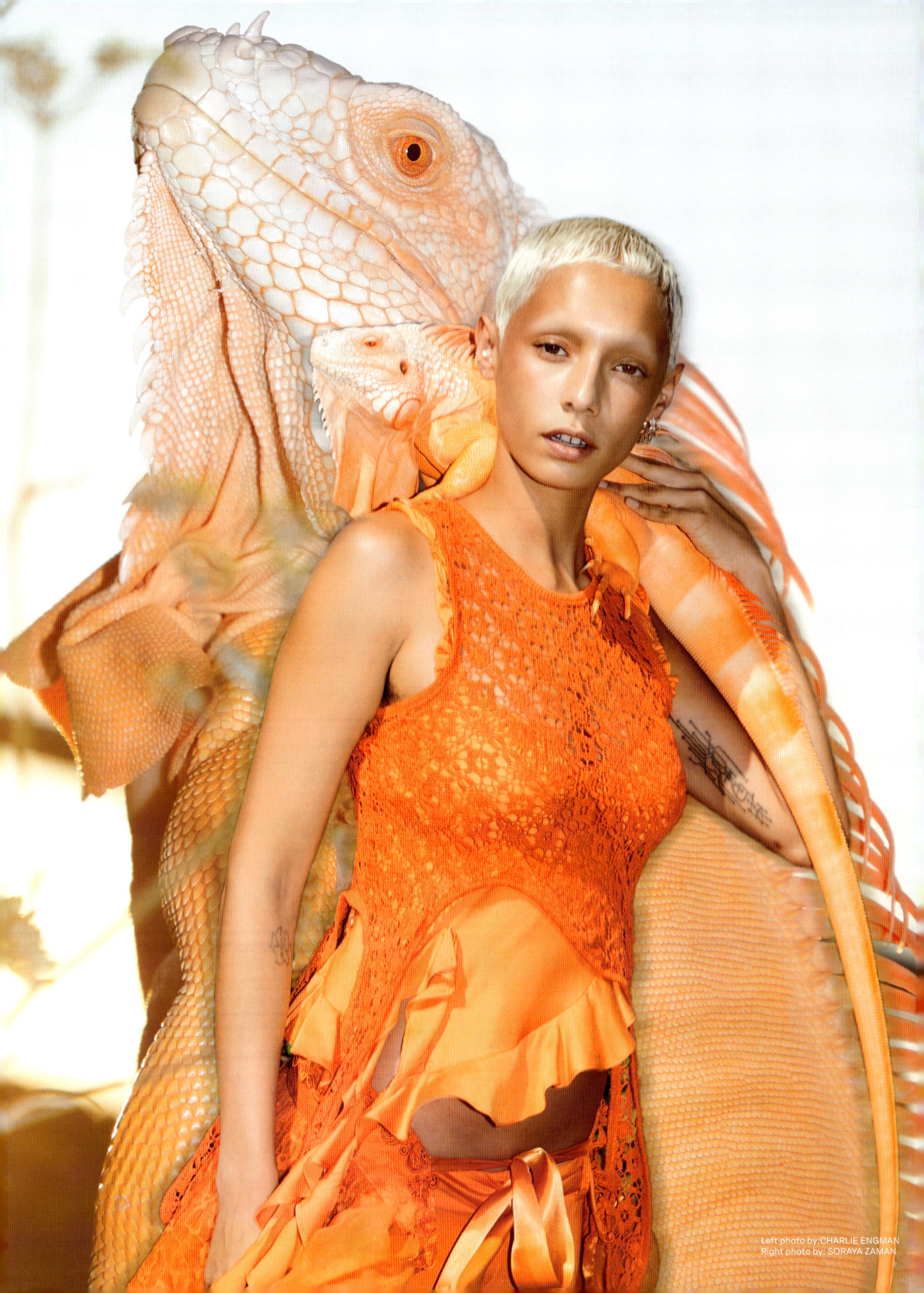

Left photo by: CHARLIE ENGMAN
Right photo by: SORAYA ZAMAN

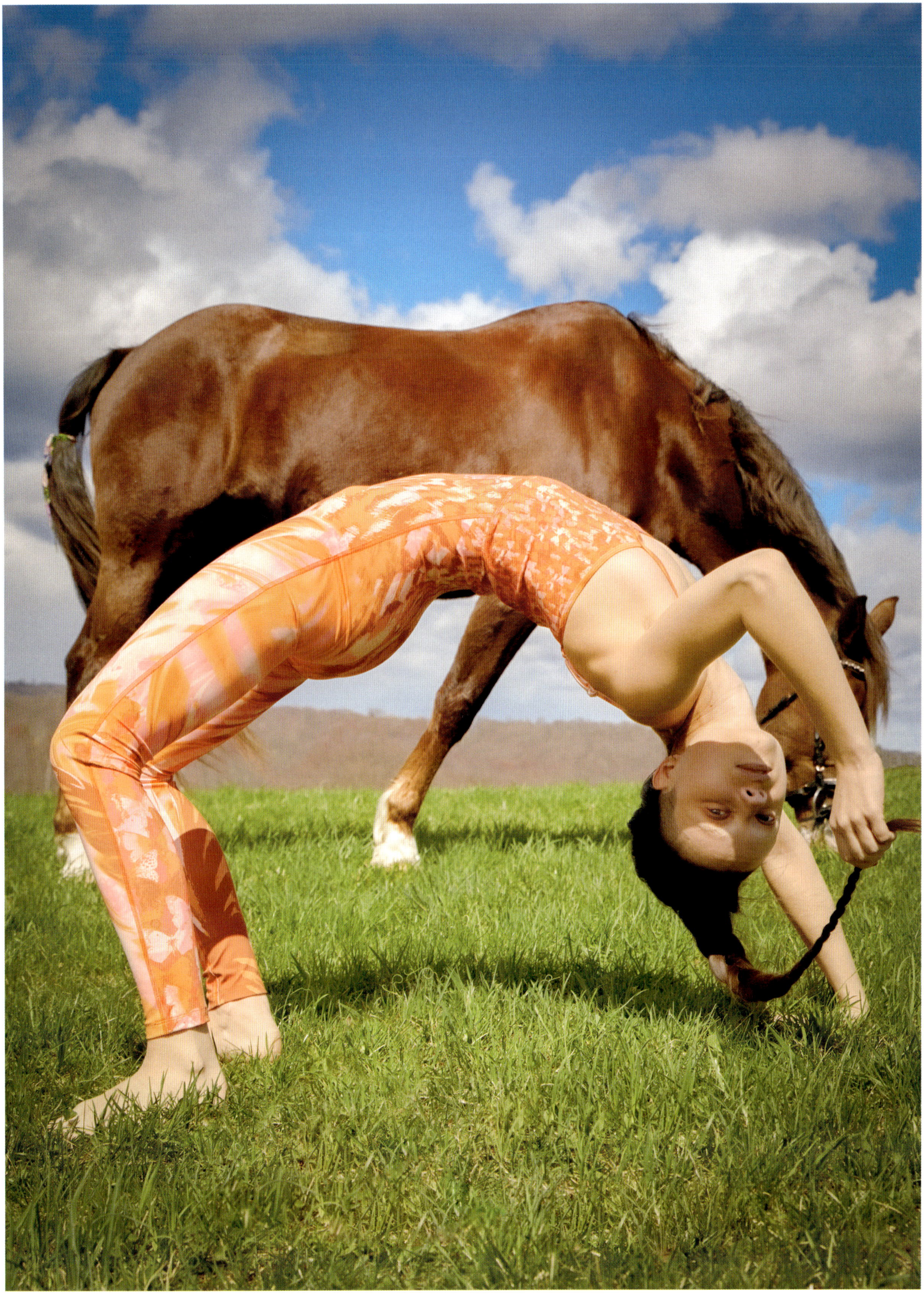

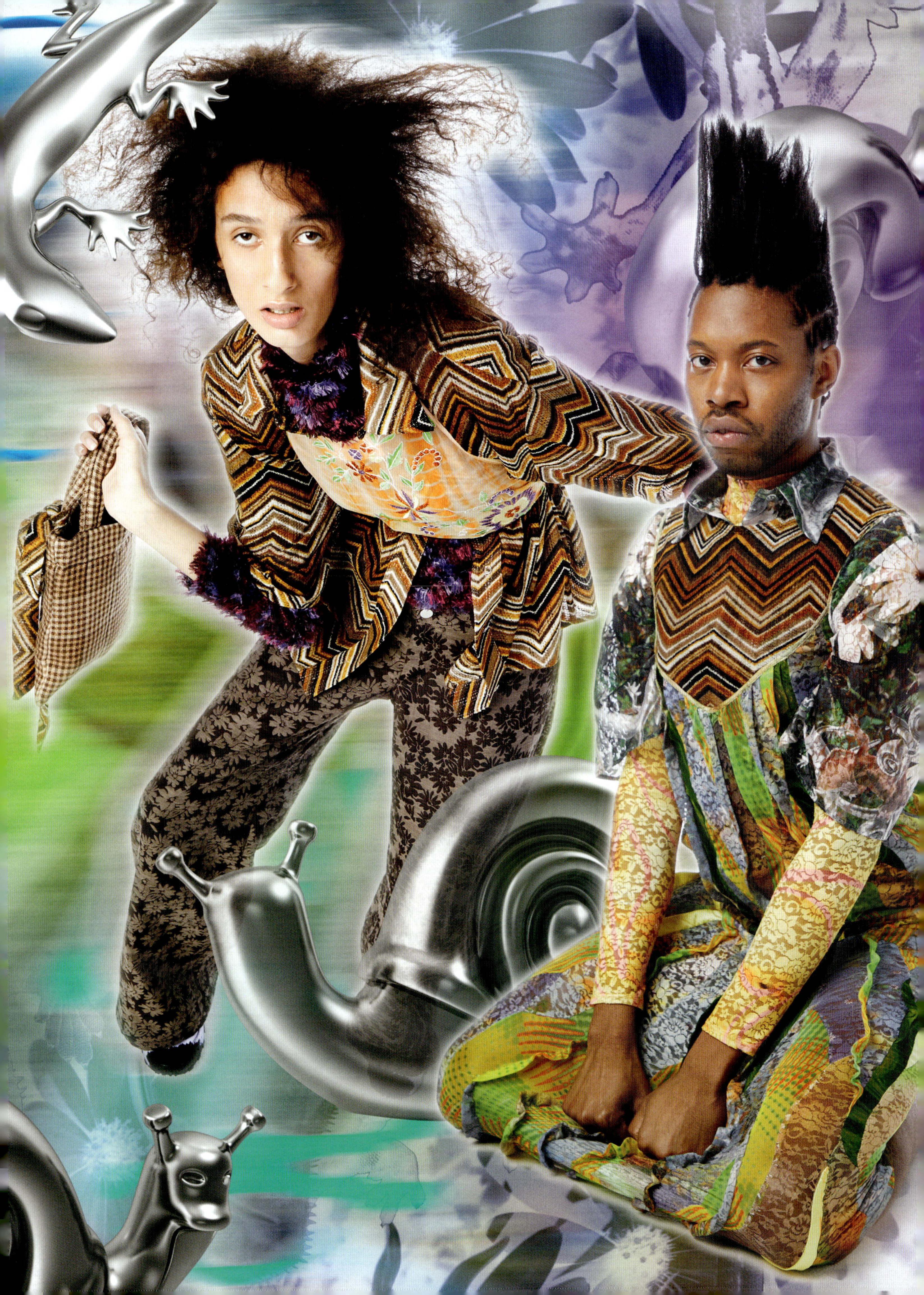

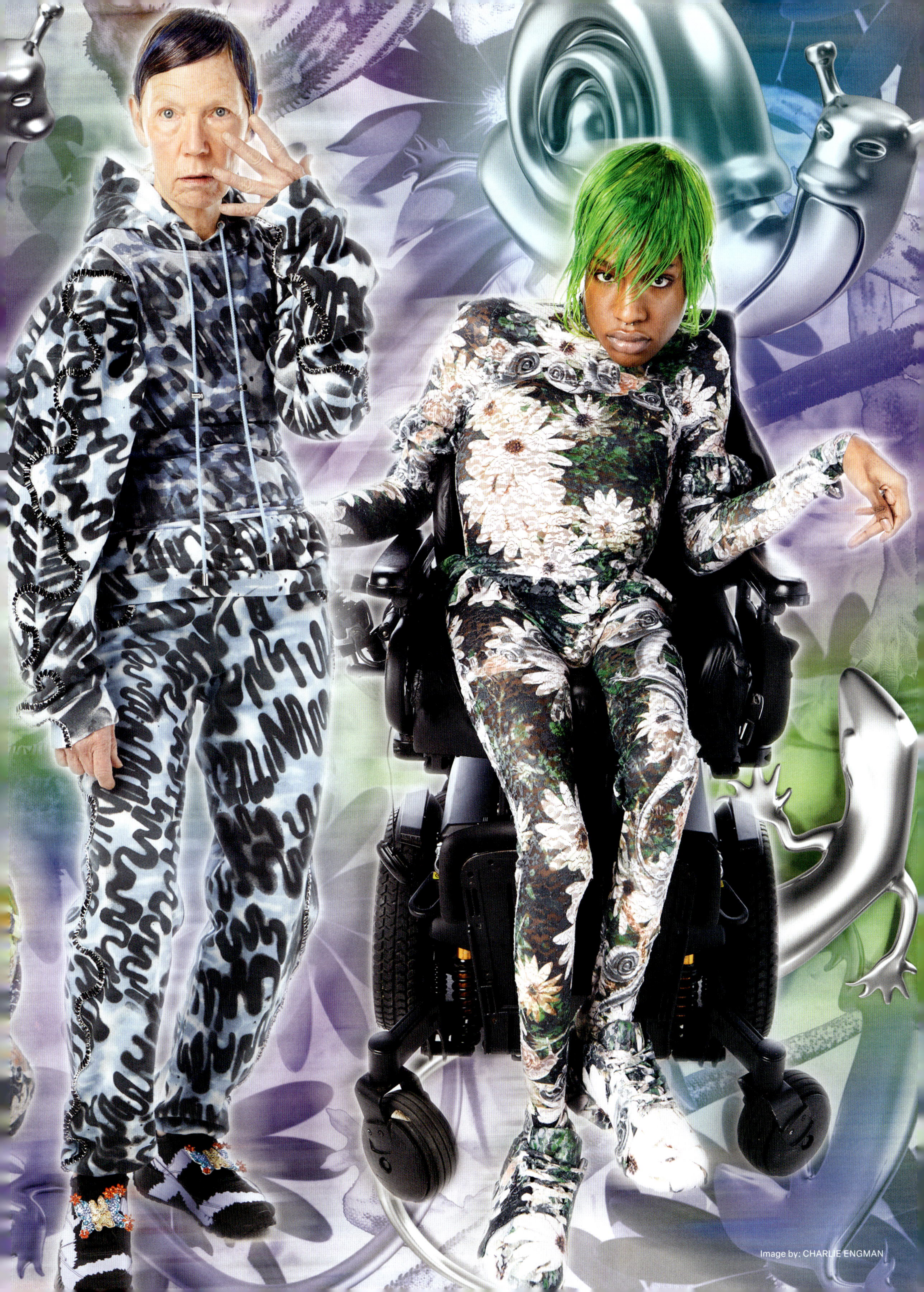

Image by: CHARLIE ENGMAN

AUTUMN WINTER 19, LOW CARBON DIET

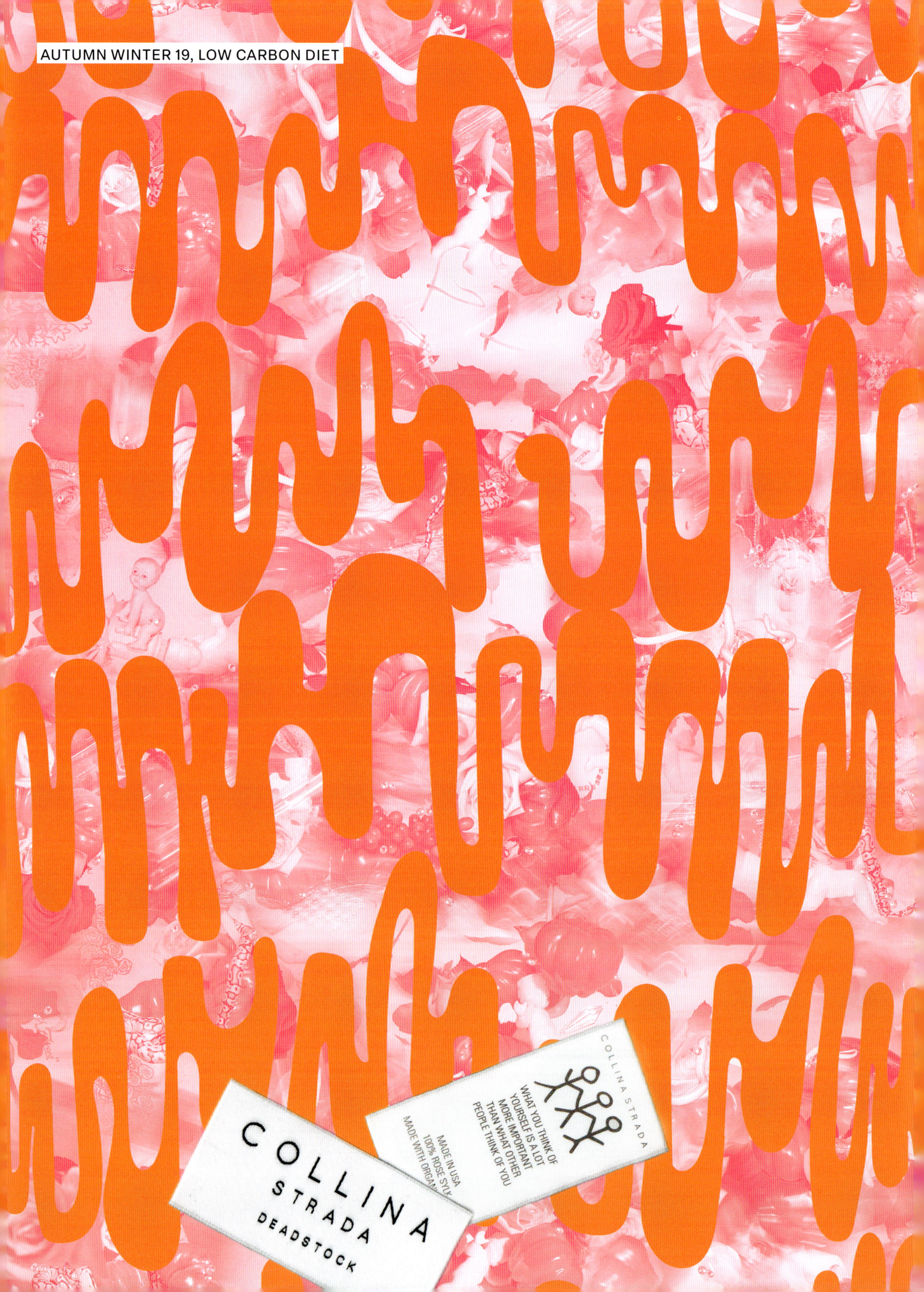

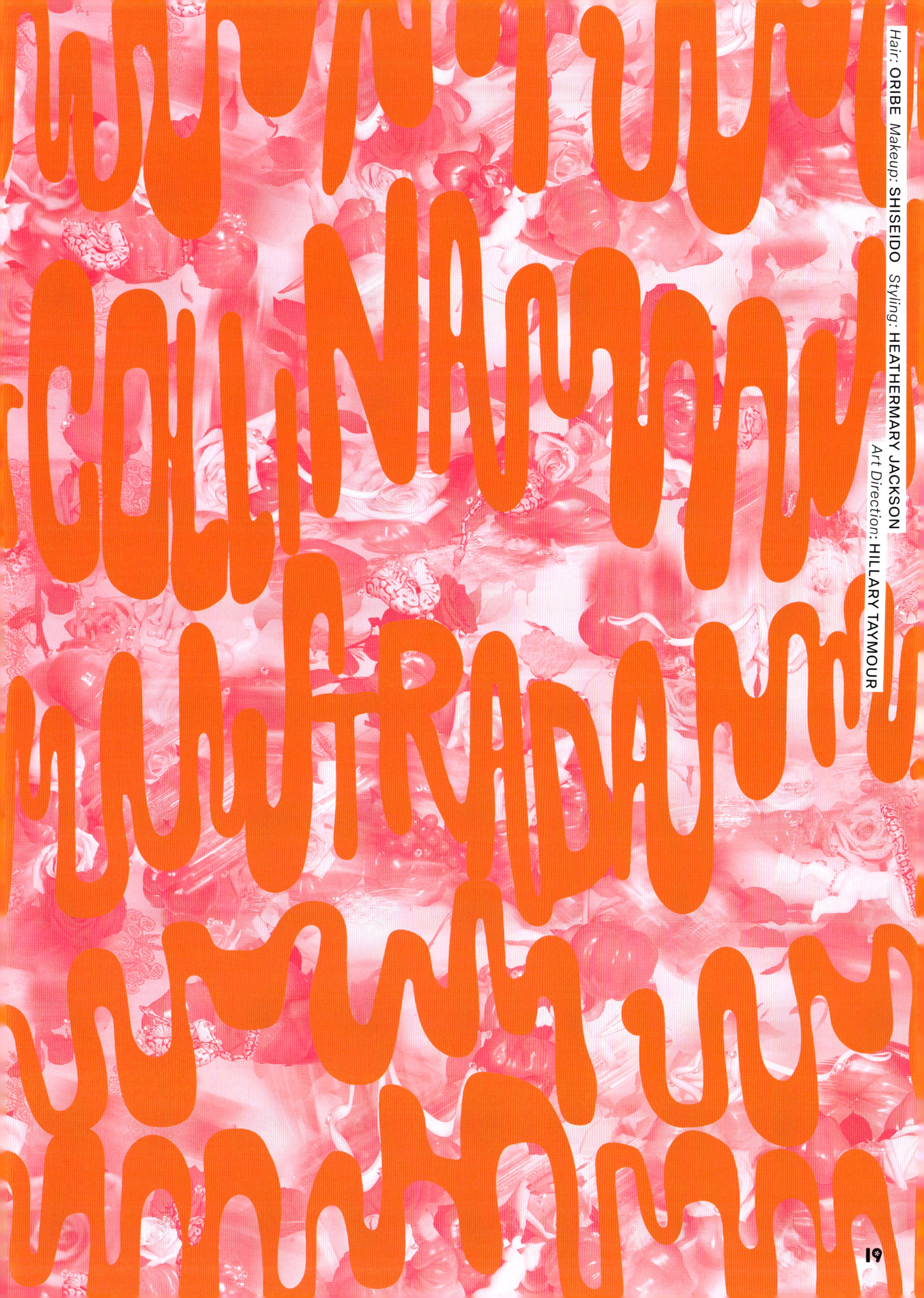

Hair: ORIBE *Makeup:* SHISEIDO *Styling:* HEATHERMARY JACKSON
Art Direction: HILLARY TAYMOUR

Low Carbon diet

AW19

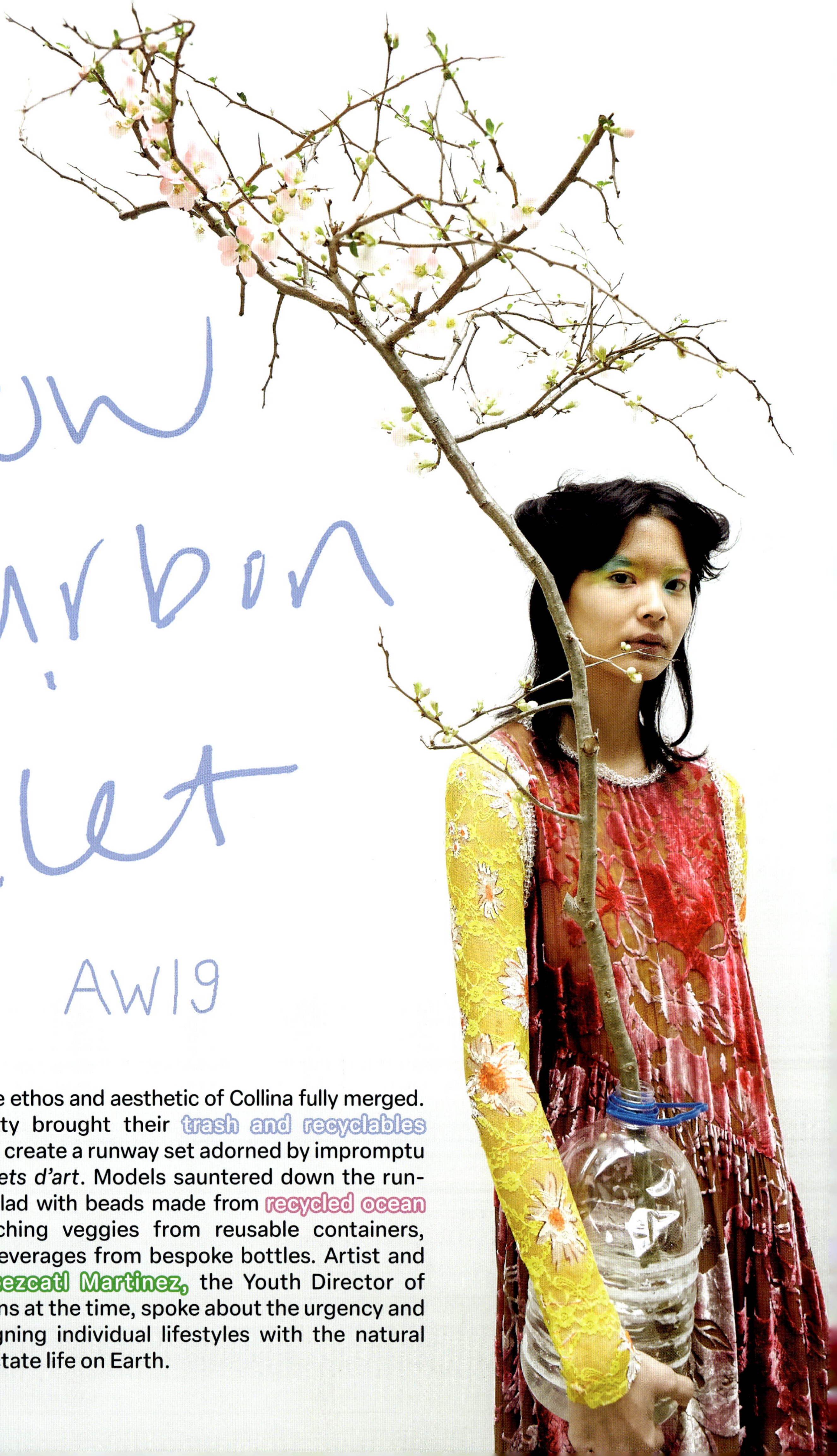

The season the ethos and aesthetic of Collina fully merged. Our community brought their trash and recyclables to the show to create a runway set adorned by impromptu vases and *objets d'art*. Models sauntered down the runway in looks clad with beads made from recycled ocean plastic, munching veggies from reusable containers, and sipping beverages from bespoke bottles. Artist and activist Xiuhtezcatl Martinez, the Youth Director of Earth Guardians at the time, spoke about the urgency and beauty of aligning individual lifestyles with the natural cycles that dictate life on Earth.

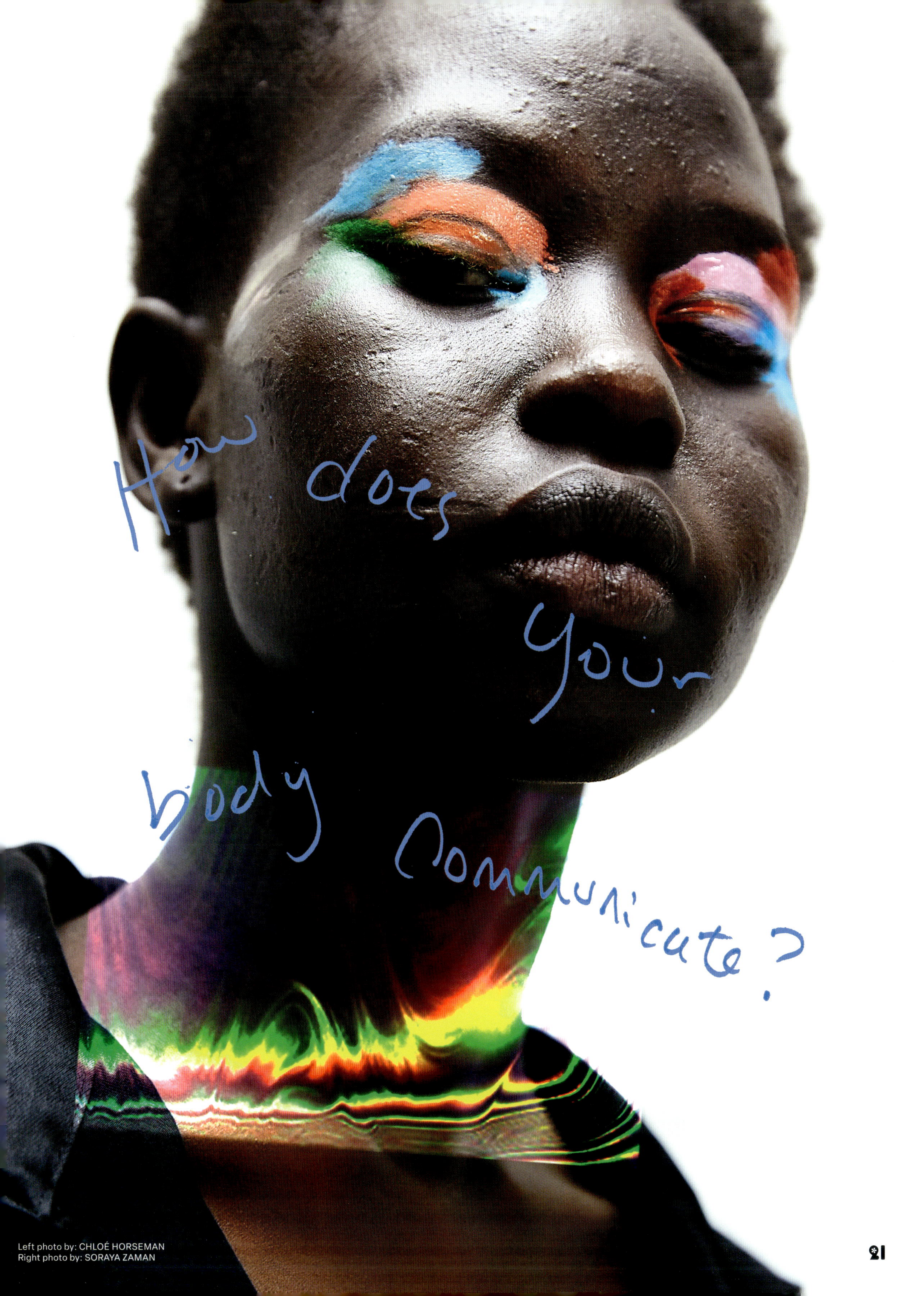

Left photo by: CHLOÉ HORSEMAN
Right photo by: SORAYA ZAMAN

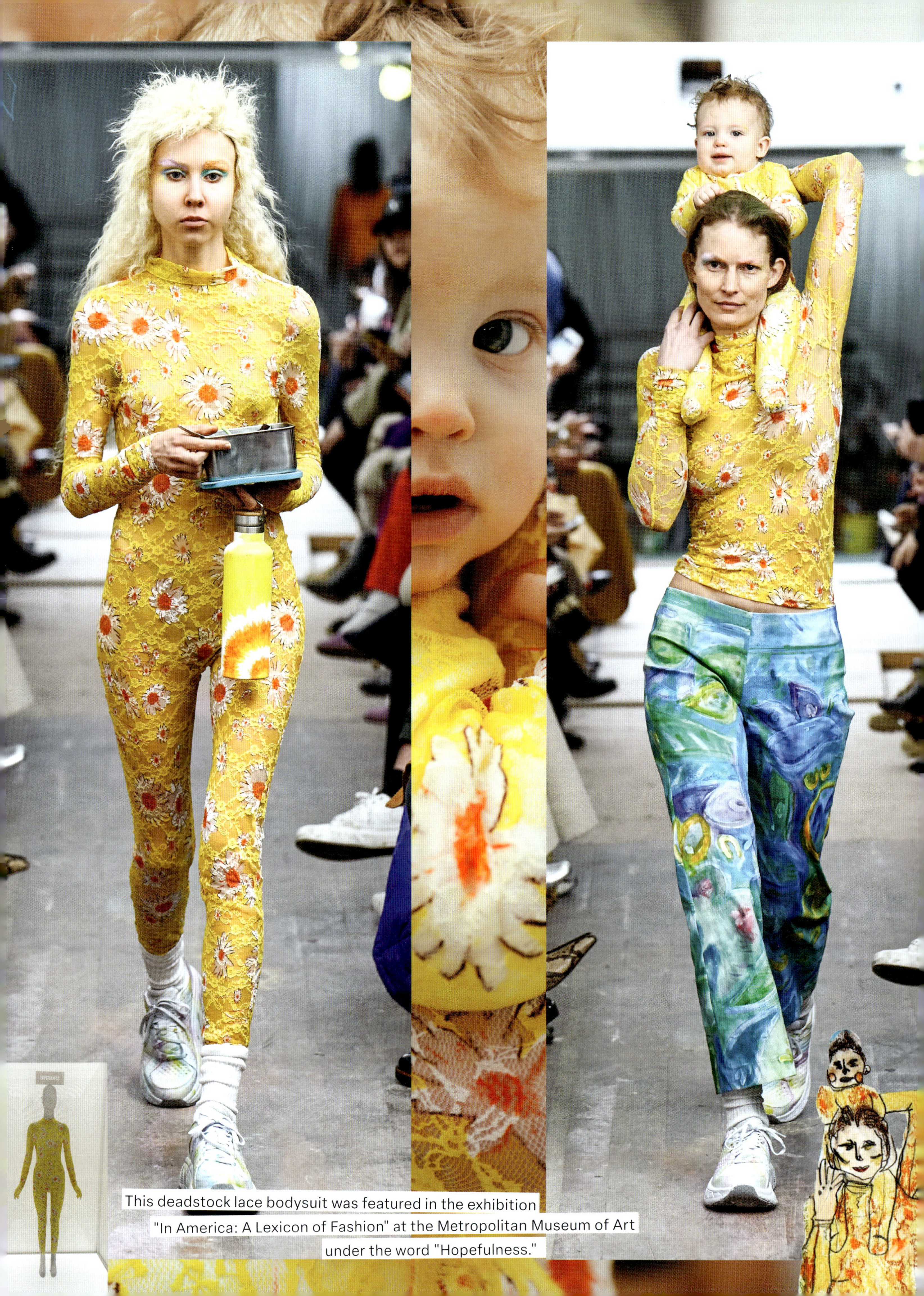

This deadstock lace bodysuit was featured in the exhibition "In America: A Lexicon of Fashion" at the Metropolitan Museum of Art under the word "Hopefulness."

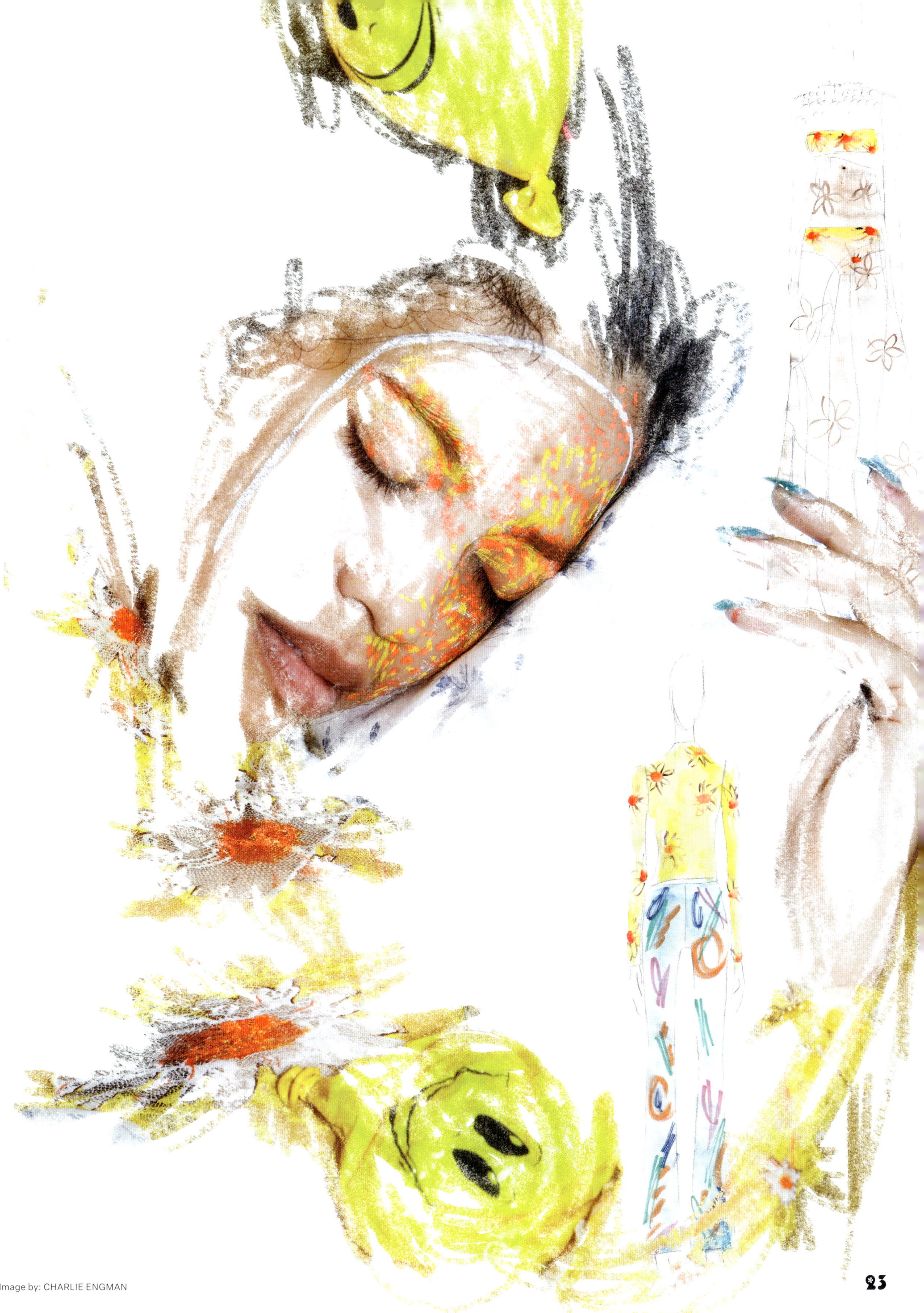

Image by: CHARLIE ENGMAN

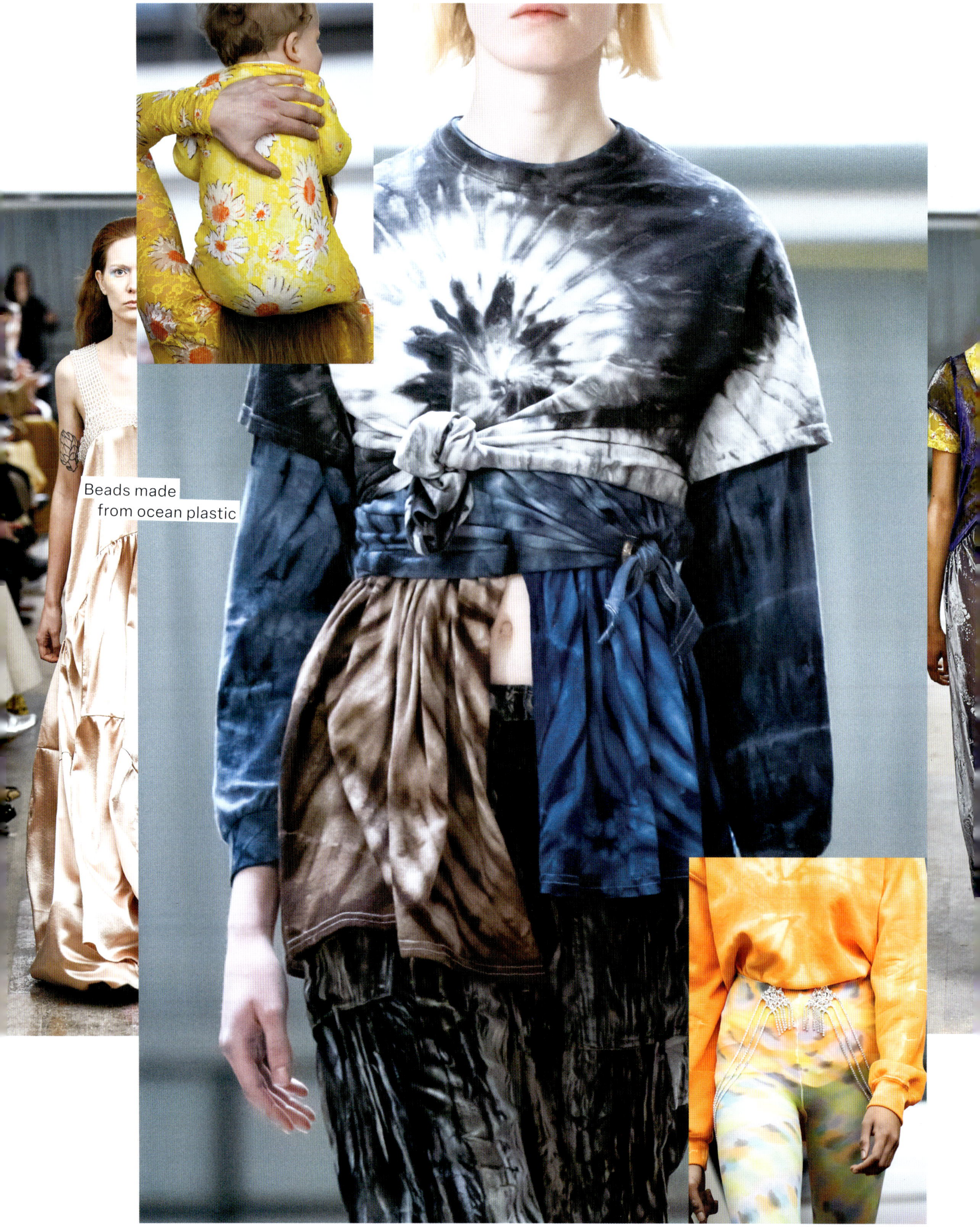

Beads made from ocean plastic

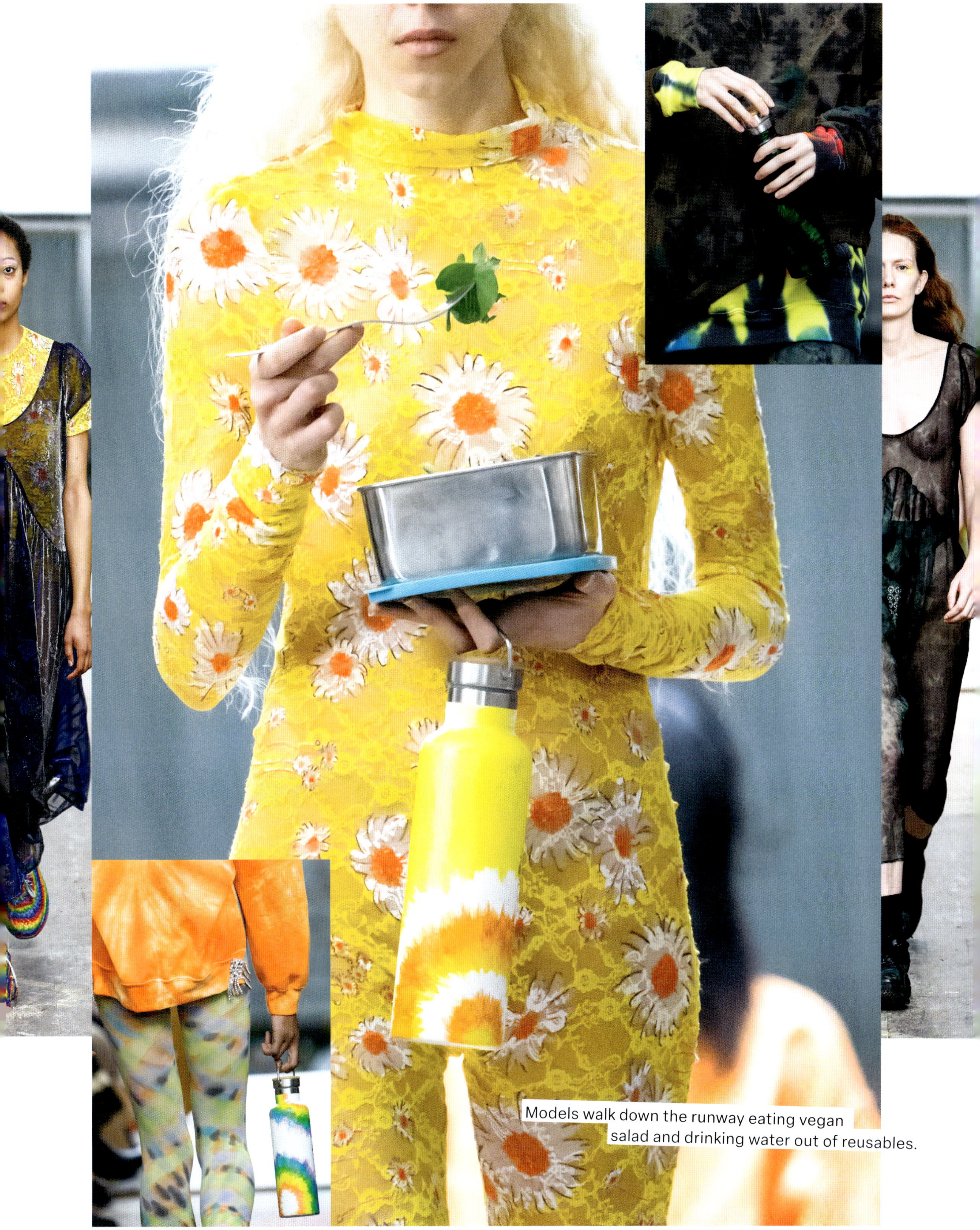

Models walk down the runway eating vegan salad and drinking water out of reusables.

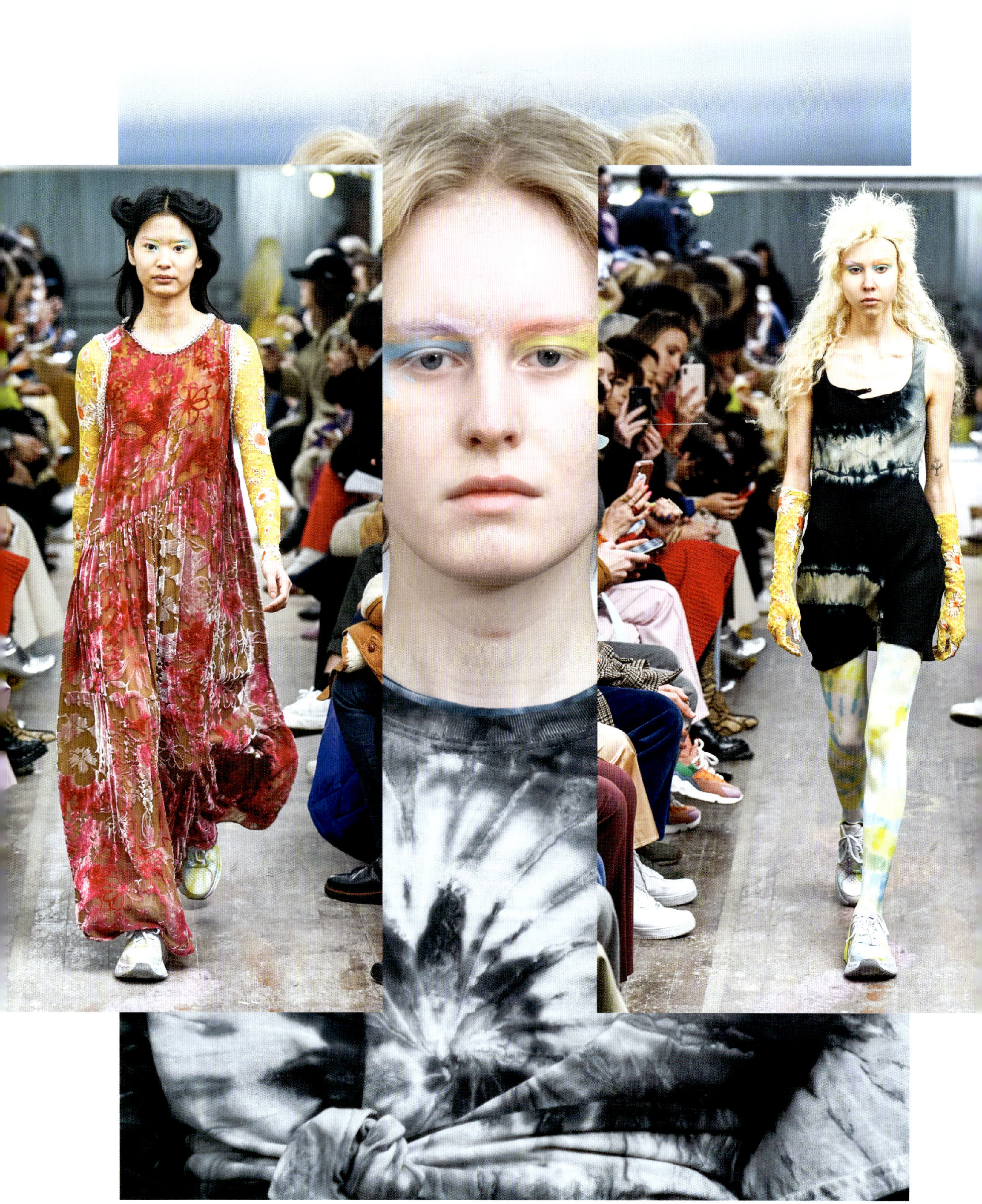

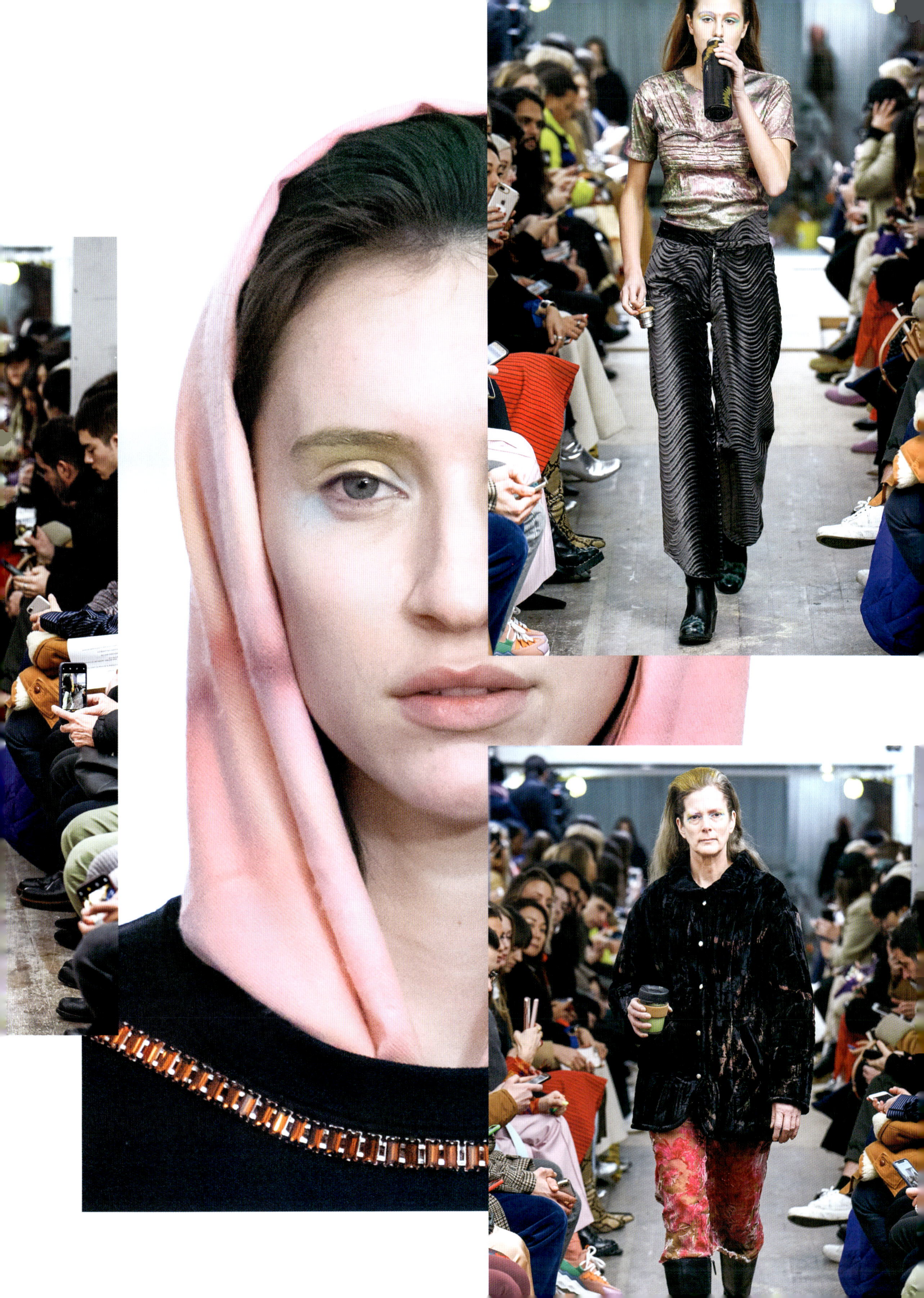

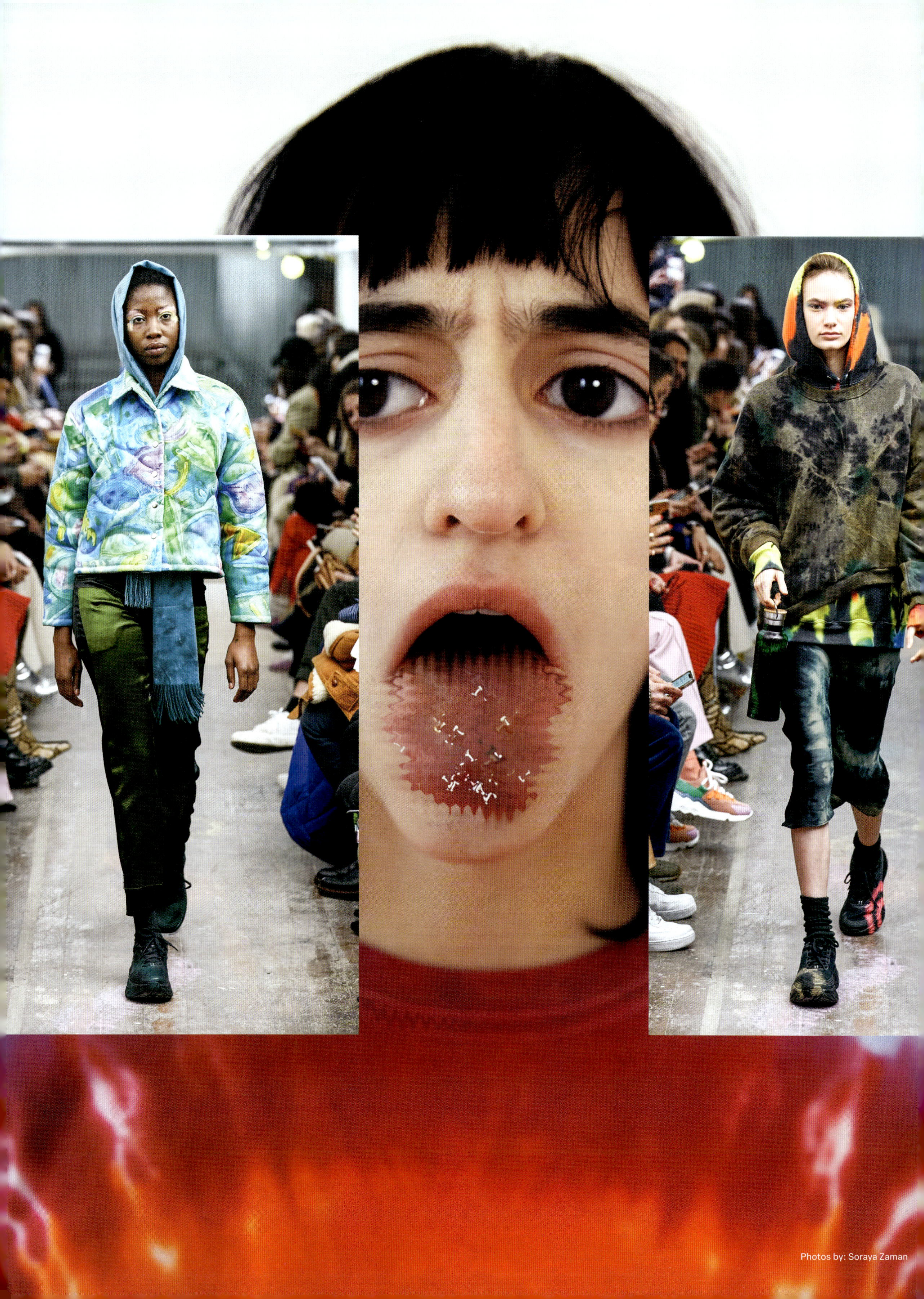

Photos by: Soraya Zaman

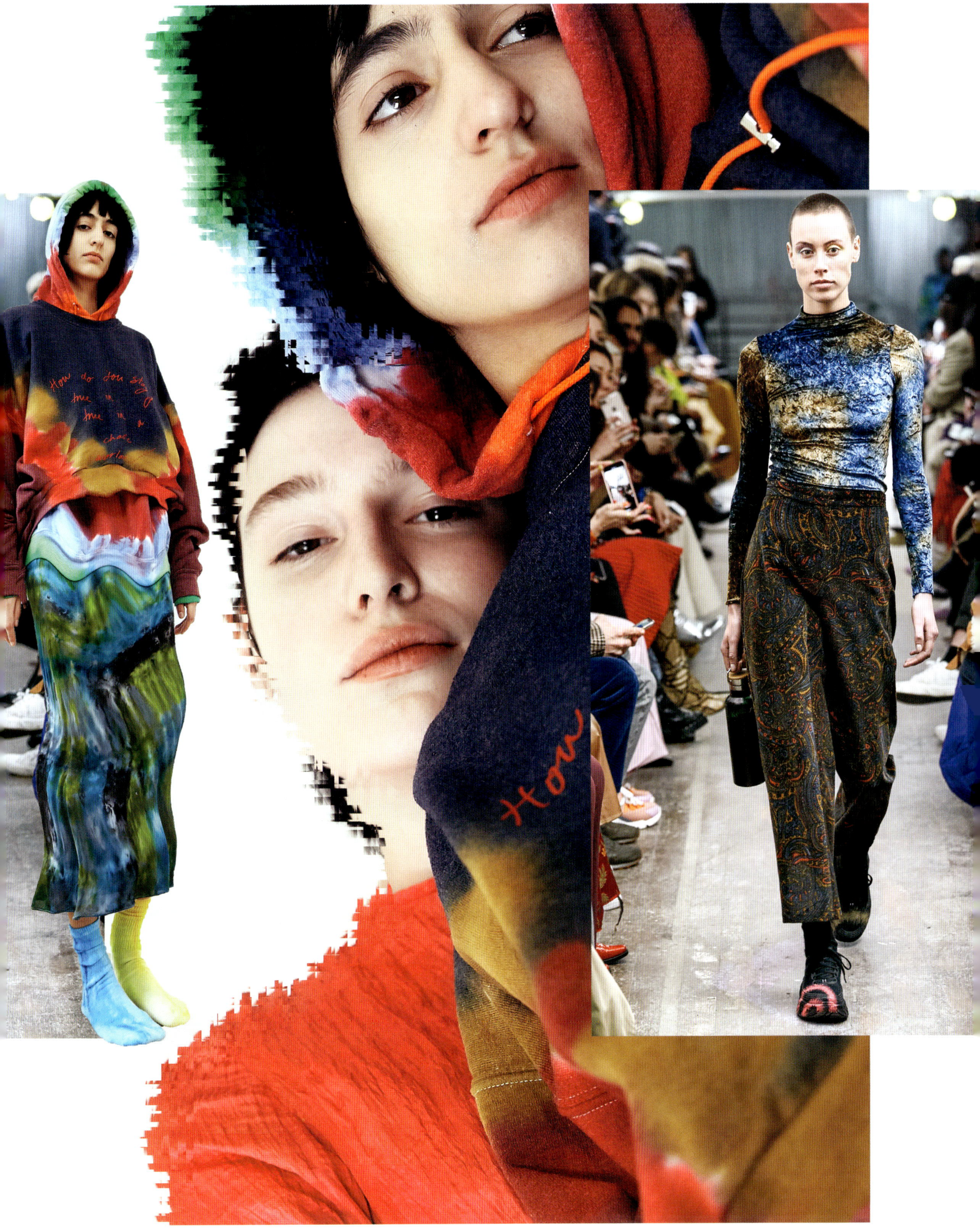

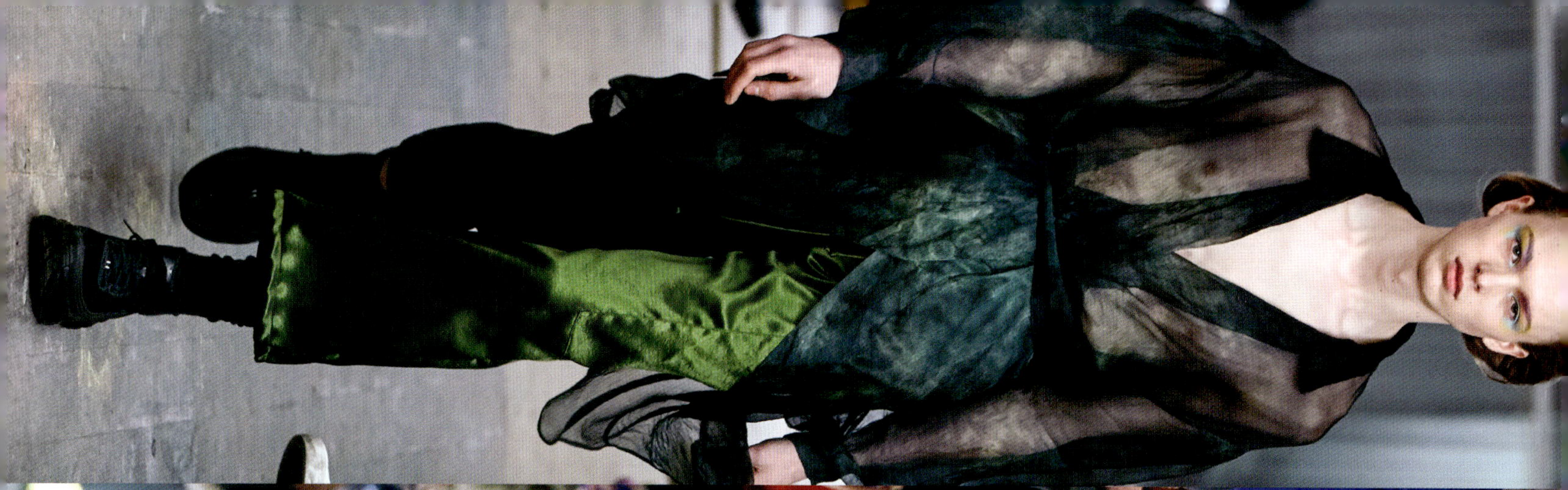
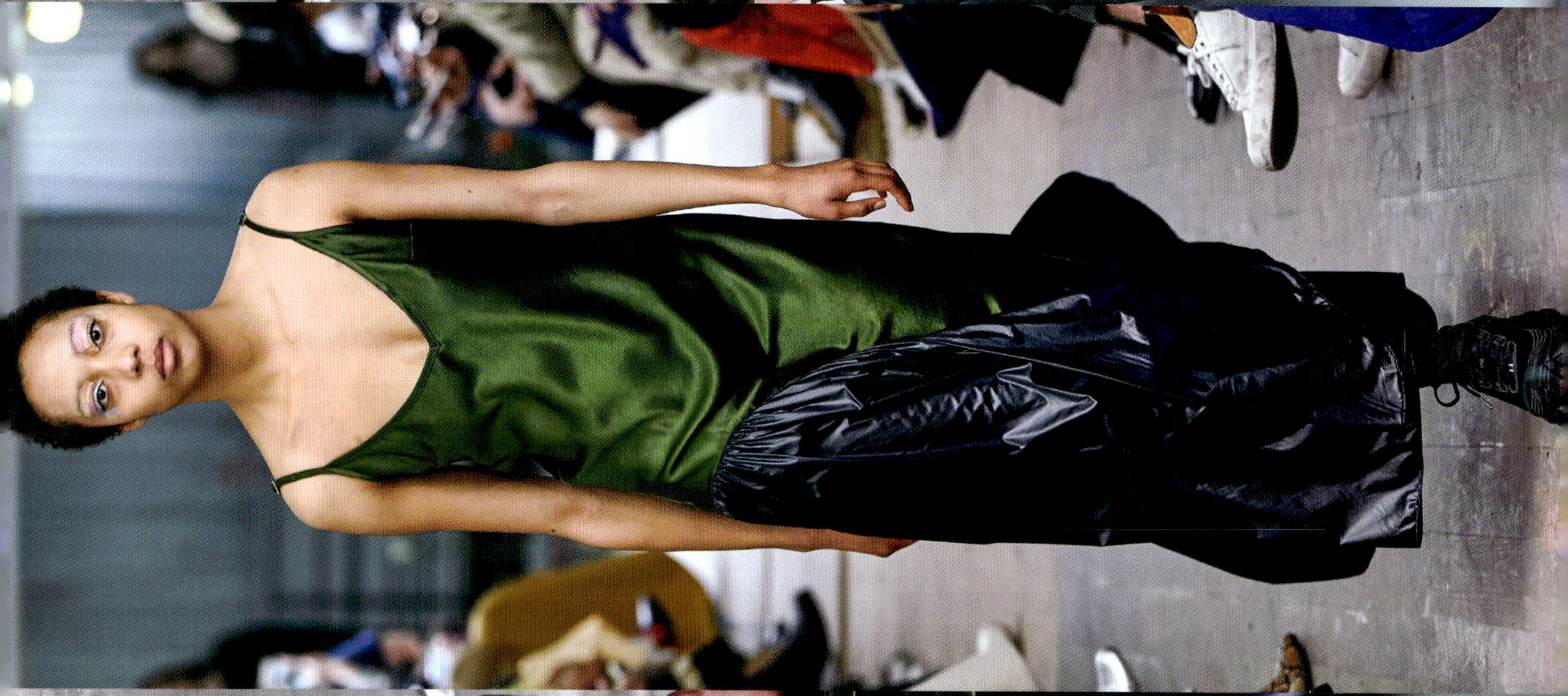
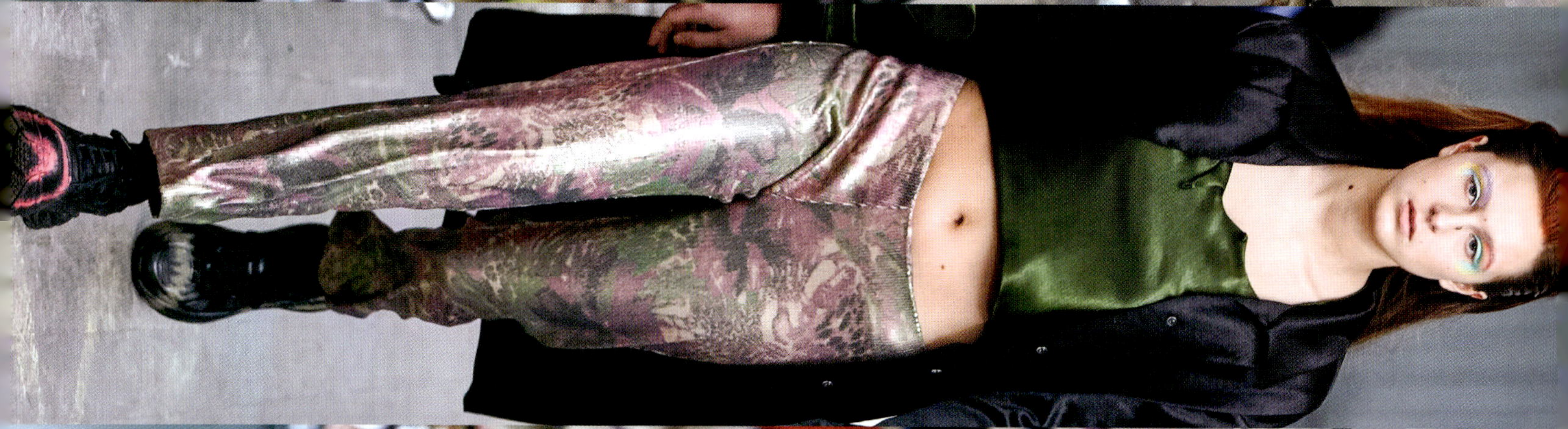
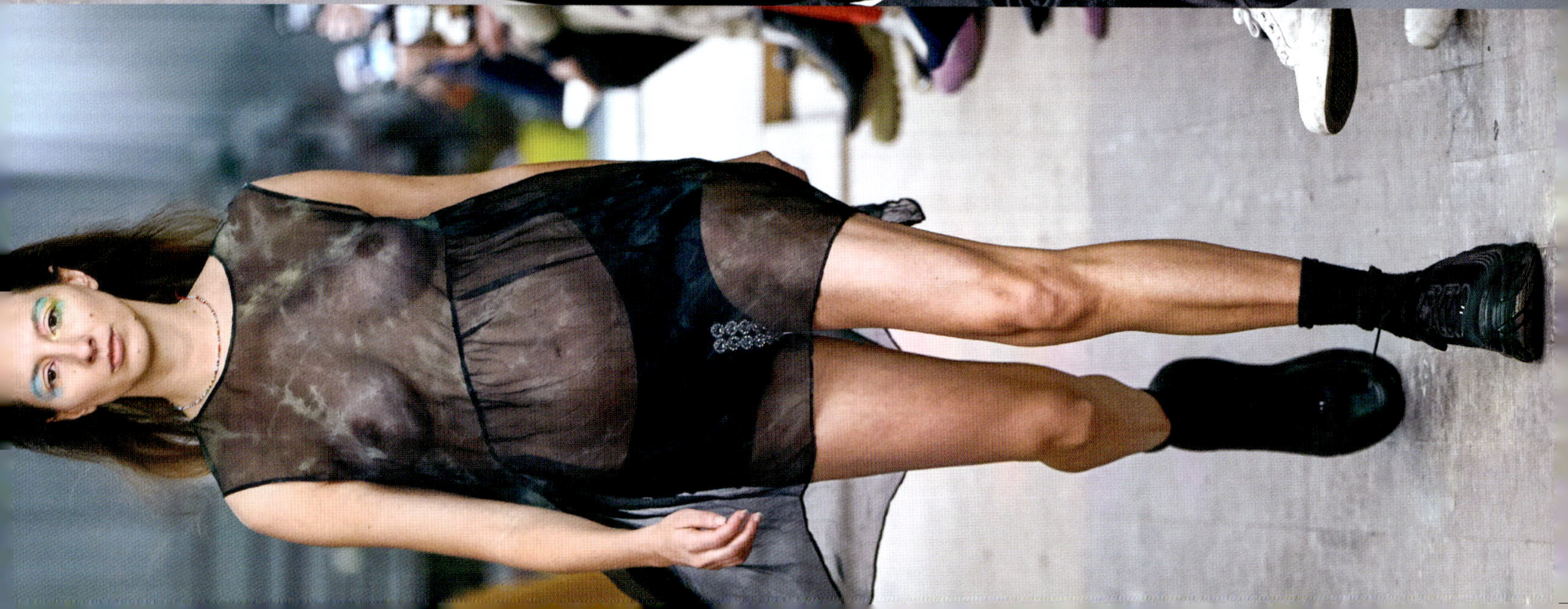

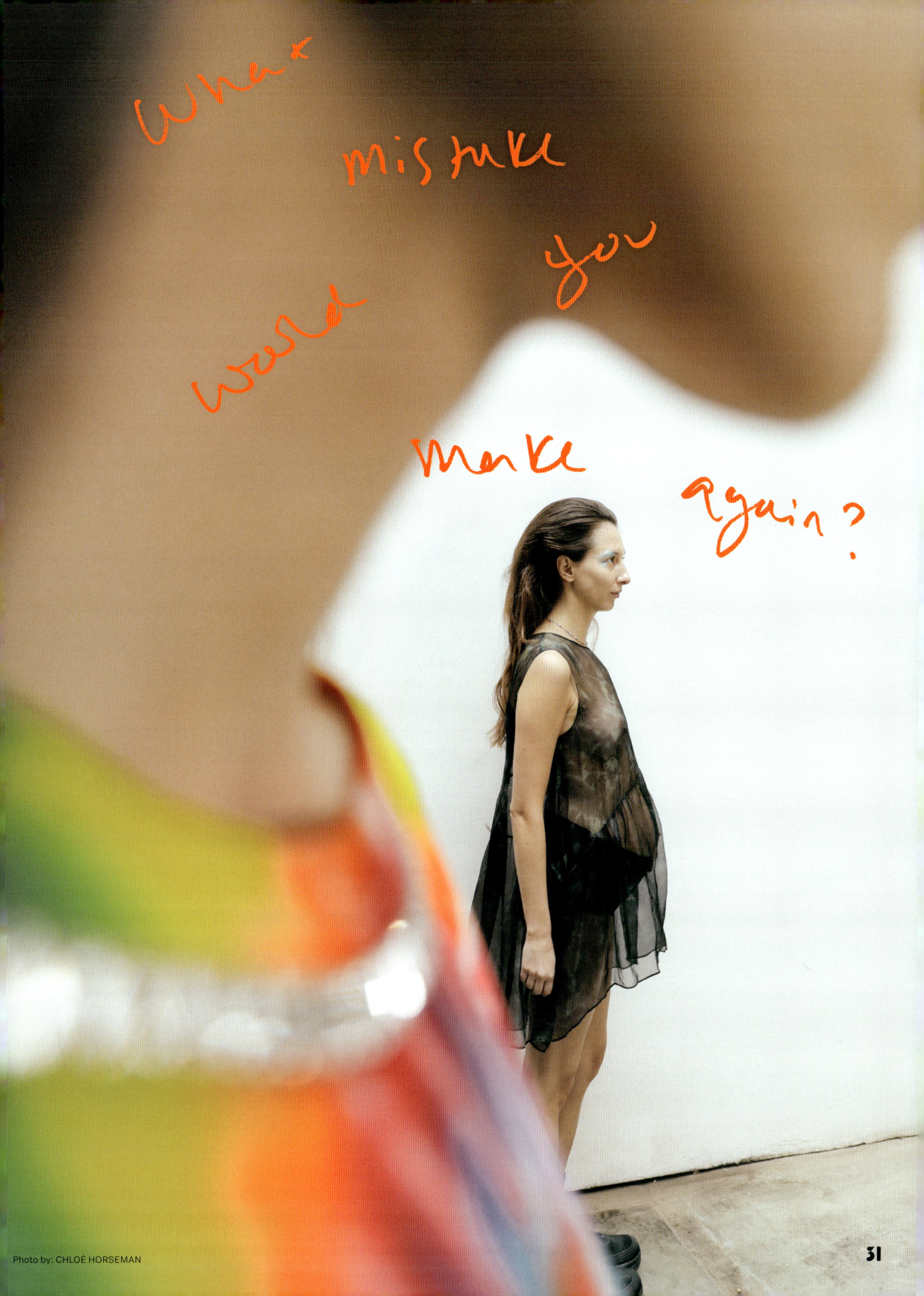

Photo by: CHLOÉ HORSEMAN

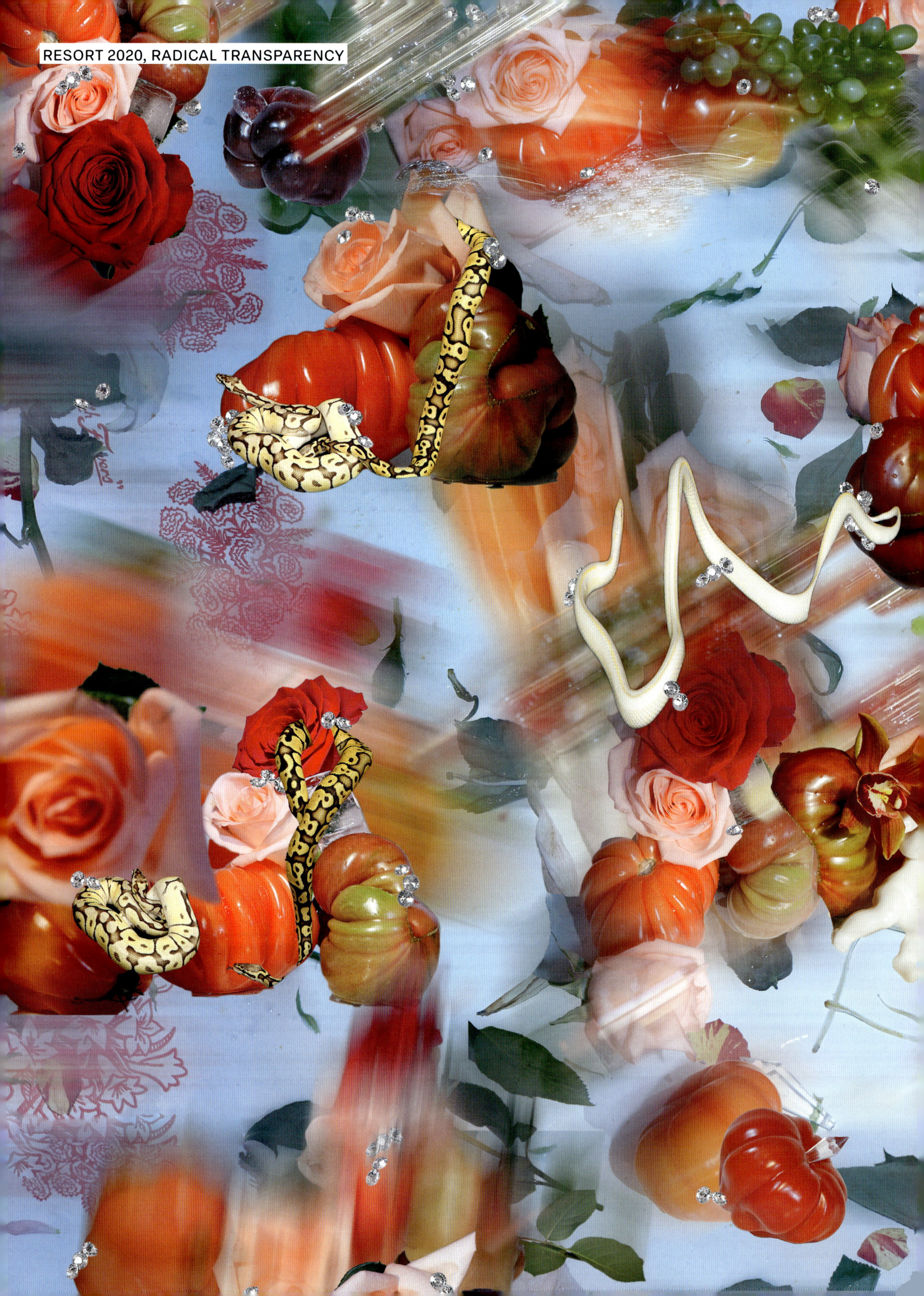

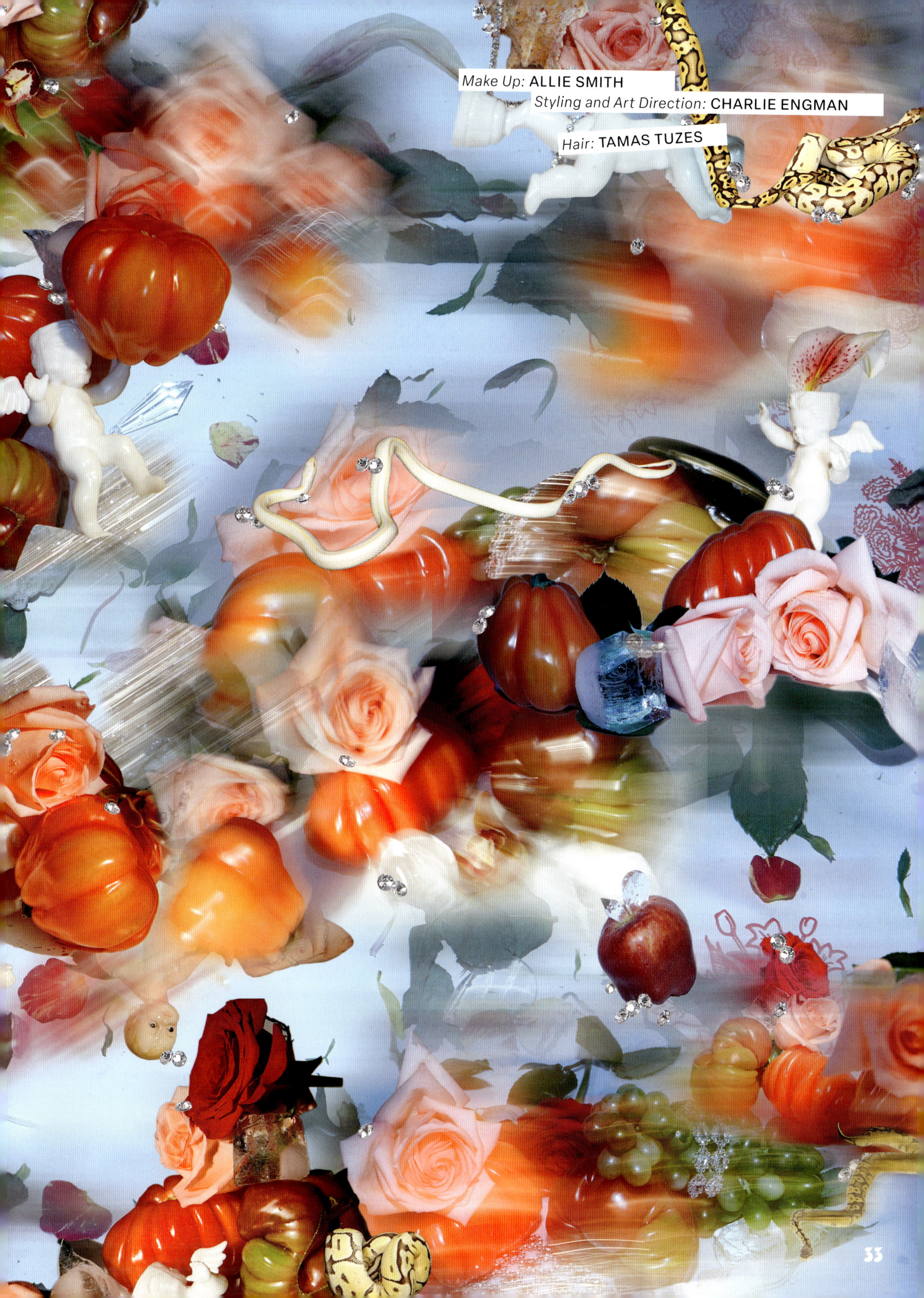

Make Up: ALLIE SMITH

Styling and Art Direction: CHARLIE ENGMAN

Hair: TAMAS TUZES

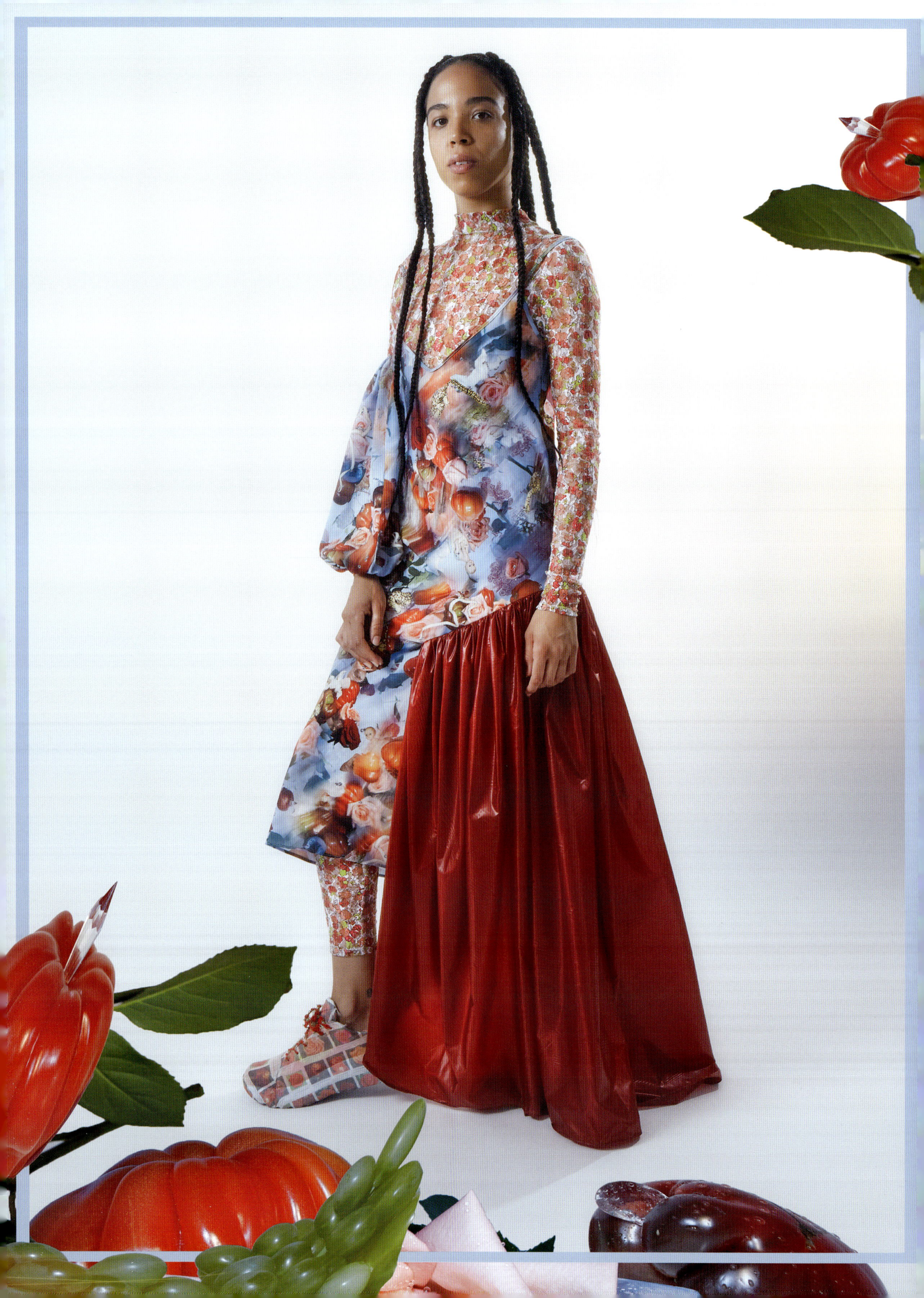

Radical Transparency

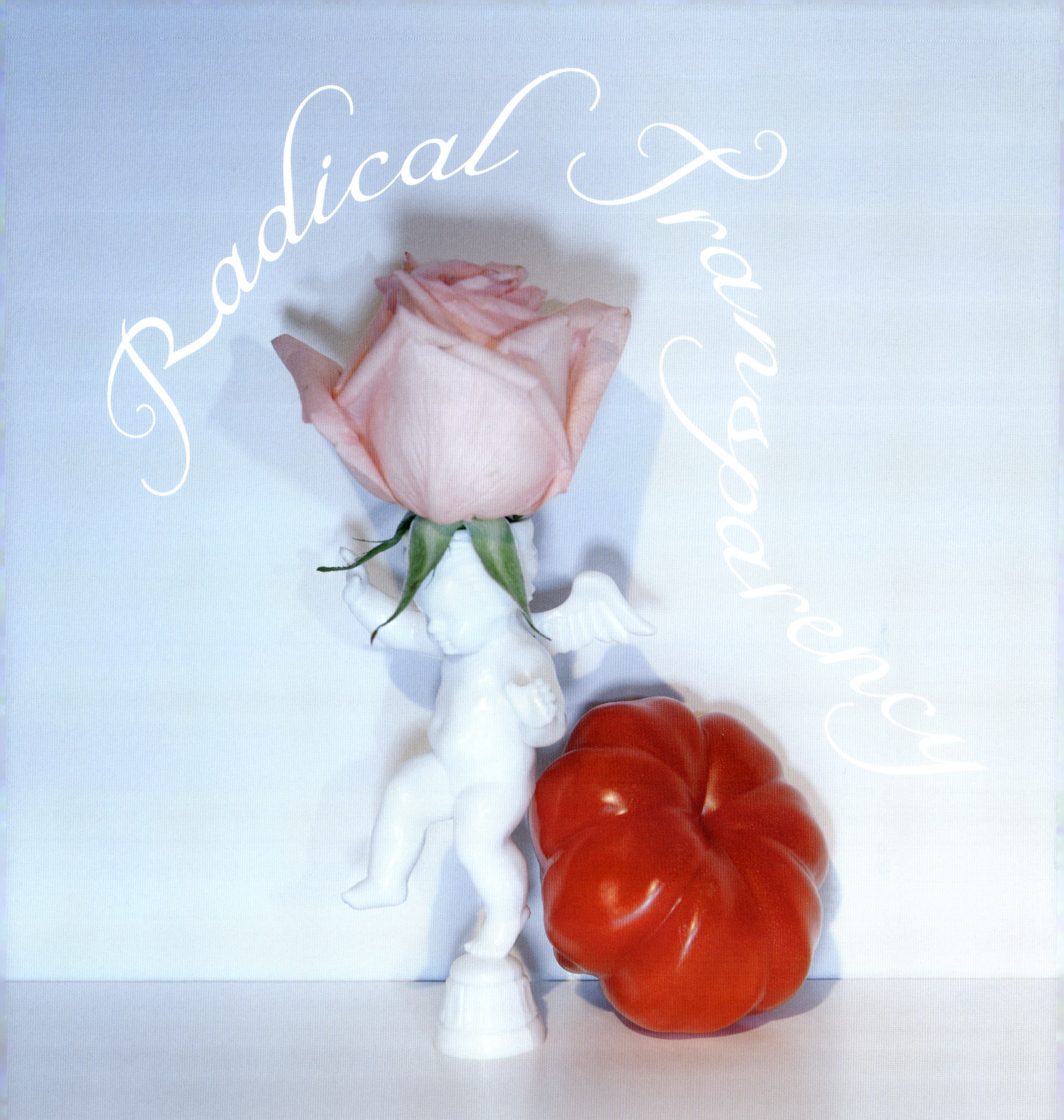

RESORT MMXX

Building on ten years of creative friendship, *Charlie Engman* and Hillary Taymour started working in tandem on all of Collina's creative elements, from design to visualization. From this collection forward, Charlie created the *custom Collina prints* from his photographs and artwork, all of which were printed on deadstock fabric. His mother, *Rustee McCain,* is the star of the show, alongside musician *Zsela* and other members of the Collina Strada universe.

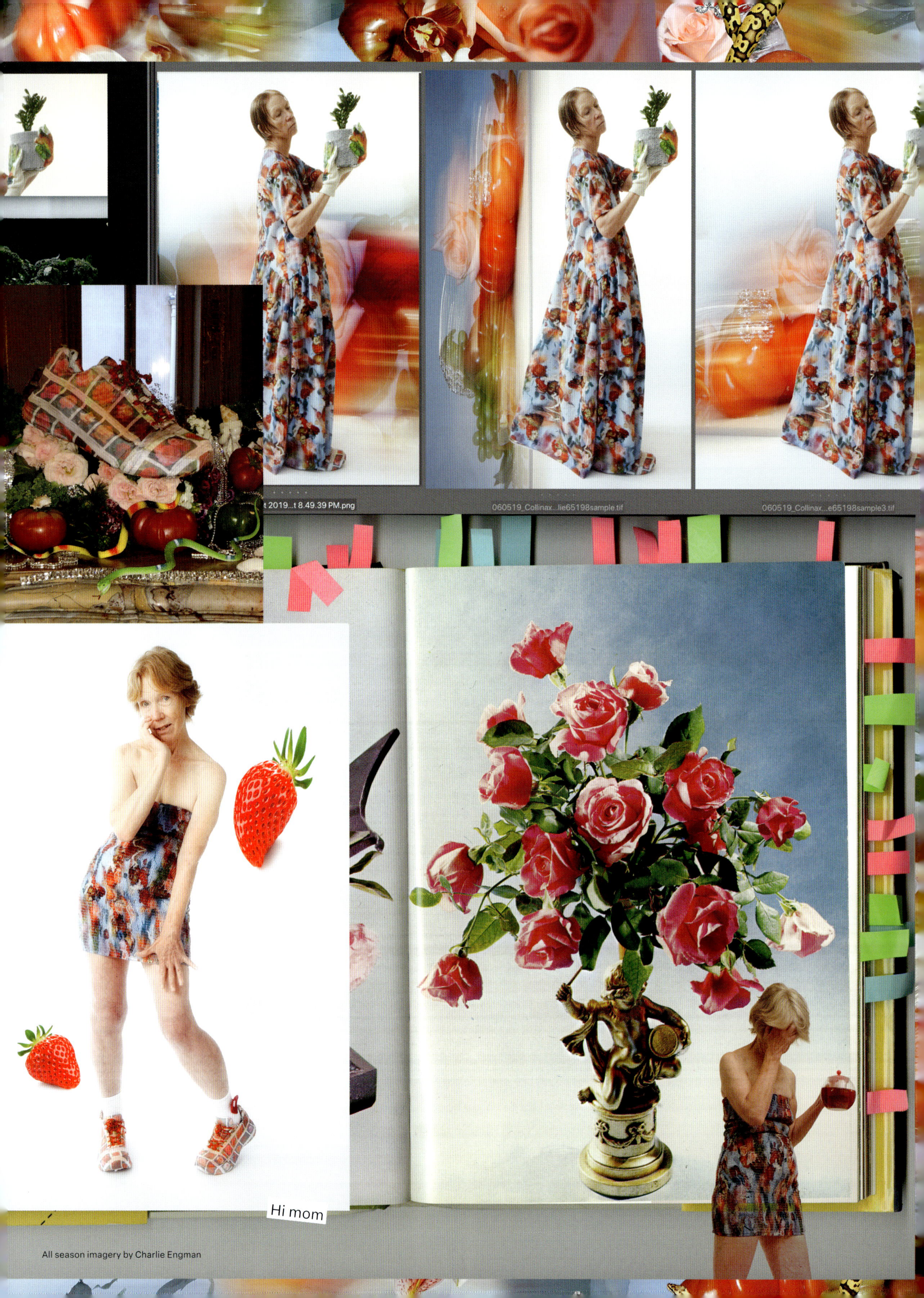

All season imagery by Charlie Engman

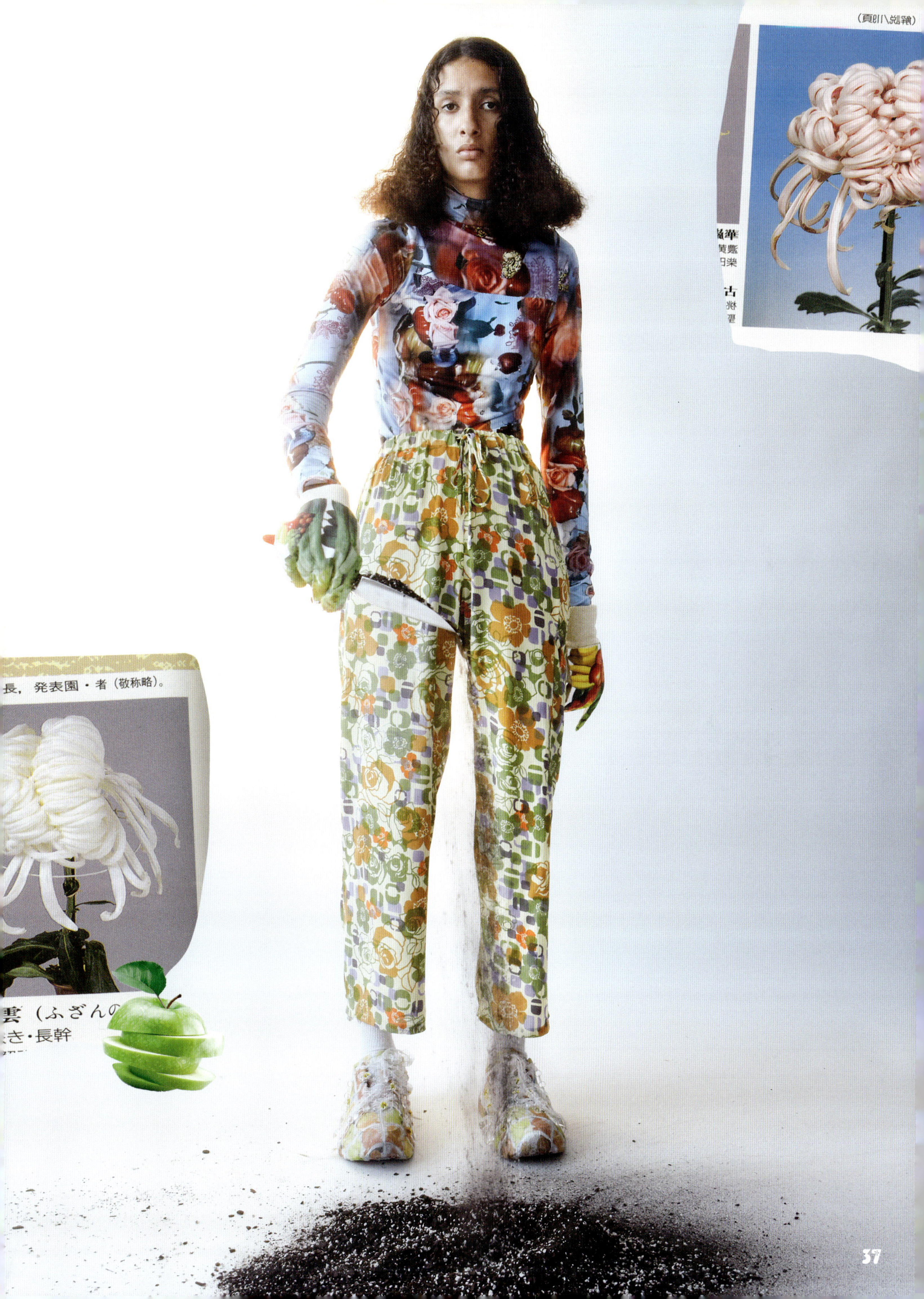
長，発表園・者（敬称略）。
雲（ふざんの
き・長幹

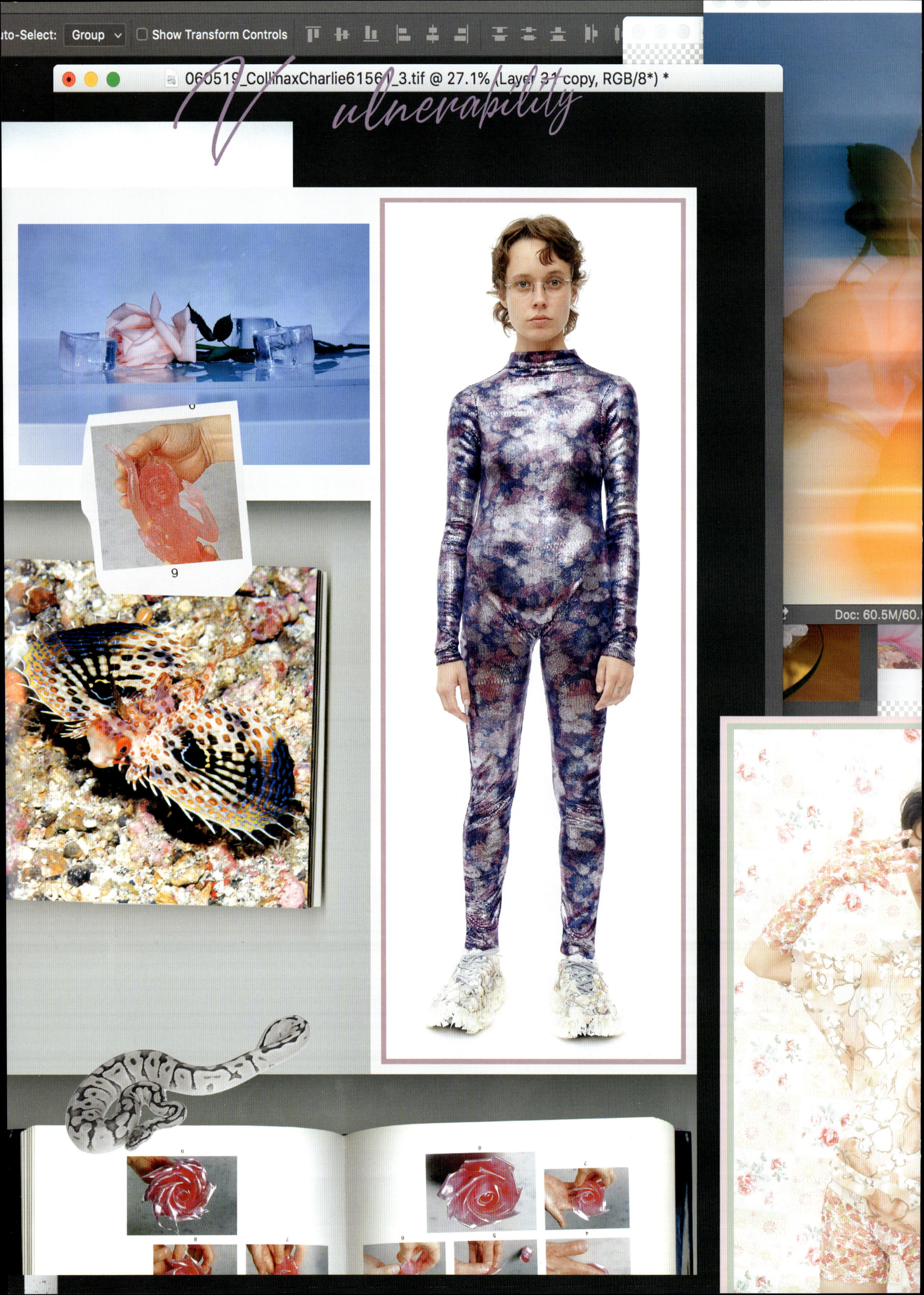
ito-Select:
Group
Show Transform Controls
060519_CollinaxCharlie61561_3.tif @ 27.1% (Layer 31 copy, RGB/8*) *
Vulnerability
9
Doc: 60.5M/60.

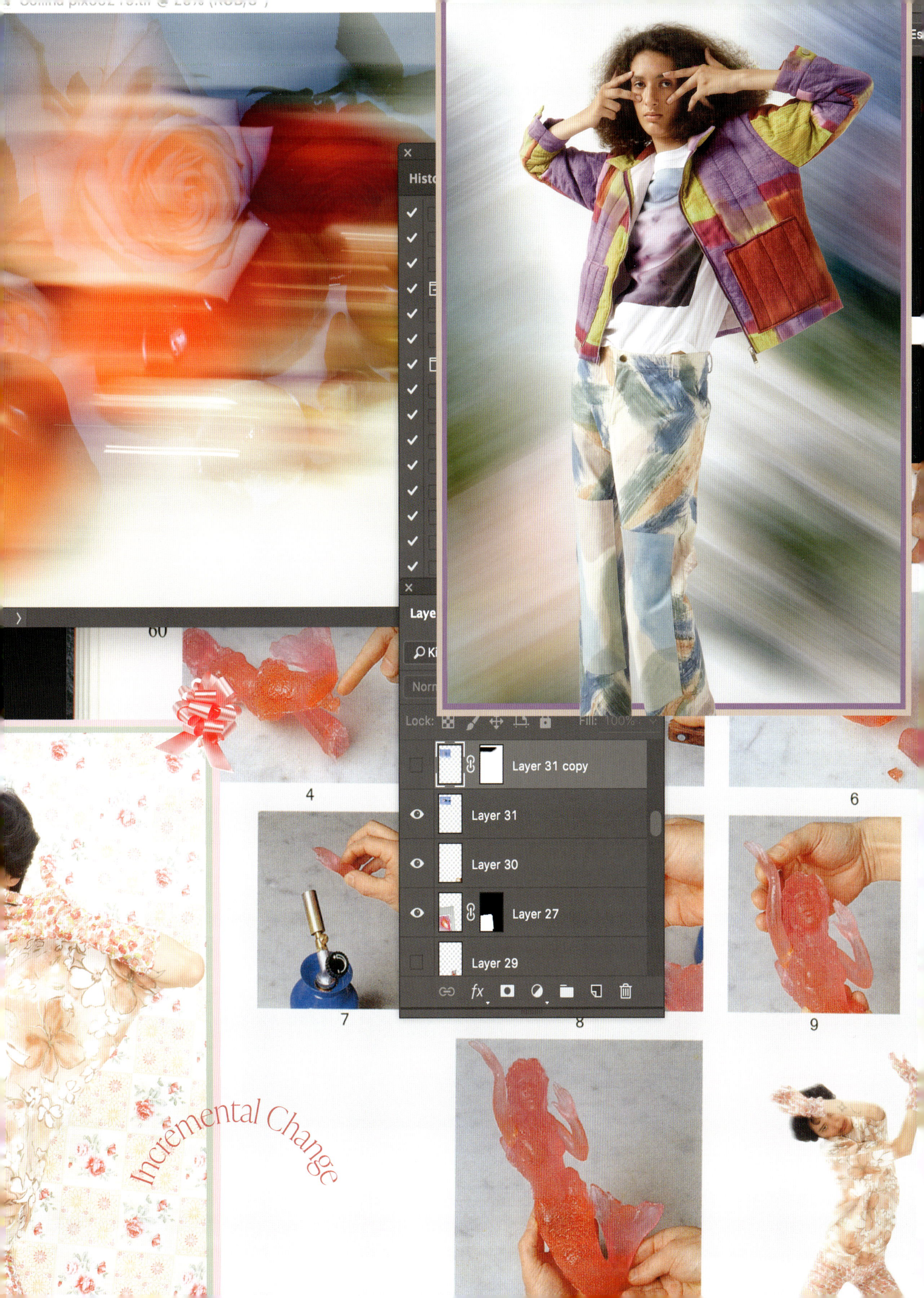
Histo
Laye
Norm
Lock:
Fill: 100%
Layer 31 copy
Layer 31
Layer 30
Layer 27
Layer 29
60
4
6
7
8
9
Incremental Change

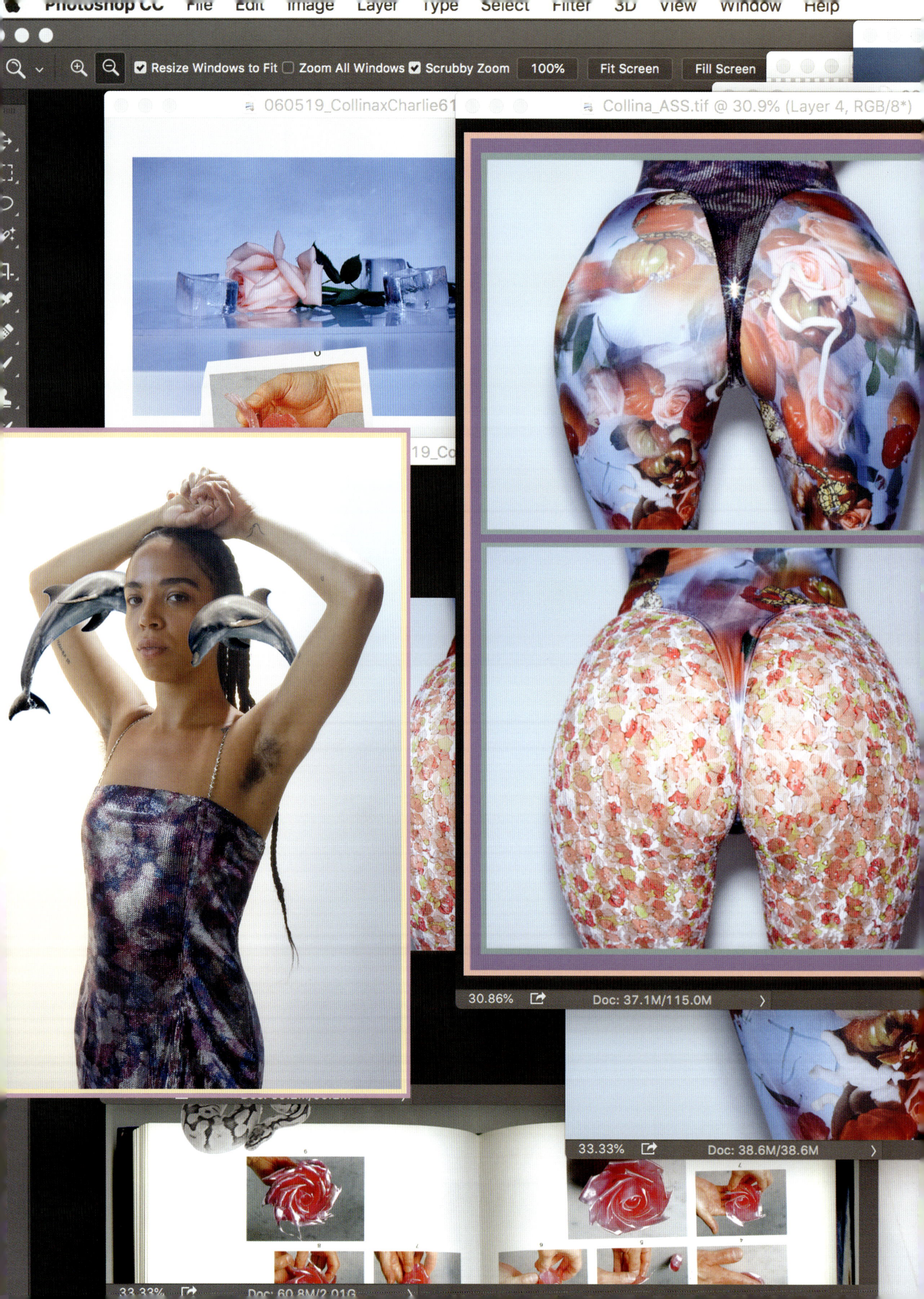
Photoshop CC
File
Edit
Image
Layer
Type
Select
Filter
3D
View
Window
Help
Resize Windows to Fit
Zoom All Windows
Scrubby Zoom
100%
Fit Screen
Fill Screen
060519_CollinaxCharlie61
Collina_ASS.tif @ 30.9% (Layer 4, RGB/8*)
30.86%
Doc: 37.1M/115.0M
33.33%
Doc: 38.6M/38.6M

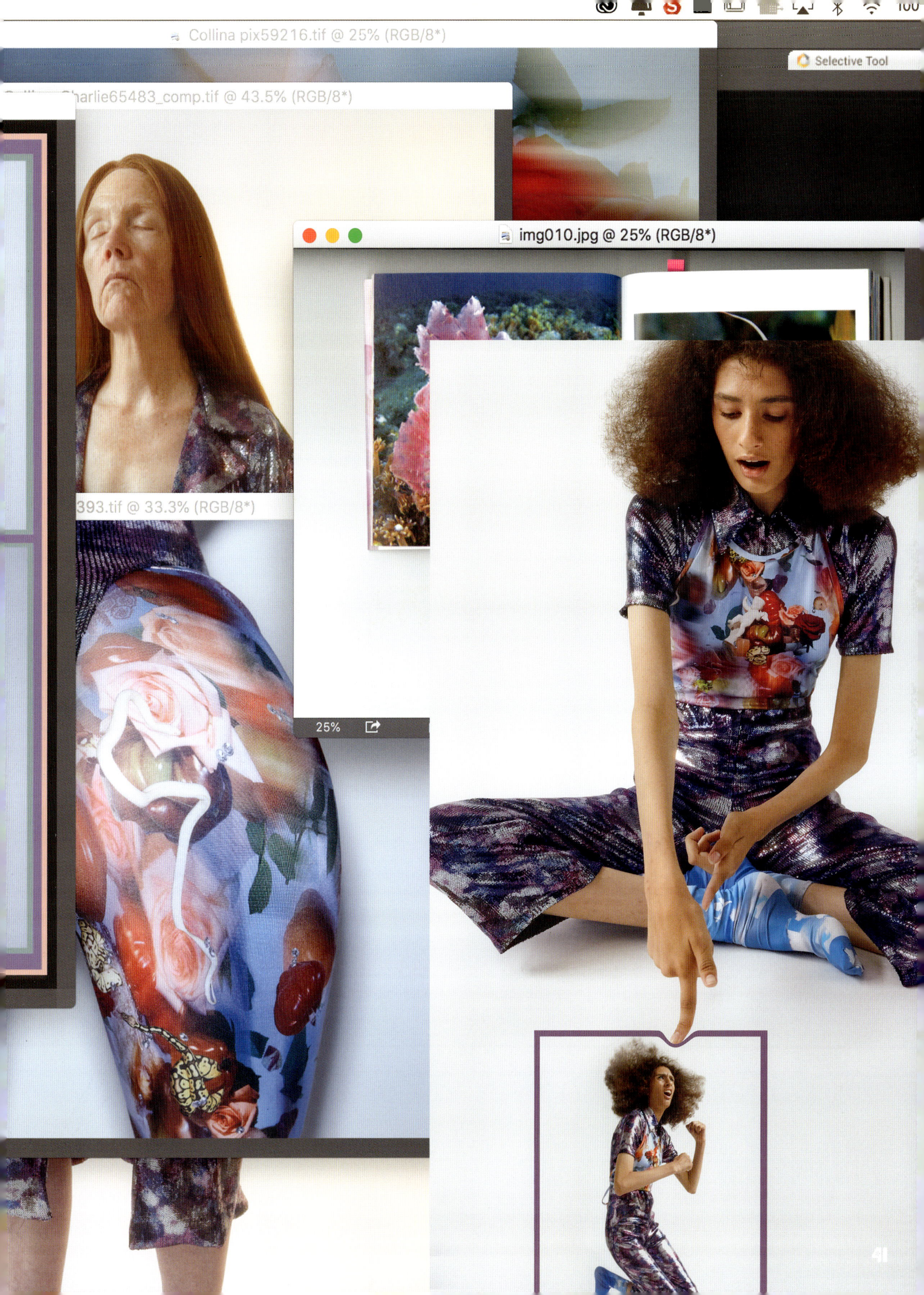
Collina pix59216.tif @ 25% (RGB/8*)
harlie65483_comp.tif @ 43.5% (RGB/8*)
Selective Tool
img010.jpg @ 25% (RGB/8*)
393.tif @ 33.3% (RGB/8*)
25%

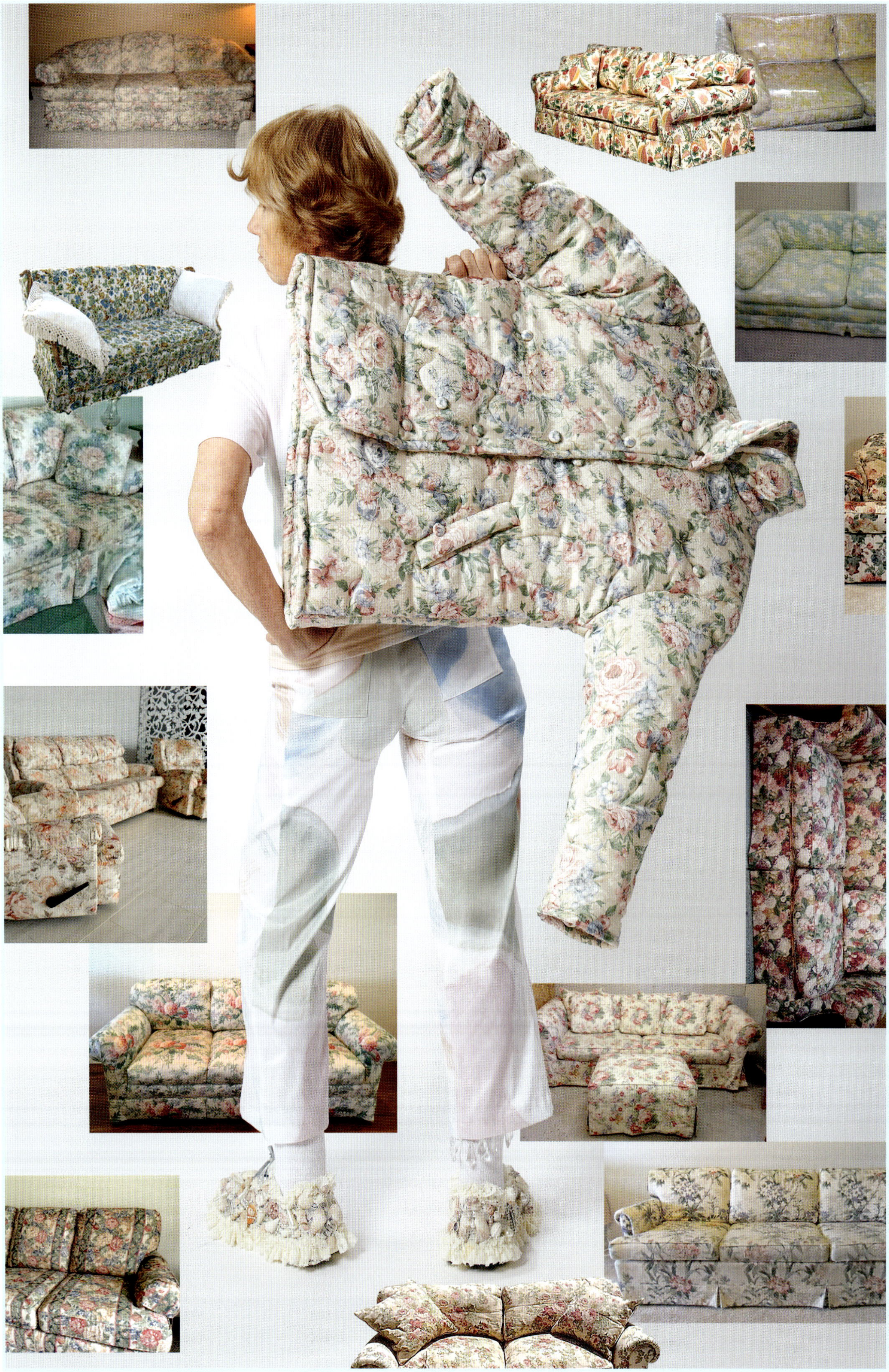

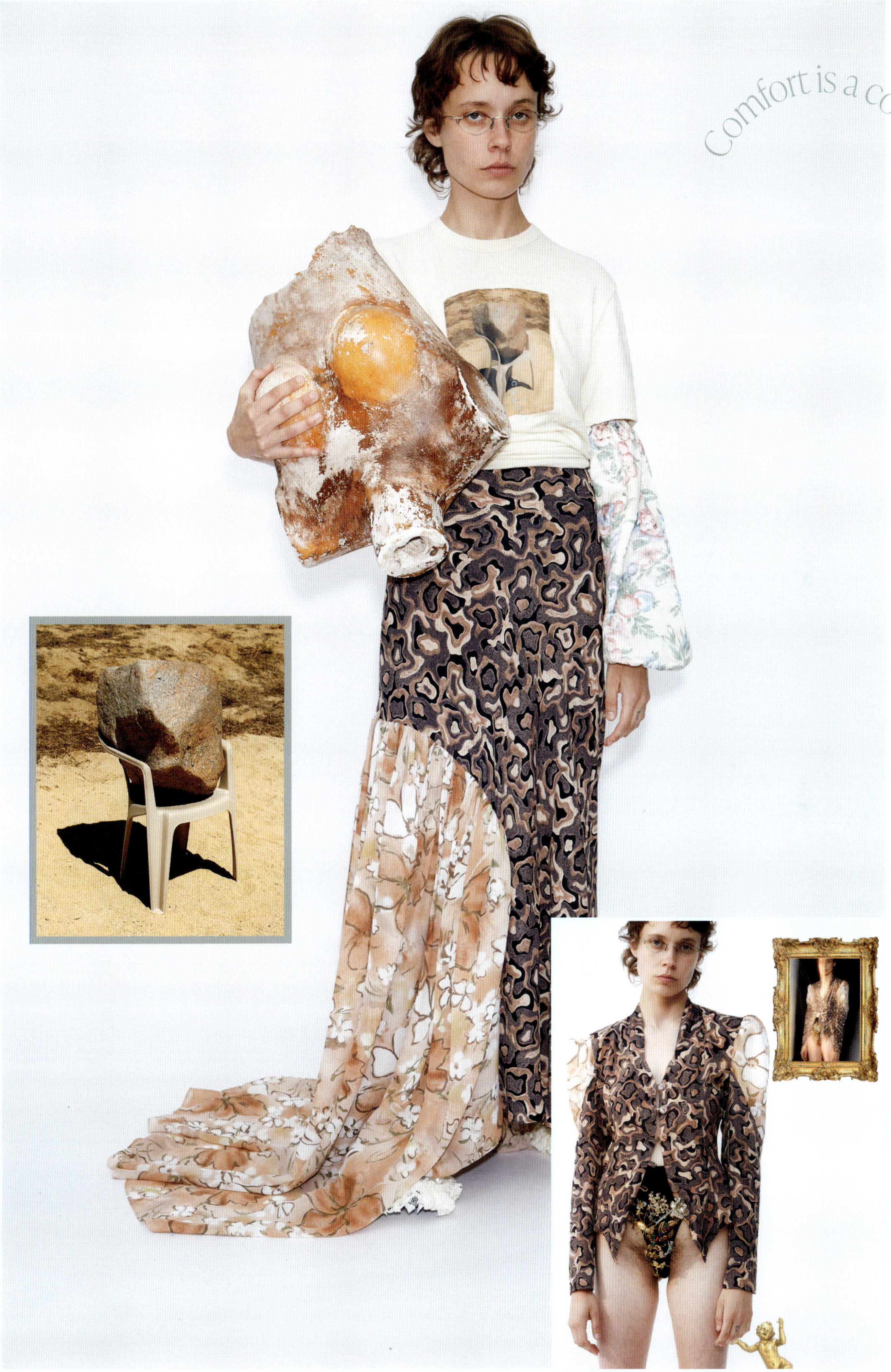

Comfort is a commodity.

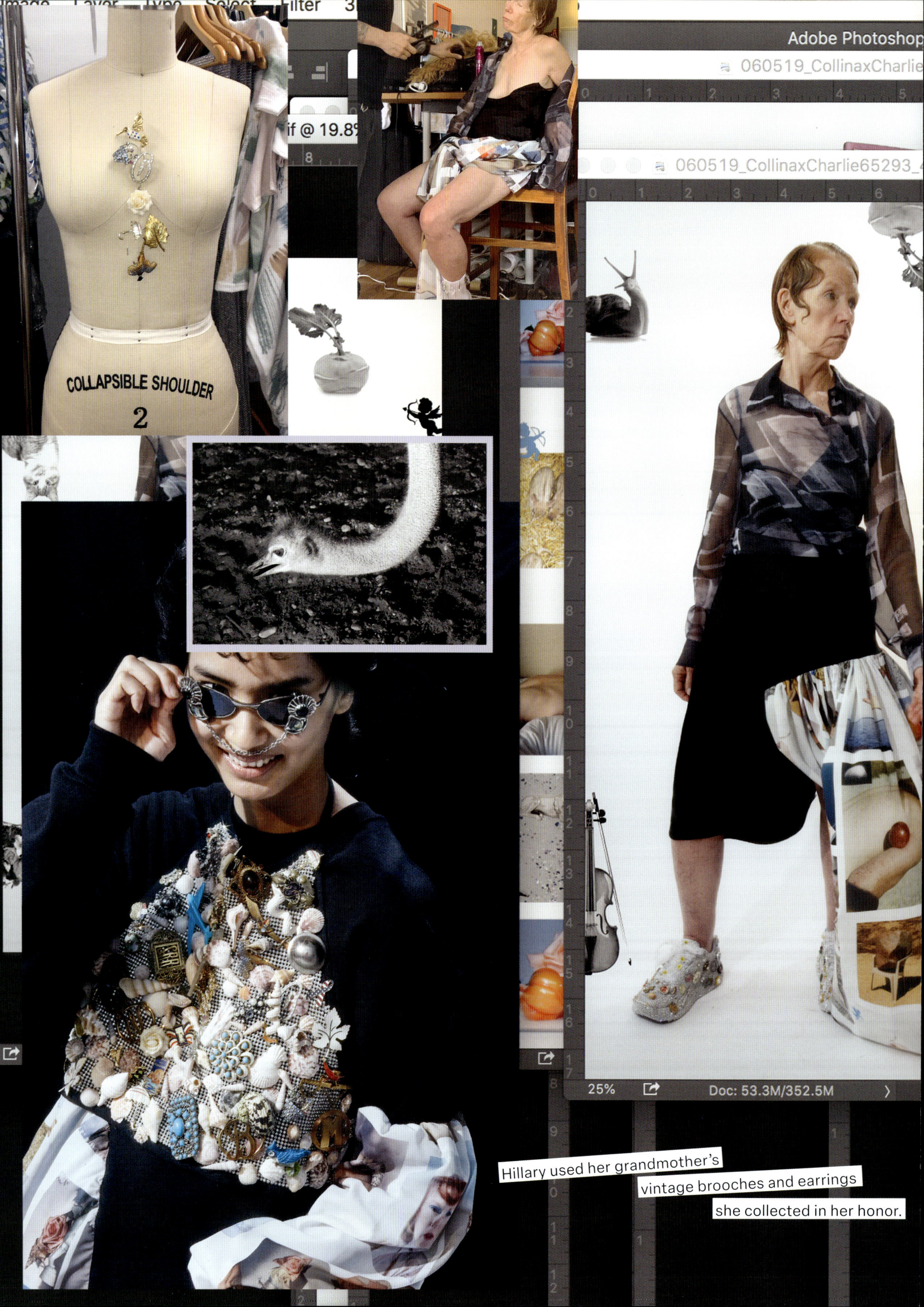

Hillary used her grandmother's vintage brooches and earrings she collected in her honor.

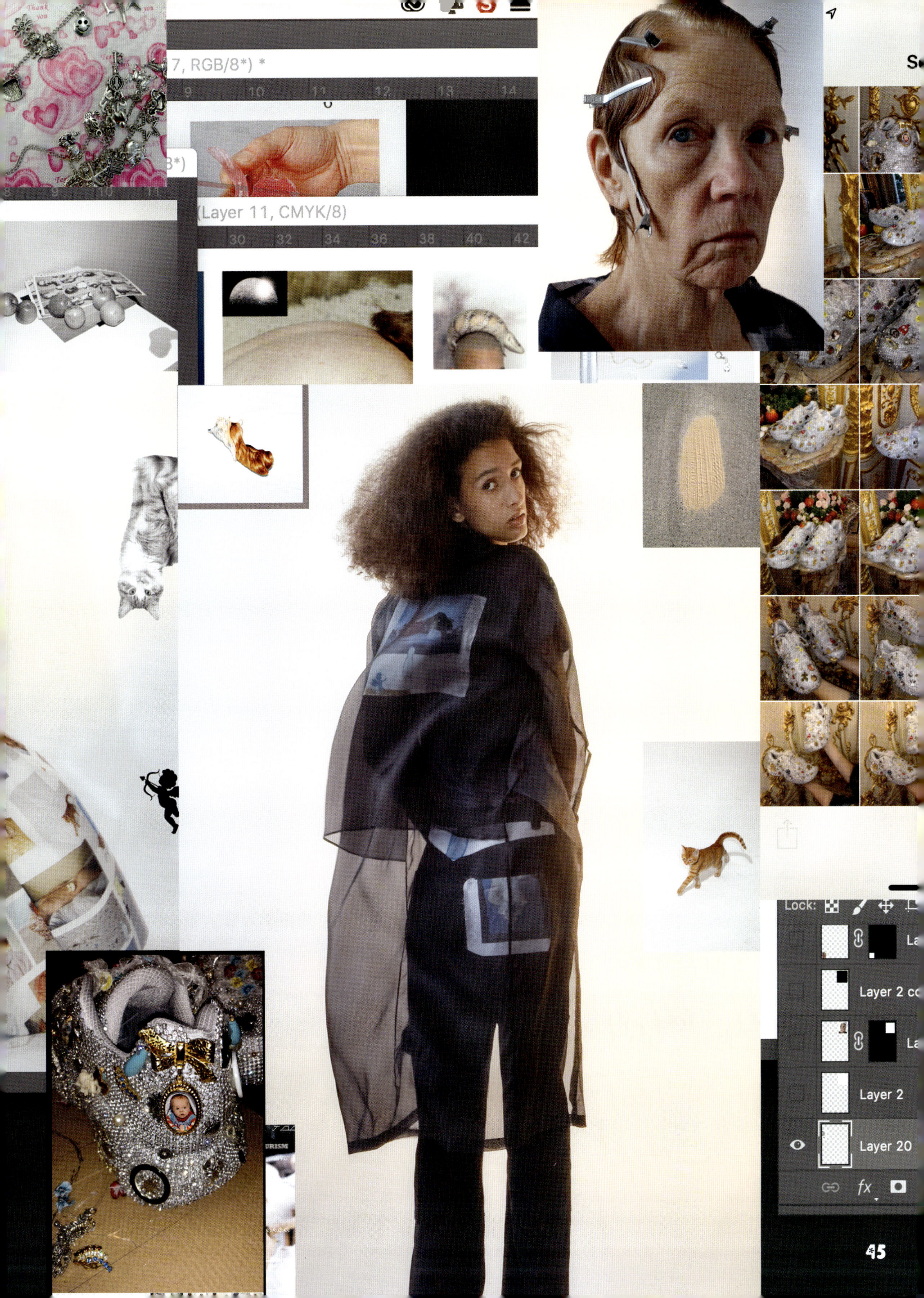
7, RGB/8*) *
(Layer 11, CMYK/8)
Lock:
Layer 2 co
Layer 2
Layer 20

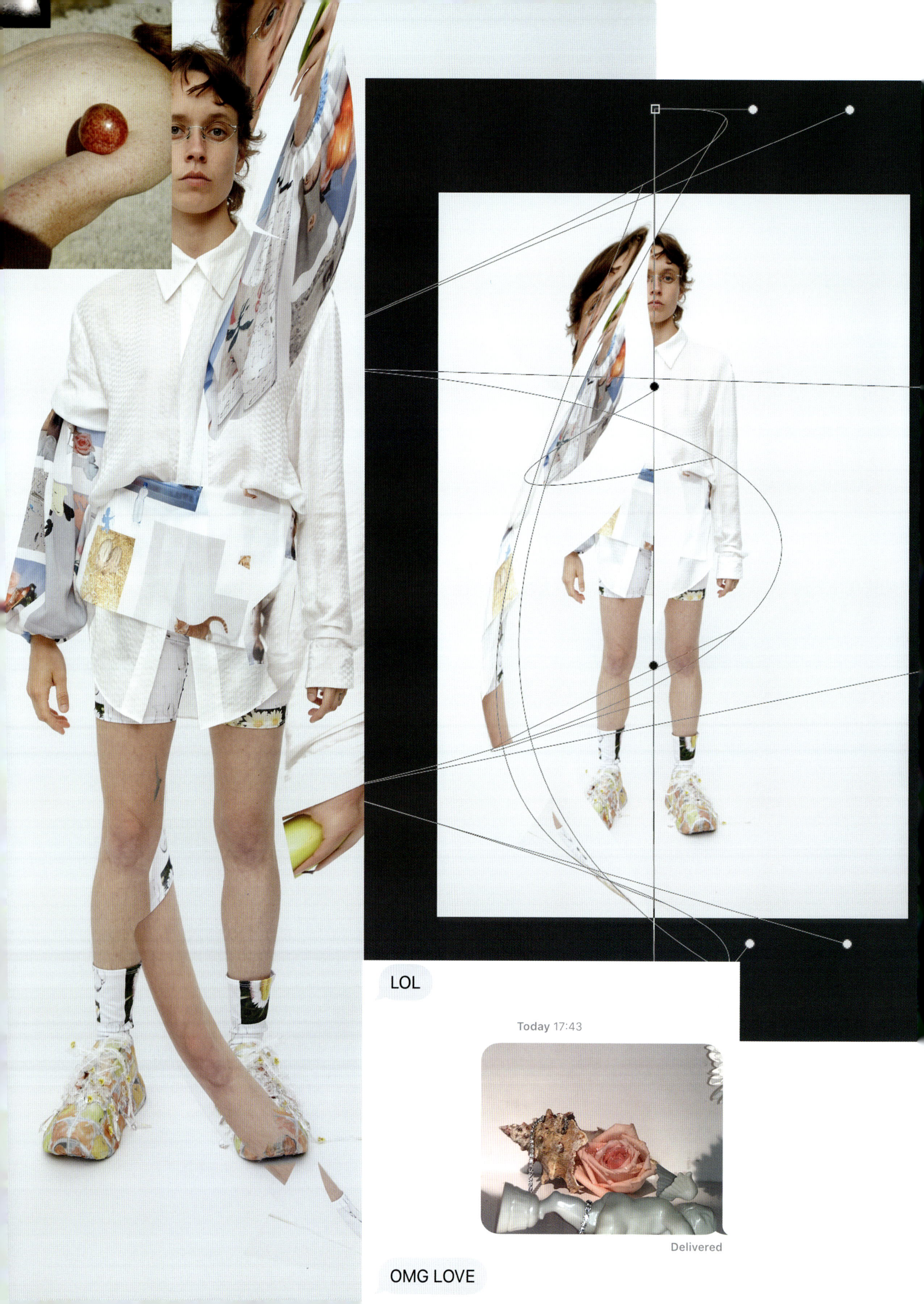
LOL
Today 17:43
Delivered
OMG LOVE

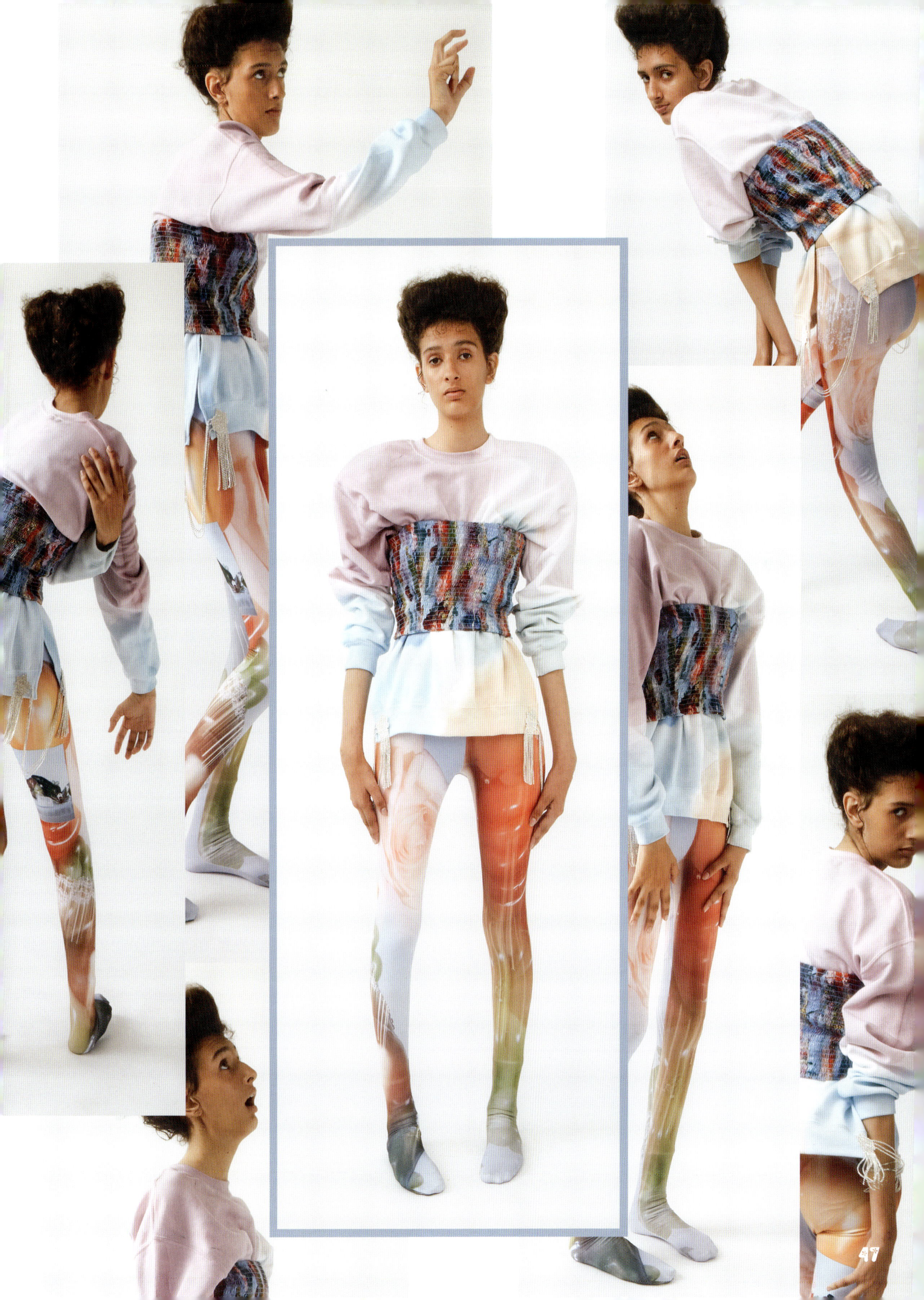

SPRING SUMMER 2020, THANK YOU VERY MUCH FOR HELPING ME

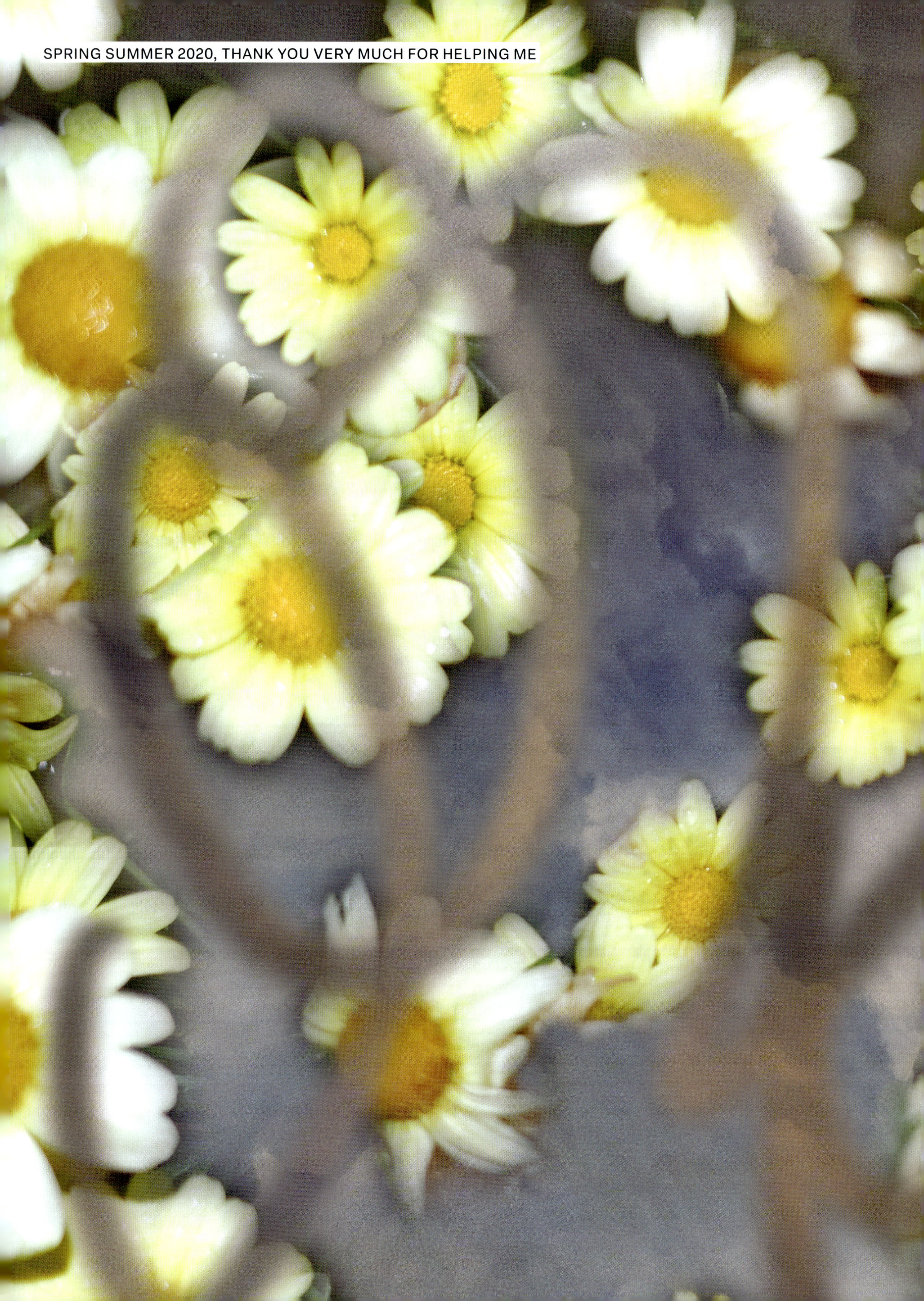

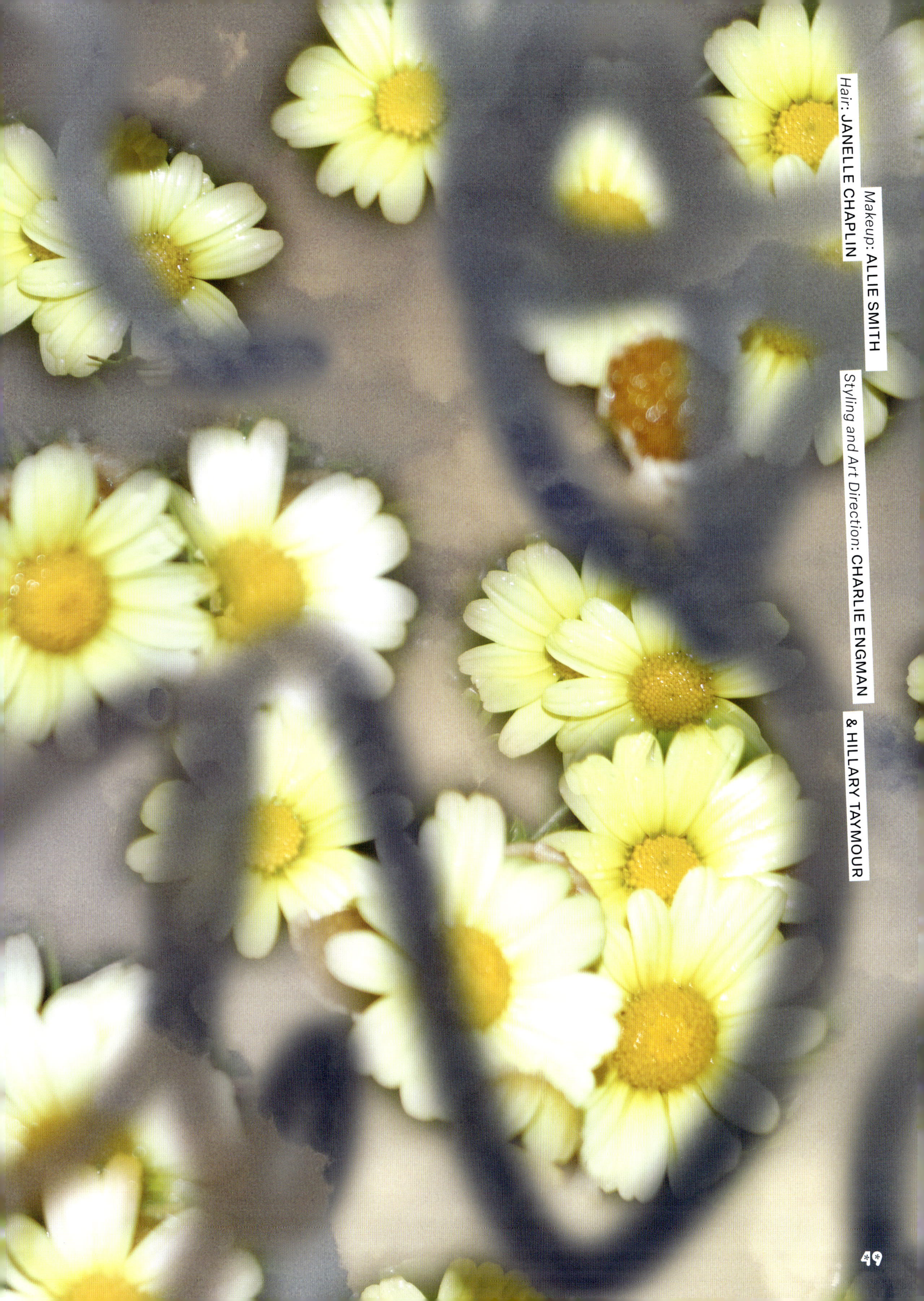

Makeup: ALLIE SMITH
Hair: JANELLE CHAPLIN
Styling and Art Direction: CHARLIE ENGMAN & HILLARY TAYMOUR

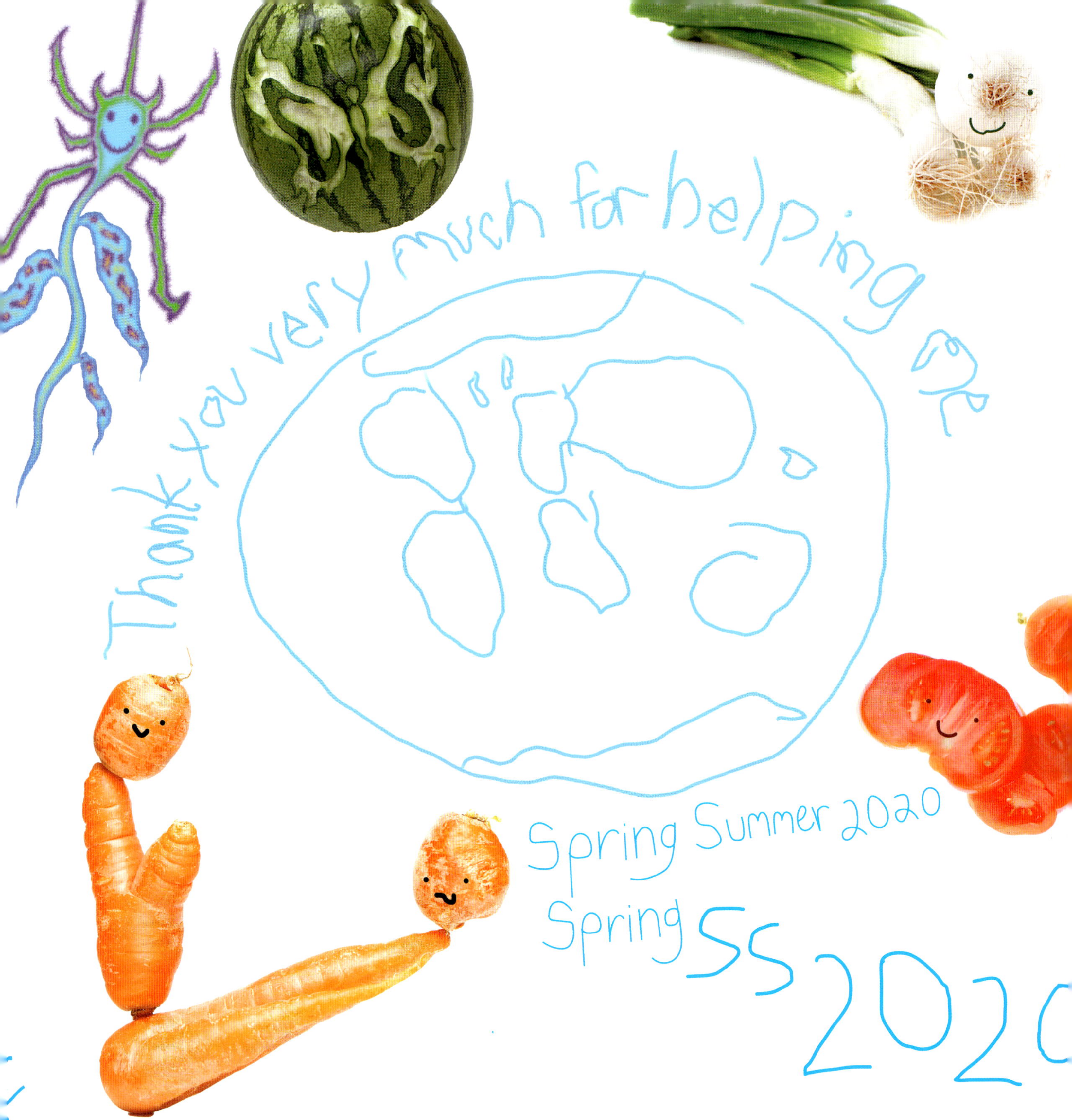

This season, we invited everyone to the ***Collina Strada Farmers Market.*** Stocked with produce deemed by the mainstream food system as too unique for consumption, we served perfectly edible treats that would otherwise have been treated as waste. Models frolicked through the bounty of resuscitated produce, while ***Zsela crooned.*** Oranges were offered to the audience, while dancing and consensual makeouts ensued. ***Tei Shi*** performed her song "Red Light" while spectators loaded up on crooked carrots. Each member of the audience was also given a ***reusable Collina grocery bag,*** so they could take home as many of the rescued morsels as they could carry.

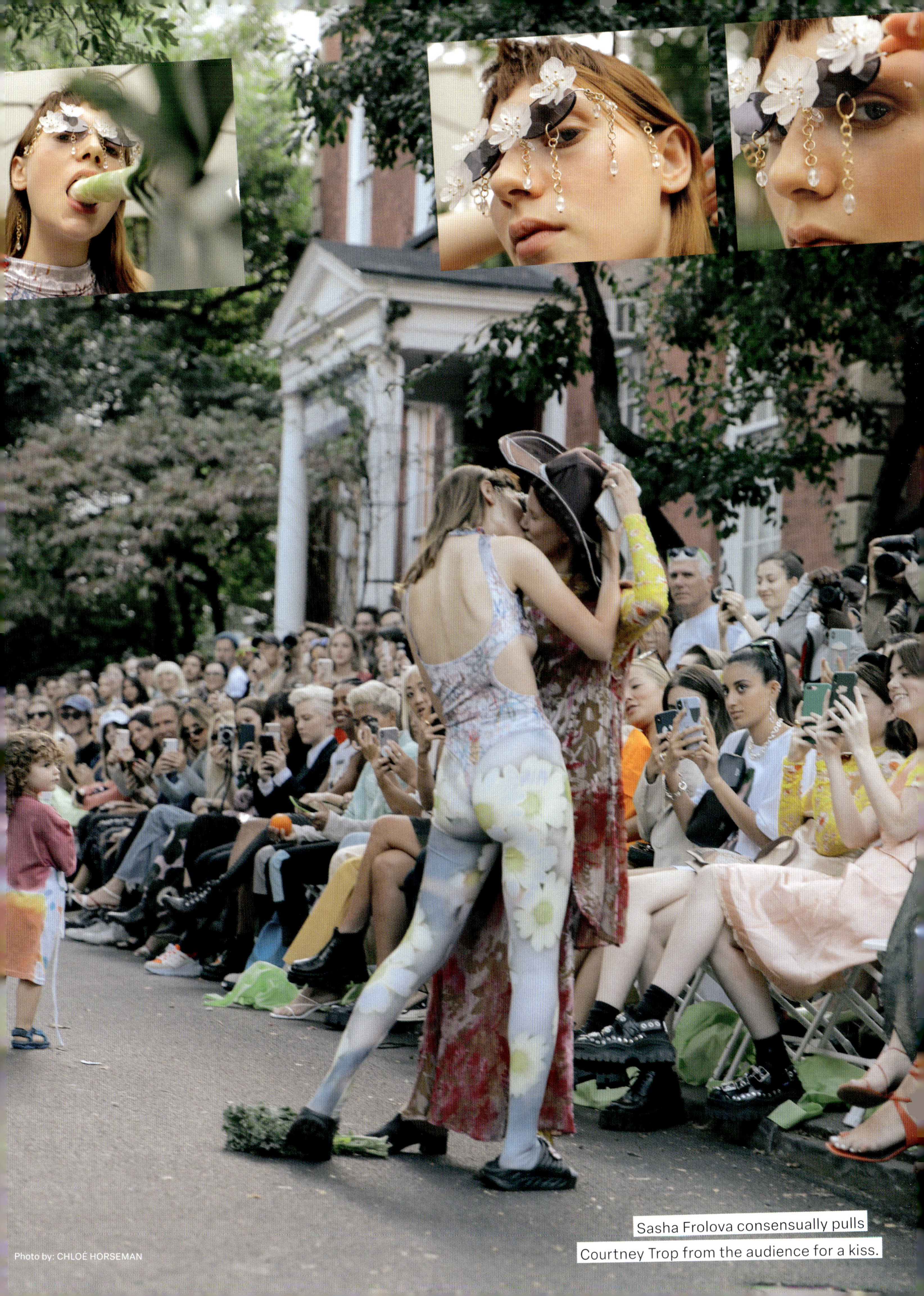

Sasha Frolova consensually pulls Courtney Trop from the audience for a kiss.

Photo by: CHLOÉ HORSEMAN

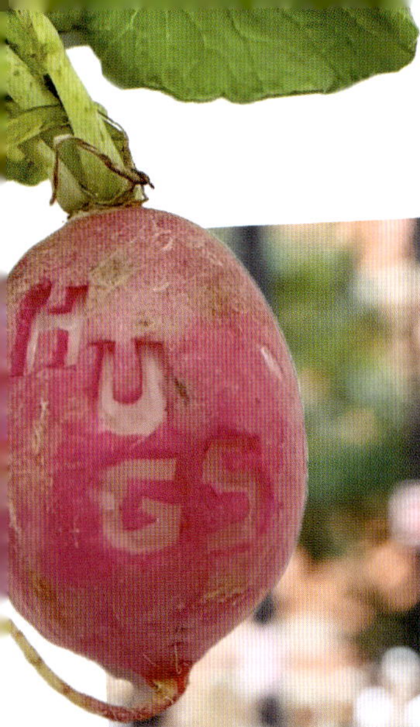

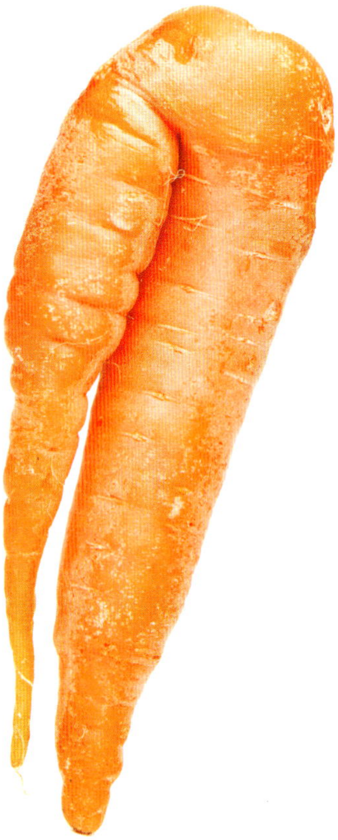

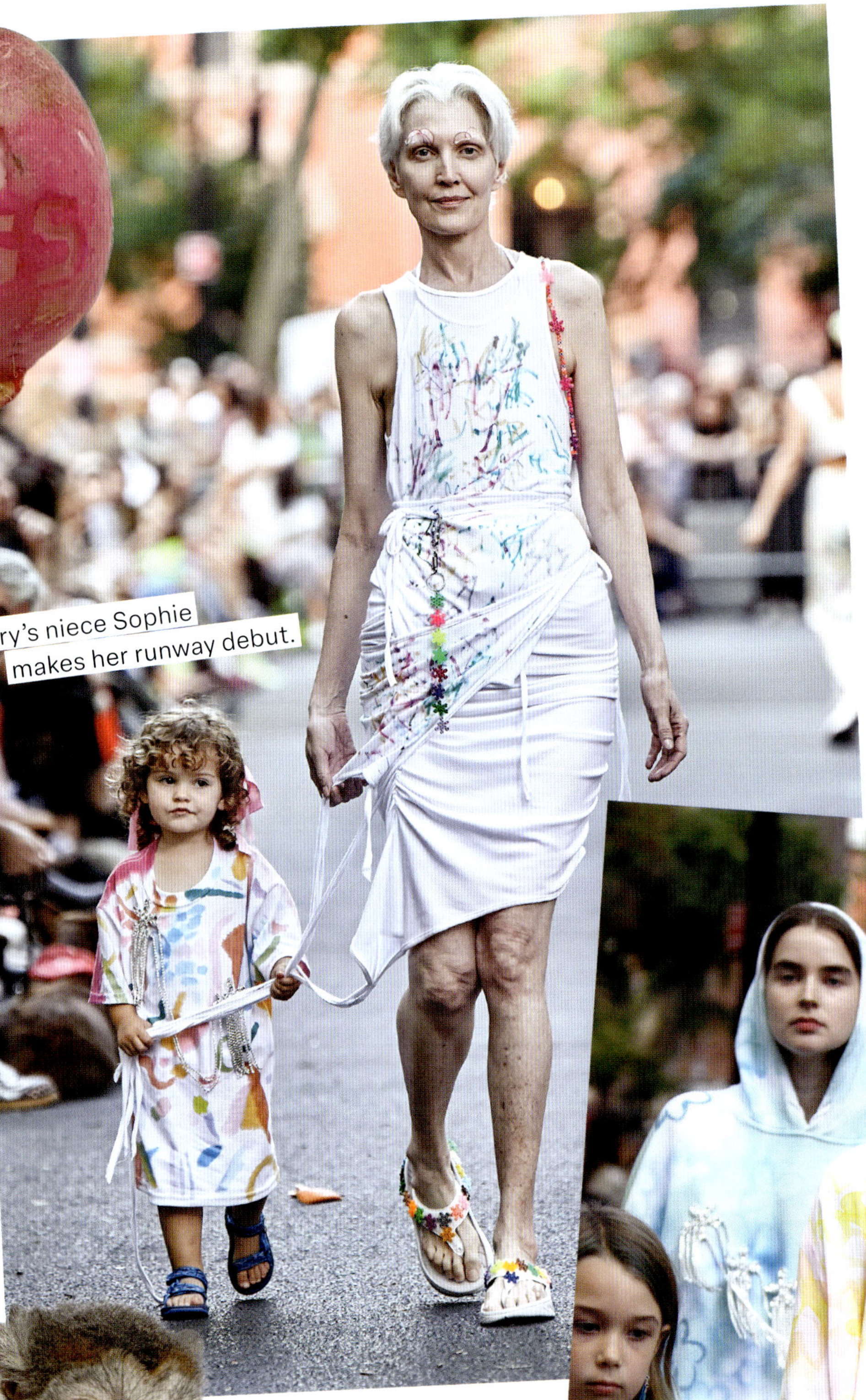

Hillary's niece Sophie makes her runway debut.

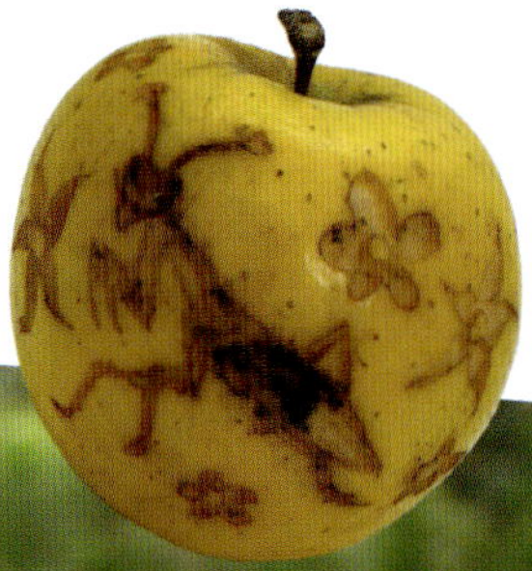

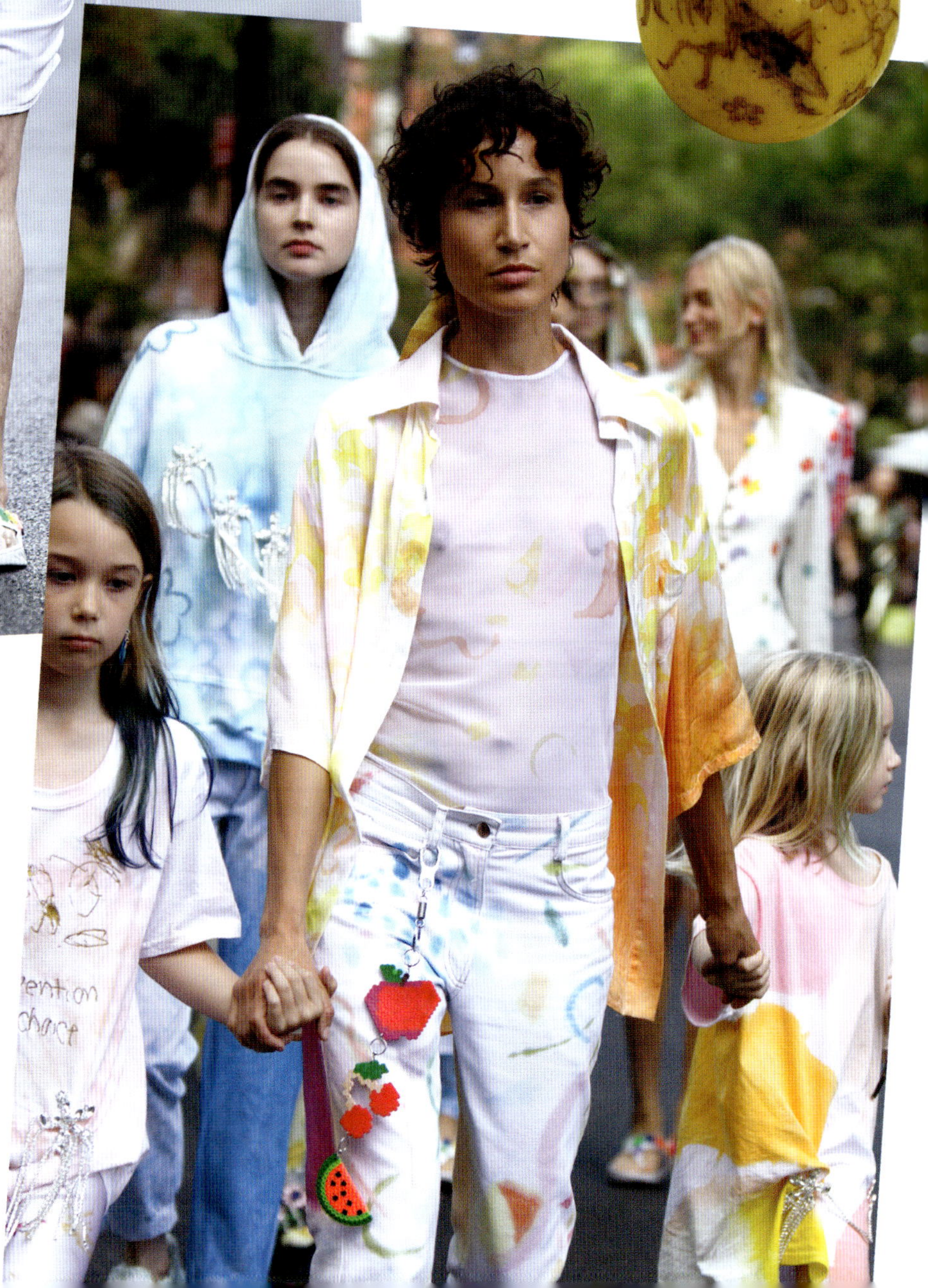

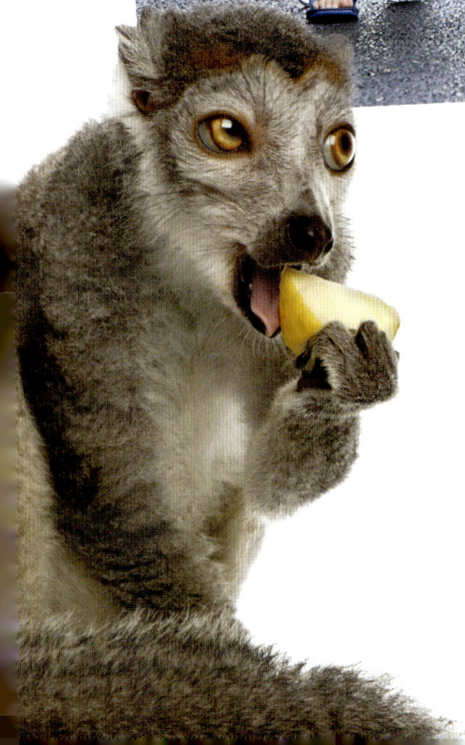

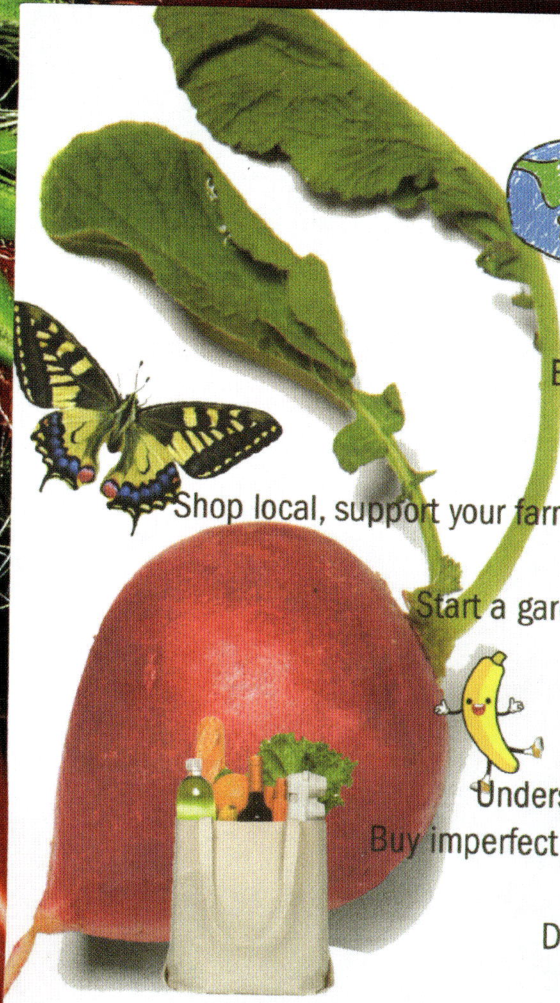
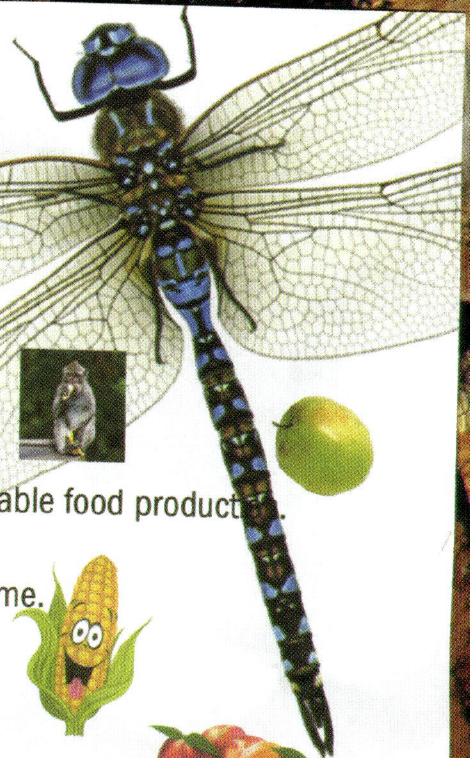

WAYS TO HELP ME

Eat less meat. Eat more plants.

Shop local, support your farmers market and small-scale sustainable food producers.

Start a garden, grow your own food. Cook at home.

Understand where your food comes from.
Buy imperfect produce that would otherwise go to waste.

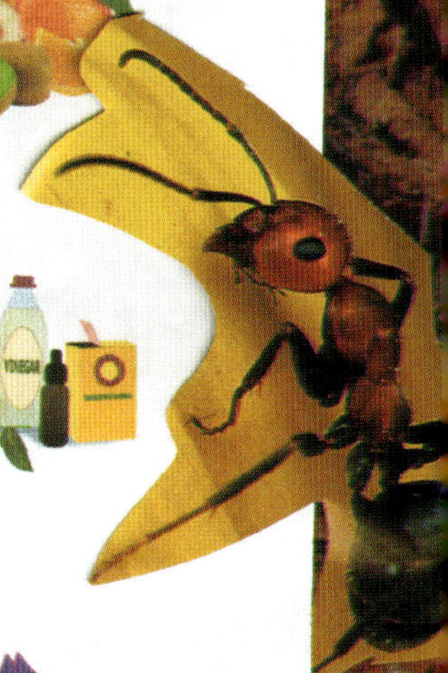

Don't accept single-use plastic.
Always bring a bag.
Avoid disposable anything.

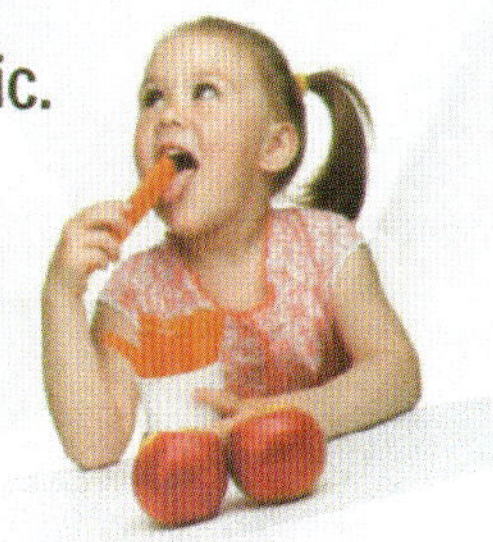

Learn to compost.

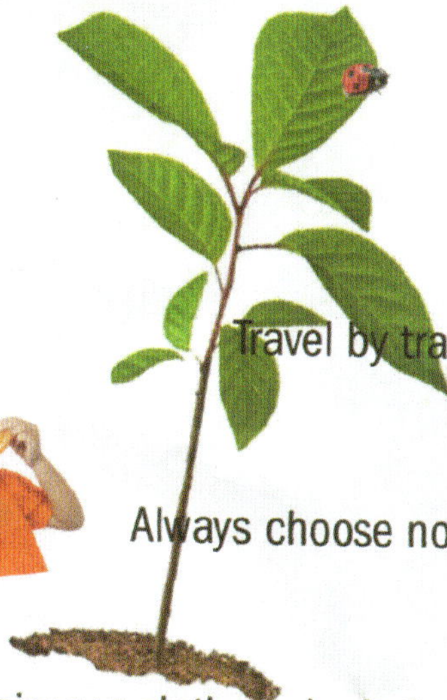

Travel by transit, ride a bike- don't drive a gas-powered car.

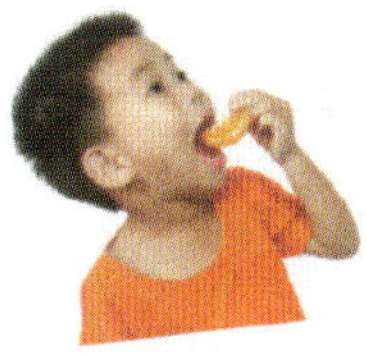

Always choose non-toxic chemicals for cleaning at home and at work.

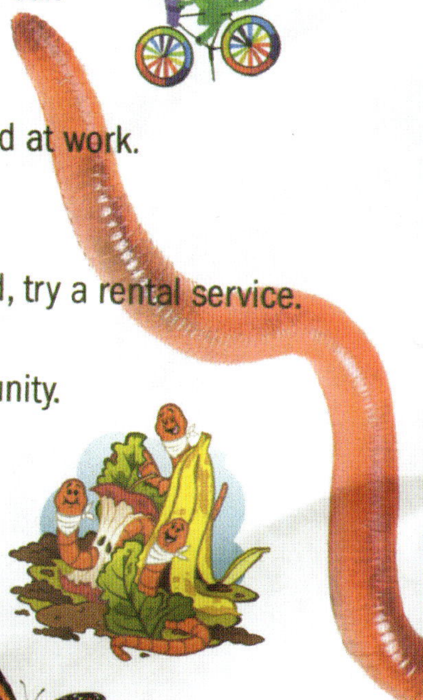

Repair your clothes, don't throw them away. Buy vintage or second hand, try a rental service.

Volunteer for clean-ups, impact your immediate community.

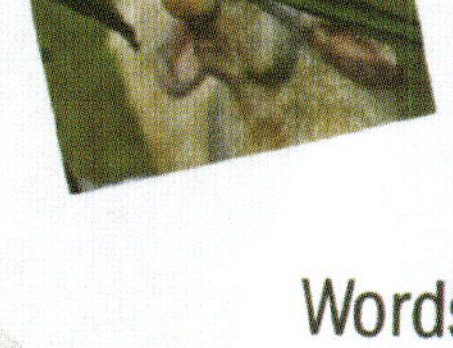

Plant a tree- plant many trees.

Words by Céline Semaan of Slow Factory

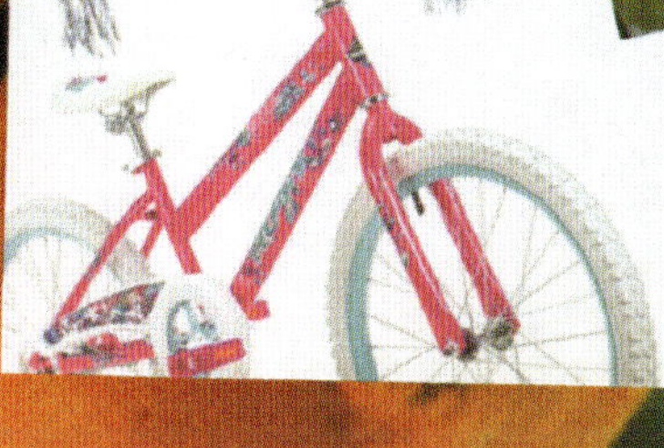
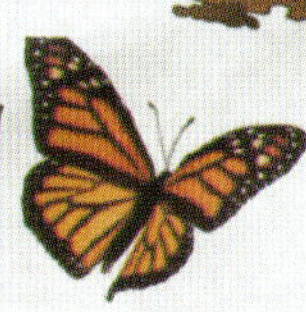

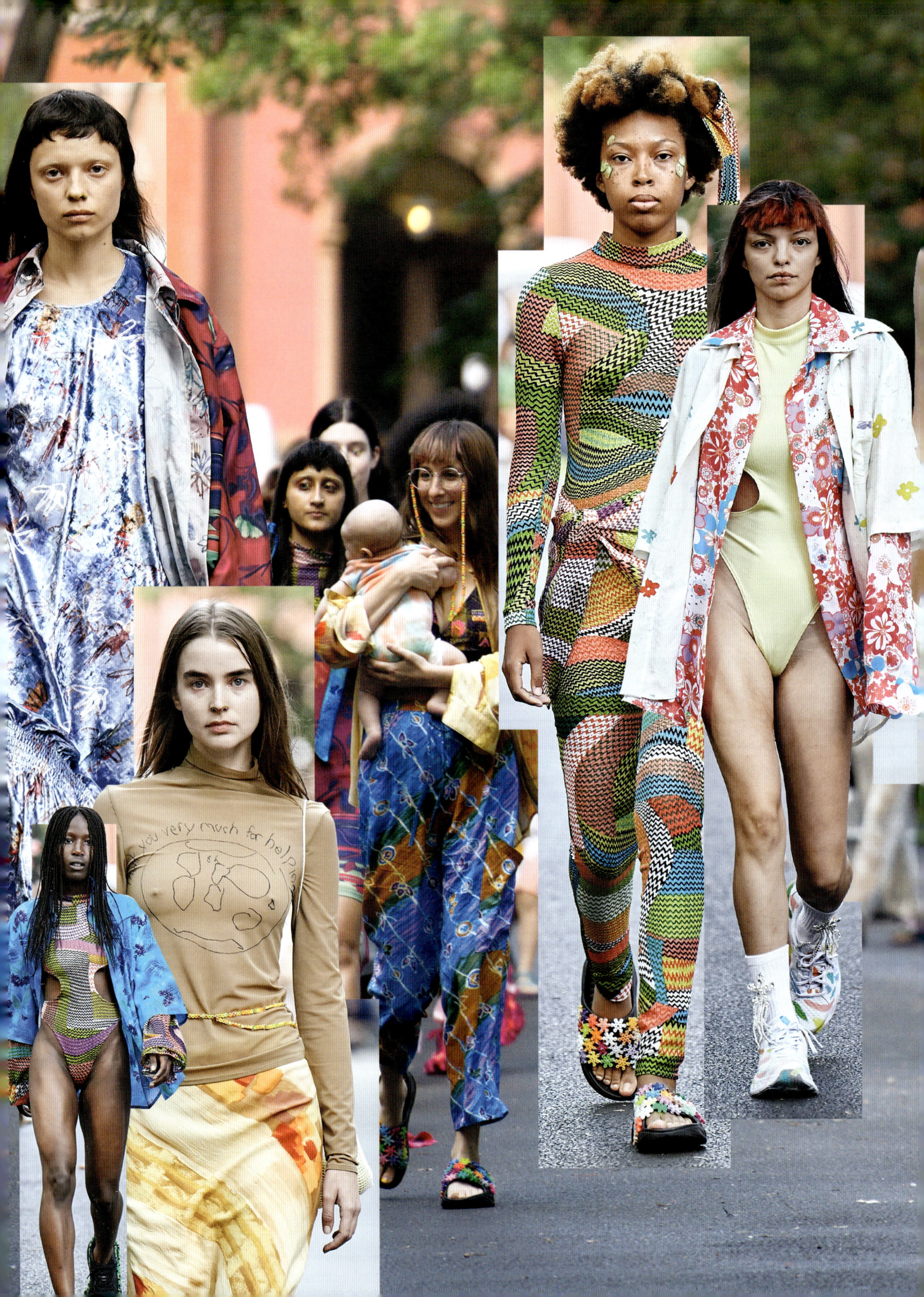
you very much for help

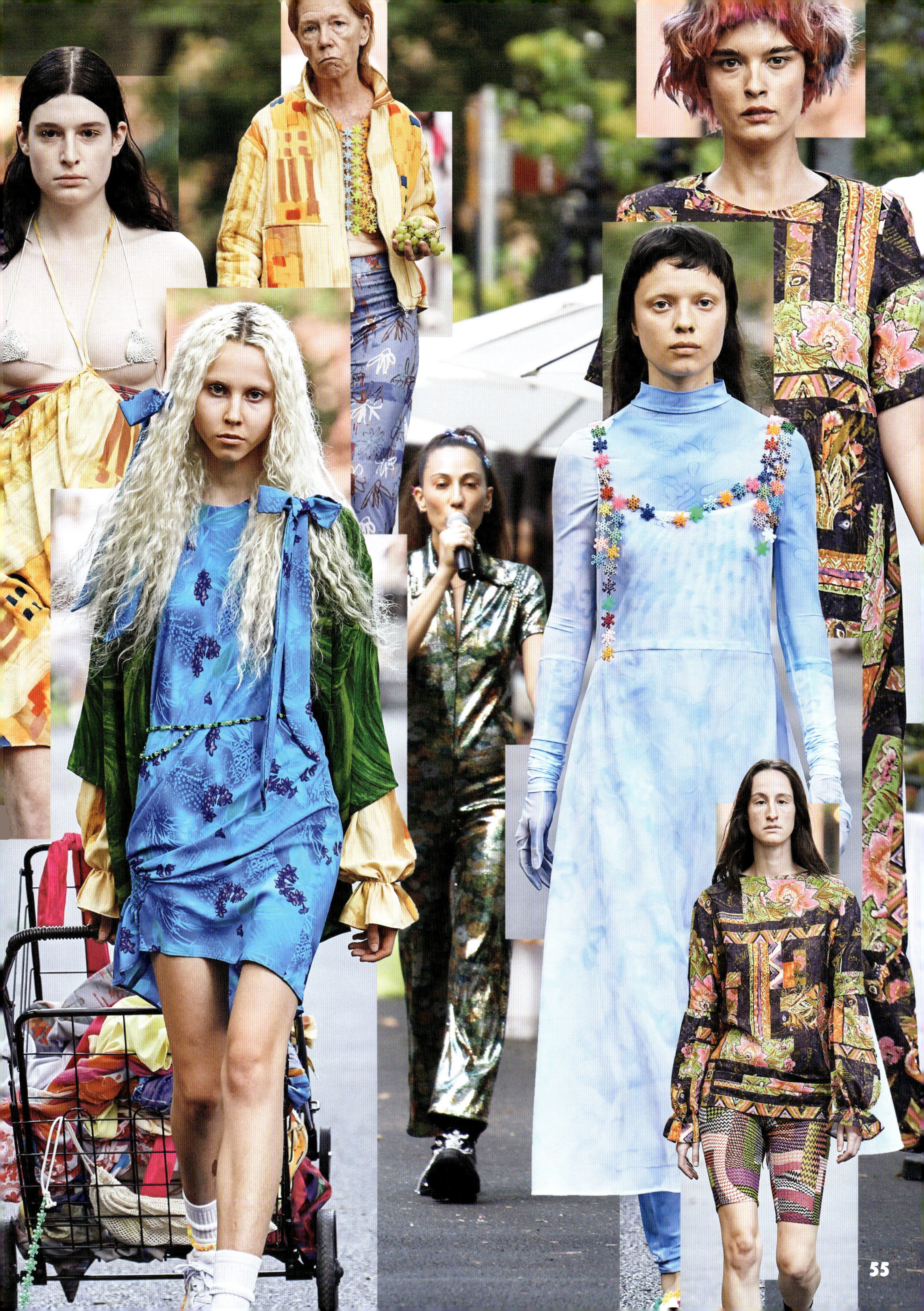

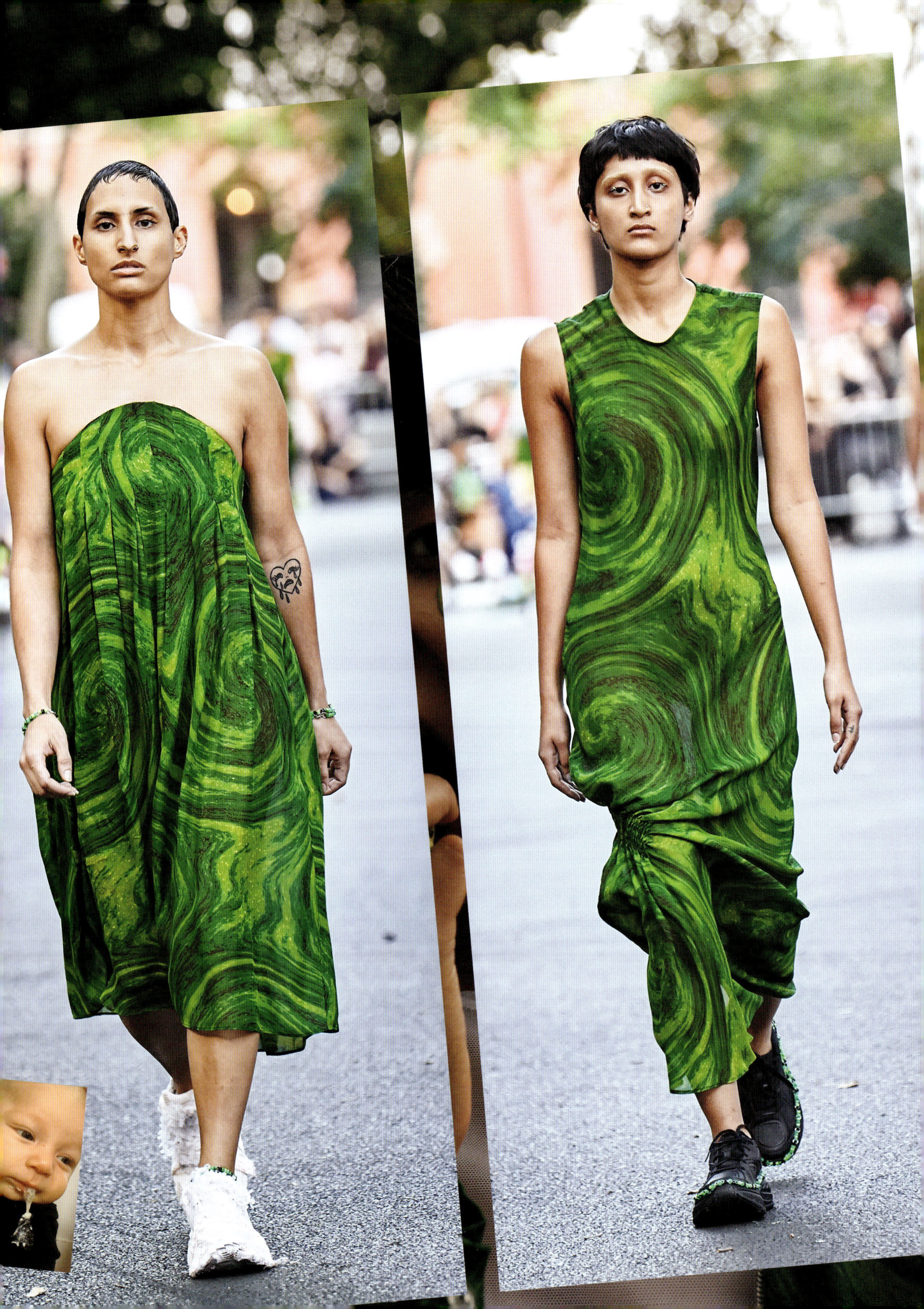

Fruit and veggies are so very nice:
they are good for skin and good for eyes.

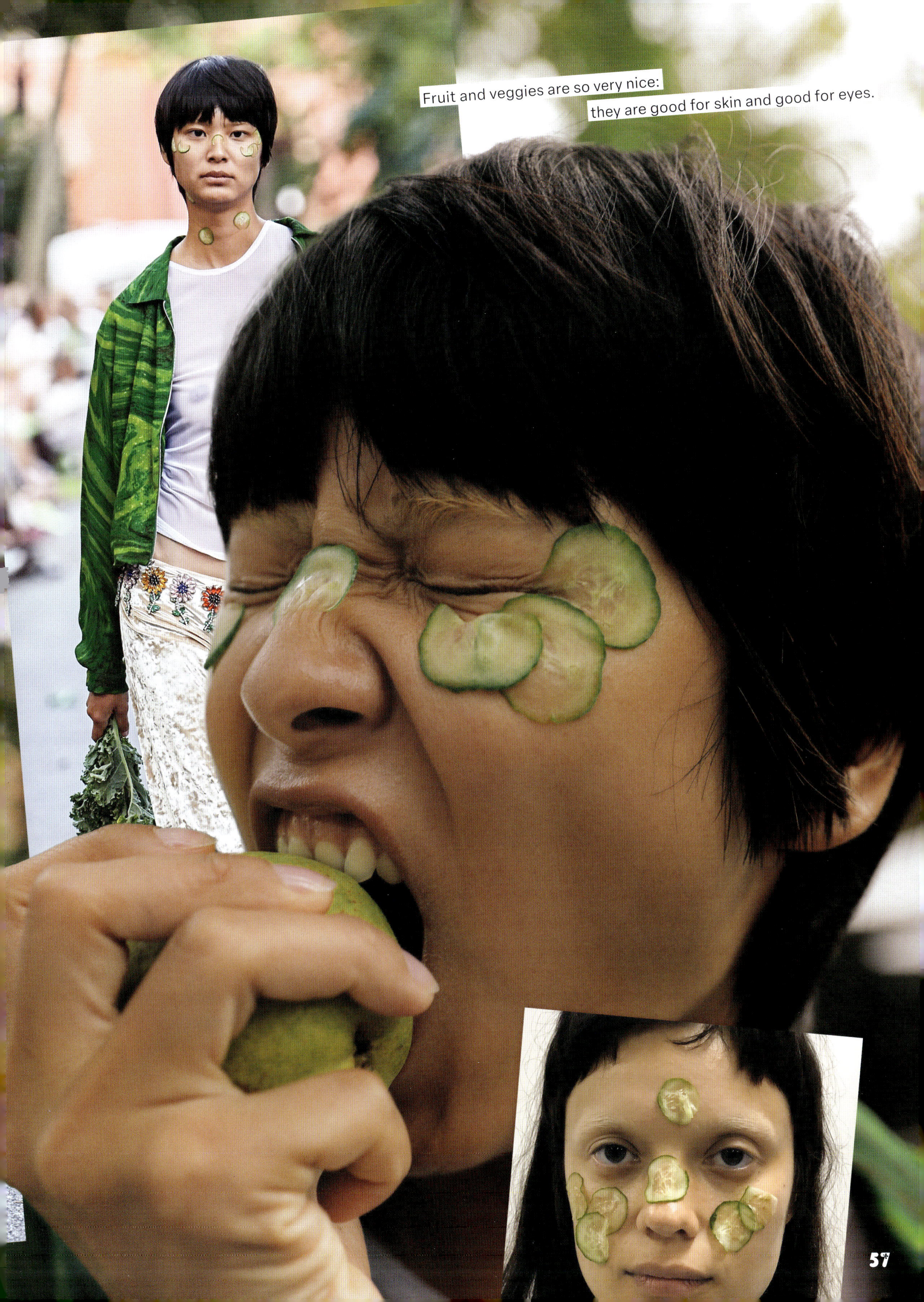

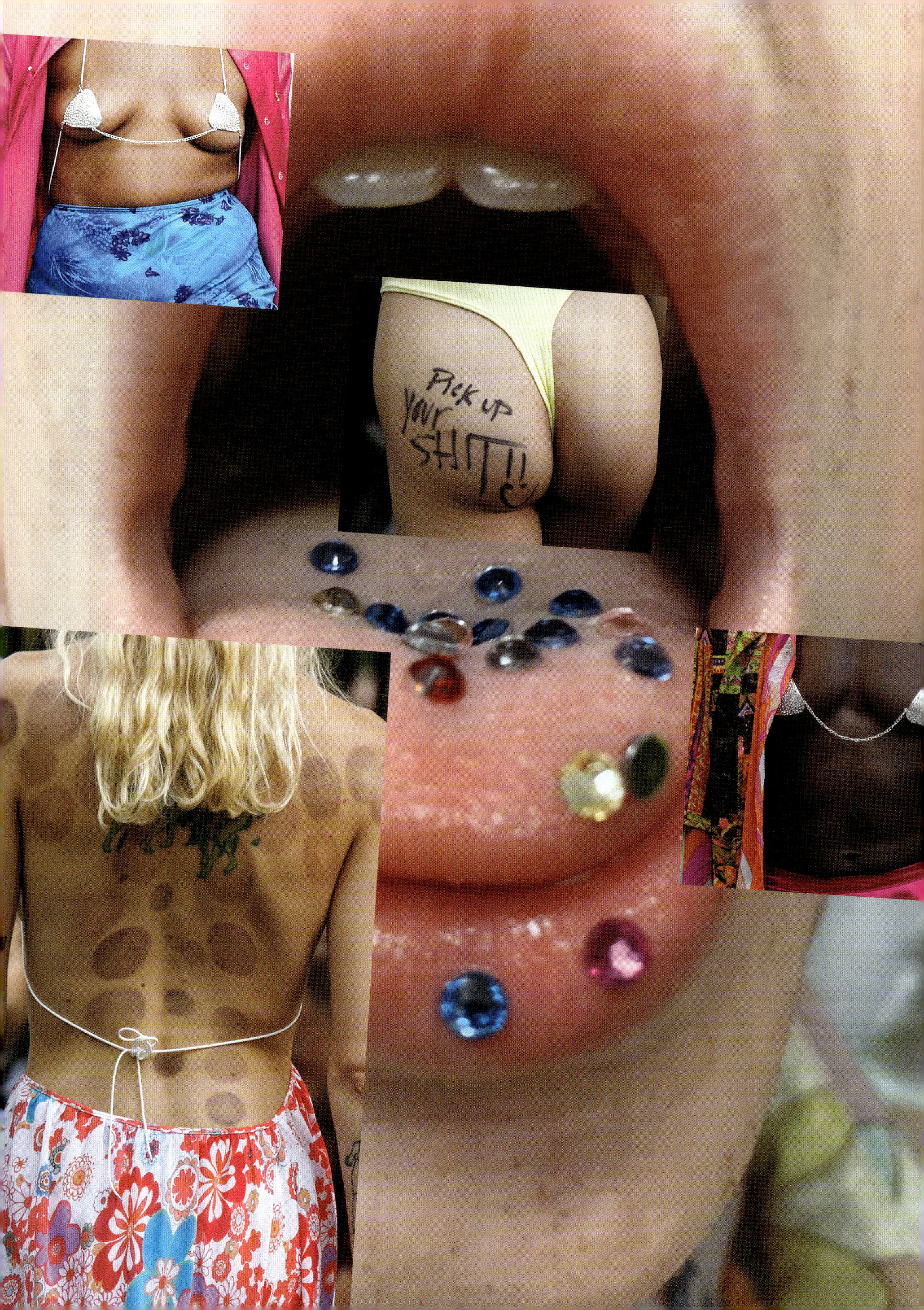
Pick up
your
SHIT!!

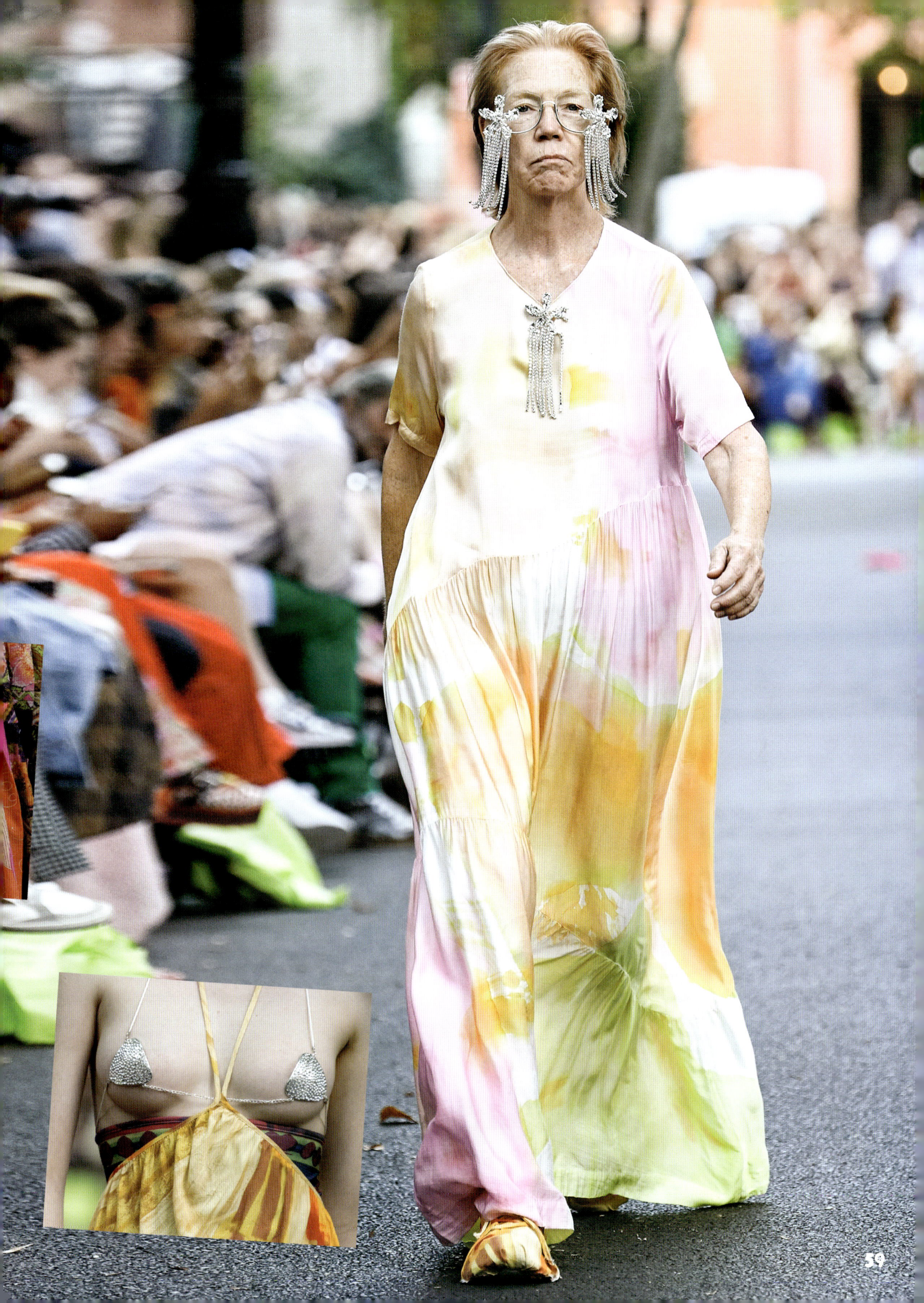

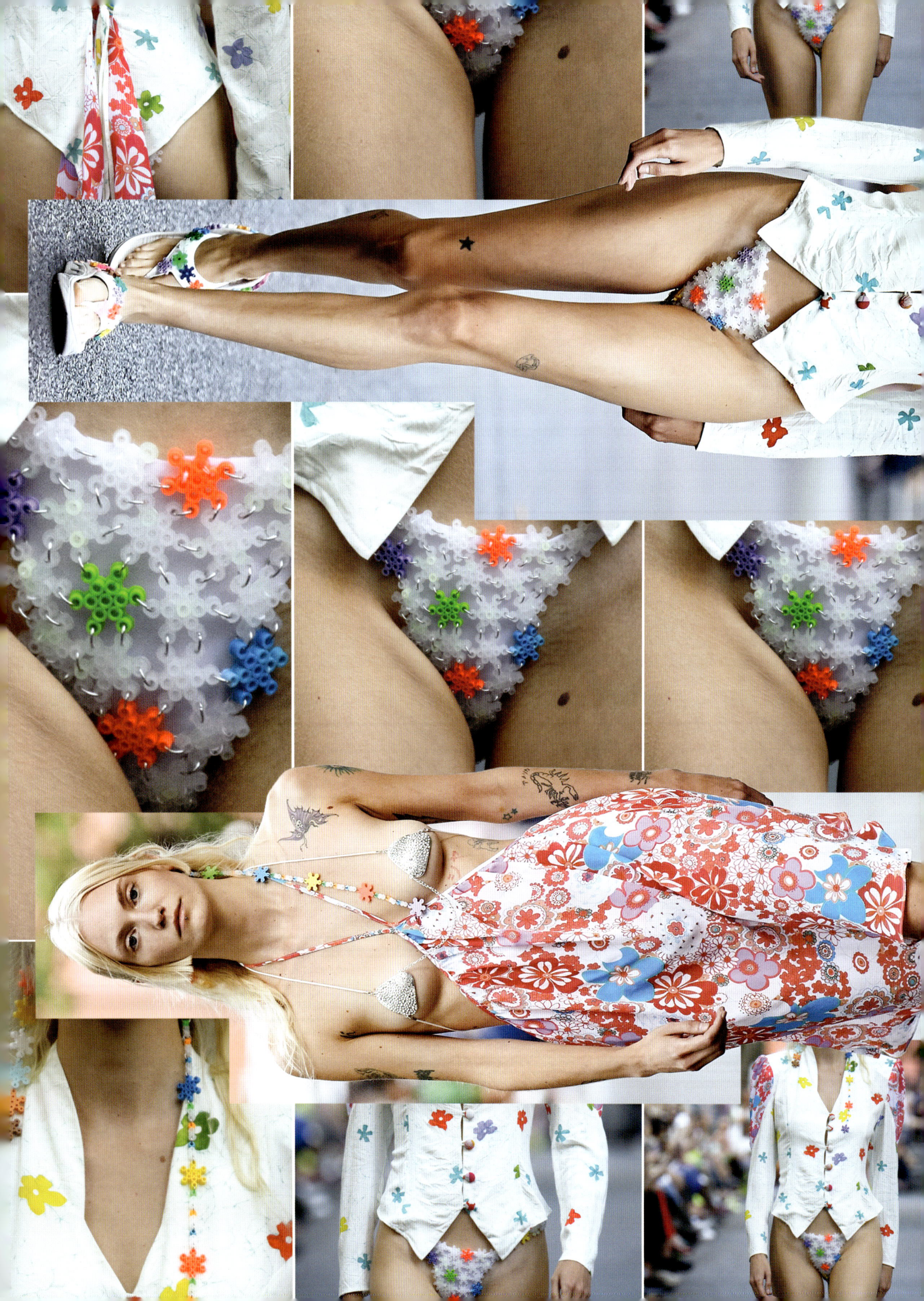

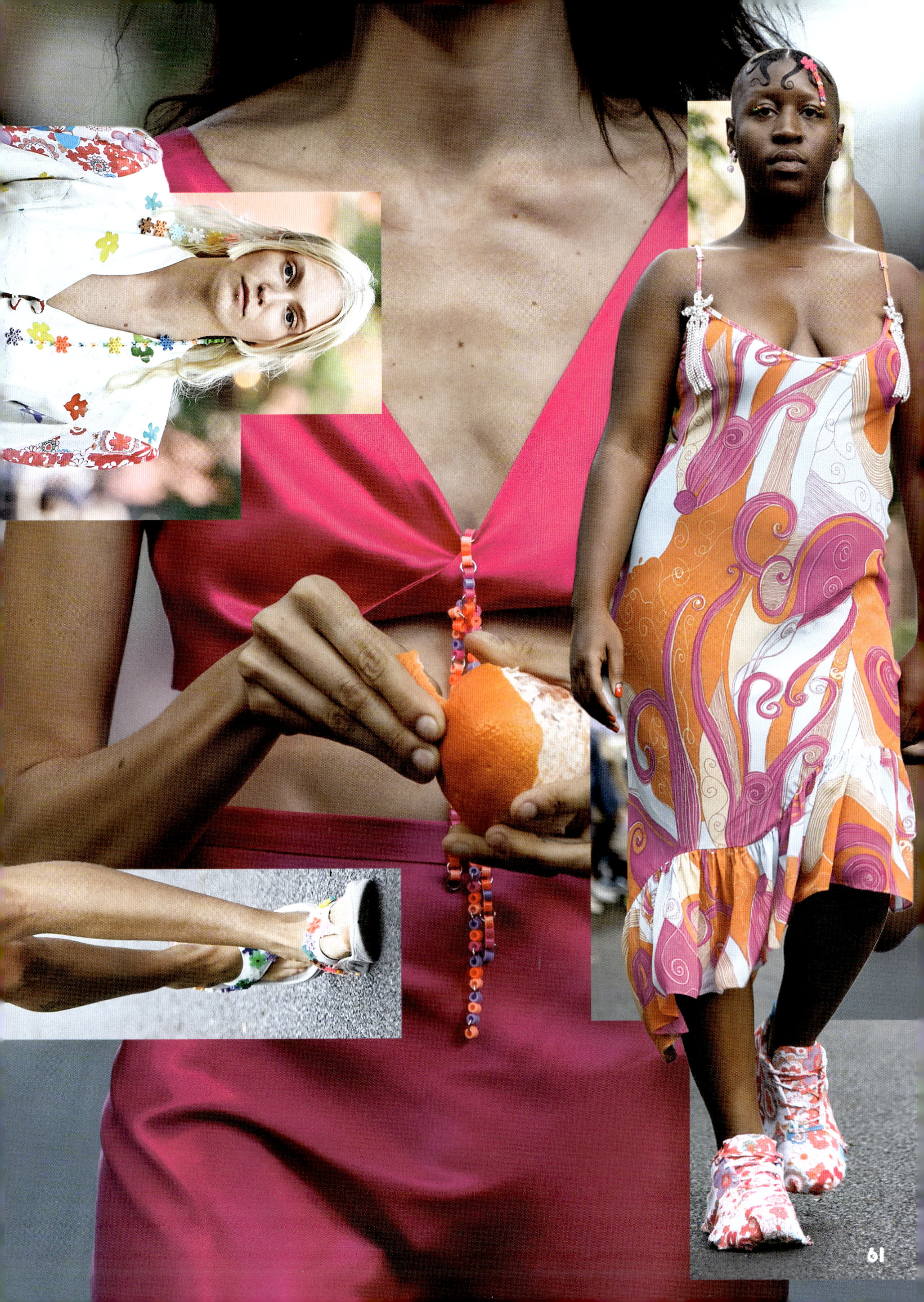

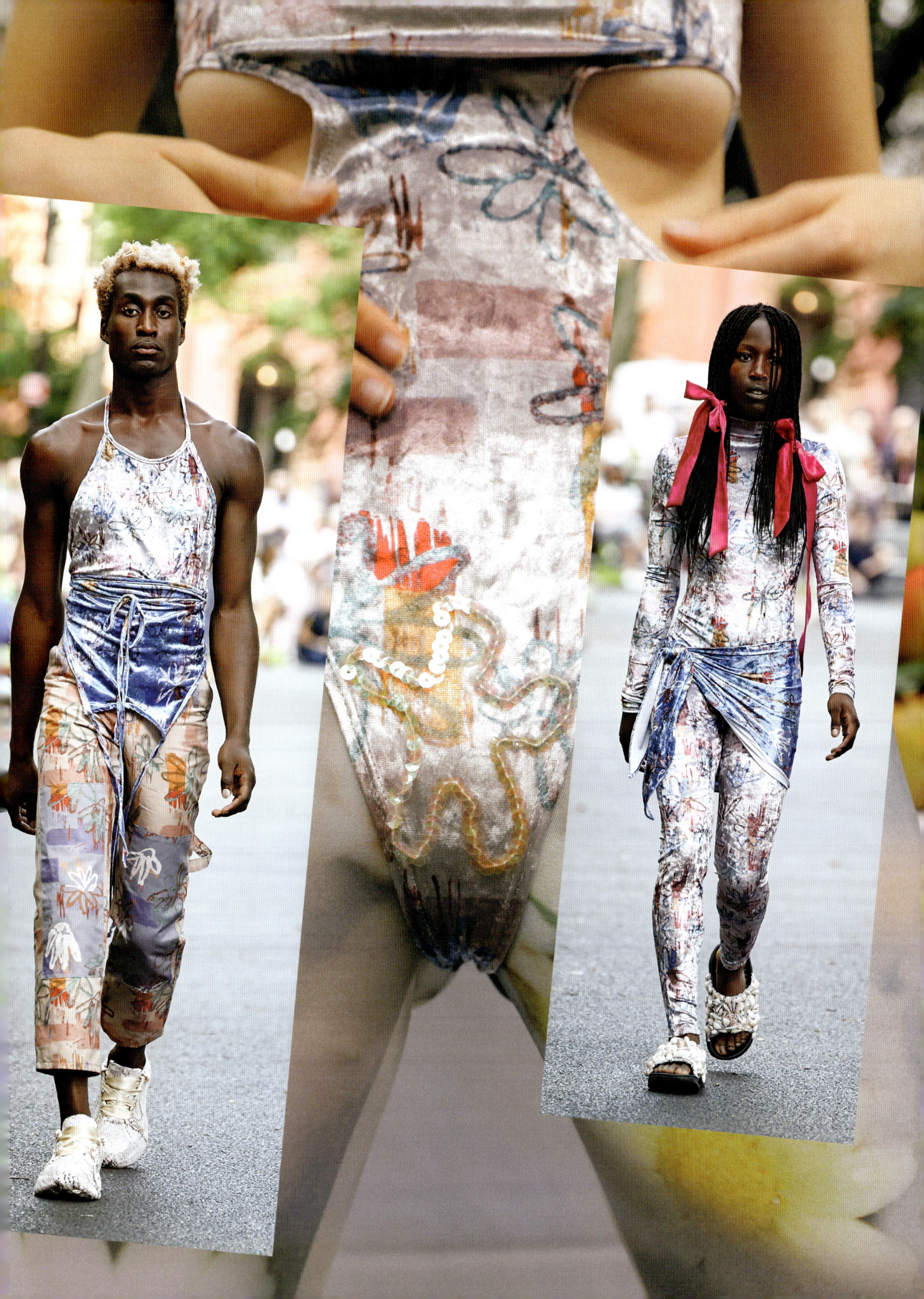

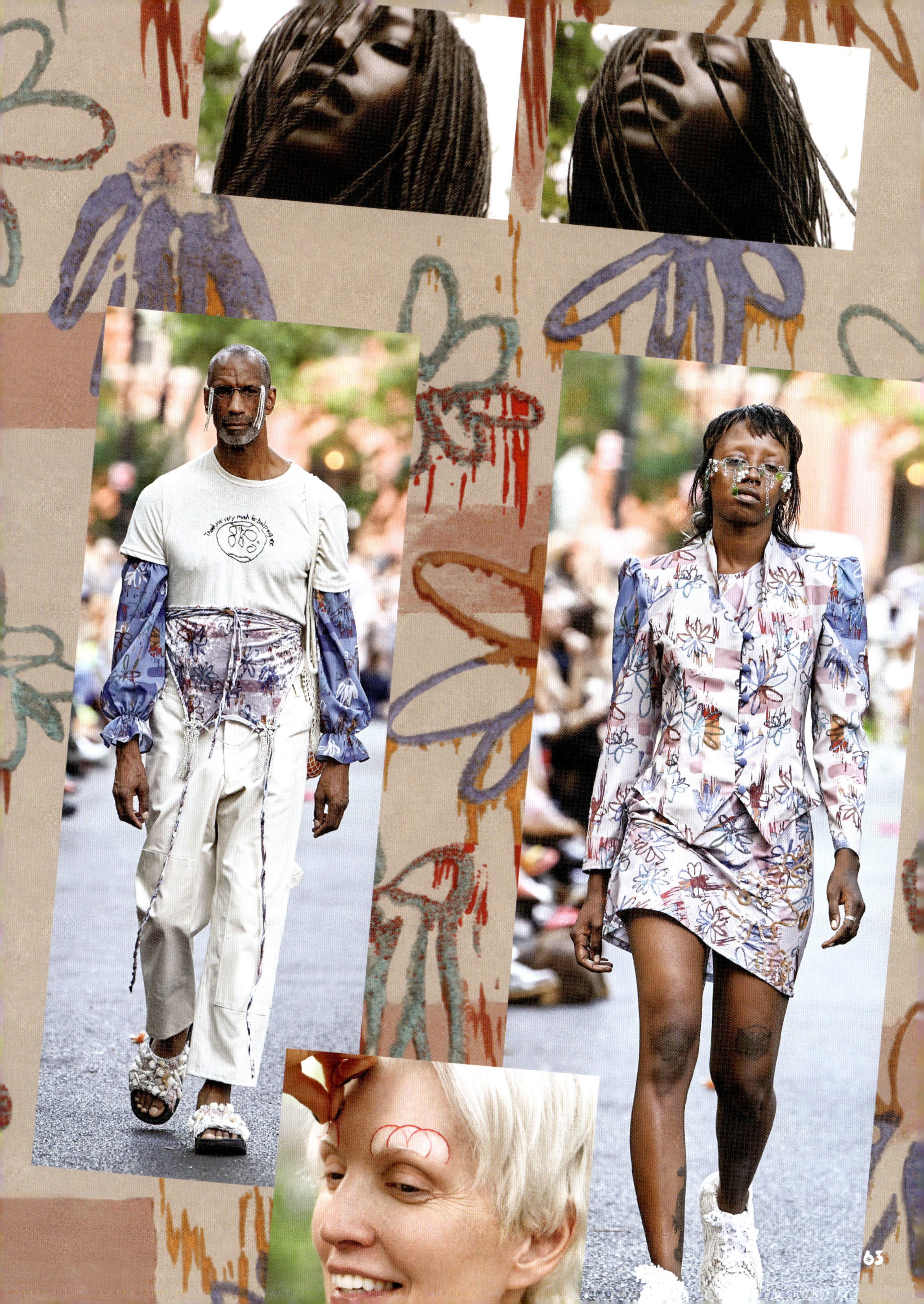

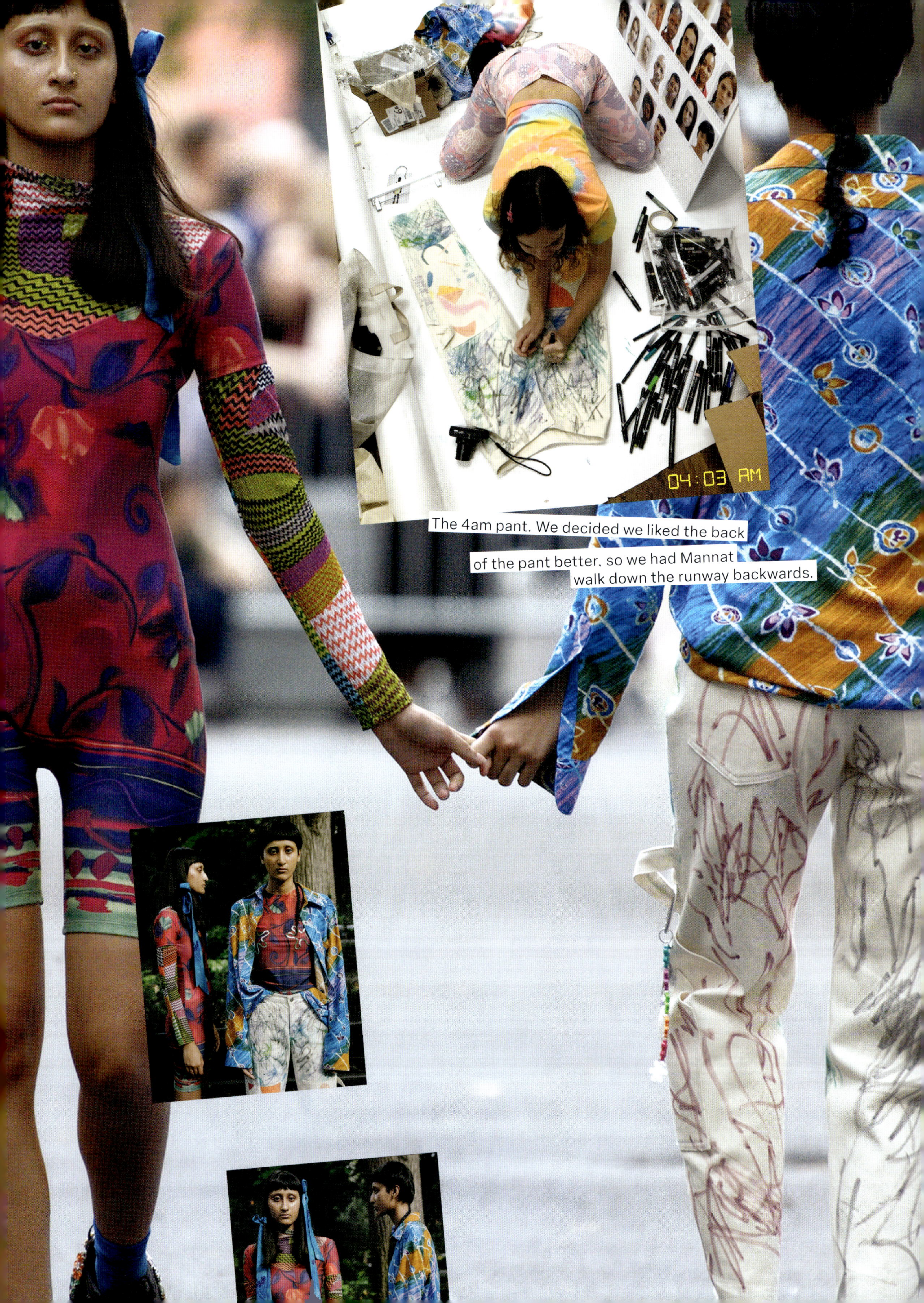

The 4am pant. We decided we liked the back of the pant better, so we had Mannat walk down the runway backwards.

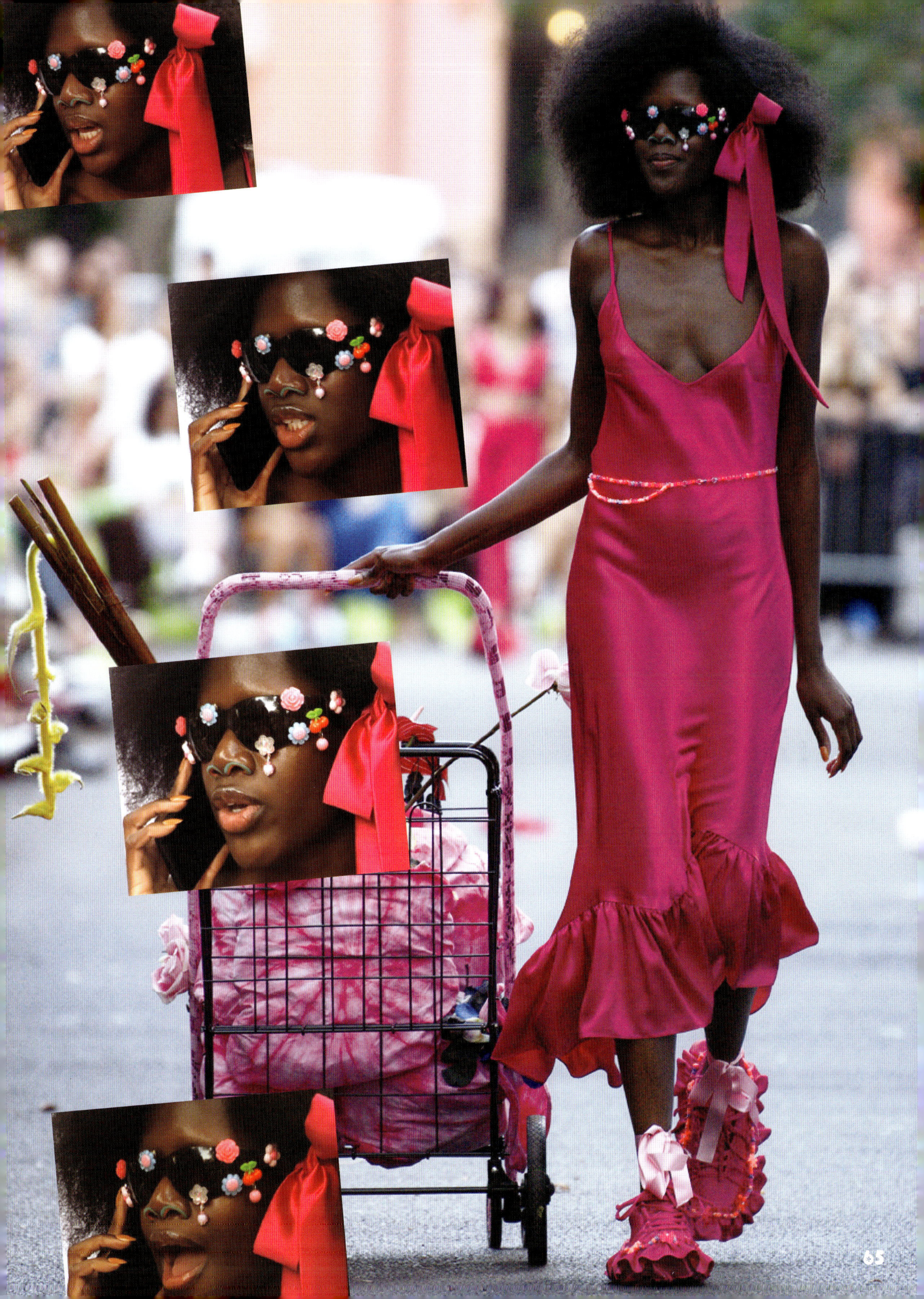

AUTUMN WINTER 2020, GARDEN HO

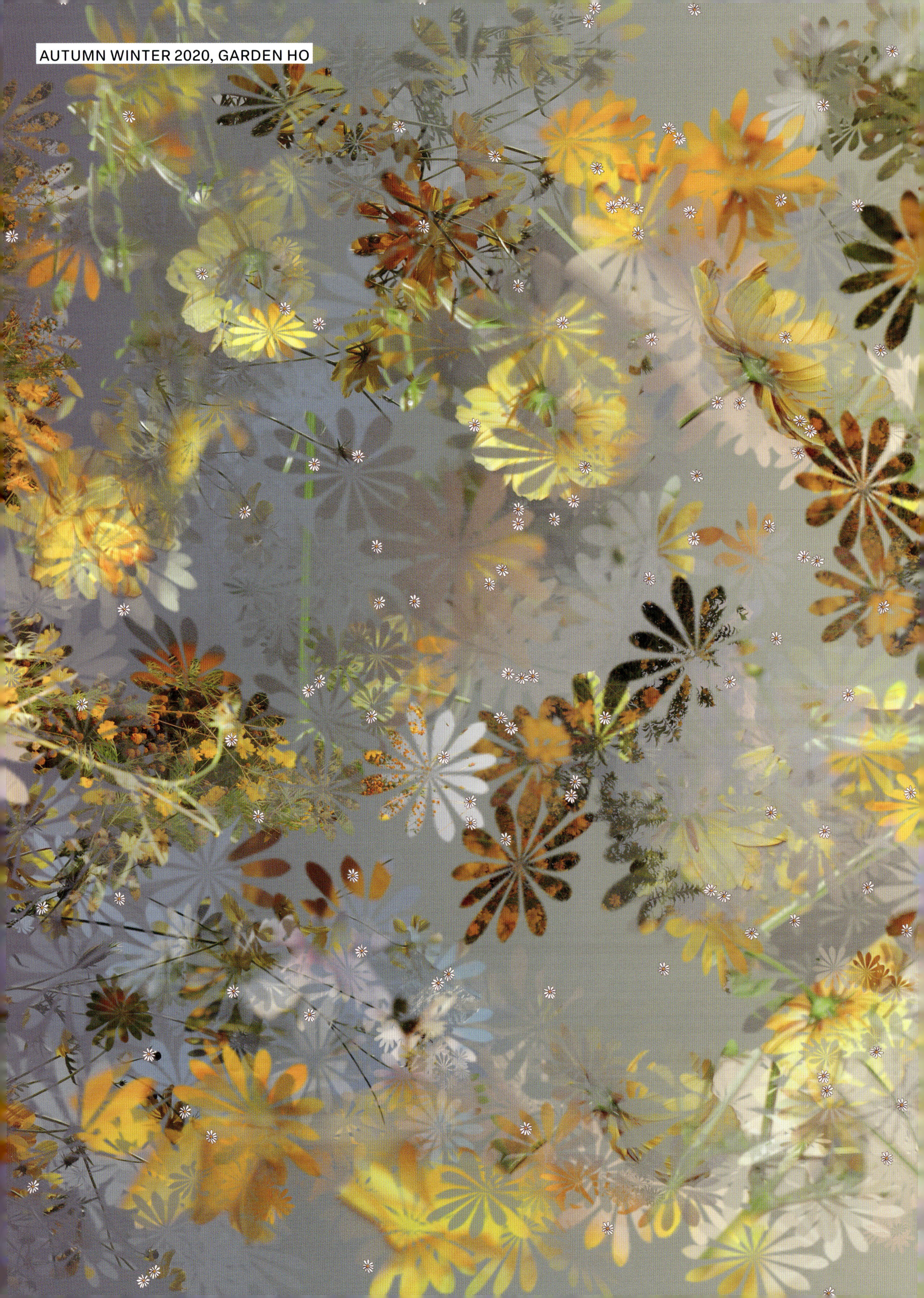

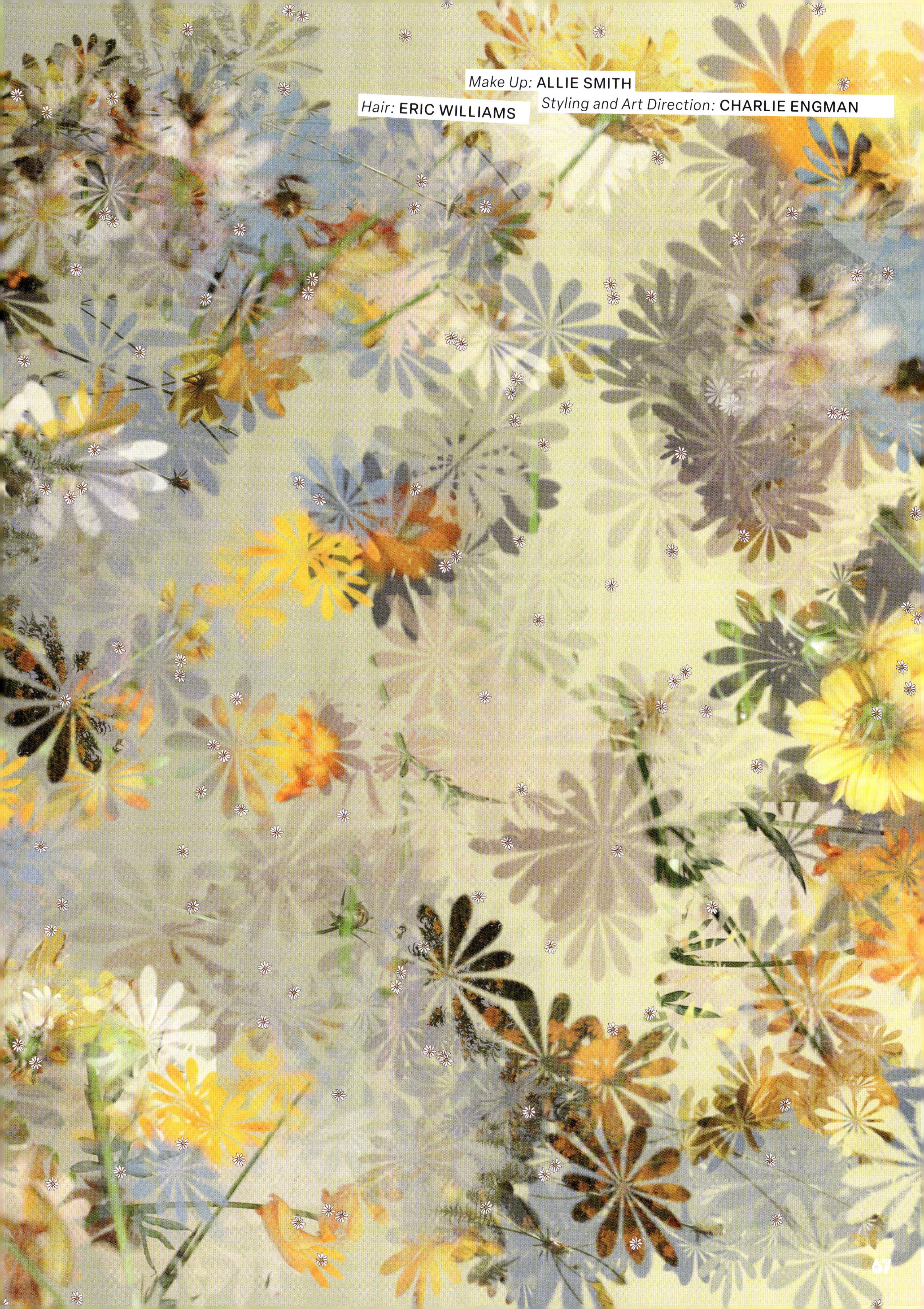

Make Up: ALLIE SMITH
Hair: ERIC WILLIAMS
Styling and Art Direction: CHARLIE ENGMAN

GARDEN HO

I know I'm not the
only flower you see

But what can I do, you are
a good looking bee

Honey, it's a job,
it's a dream come true

You're my favorite flower,
when I'm intimate with you

At Collina Strada we encourage a DIY approach that pertains not only to what you put on your body but also to what you put in your body. *Bedazzle your closet,* and grow your own food. This season, models worked a runway flanked with family-sized vegetable gardens atop a lush bed of replantable natural grass. *Hayley Williams* debuted her single "Simmer" while the cast backup-danced in the dirt. After the show, all of the set pieces were donated to the Elizabeth Street Community Garden, where the Collina team *replanted* the grass.

GET OUTSIDE AND BE A GARDEN HO.

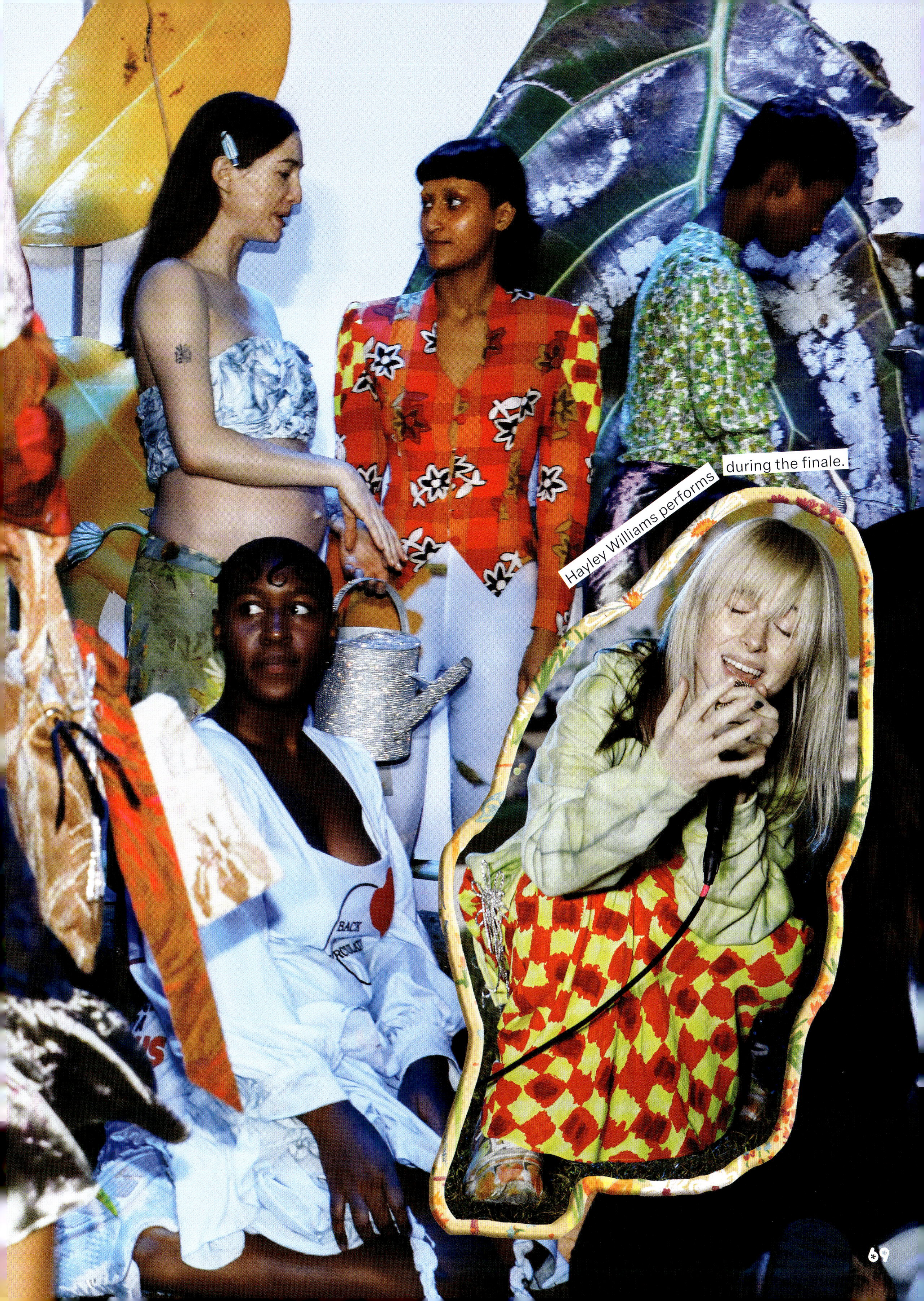

Hayley Williams performs during the finale.

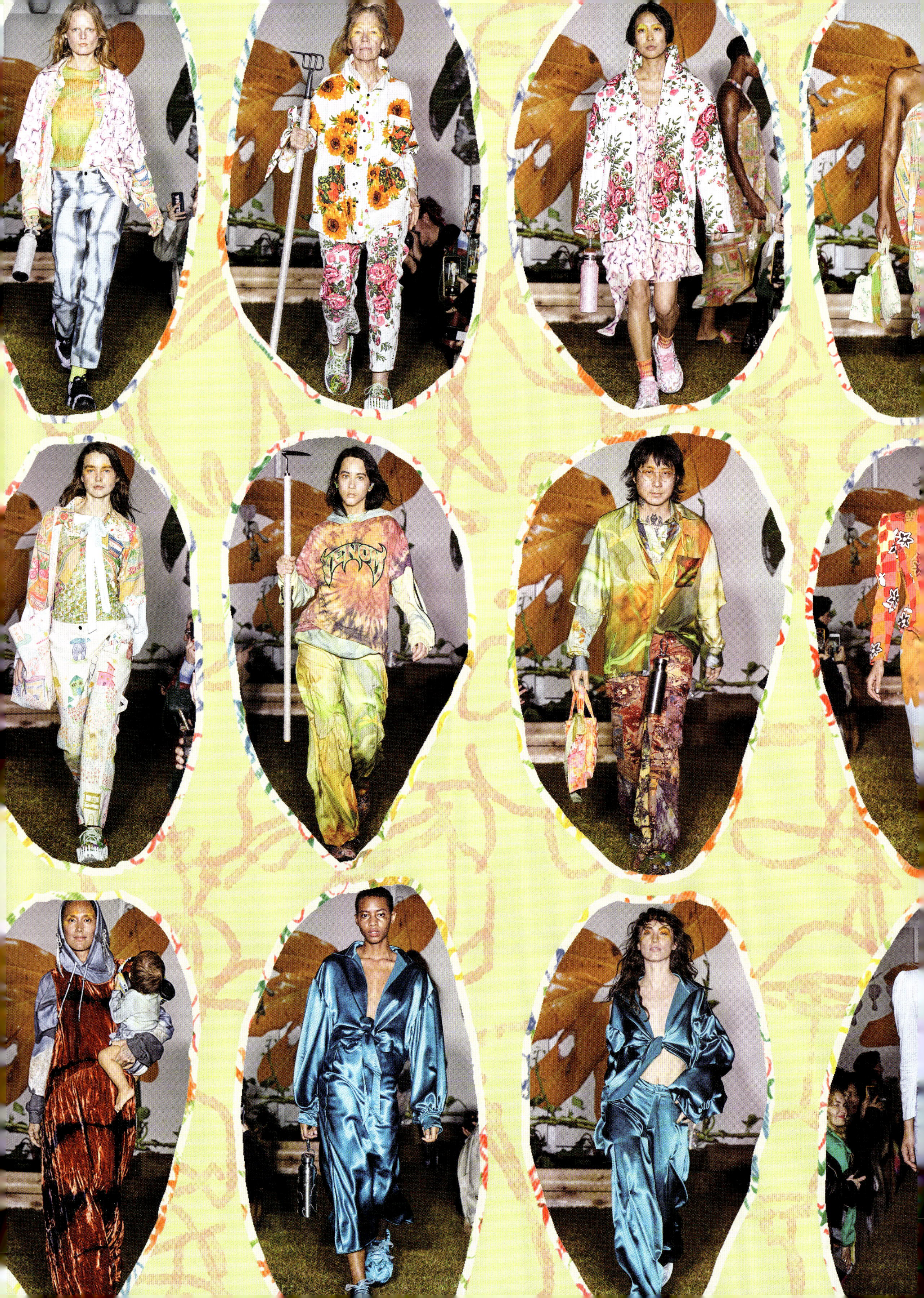

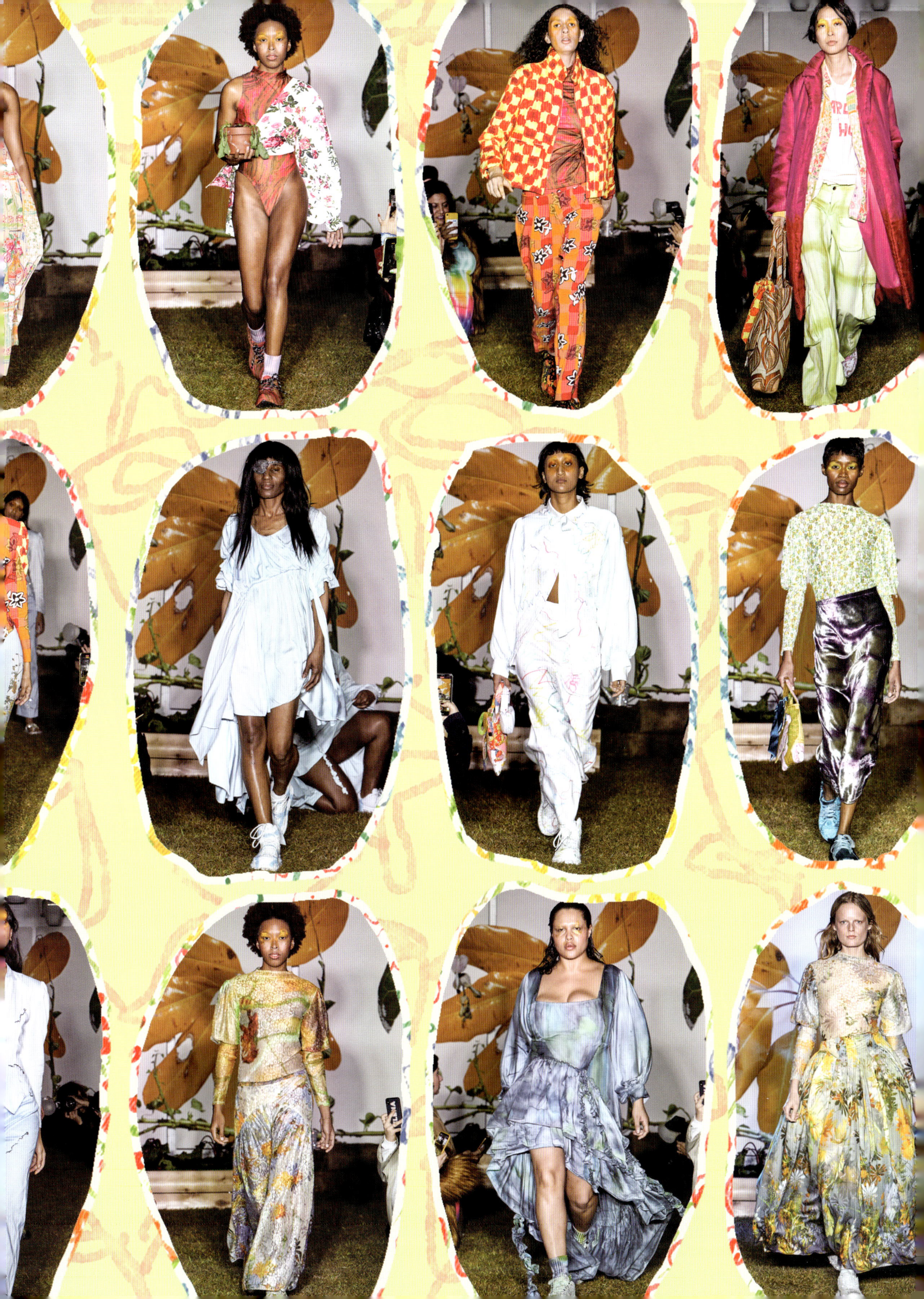

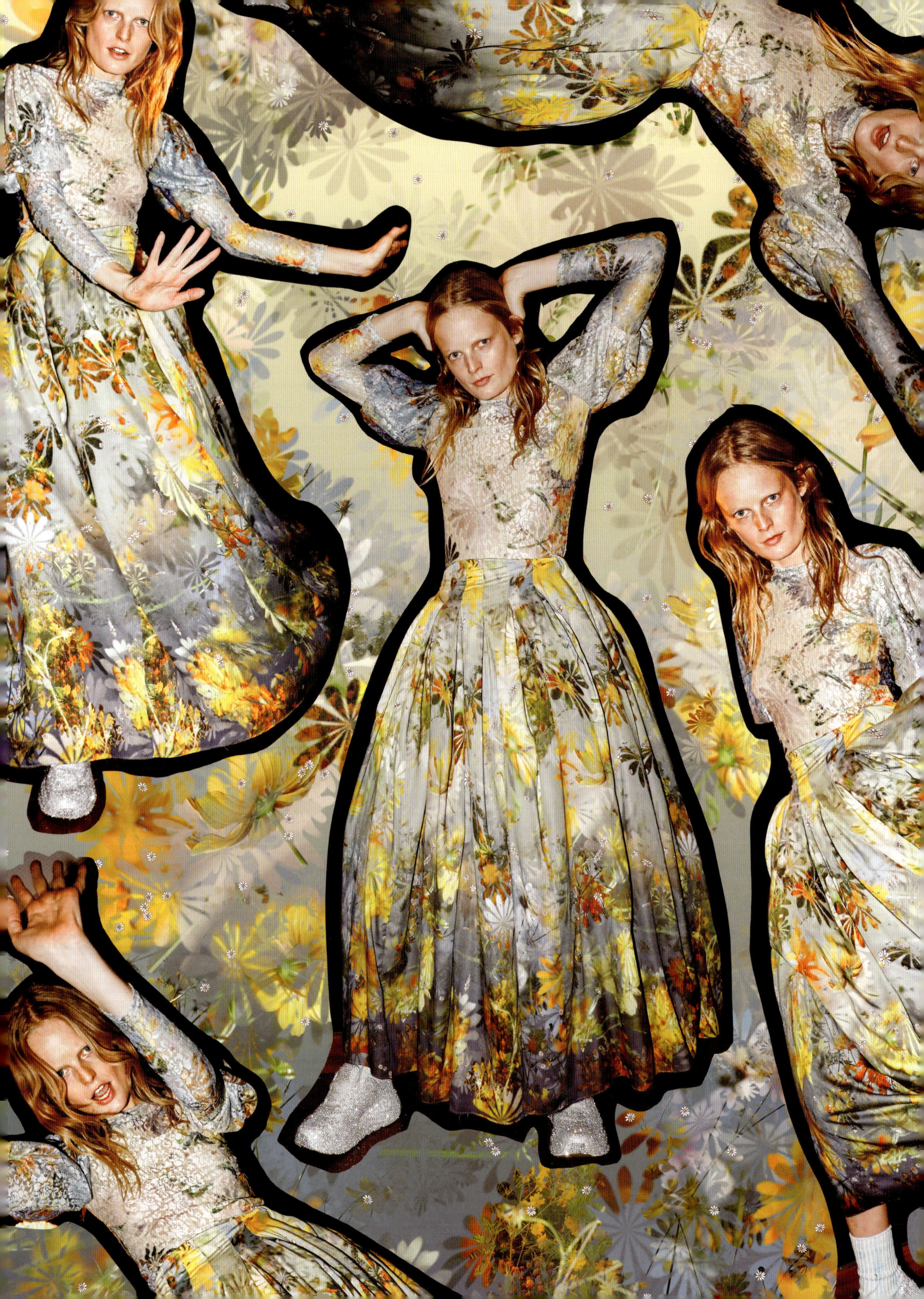

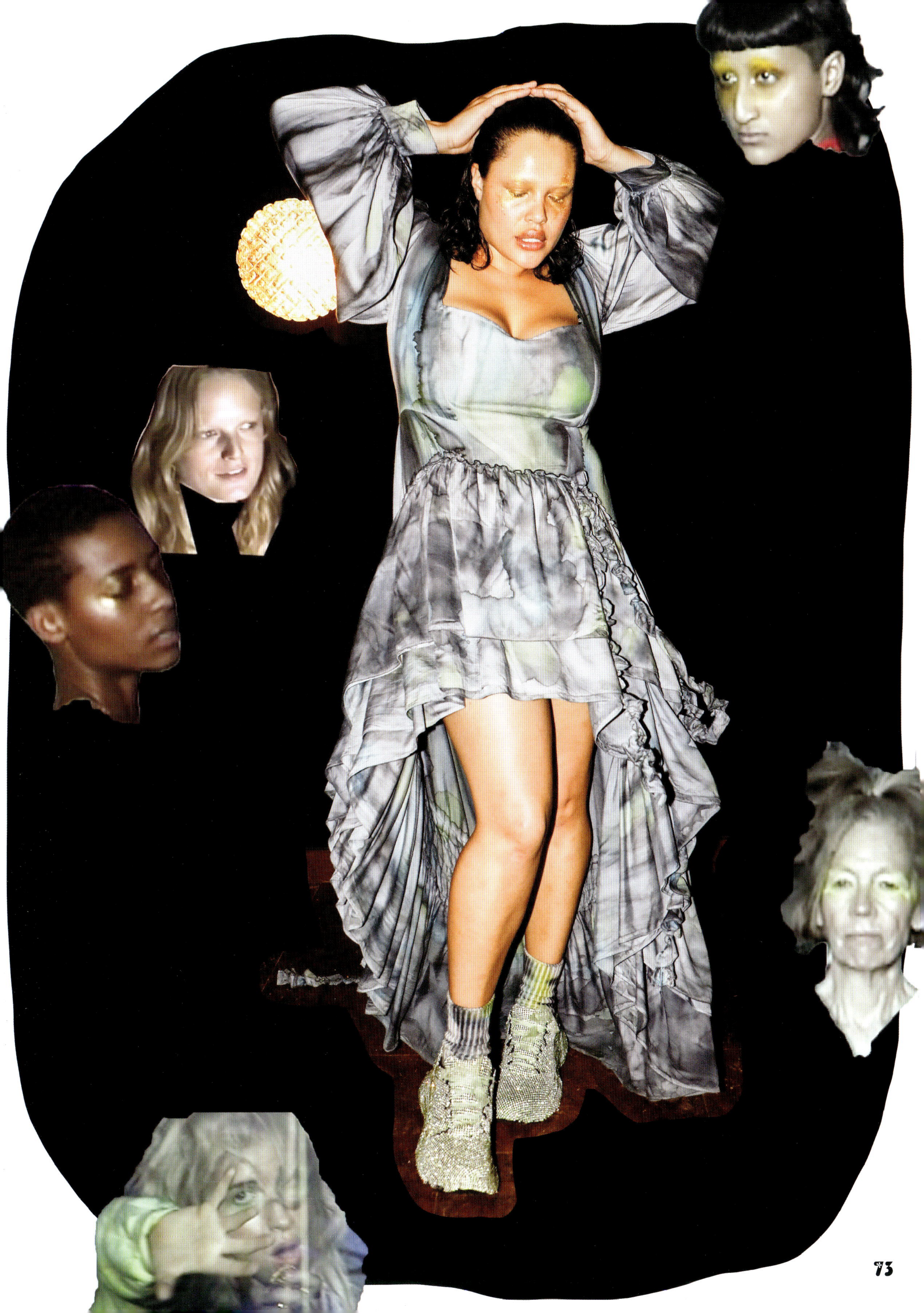

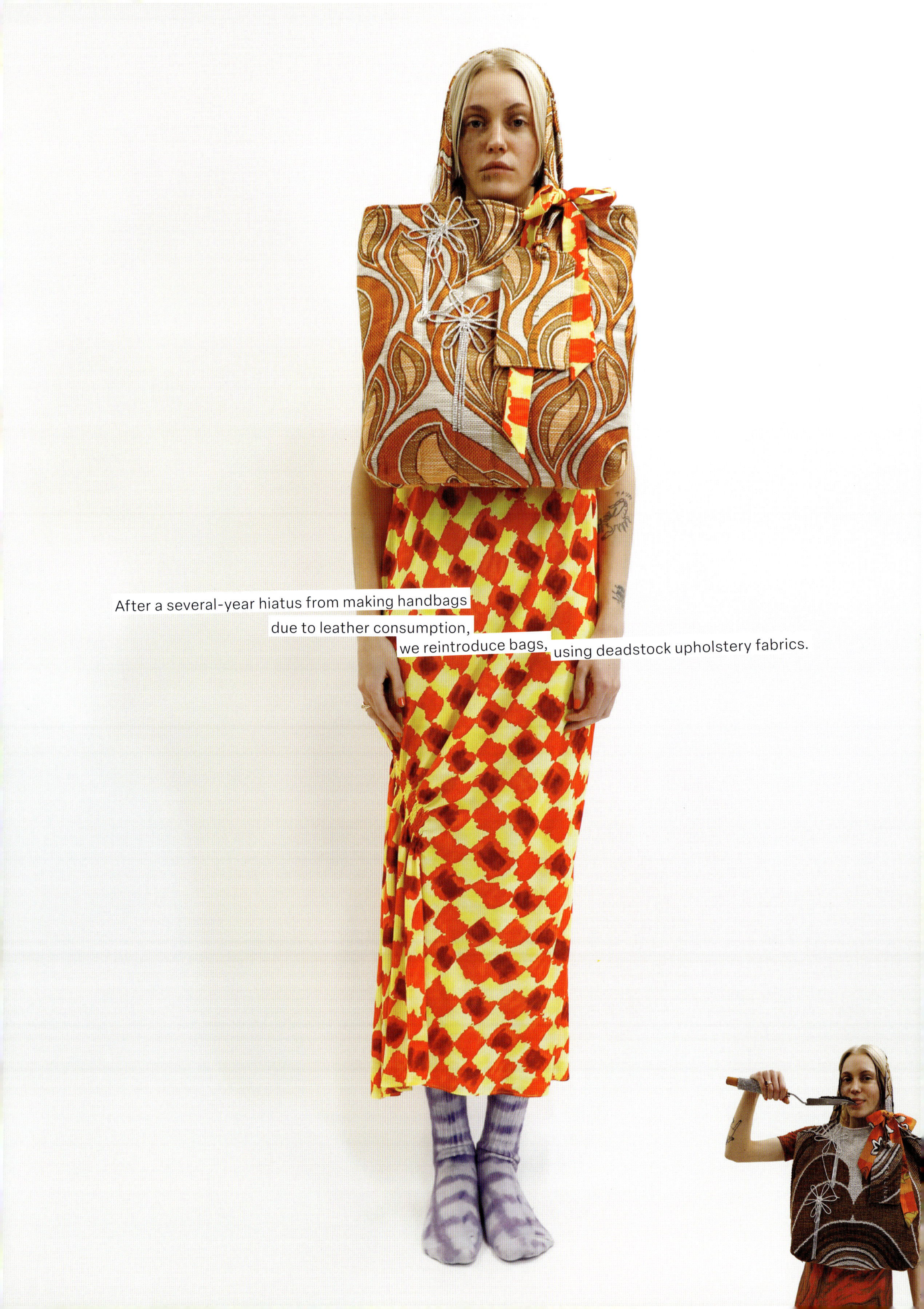

After a several-year hiatus from making handbags due to leather consumption, we reintroduce bags, using deadstock upholstery fabrics.

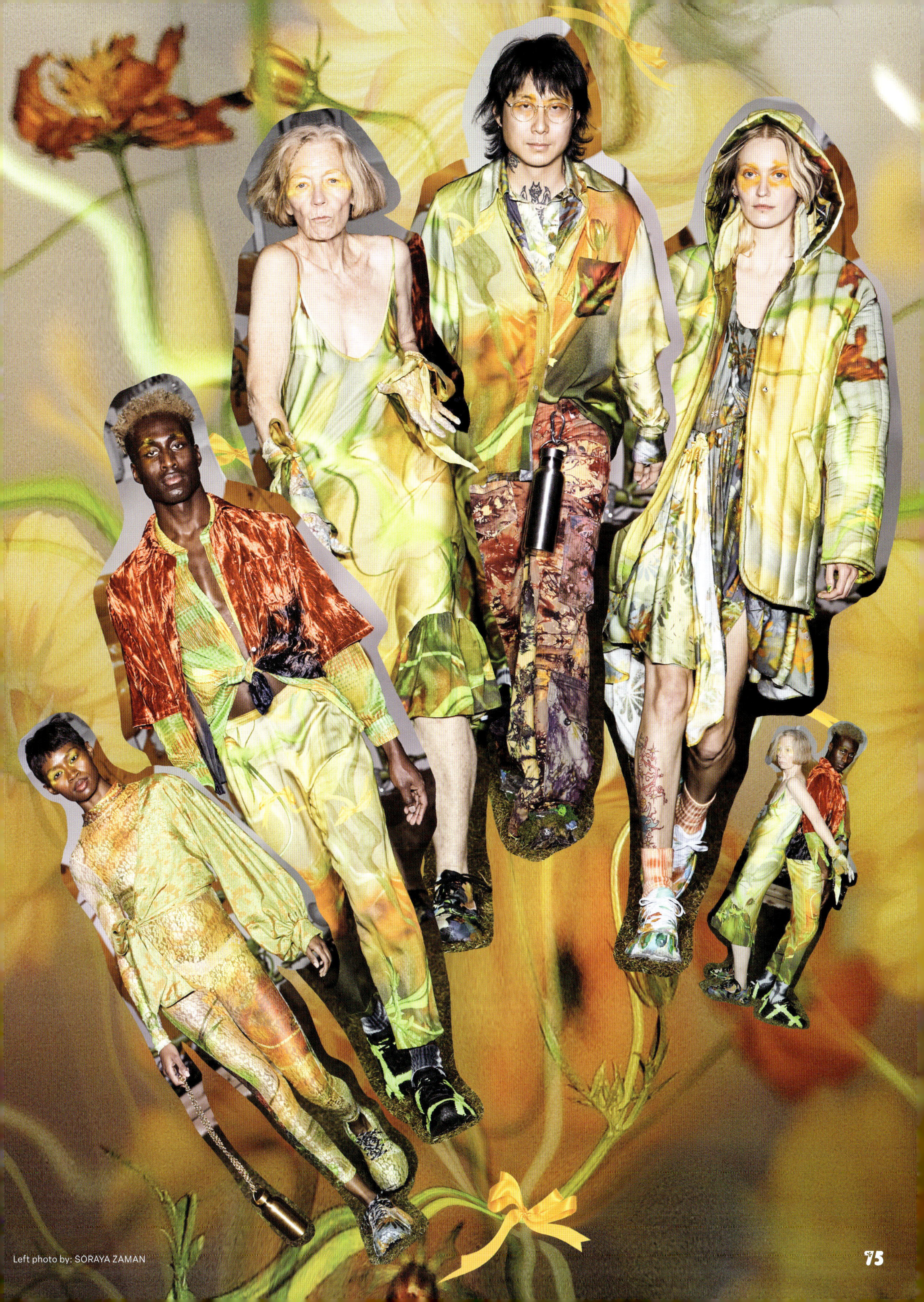

Left photo by: SORAYA ZAMAN

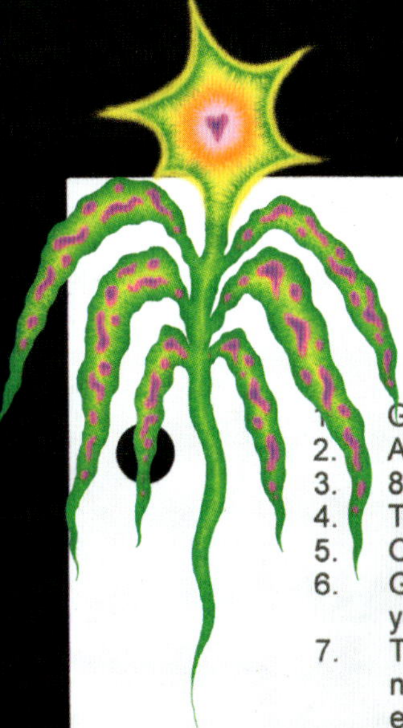

- you can hear them grow, they pop

1. Giant bamboo plants can grow up to 9 inches a day.
2. An area of a rainforest the size of a football field is being destroyed each second.
3. 80% of the flowers in the Australian rainforests are not found anywhere else in the world.
4. The Amazon rainforest produces half the world's oxygen supply.
5. One large tree can provide a day's supply of oxygen for up to four people.
6. Ginkgo (Ginkgo biloba) is one of the oldest living tree species, it dates back to about 250 million years ago.
7. The oldest known living tree … Mountains of California named Methuselah. A drill c… estimate its age at 5,060 ye…
8. Oak trees are struck by ligh…
9. In one day, one large tree c… …t into the air.
10. Trees reduce stormwater r… water into the atmosphere…
11. The locations of the world'… …ls damaging them and their…
12. Since 1981, every Chines…
13. 96 percent of ancient red… …en cut down
14. There are Eucalyptus tre…
15. Roadside trees reduce r…
16. Justin Timberlake had a… …ve trees and bushes planted in t…
17. The tallest tree currentl… …11 metres (380 feet 1 inch…
18. Scientists have found … …er repay them back when they…
19. In New York City, trees…
20. Trees remove pollutio… …Los Angeles, trees remov…
21. A study of 10 cities fo… …New York City, trees save an a…
22. Some species of bar…
23. Office workers with … …n.
24. In 1997, New York C… …ies New City's drinking… …shed. A …n plant large… …ore than $6 billion dollars.
25. In one year, an ac… …driven 26,000 miles.
26. 85% of plant life is…
27. Trees properly pla… …nd can save 20–50% in energ…
28. In New York City, it has bee… …efits for every dollar spent on tree planting and care.
29. Trees prevent floods.
30. Neighborhoods with more trees have less crime.
31. Trees also prevent droughts.
32. There is a plant called "Electric Daisy" whose leaves will make you salivate uncontrollably.
33. National Arbor Day of 2020 is April 24th
34. 40 Liters of Tree Sap produce One Liter of Maple Syrup
35. 90% of the foods we eat come from 30 plants. Out of all the plants that we could eat, we eat less than 5% of the total amount of plants. … are able to communicate and defend themselves against attacking insects.
36. Rainforests help to regulate the temperatures around the world and the weather patterns as well.
37. The rings in a cut tree don't just reveal its age. They can also show signs of environmental changes, like a volcanic eruption or severe drought.

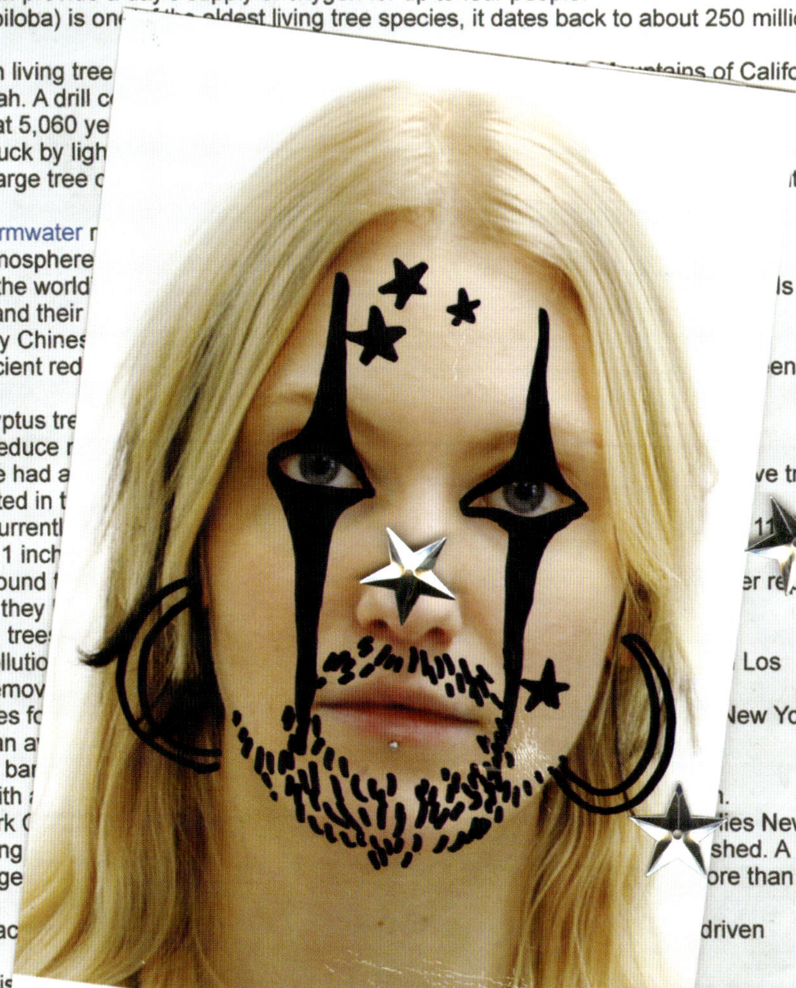

SASHA MEL

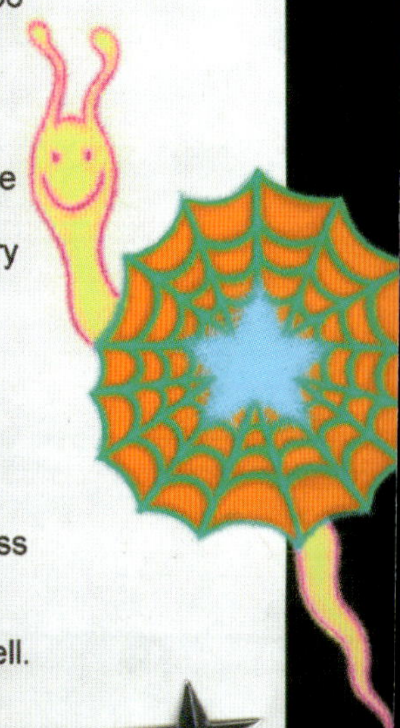

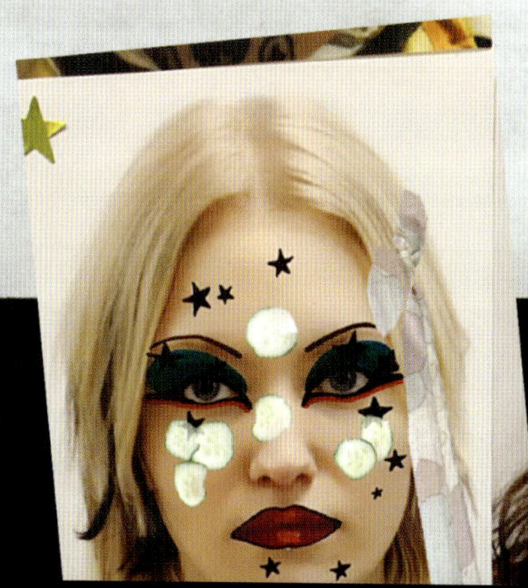

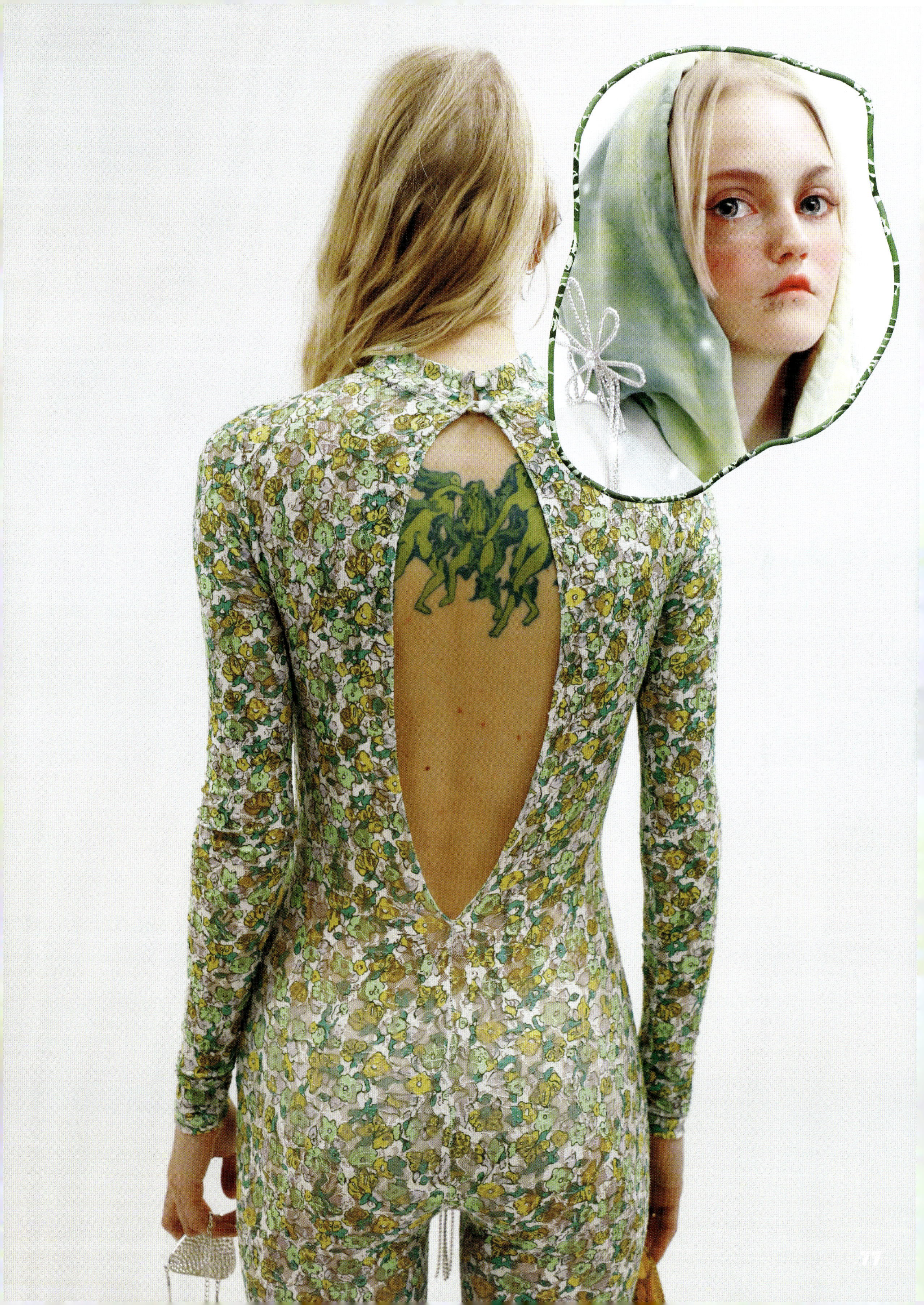

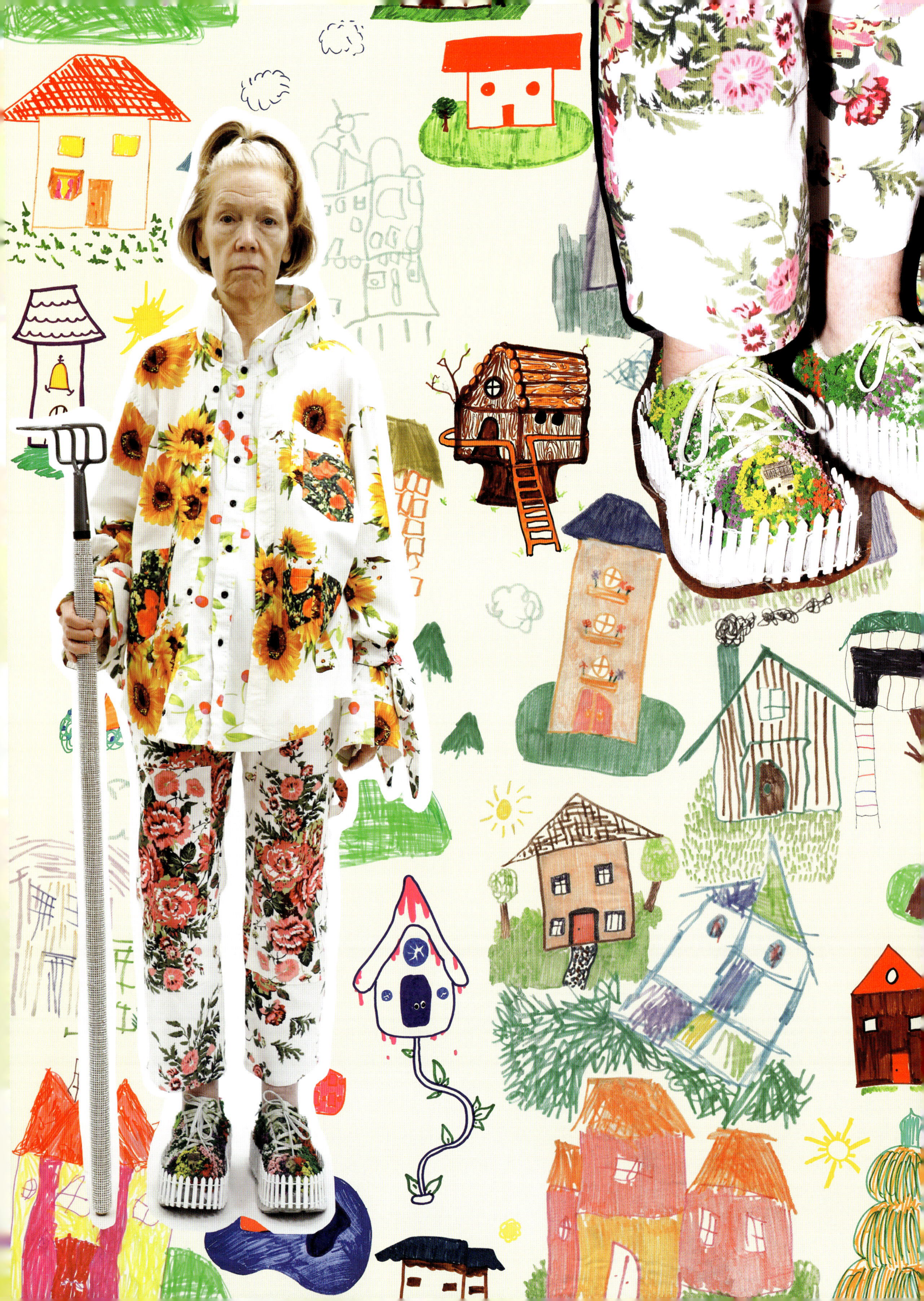

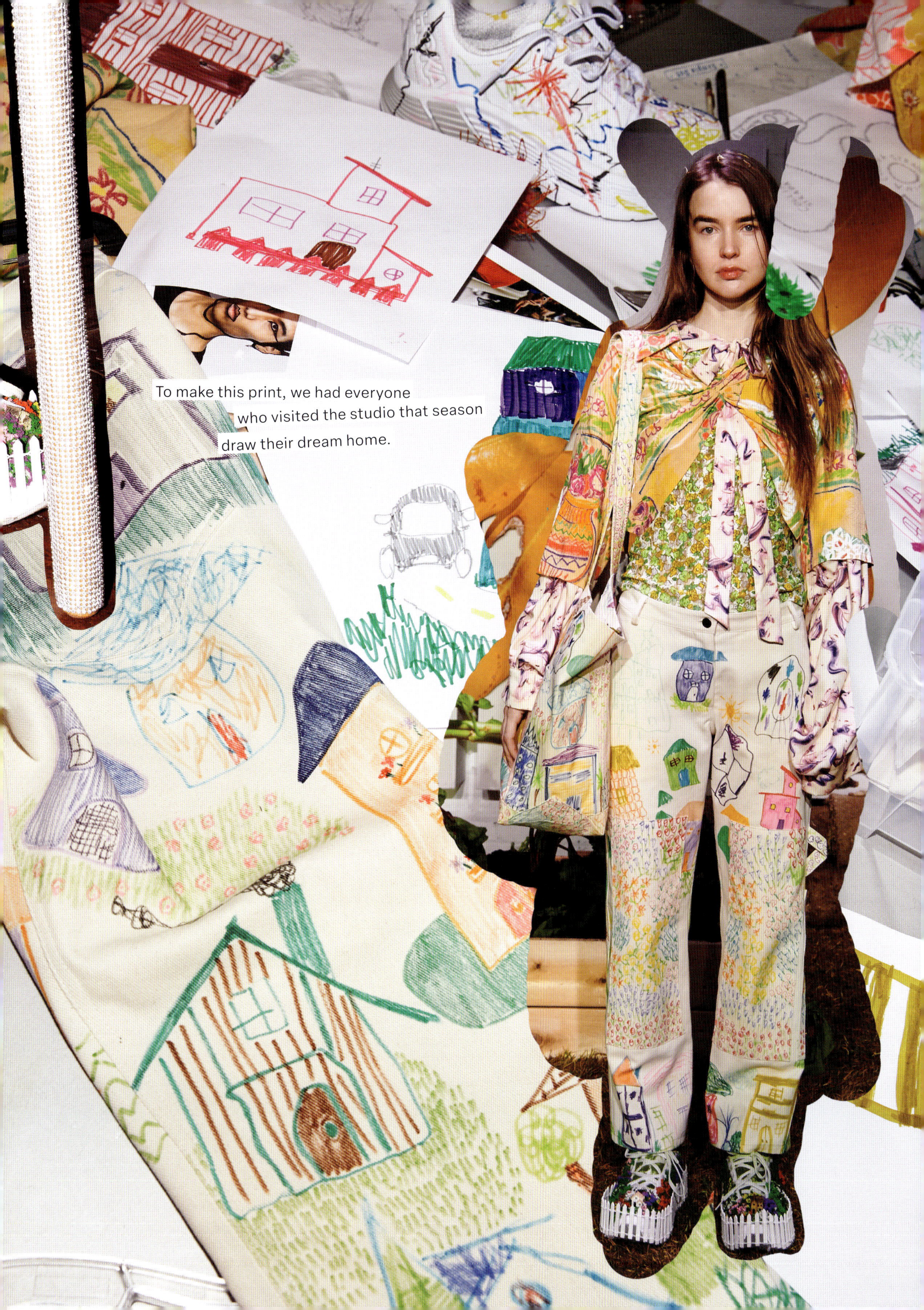

To make this print, we had everyone who visited the studio that season draw their dream home.

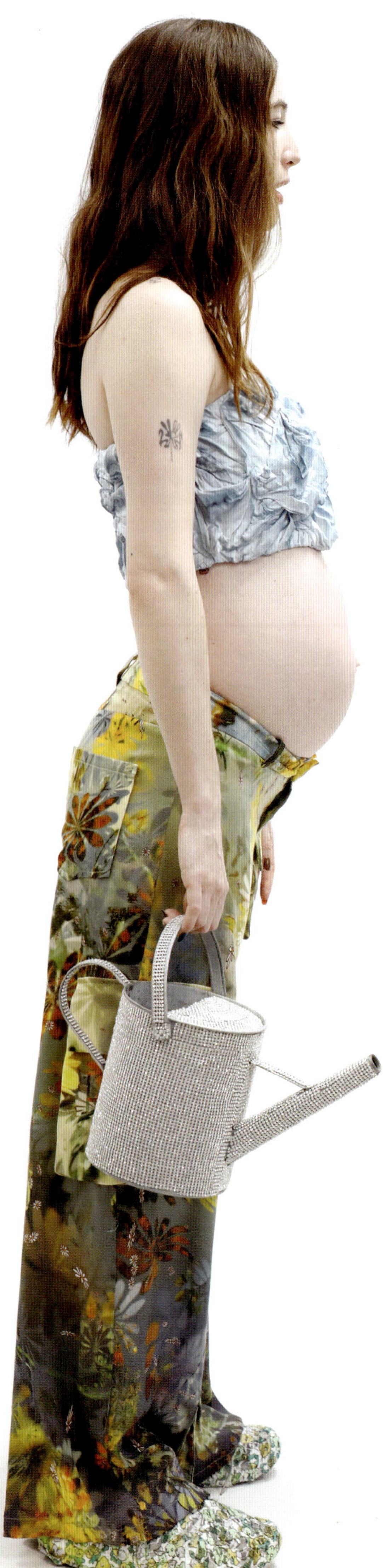

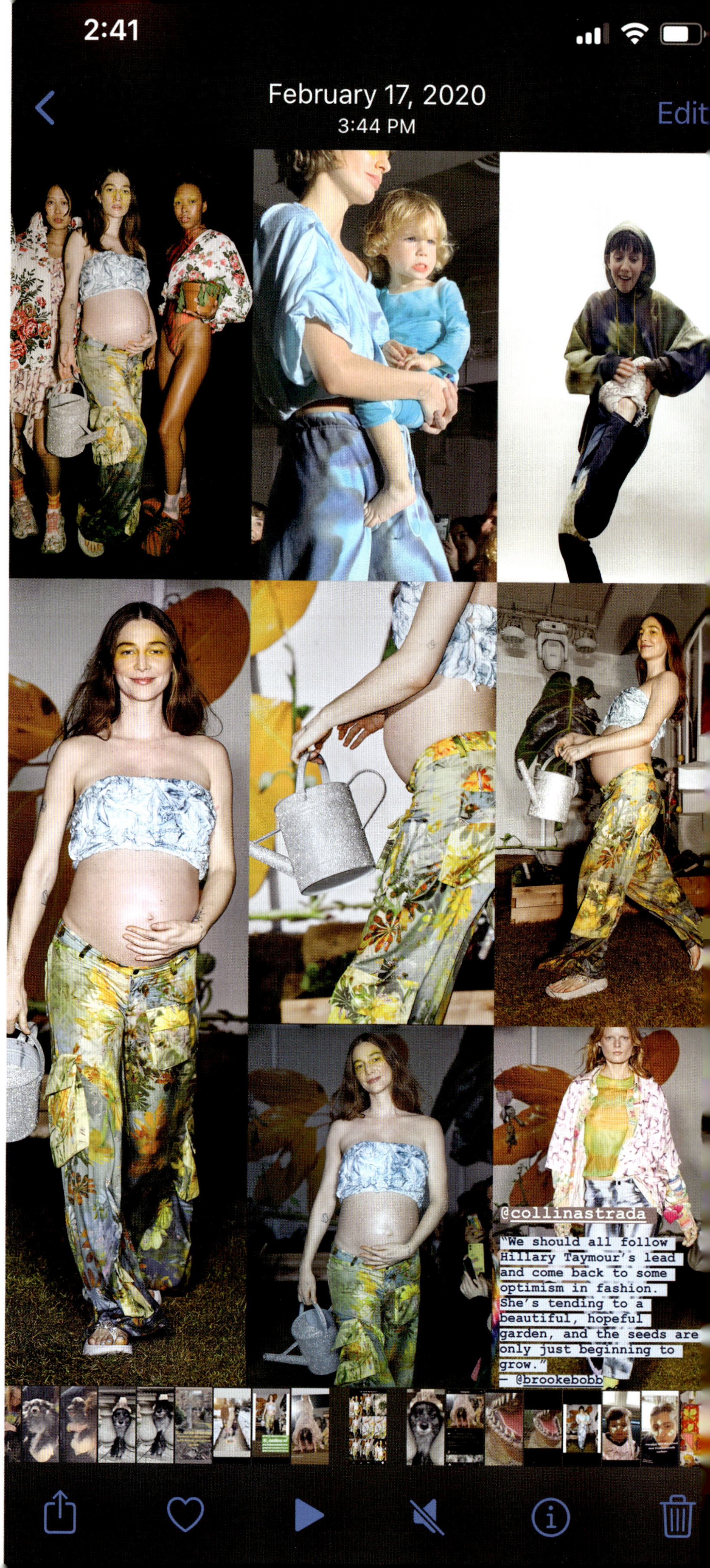
2:41
February 17, 2020
3:44 PM
Edit
@collinastrada
"We should all follow Hillary Taymour's lead and come back to some optimism in fashion. She's tending to a beautiful, hopeful garden, and the seeds are only just beginning to grow."
– @brookebobb

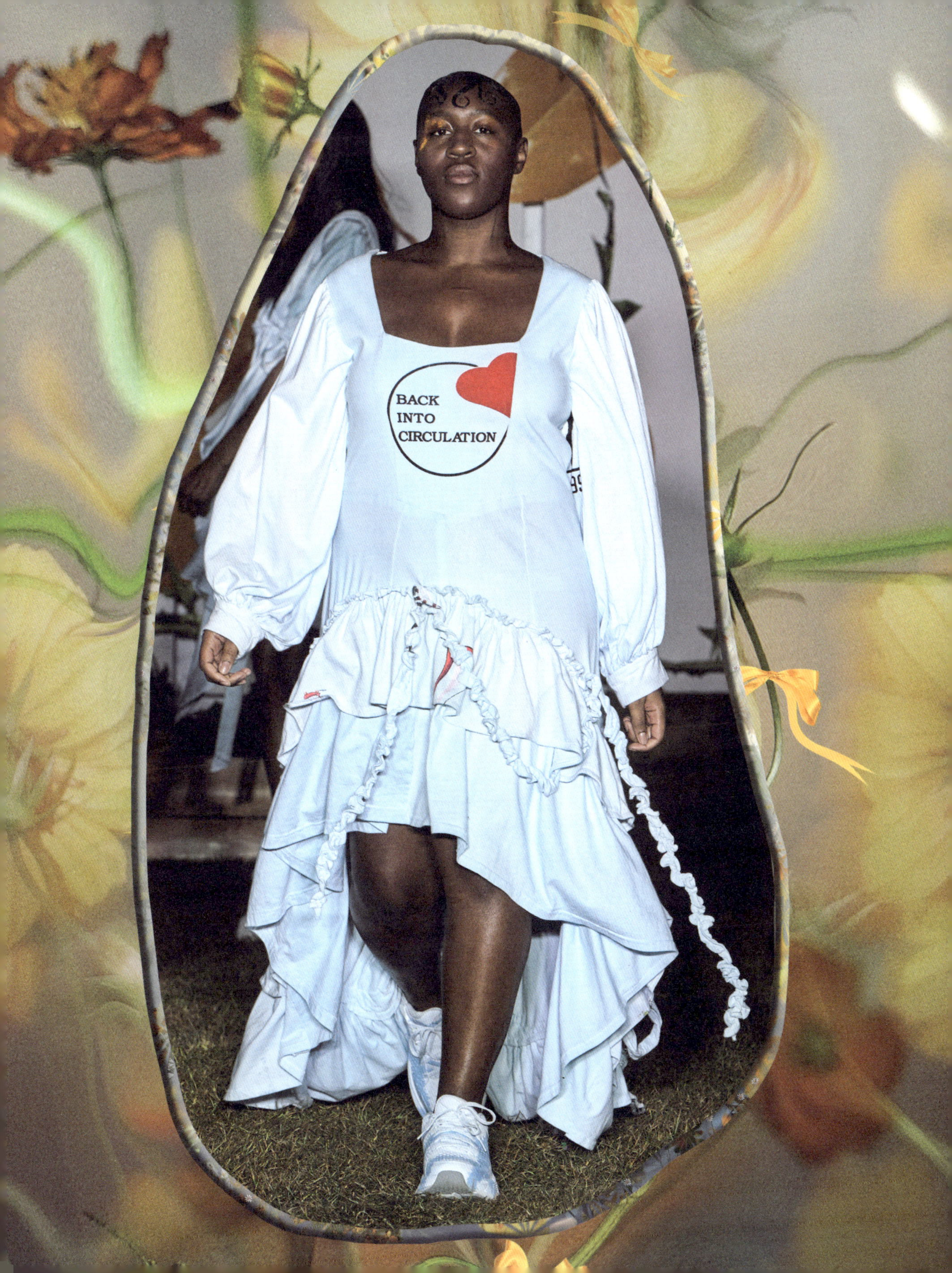
BACK
INTO
CIRCULATION

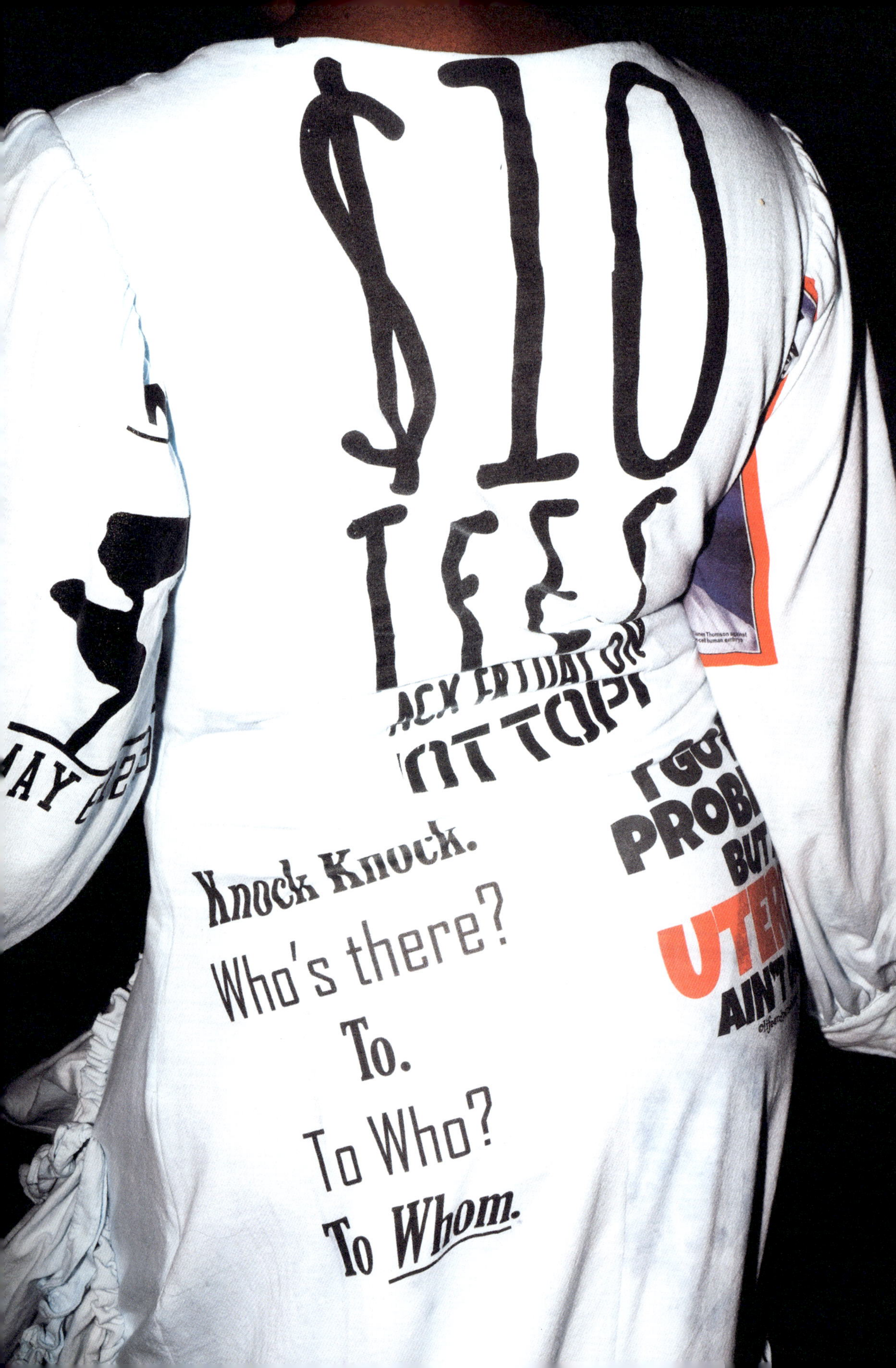
$10
Knock Knock.
Who's there?
To.
To Who?
To Whom.
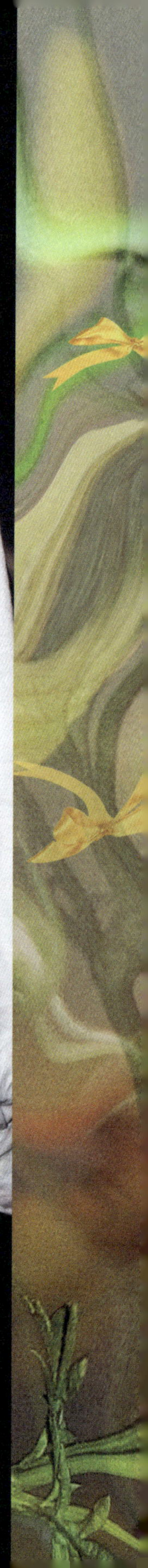

The Or Foundation

With our Fall 2020 collection, in partnership with The Or Foundation, a non-profit based between Ghana and the US, we introduce our ongoing program of garments made from upcycled waste shirts sourced from Ghana.

Accra, Ghana, is home to Kantamanto Market, the world's largest secondhand clothing market. In the guise of "donations," approximately 15 million items of unwanted clothing—primarily fast-fashion and single-use t-shirts—are sent to Ghana from the Global North every week, about 40% of which is immediately discarded as waste due to poor quality. The remaining garments soon join that waste as they overflow the market, causing toxic landfill fires, polluting the streets and beaches, and forcing many Ghanaians into debt- and wage-slavery due to the predatory imbalance between supply and demand. This is a cycle of waste colonialism that plays out in similar ways in many other places across the Global South. We believe the people working in and around places like Kantamanto Market are resilient, innovative, and necessary leaders in the sustainable fashion movement.

For our first program, we worked with The Or Foundation to source used t-shirts directly from Kantamanto Market, and now we use waste shirts bound for Ghana before they leave the US in the first place. We cut the shirts back into fabric swatches and dye and re-fashion them into new garments, embracing the quirks and imperfections of the original material to allow each piece to be unique.

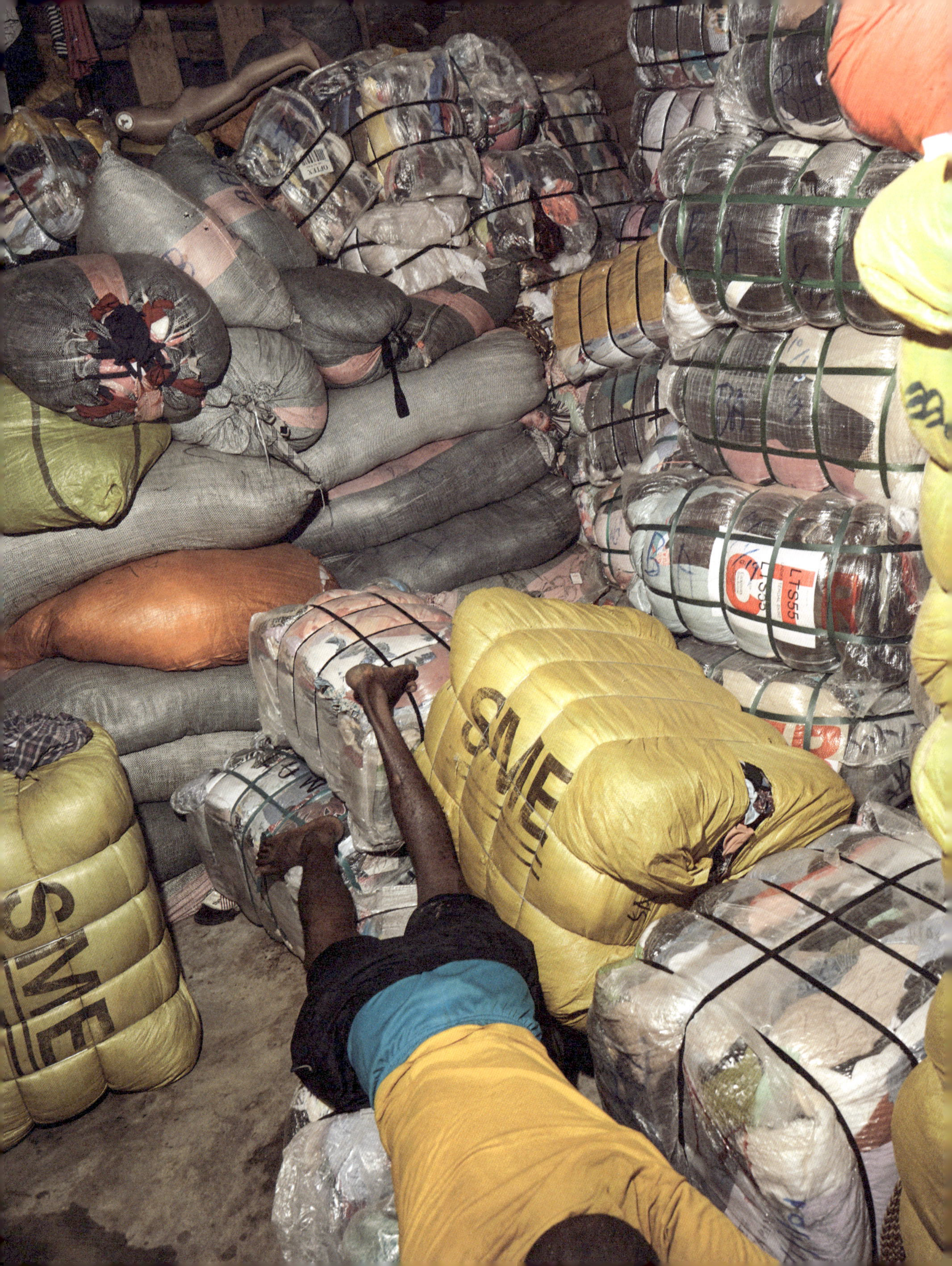
SME
SME
LTS55

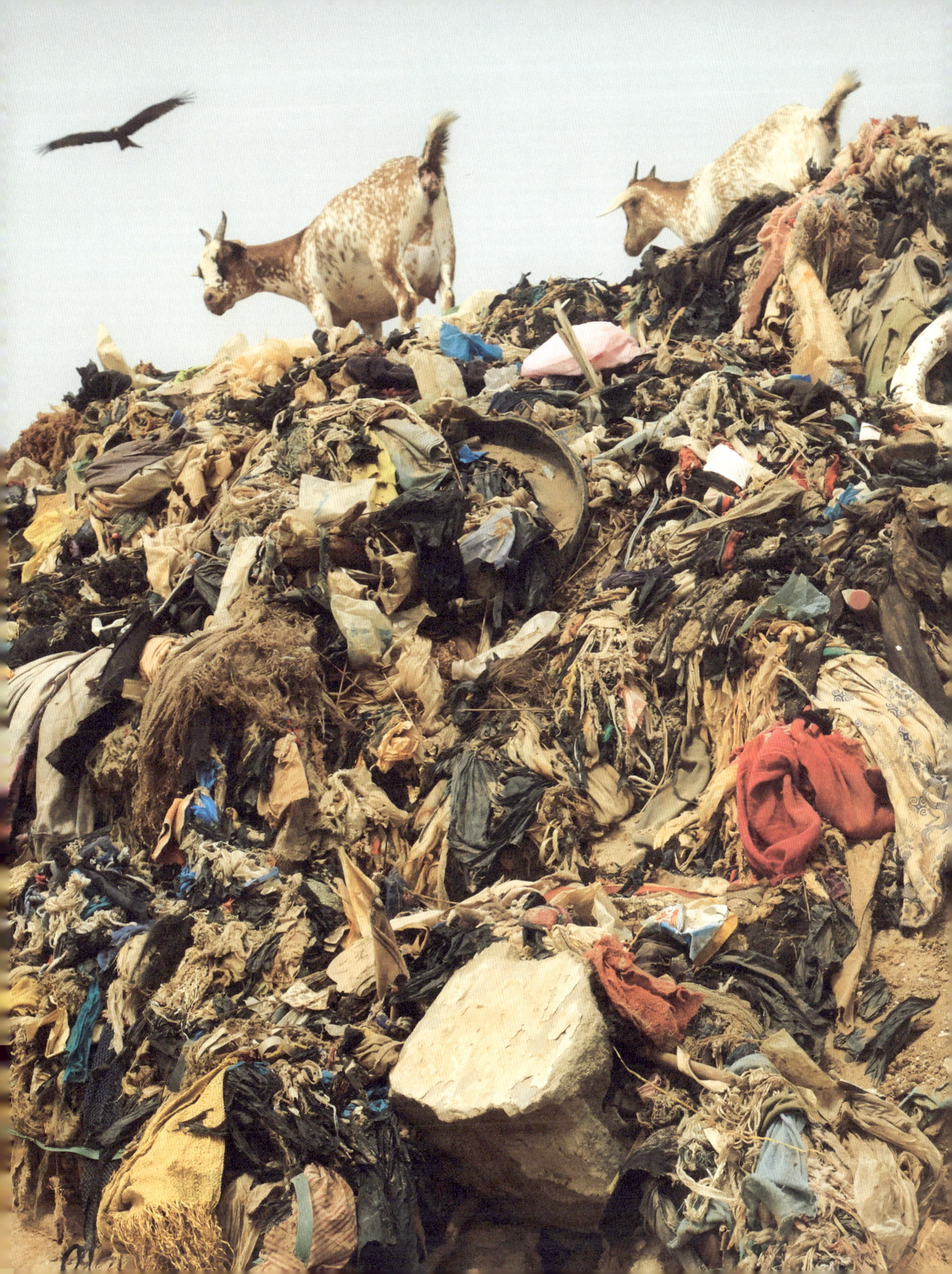

Please visit The Or Foundation's website for more information and resources about fashion's waste crisis as exemplified through the situation in Ghana.

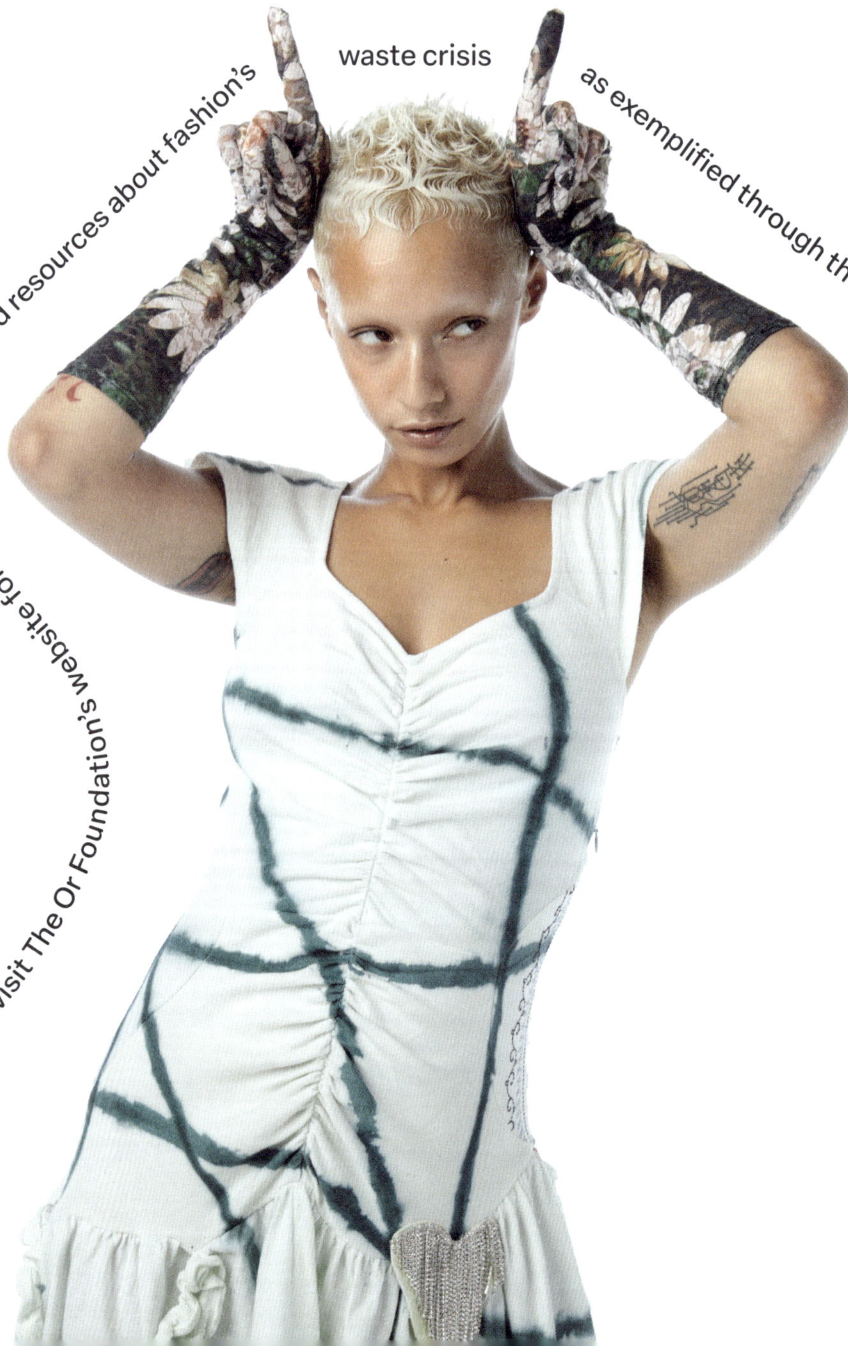

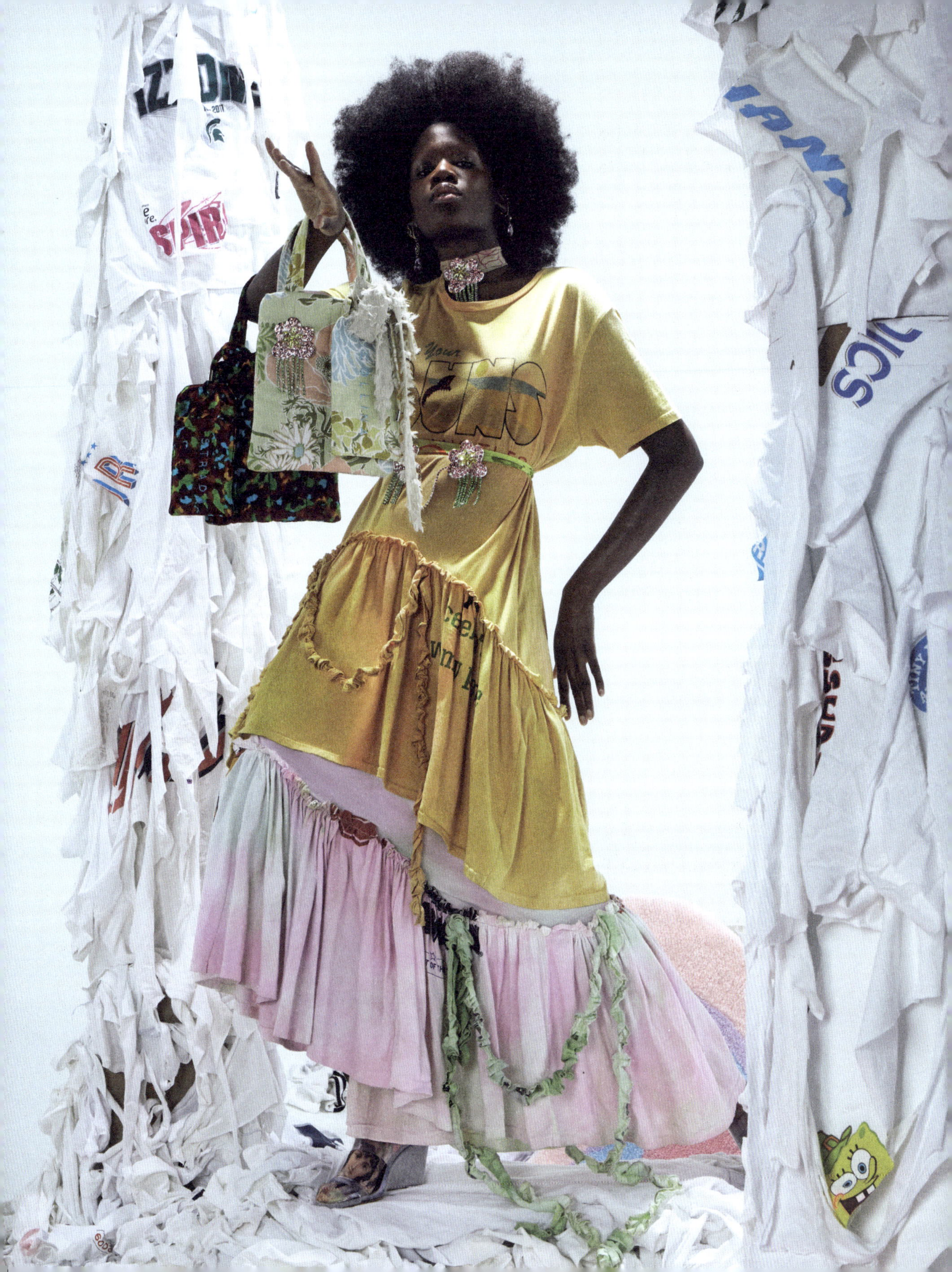

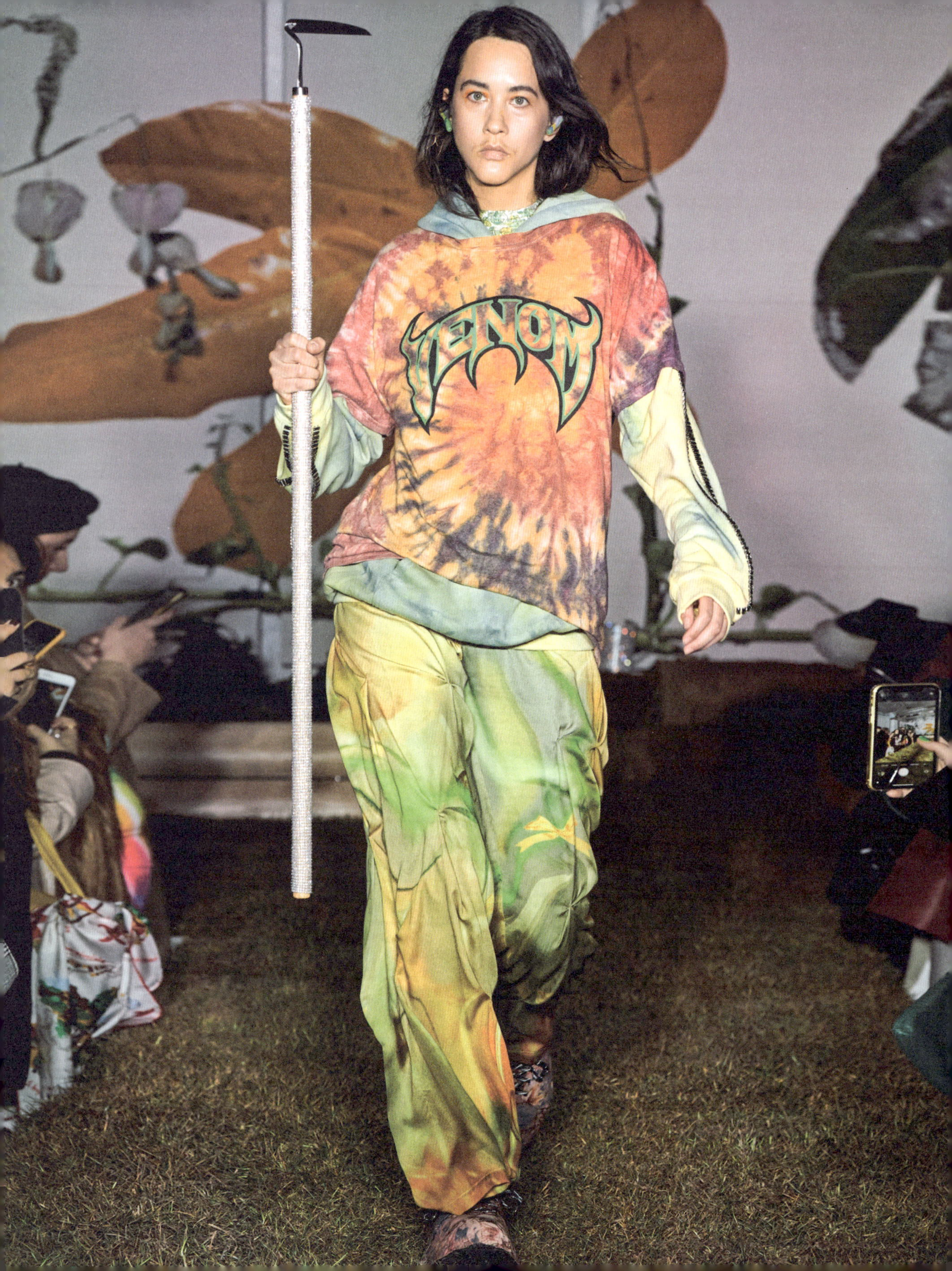
VENOM

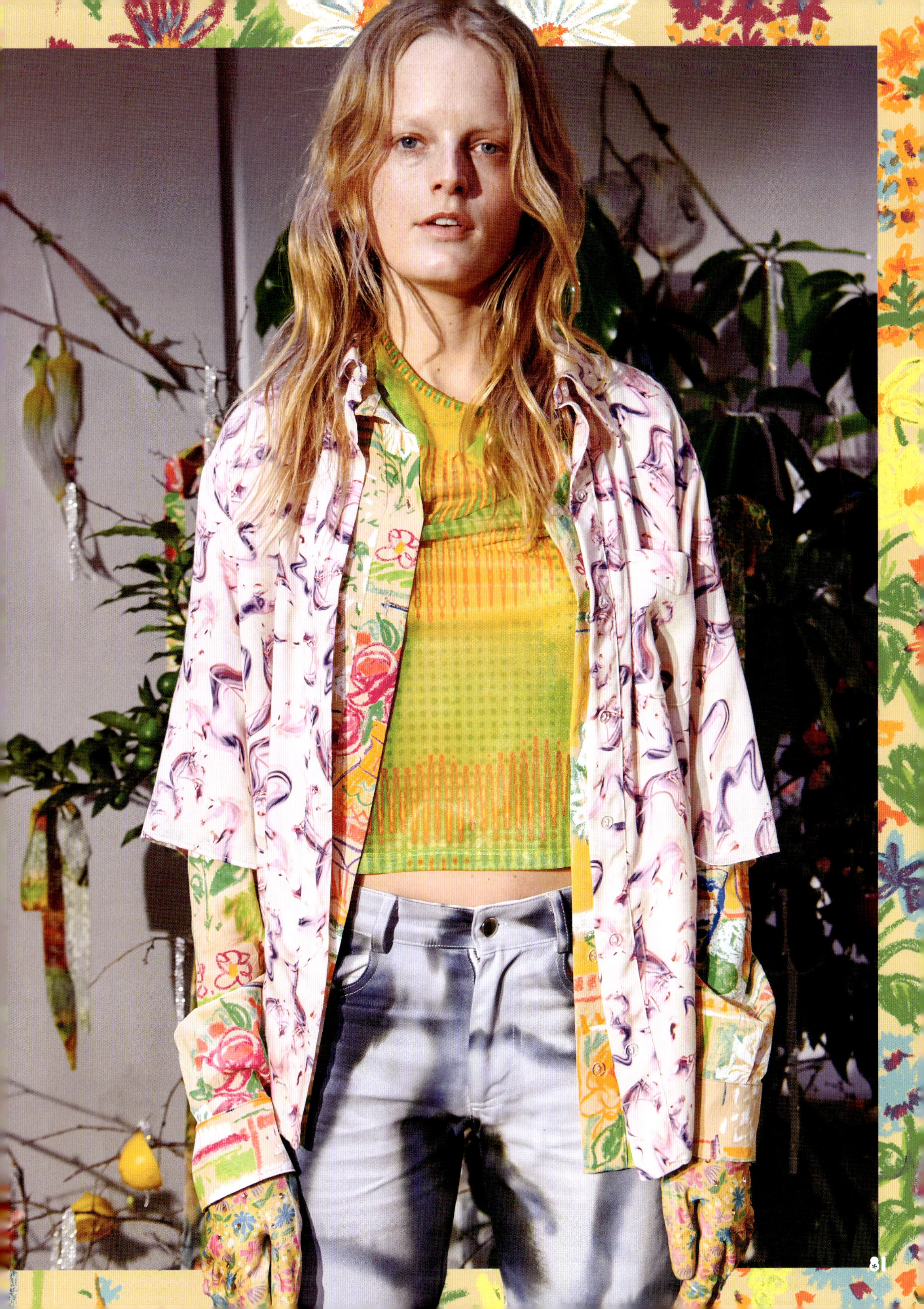

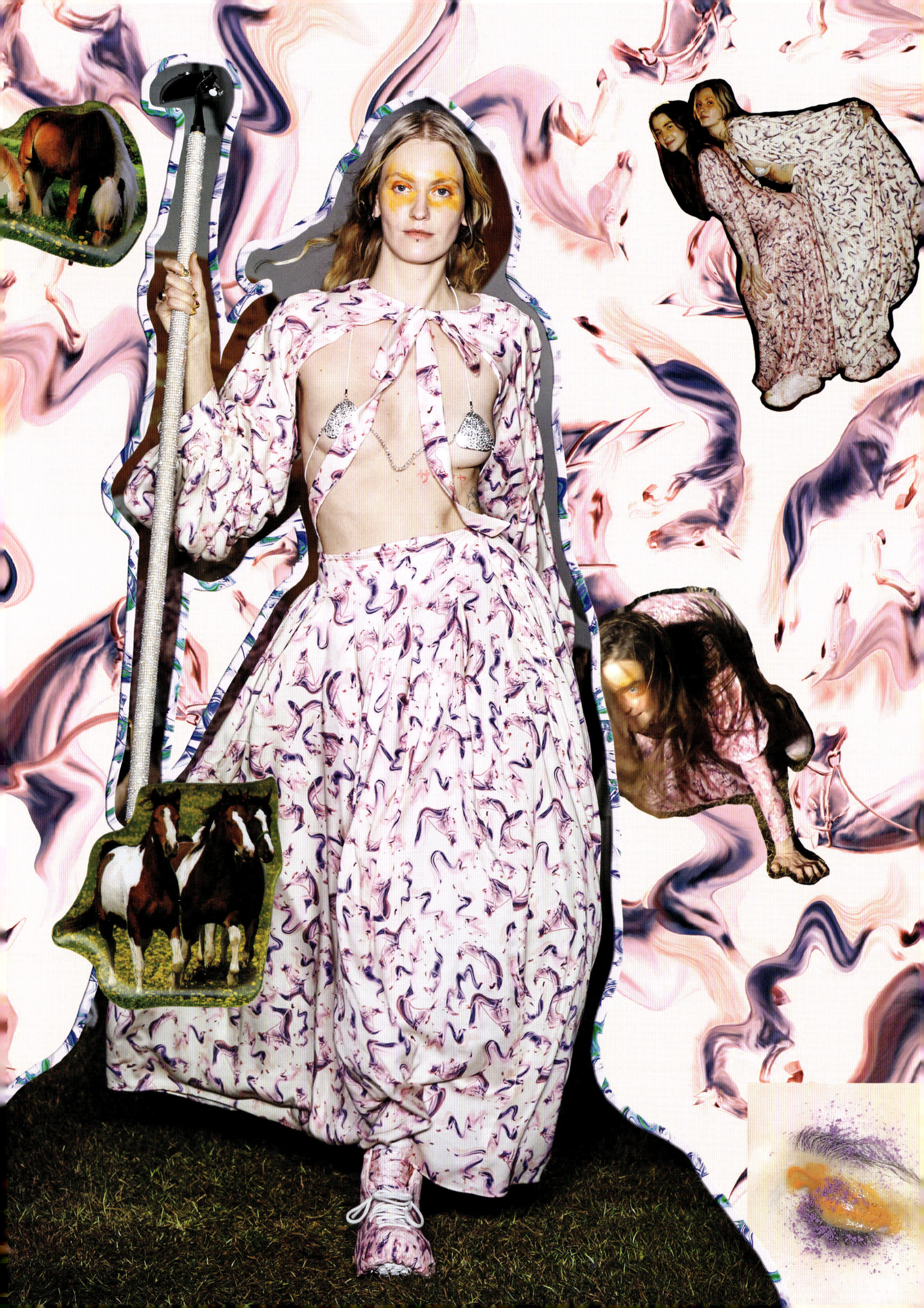

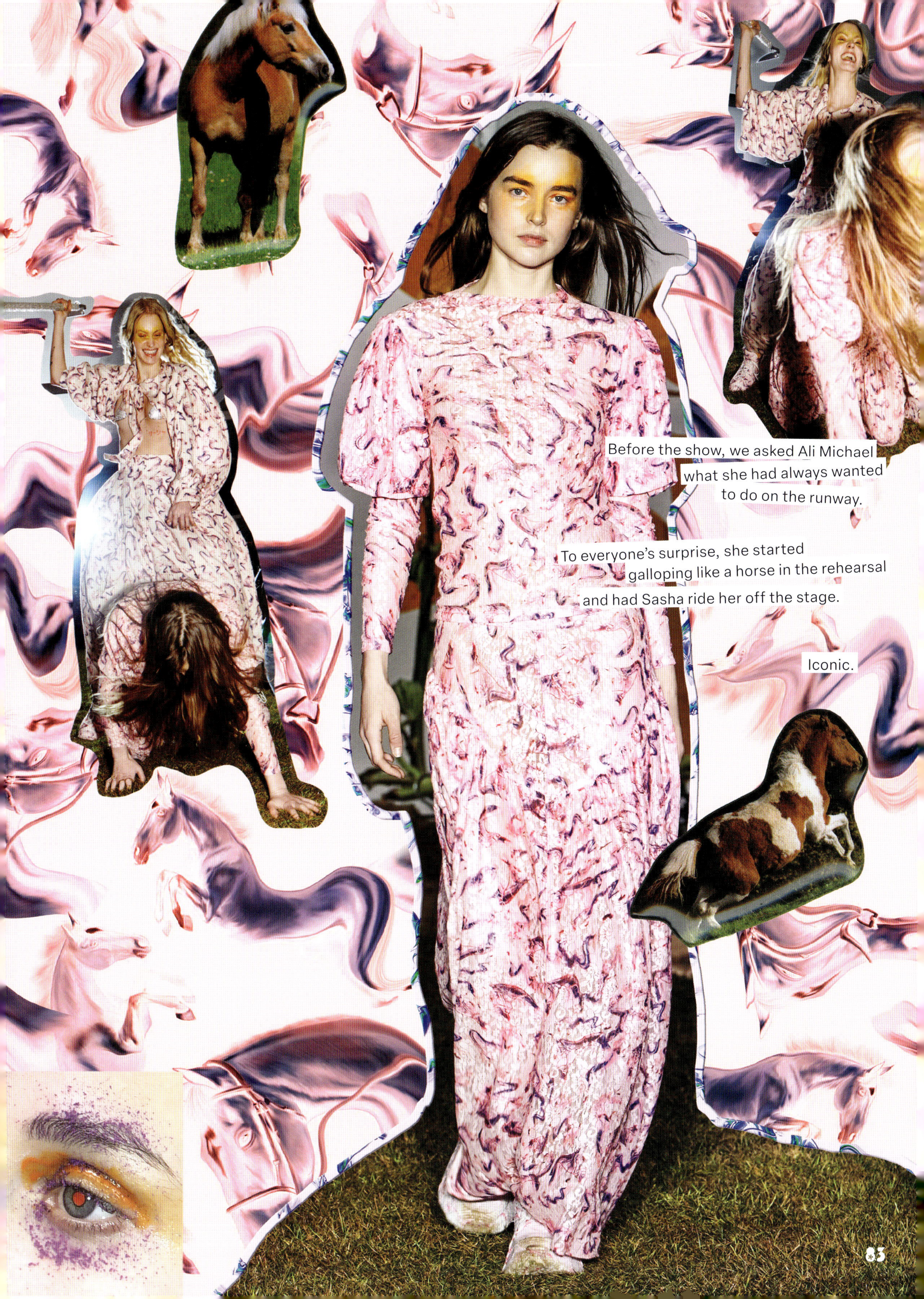

Before the show, we asked Ali Michael what she had always wanted to do on the runway.

To everyone's surprise, she started galloping like a horse in the rehearsal and had Sasha ride her off the stage.

Iconic.

SPRING SUMMER 2021, CHANGE IS CUTE

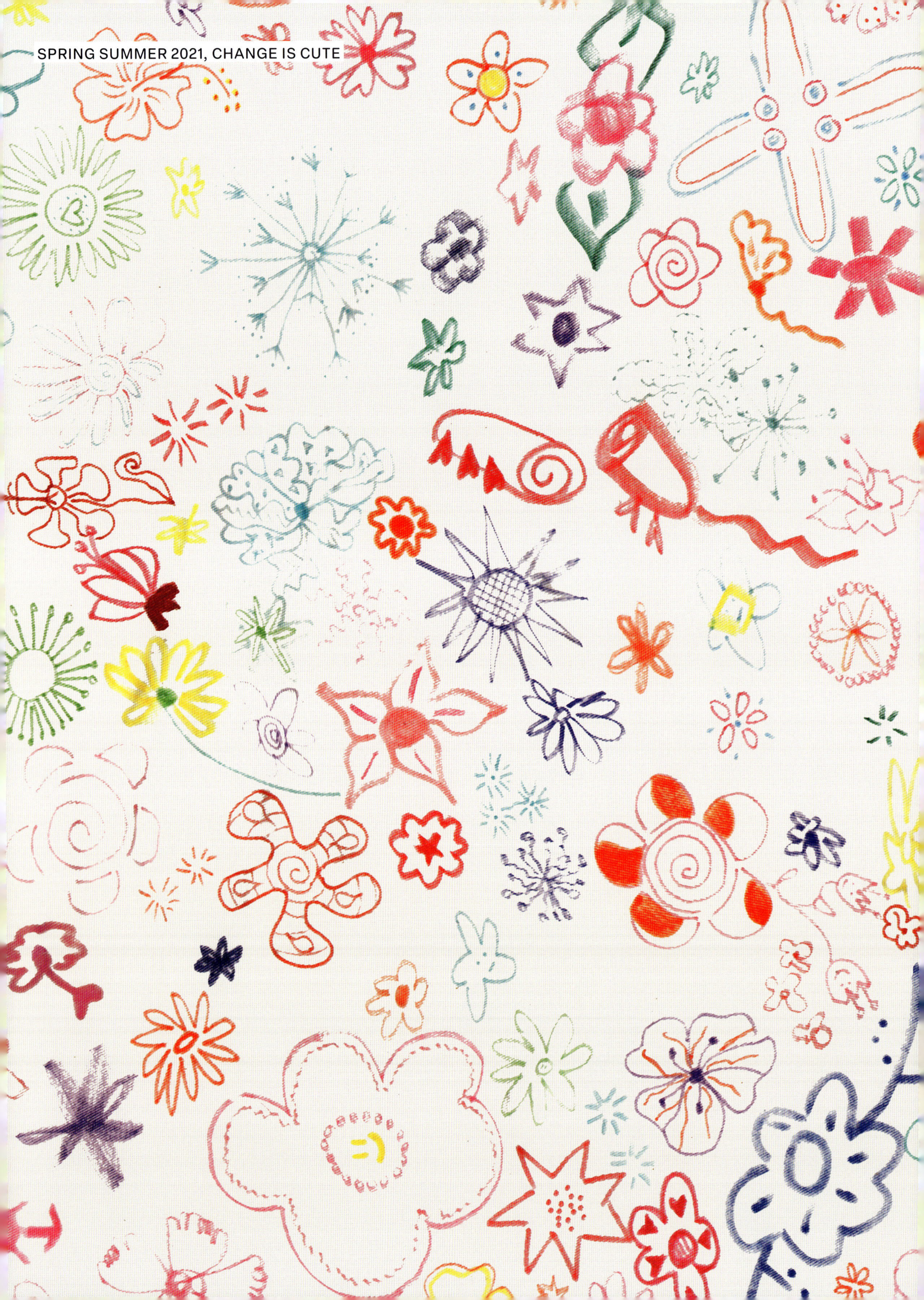

Directors: CHARLIE ENGMAN AND HILLARY TAYMOUR
3D Animation: JEFFERSON WENZEL
Make Up: ALLIE SMITH
Hair: CHIKA NISHIYAMA
Styling: CHARLIE ENGMAN and SASHA MELNYCHUK
Wigs: TOMIHIRO KONO

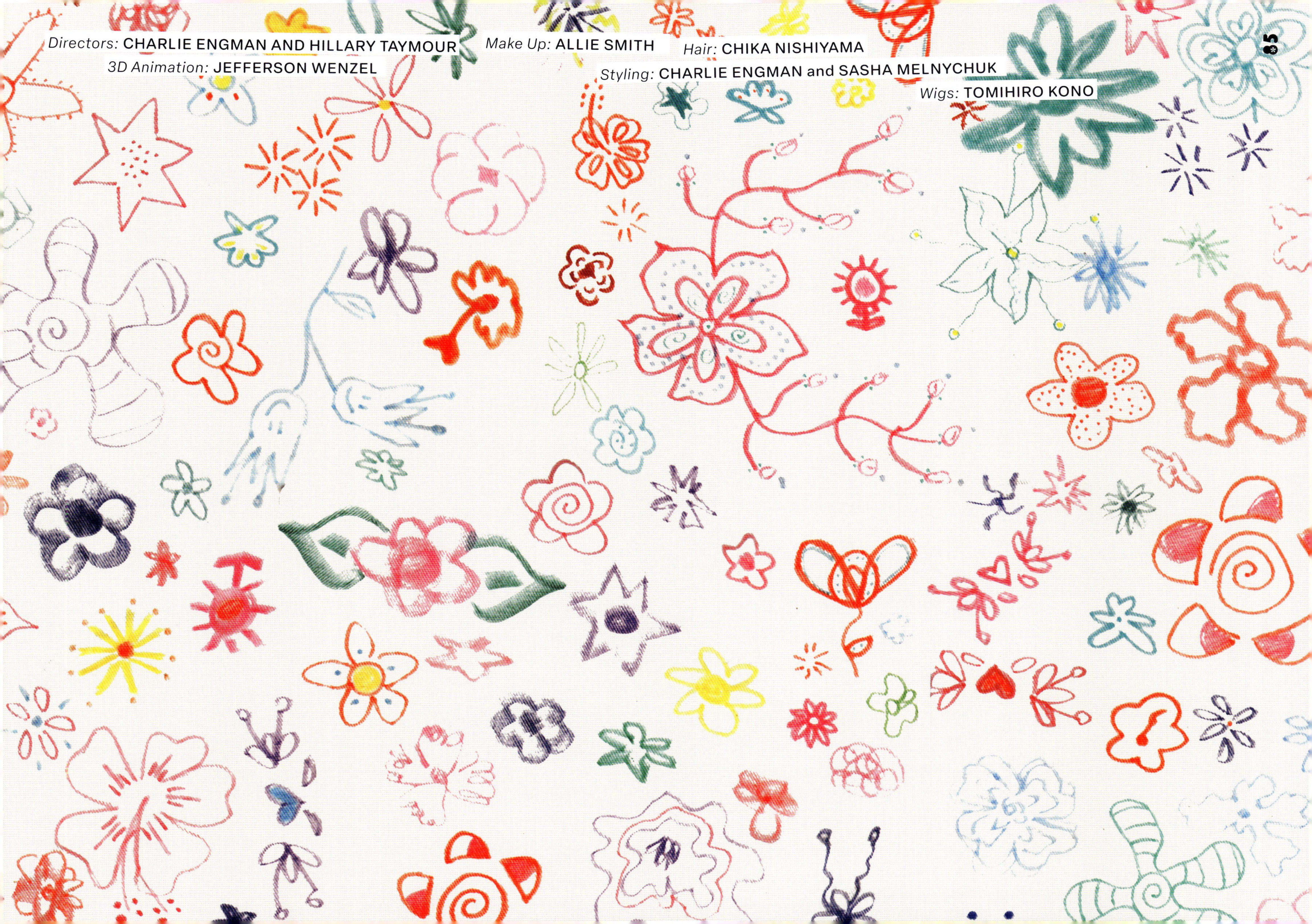

Spring Summer 2021

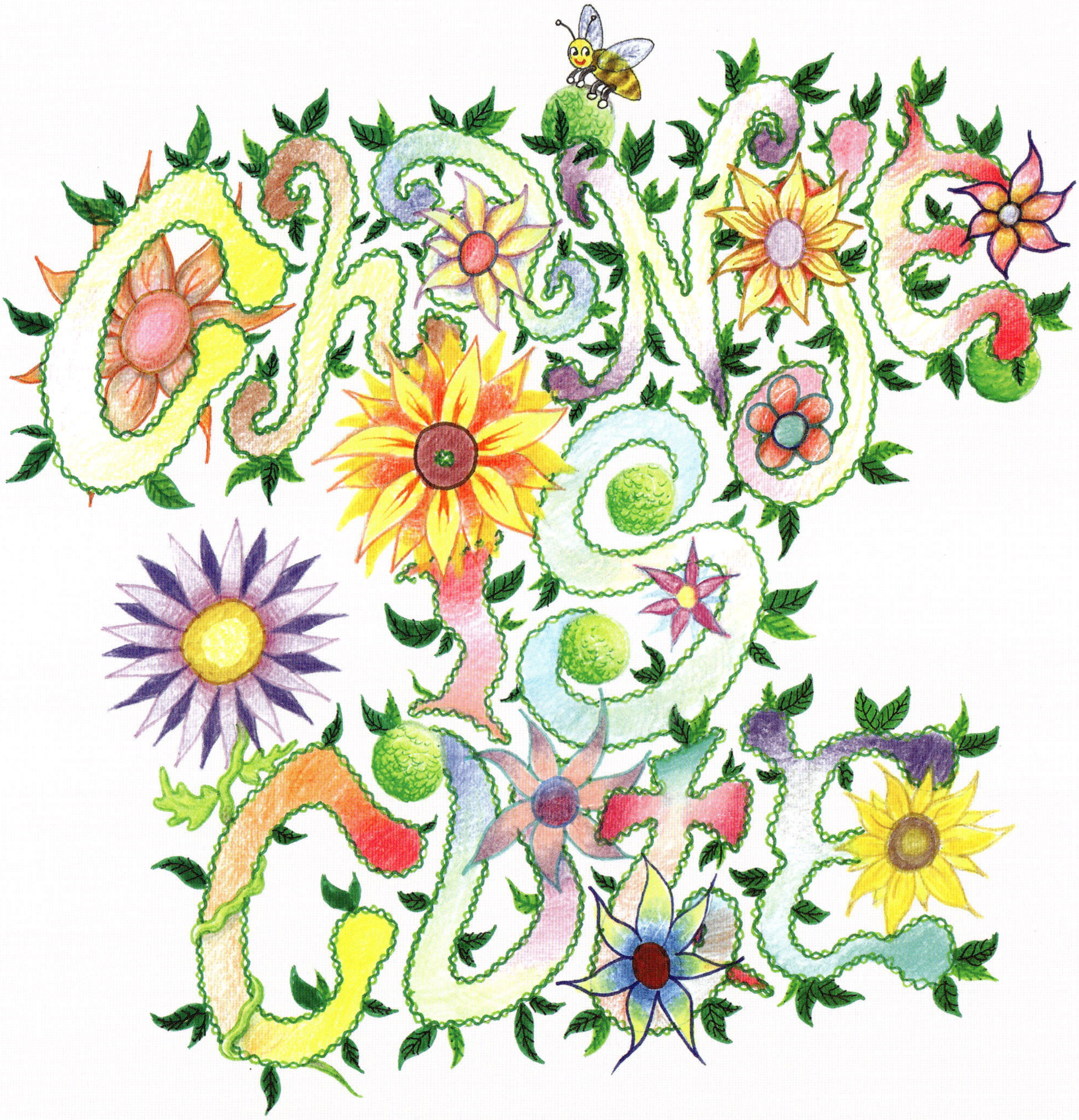

When the COVID-19 Pandemic forced us all into social distancing and collective introspection, many of us turned to screens to connect. This shift led to the imagining of a hybrid digital-reality: *Collina Utopia.* We enlisted friend and artist *Sean-Kierre Lyons* to create custom floral illustrations and *Alicia Mersy,* whose multimedia work focuses on political resistance, and animated their visions with the direction of 3D virtual artist *Jefferson Wenzel.* The resulting dreamscape was filled with tie-dyed cornfields, floating gardens, giant turnips from space, and a Collina-print rainbow waterfall, which set the scene for the season's *farm-tastic show.*

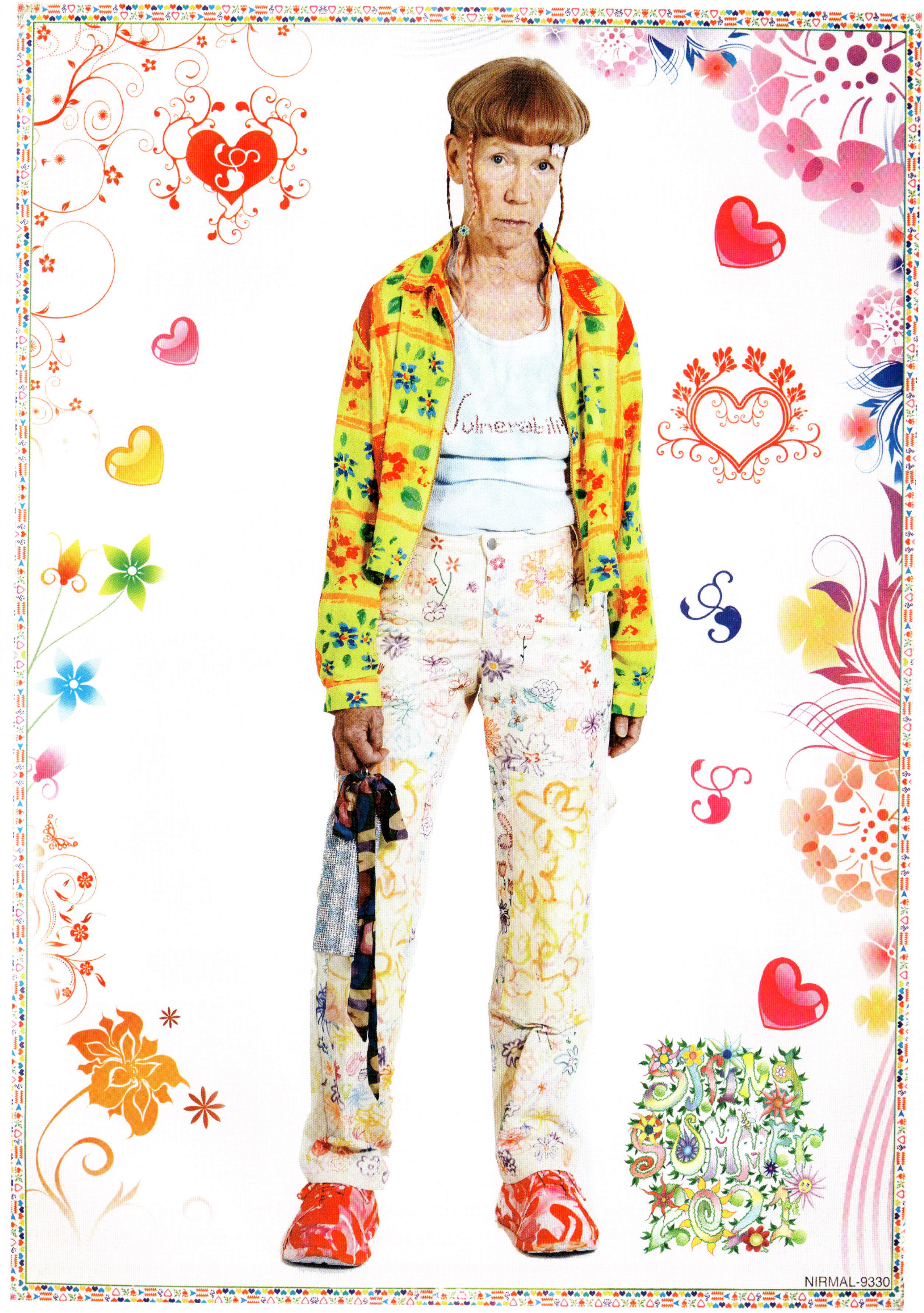
Vulnerabili
SUMMER
2021
NIRMAL-9330

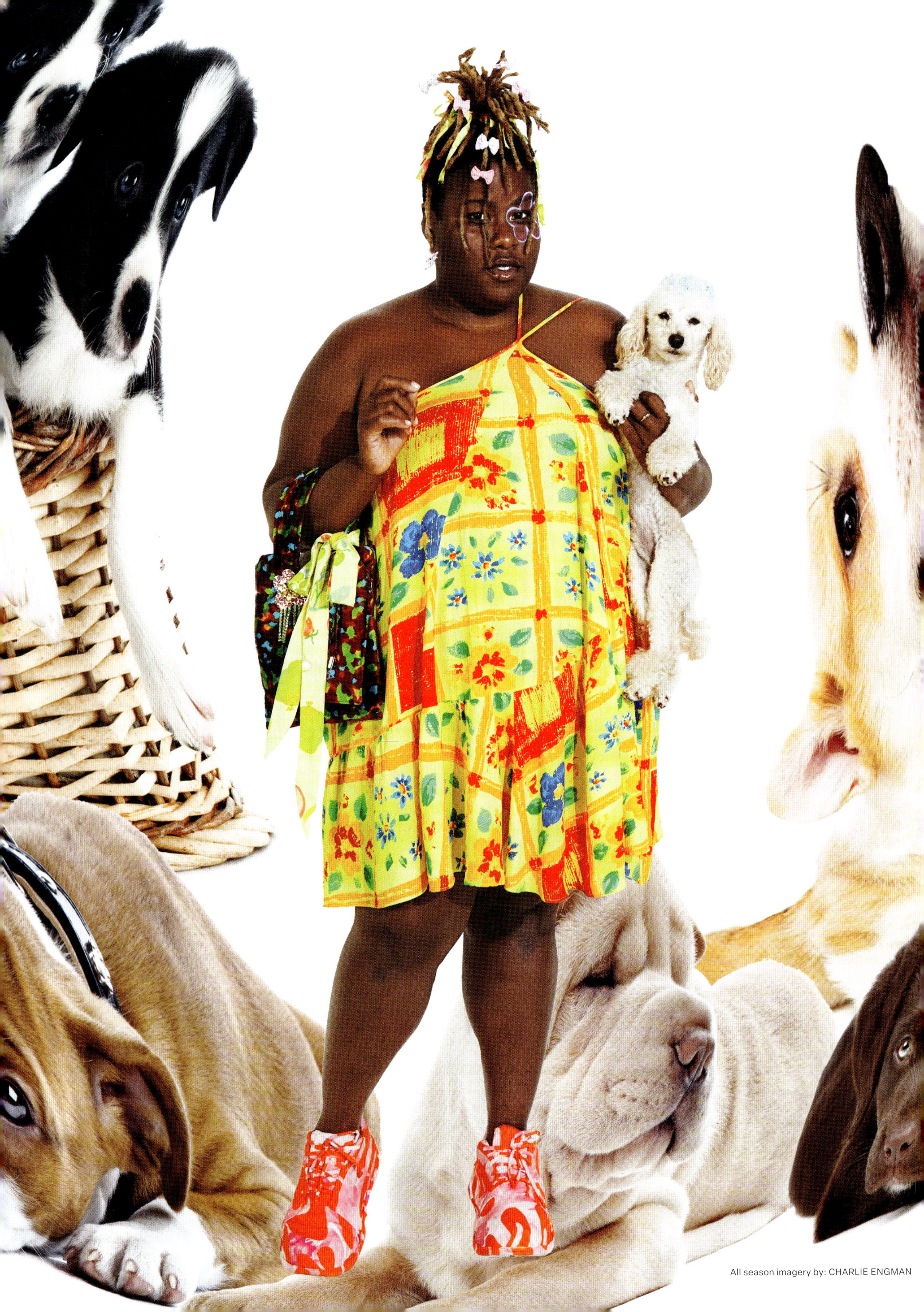

All season imagery by: CHARLIE ENGMAN

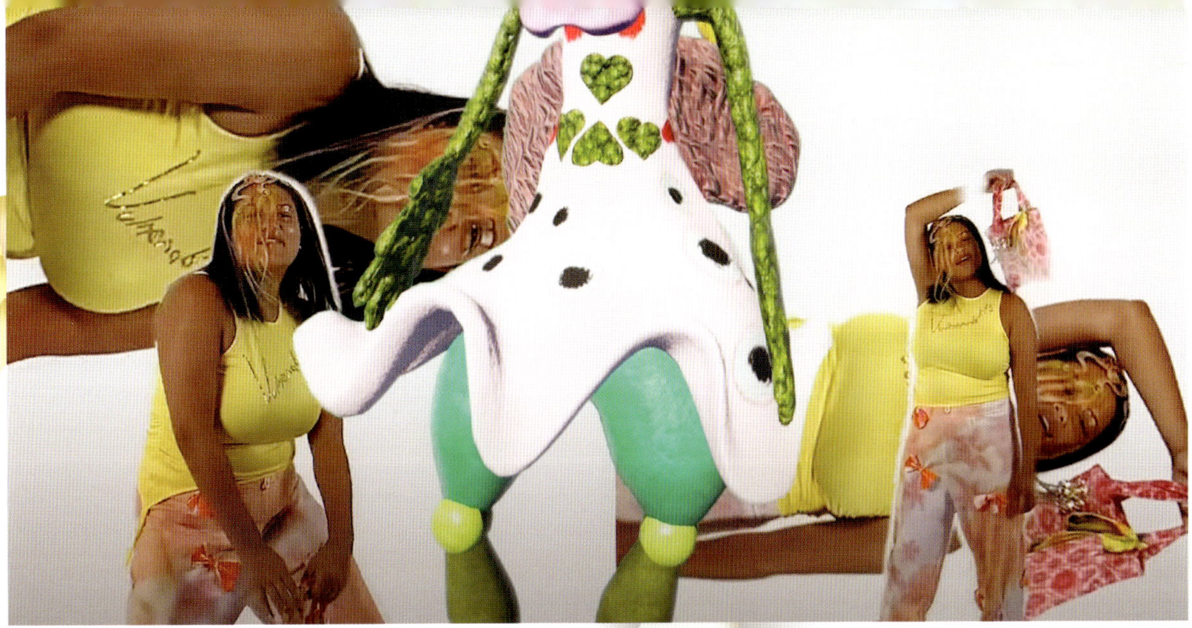

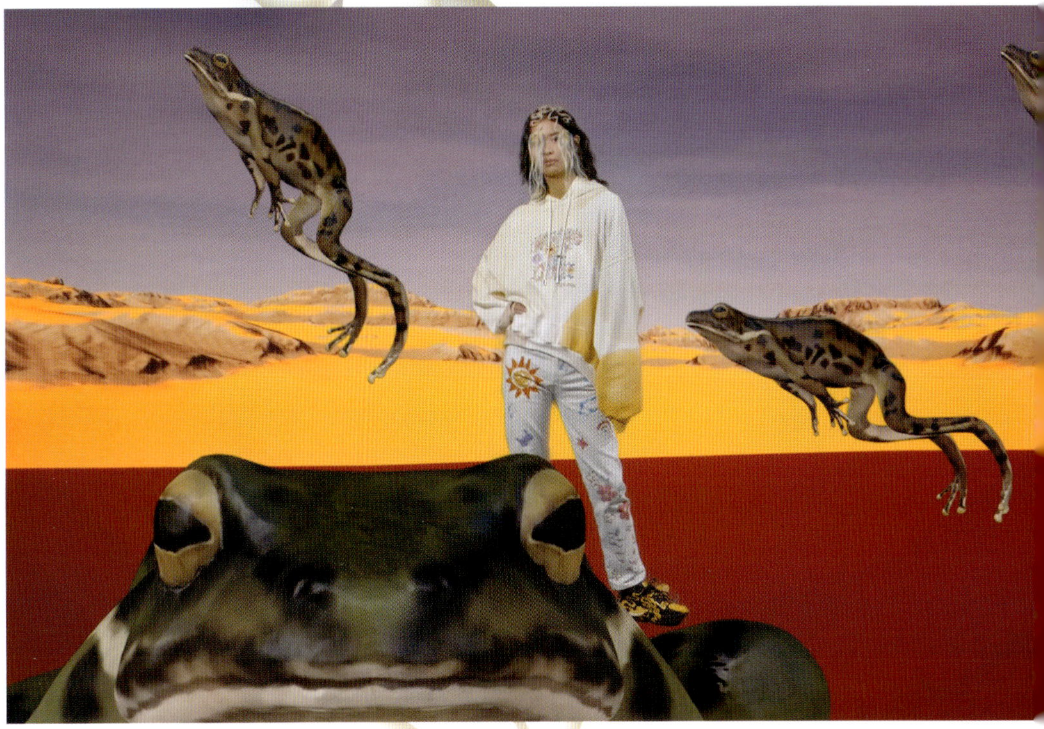

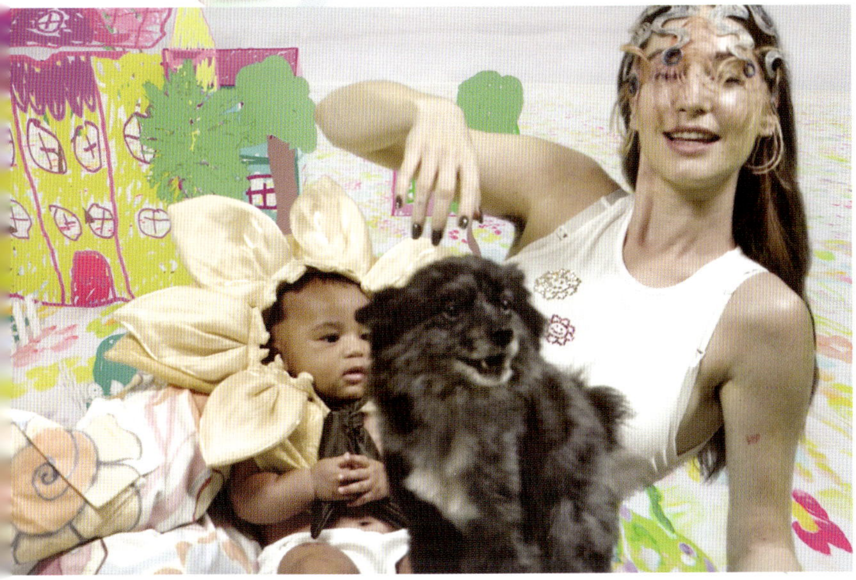

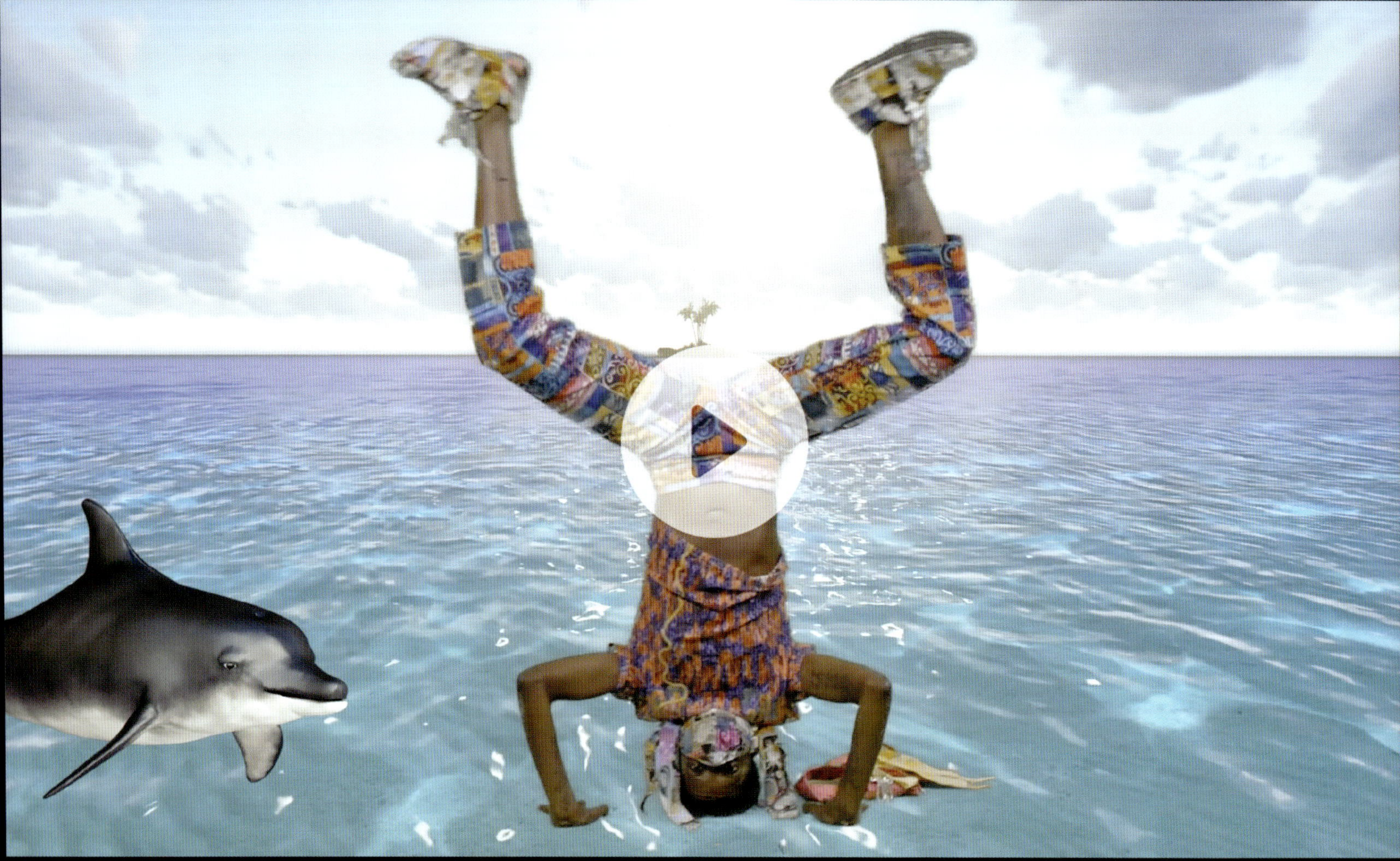

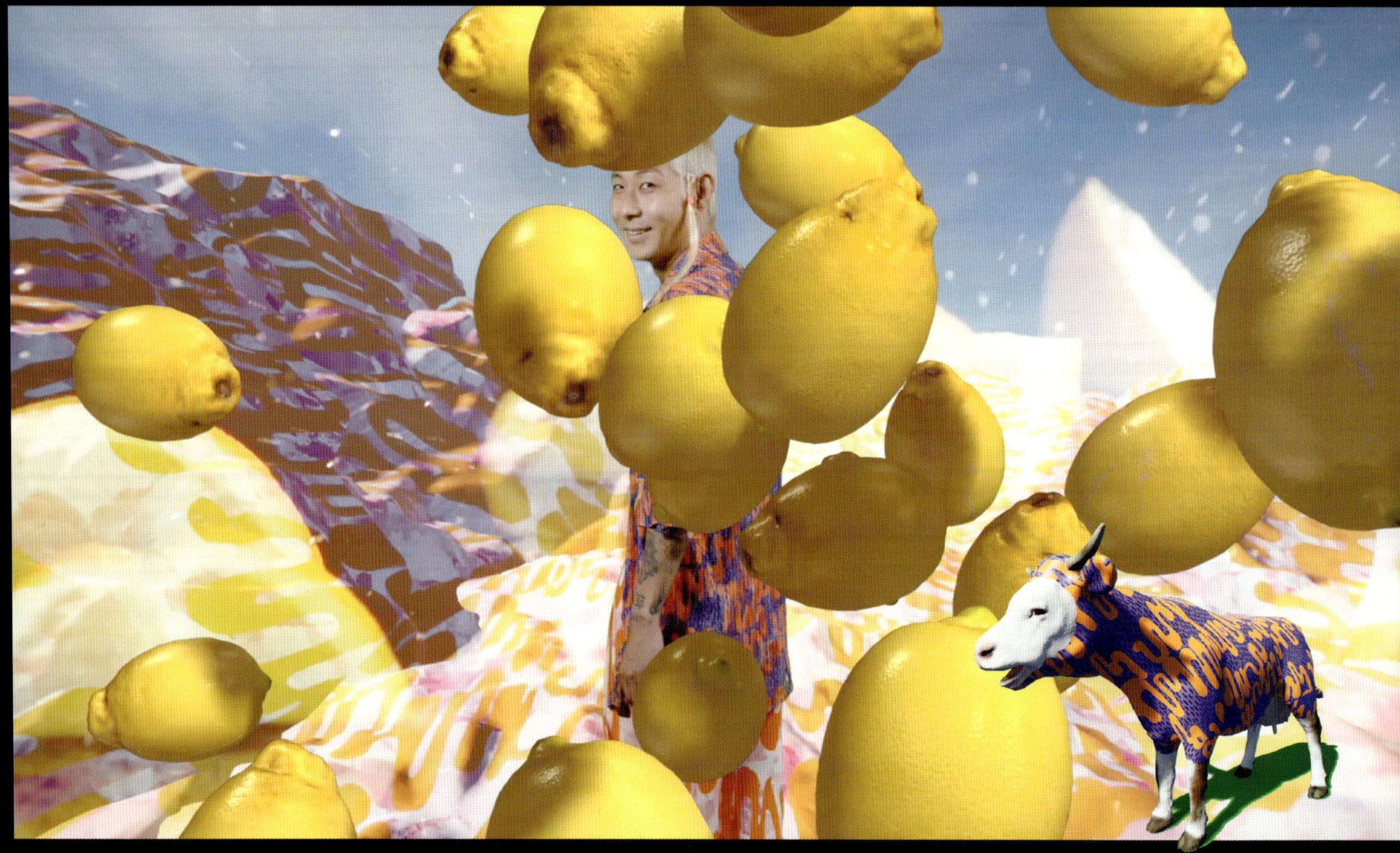

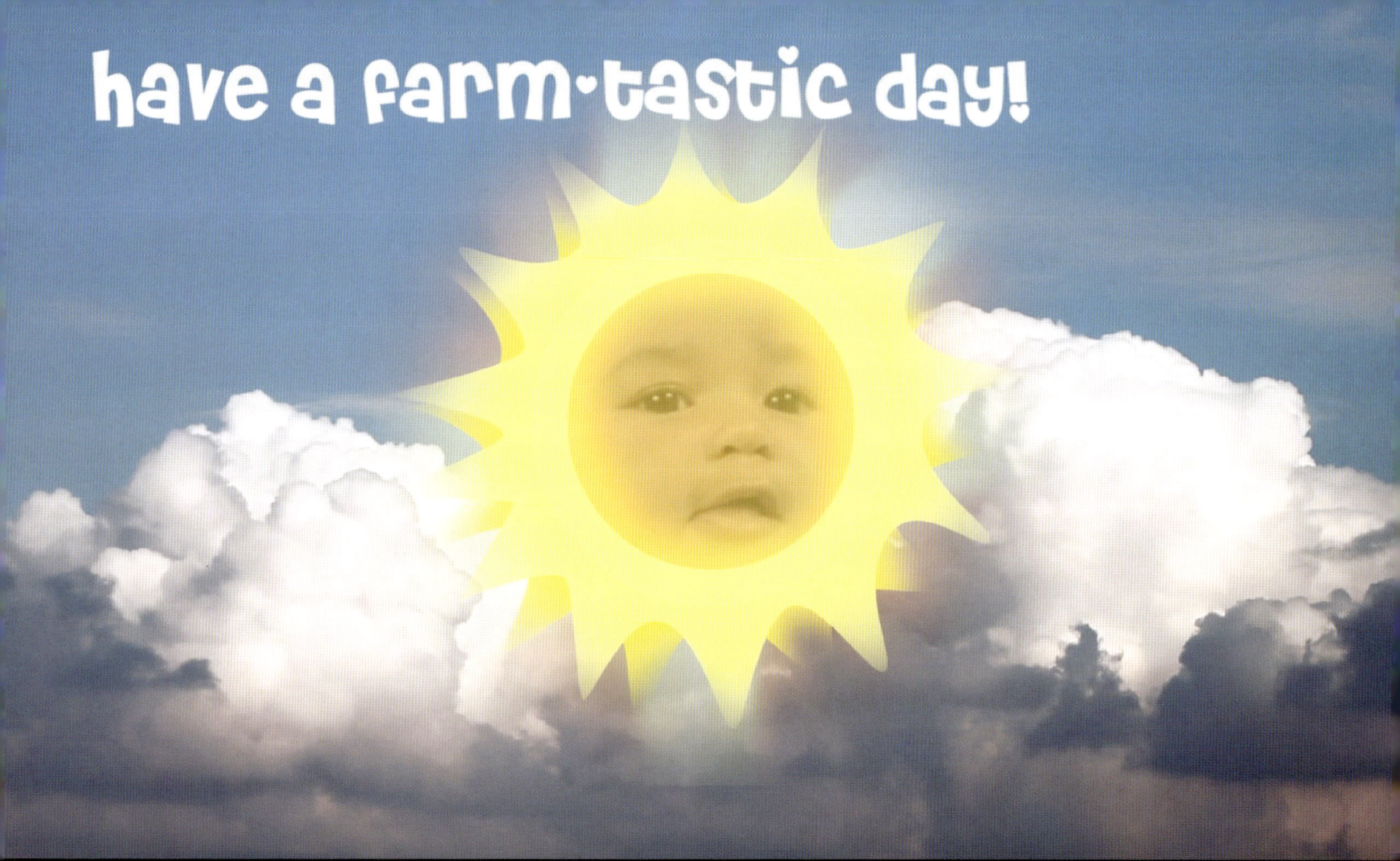
have a farm·tastic day!

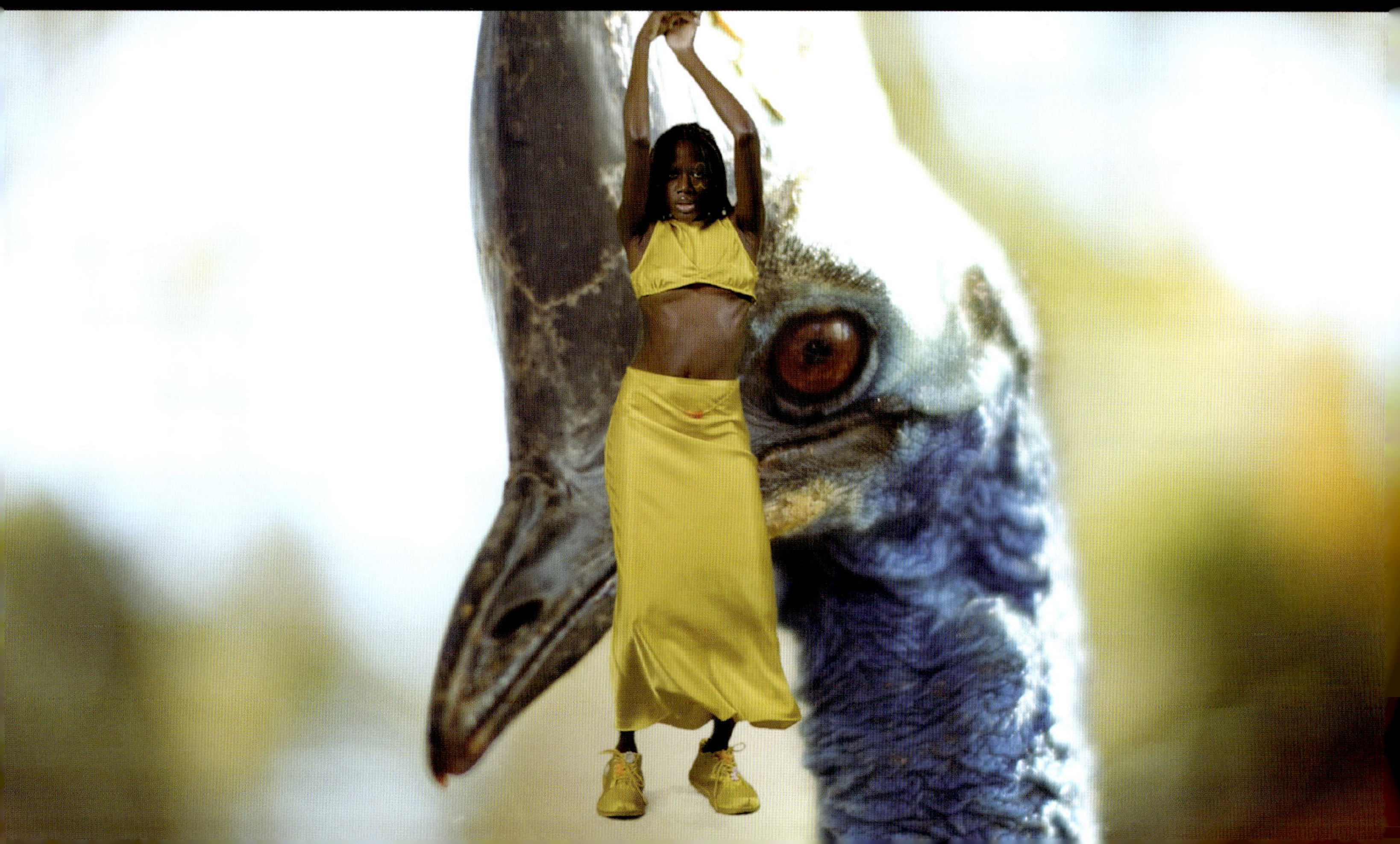

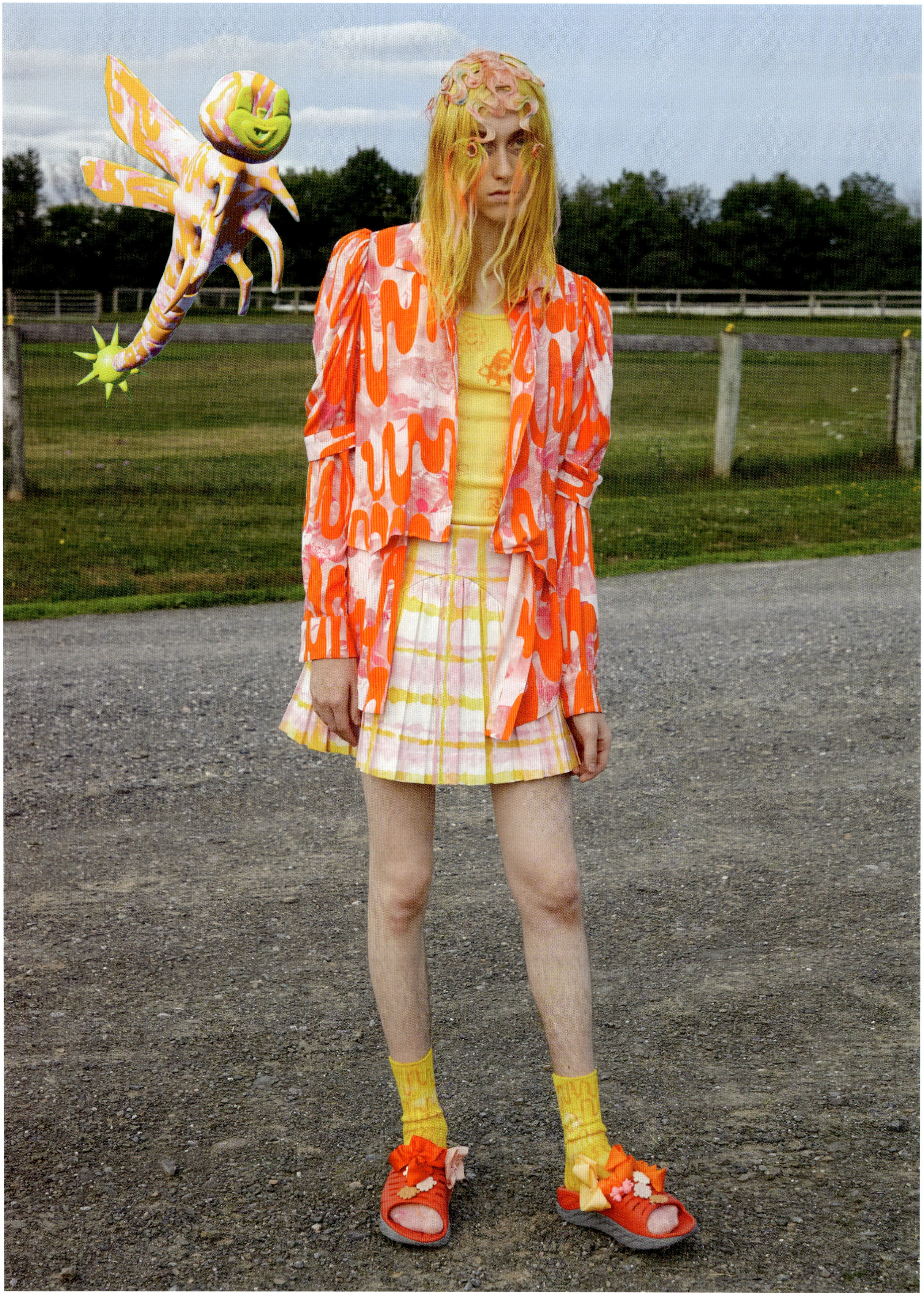

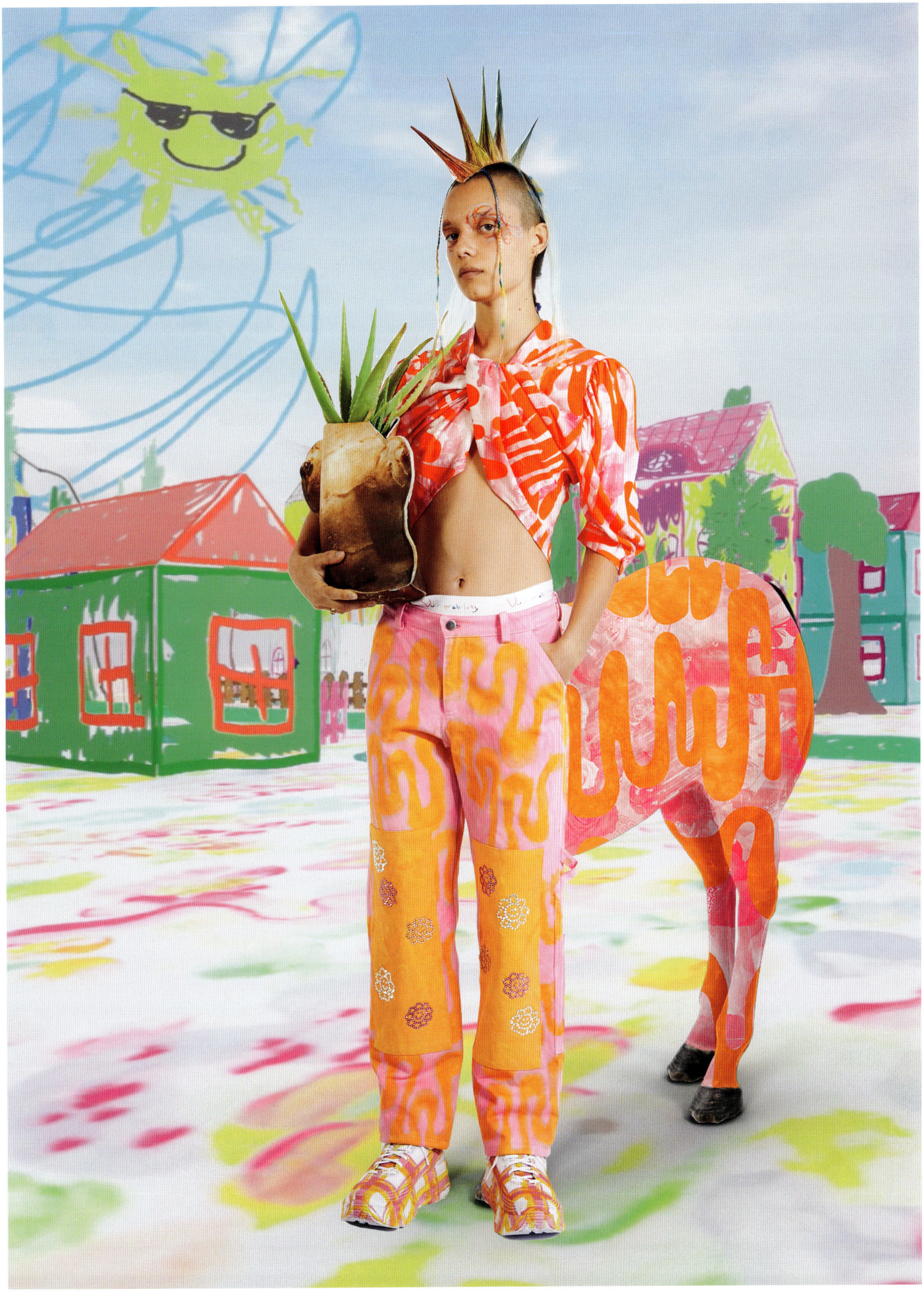

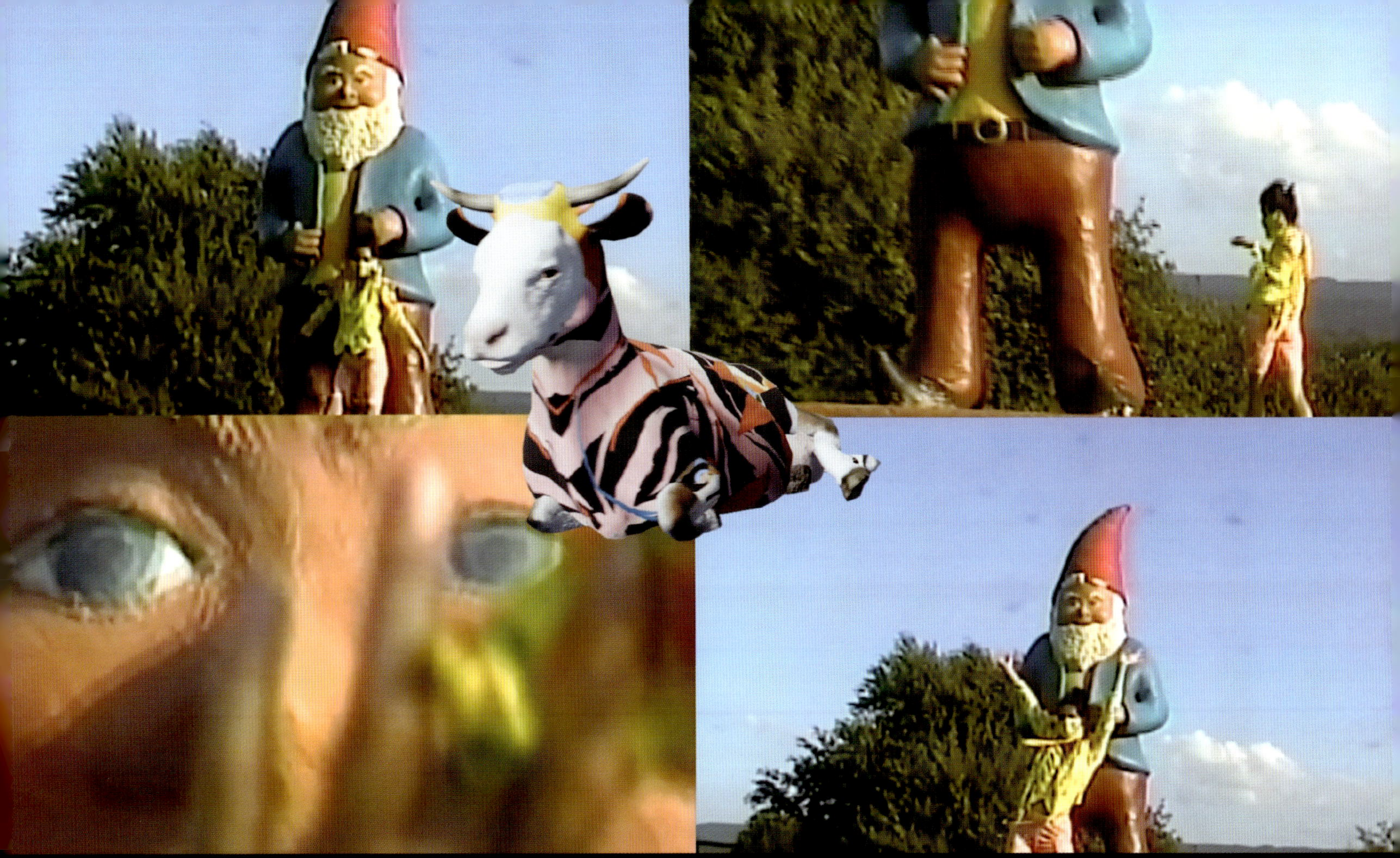

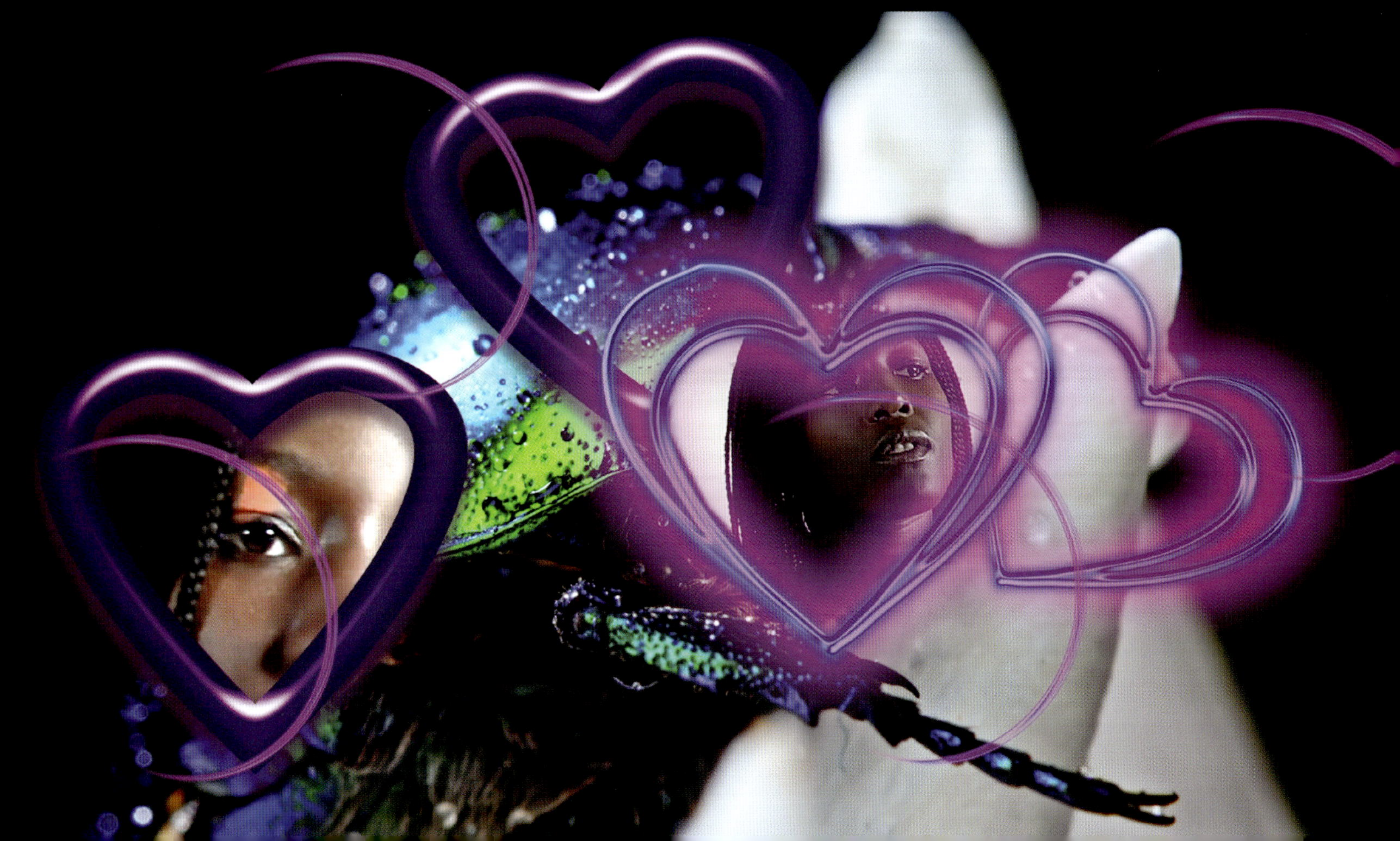

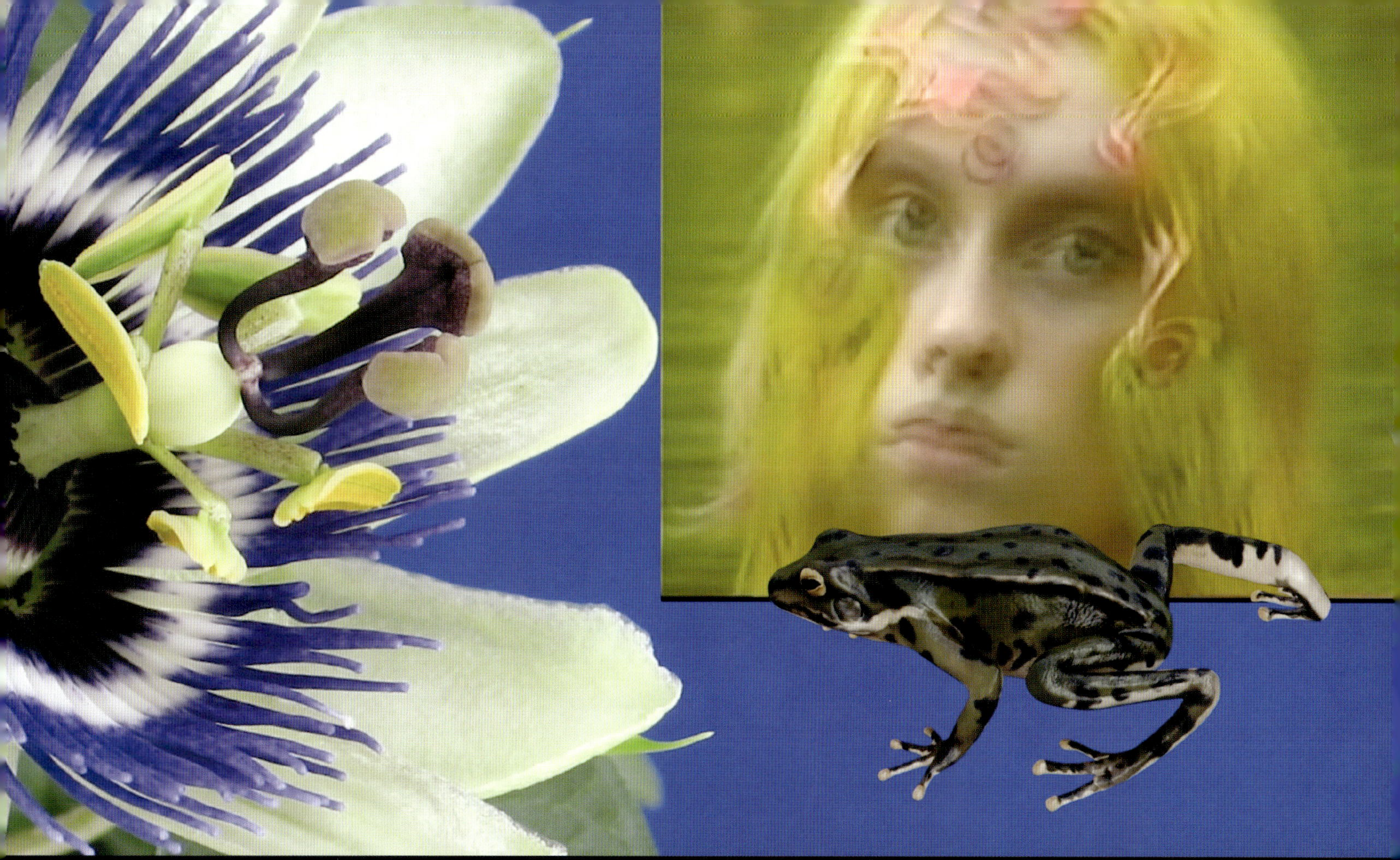

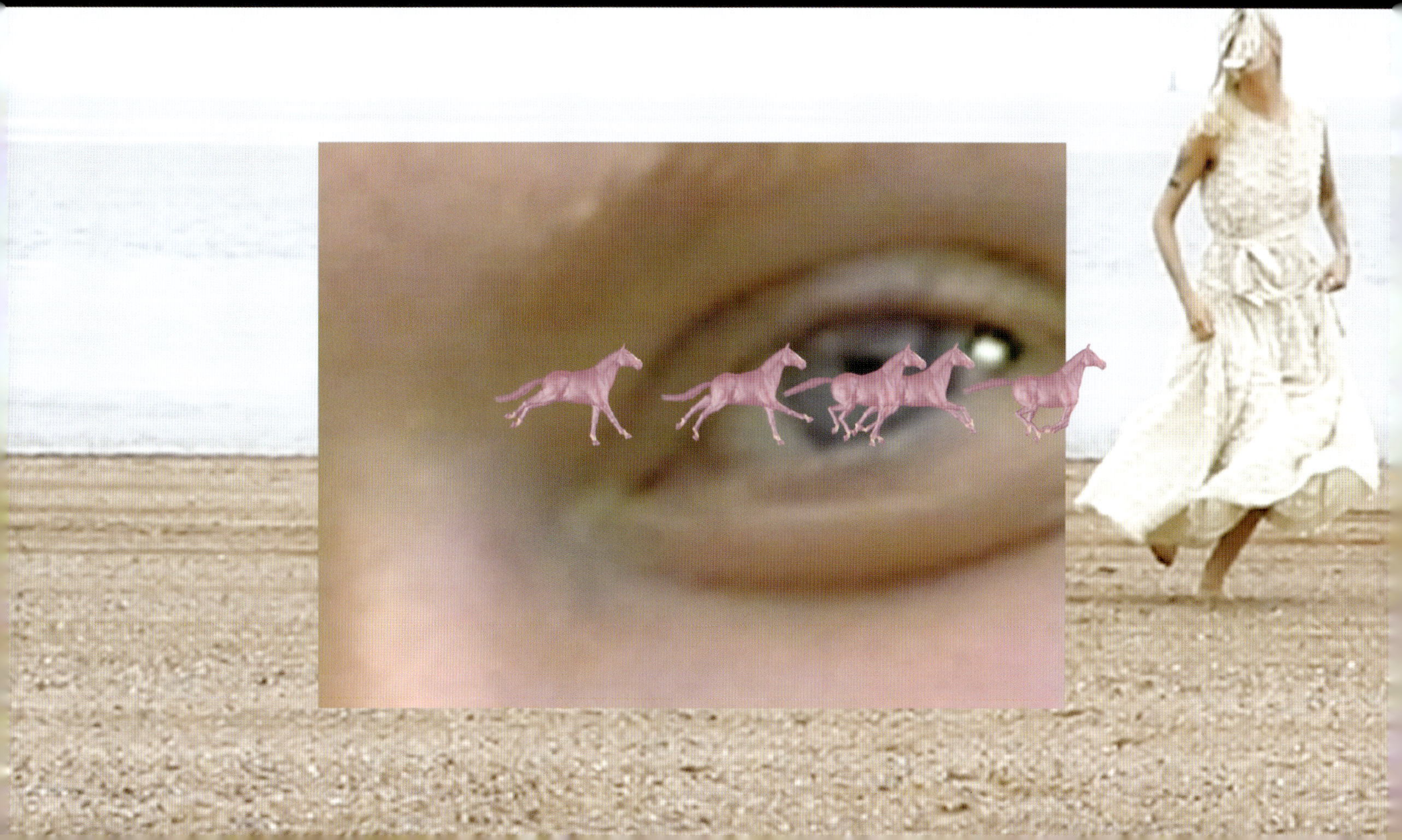

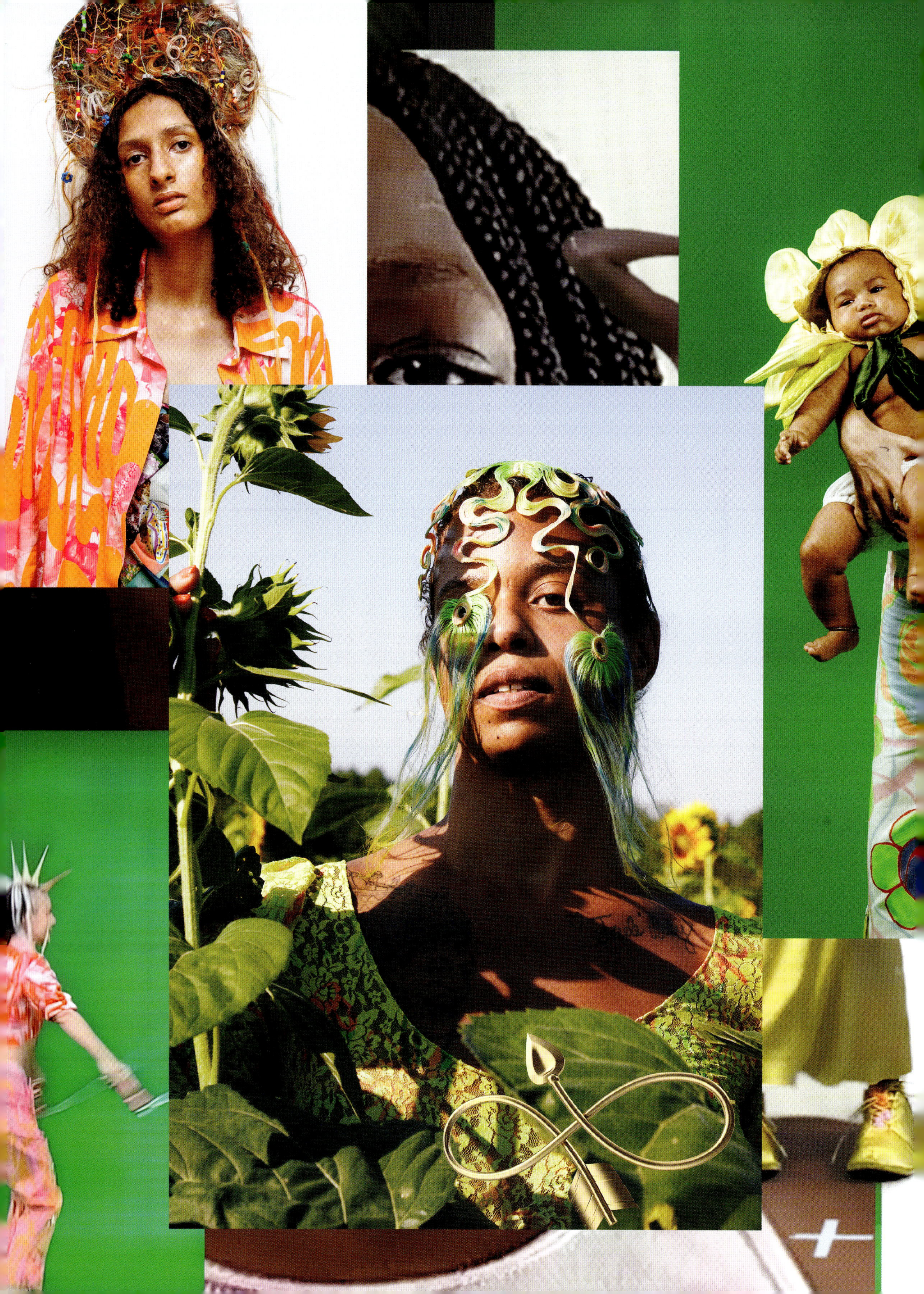

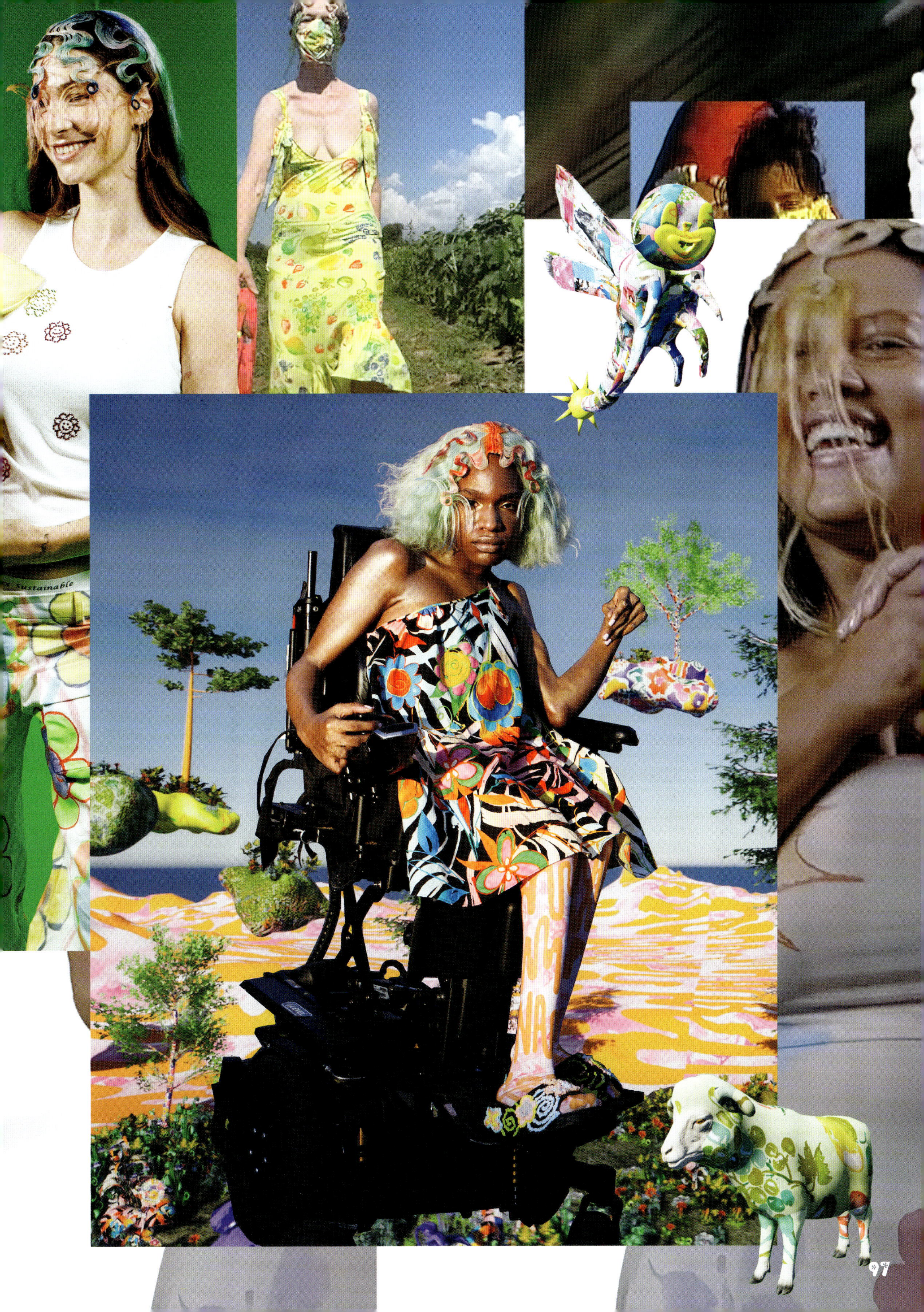
Sustainable

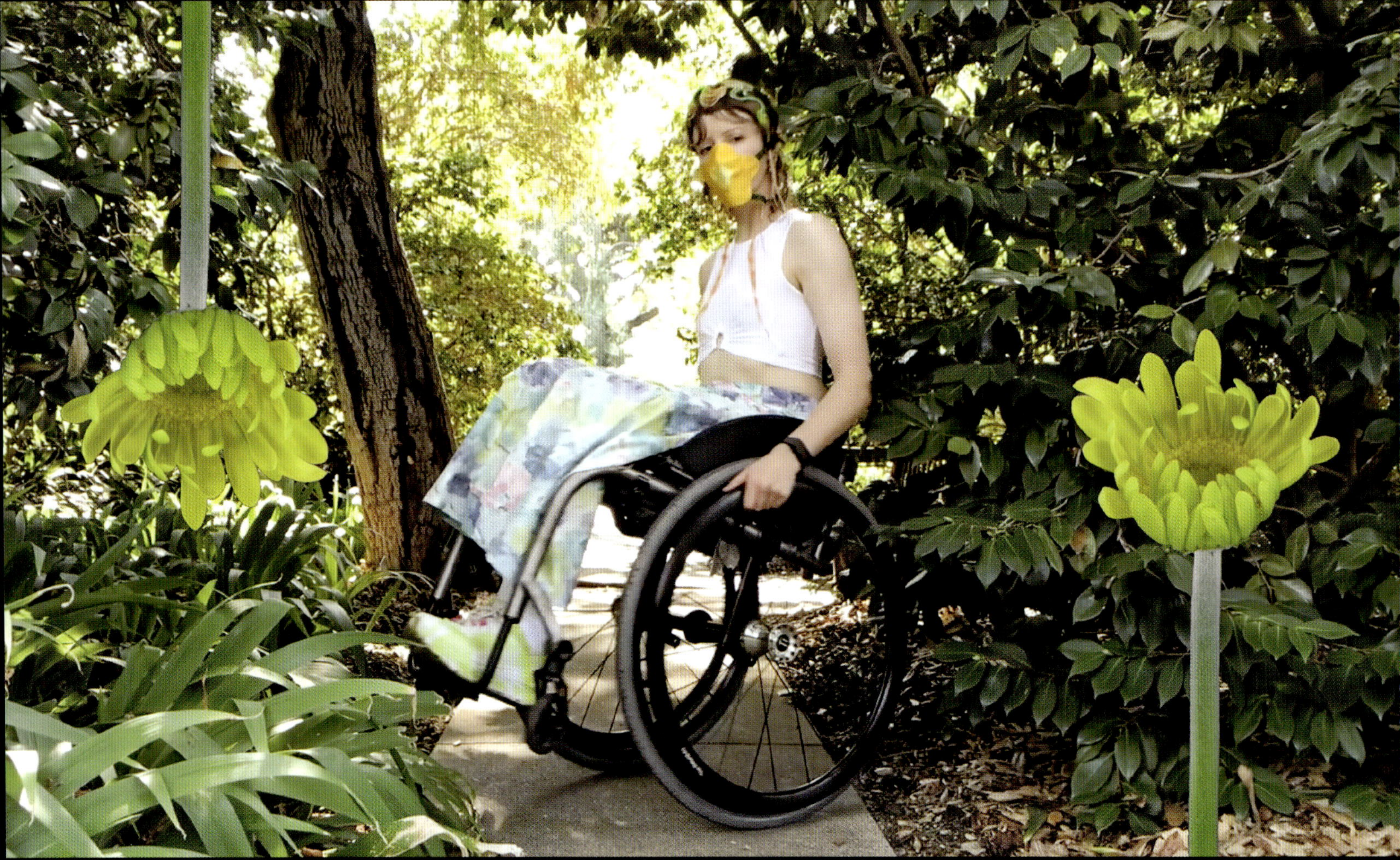

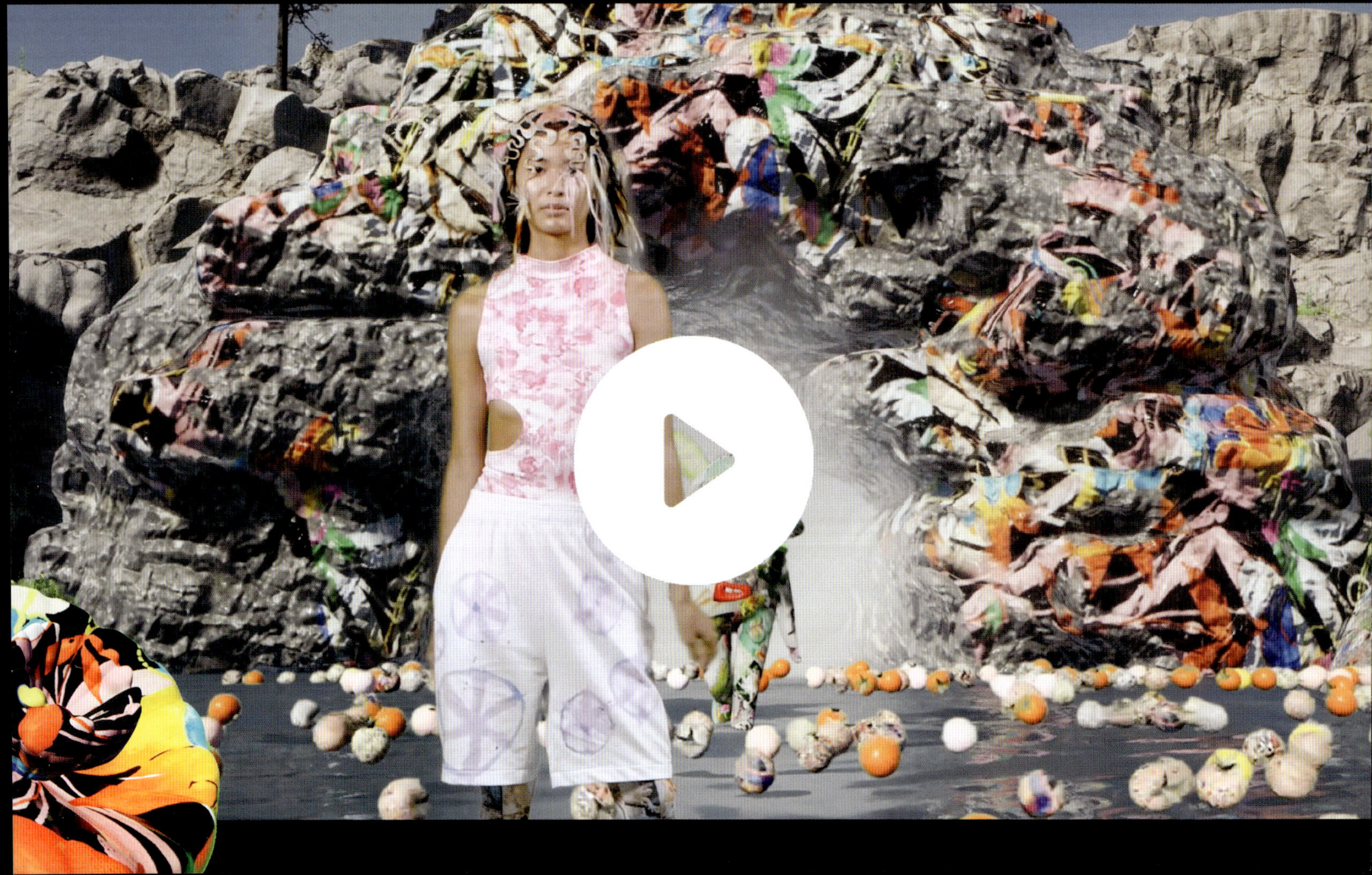

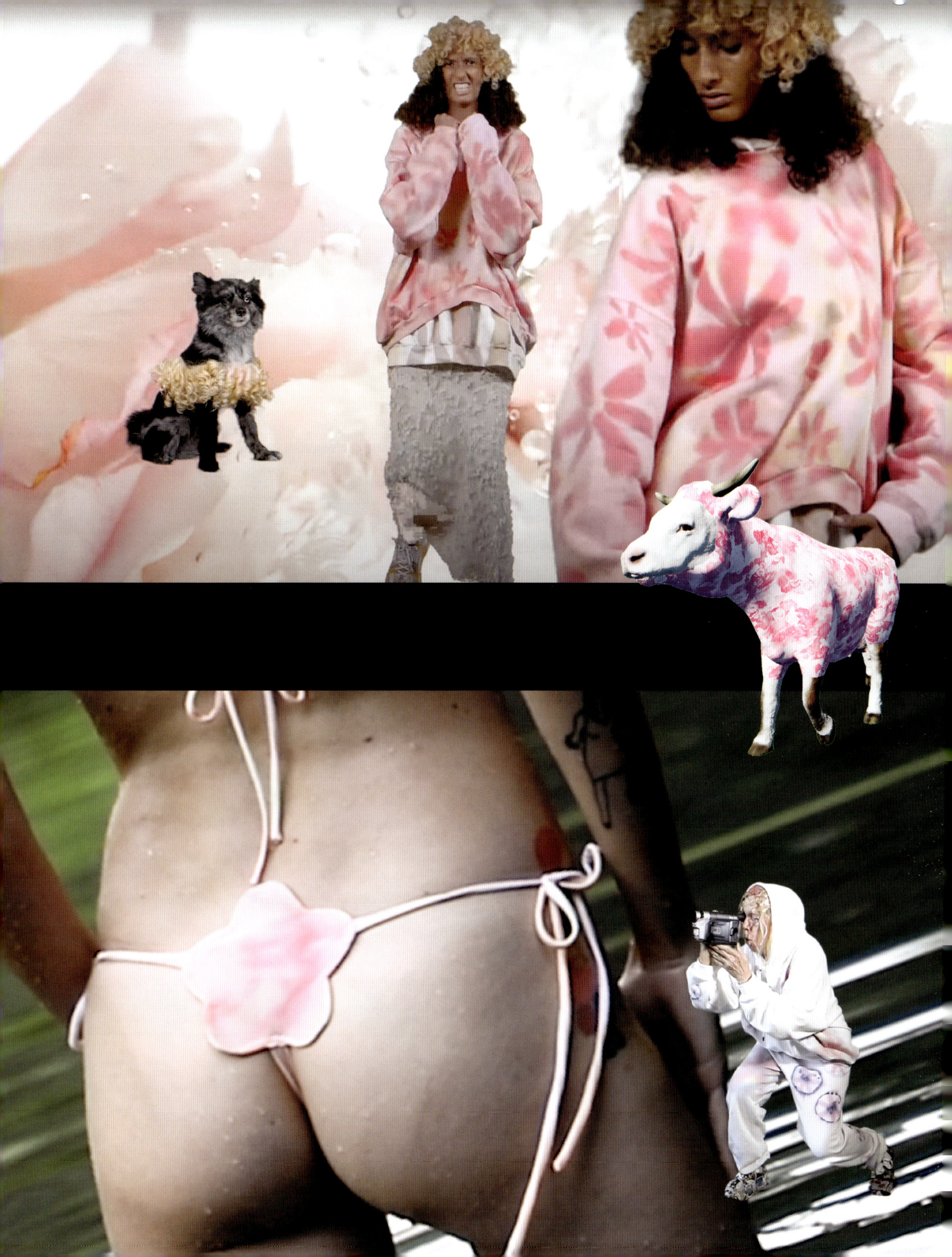

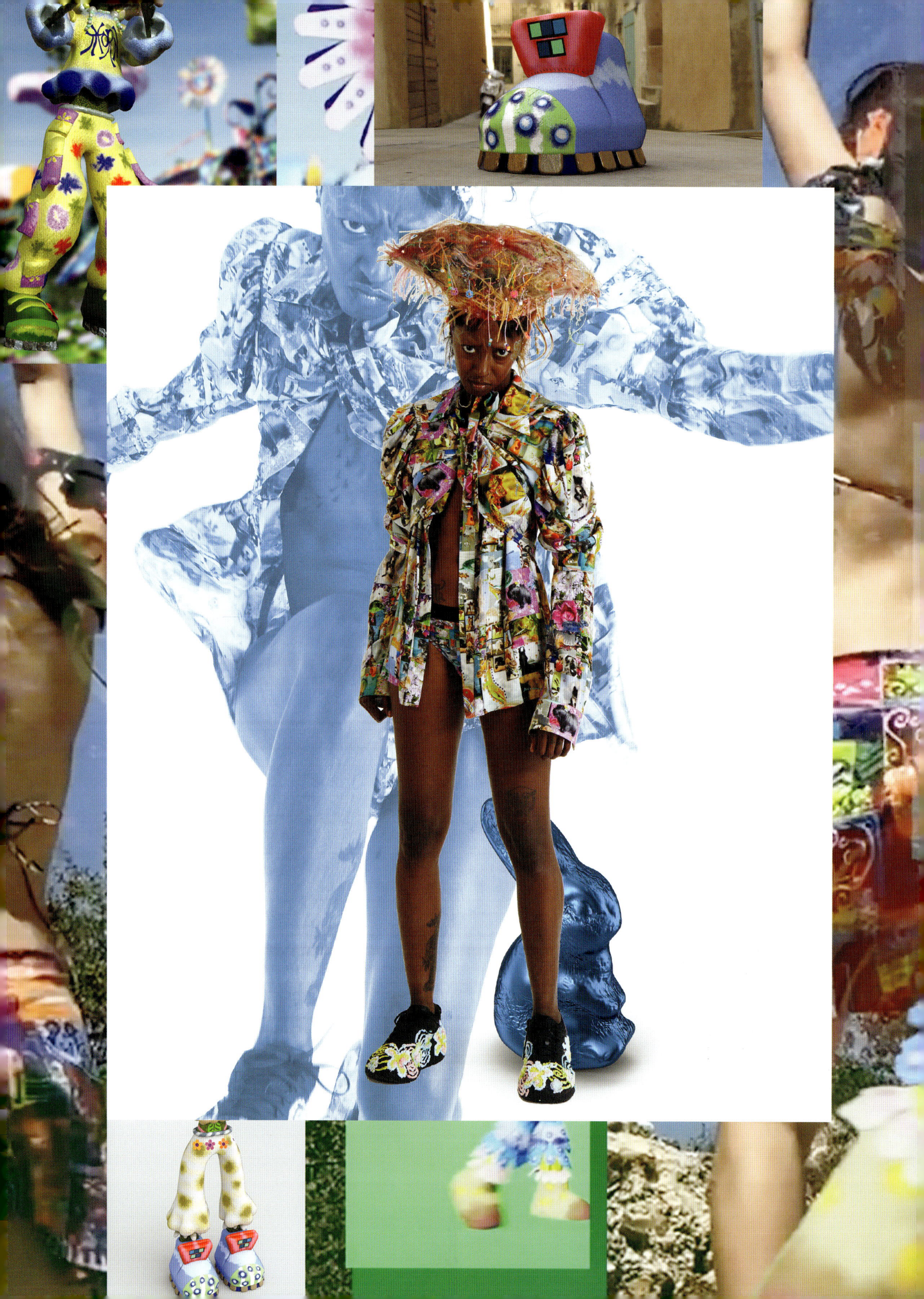

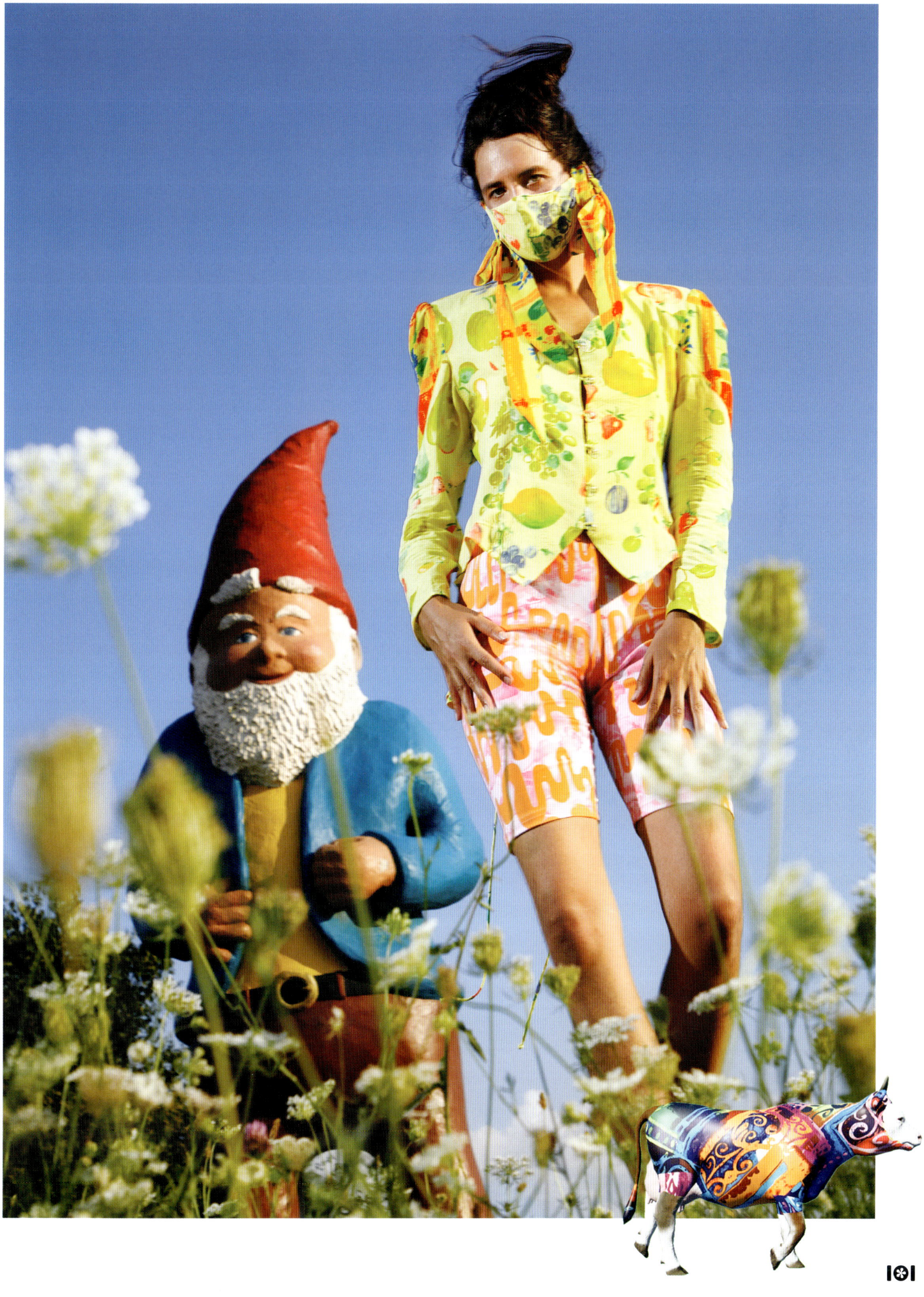

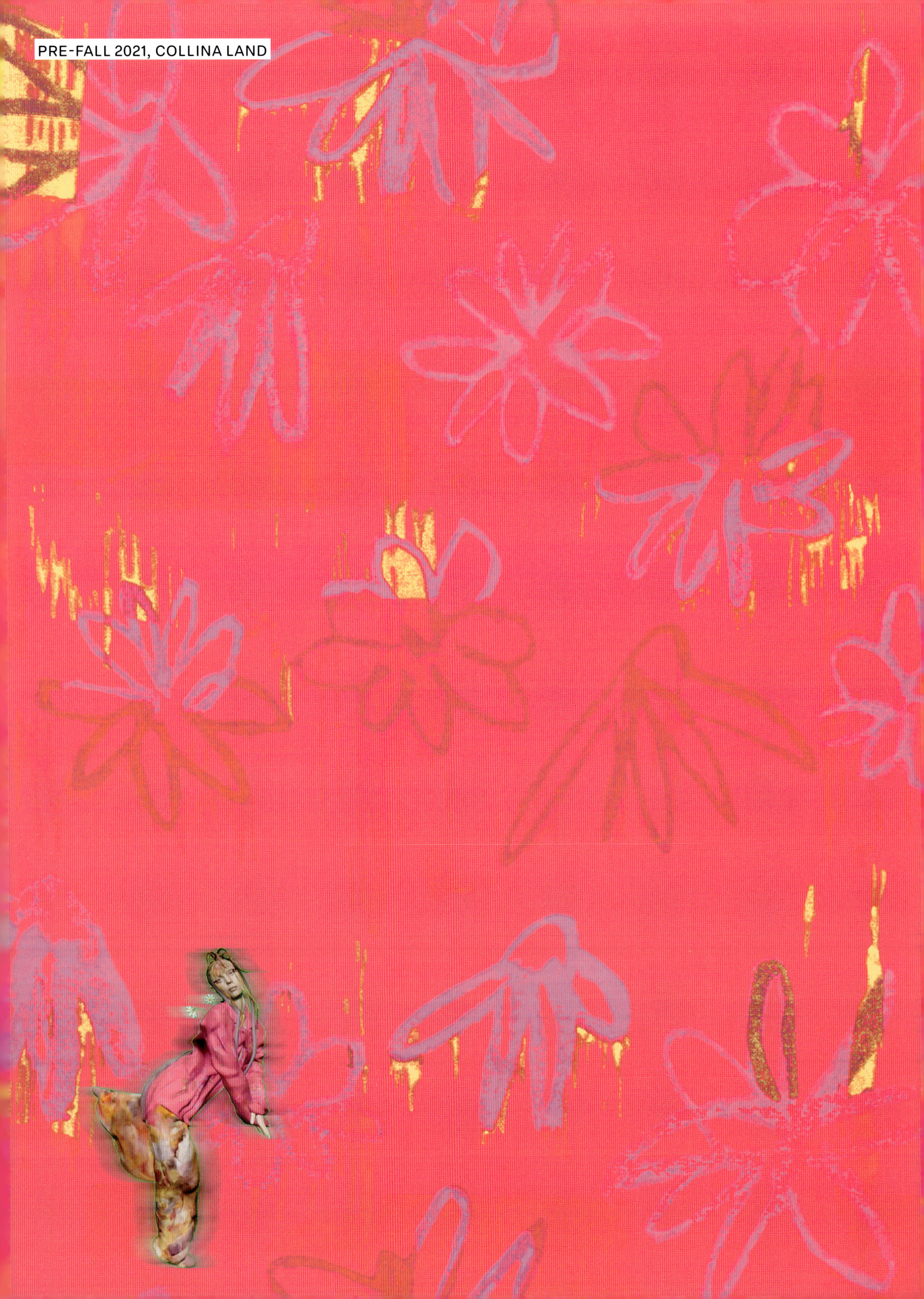

PRE-FALL 2021, COLLINA LAND

Hair: CHARLIE LE MINDU *Makeup:* ALLIE SMITH *Styling and Art Direction:* CHARLIE ENGMAN
Nails: JUAN ALVEAR *Game Design:* JEFFERSON WENZEL *Visual FX:* FREEKA TET

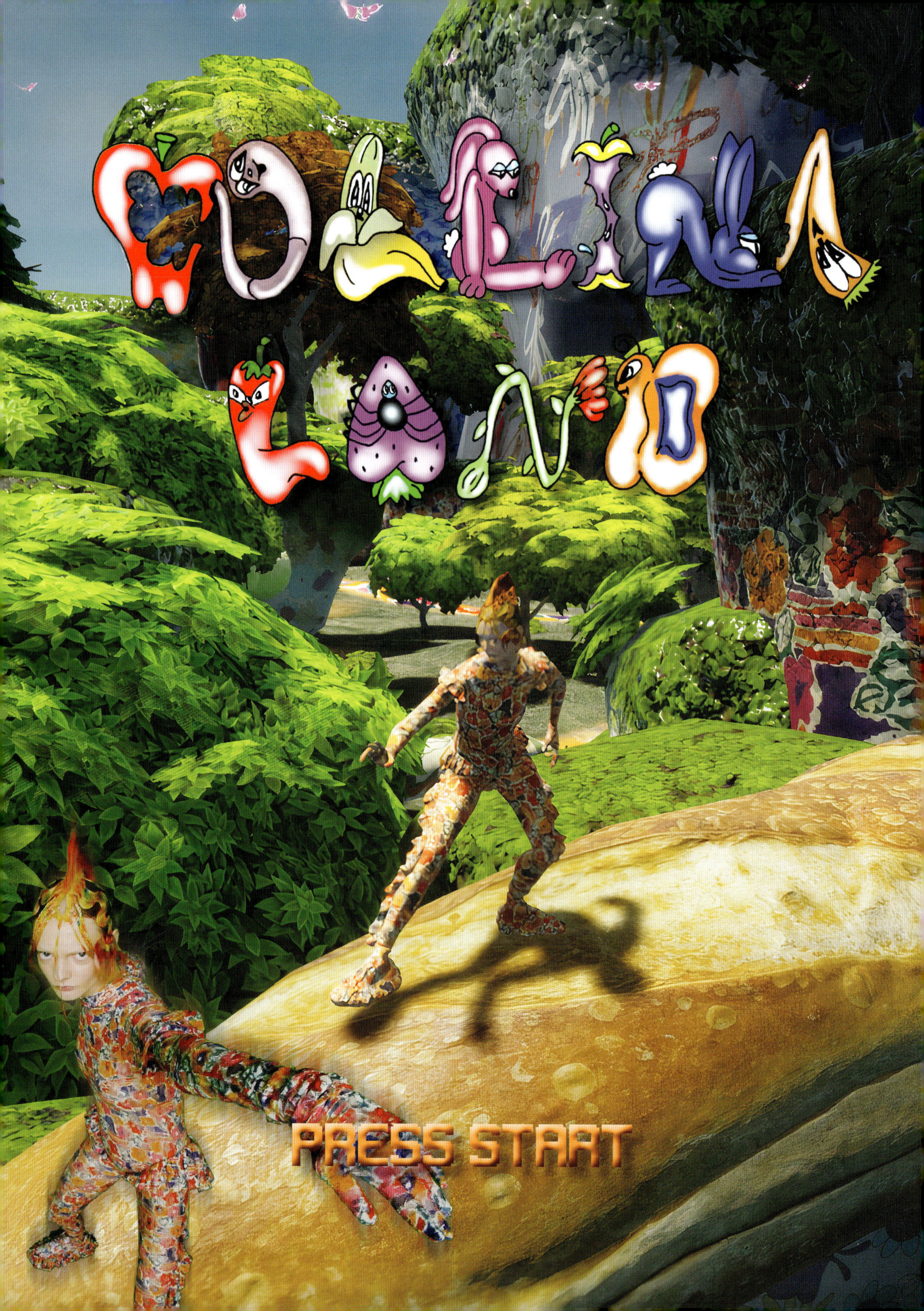
PRESS START

12,687 13,458 2,250

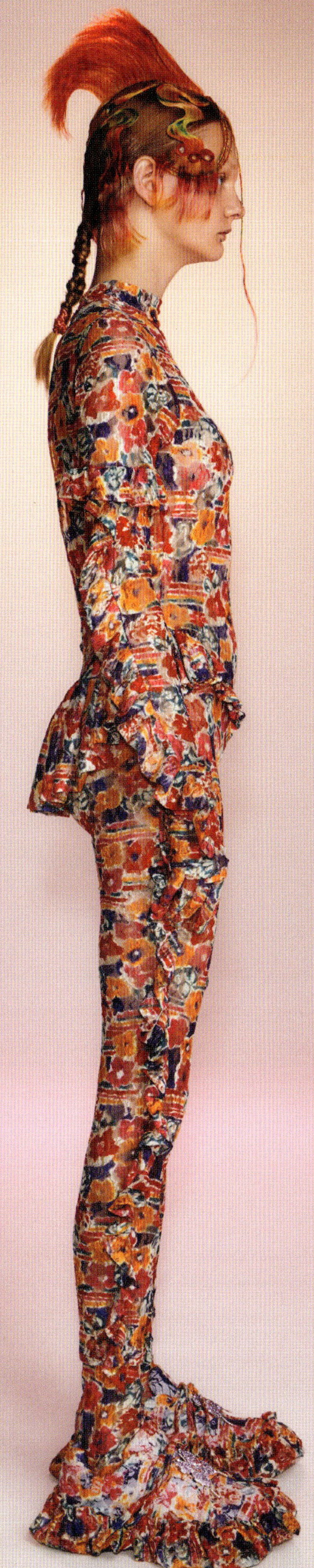

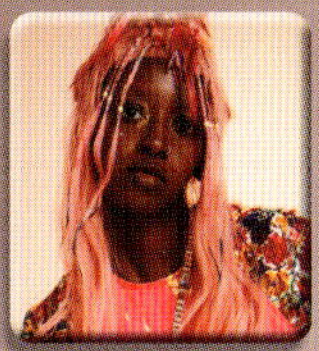

DACHI

Having already laid the foundation for a virtual Collina world, we delved even deeper into the DIGI-VERSE and created Collina-Land, a fully playable video game, for GUCCIFEST2020. Architected by JEFFERSON WENZEL, the game tasks players with saving Collina-Land from climate catastrophe.

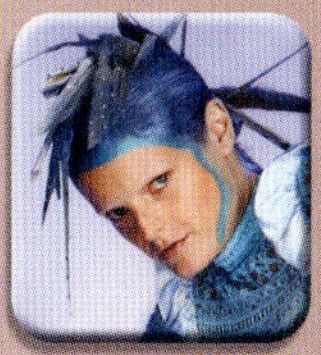

HANNE

We 3D-SCANNED our models and outfitted them with the powers and accessories they need to traverse the 5 REALMS of Collina-Land: the Drawing World, the Desert World, the Farm World, the Ice World, and the Water World.

PRE-FALL 2021

All season imagery by CHARLIE ENGMAN unless noted otherwise.

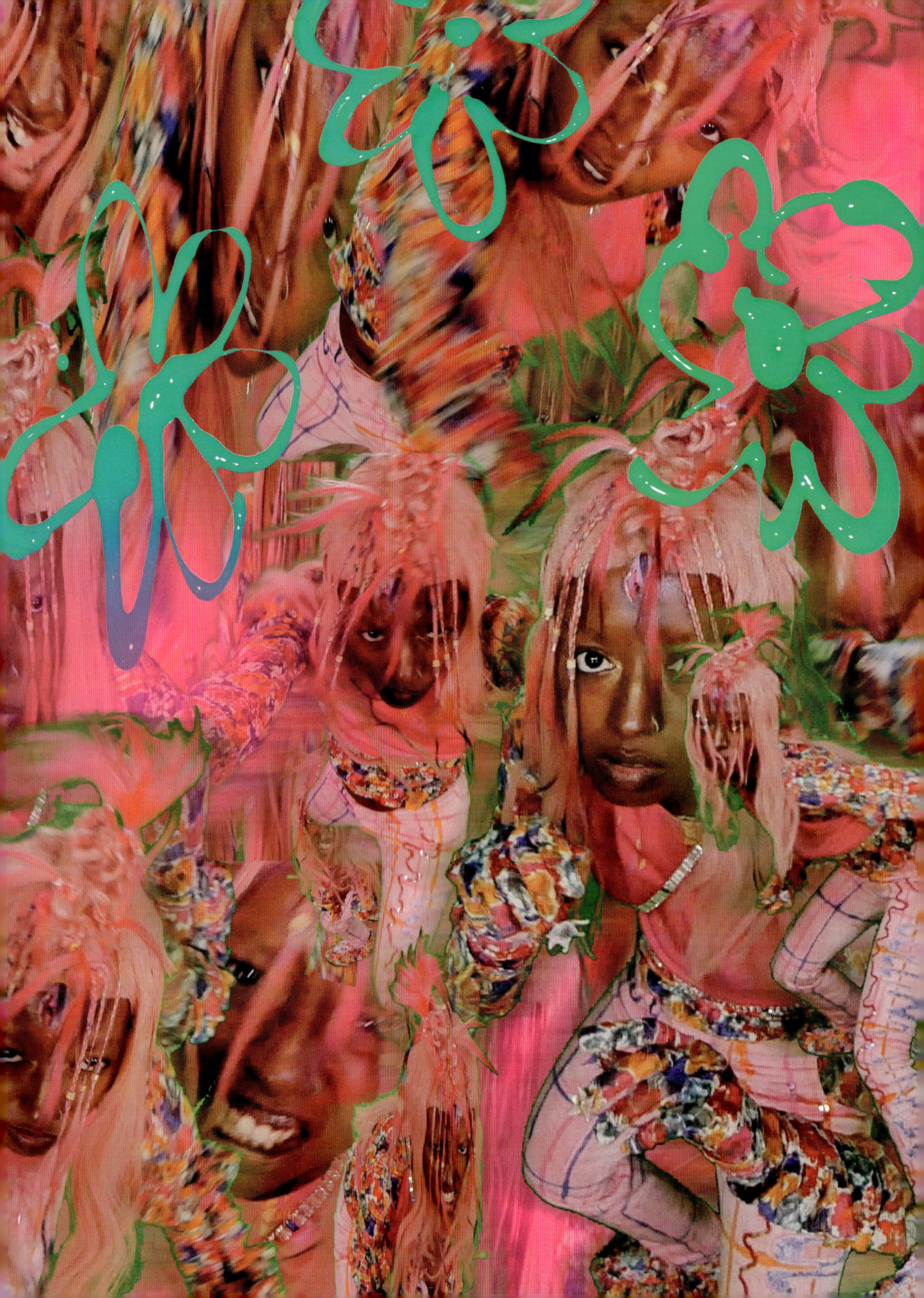

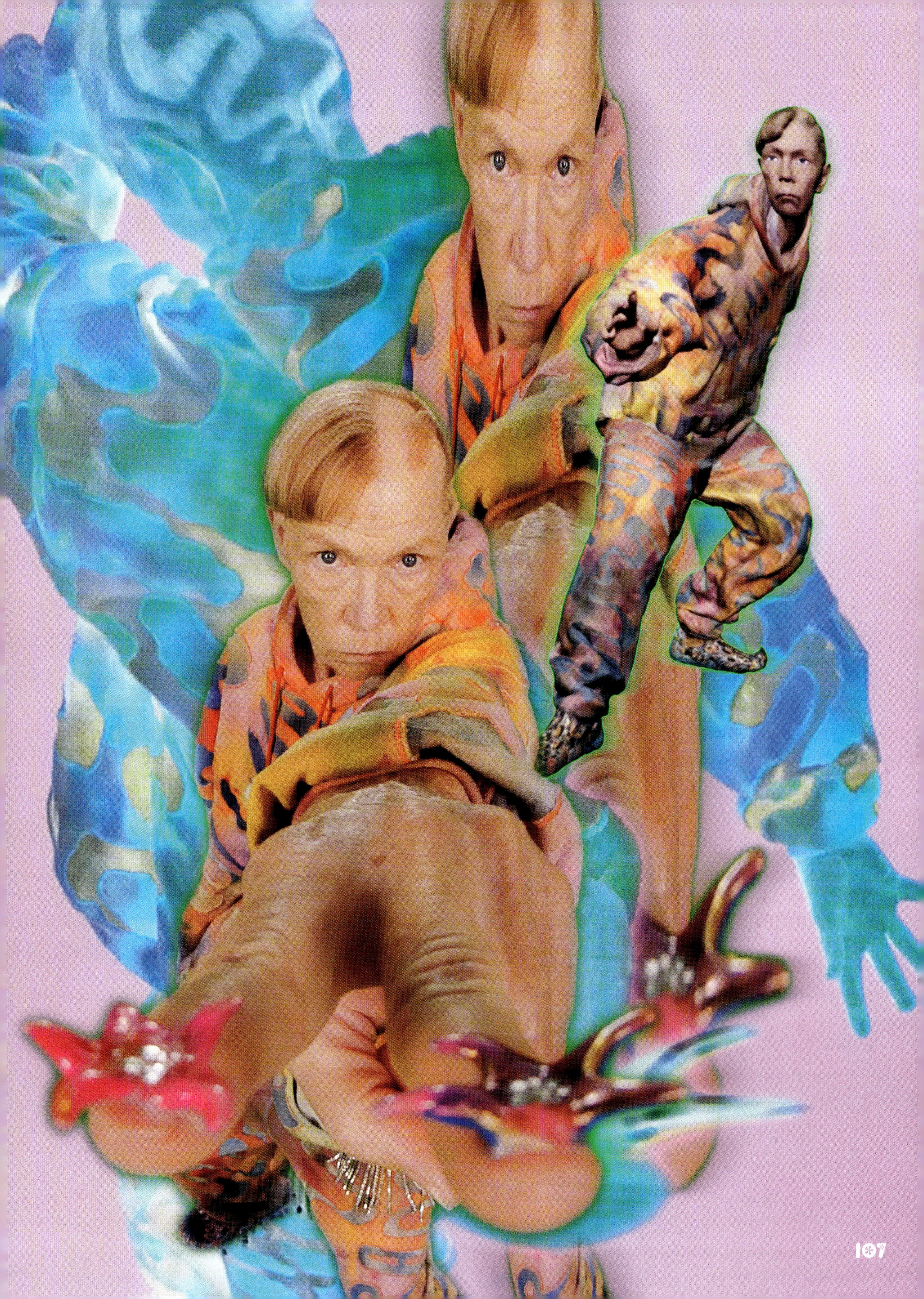

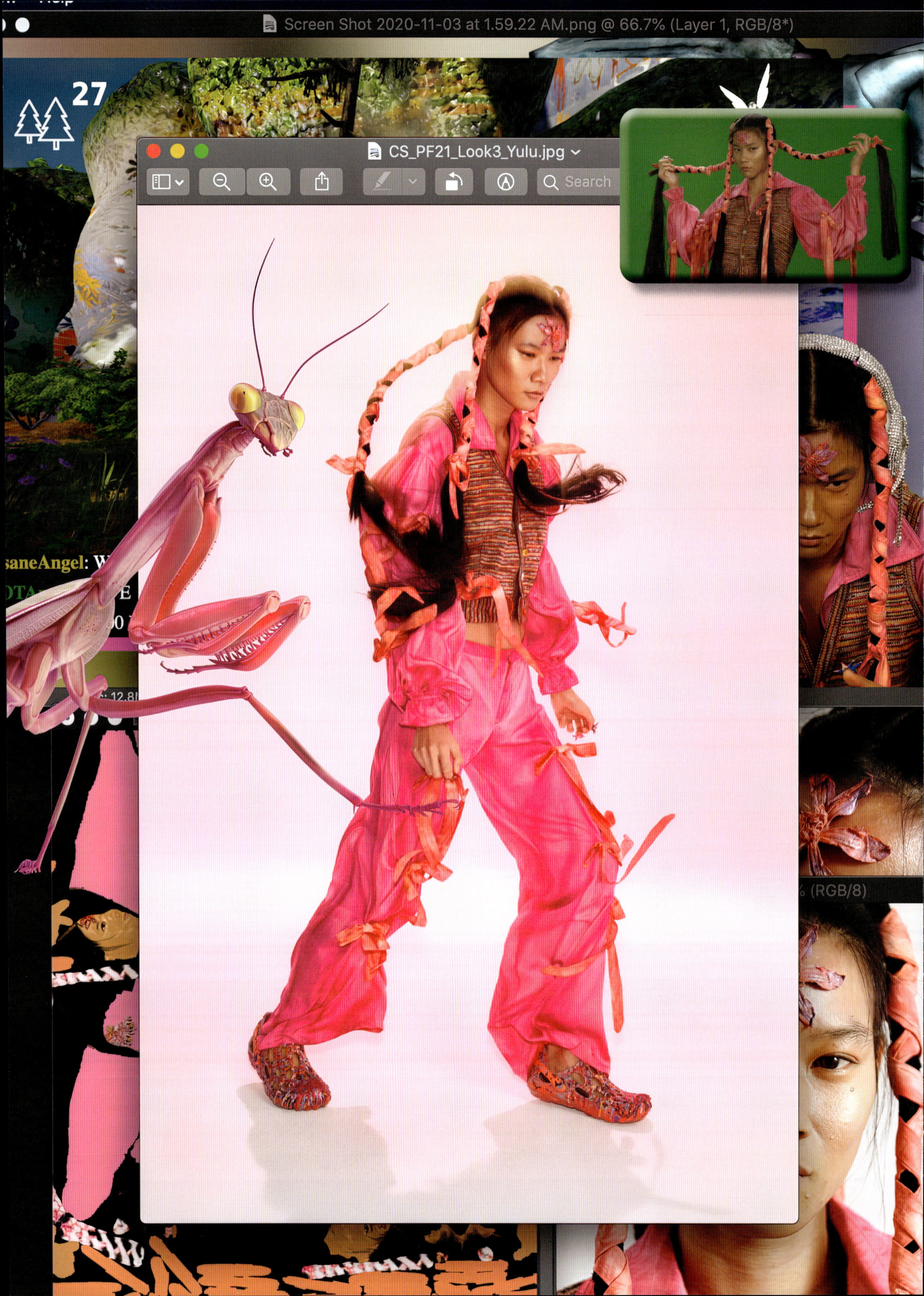
Screen Shot 2020-11-03 at 1.59.22 AM.png @ 66.7% (Layer 1, RGB/8*)
27
CS_PF21_Look3_Yulu.jpg
Search
(RGB/8)

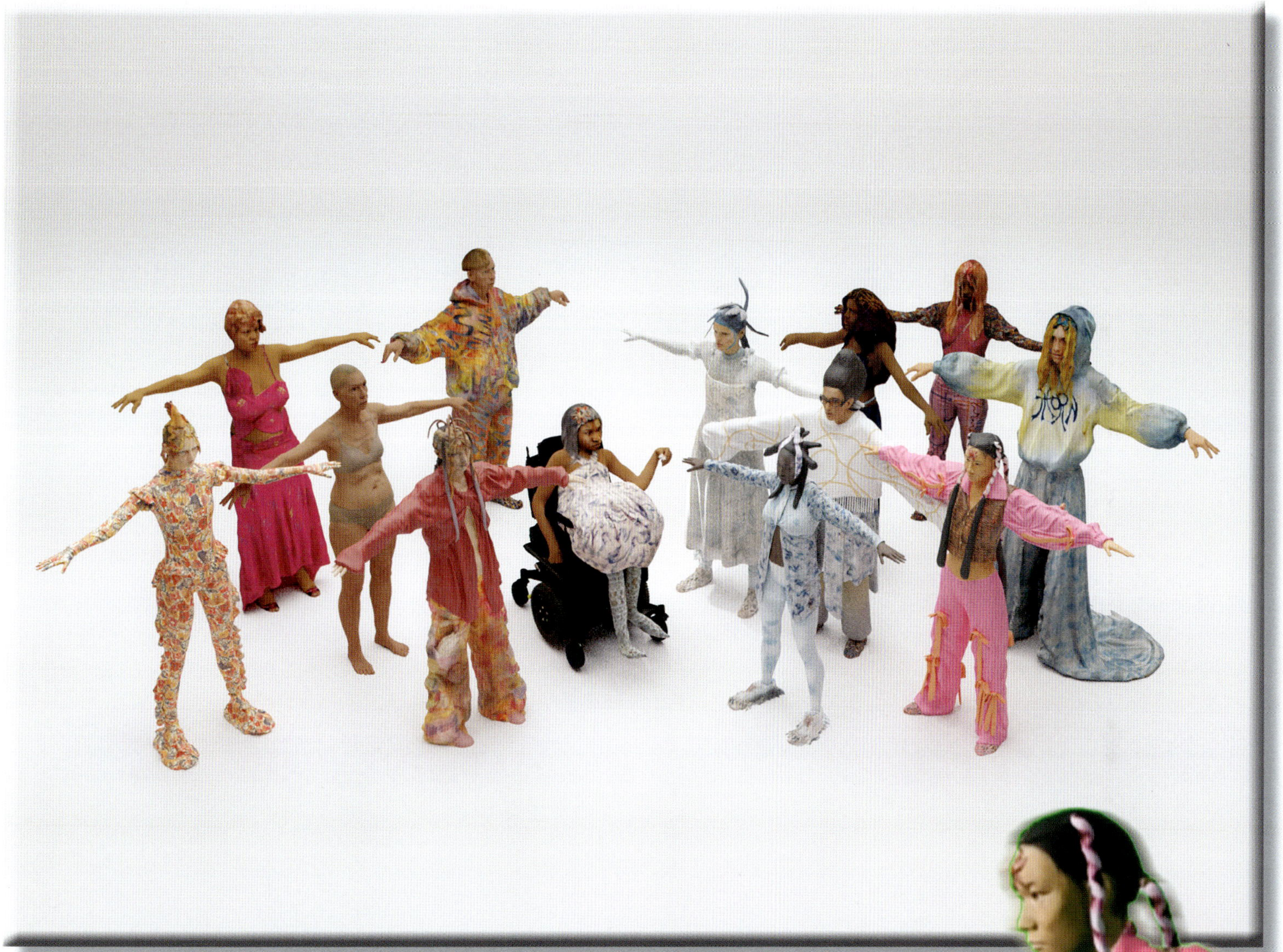

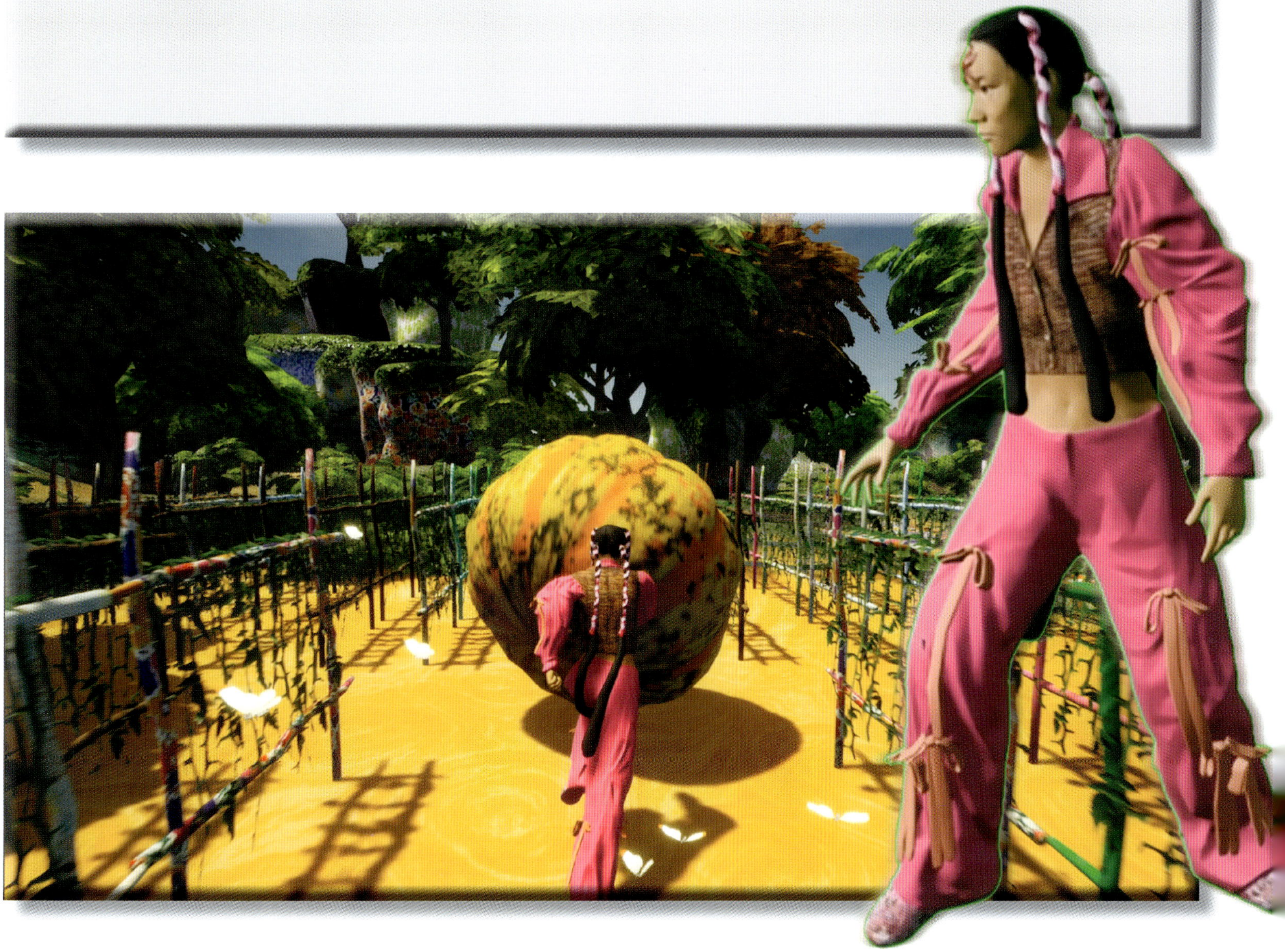

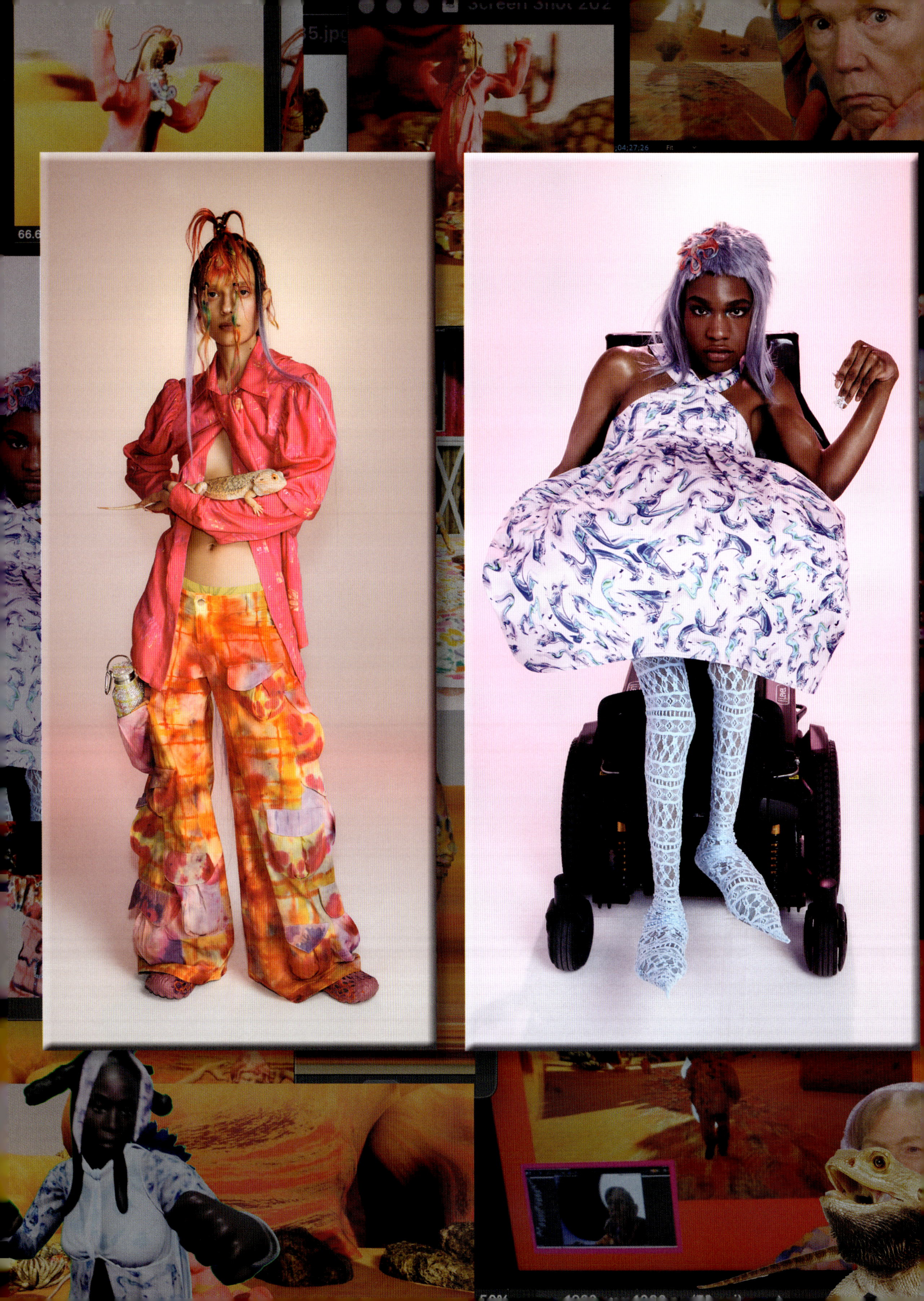
5.jpg

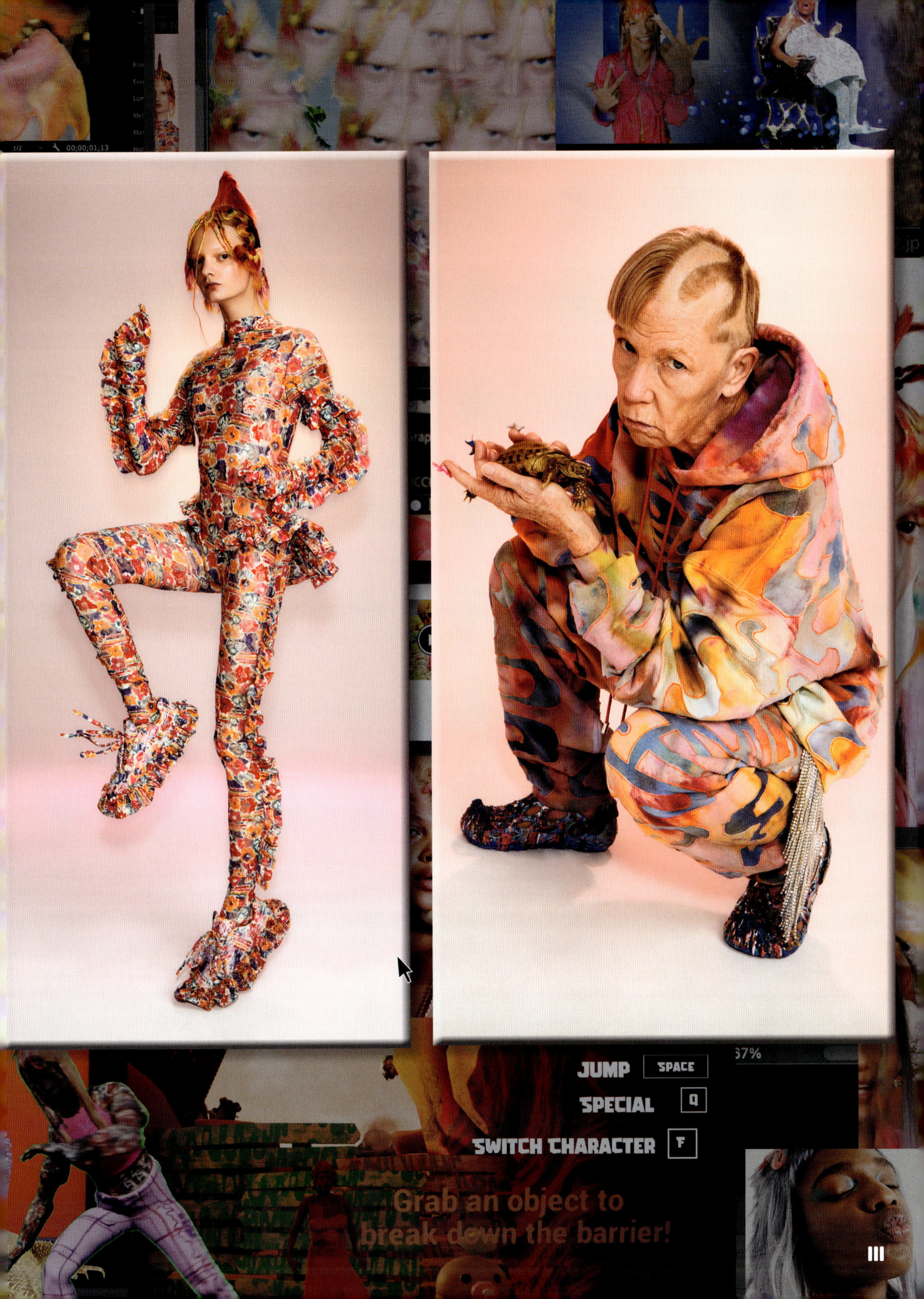
JUMP SPACE
SPECIAL Q
SWITCH CHARACTER F
Grab an object to break down the barrier!

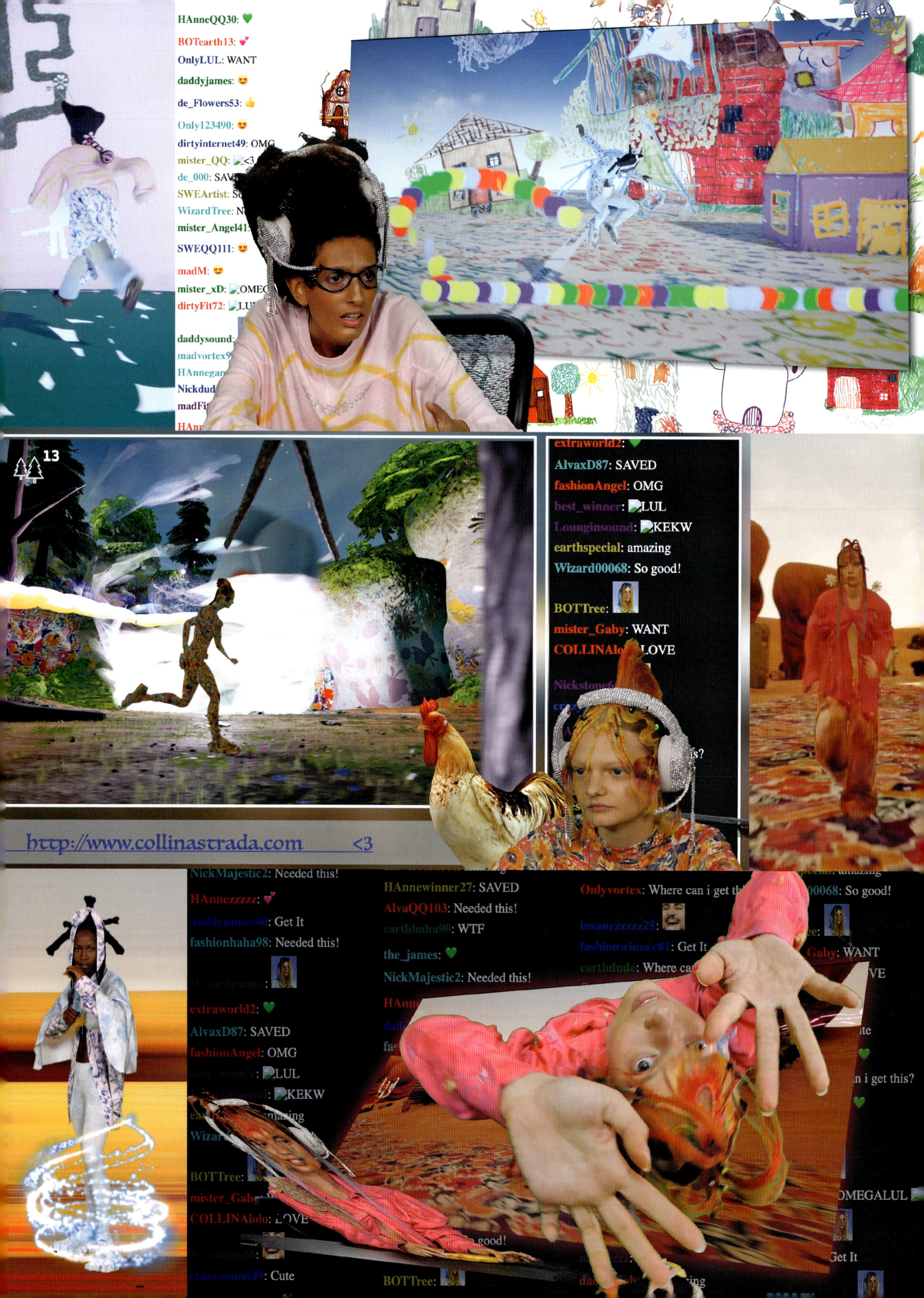
HAnneQQ30:
BOTearth13:
OnlyLUL: WANT
daddyjames:
de_Flowers53:
Only123490:
dirtyinternet49: OMG
mister_QQ: <3
de_000:
SWEArtist:
WizardTree:
mister_Angel41:
SWEQQ111:
madM:
mister_xD: OMEG
dirtyFit72:
daddysound:
13
extraworld2:
AlvaxD87: SAVED
fashionAngel: OMG
best_winner: LUL
Lounginsound: KEKW
earthspecial: amazing
Wizard00068: So good!
BOTTree:
mister_Gaby: WANT
COLLINAlo LOVE
http://www.collinastrada.com <3
NickMajestic2: Needed this!
HAnnezzzzz:
daddyjames40: Get It
fashionhaha98: Needed this!
extraworld2:
AlvaxD87: SAVED
fashionAngel: OMG
LUL
KEKW
BOTTree:
COLLINAlolo: LOVE
crazysound49: Cute
HAnnewinner27: SAVED
AlvaQQ103: Needed this!
earthhaha90: WTF
the_james:
NickMajestic2: Needed this!
BOTTree:
Onlyvortex: Where can i get th
insanezzzzz25:
fashionwinner81: Get It
earthdude: Where ca
00068: So good!
Gaby: WANT
n i get this?
OMEGALUL
Get It

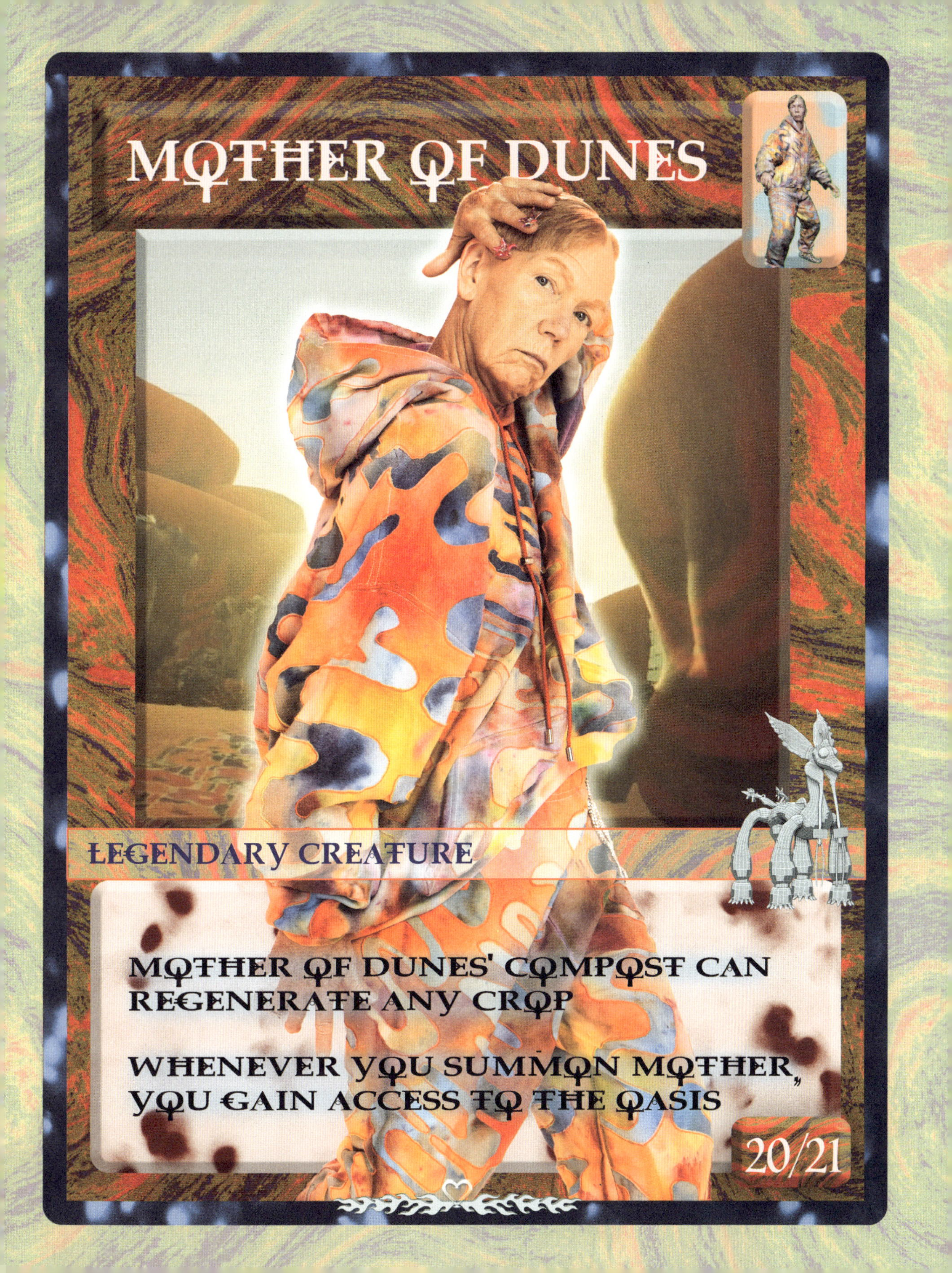
MOTHER OF DUNES
LEGENDARY CREATURE
MOTHER OF DUNES' COMPOST CAN REGENERATE ANY CROP
WHENEVER YOU SUMMON MOTHER, YOU GAIN ACCESS TO THE OASIS
20/21

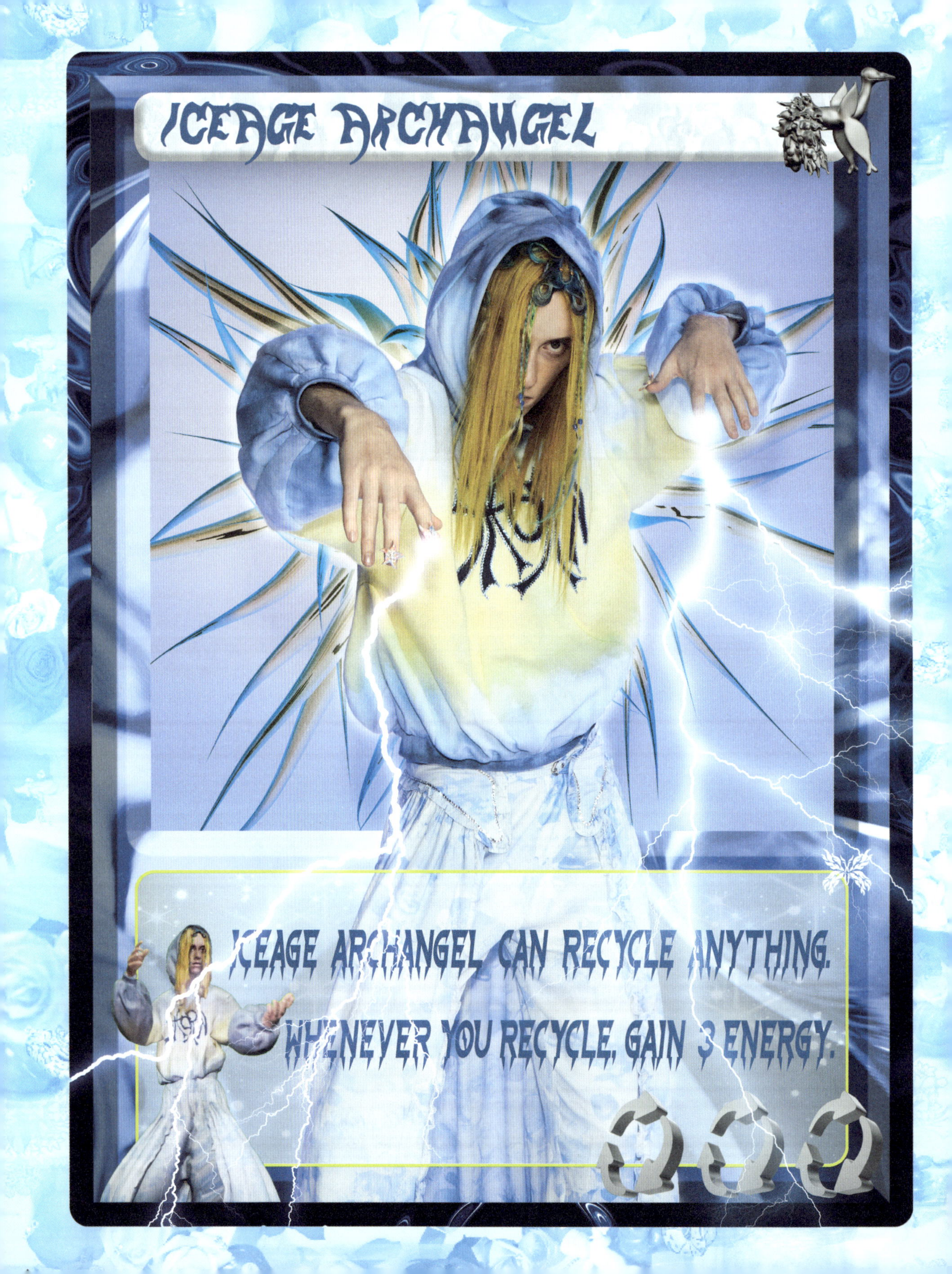
ICEAGE ARCHANGEL
ICEAGE ARCHANGEL CAN RECYCLE ANYTHING.
WHENEVER YOU RECYCLE, GAIN 3 ENERGY.

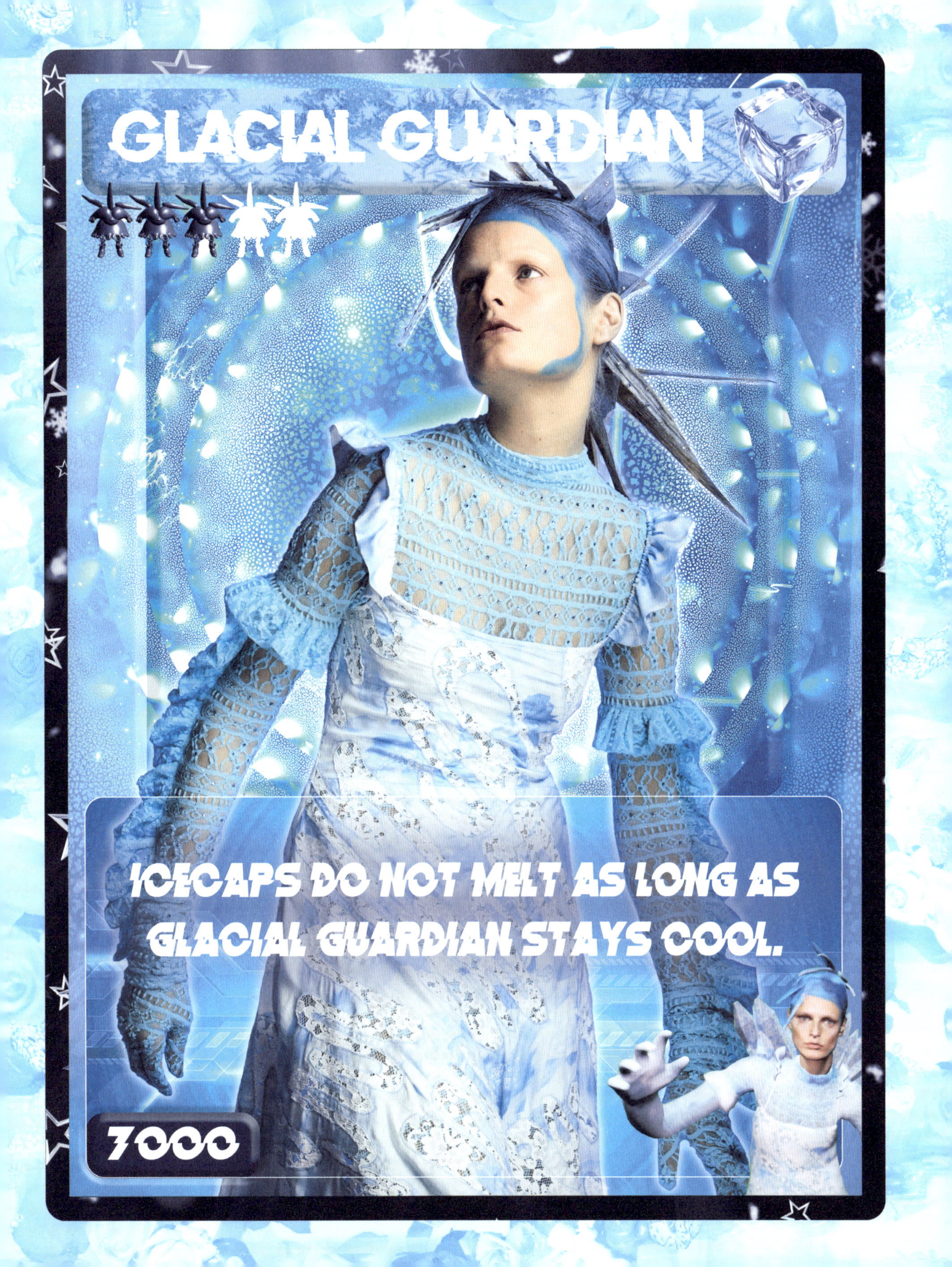
GLACIAL GUARDIAN
ICECAPS DO NOT MELT AS LONG AS GLACIAL GUARDIAN STAYS COOL.
7000

hawa from heaven

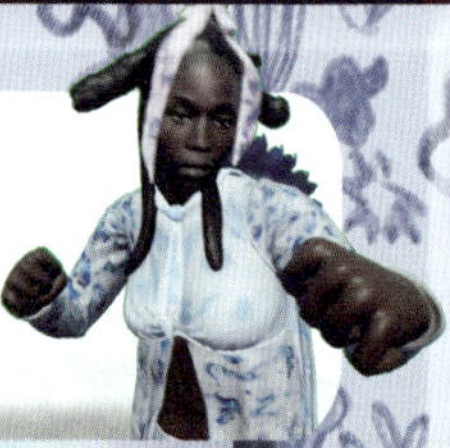

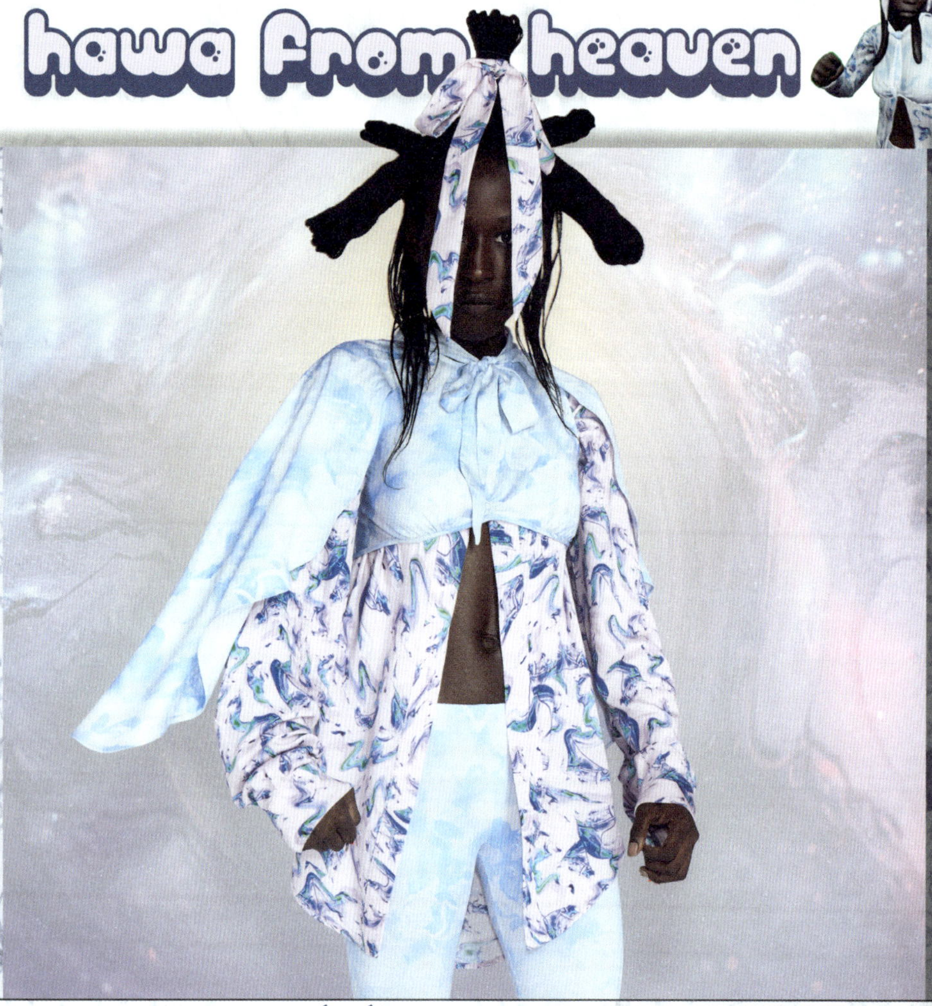

summon spirit

when hawa from heaven enters the drawing world, add three colors to your palette.

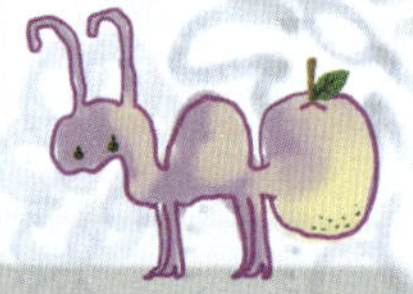

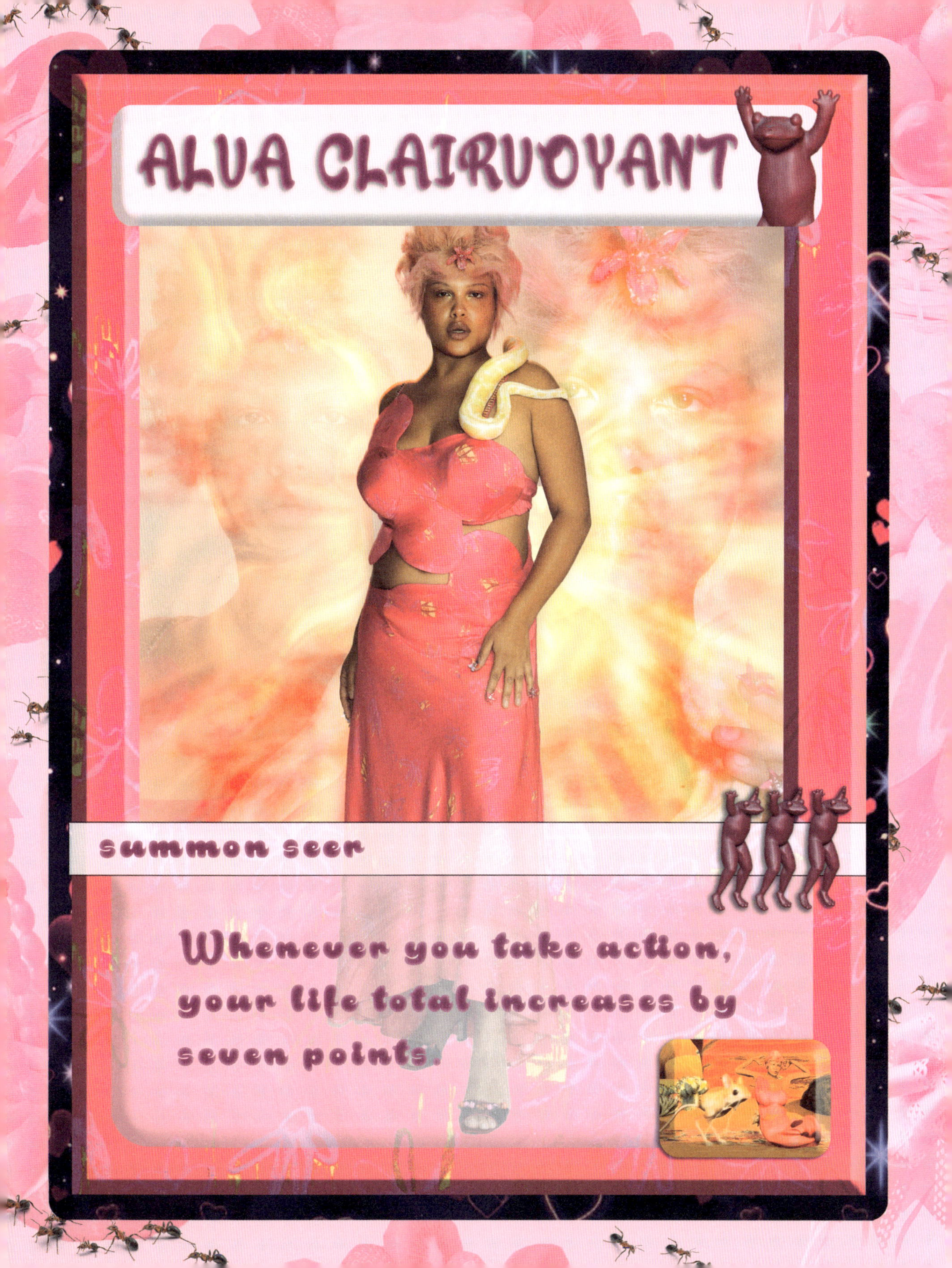
ALVA CLAIRVOYANT
summon seer
Whenever you take action, your life total increases by seven points.

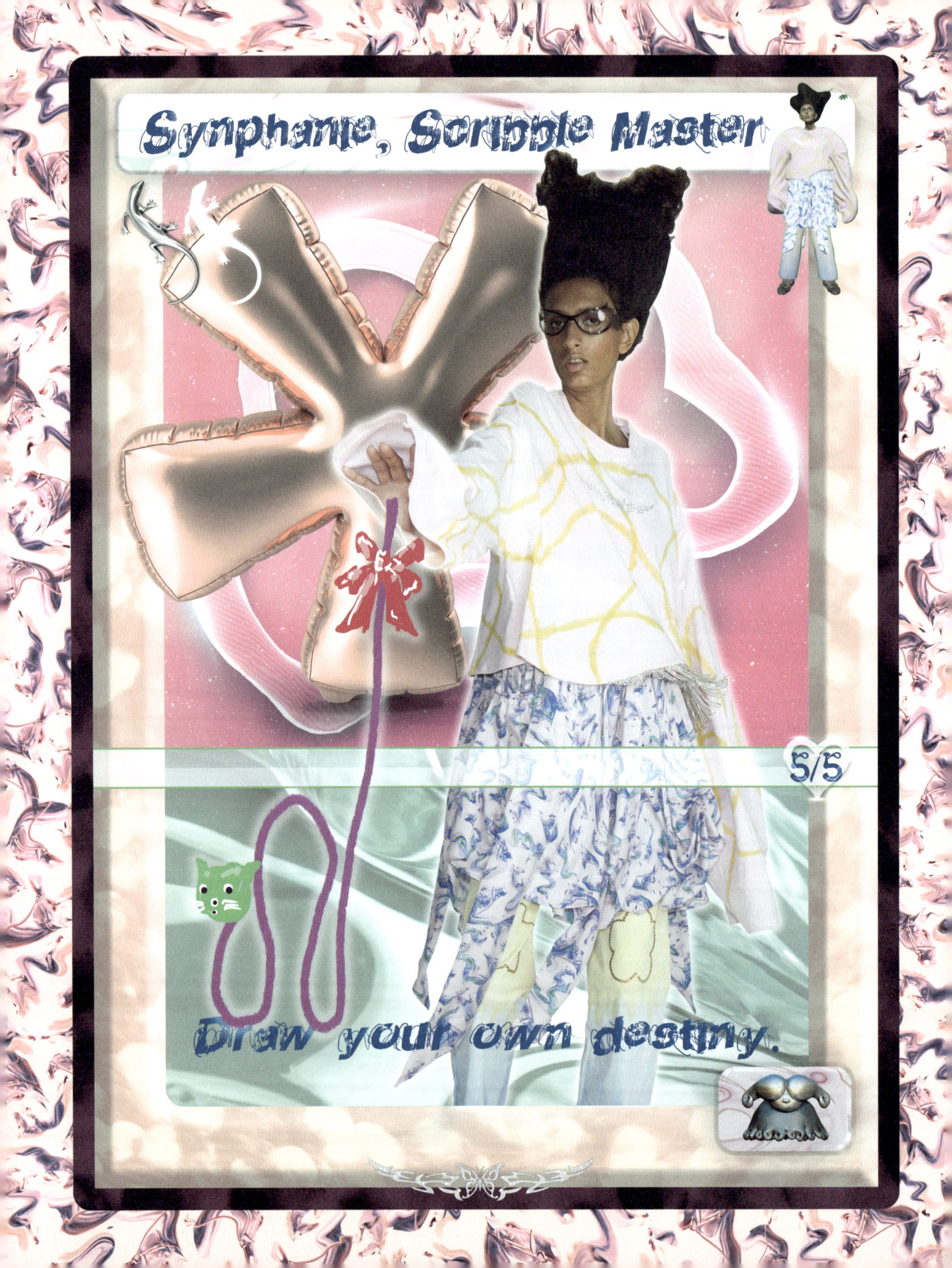
Synphanie, Scribble Master
5/5
Draw your own destiny.

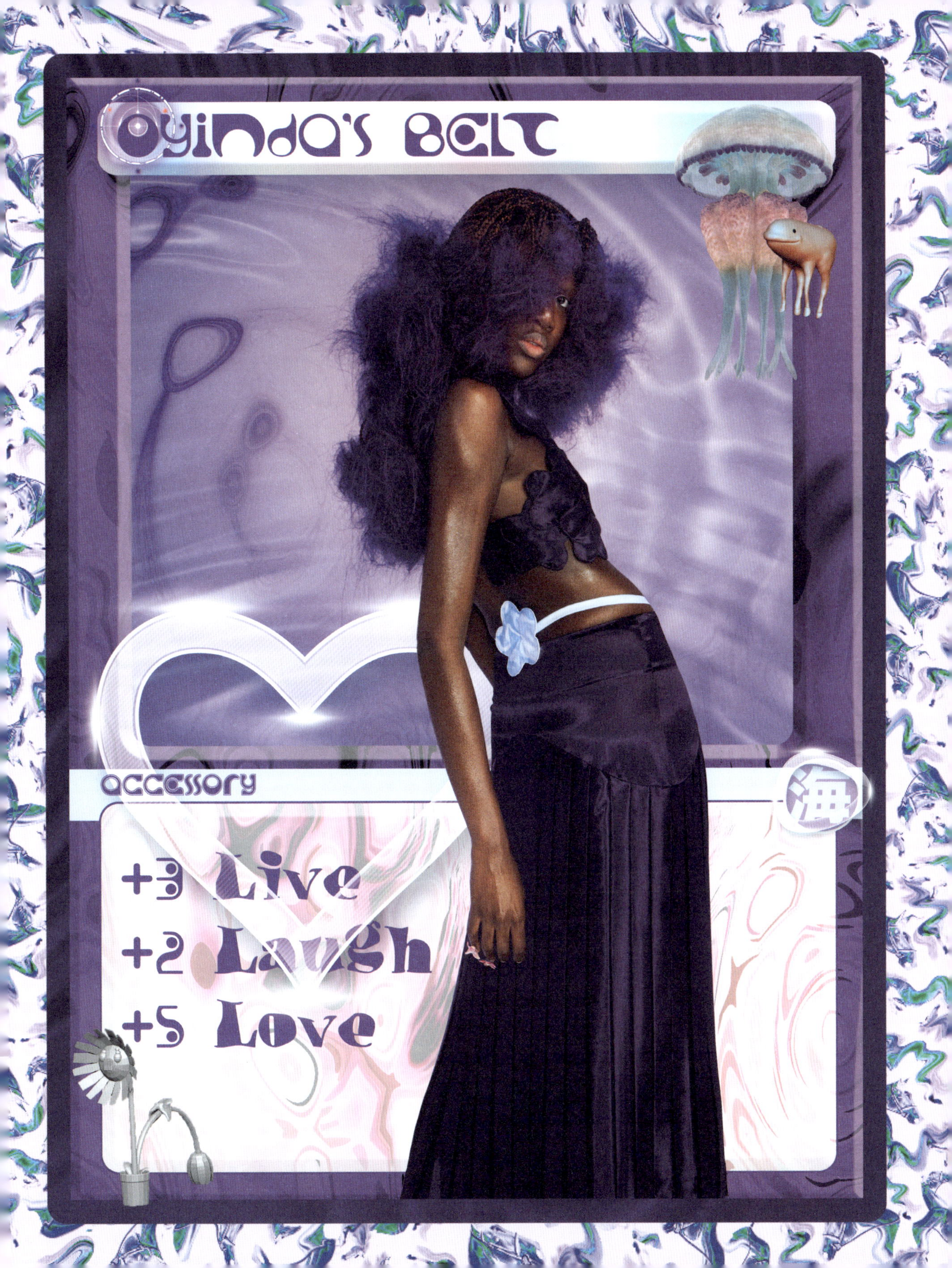
Oyinda's Belt
accessory
海
+3 Live
+2 Laugh
+5 Love

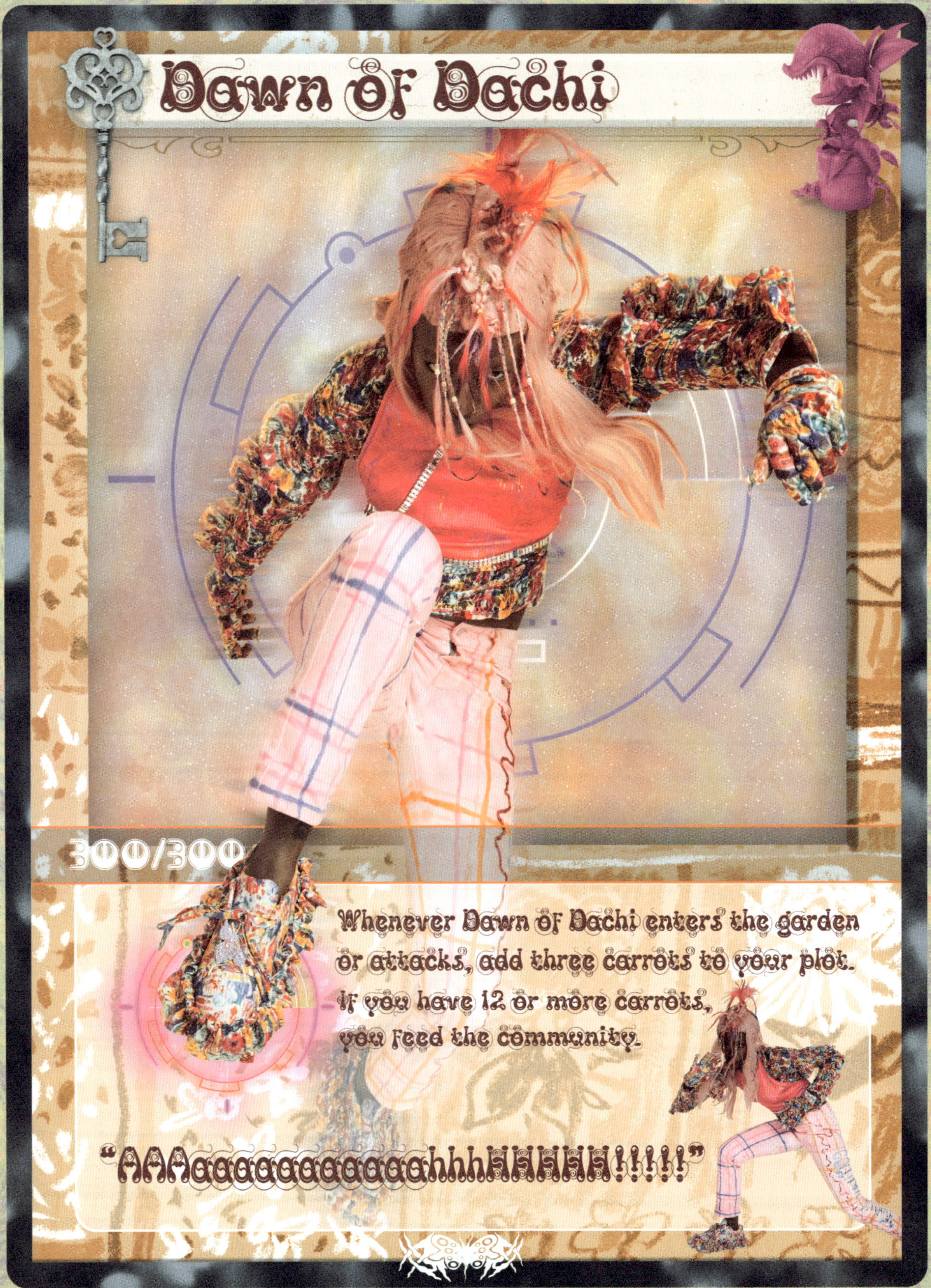
Dawn of Dachi
300/300
Whenever Dawn of Dachi enters the garden or attacks, add three carrots to your plot.
If you have 12 or more carrots, you feed the community.
“AAAaaaaaaaaaahhhHHHHHH!!!!!”

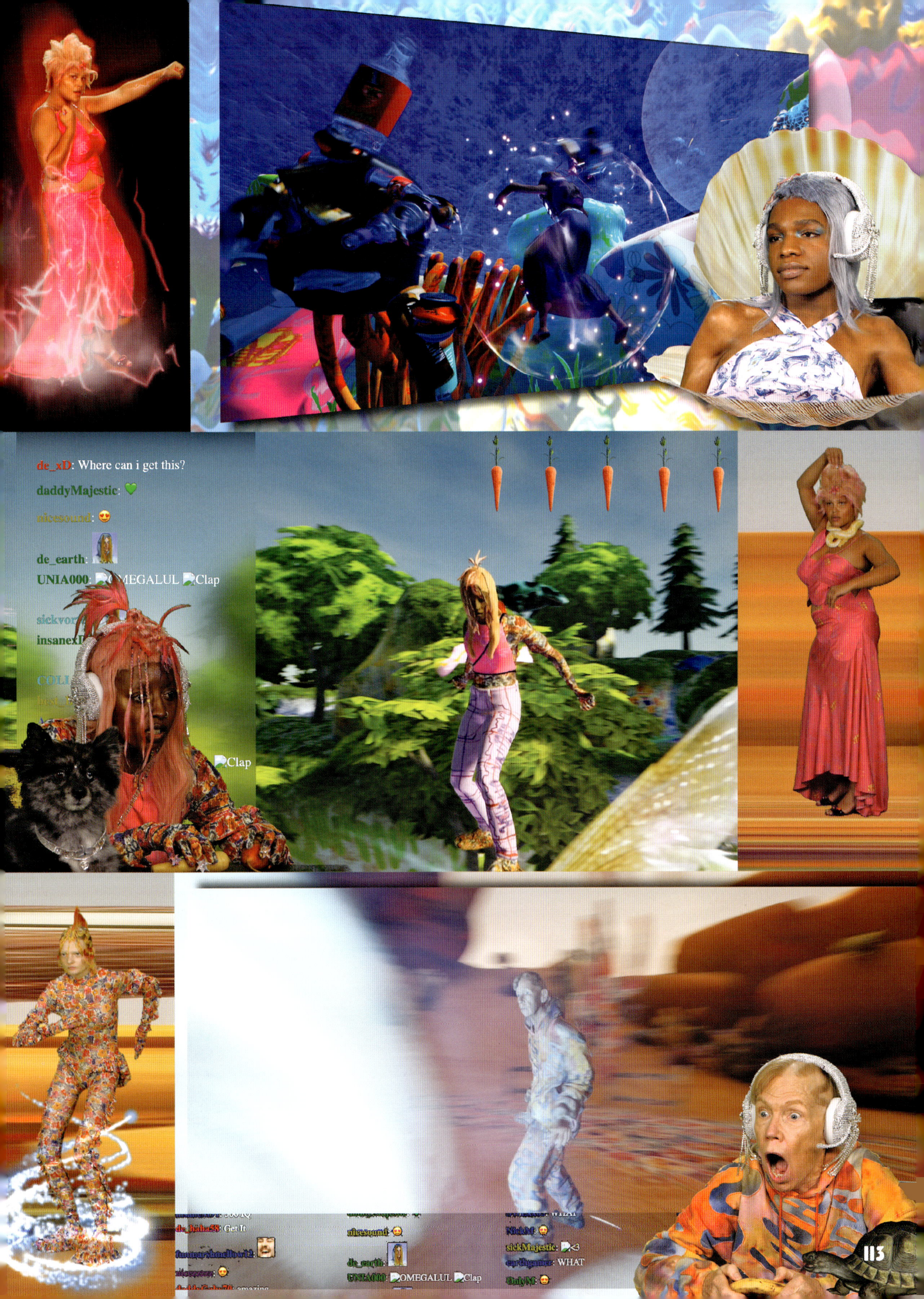
de_xD: Where can i get this?
daddyMajestic:
nicesound:
de_earth:
UNIA000: OMEGALUL Clap
Clap
de_haha58: Get It
funmarshmellow12:
nicesound:
de_earth:
UNIA000: OMEGALUL Clap
NickM:
sickMajestic: <3
earthgamer: WHAT
OnlyM:

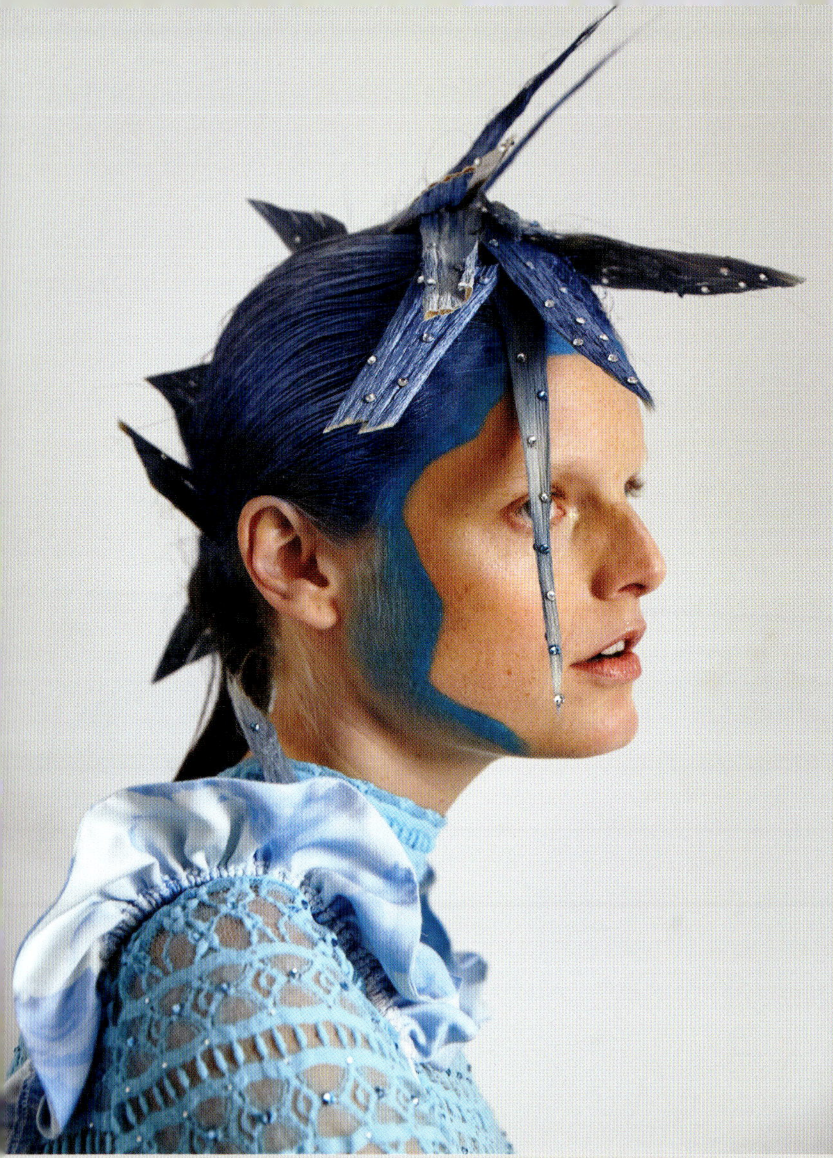
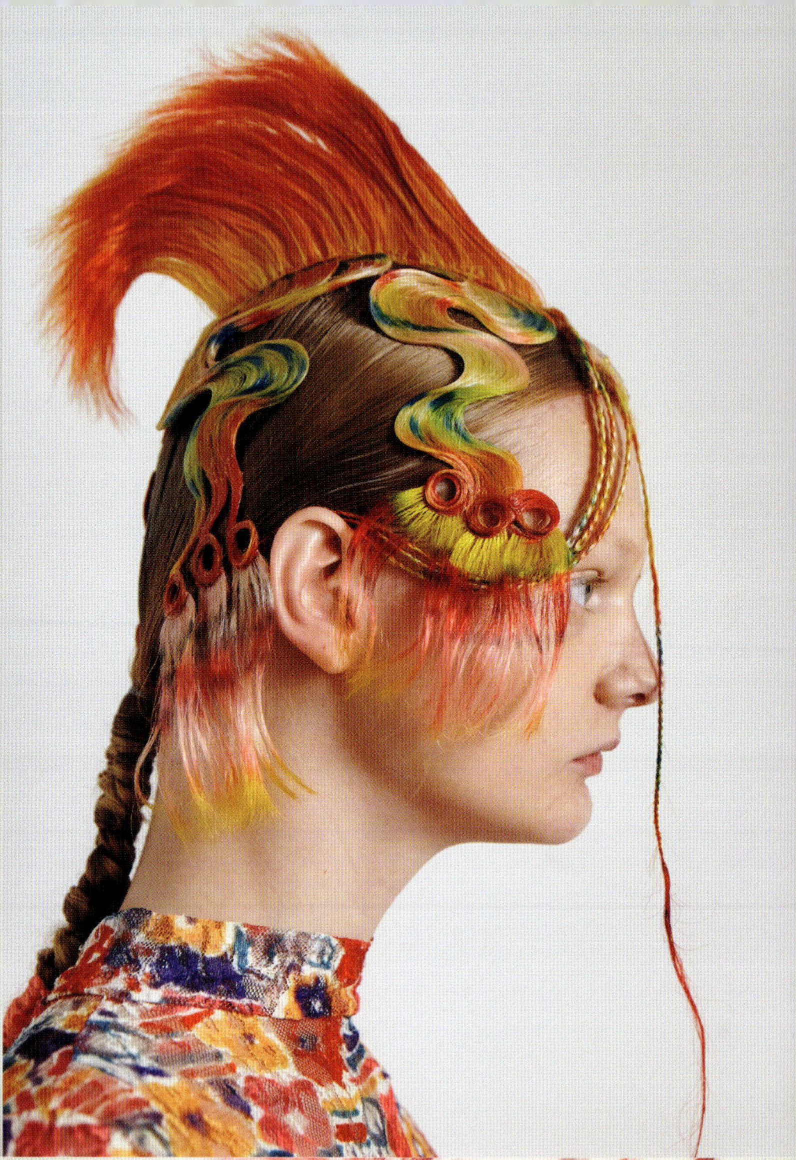
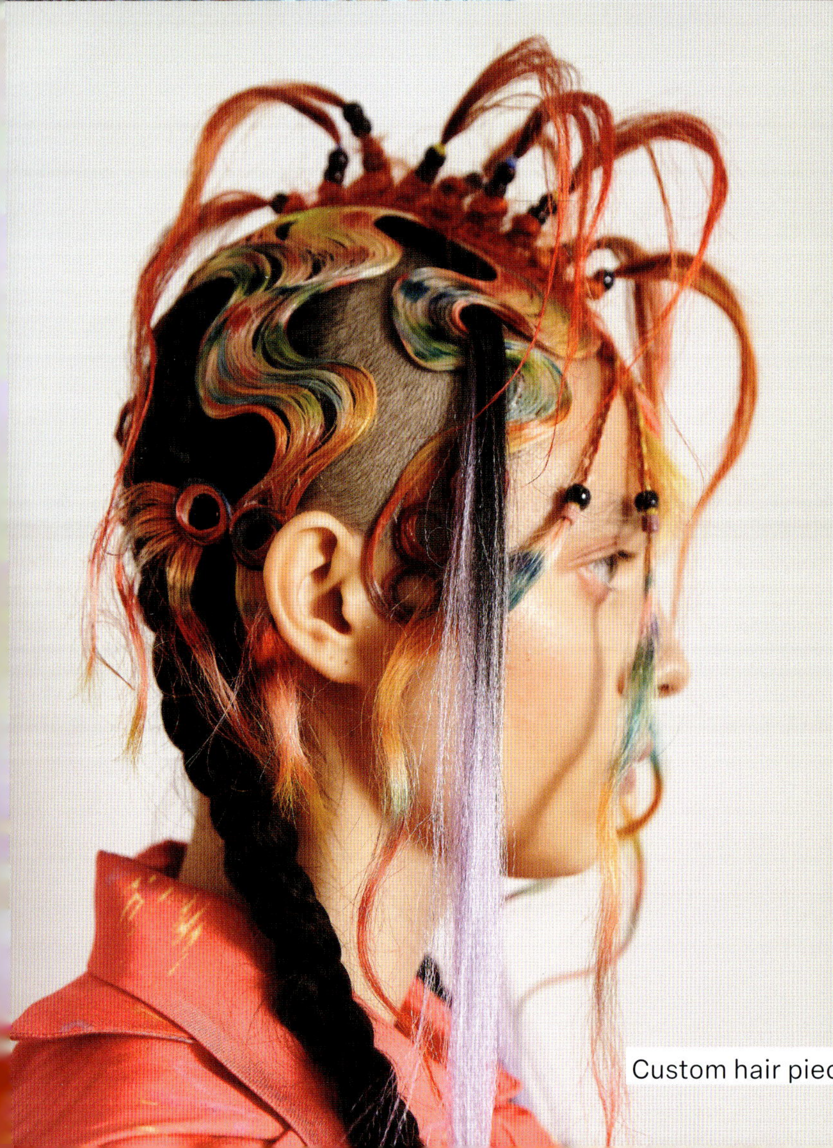
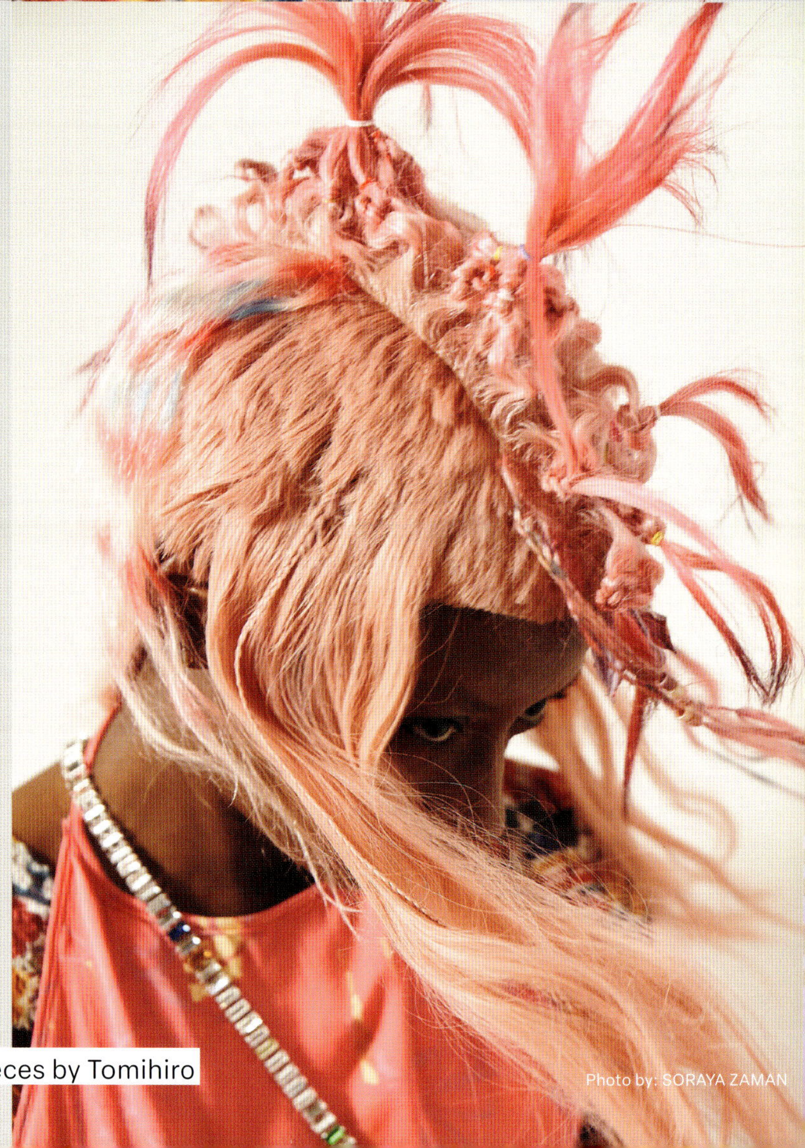

Custom hair pieces by Tomihiro

Photo by: SORAYA ZAMAN

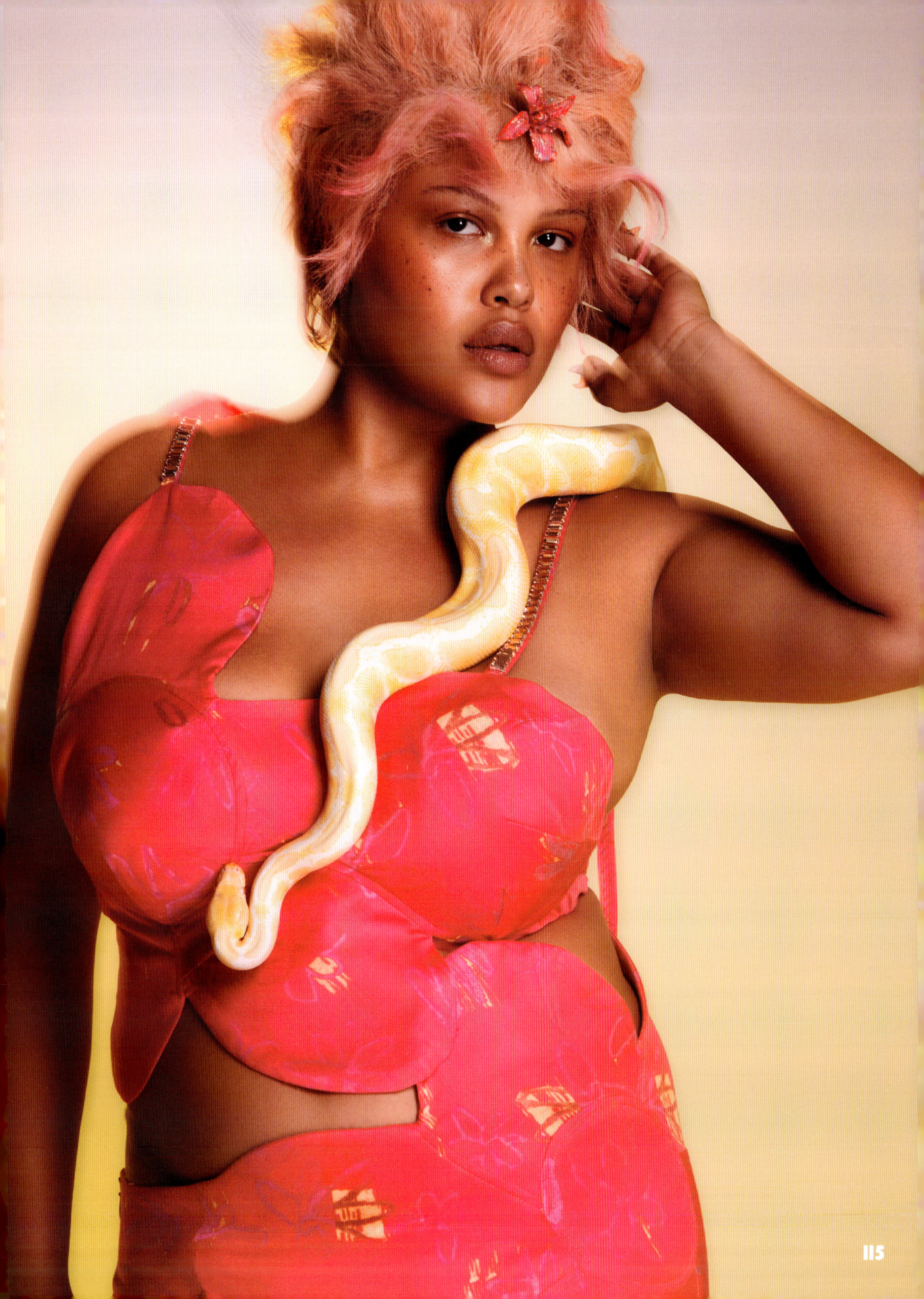

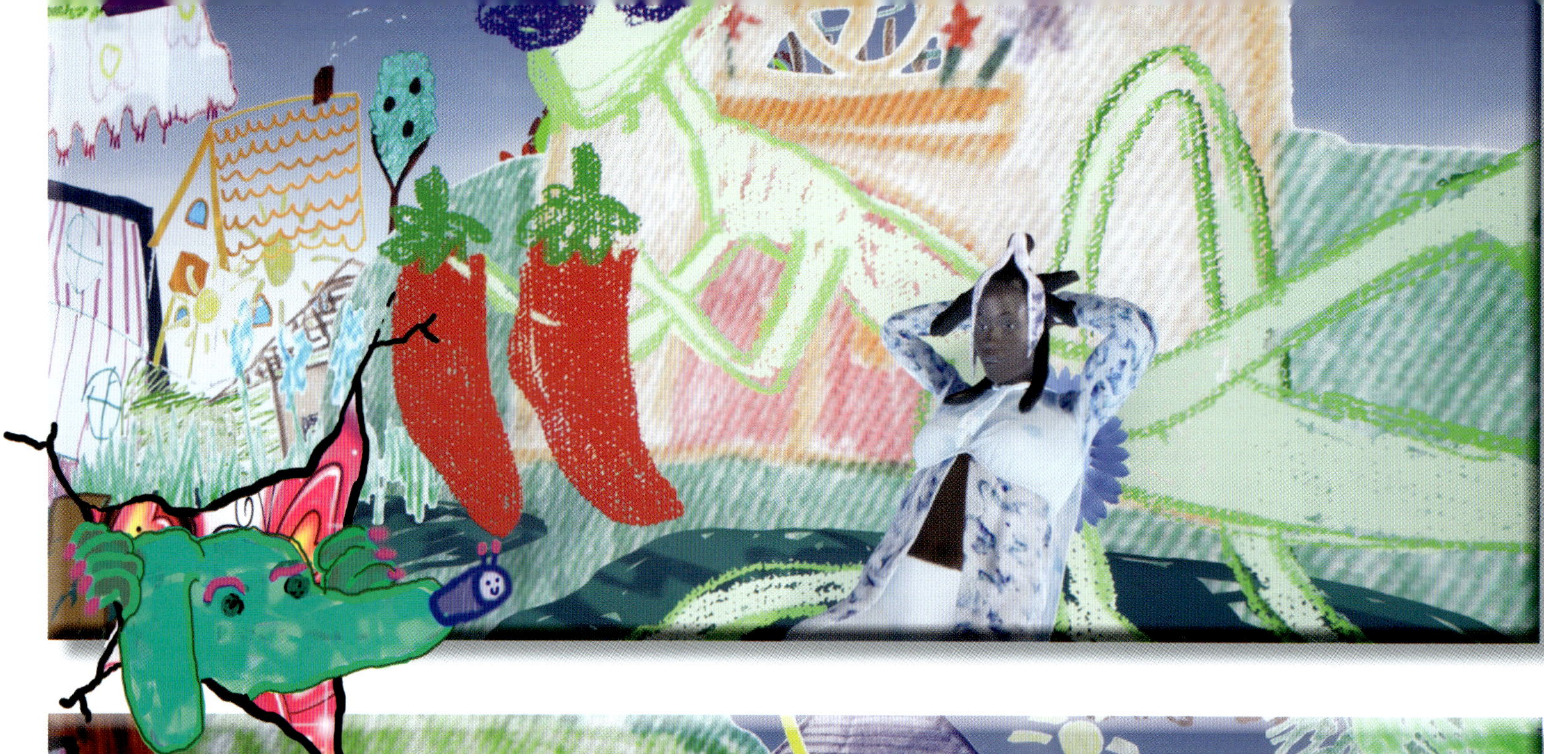
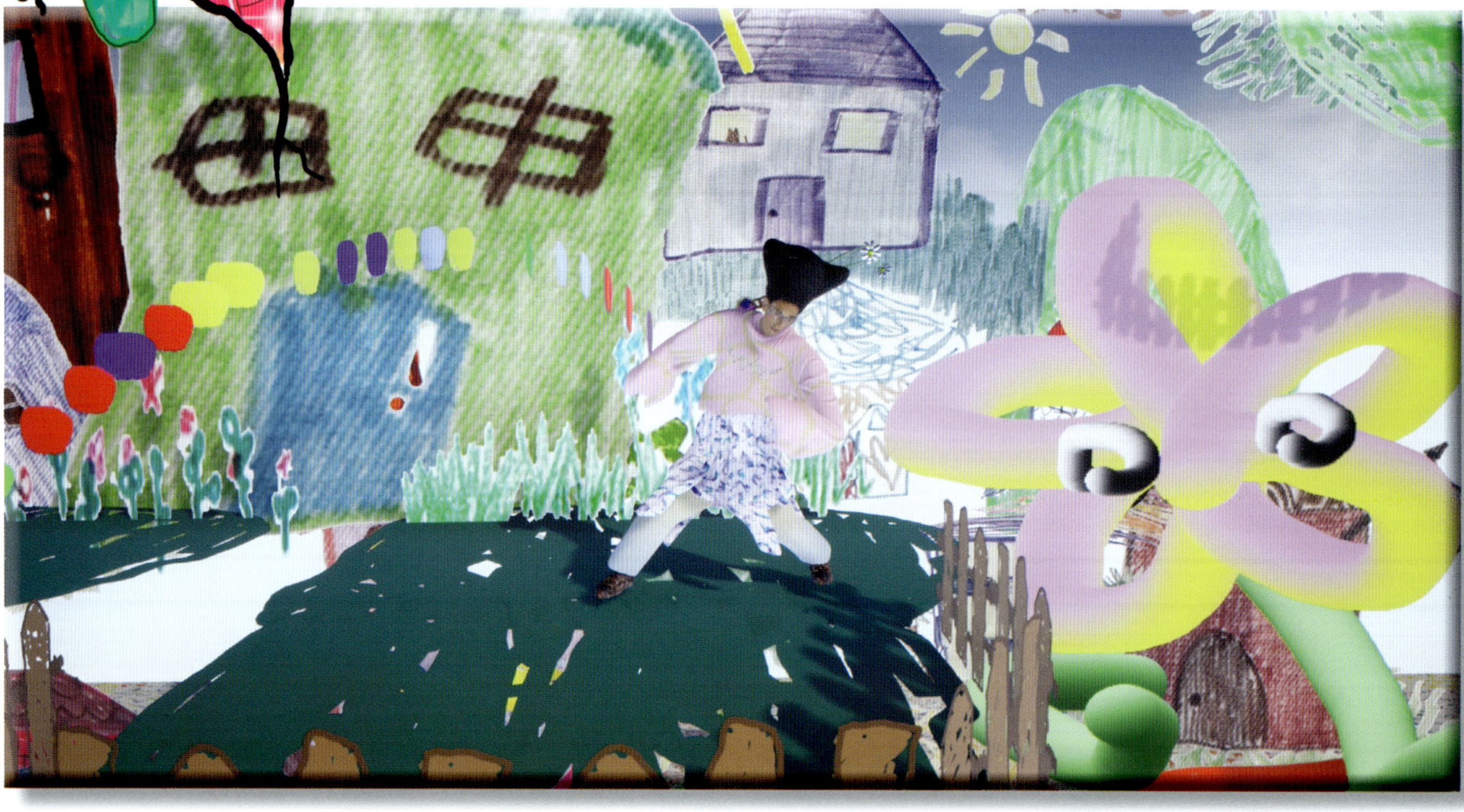
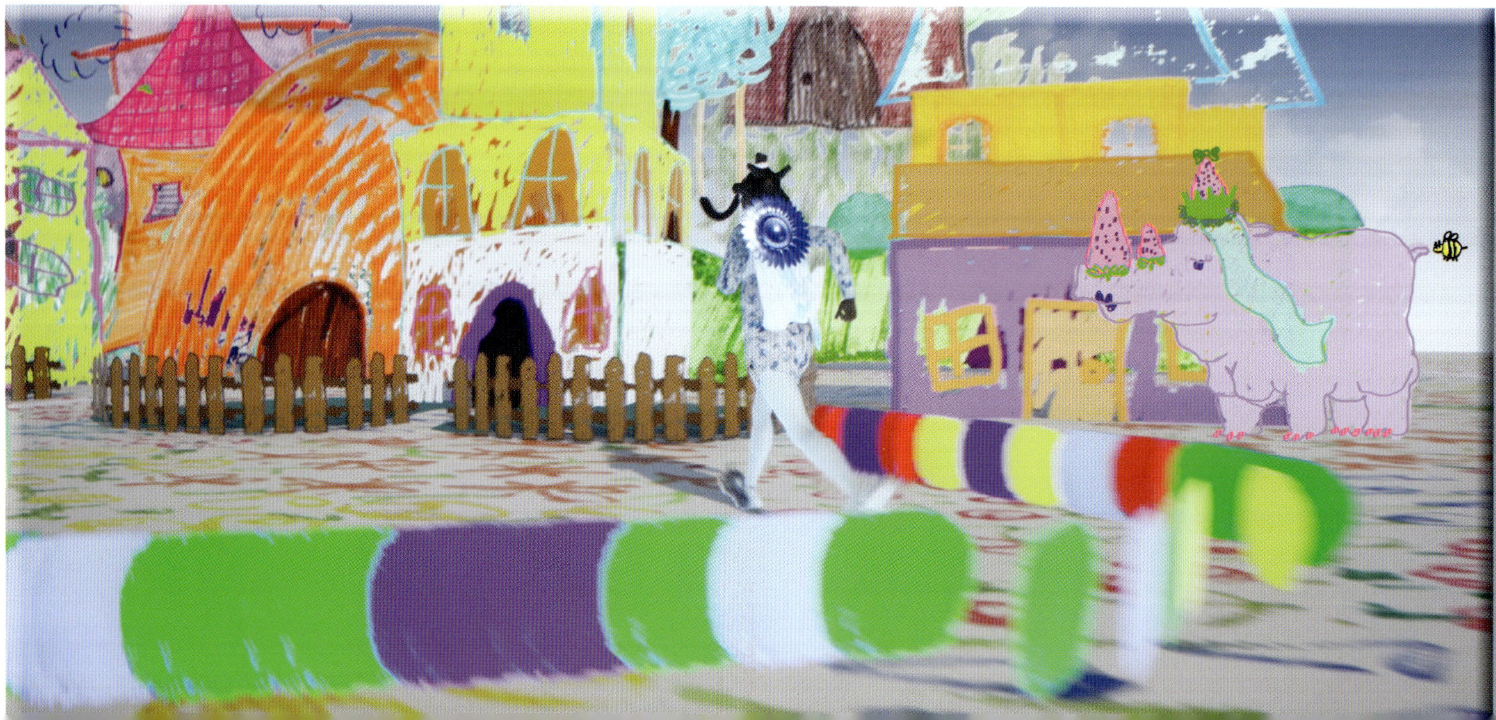

DRAWING WORLD

Your avatar needs to harness their creative energies to ascend the scribble steps and save the princess from pencil prison.

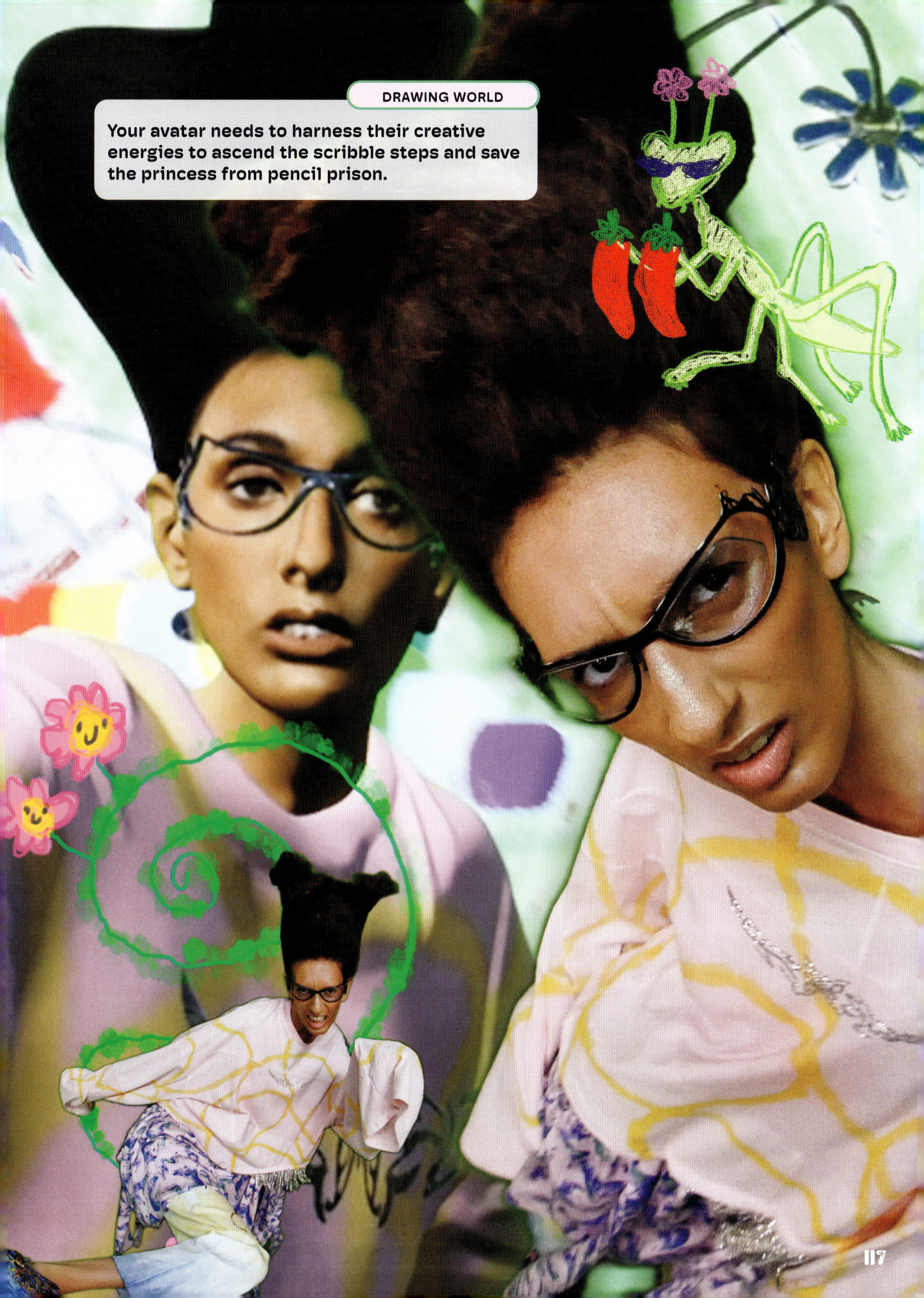

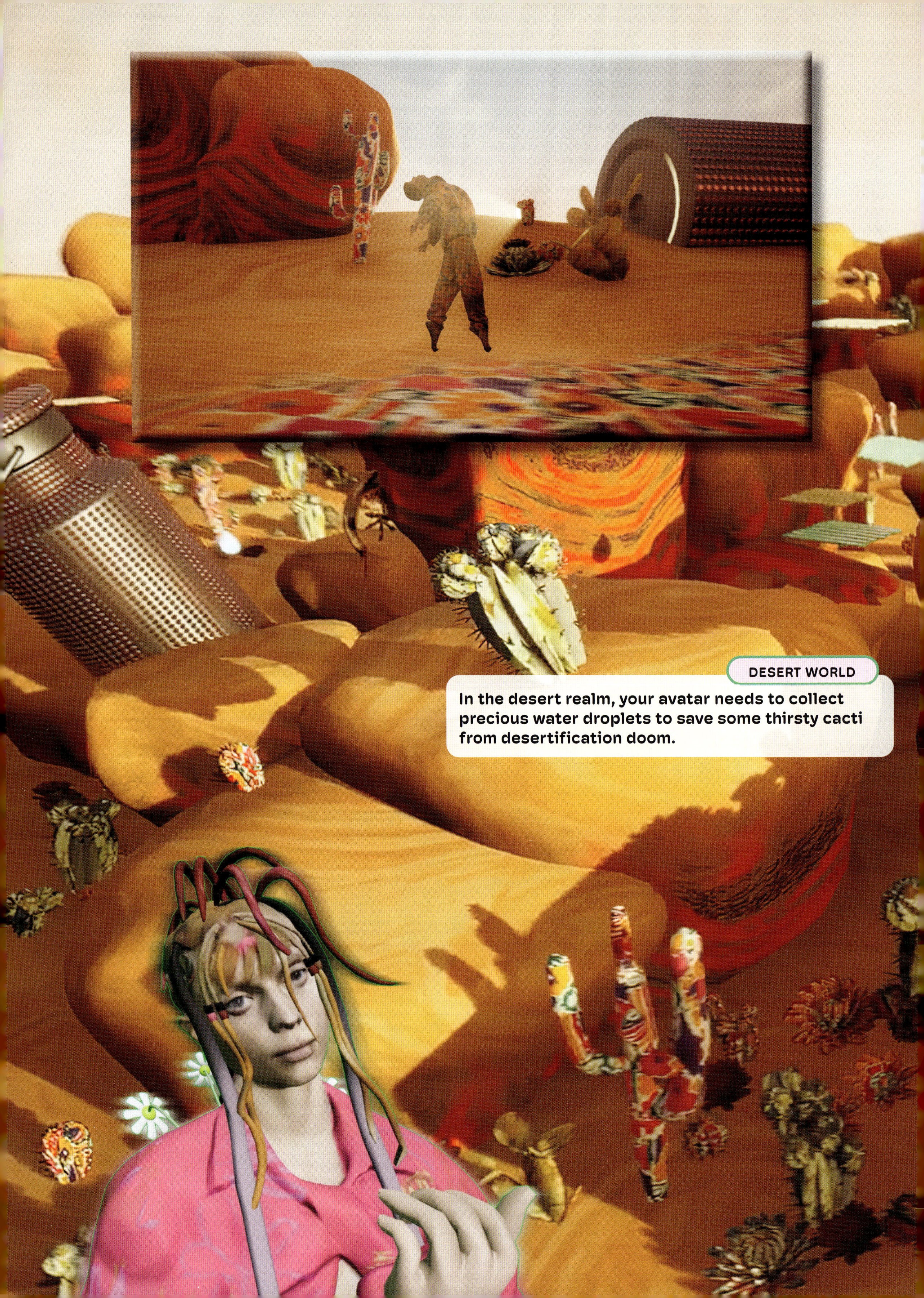

DESERT WORLD

In the desert realm, your avatar needs to collect precious water droplets to save some thirsty cacti from desertification doom.

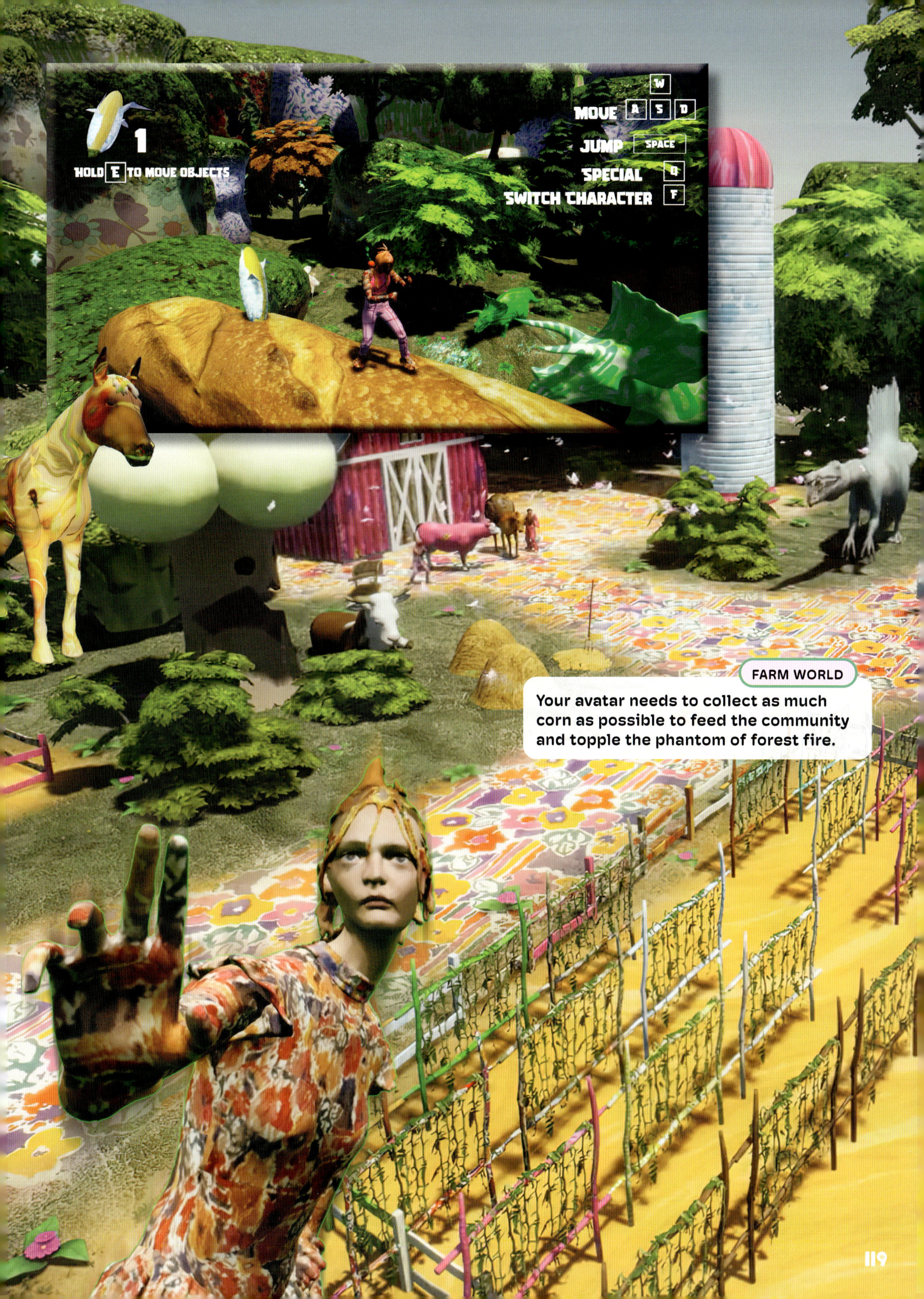

FARM WORLD

Your avatar needs to collect as much corn as possible to feed the community and topple the phantom of forest fire.

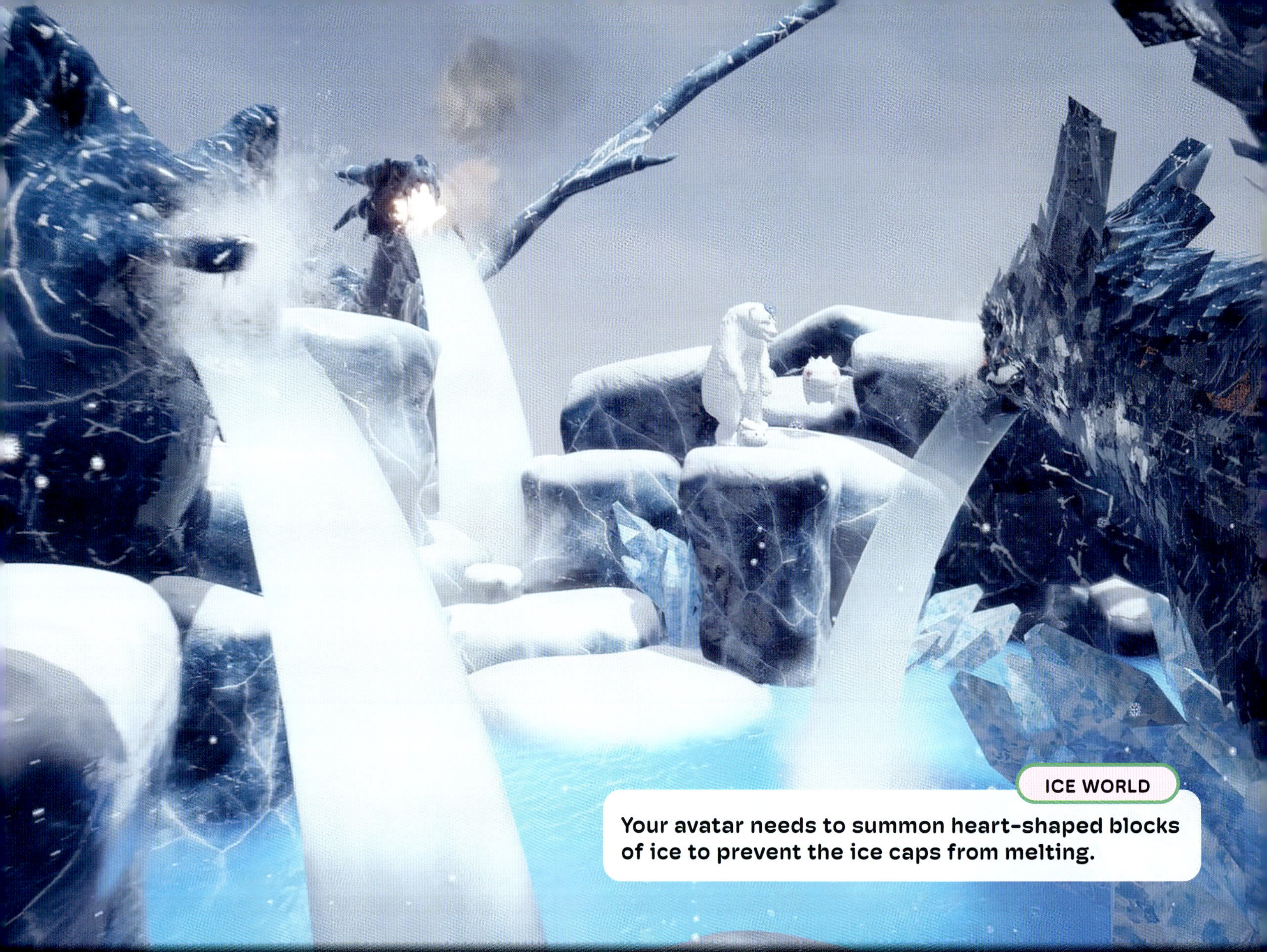

ICE WORLD

Your avatar needs to summon heart-shaped blocks of ice to prevent the ice caps from melting.

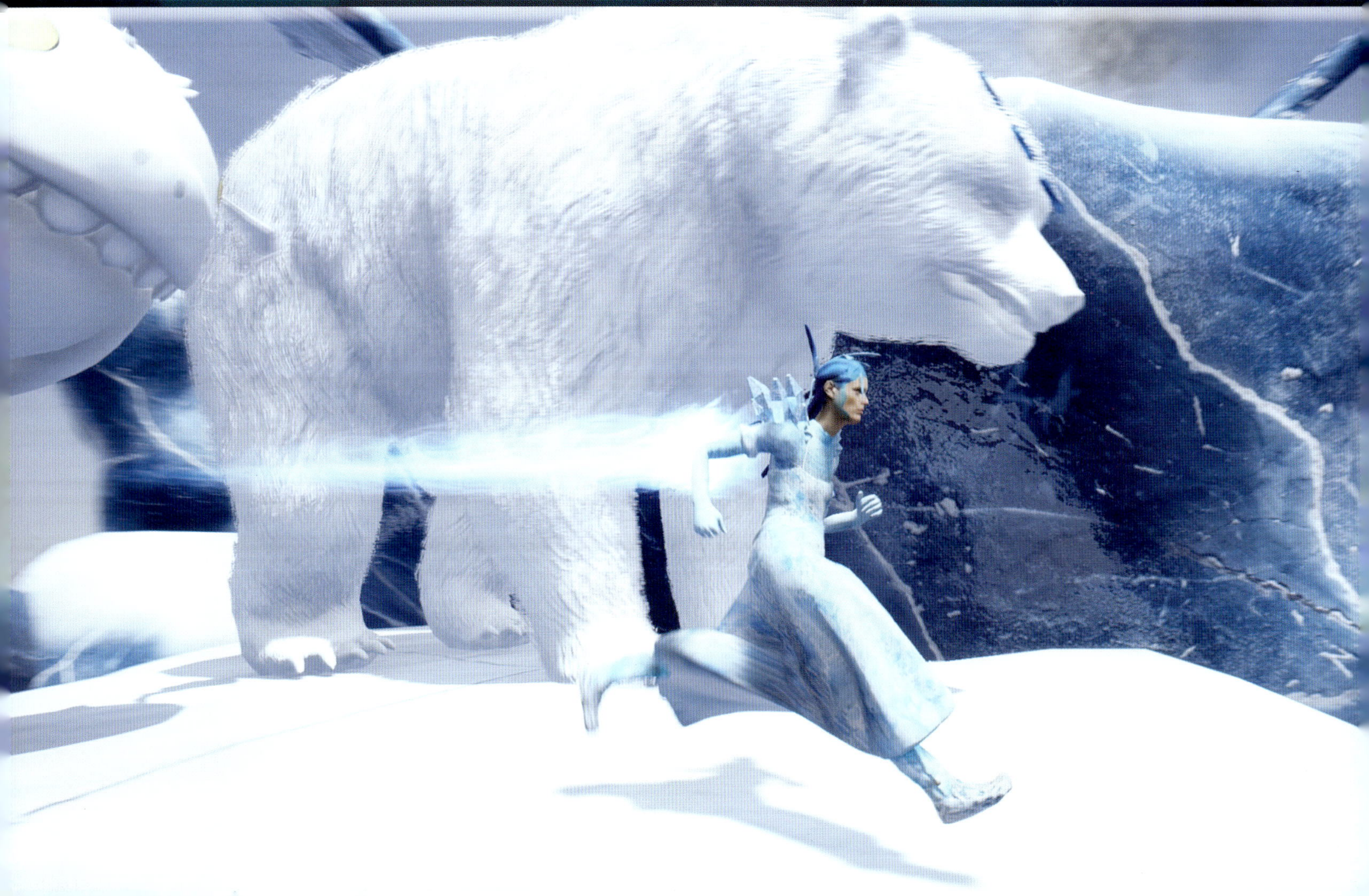

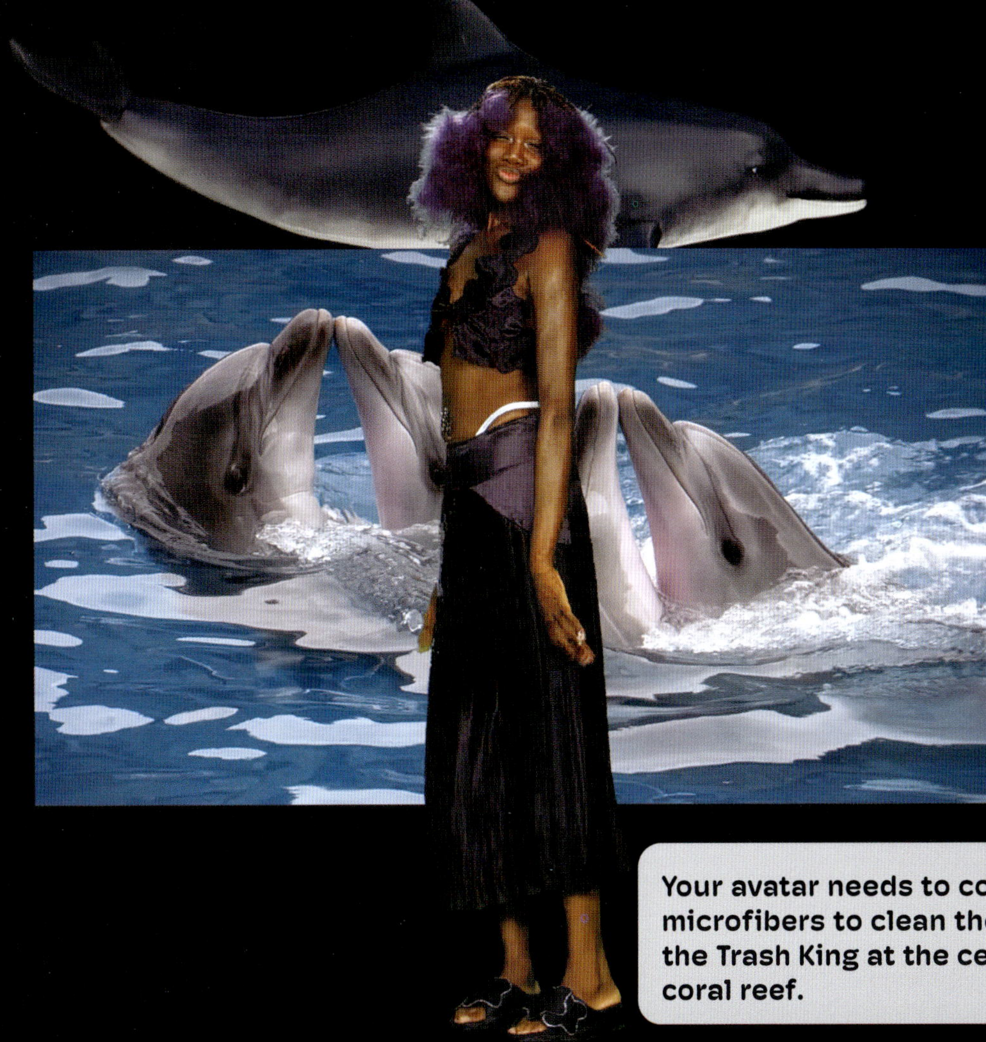

WATER WORLD

Your avatar needs to collect spools of microfibers to clean the ocean and defeat the Trash King at the center of the Collina coral reef.

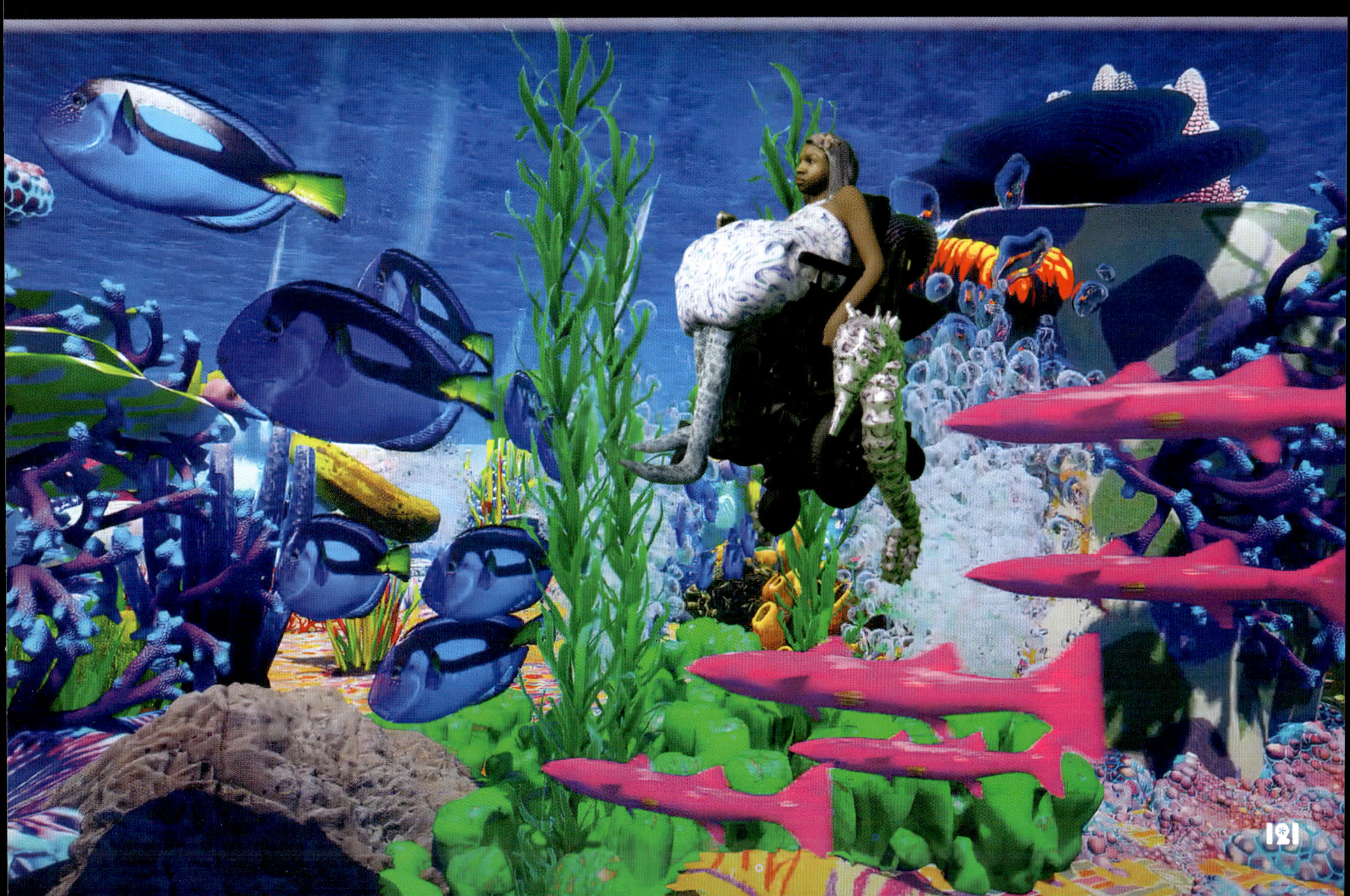

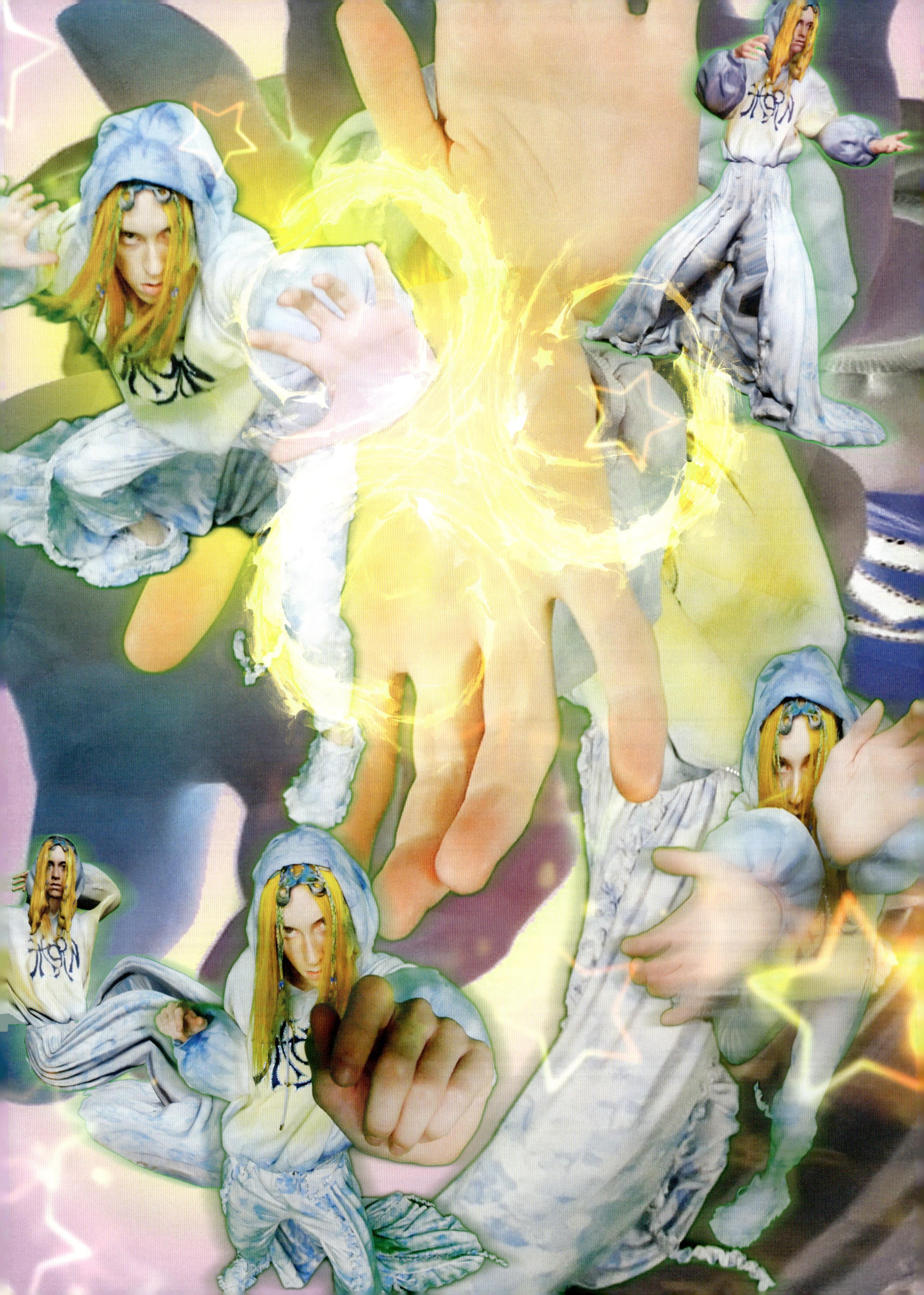

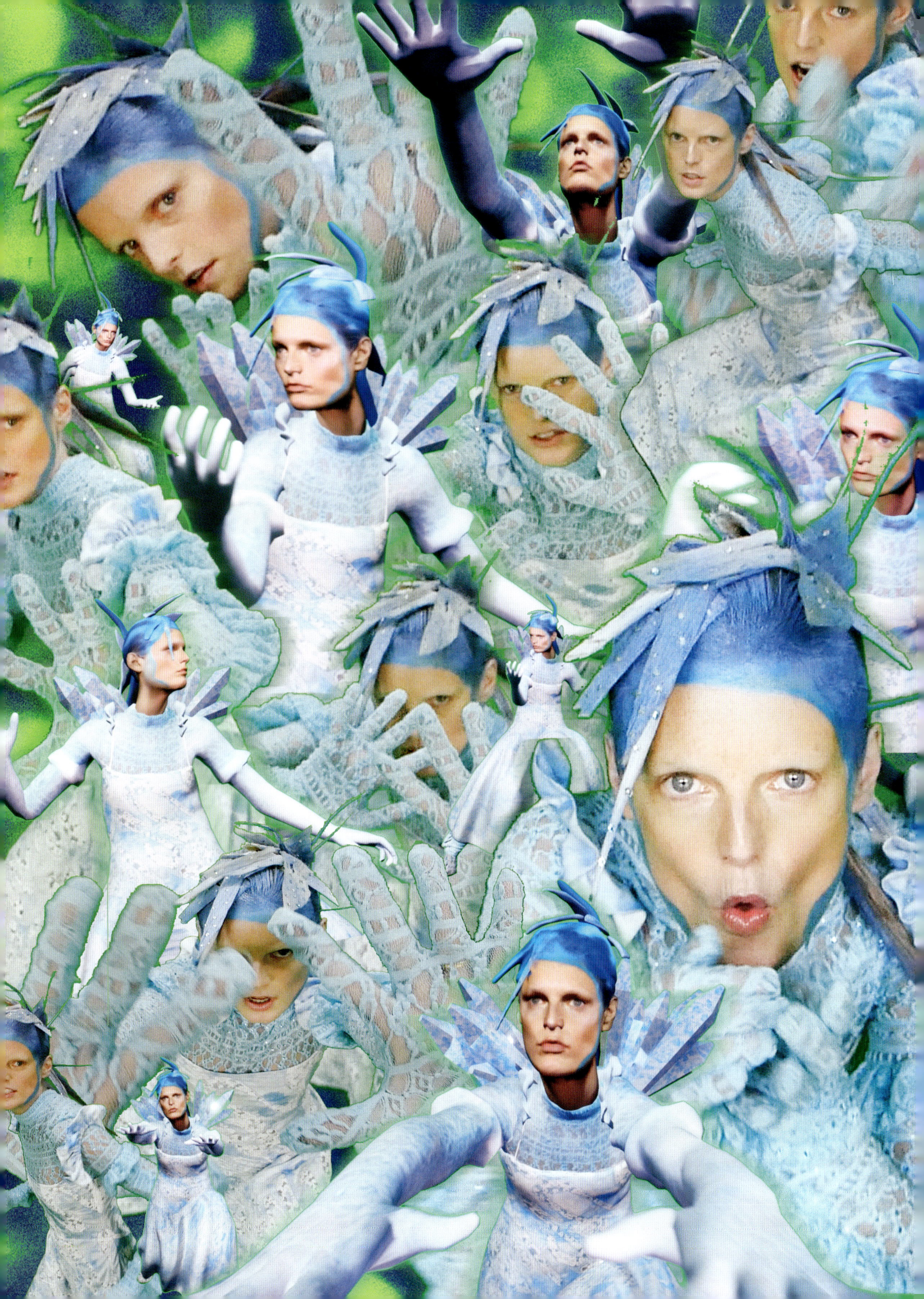

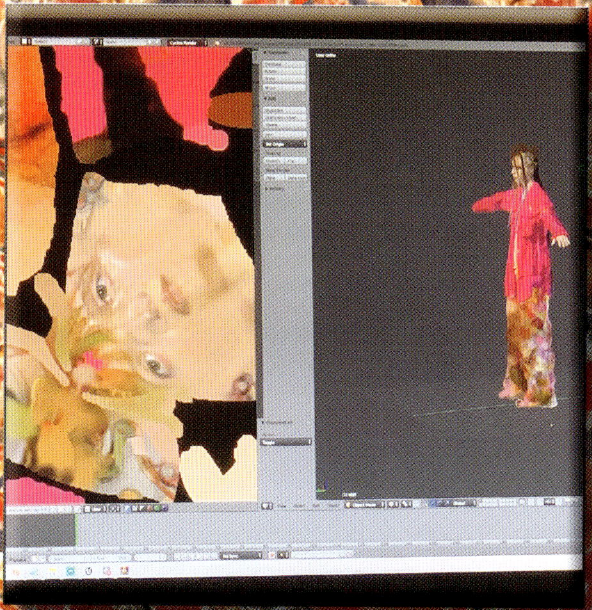

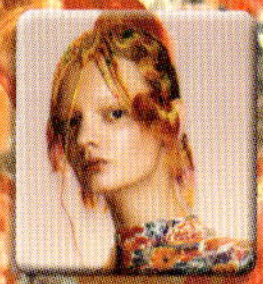

UNIA

These are some examples of the **TEXTURE MAPS** we used to create the video game characters. Once we 3D-scanned our talent, we wrapped the resulting 3D models in these flat images of their skin and clothing to give them their final looks, like peeling an orange and laying the skin out flat, only in reverse.

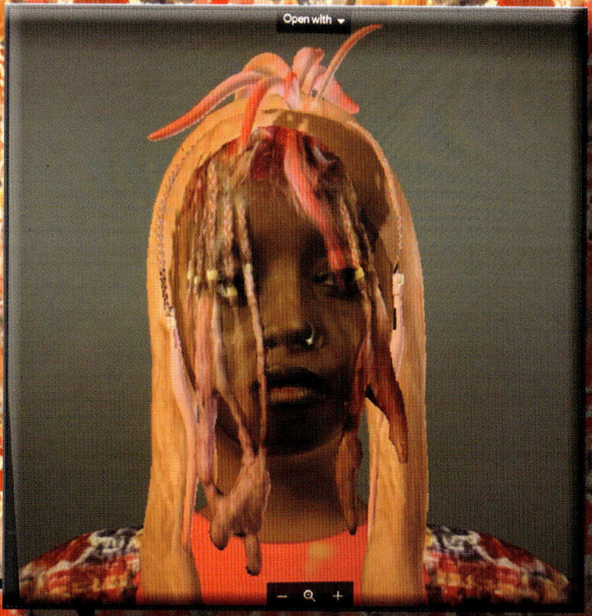

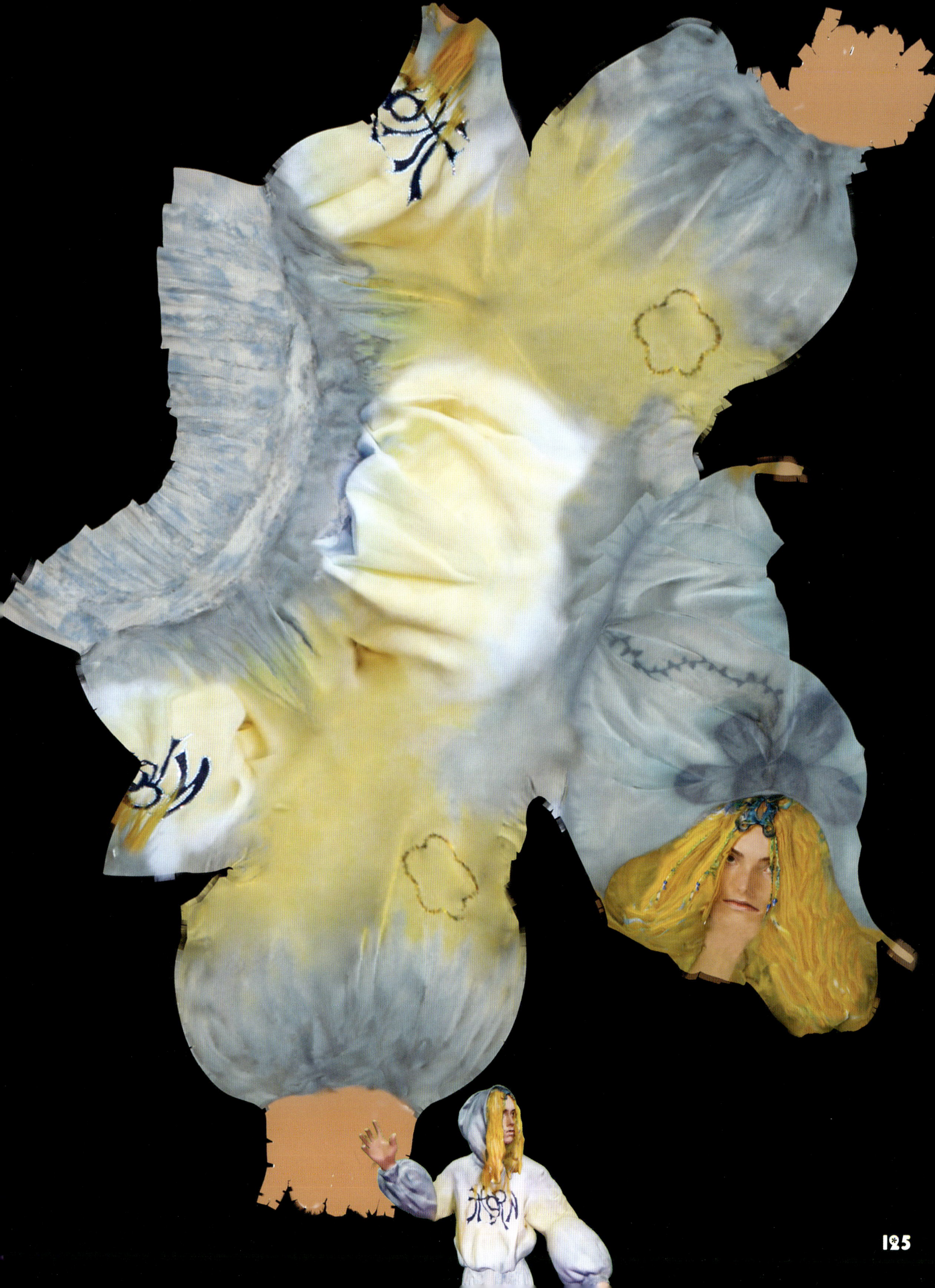

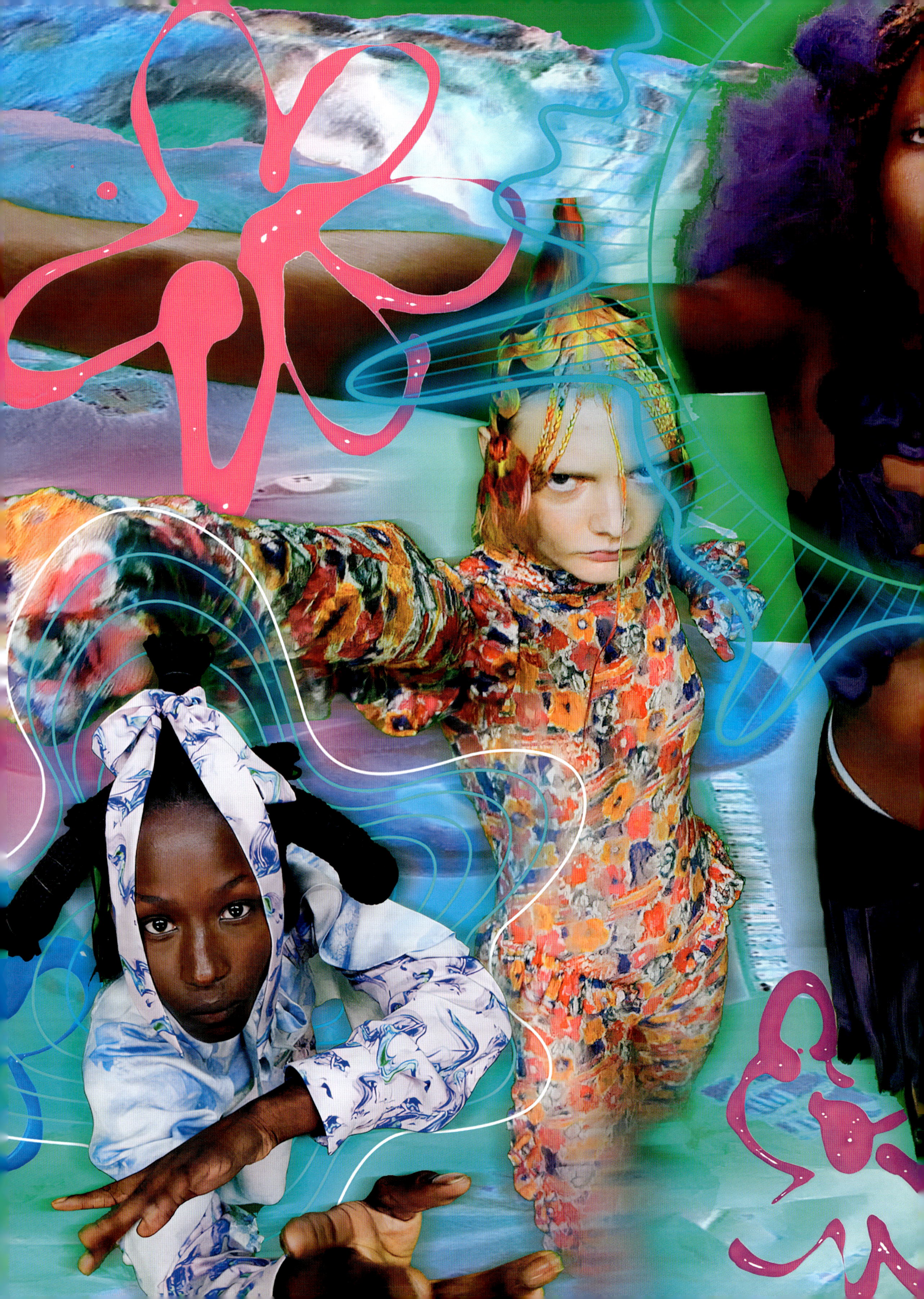

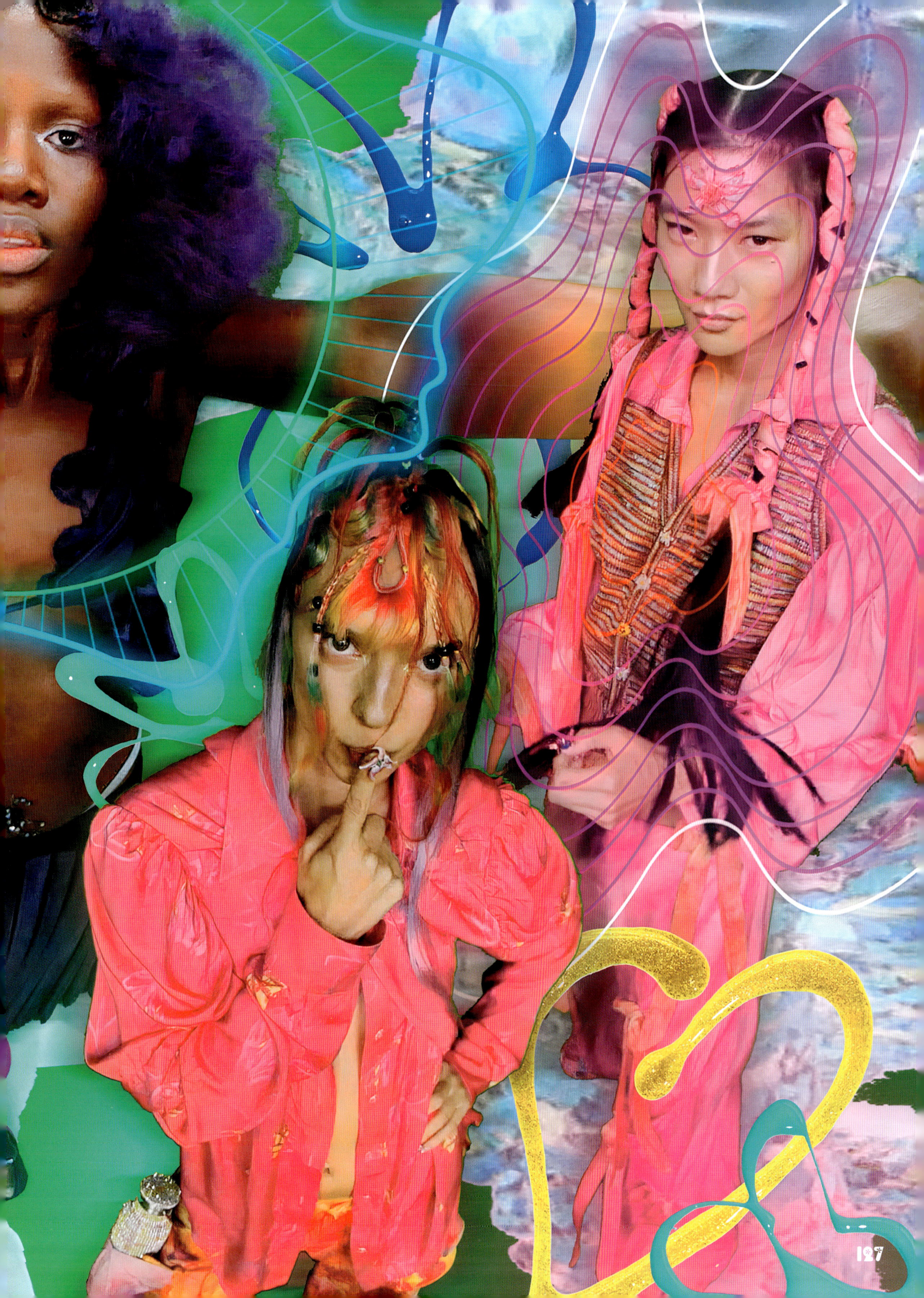

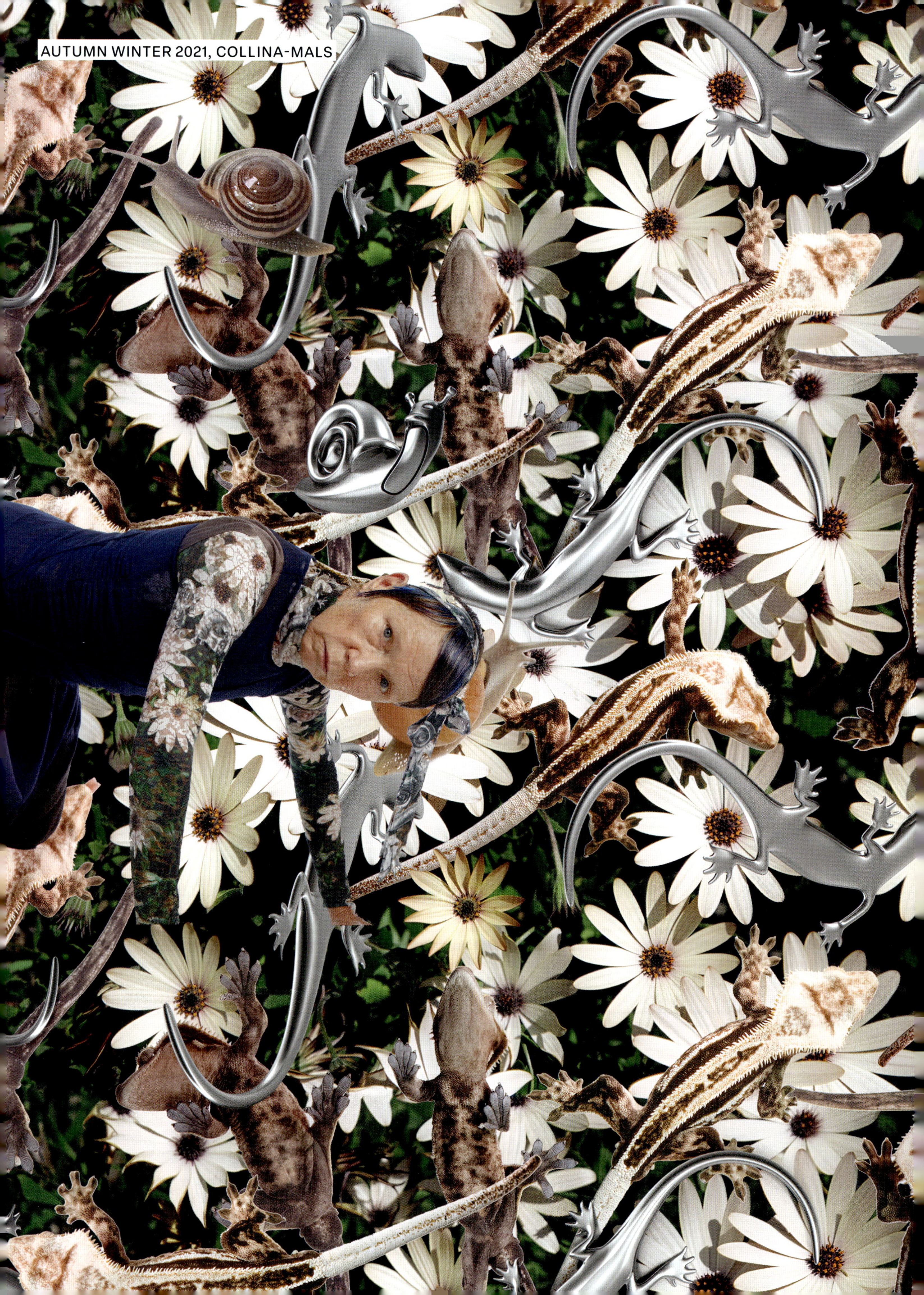

AUTUMN WINTER 2021, COLLINA-MALS

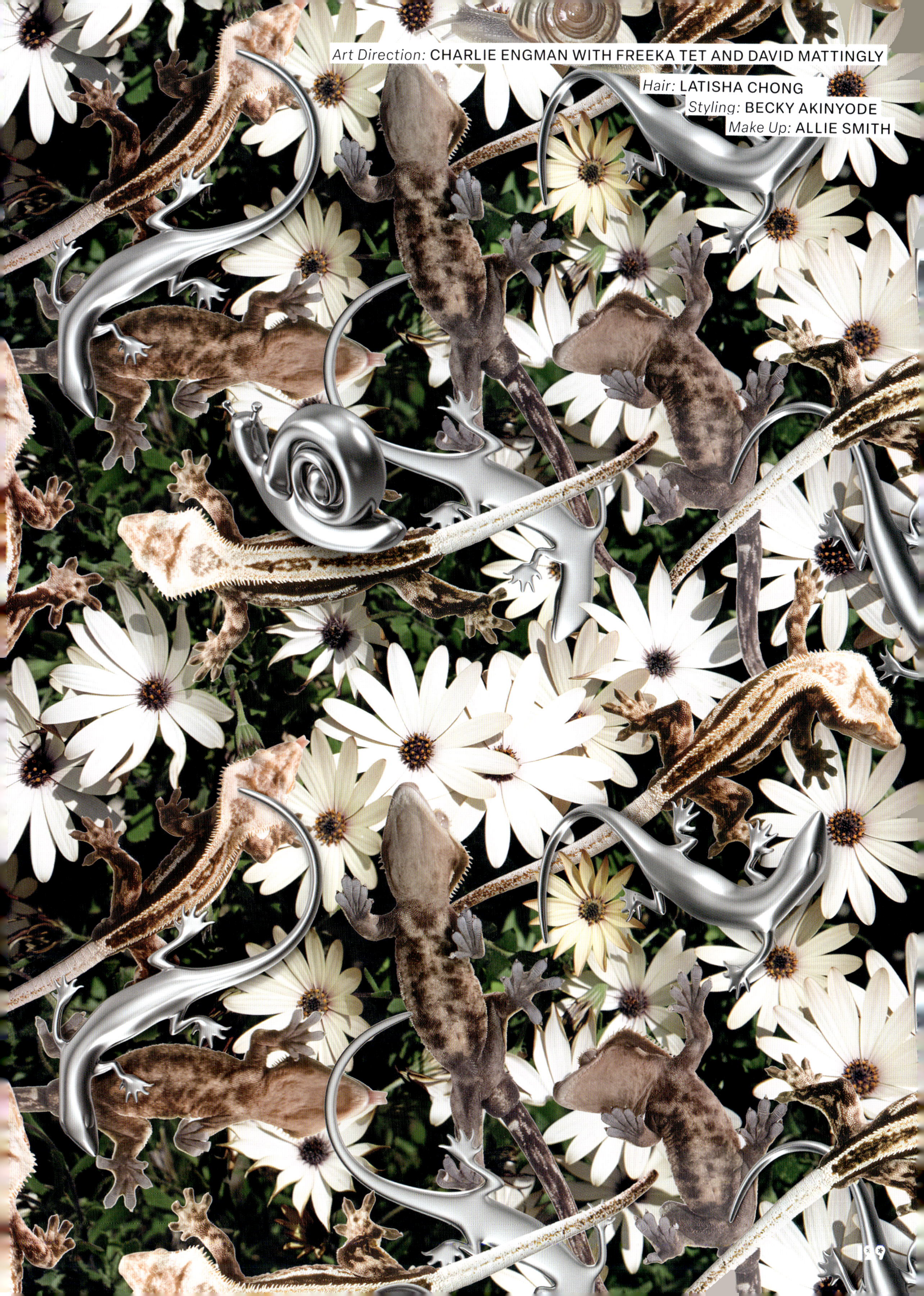

Art Direction: CHARLIE ENGMAN WITH FREEKA TET AND DAVID MATTINGLY

Hair: LATISHA CHONG
Styling: BECKY AKINYODE
Make Up: ALLIE SMITH

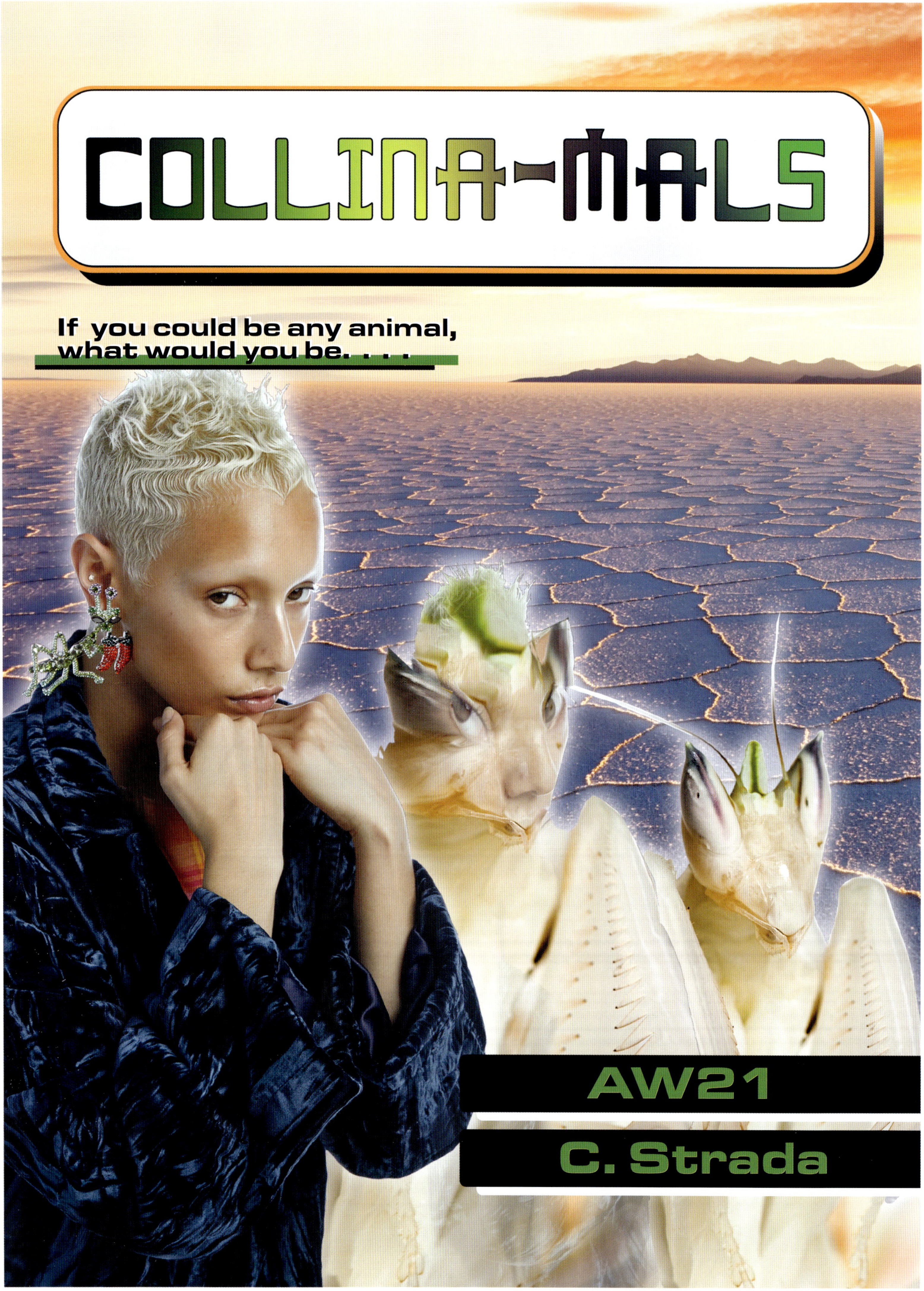
COLLINA-MALS
If you could be any animal,
what would you be. . . .
AW21
C. Strada

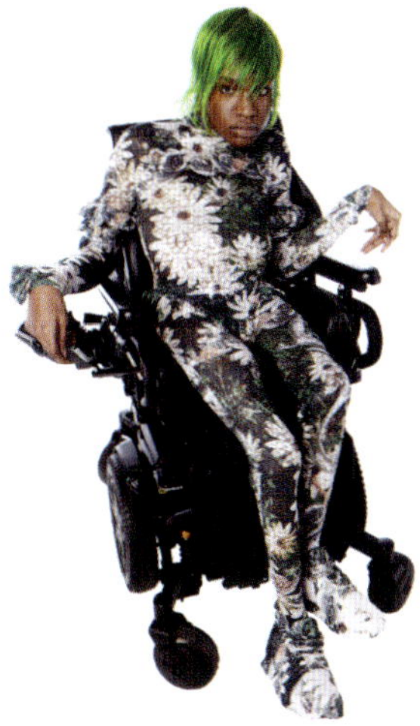

Autumn Winter '21

Beyond the campy covers that depict kids transforming into hawks, butterflies, and spiders, ***Animorphs*** was about metamorphosis—between human and animal, between childhood and adulthood, between a carefree existence and the weight of responsibility. ***K.A. Applegate's*** books were not only a cherished part of our late-90s youth and nascent environmentalism, but also an analogue that mirrored the evolution of our own lives. Using the series as an inspiration for this season, we granted our models the superpower to change into their favorite animals. Each model chose their critter—ranging from classic kitties to puppy-pony hybrids to balloon animals (all animals welcome :-))—and we birthed a beautiful menagerie. The process included working directly with ***David Mattingly***, the artist who created the original *Animorphs* cover art. David lent us his expertise on which poses and techniques make for the best morphs, and, from there, digital artist ***Freeka Tet*** created a machine-learning formula to give our models their wings.

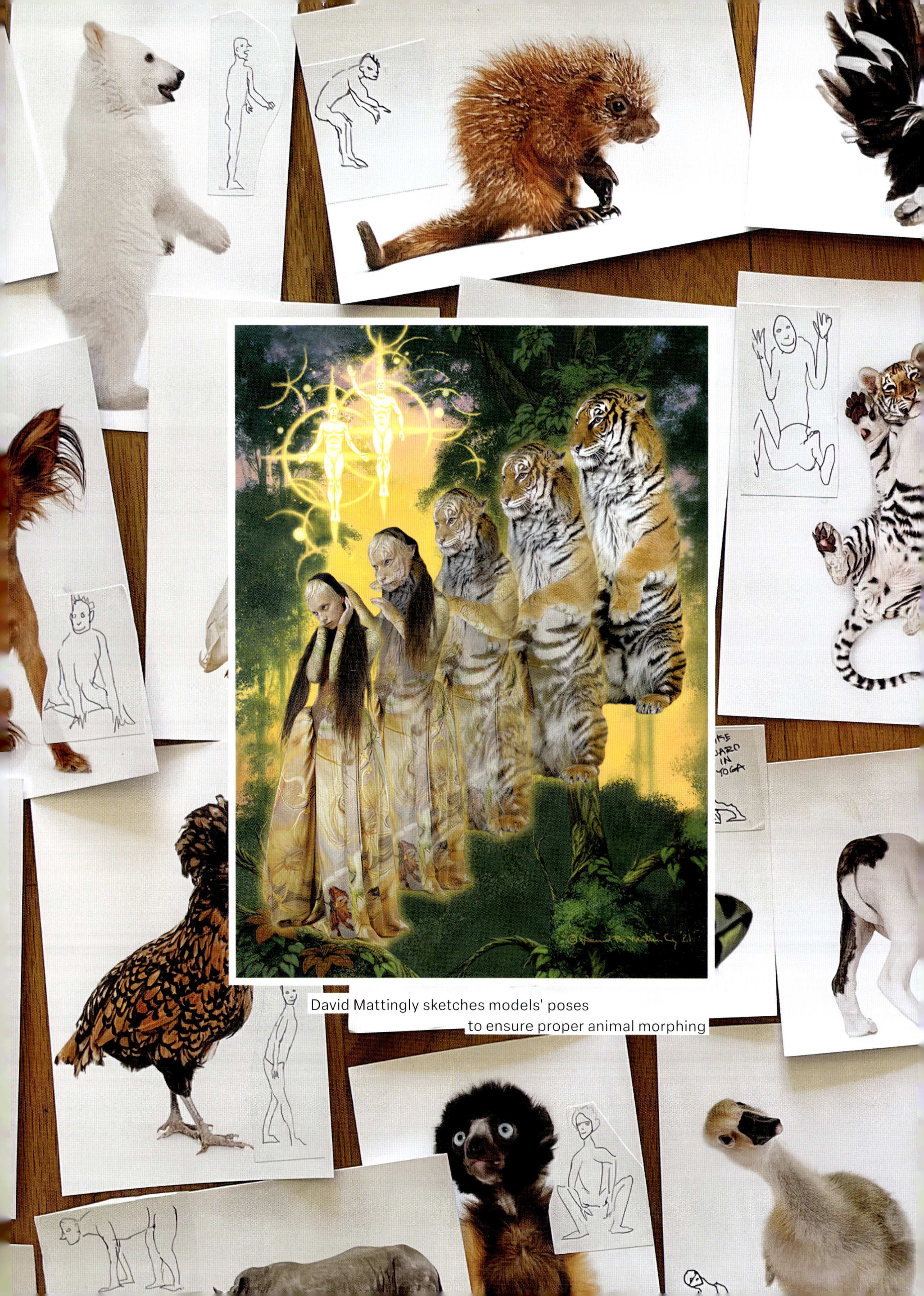

David Mattingly sketches models' poses
to ensure proper animal morphing

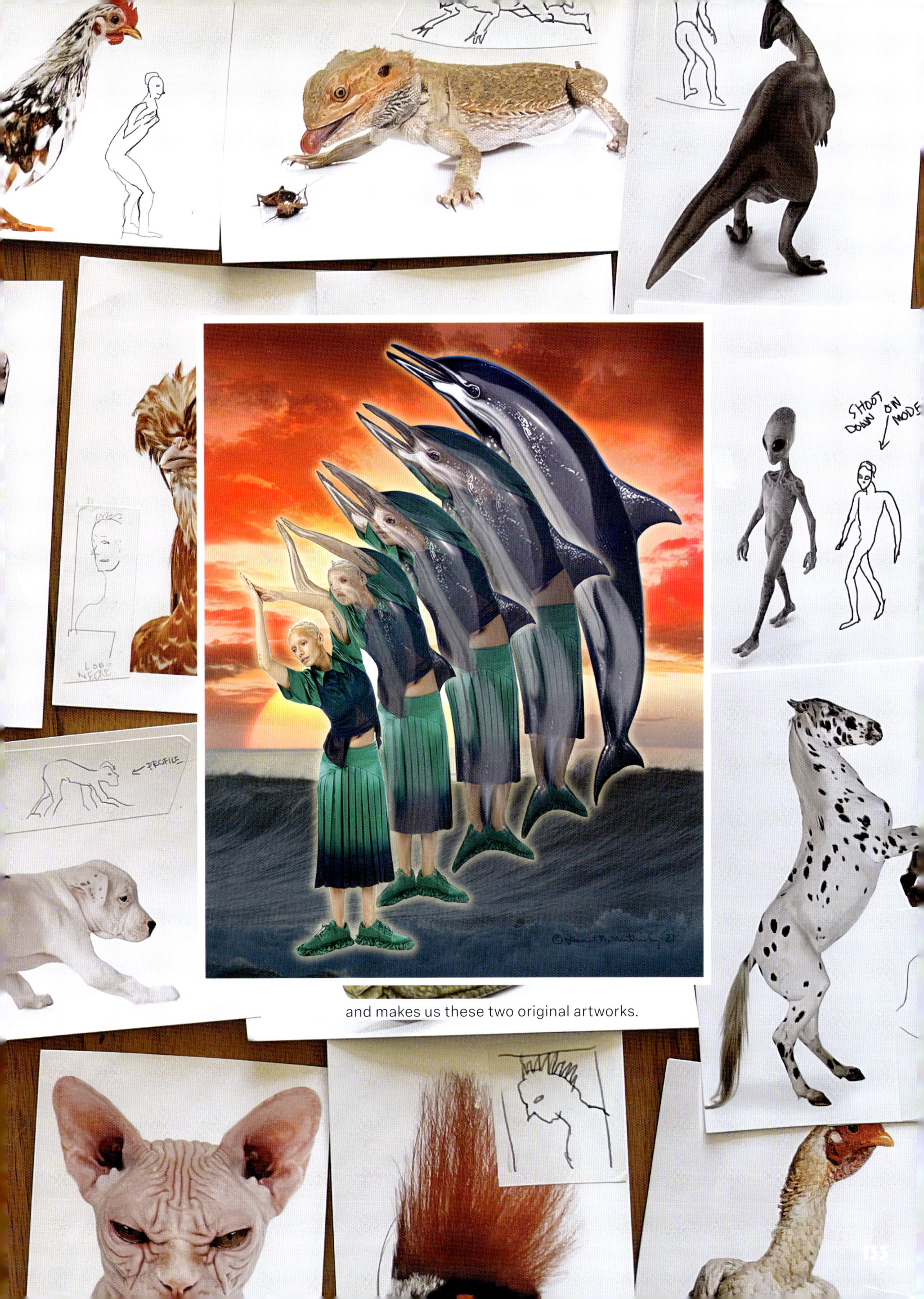

and makes us these two original artworks.

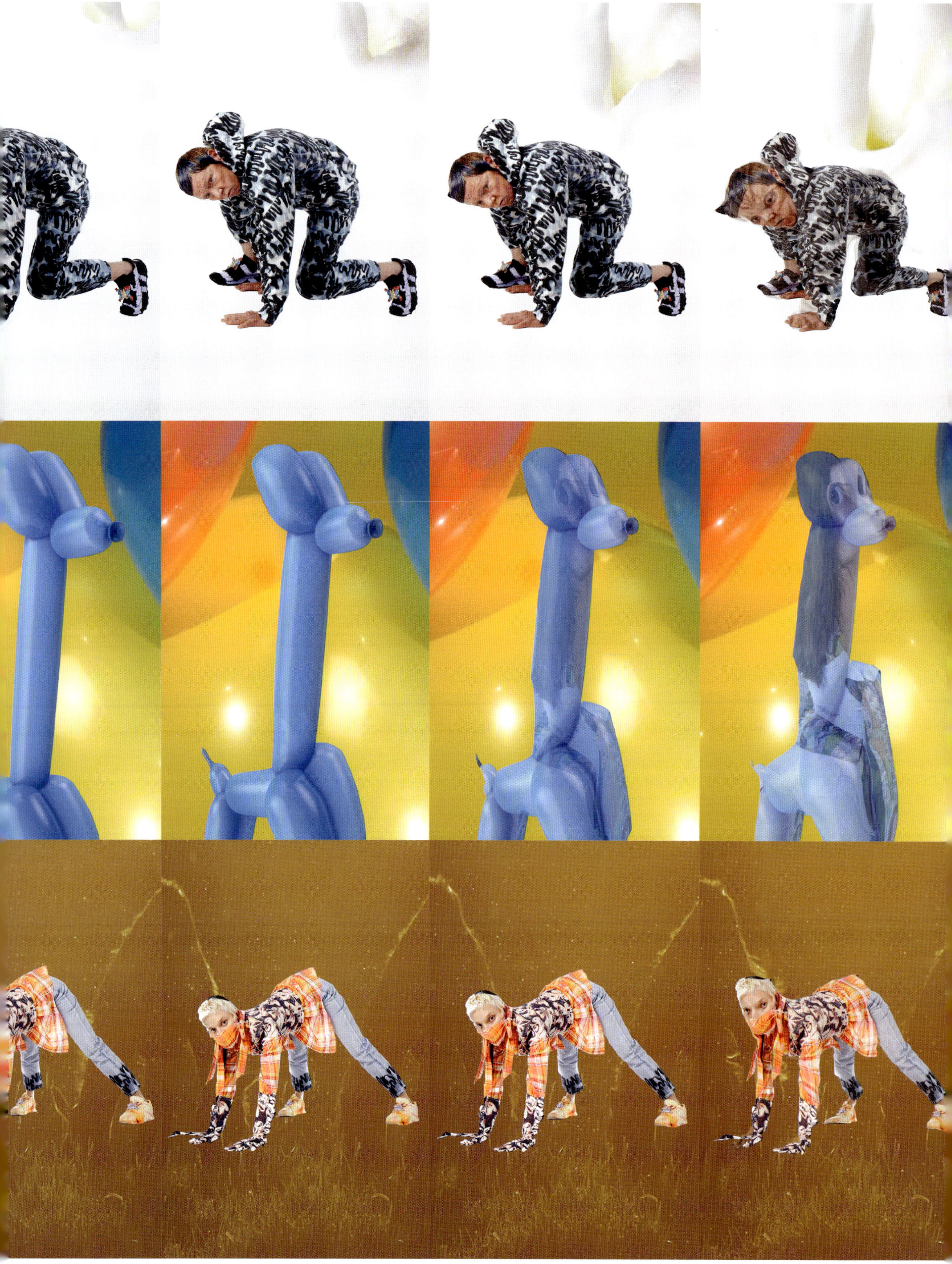

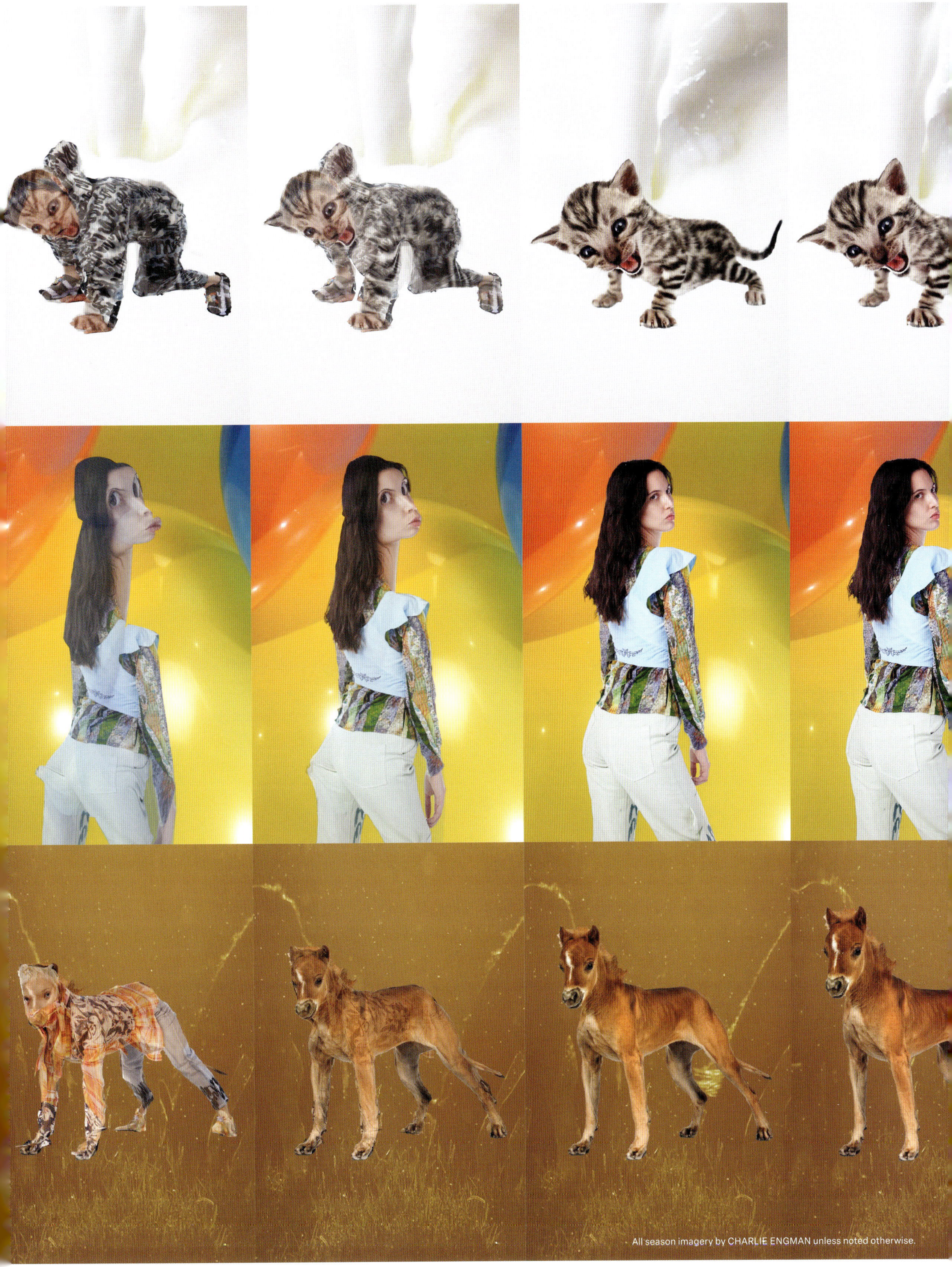

All season imagery by CHARLIE ENGMAN unless noted otherwise.

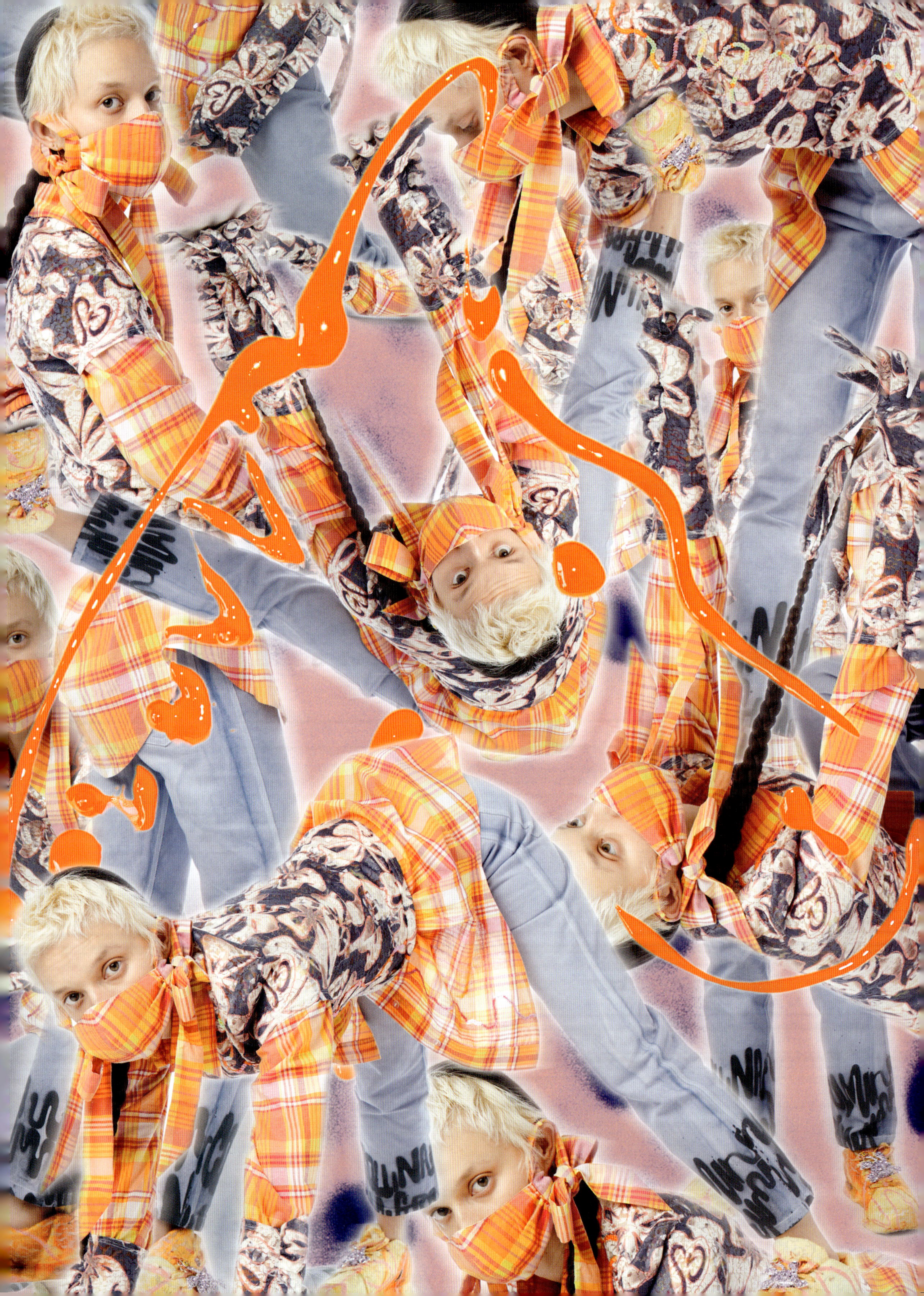

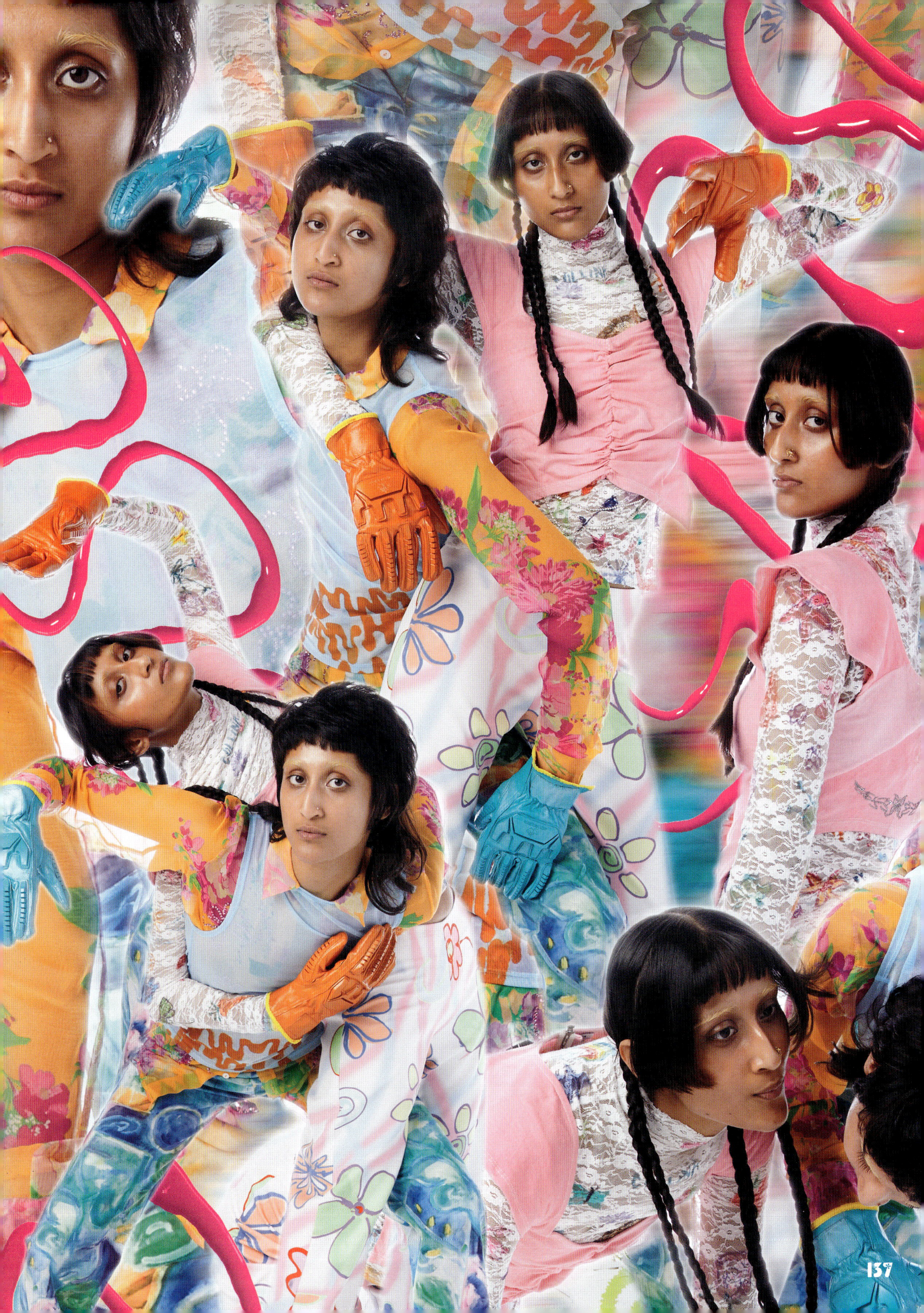

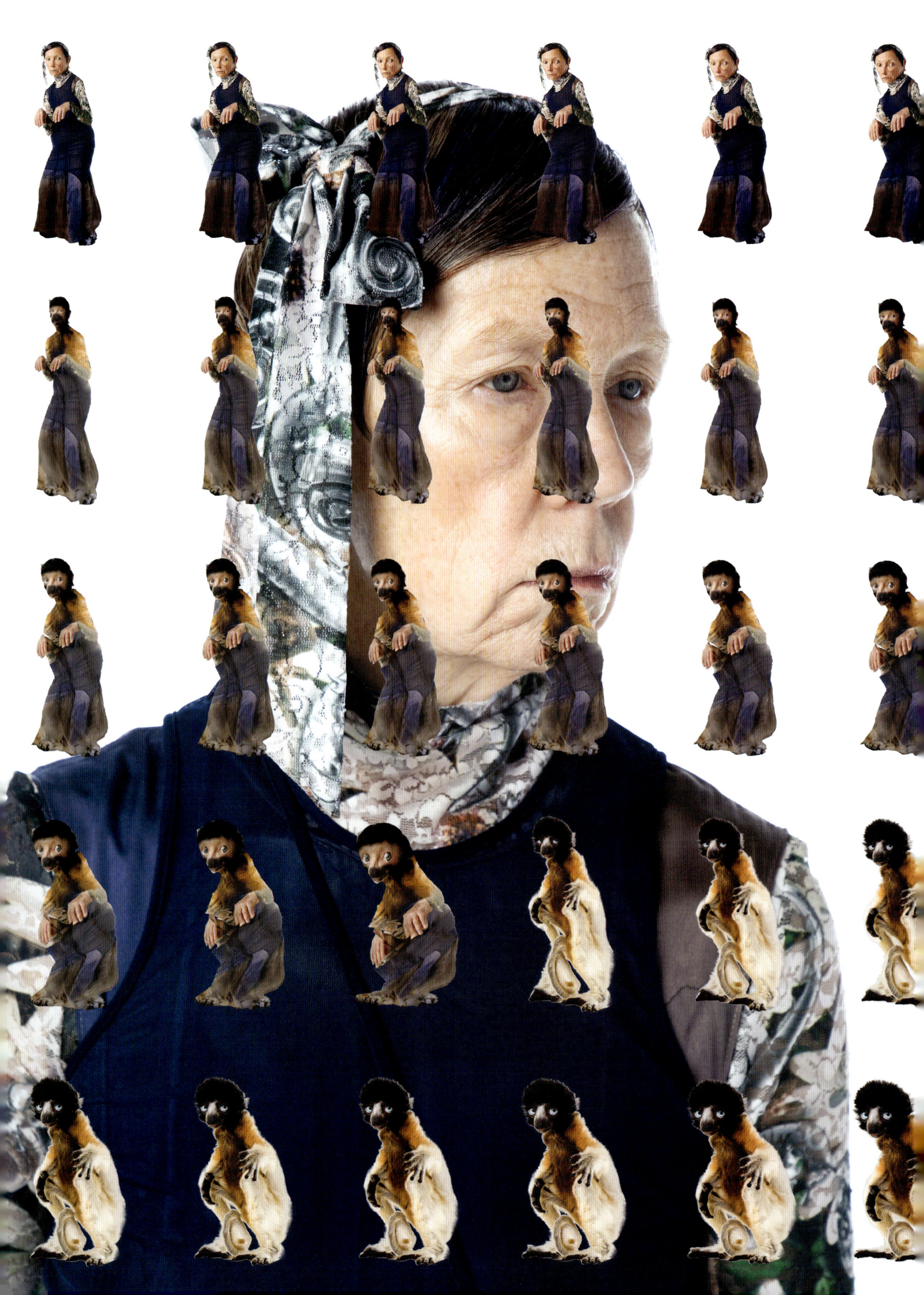

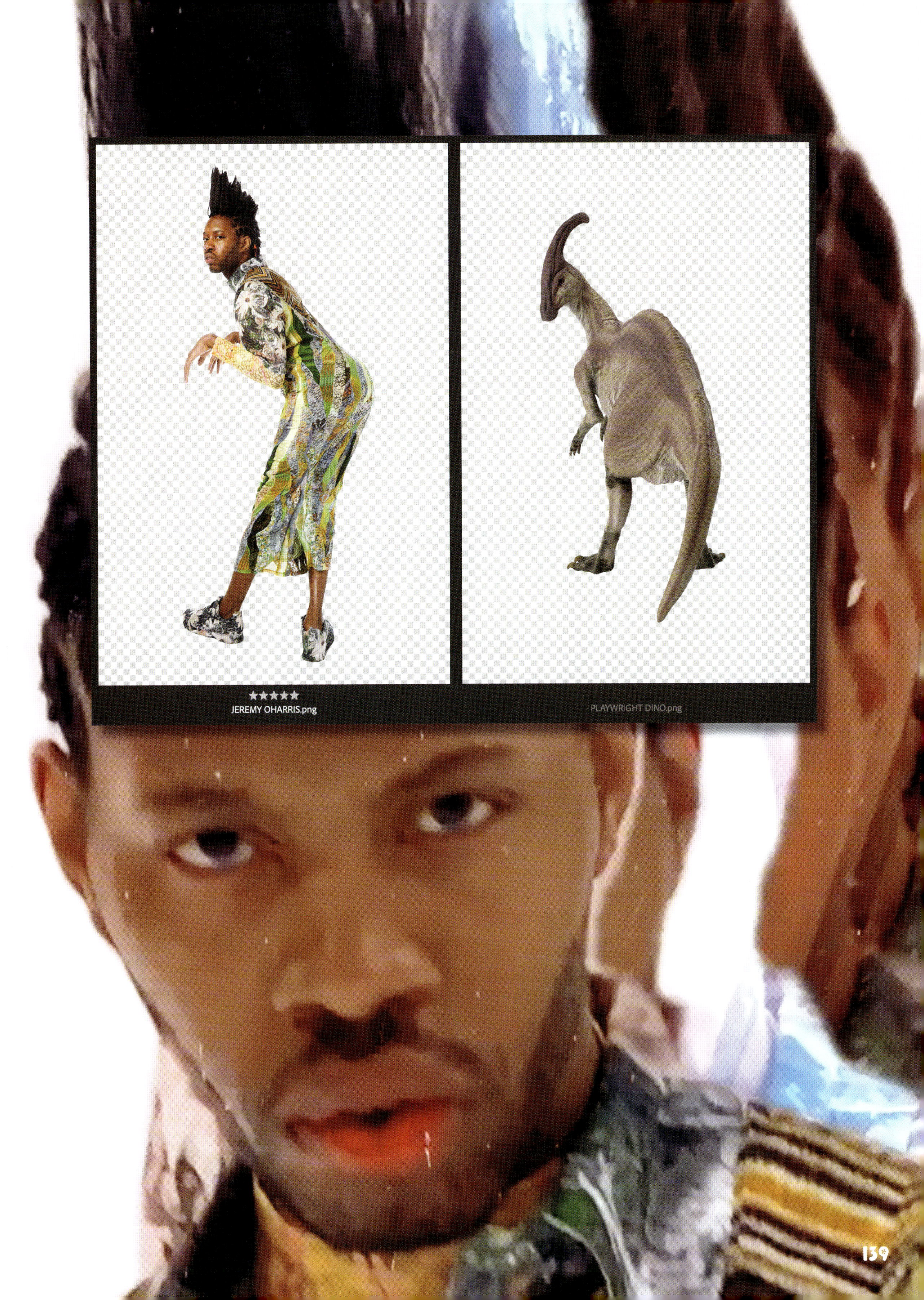
★★★★★
JEREMY OHARRIS.png
PLAYWRIGHT DINO.png

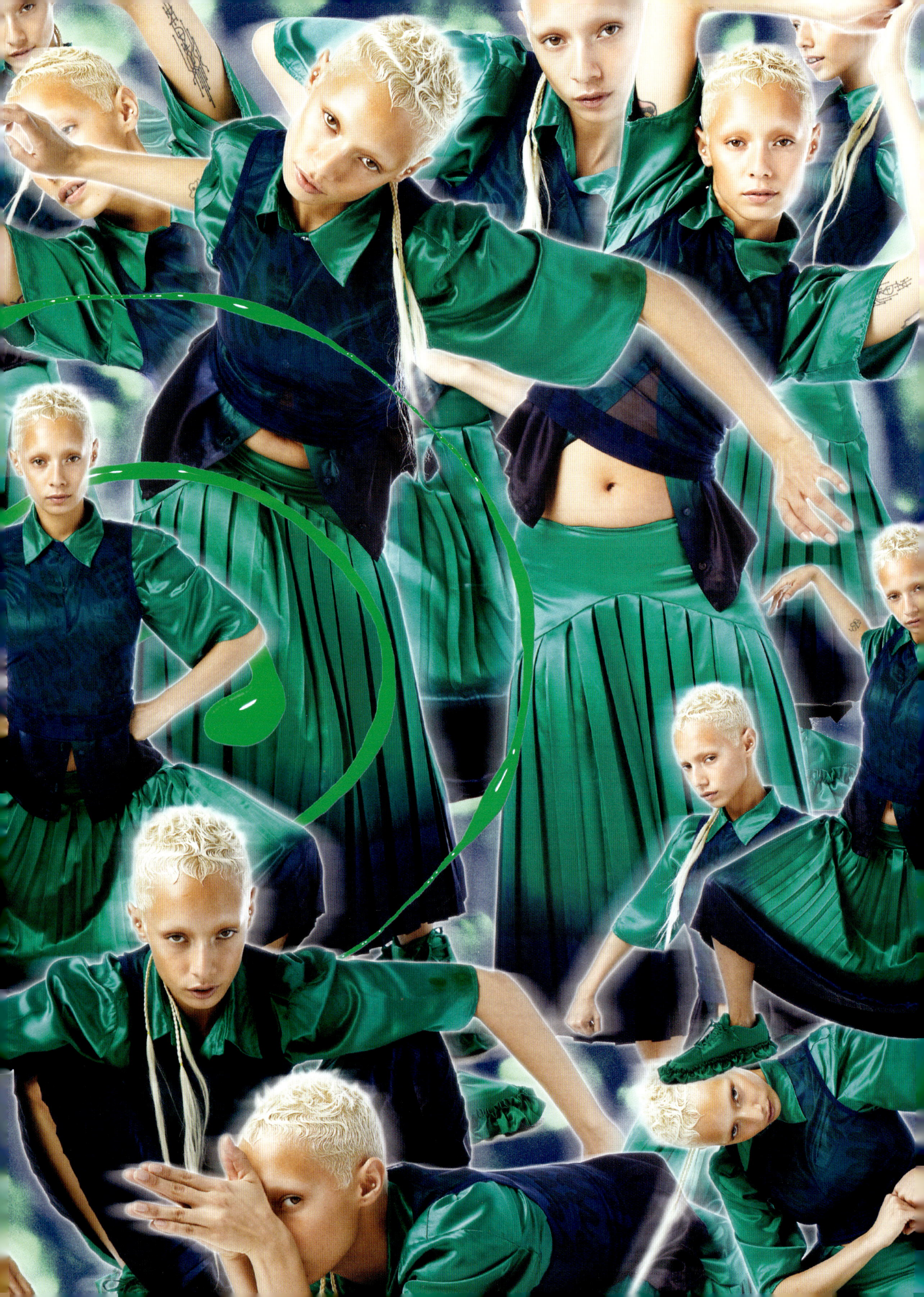

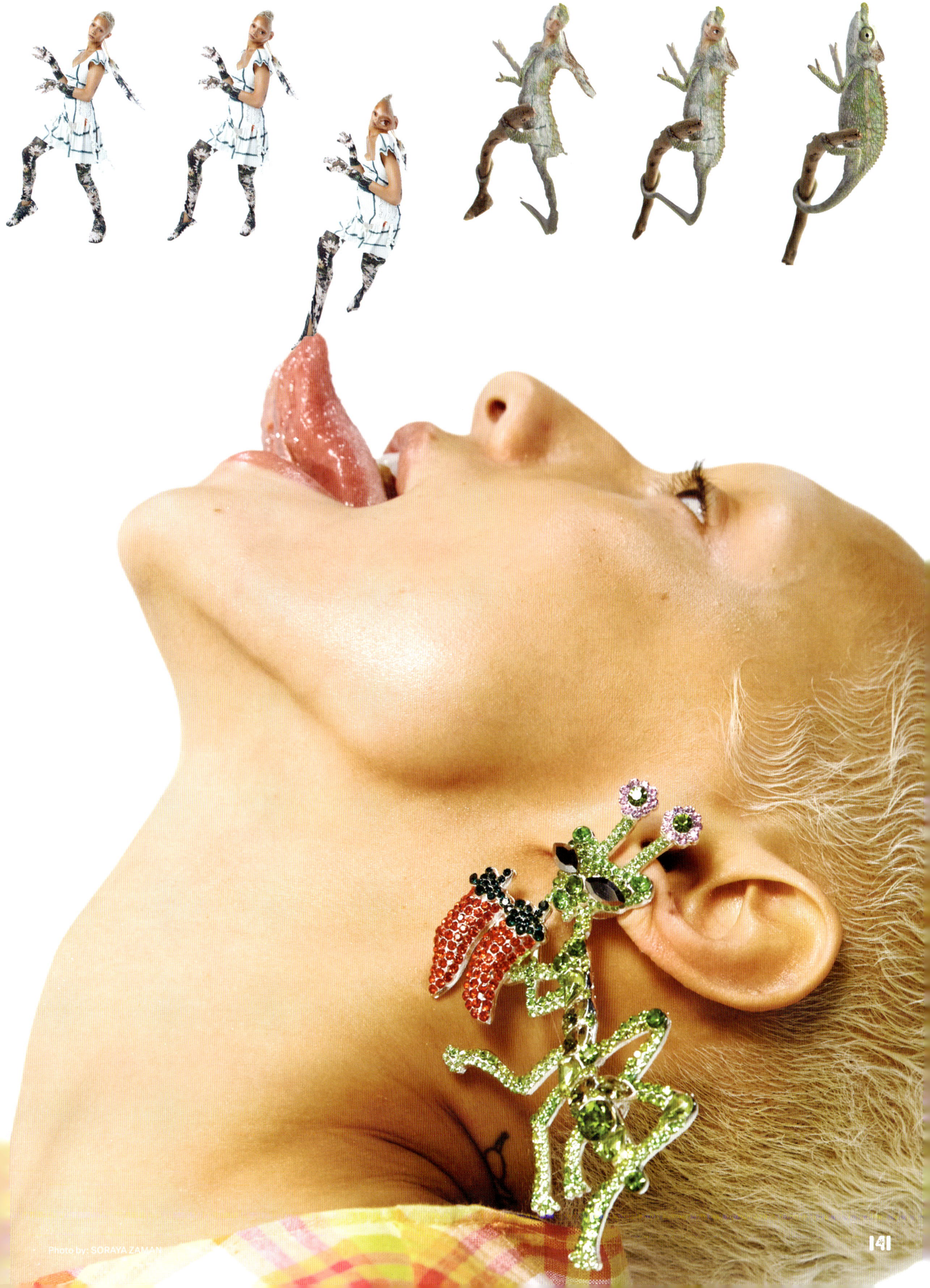

Photo by: SORAYA ZAMAN

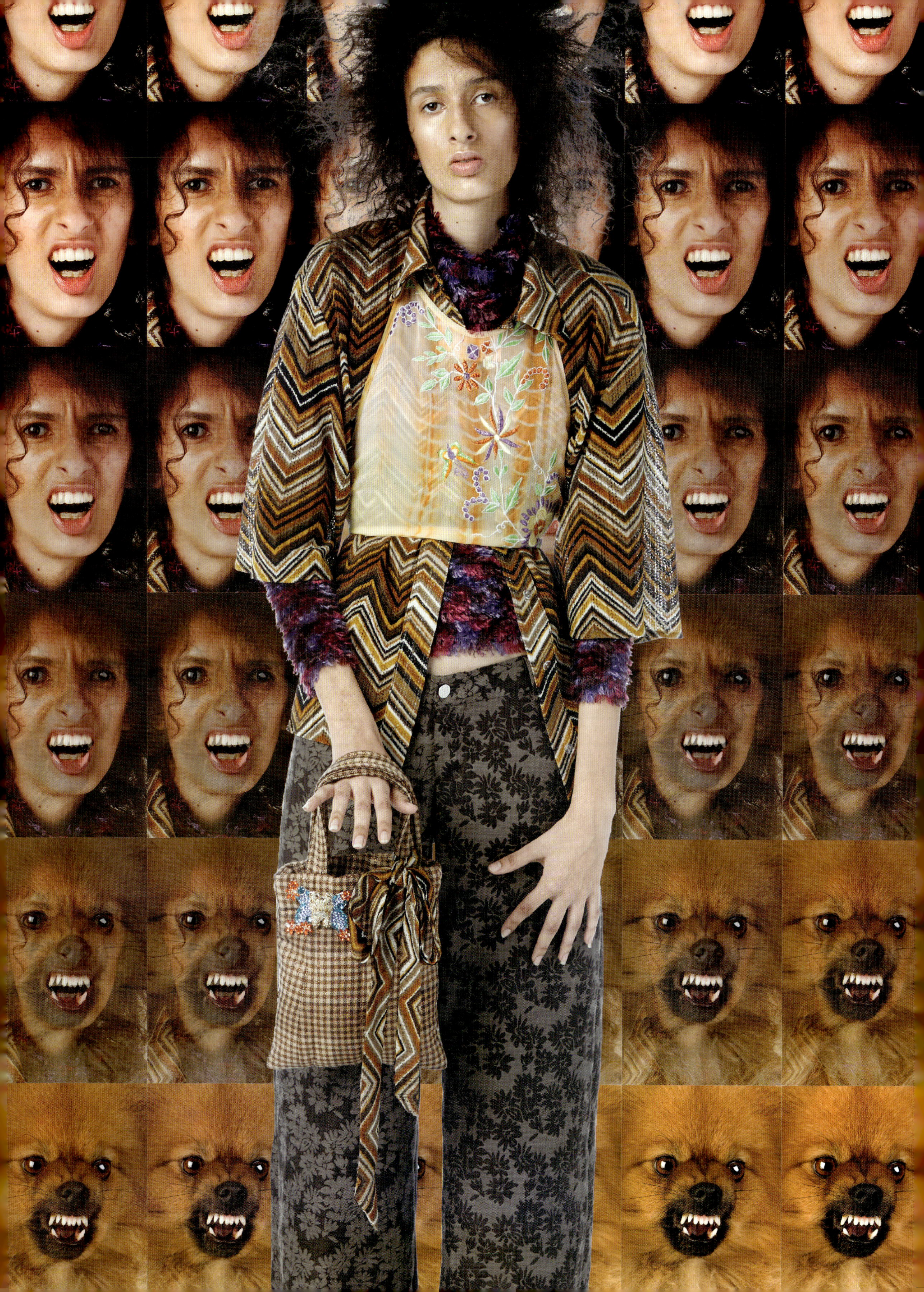

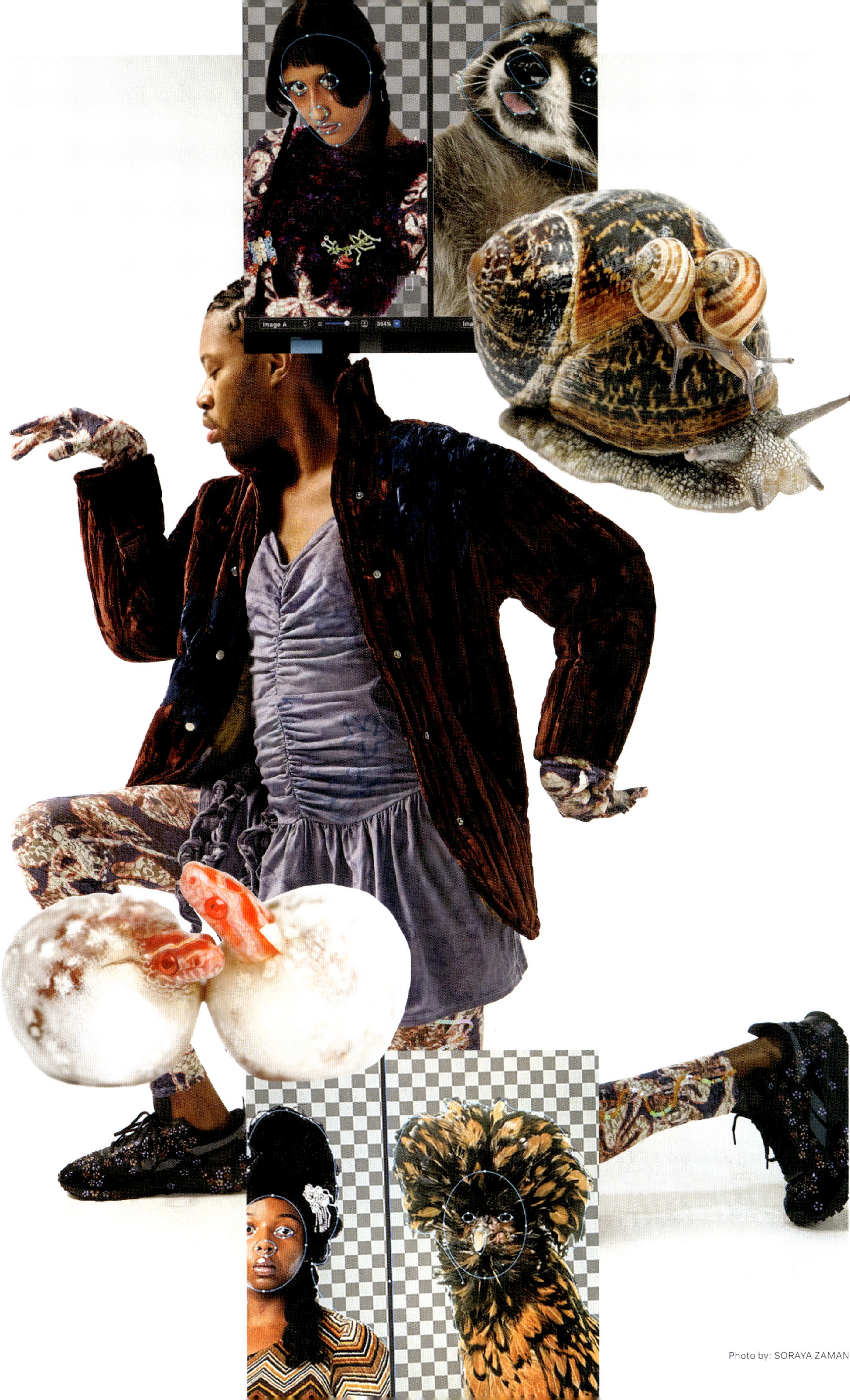

Photo by: SORAYA ZAMAN

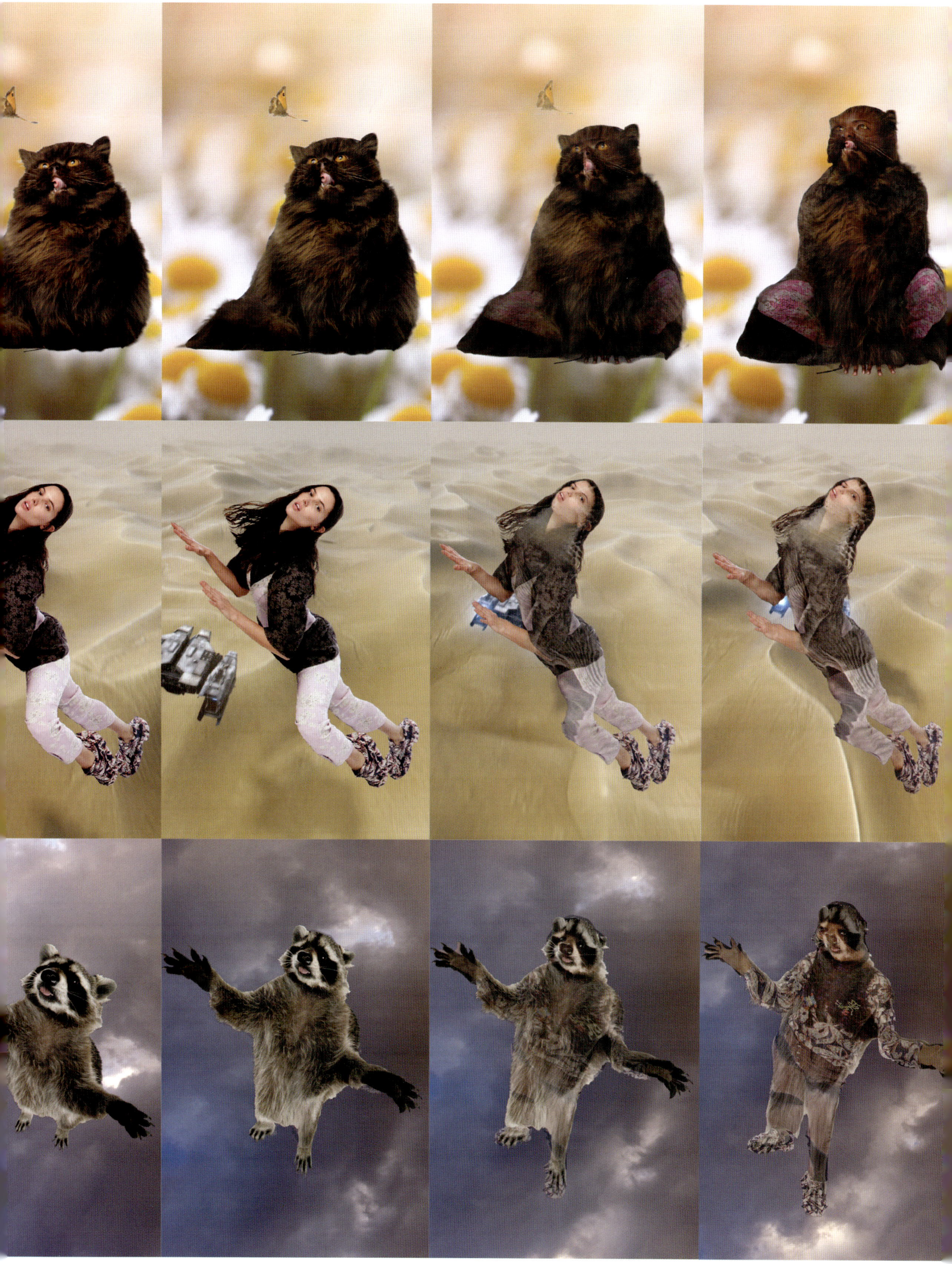

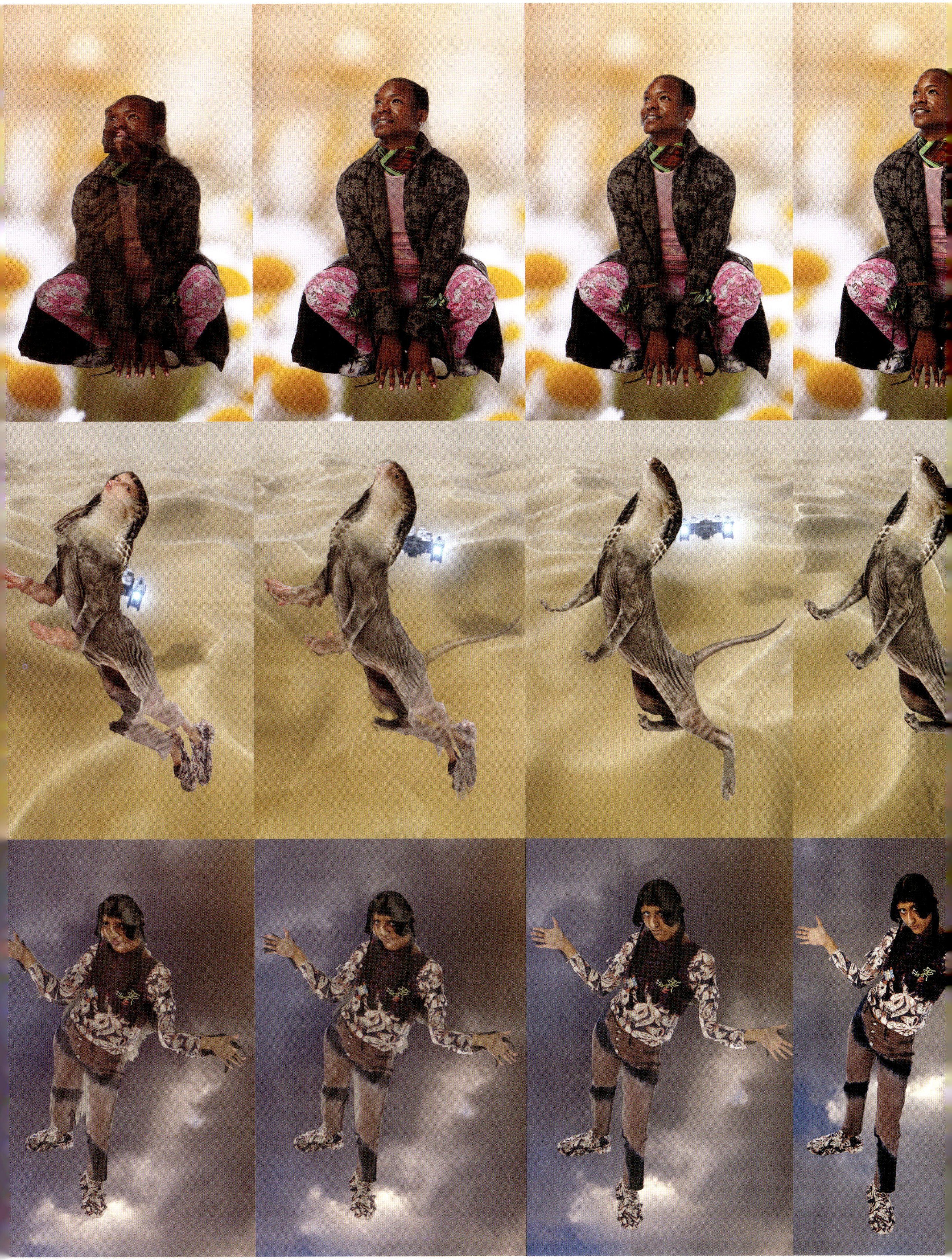

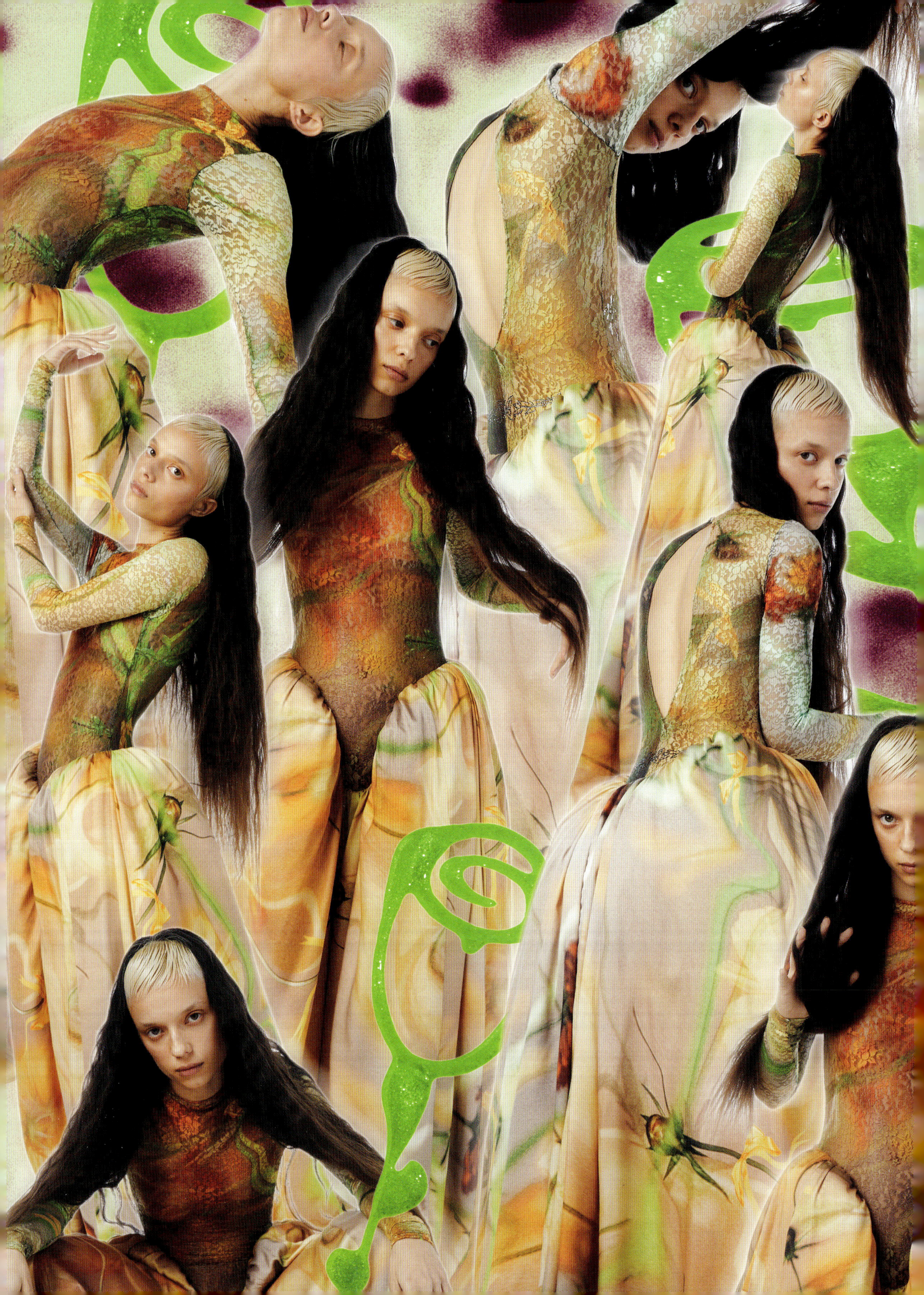

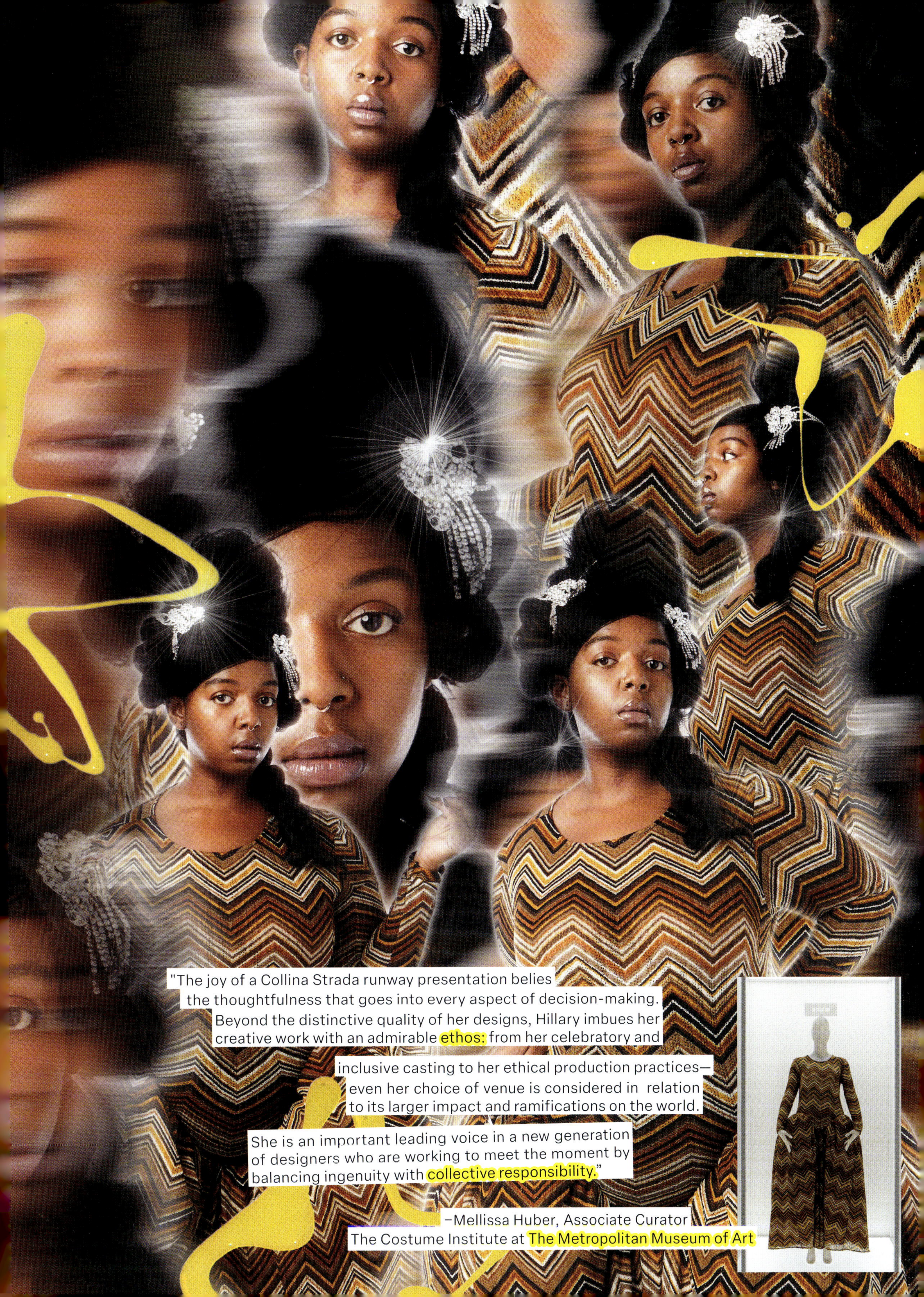

"The joy of a Collina Strada runway presentation belies the thoughtfulness that goes into every aspect of decision-making. Beyond the distinctive quality of her designs, Hillary imbues her creative work with an admirable ethos: from her celebratory and inclusive casting to her ethical production practices—even her choice of venue is considered in relation to its larger impact and ramifications on the world.

She is an important leading voice in a new generation of designers who are working to meet the moment by balancing ingenuity with collective responsibility."

–Mellissa Huber, Associate Curator
The Costume Institute at The Metropolitan Museum of Art

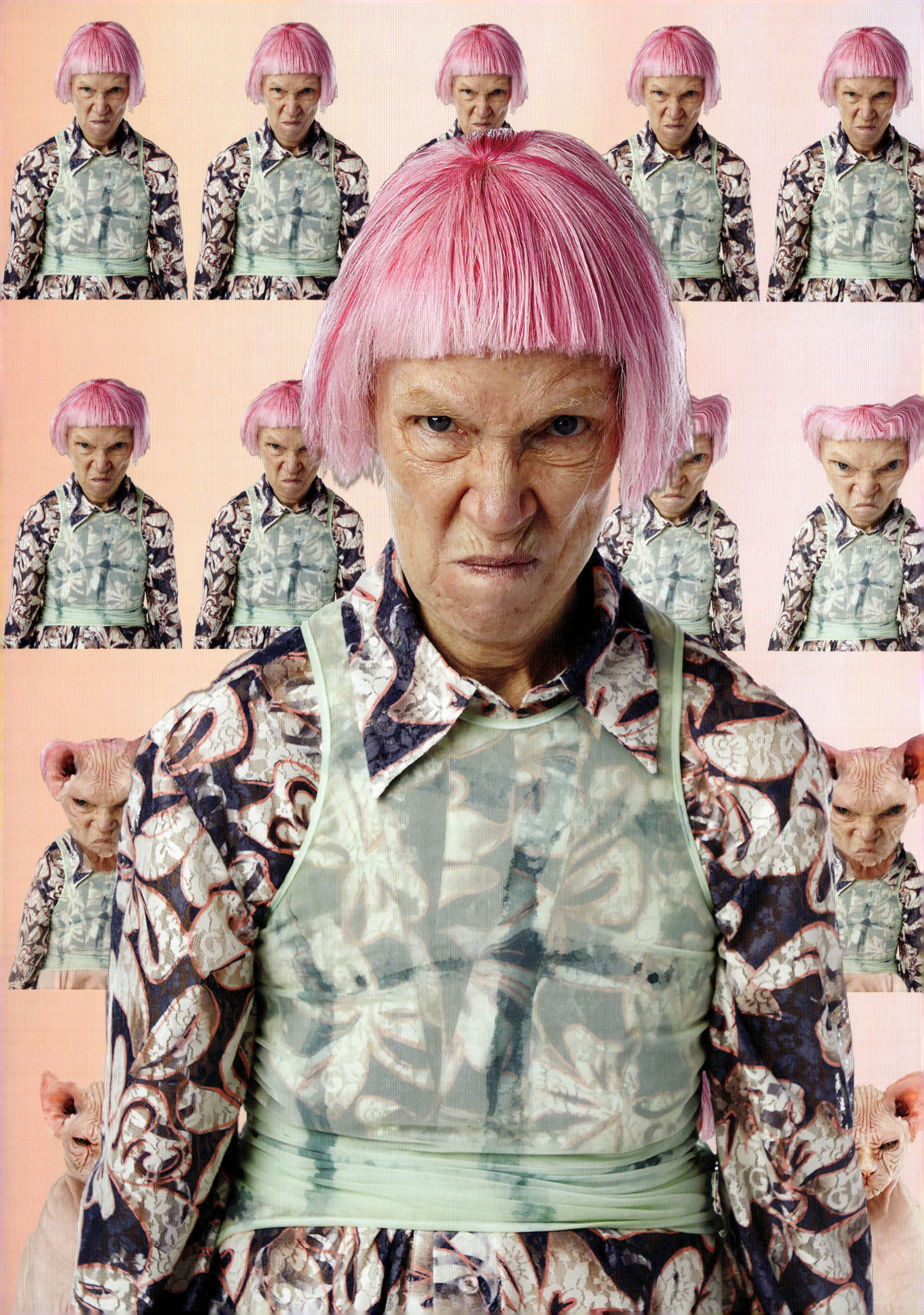

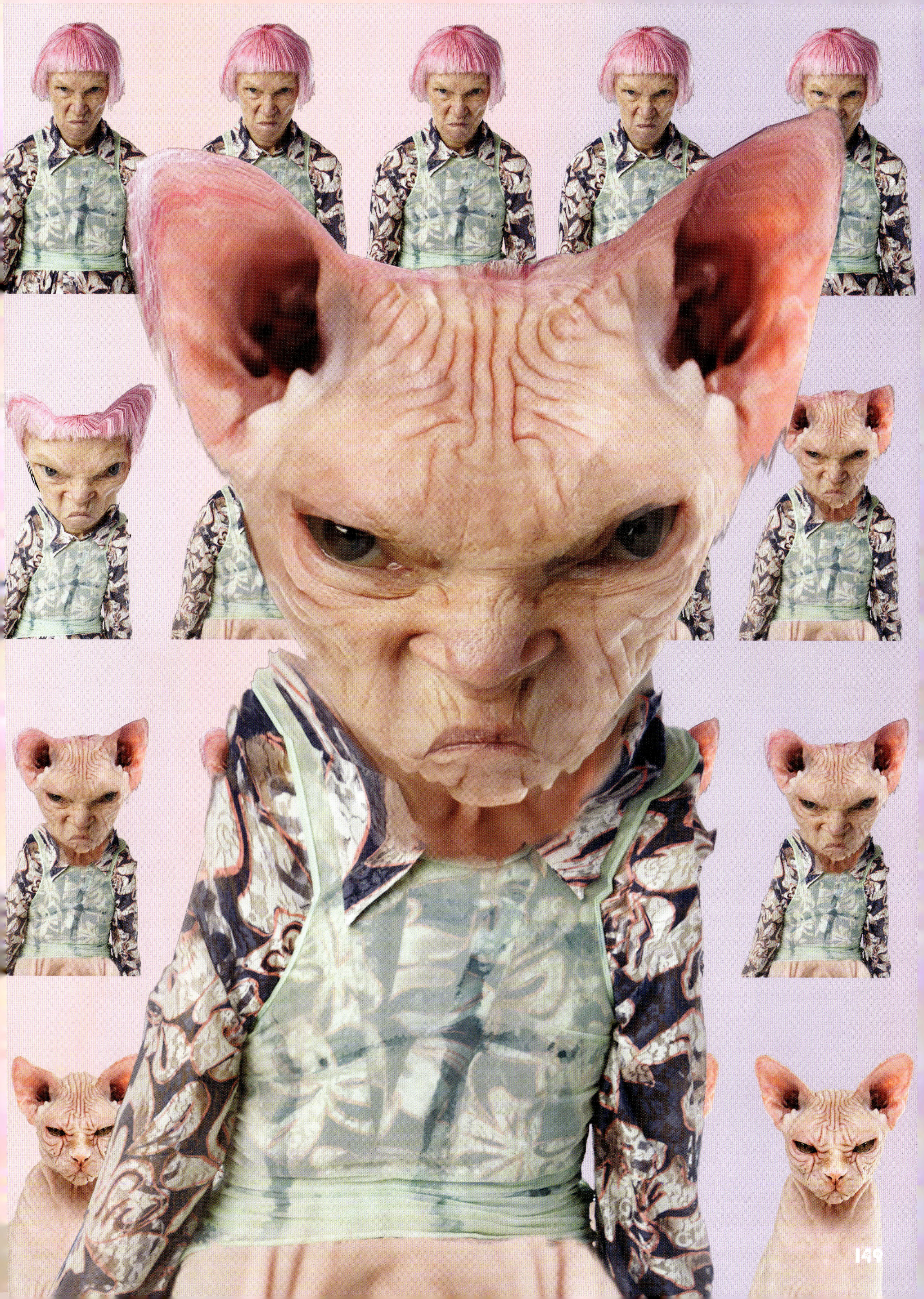

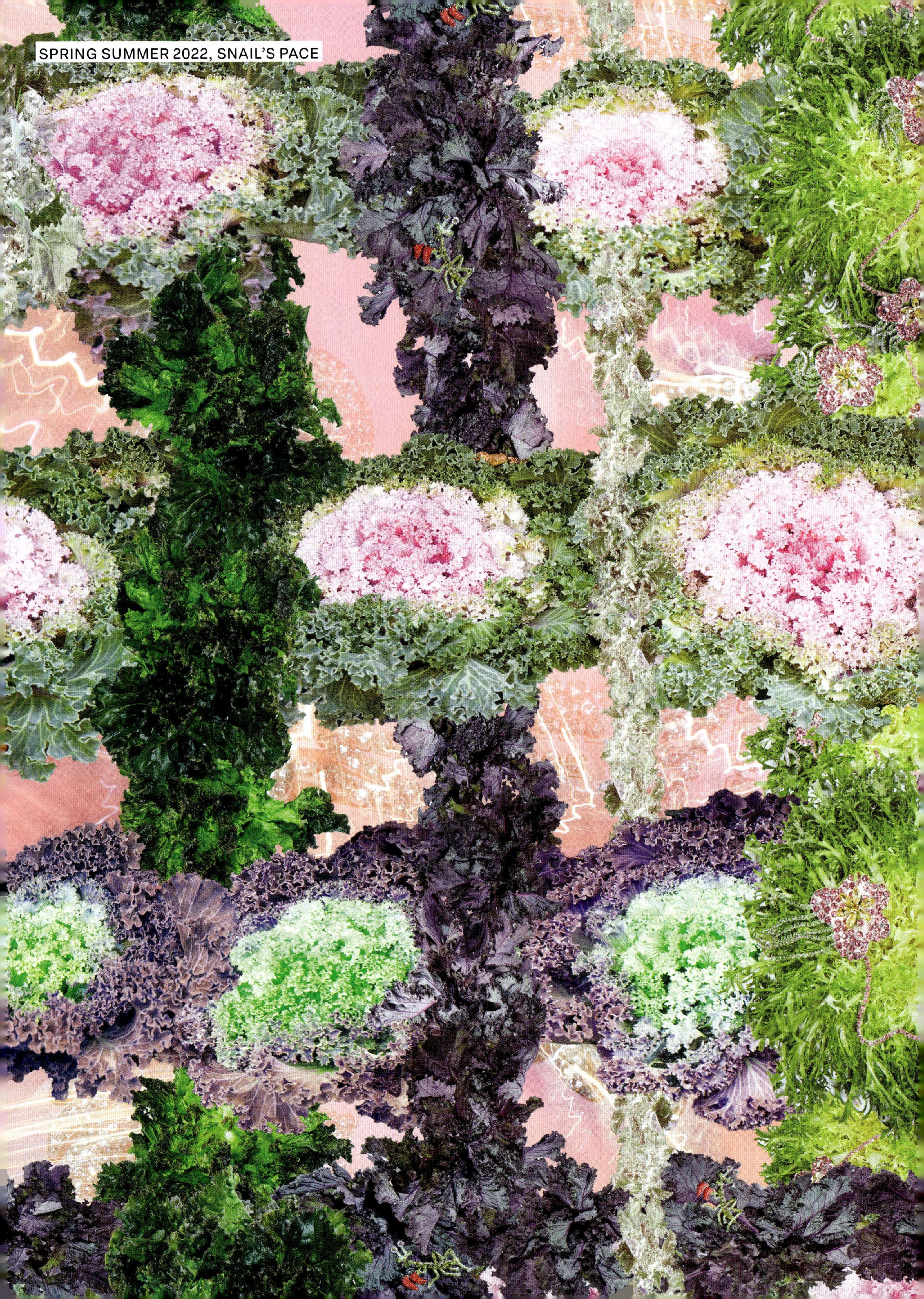

Art Direction and Styling: CHARLIE ENGMAN AND HILLARY TAYMOUR

Hair: EVANIE FRAUSTO

Makeup: ALLIE SMITH

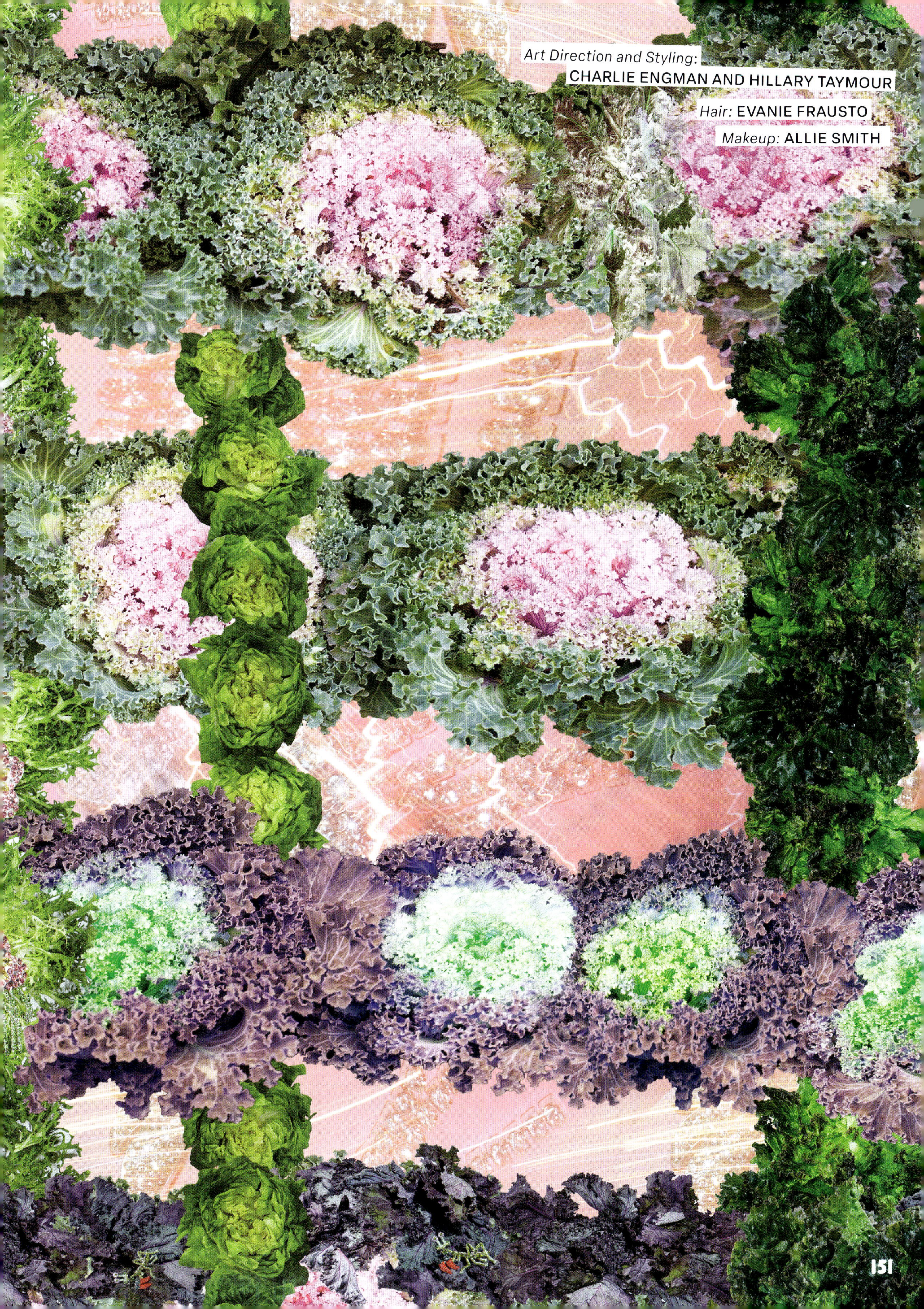

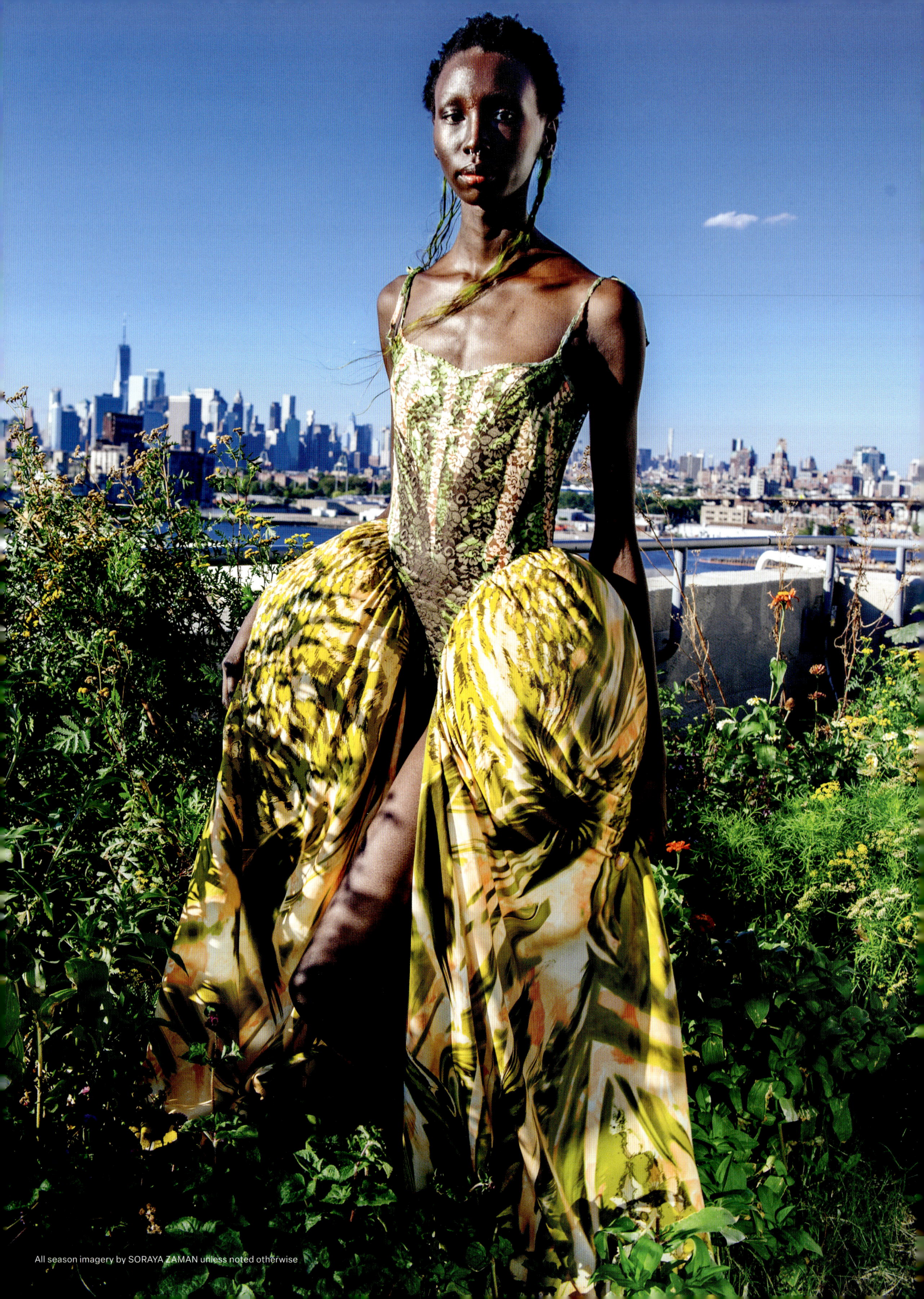

All season imagery by SORAYA ZAMAN unless noted otherwise

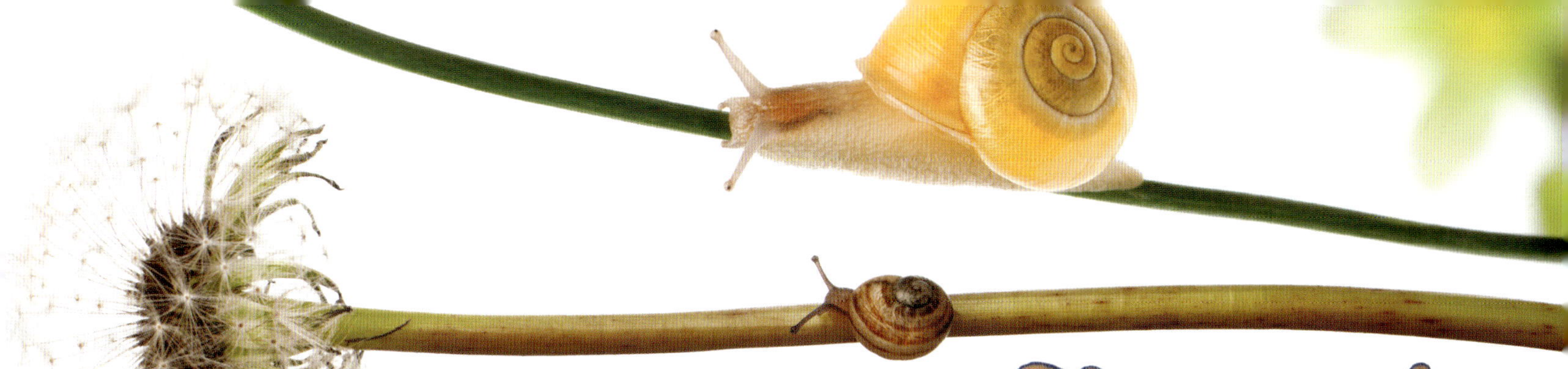

Snails Pace

SS22

It's a chaotic time.

The world is changing, and so are you.

You dress for the mess: print on print, layer on layer. Your mind is everywhere.

You lose concentration and break your arm while learning how to skateboard. You sleep it off in a sk8r boi's bed wearing an old wedding dress dyed green from rolling in the grass.

You wake up and throw on said sk8r's cargo shorts to make your timeslot at the community garden.

En route, you pick up a nugget of trash that might make a good belt buckle l8r.

After watering your tomatoes, you meet up with Mom for dinner. She's looking a little chaotic, too.

It suits you both.

As the first live runway show in New York after the pandemic lockdown, in which so many of us were physically separated,

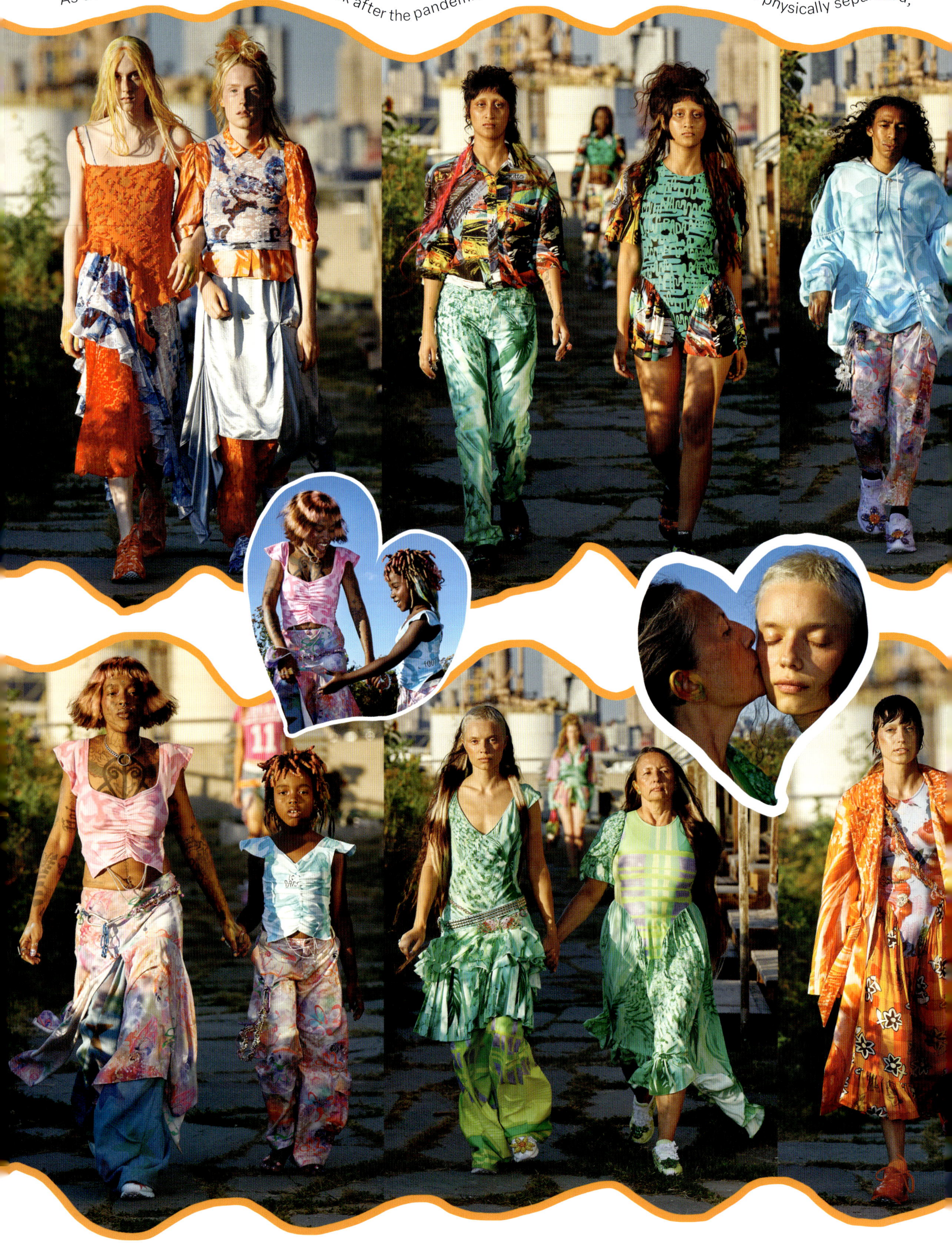

we cast longtime collaborators alongside their loved ones in a celebration of togetherness

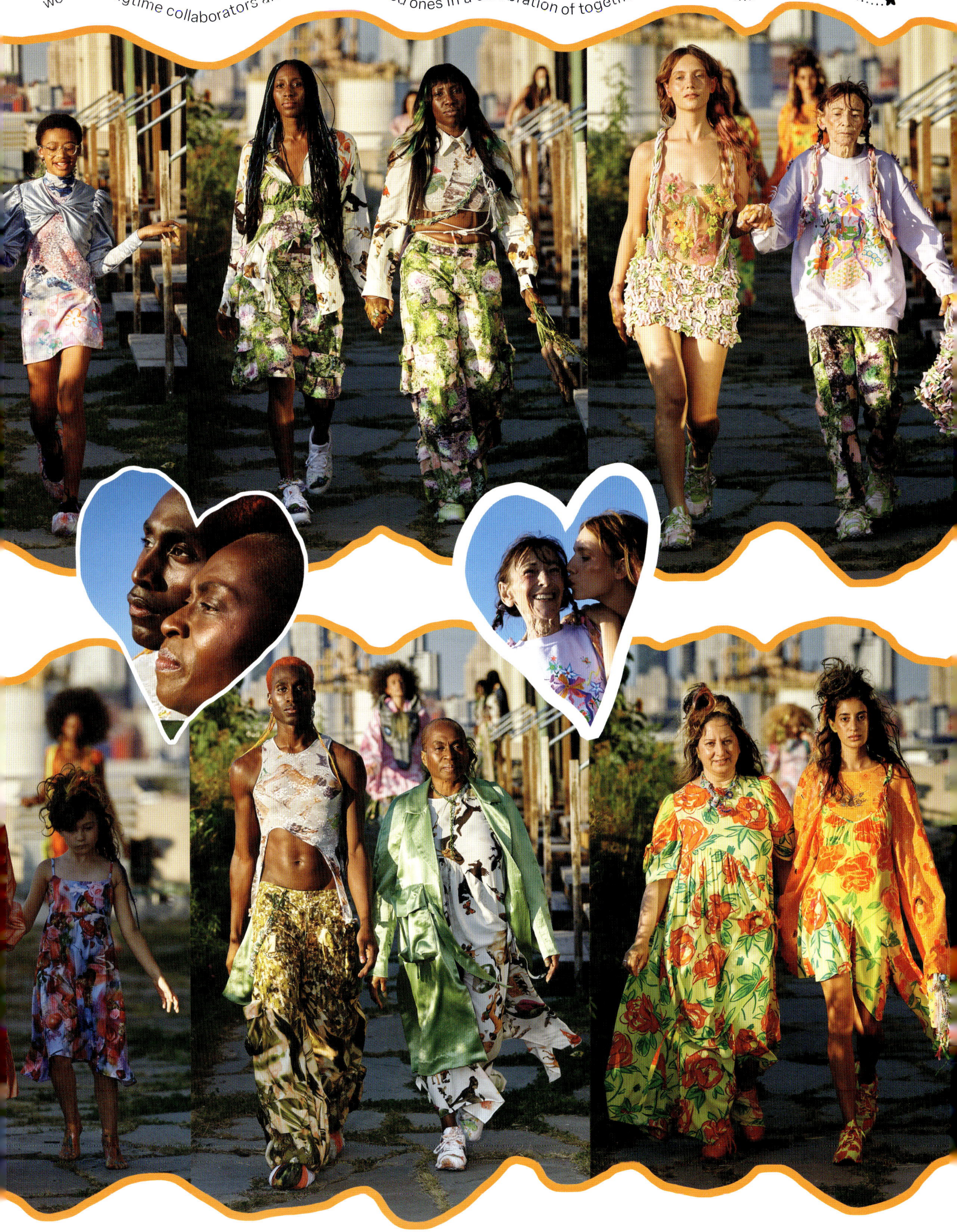

MORE LAWNS SHOULD LOOK LIKE THIS

MORE LAWNS SHOULD LOOK LIKE THIS

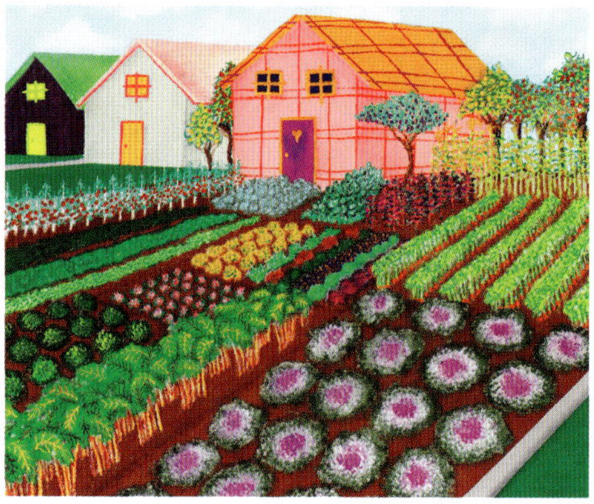

To whom it may concern,

I'm writing to urge you to implement green infrastructure in our building. Here is just a partial list of reasons why it's important and beneficial to do this now.

In addition to the city's Green Roof Tax Abatement program, New York City's Department of Environmental Protection (DEP) offers a Green Infrastructure Grant to subsidize the costs of implementation and maintenance.

Adding energy efficiency will also help building owners avoid fines and comply with local laws like NYC LL 92/94 and 97, while conforming to the latest NYC Department of Buildings Zoning Resolutions and Construction Codes.

Green infrastructure is also a smart way to re-invest in your building. It protects the building's roof membrane, reduces energy bills, and boosts property value, all while increasing the city's biodiversity, sequestering carbon, reducing greenhouse gas (GHG) emissions, and creating a unique outdoor amenity space—which is vital to tenants' mental health after periods of lockdowns that have caused many to spend more time at home. Rooftop gardens also reduce stormwater runoff. Some green solutions can keep as much as 55% of stormwater out of the city's sewer system. This is more important than ever, as the city still reels from the water damage of multiple recent hurricanes.

In short, going green has never been better supported—or more urgently needed—in New York City. We urge you to help implement green infrastructure in our building now.

Sincerely,

XOXO

The runway for this season was Brooklyn Grange, New York City's largest rooftop farm. We gave each attendee a letter template to advocate for a green roof in their own building to help spread the idea of green rooftops around the city.

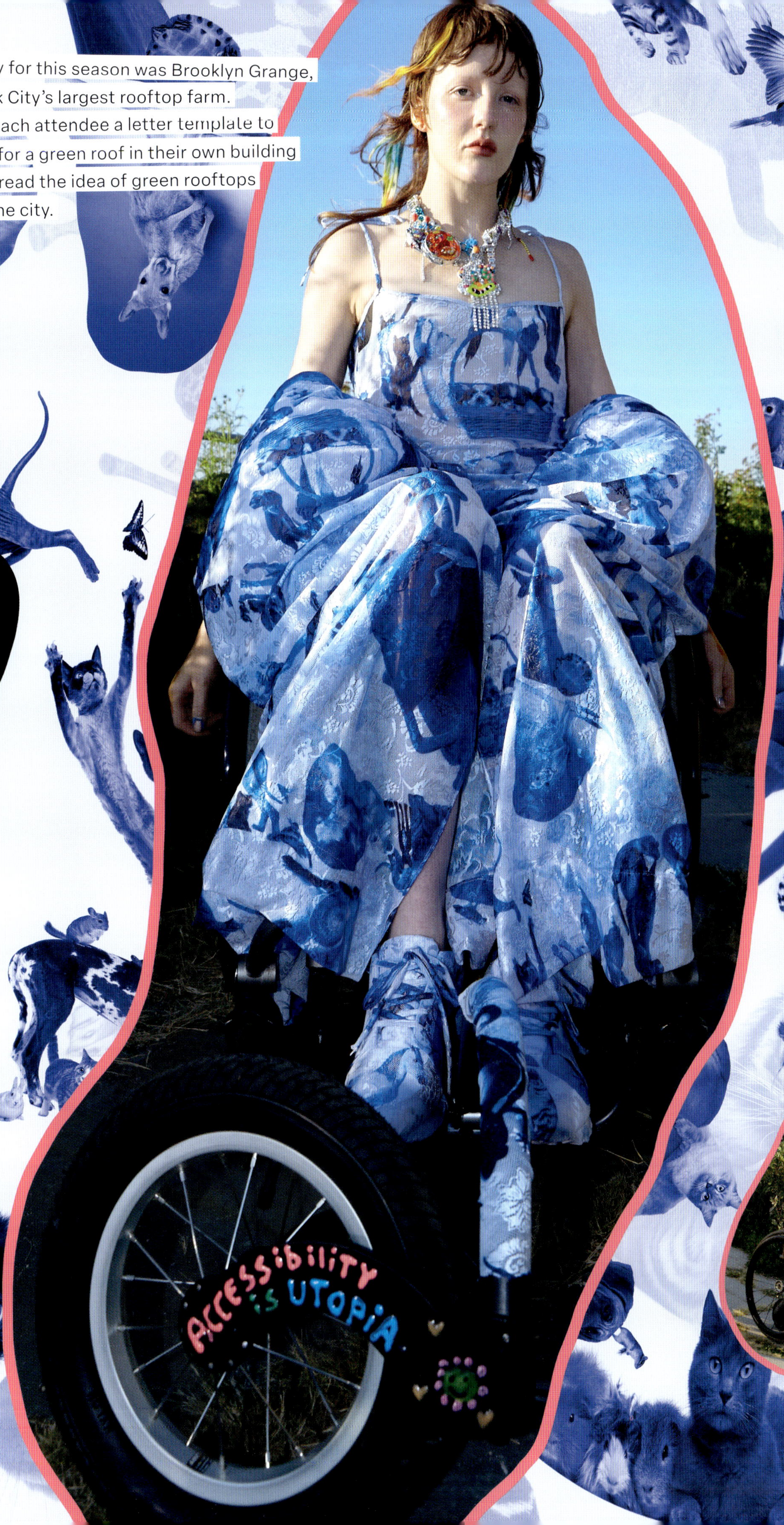

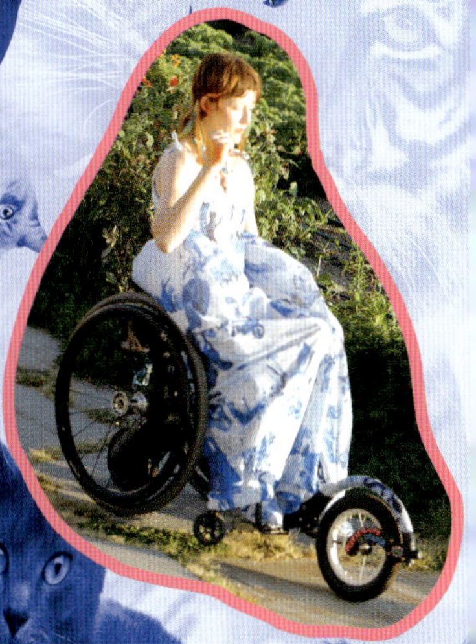

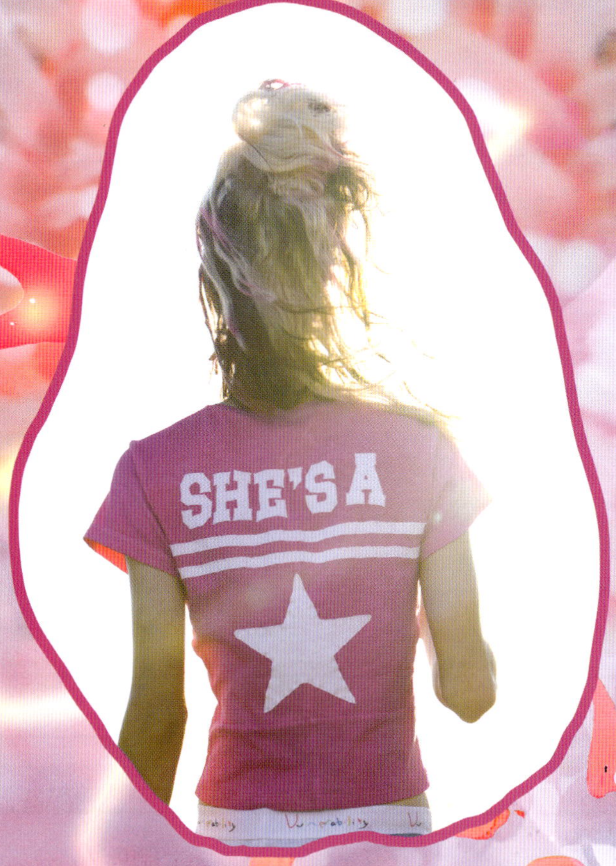

The world makes me kinda scared....Seems like no one wants to share...Sometimes don't know what to wear...But that's life when you're a snail. Wake up each day, put my shell on...Look around me, the fuc is going on...Life in the city's hard...I'll keep slugging along in the dark...Where do we go when Earth is no more?..I don't know where to go...Don't think I can handle what we have in store. Wouldn't life be better at a snail's pace..I think that we should try it...It's time to slow it down.........Or we'll burn it to the ground...Let's listen to what nature has to say...Life is simpler at a snail's pace...I think...that we should try it...It's time to slow it down...Or we'll burn it to the ground...Let's listen to what nature has to say. I'll take it slow on the runway.......... Talked to God, she said we'll be okay...The world is so big, wish it was smaller...Burning coal makes us live in squalor... RAAAAAH..... Don't want to be lavish...I'll just...live among the cabbage... Kick back and drink some kava...And wear Collina Strada

Custom song by Frost Children, "Snails Pace"

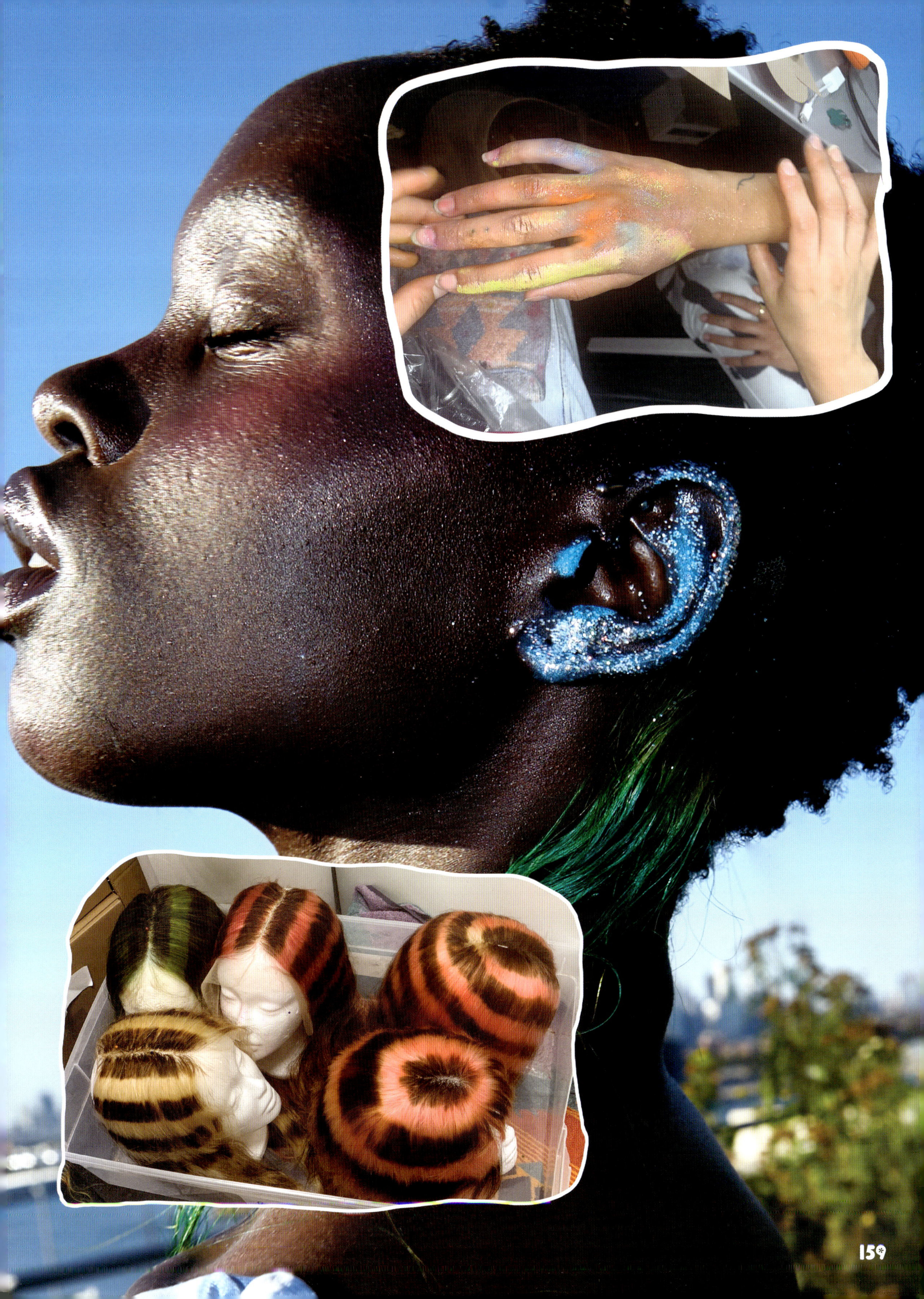

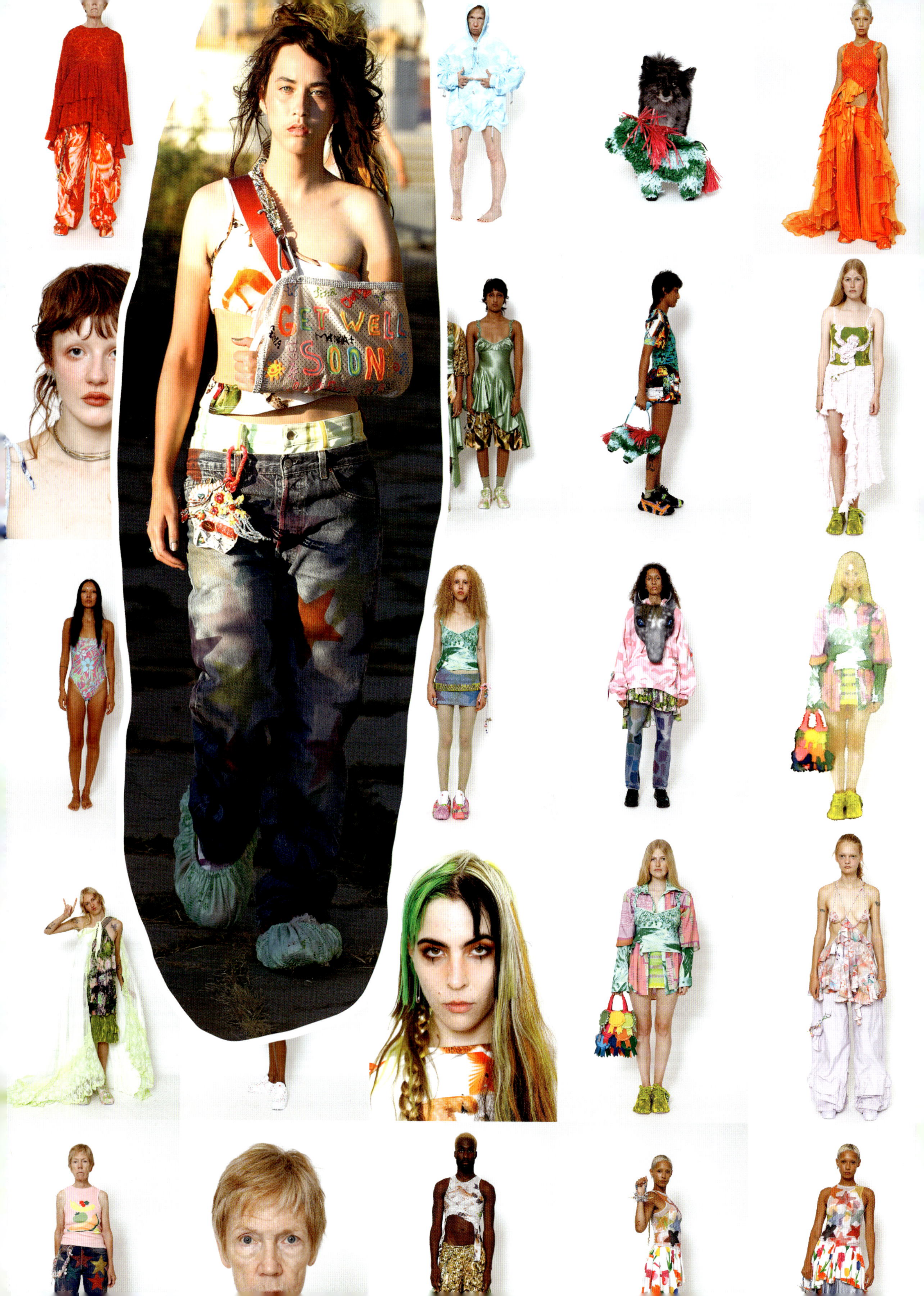
GET WELL
SOON

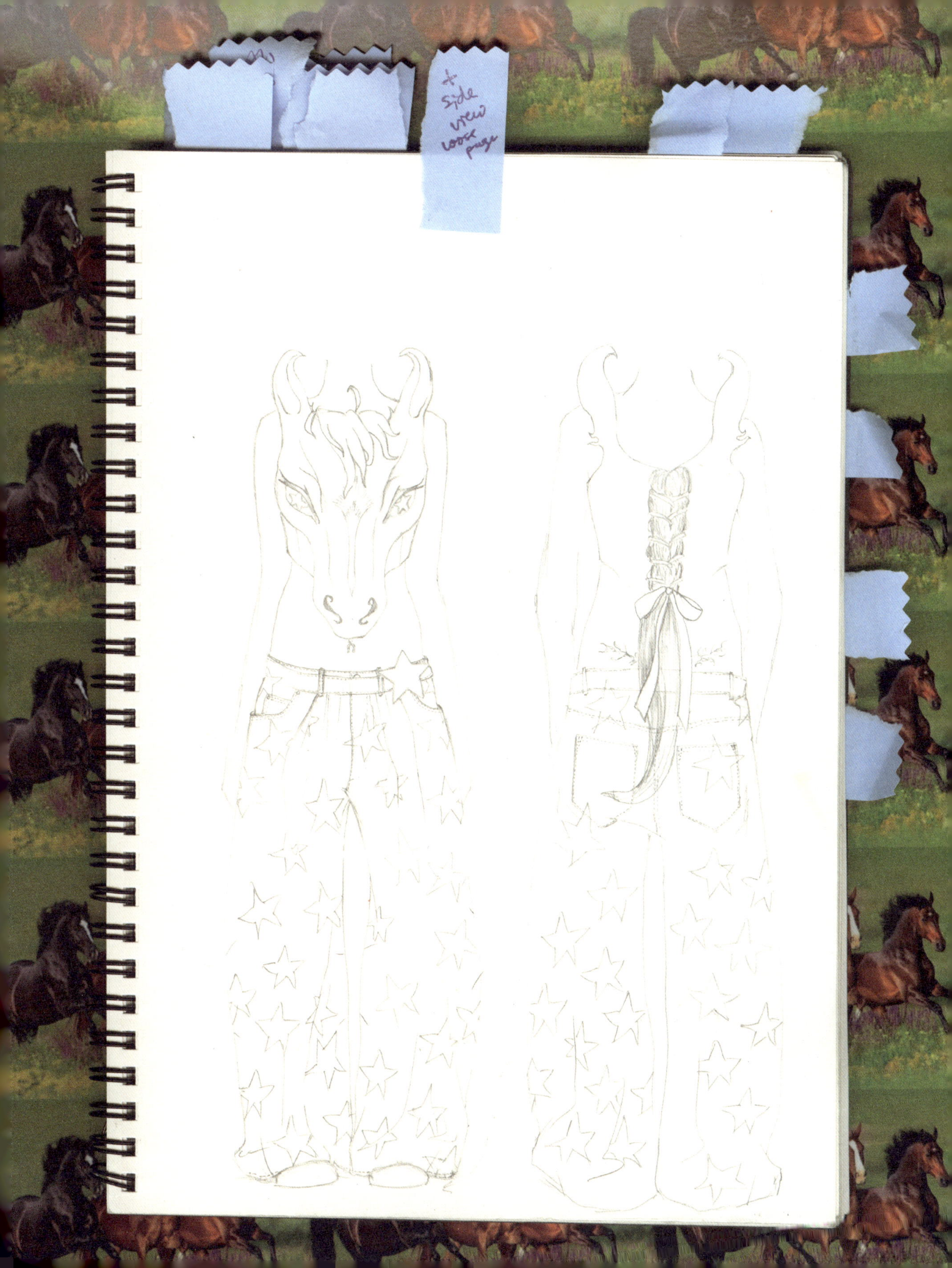
+ side view loose page

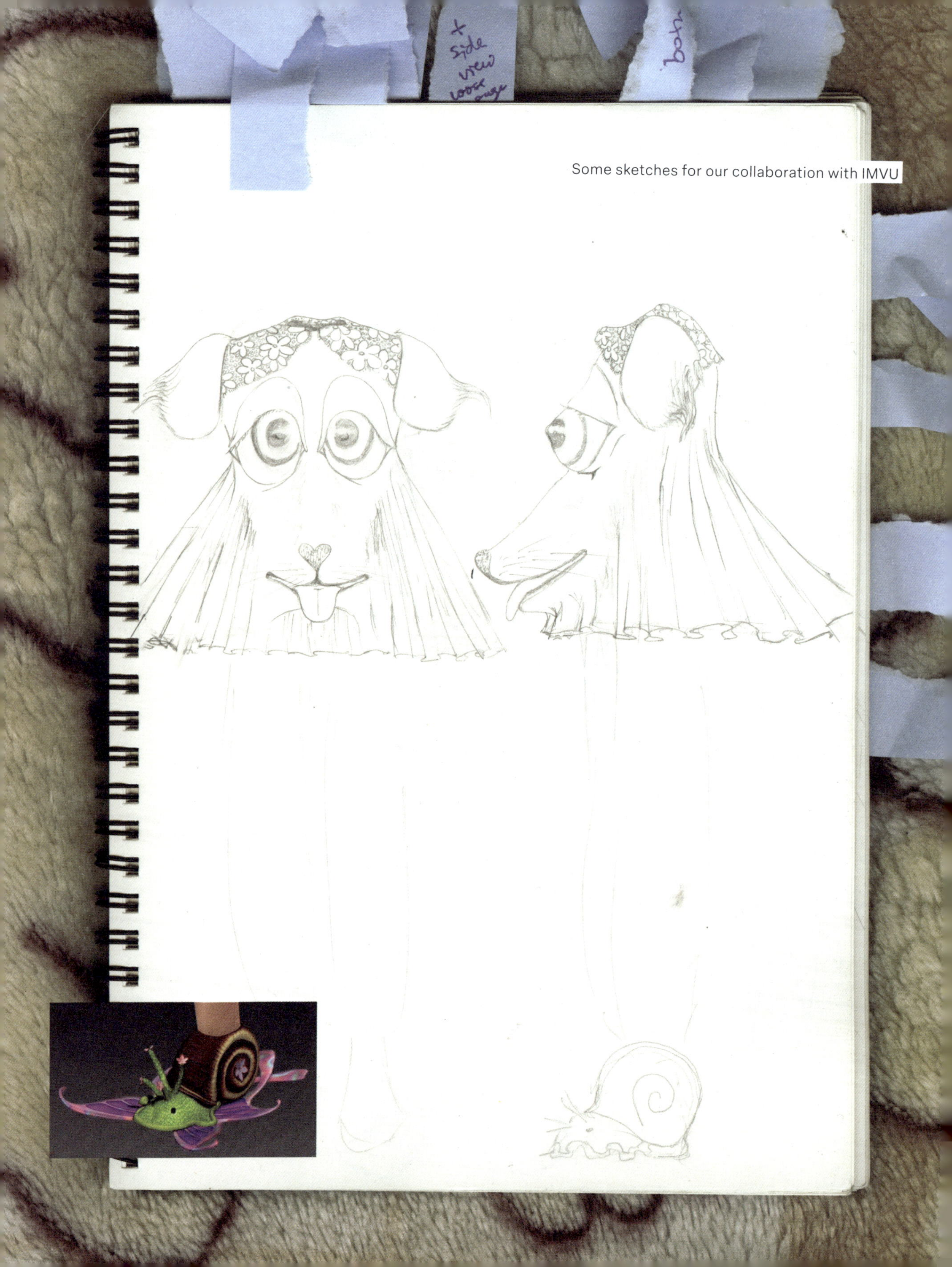

Some sketches for our collaboration with IMVU

Sketches by Regina Mun

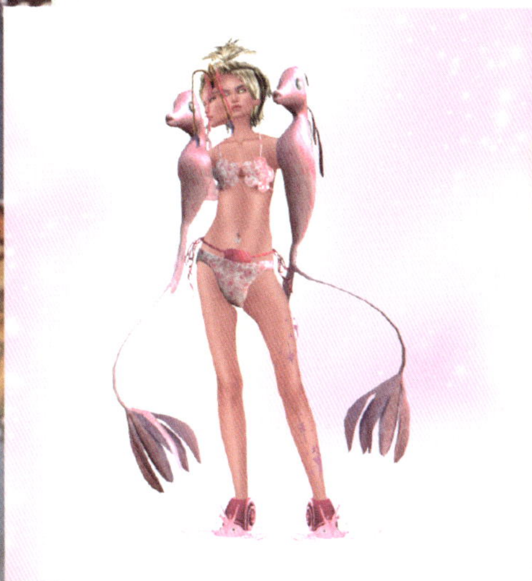

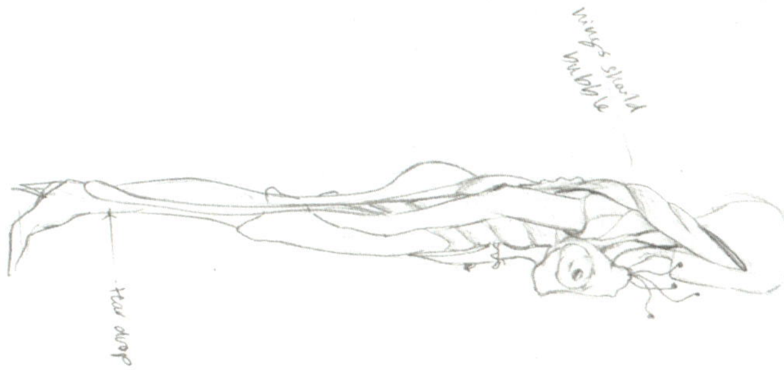

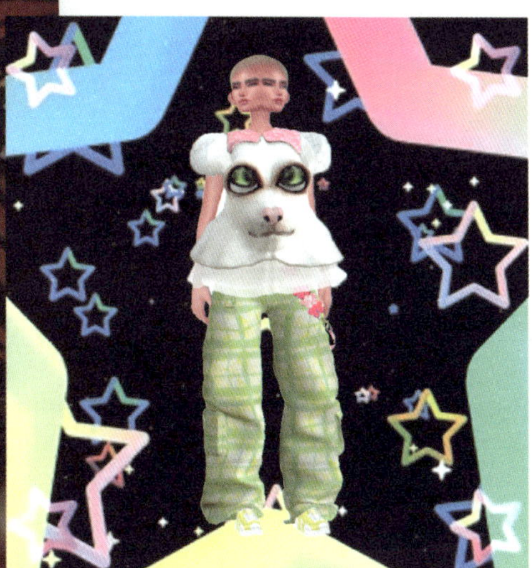

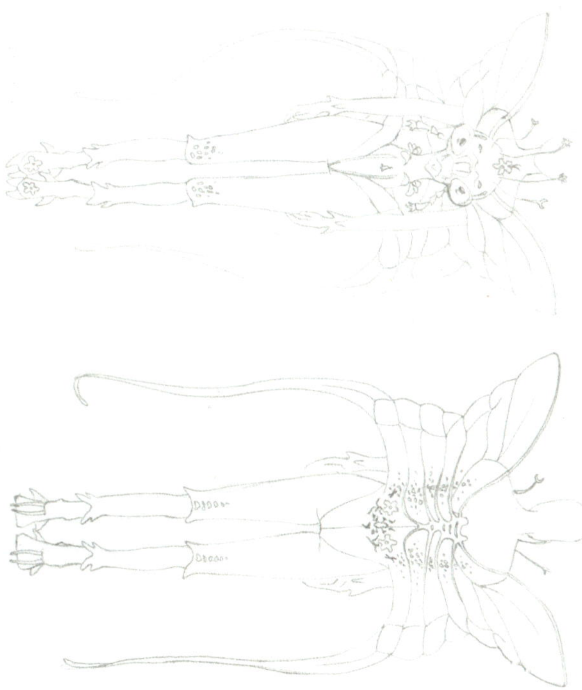

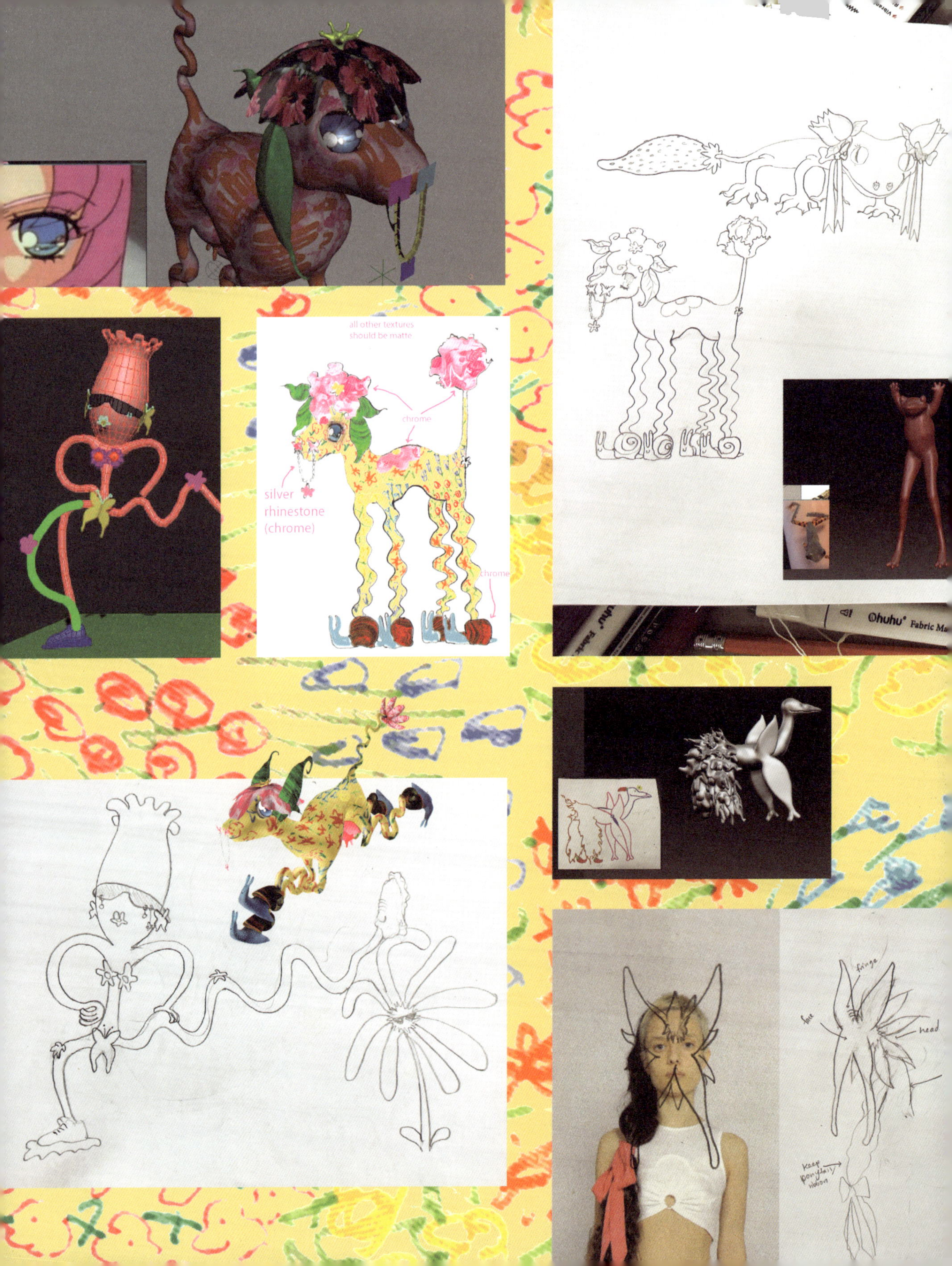
all other textures
should be matte
chrome
silver
rhinestone
(chrome)
chrome
Ohuhu Fabric Ma
fringe
head

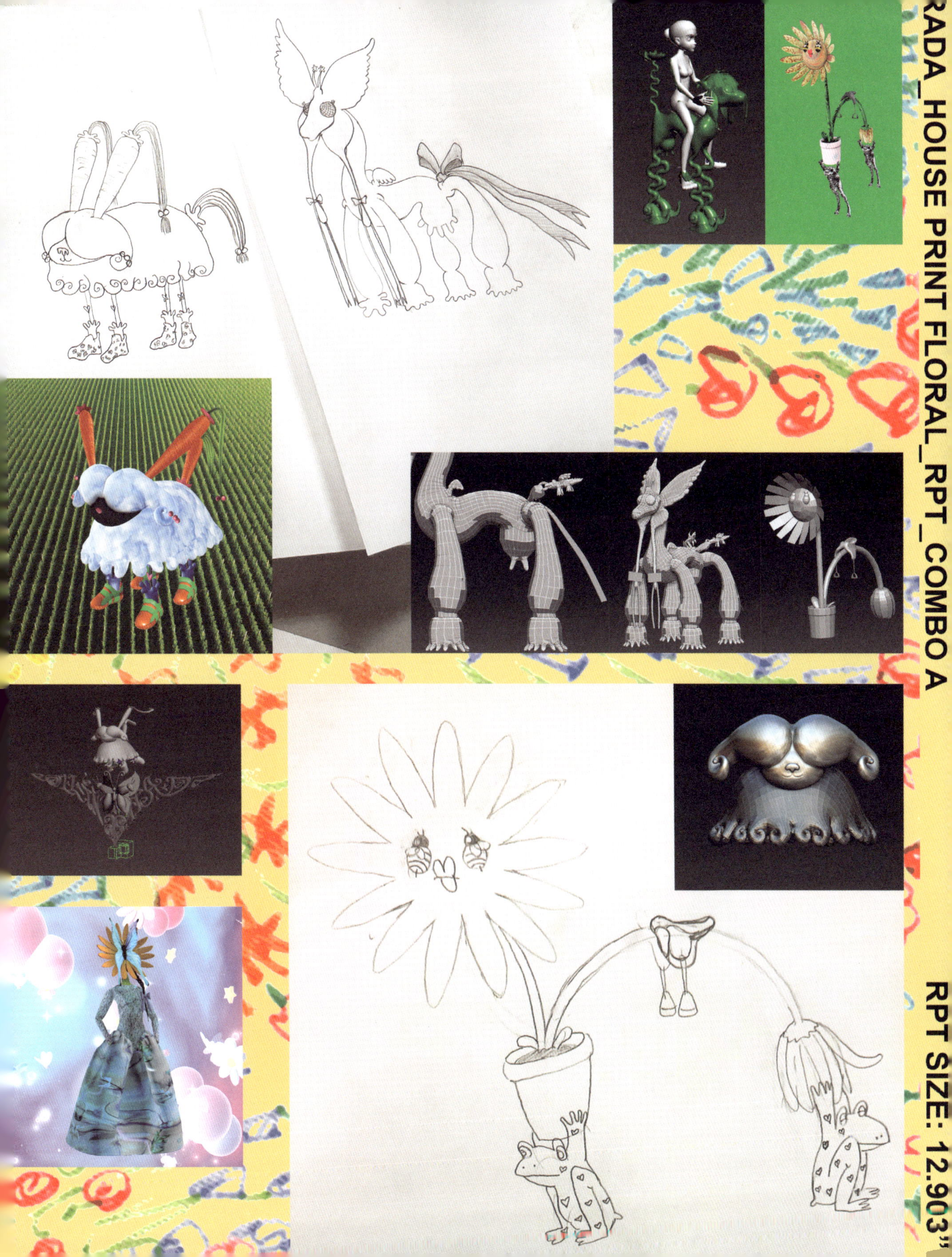

RADA_HOUSE PRINT FLORAL_RPT_COMBO A
RPT SIZE: 12.903"

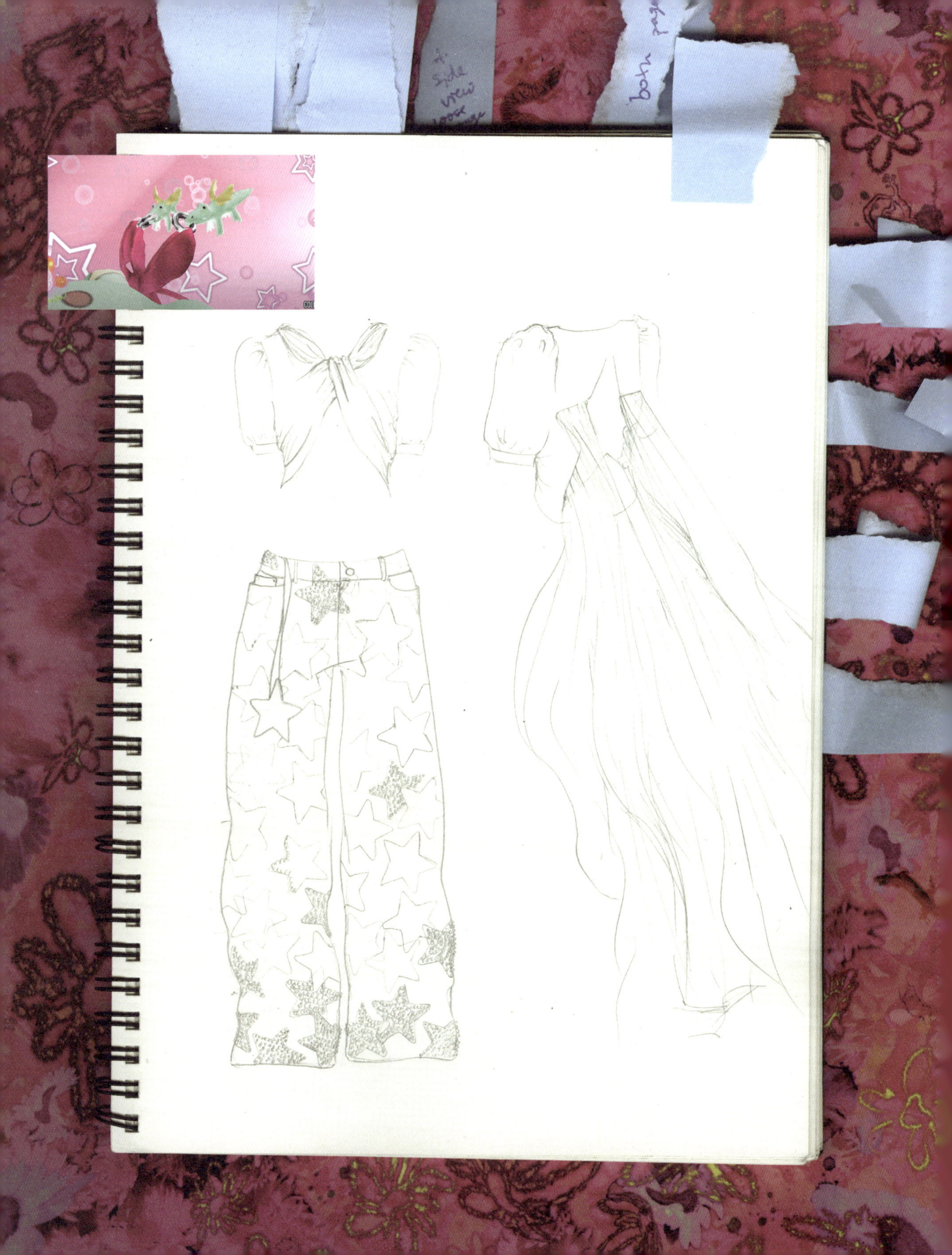

side view
both

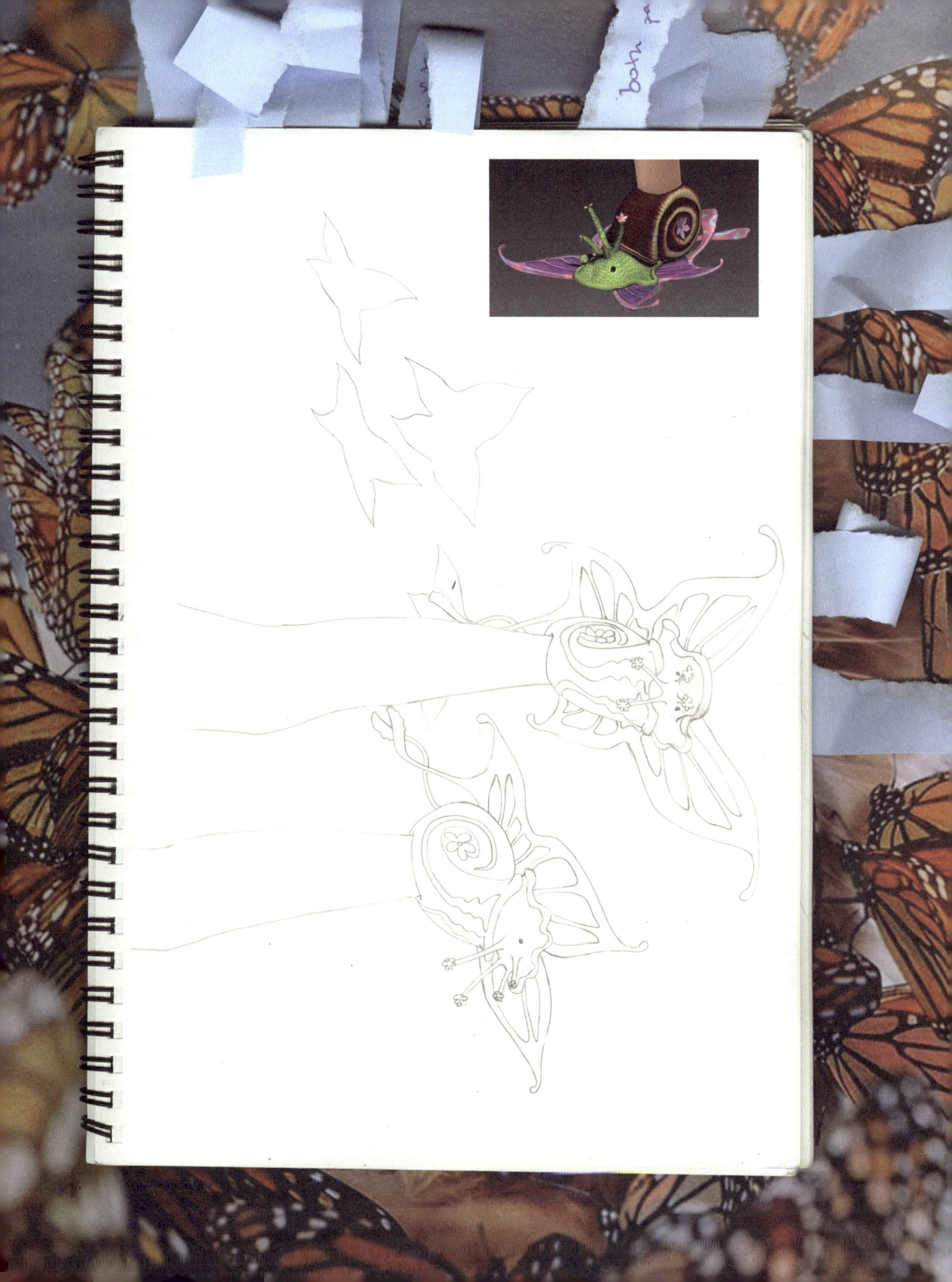

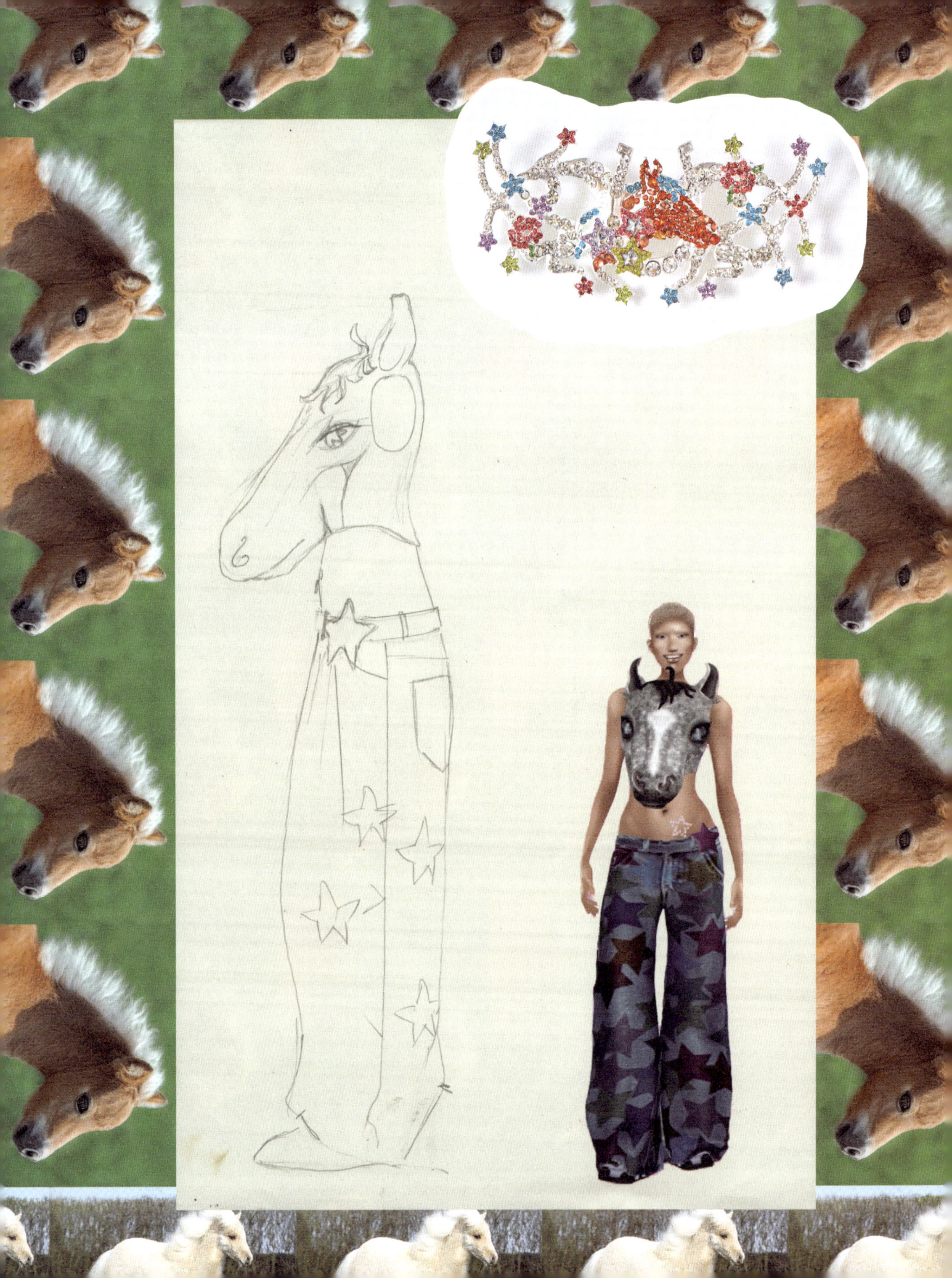

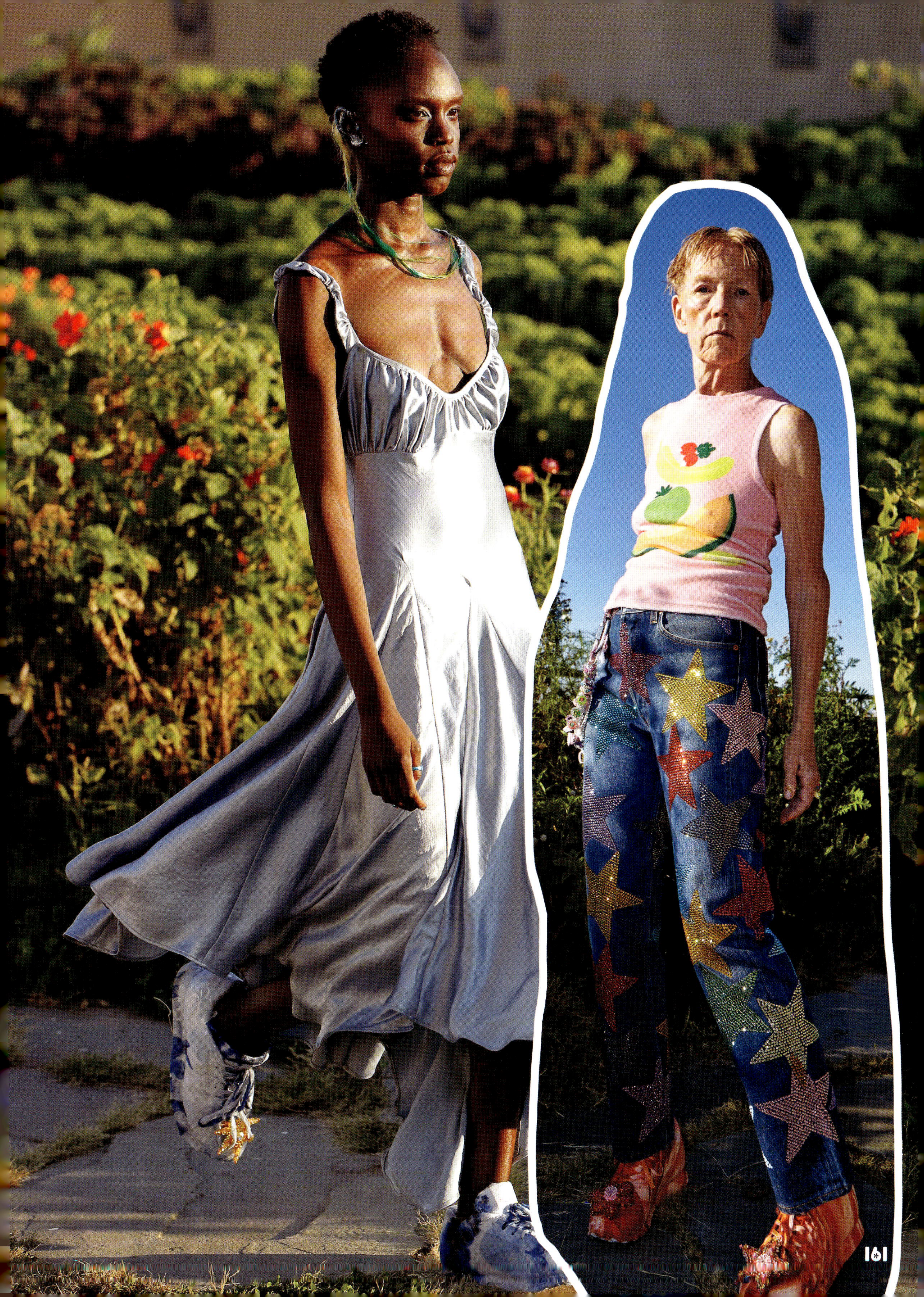

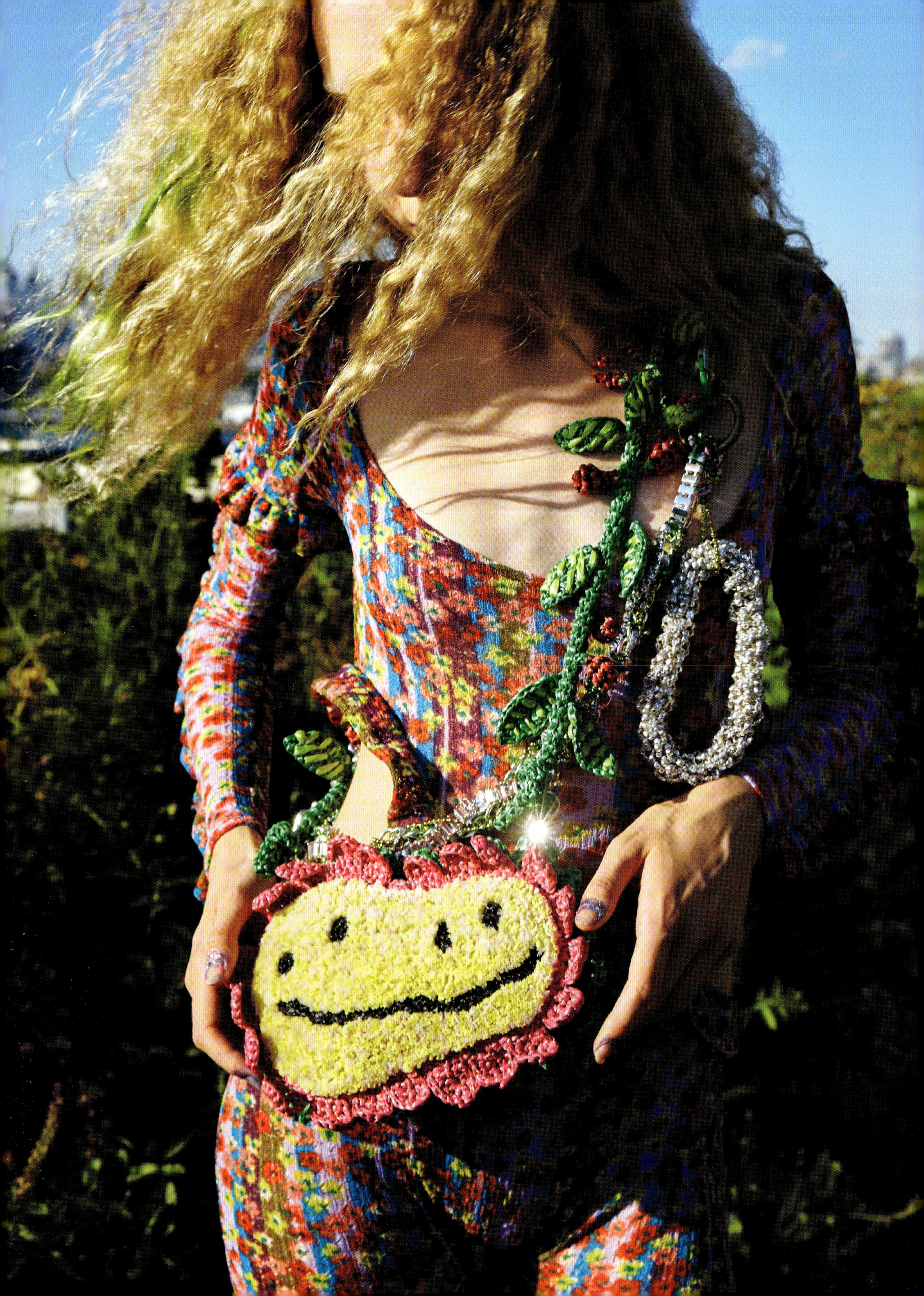

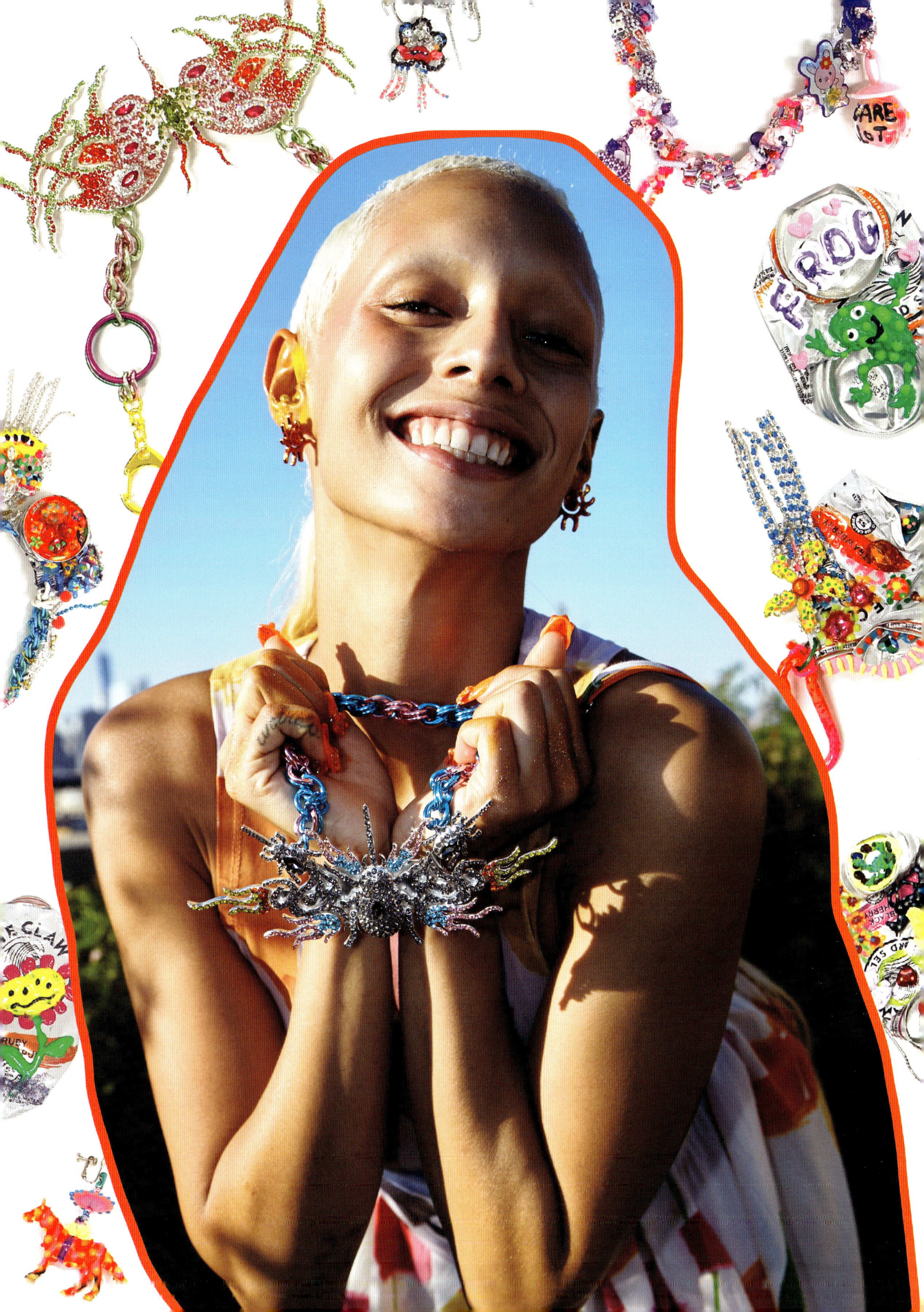
FROG

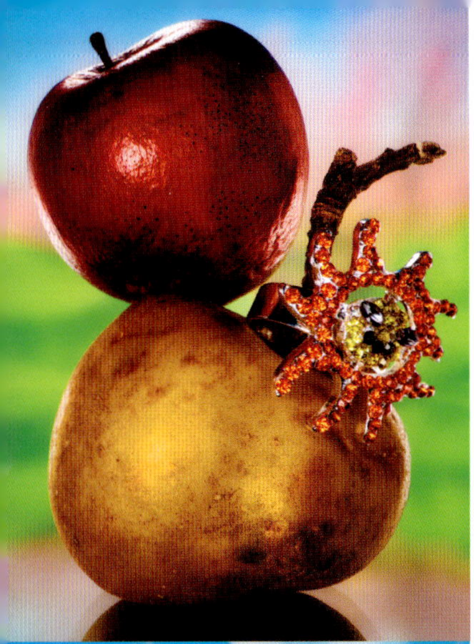

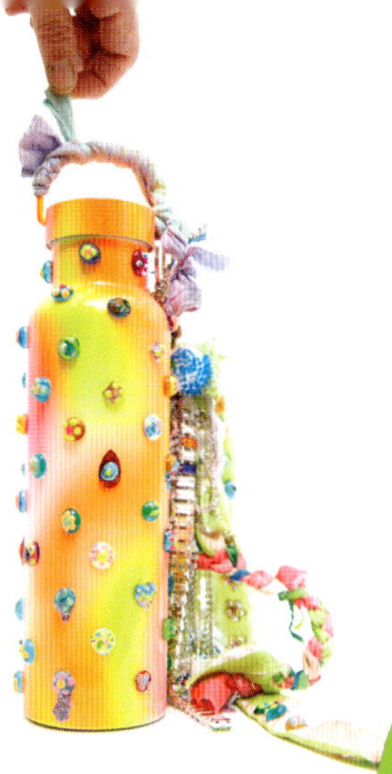

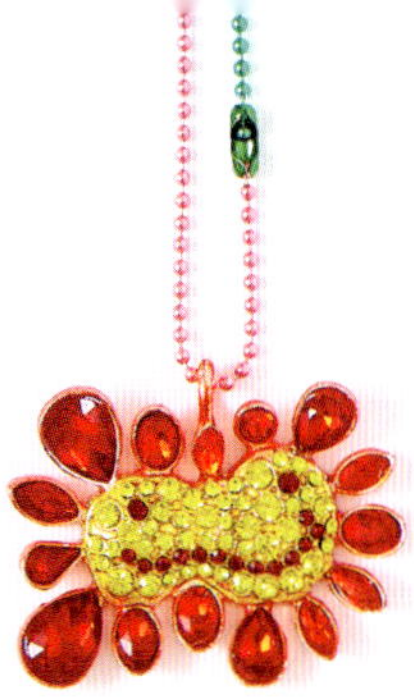

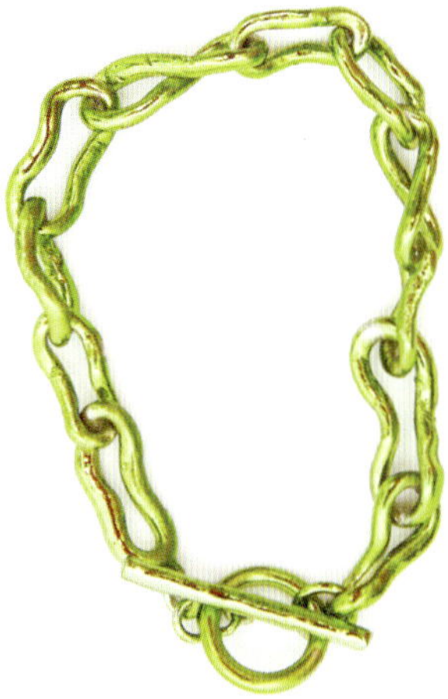

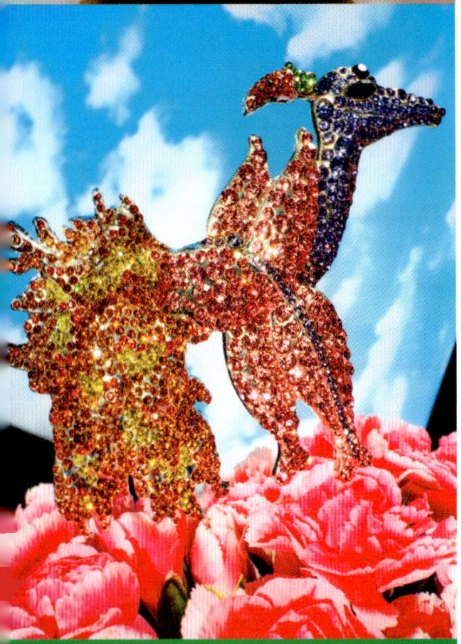

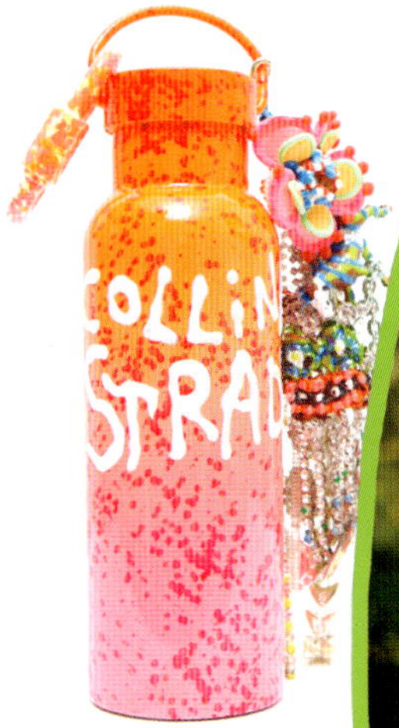
OLLIN
STRAD

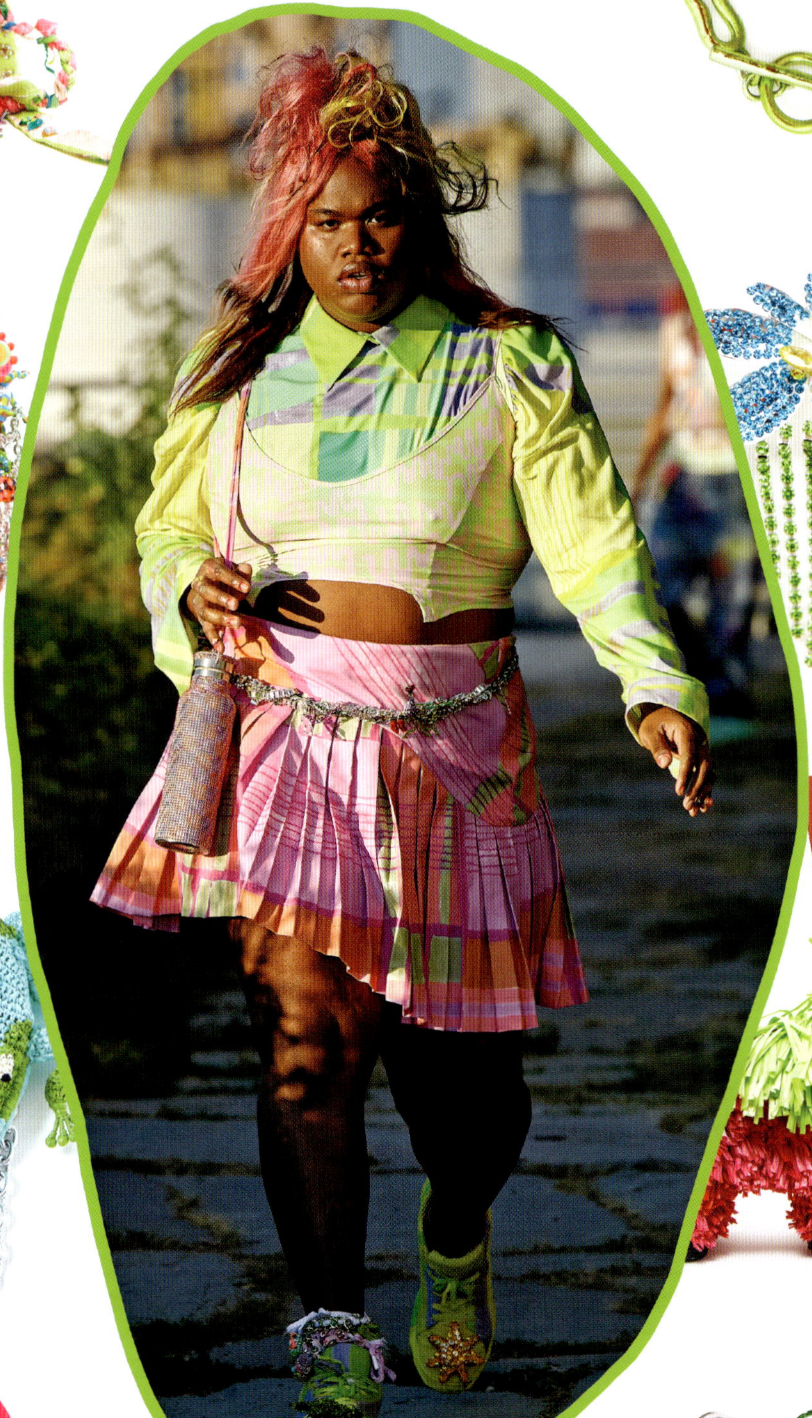

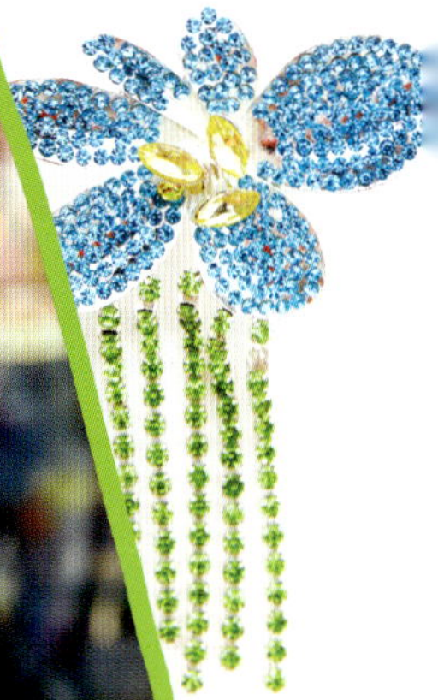

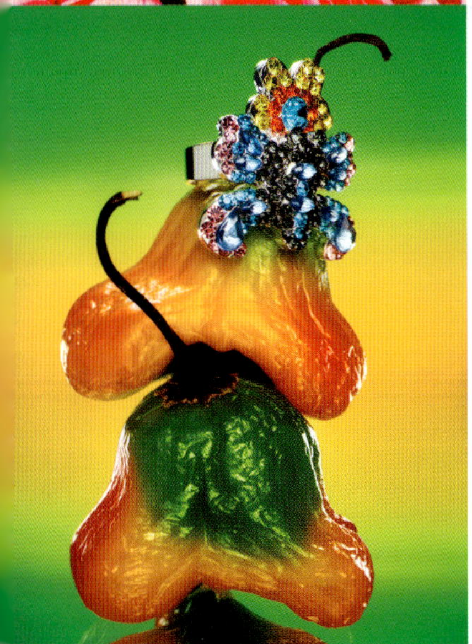

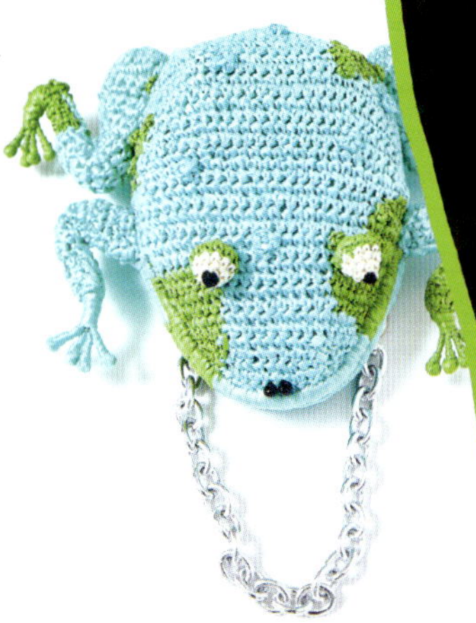

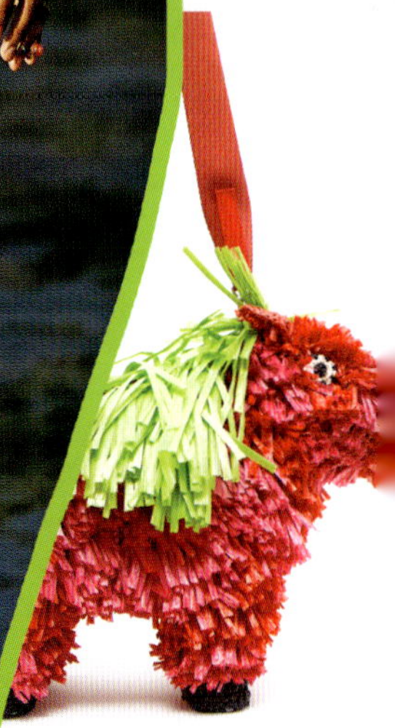

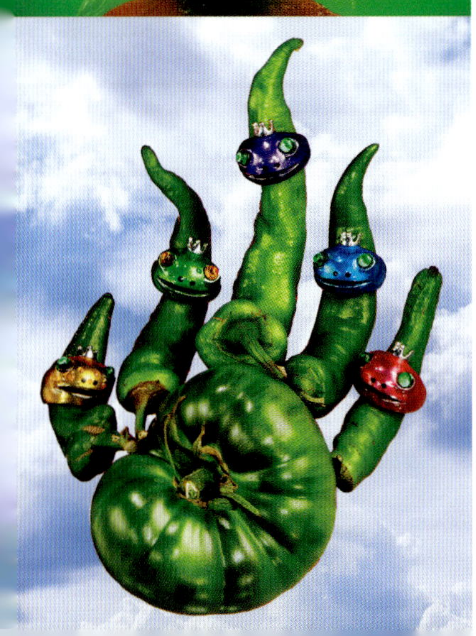

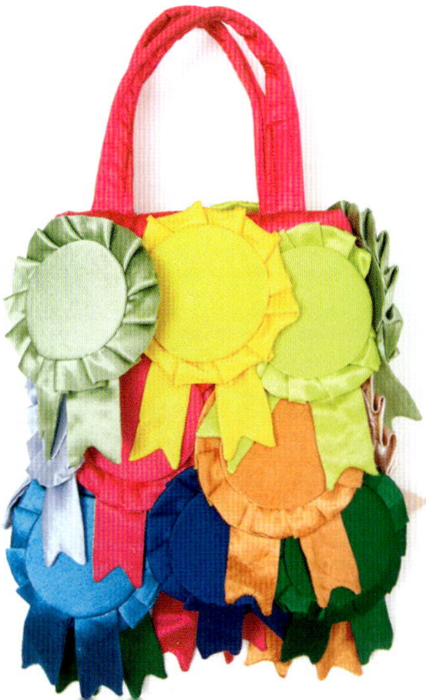

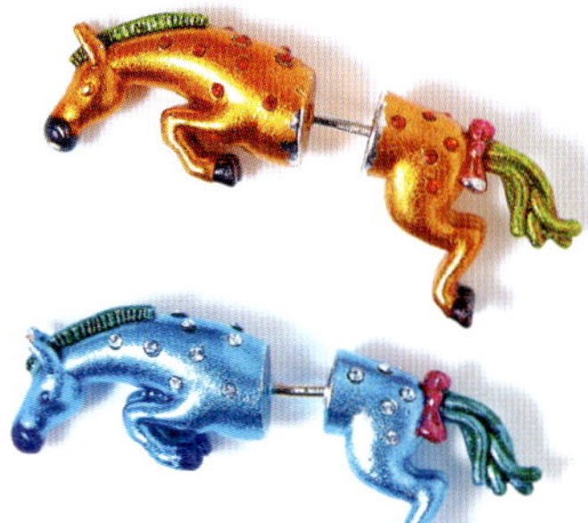

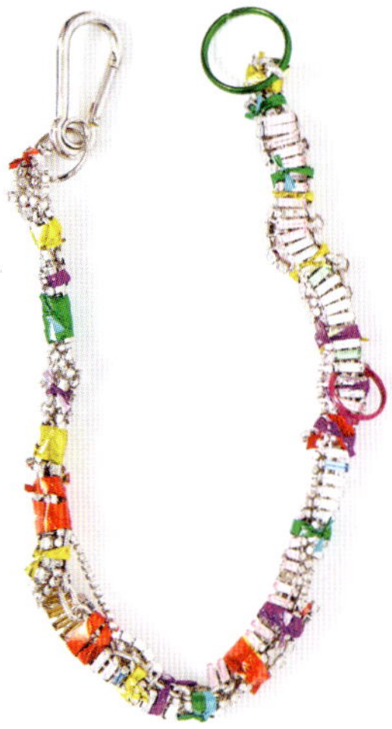

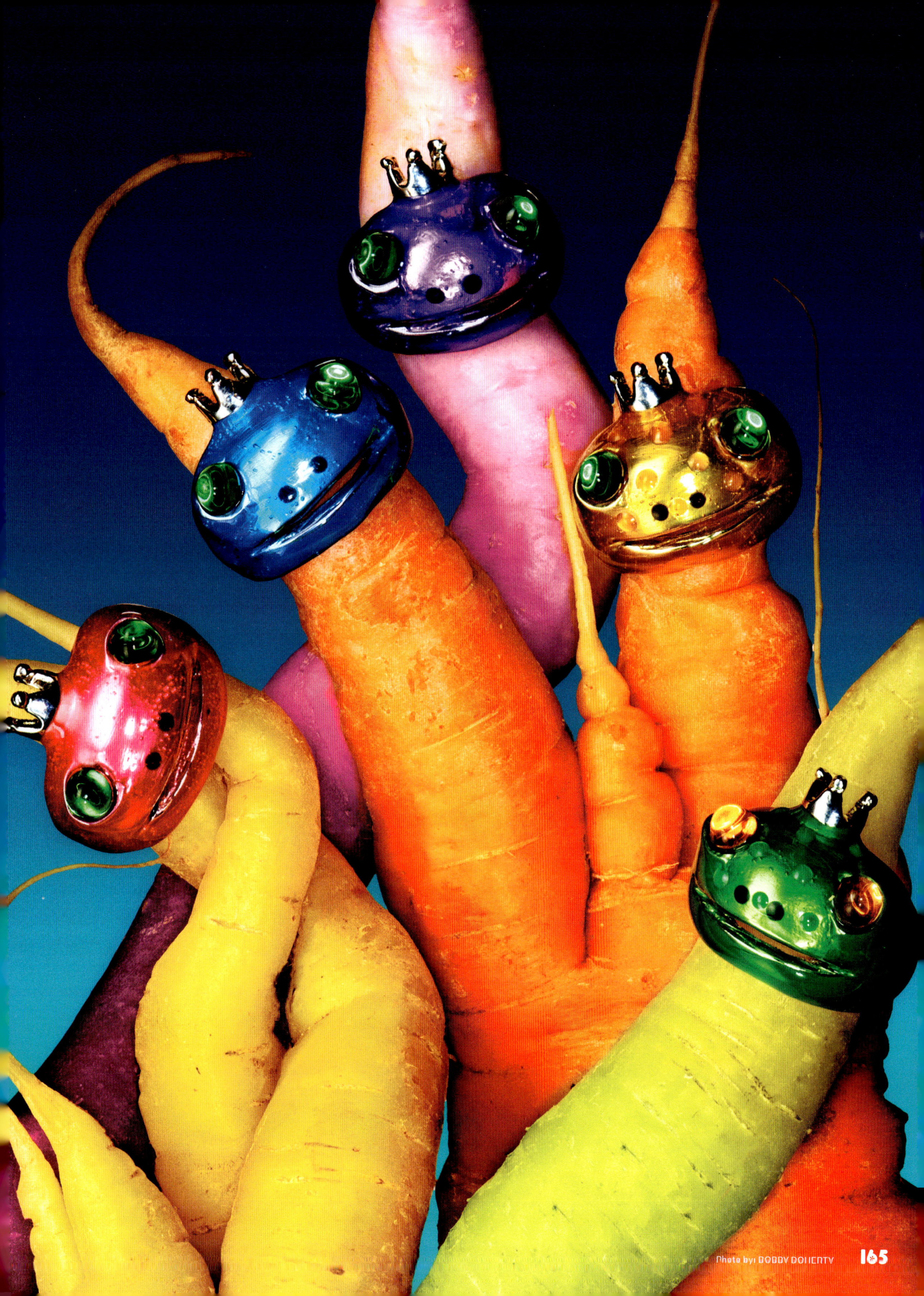

Photo by: BOBBY DOHERTY

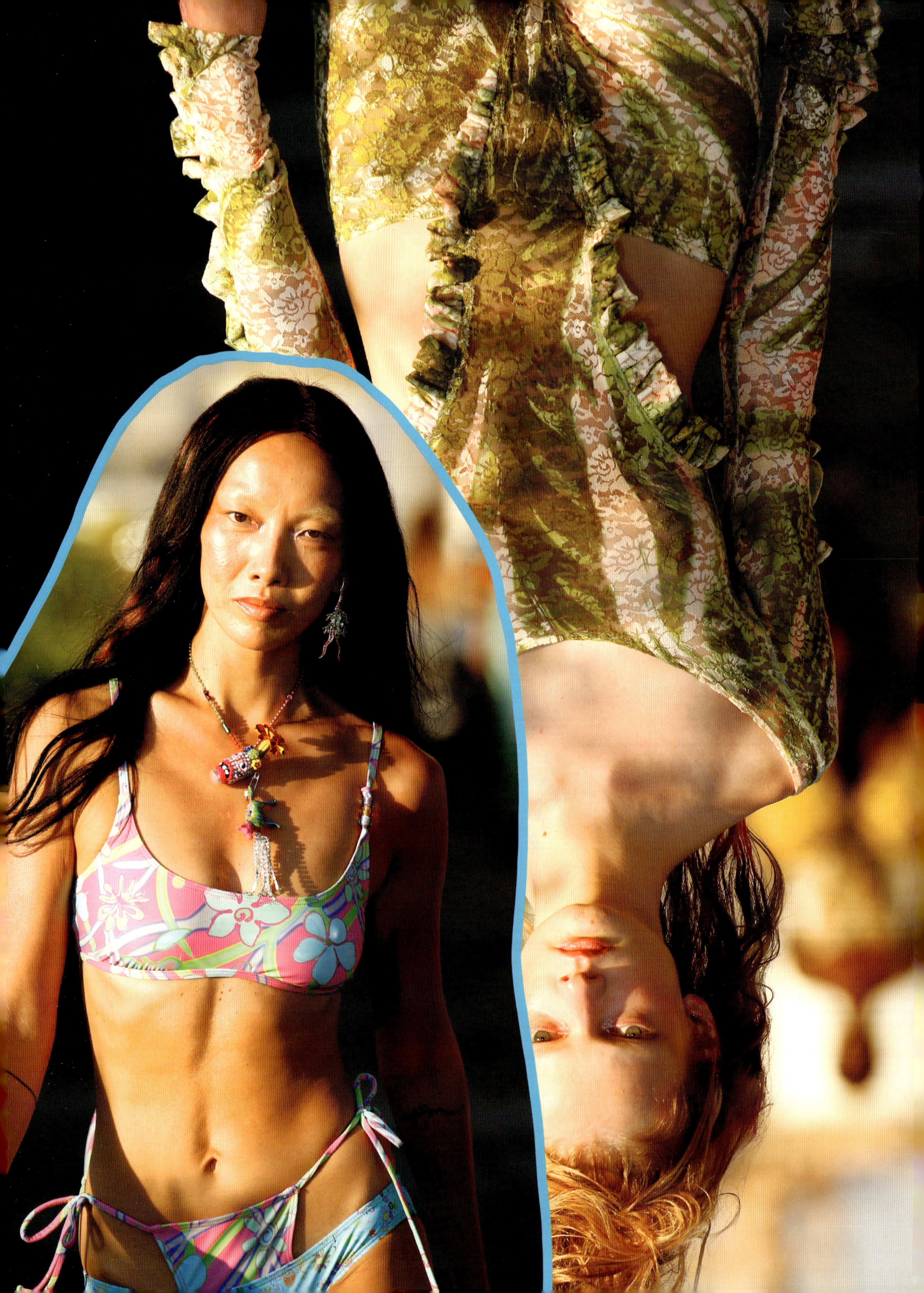

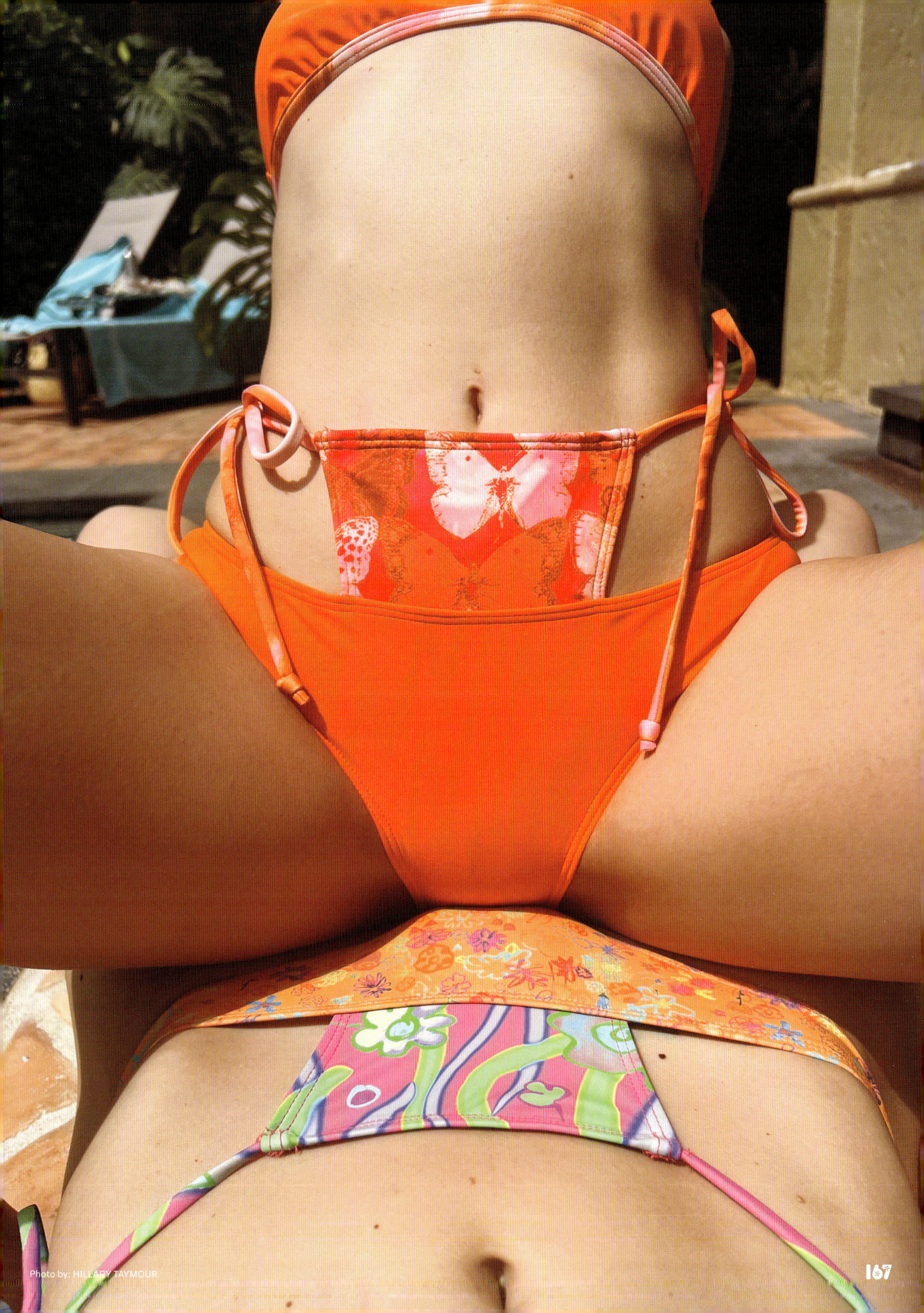

Photo by: HILLARY TAYMOUR

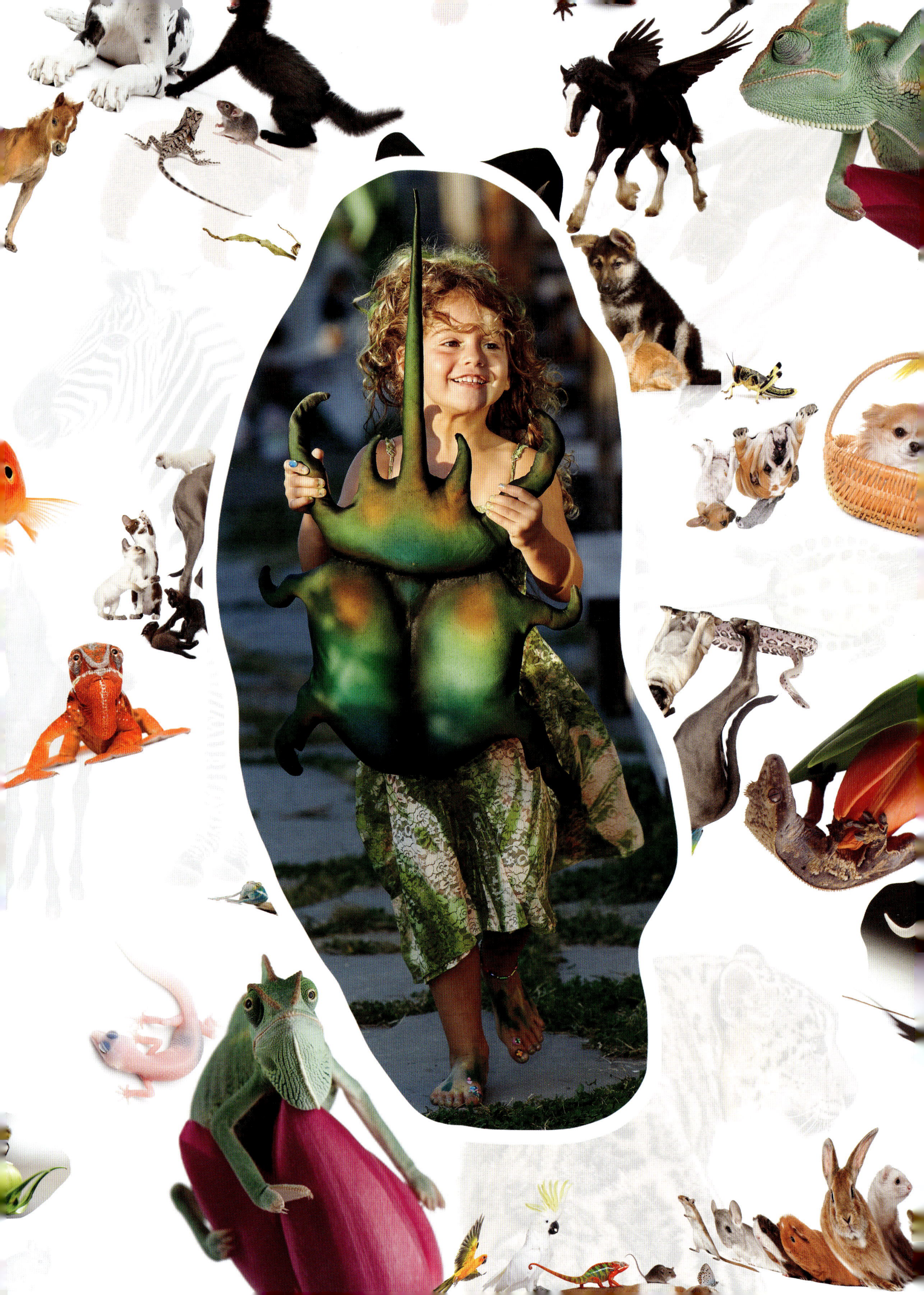

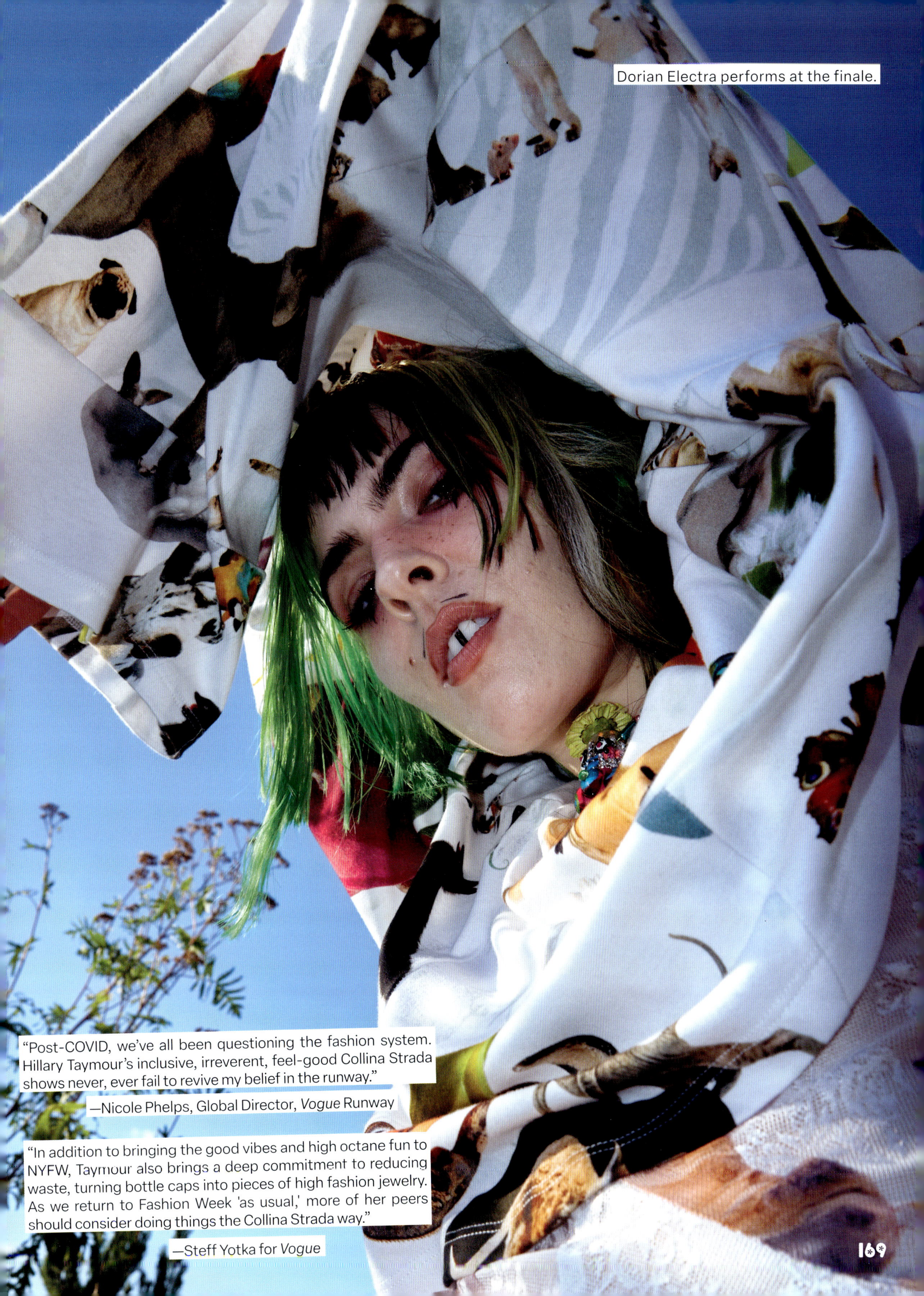

Dorian Electra performs at the finale.

"Post-COVID, we've all been questioning the fashion system. Hillary Taymour's inclusive, irreverent, feel-good Collina Strada shows never, ever fail to revive my belief in the runway."

—Nicole Phelps, Global Director, *Vogue* Runway

"In addition to bringing the good vibes and high octane fun to NYFW, Taymour also brings a deep commitment to reducing waste, turning bottle caps into pieces of high fashion jewelry. As we return to Fashion Week 'as usual,' more of her peers should consider doing things the Collina Strada way."

—Steff Yotka for *Vogue*

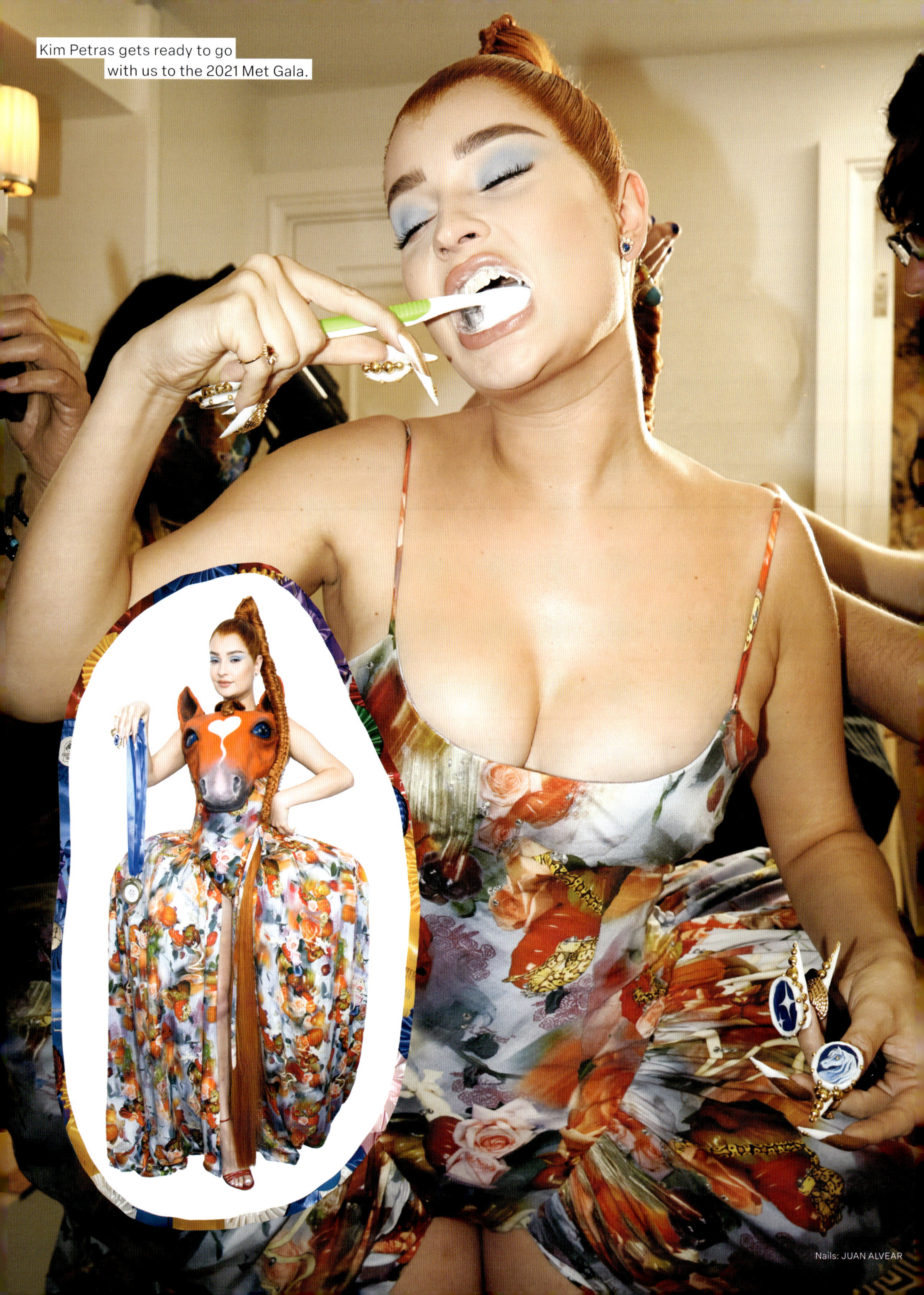

Kim Petras gets ready to go with us to the 2021 Met Gala.

Nails: JUAN ALVEAR

"I'll never forget running into Hillary at a Met Gala afterparty in 2021. She was wearing a 3D horse head bustier, and we took turns donning the horse on the dance floor as a curious crowd gathered around to take photos. It was no surprise when we realized a few hours later that her Met look had gone mega viral. It was pure Collina, after all, with DIY energy and a totally joy-inducing effect."

–Sam Hines, Editor at GQ

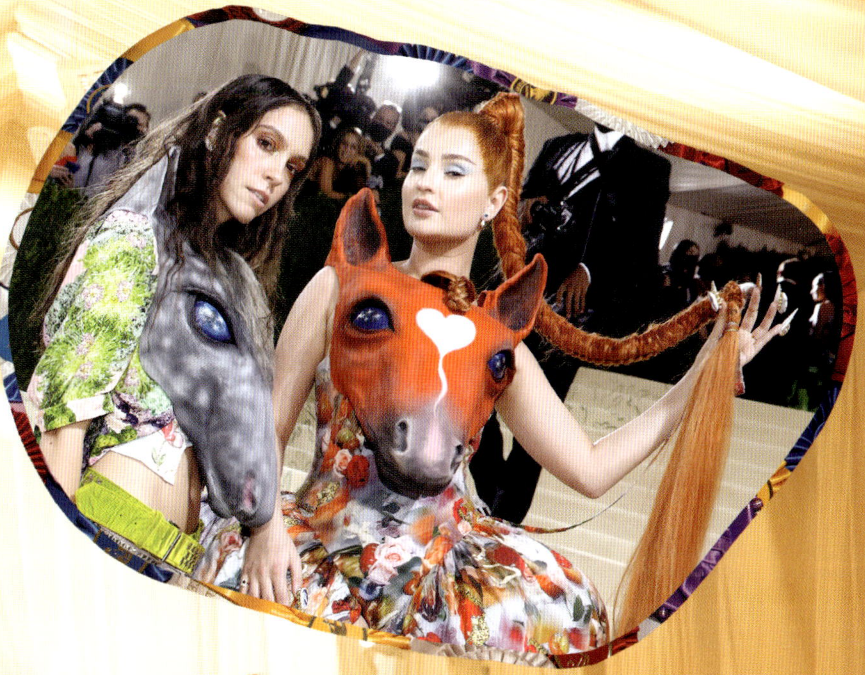

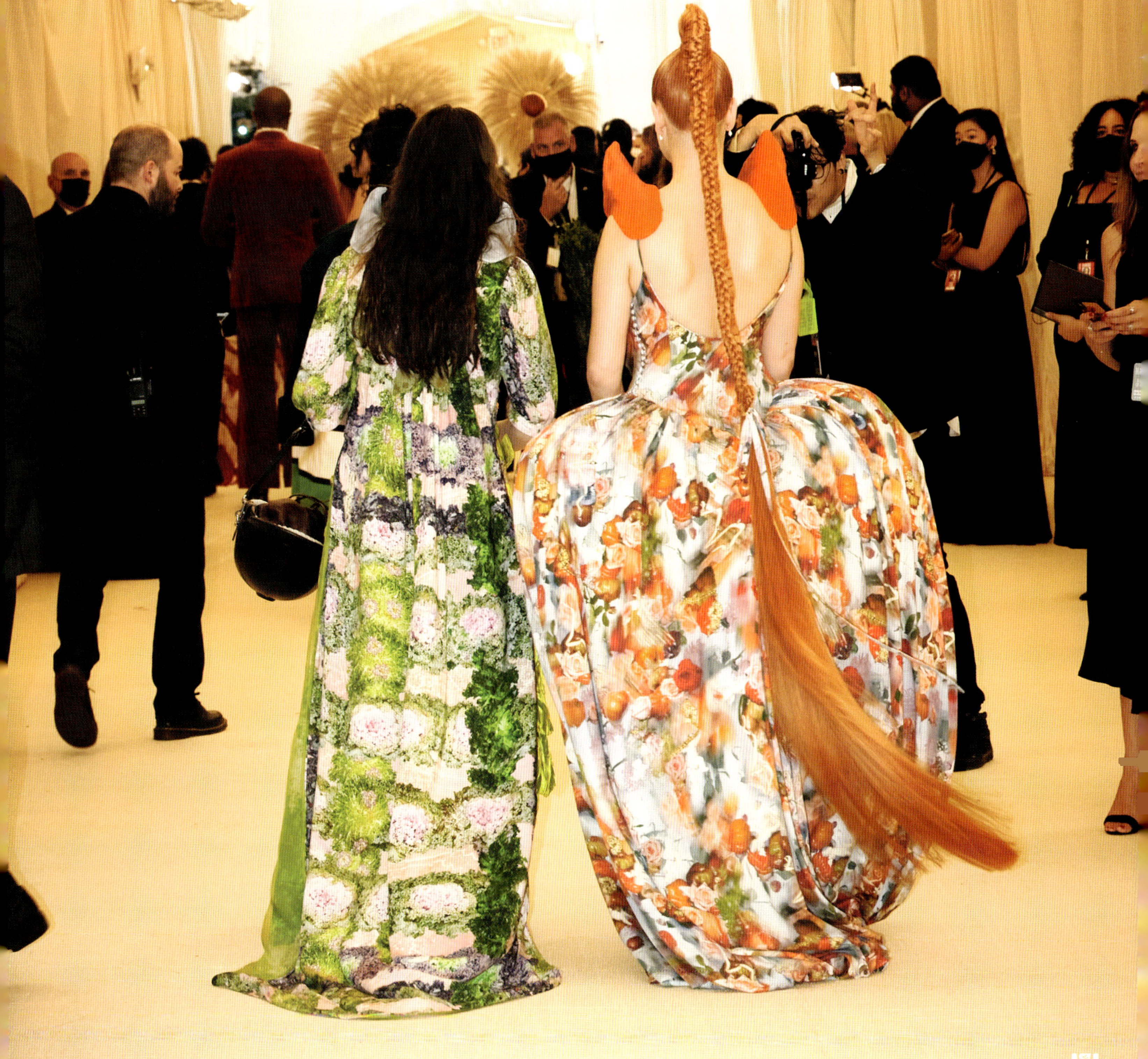

Photo by: SORAYA ZAMAN

AUTUMN WINTER 2022, THE COLLINAS

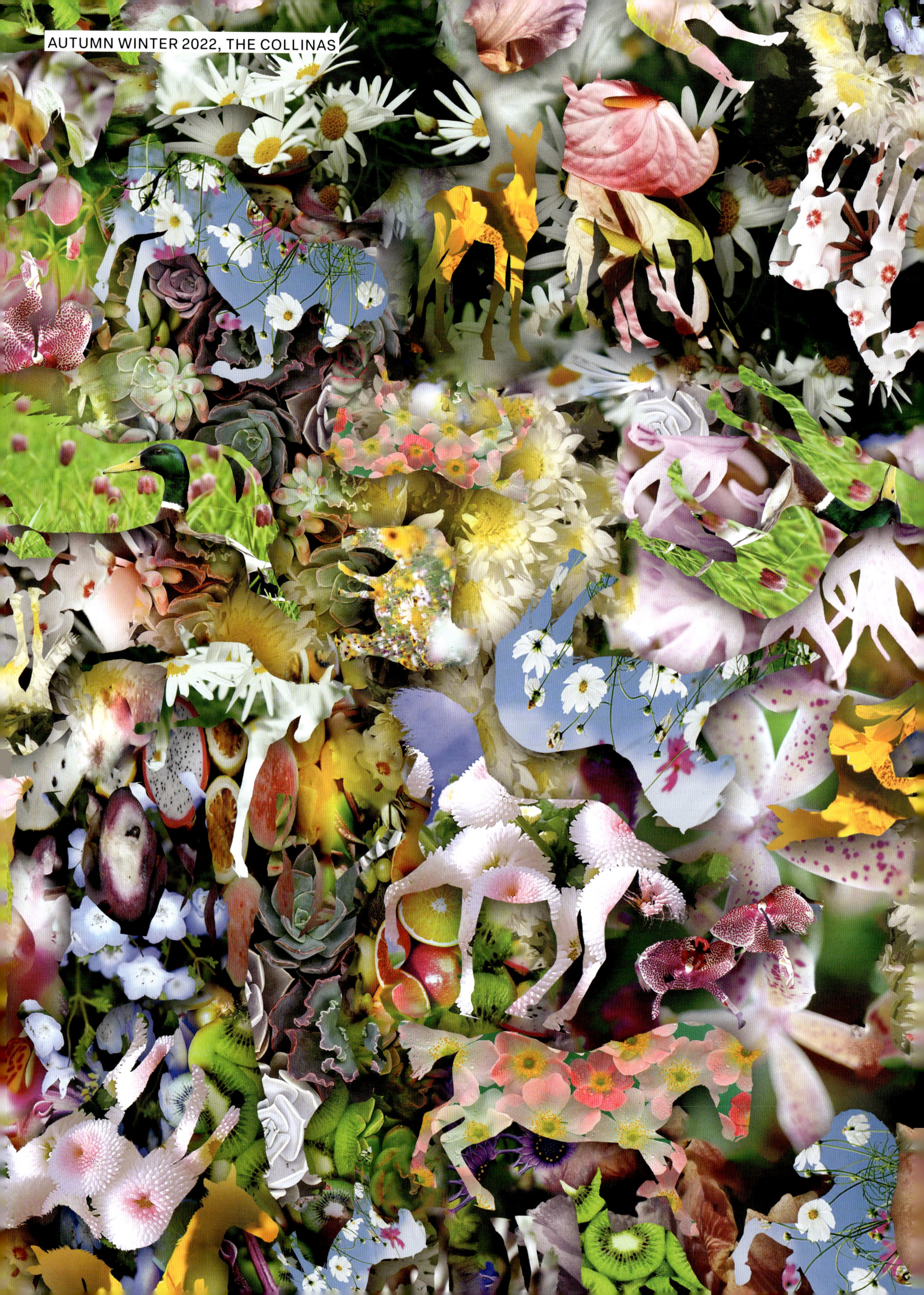

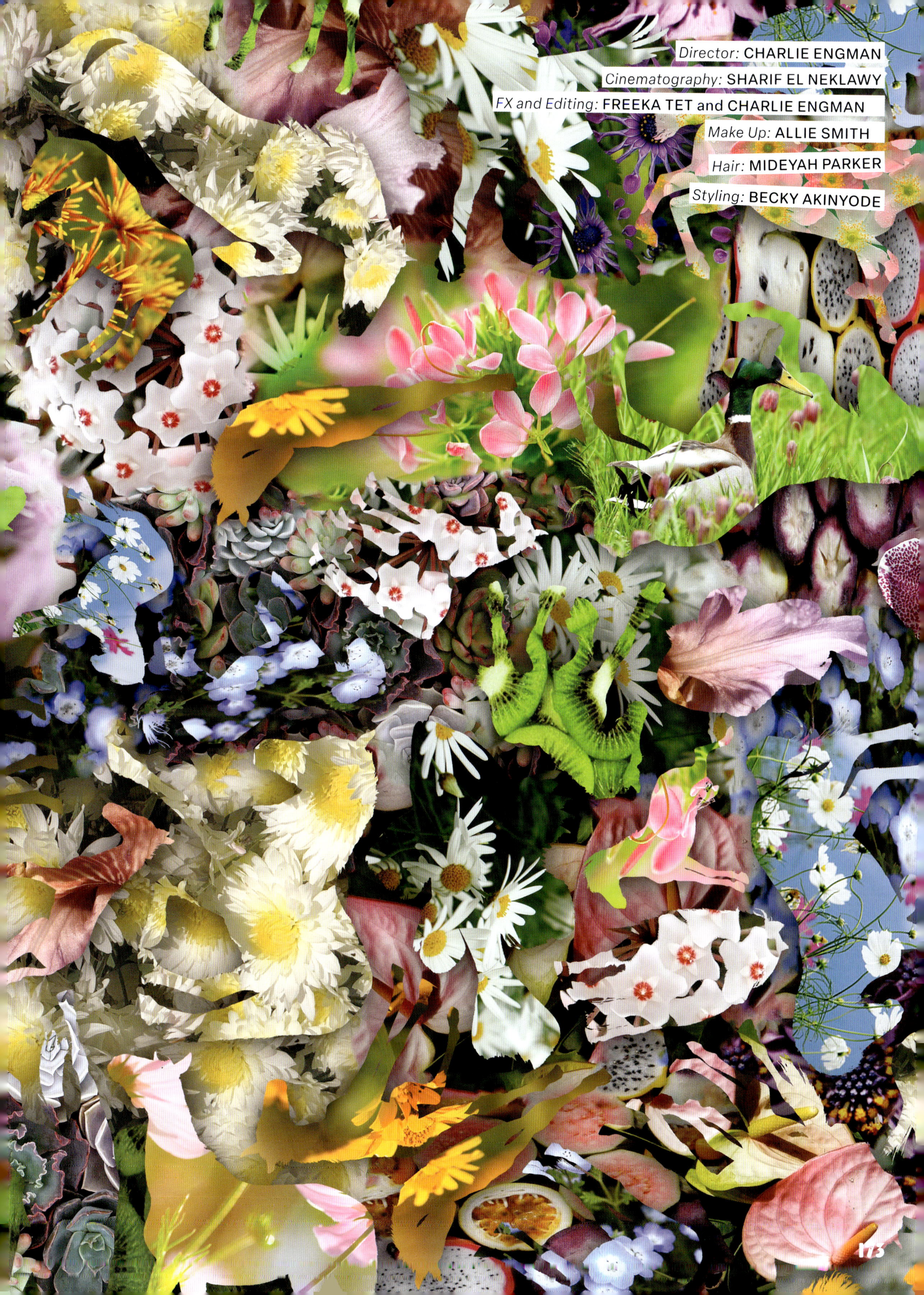

Director: CHARLIE ENGMAN
Cinematography: SHARIF EL NEKLAWY
FX and Editing: FREEKA TET and CHARLIE ENGMAN
Make Up: ALLIE SMITH
Hair: MIDEYAH PARKER
Styling: BECKY AKINYODE

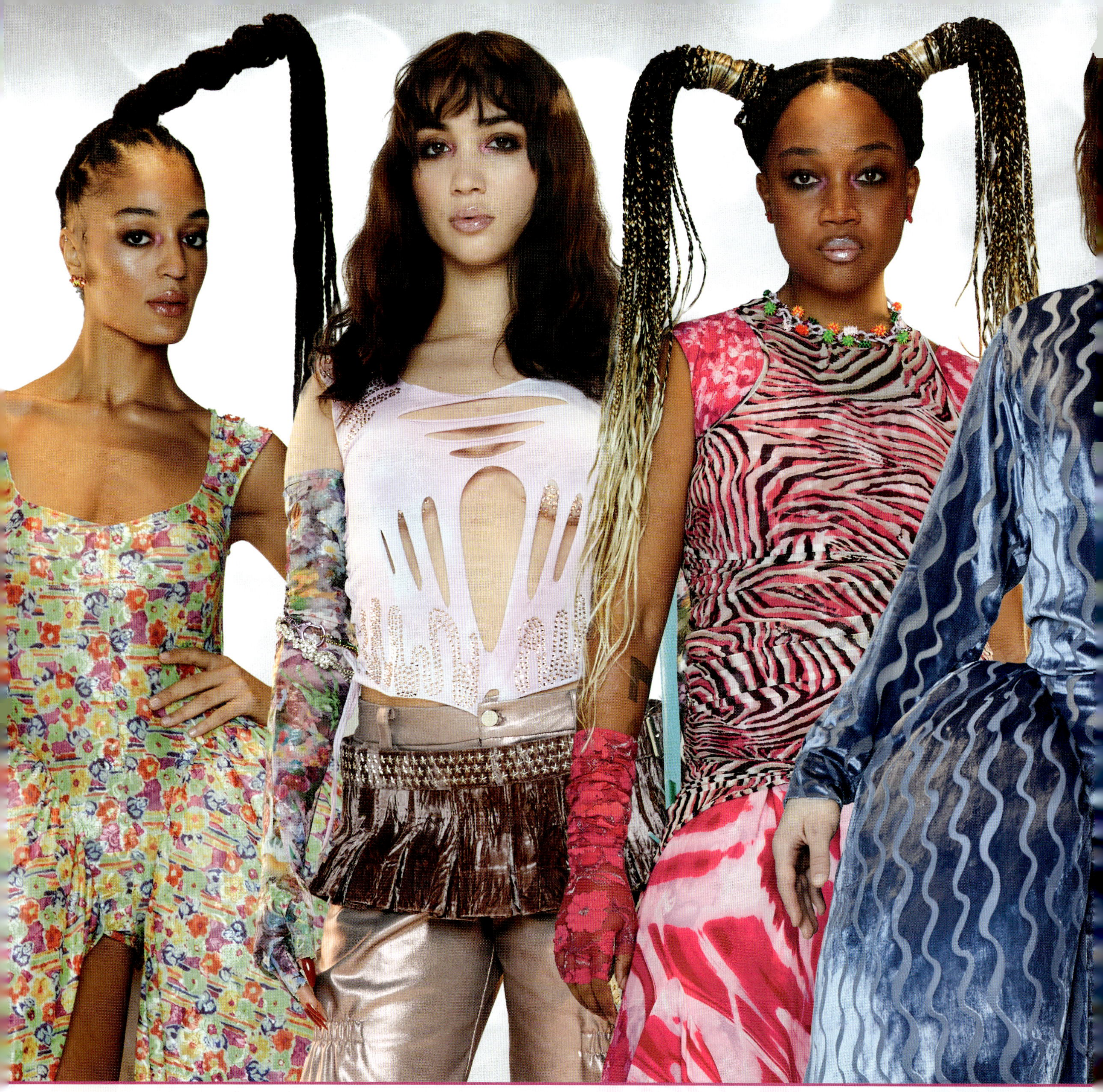

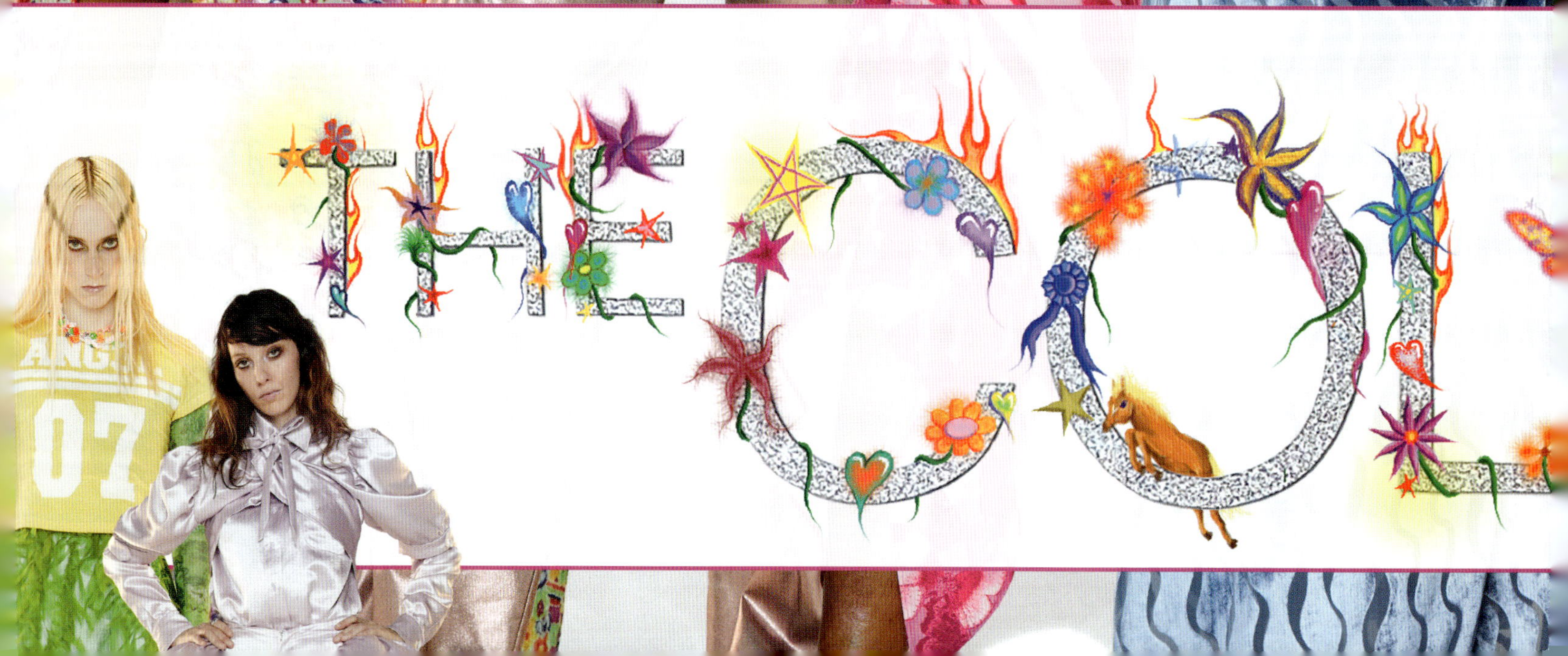
THE COL

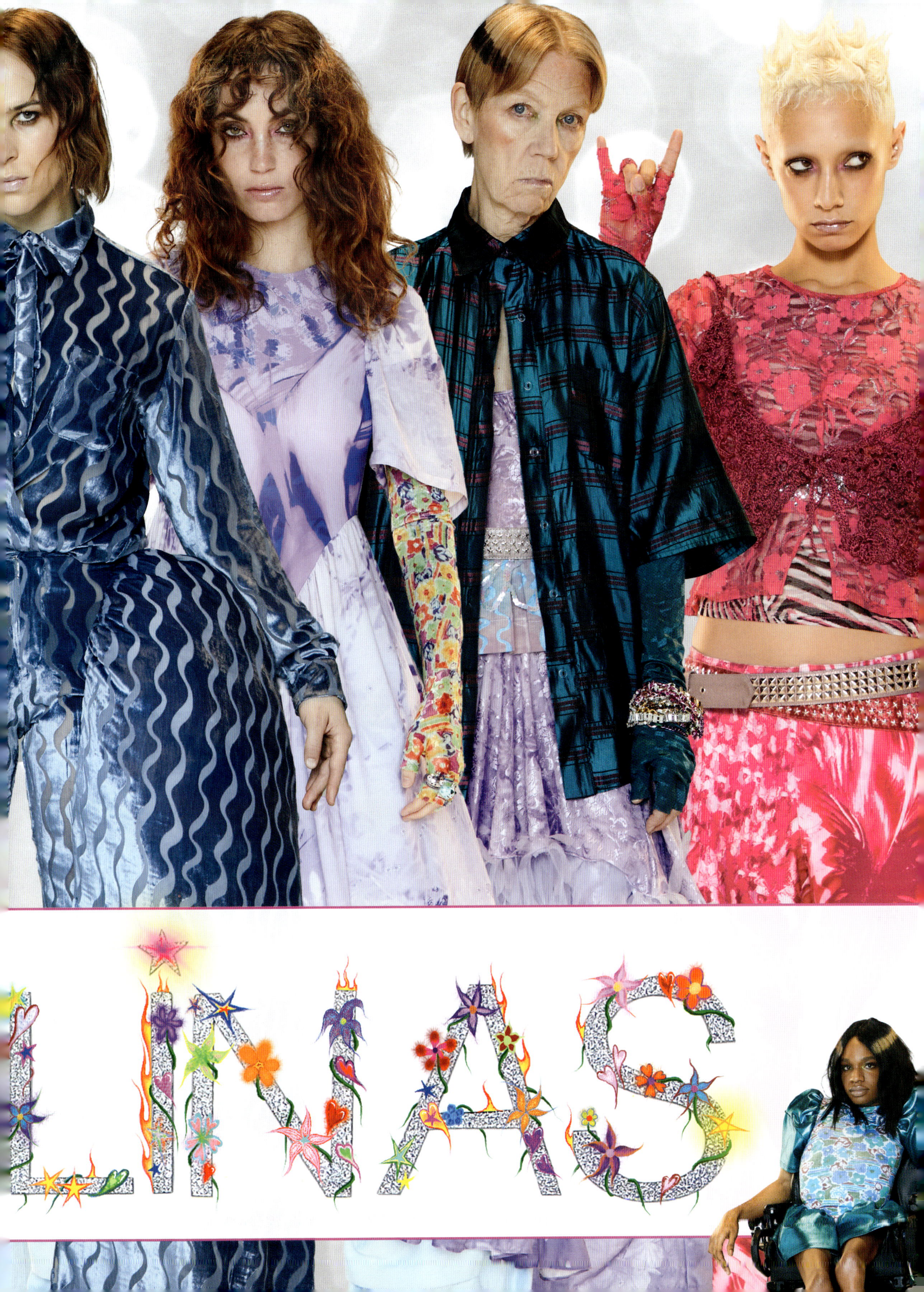
LINAS

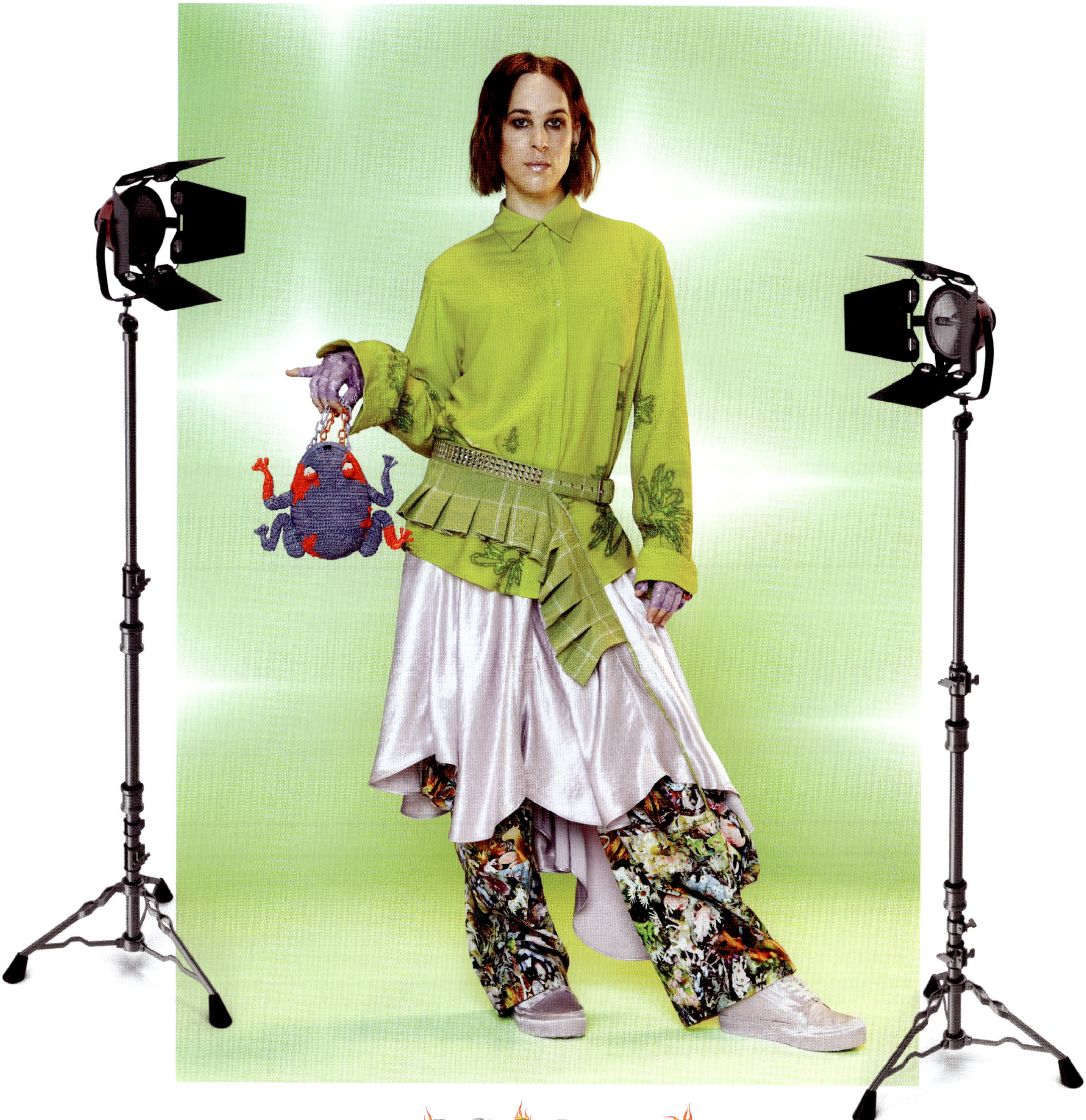

AW22

On the premier episode of *The Collinas*, Tommy Dorfman heads to New York for the opportunity of a lifetime to work at Collina Strada. But when she struggles to adapt to the workplace culture and a plant-based diet, her dream job turns into a wake-up call. Can Tommy make it in the high-stakes world of sustainable fashion?

EXT. NEW YORK STREET - DAY

Tommy and Eva are walking to work.

INT. COLLINA STRADA STUDIO - DAY

TOMMY
Wow. What a crazy day.

EVA
It's always like this.
(reassuringly)
But you'll get used to it.

TOMMY
I hope so.
(brightening up)
So...what are we *getting into* after work? I'm thinking about checking out this Brooklyn place.

EVA
Which Brooklyn place?

TOMMY
(beat)
Brooklyn.

Mannat walks up.

MANNAT
I need you both to trace 150 stars in these t-shirt scraps before you leave today.

Tommy and Eva exchange dismal glances.

TOMMY
There's gotta be an easier way.

EVA
Not if you want to recycle t-shirt scraps.

TOMMY
Sustainability is hard work.

INT. SHOWROOM - DAY

Tommy is with LYNETTE and GABY, who are inspecting t-shirt scraps.

NARRATOR (V.O.)
Next time on "The Collinas"...

All season imagery by CHARLIE ENGMAN unless noted otherwise

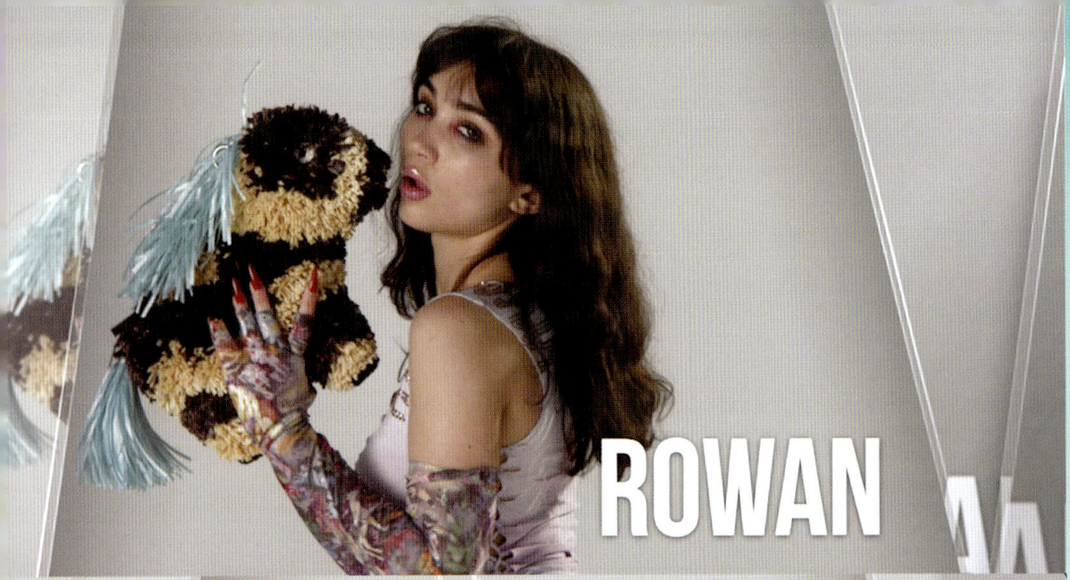
ROWAN

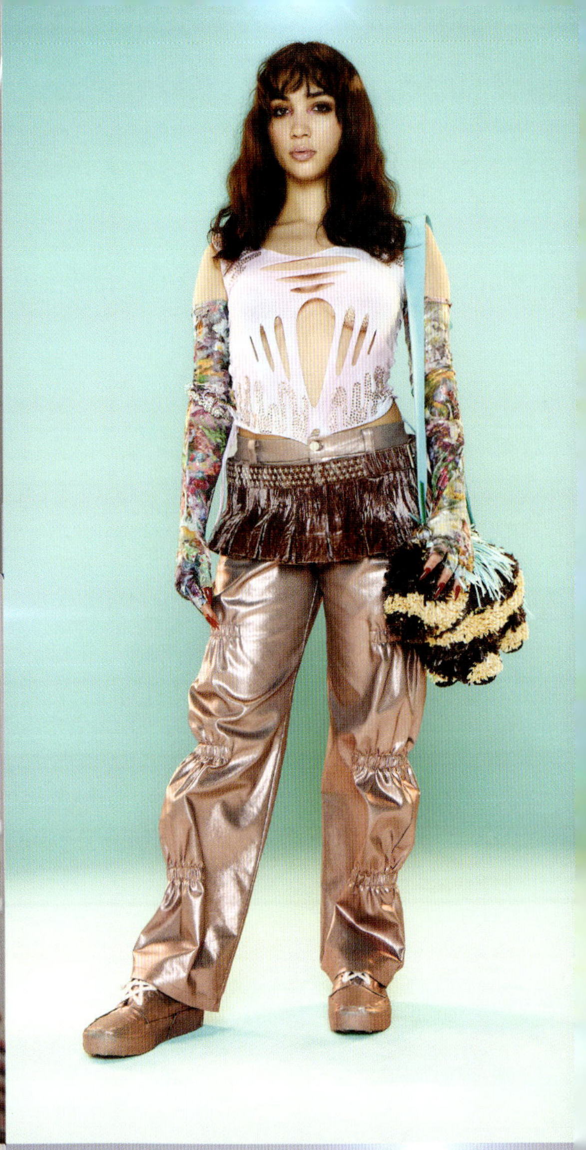

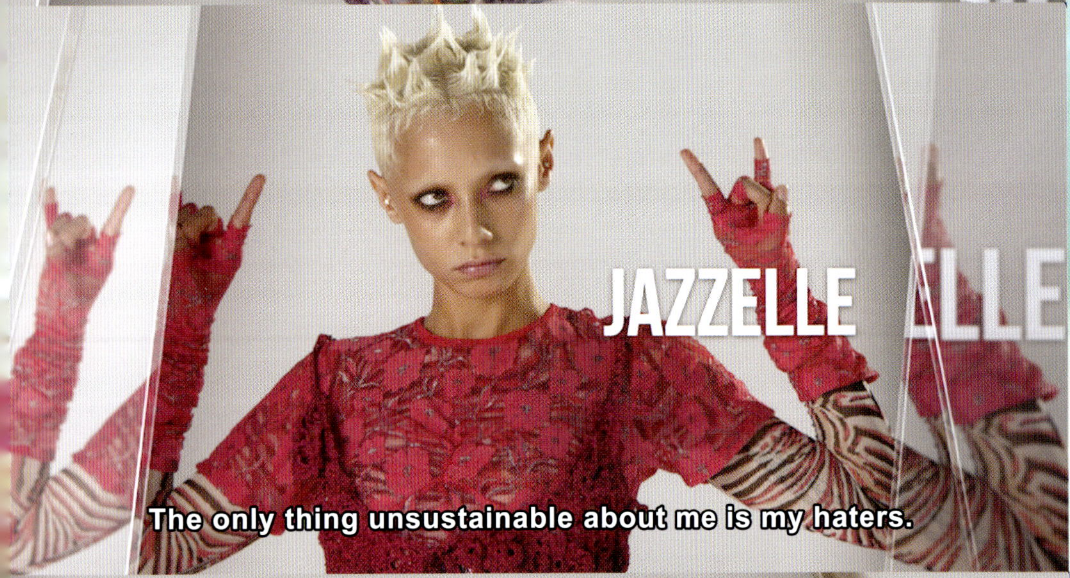
JAZZELLE
The only thing unsustainable about me is my haters.

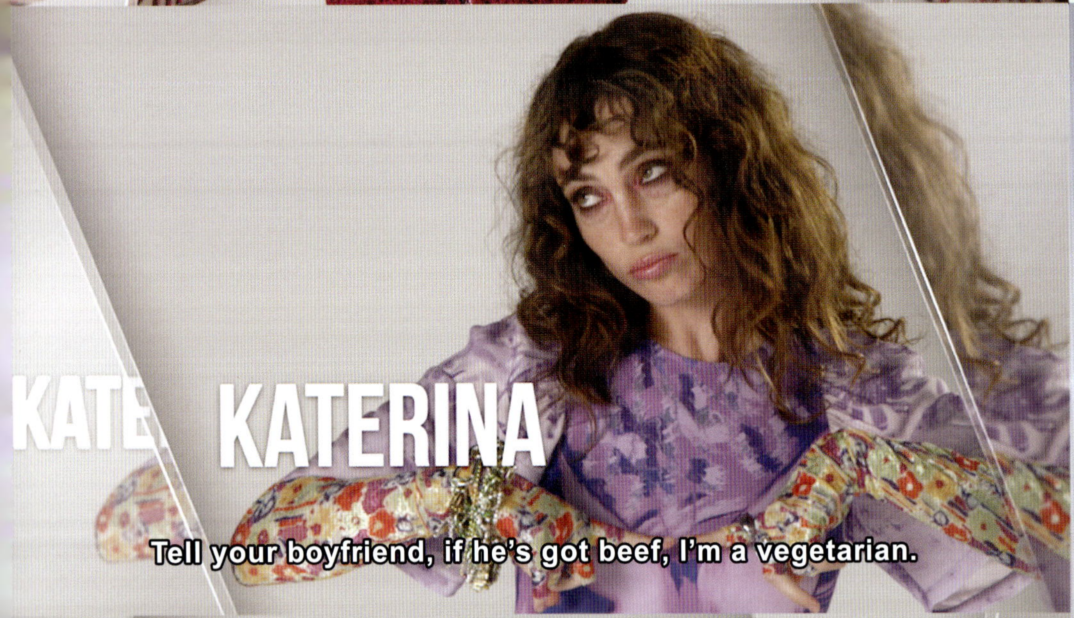
KATERINA
Tell your boyfriend, if he's got beef, I'm a vegetarian.

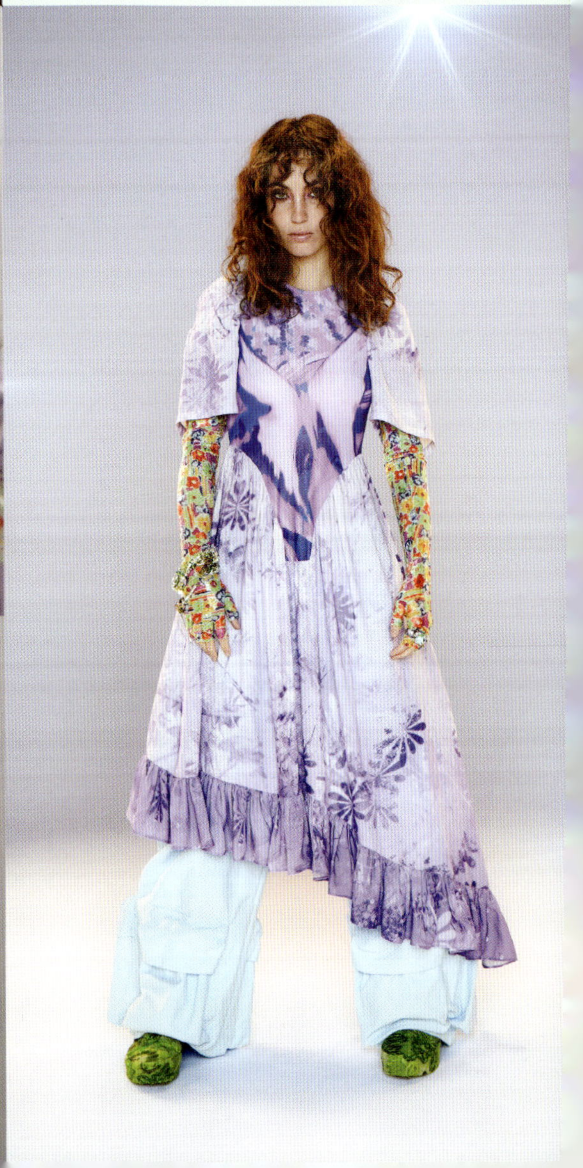

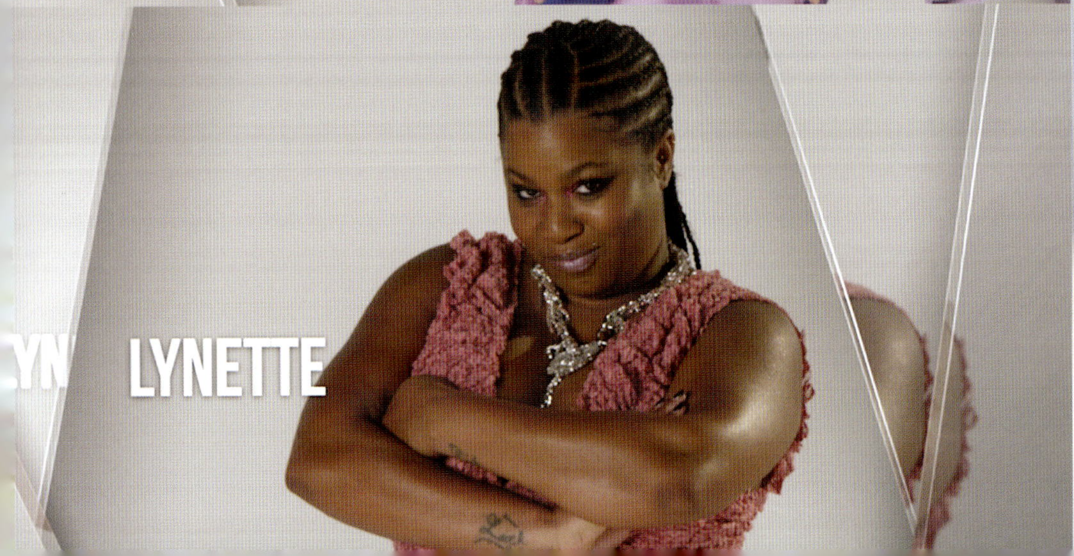
LYNETTE

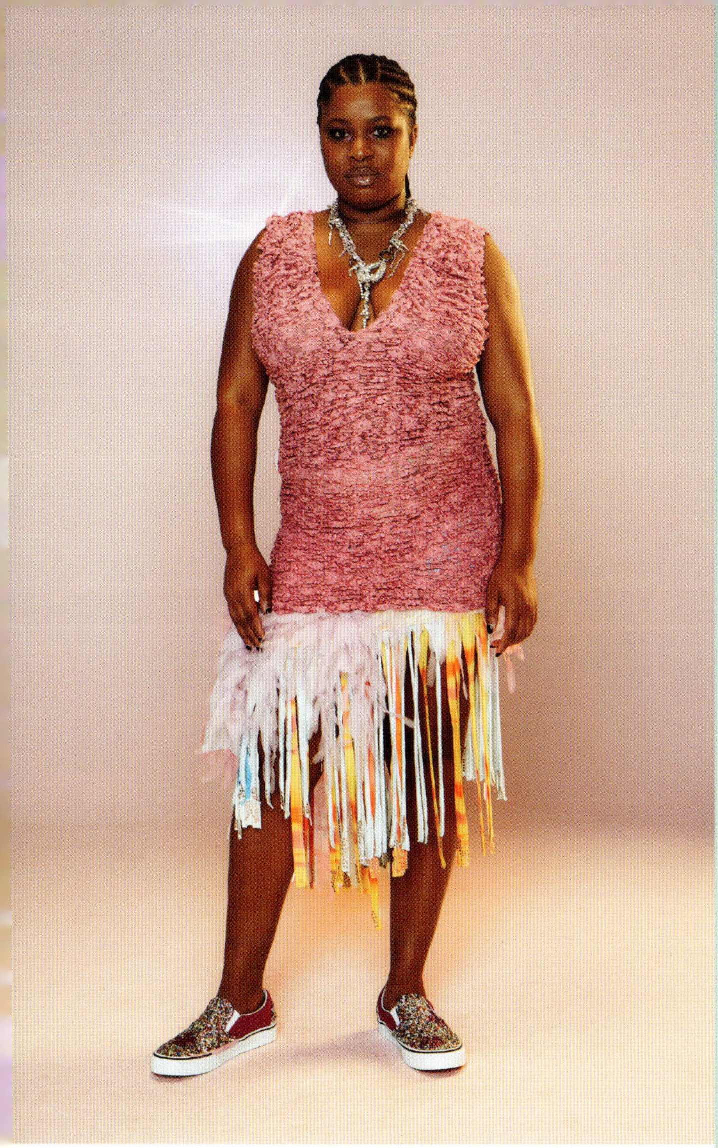

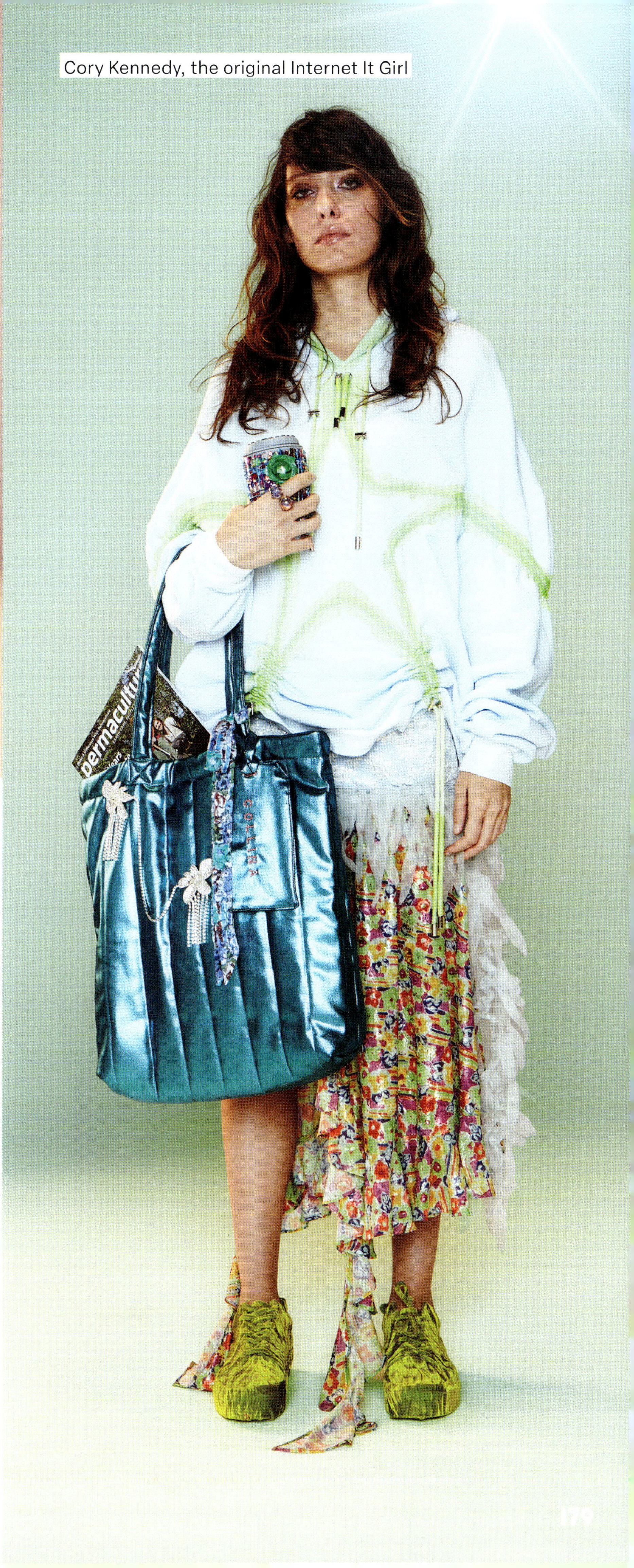

Cory Kennedy, the original Internet It Girl

"The eye doesn't always know where to settle. On the purple-and-orange wicker purse in the shape of a frog? On the rhinestone horns stuck to the tops of lime-green sneakers? On the protruding, heart-shaped hips of a pink velvet gown, formed by old-fashioned side hoops?

Visiting the set of a Collina Strada shoot is not unlike being greeted by a delegation from another planet. The models, in their layers of mismatched candy-colored clothing, are a new species, bred from goth mall rats and granola girls. They don't strut and pose. They frolic and stomp.

On this Monday in February, they have been plucked from their grungy fantasyland and dropped into a rented film studio in South Brooklyn. Here, the brand is working on a project bridging our world and theirs: a parody of the mid-2000s reality show *The Hills* (Collina translates to 'hill' in Italian) with some *Real Housewives energy*."

- Jessica Testa for *The New York Times*

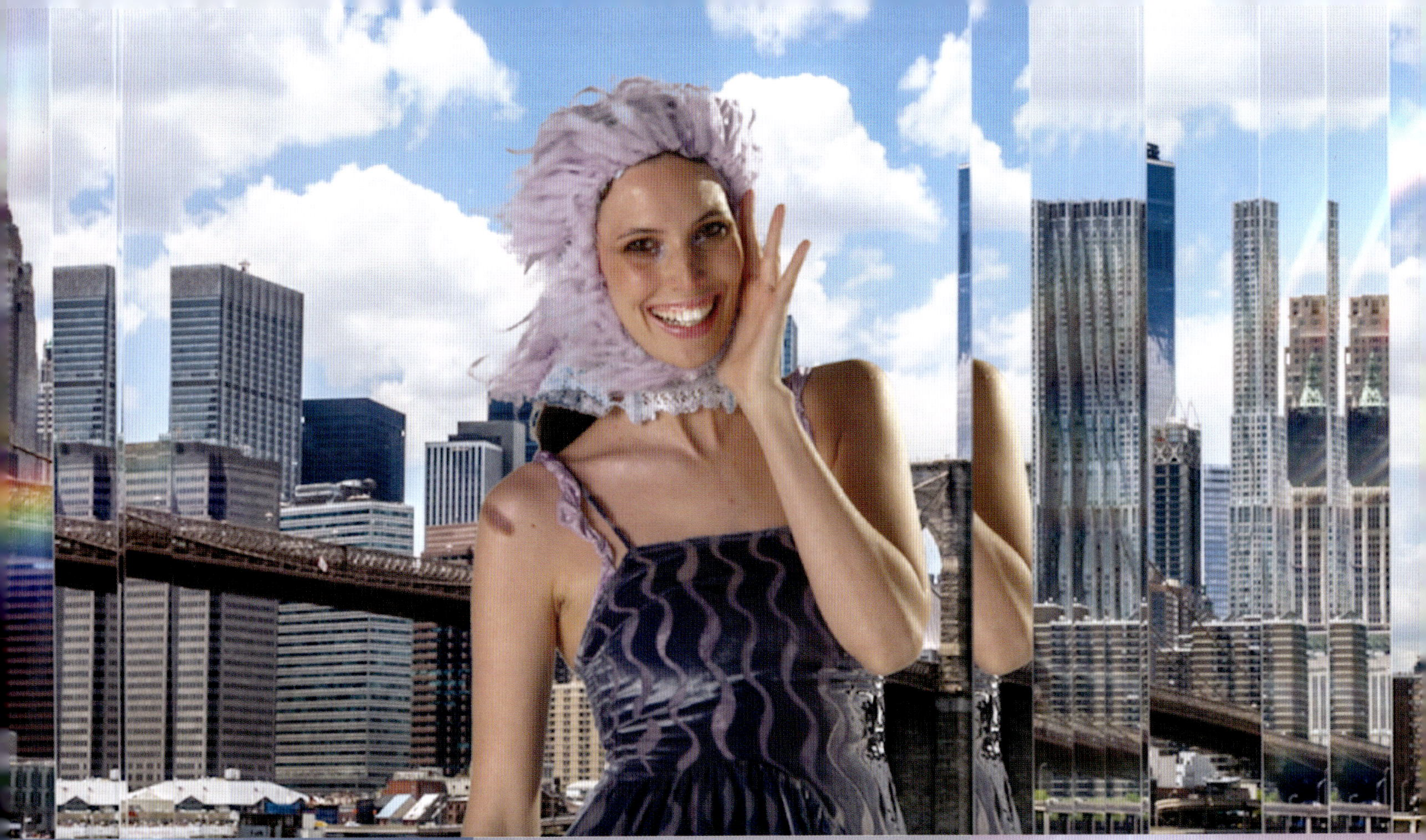

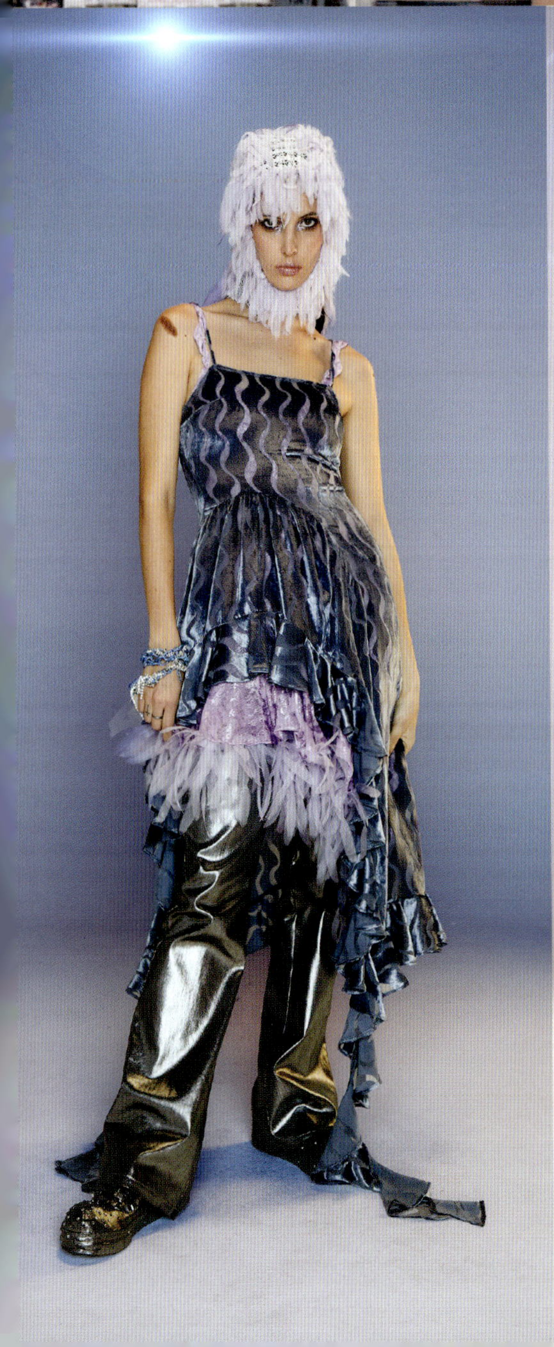

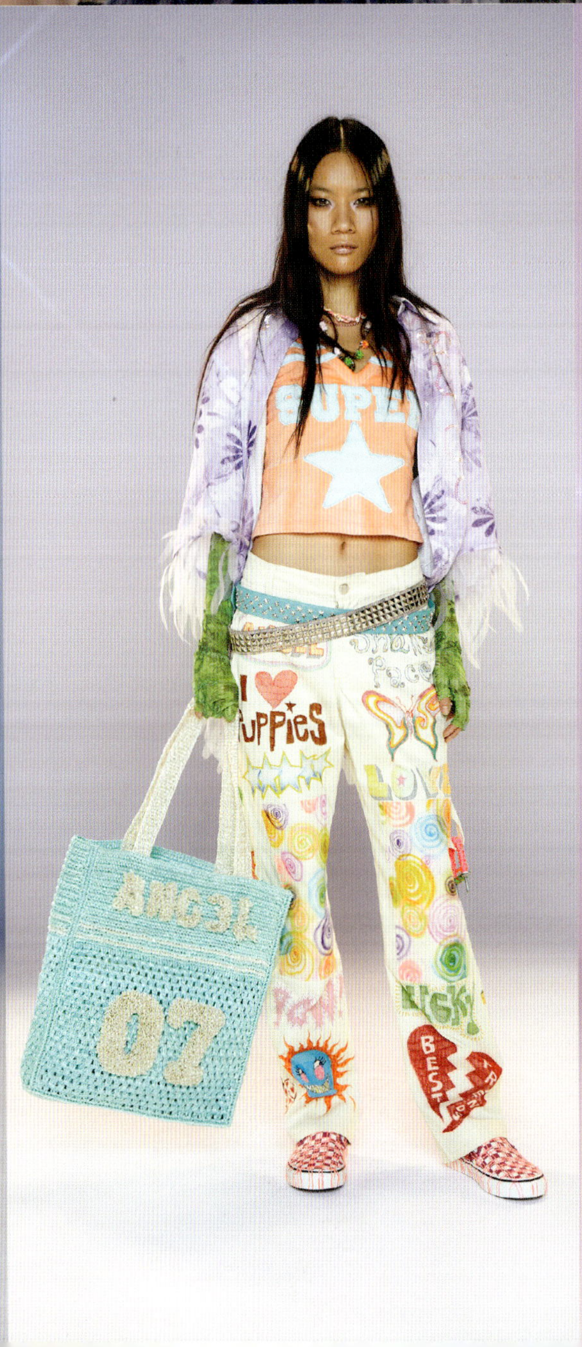
07

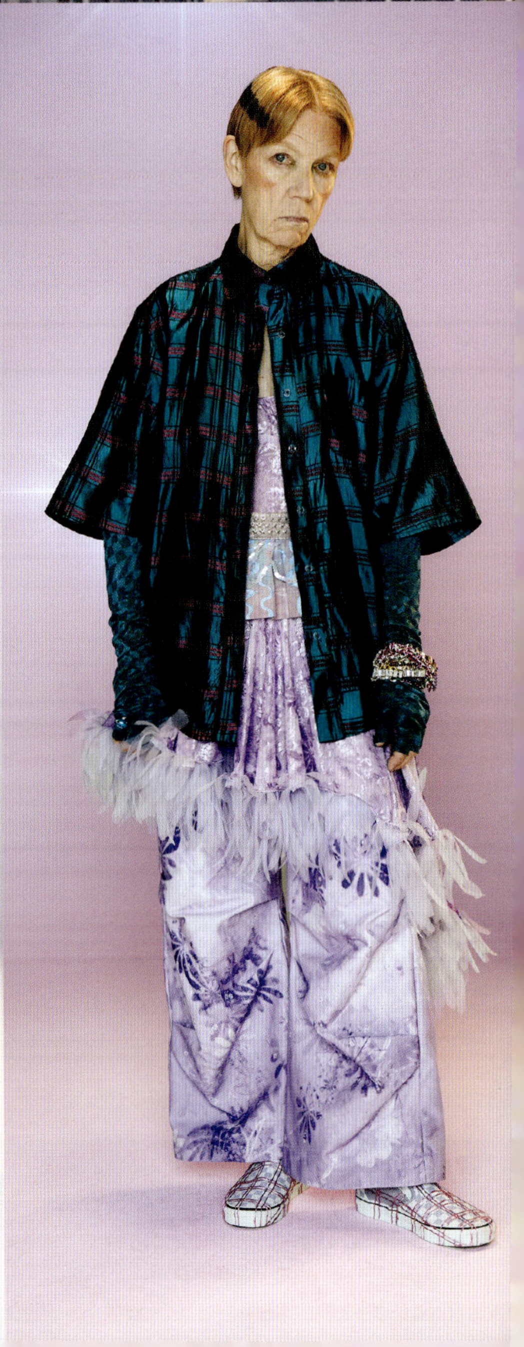

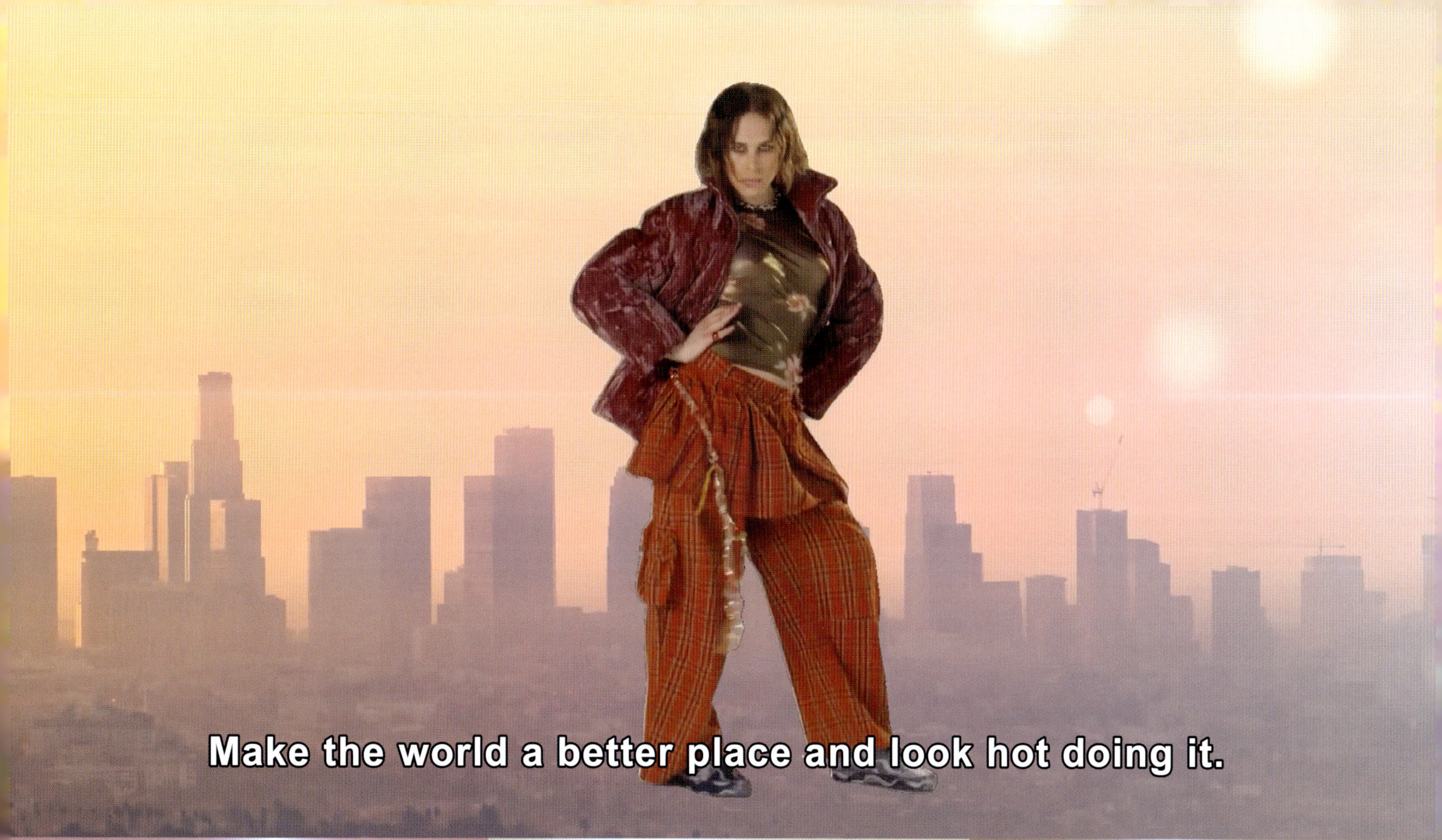
Make the world a better place and look hot doing it.

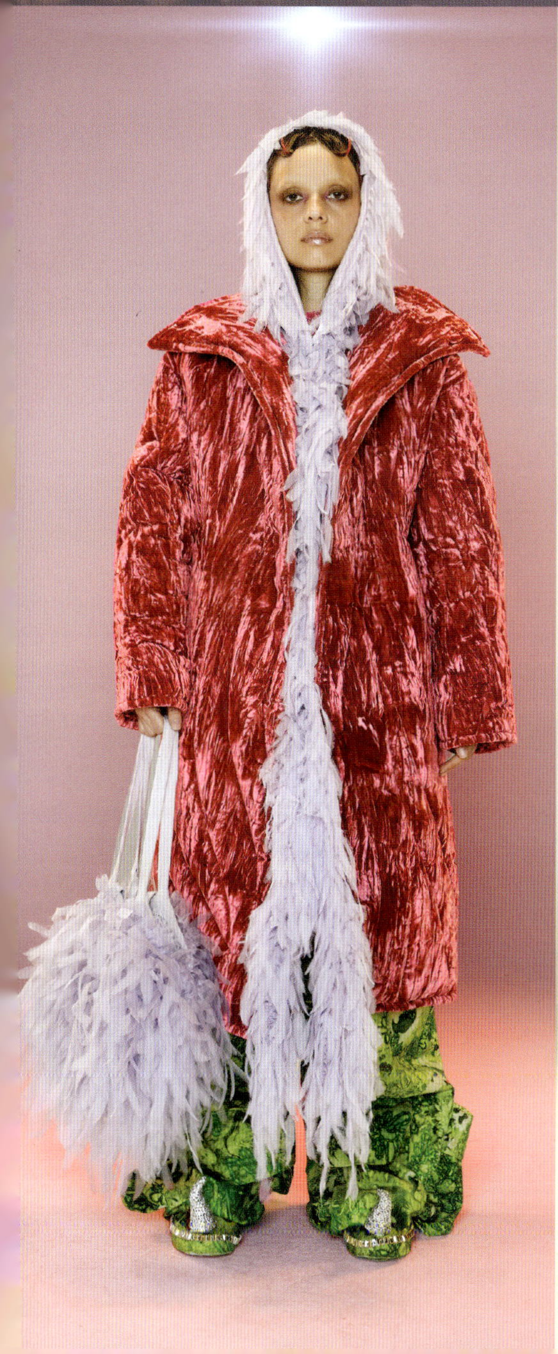

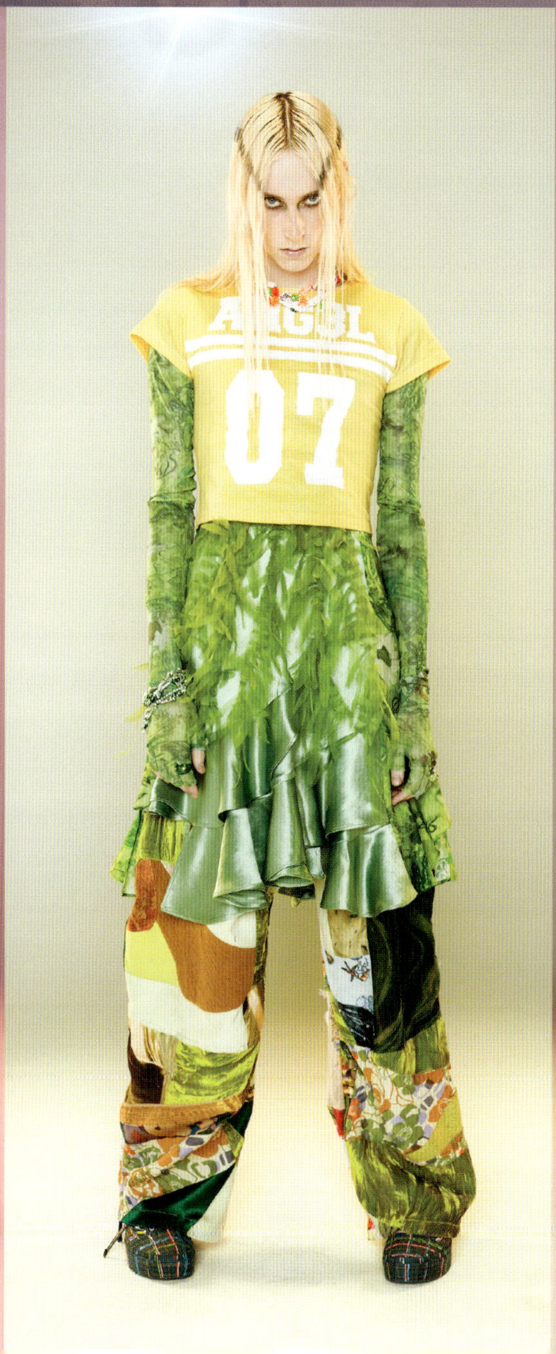
07

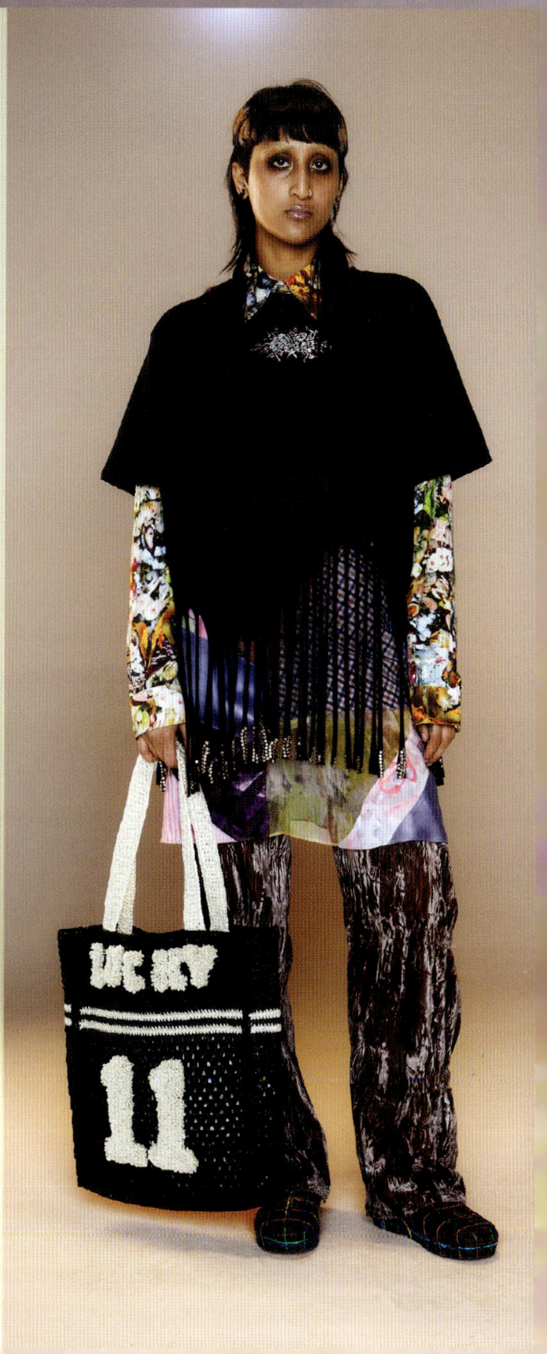
11

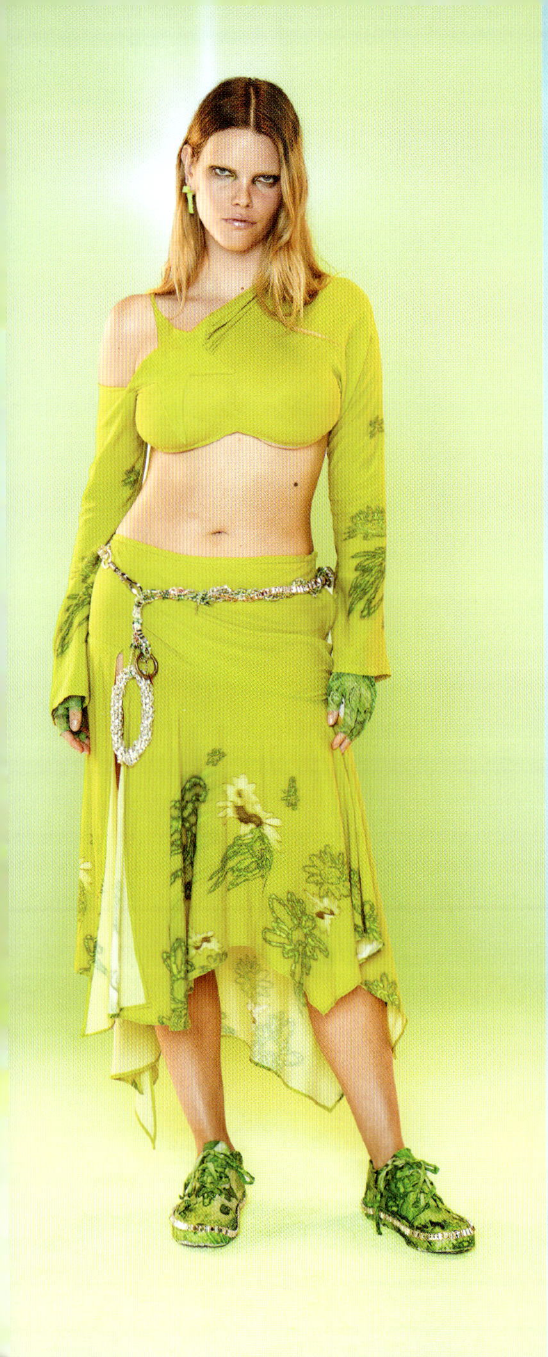
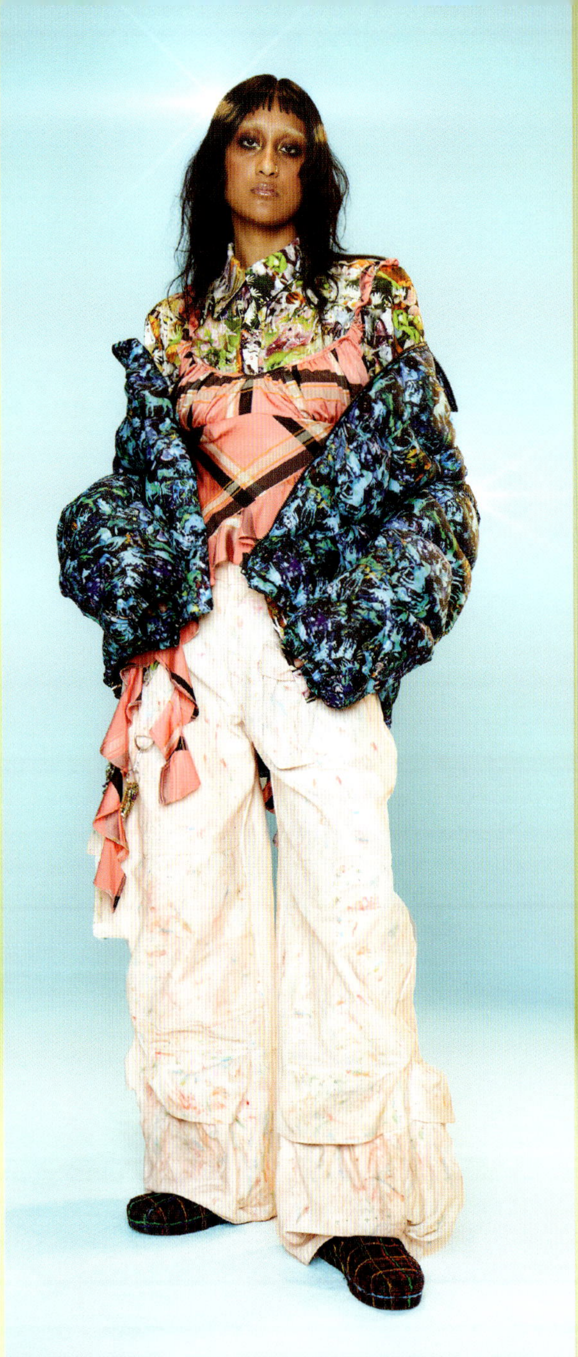
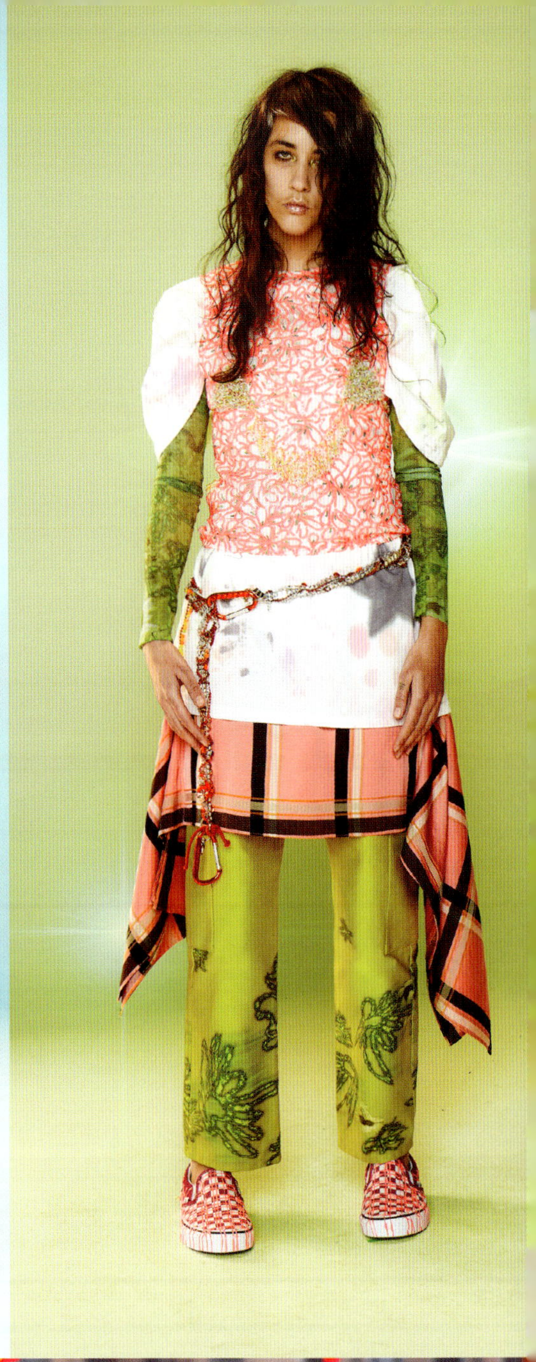
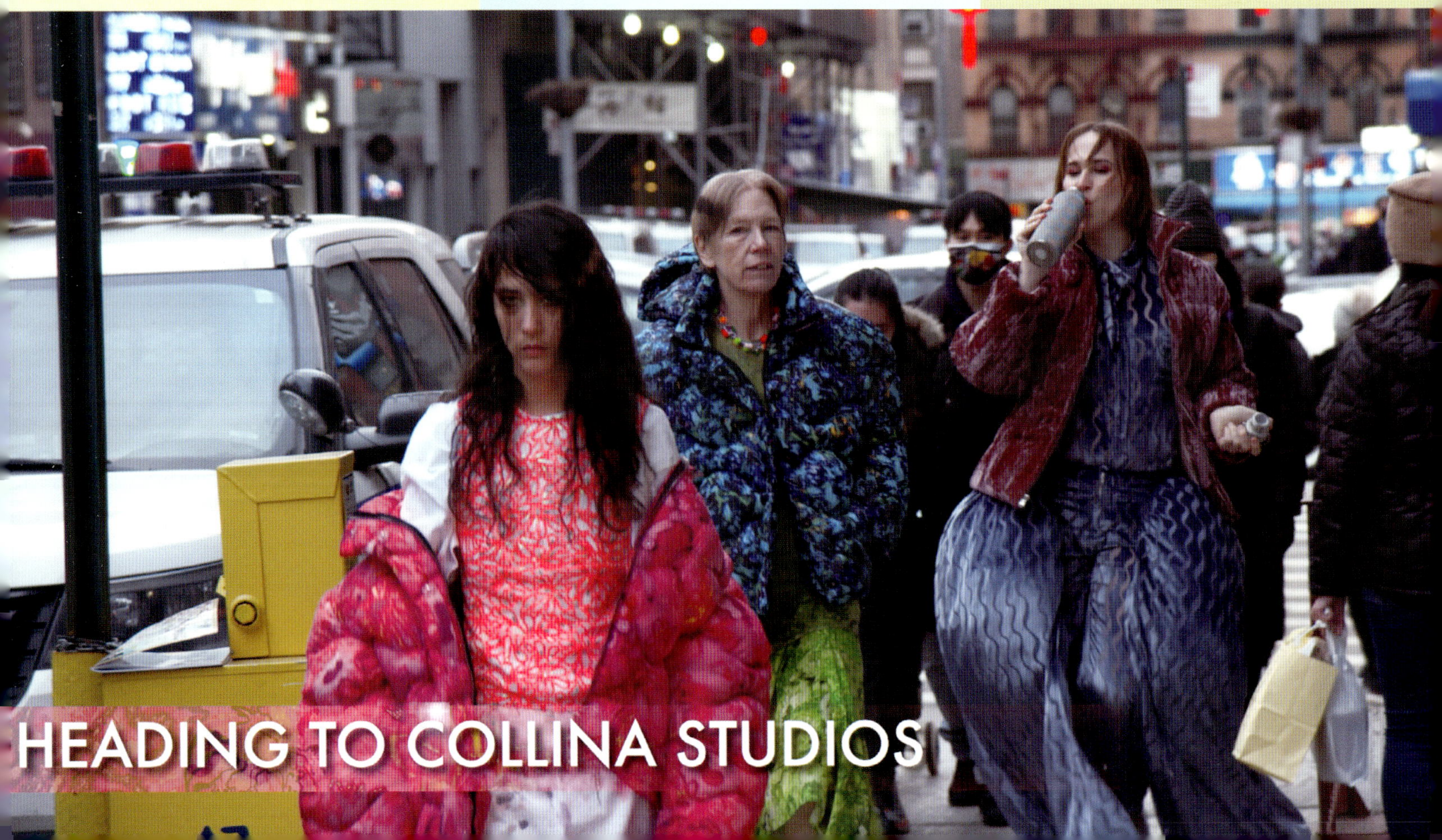

HEADING TO COLLINA STUDIOS

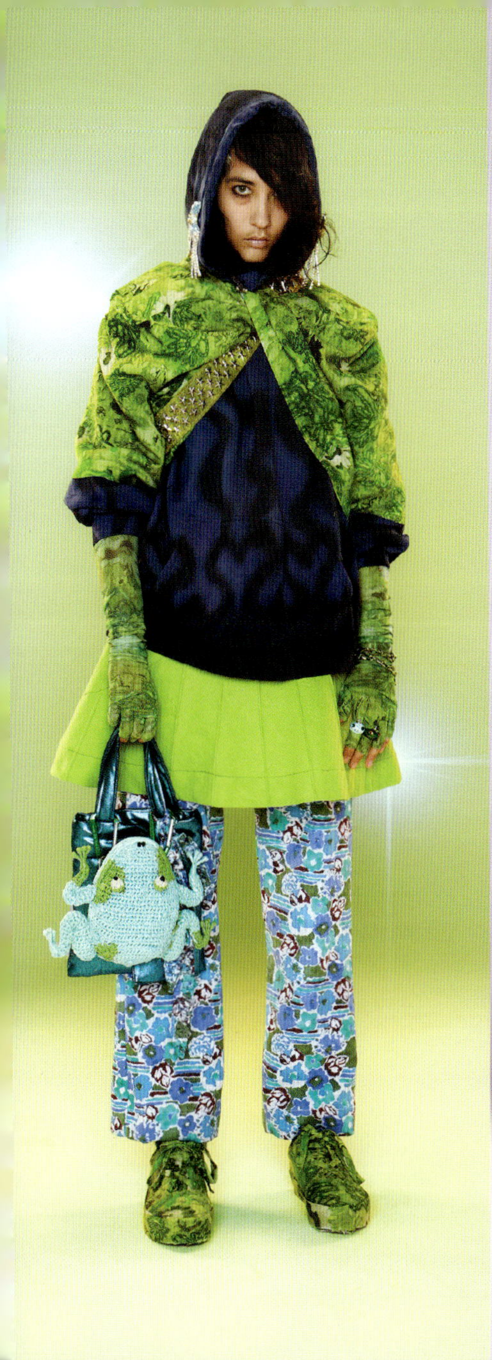
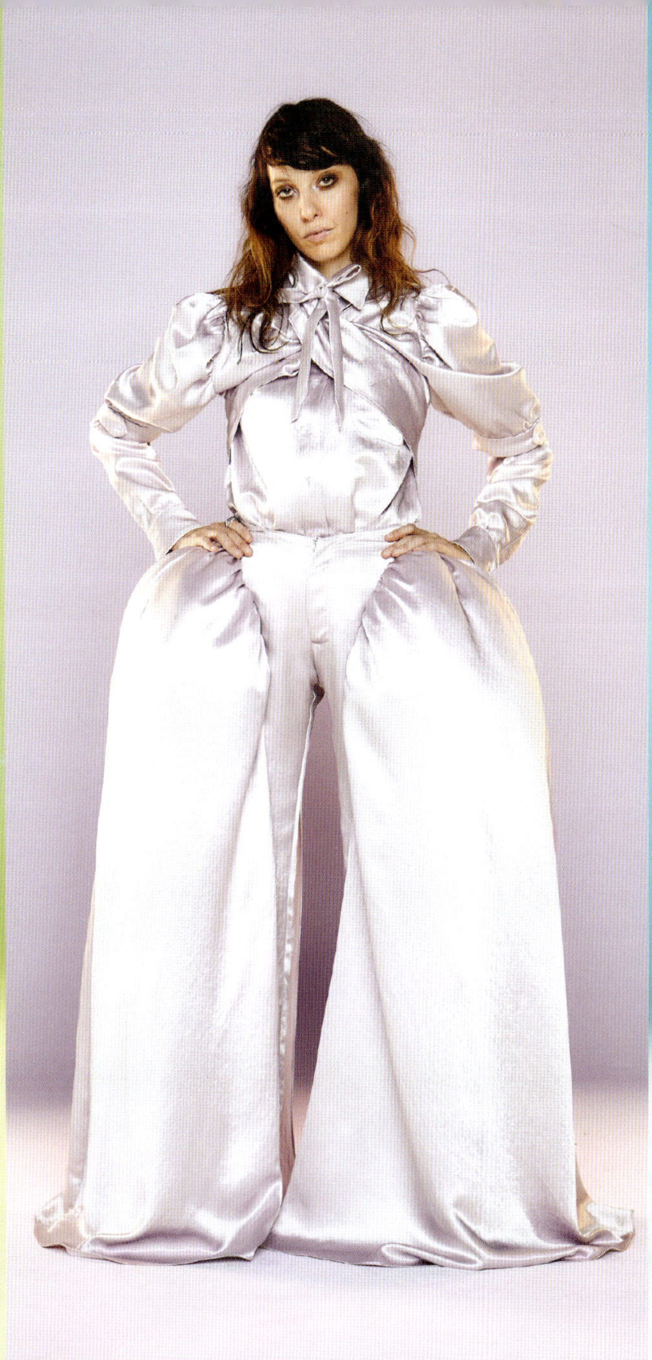
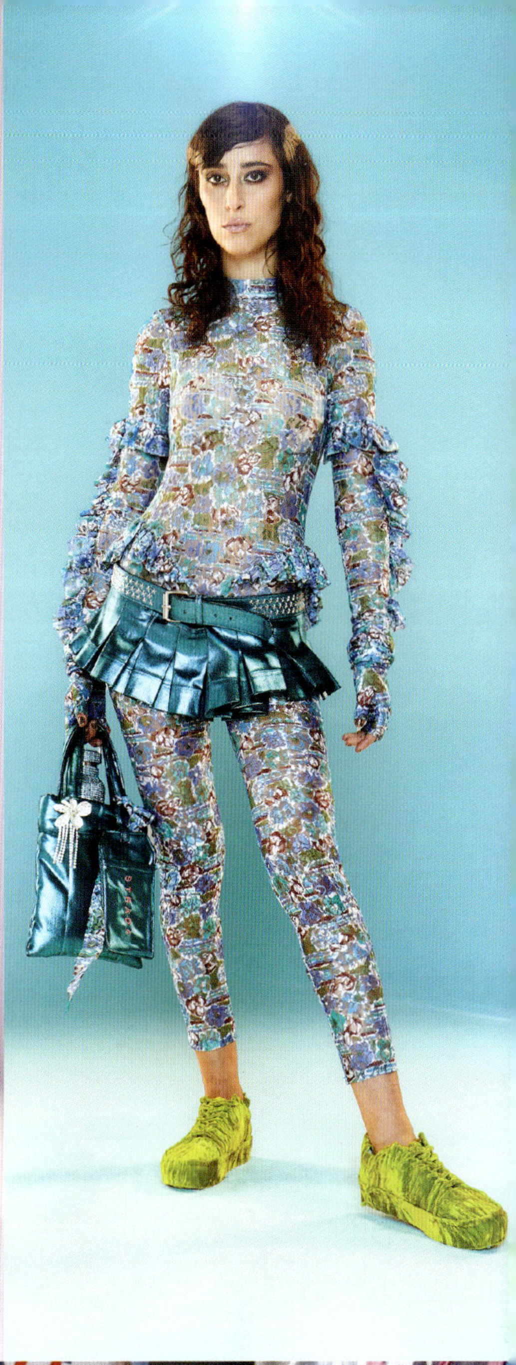
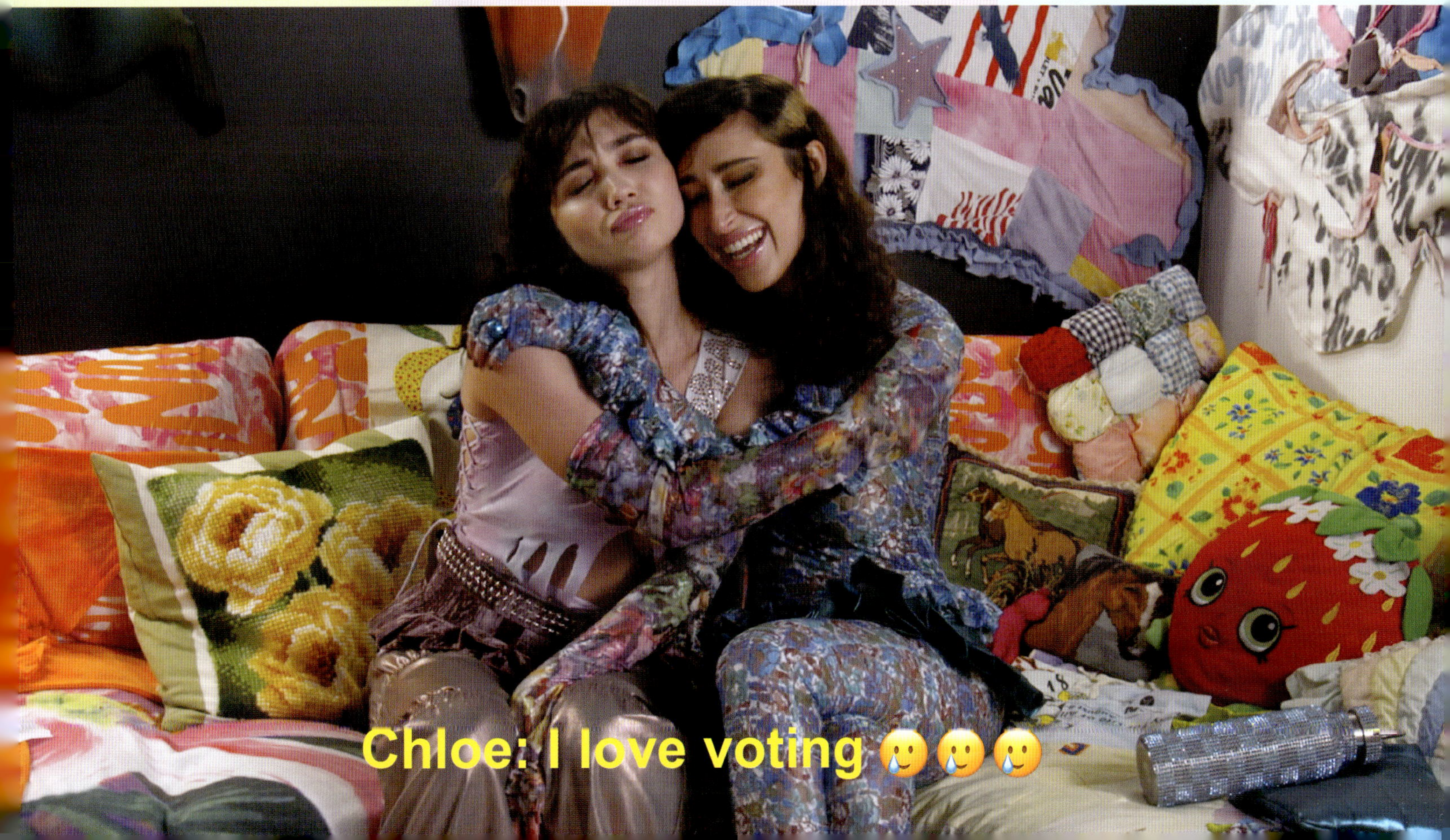
Chloe: I love voting 🥲🥲🥲

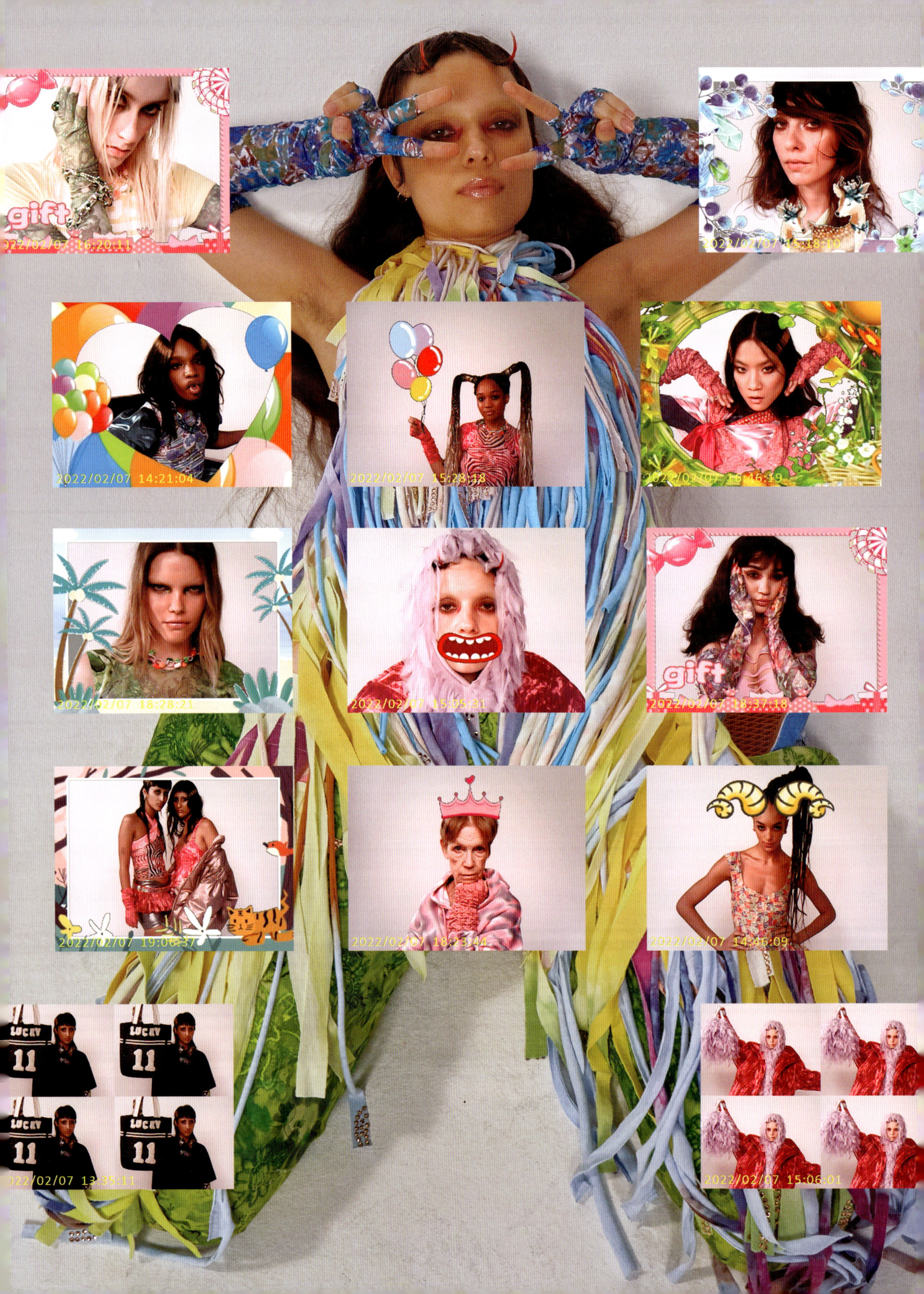
gift
2022/02/07 14:21:04
2022/02/07 15:28:18
gift
2022/02/07 14:46:09
LUCKY
11
2022/02/07 15:06:01

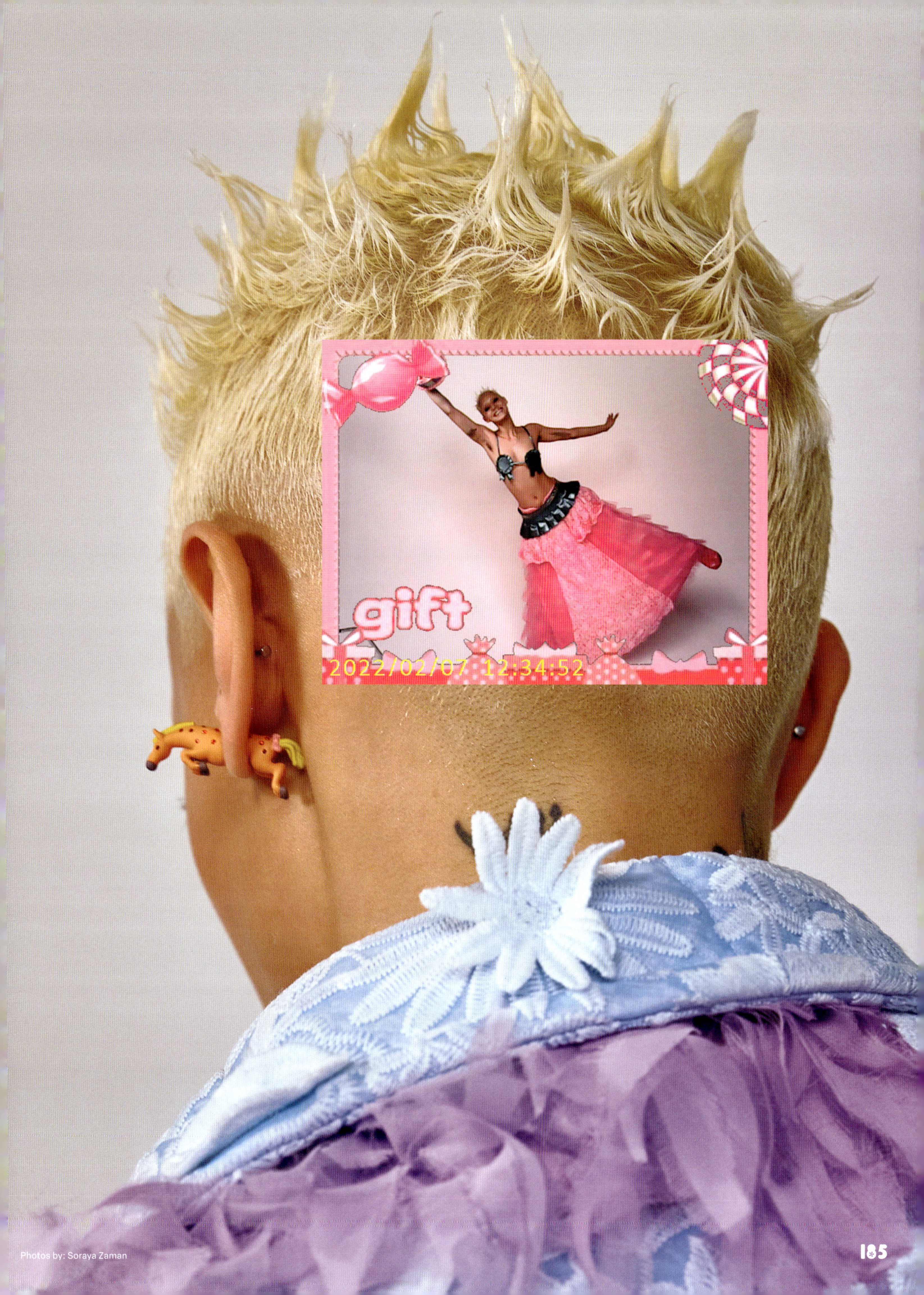

Photos by: Soraya Zaman

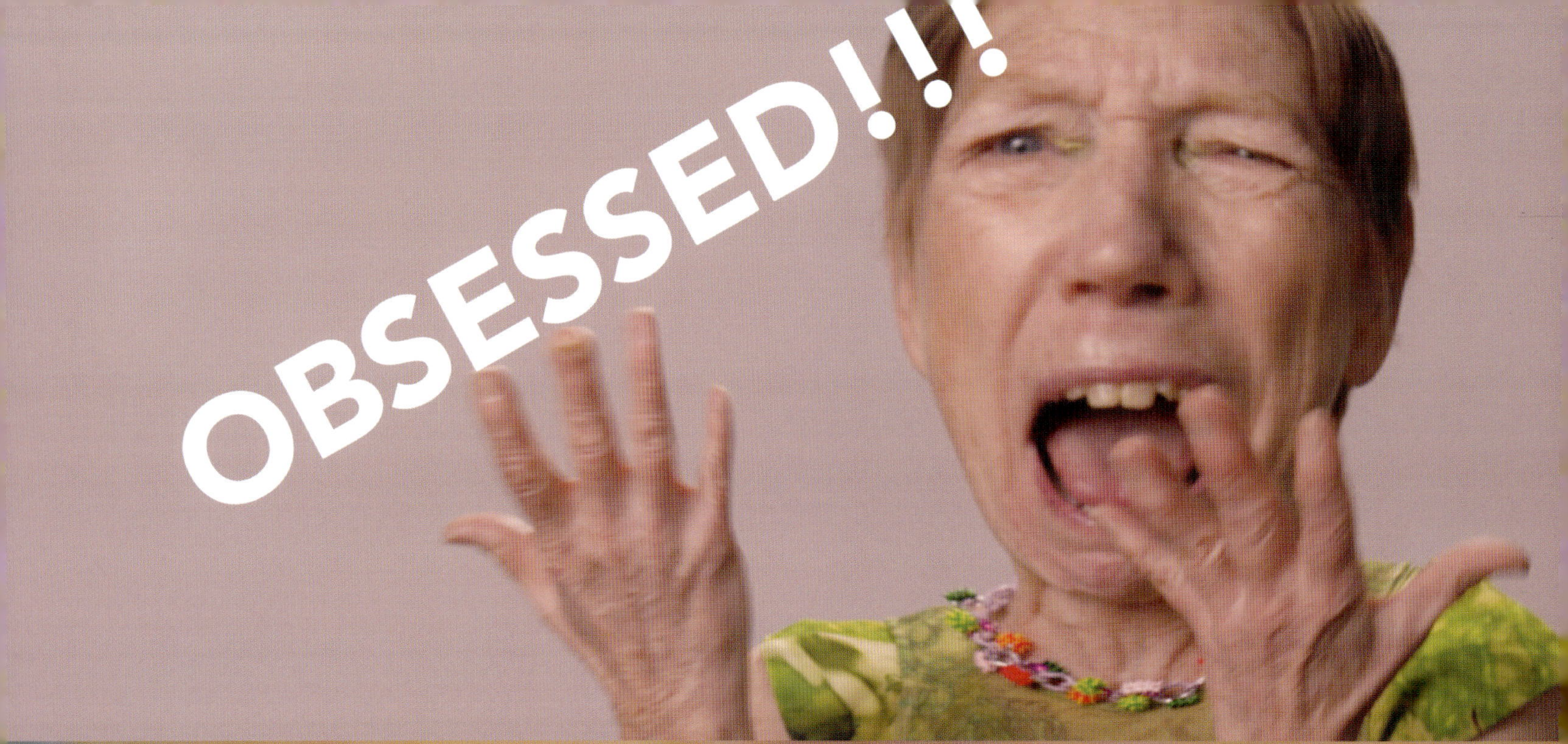
OBSESSED!!!

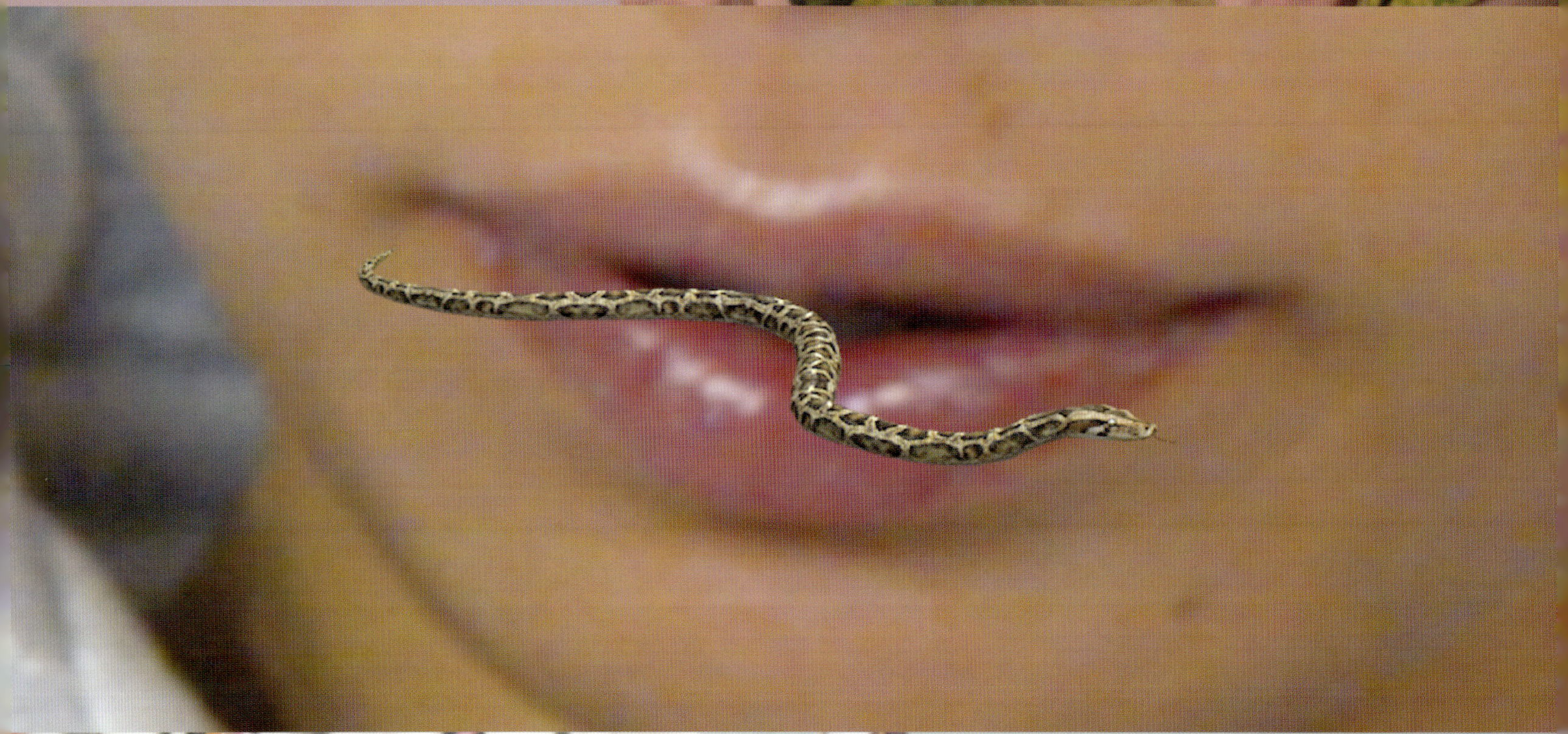

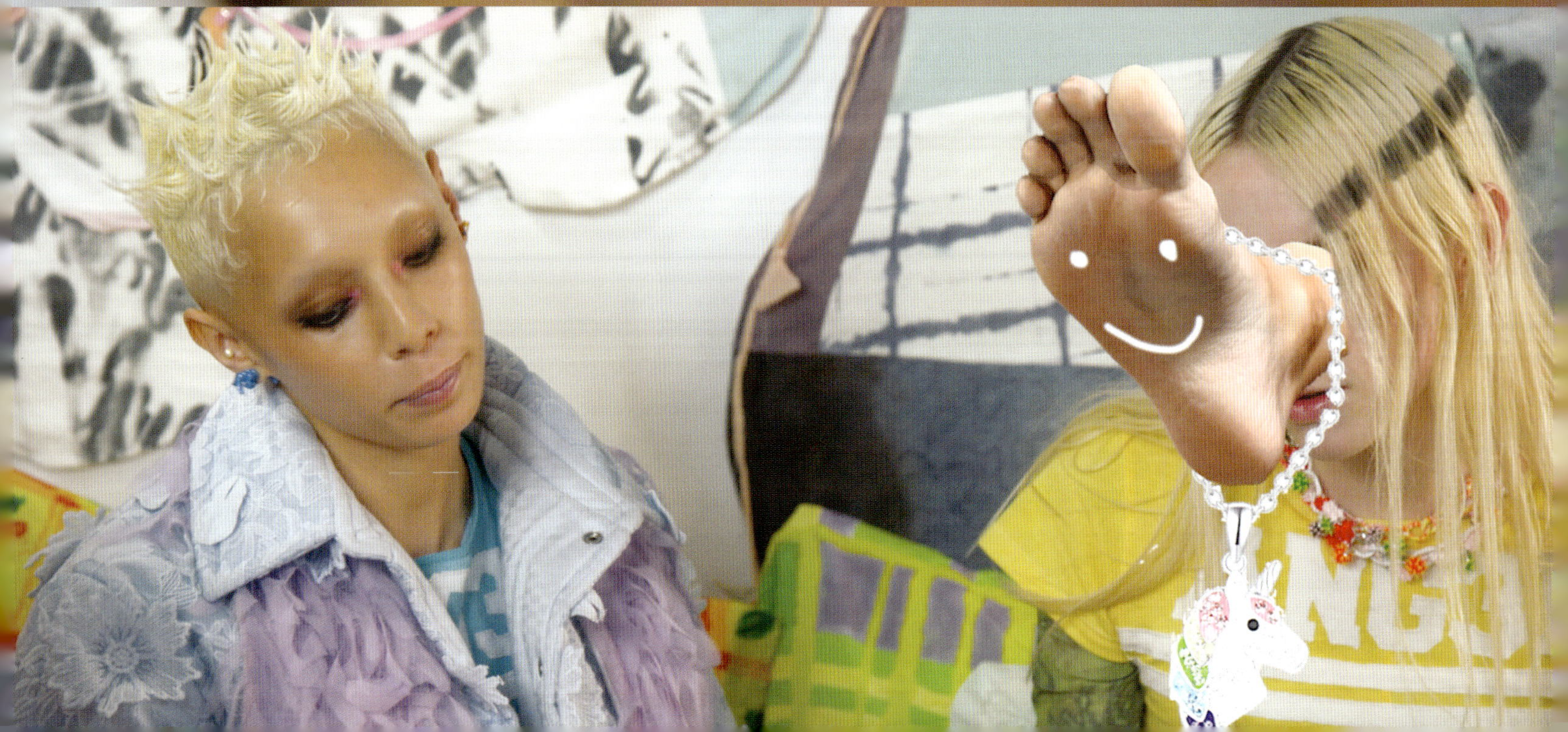

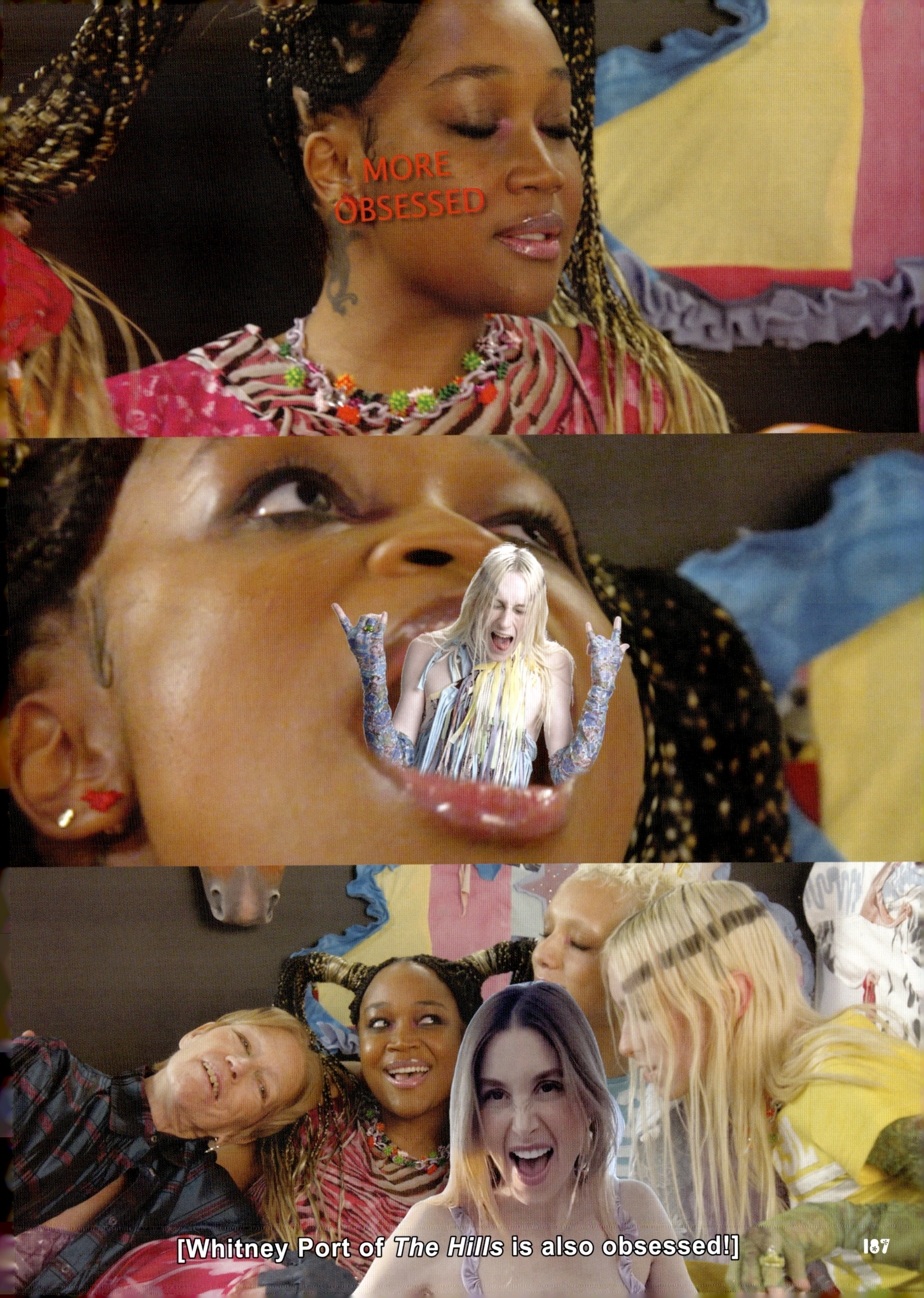
MORE
OBSESSED
[Whitney Port of *The Hills* is also obsessed!]

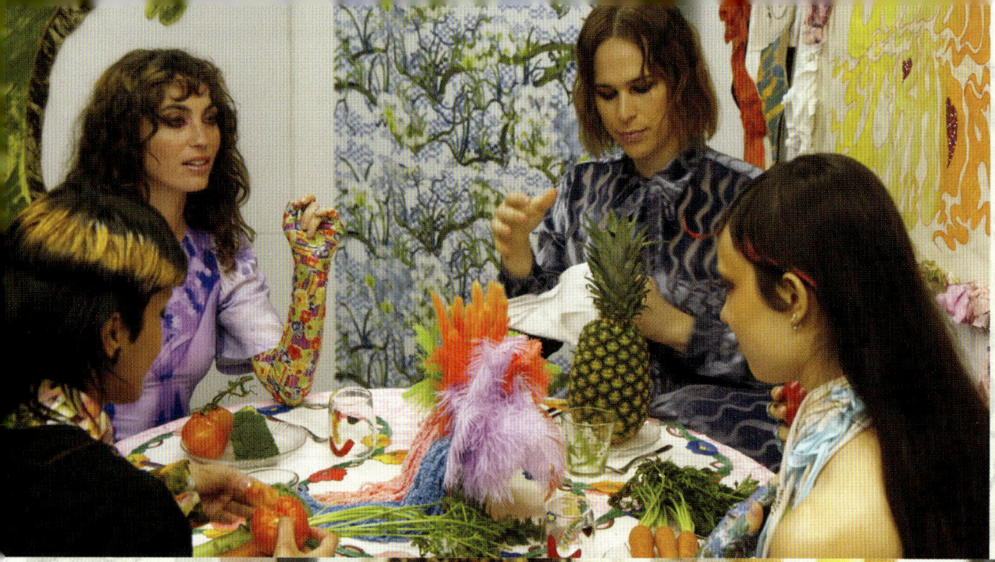

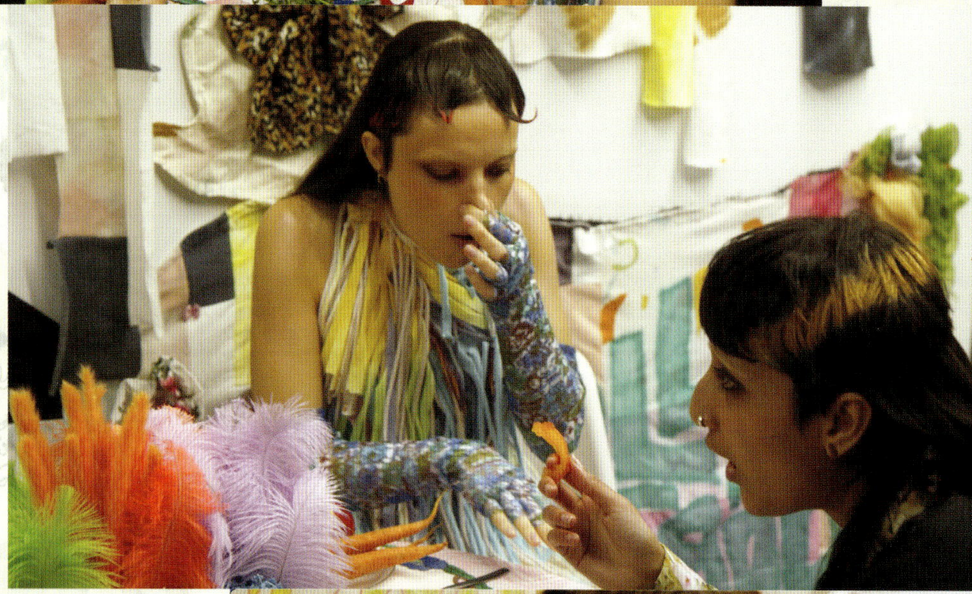

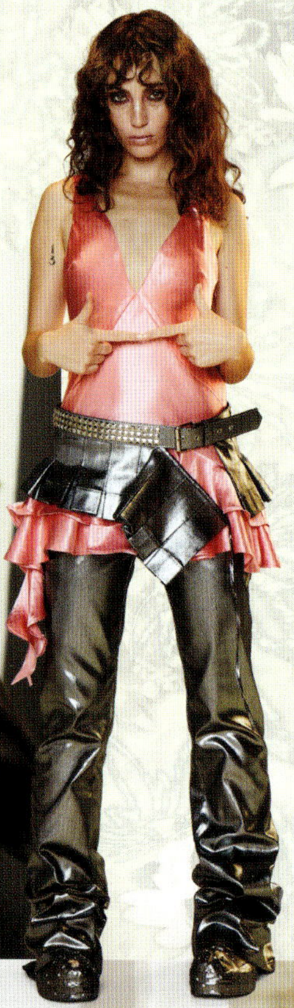

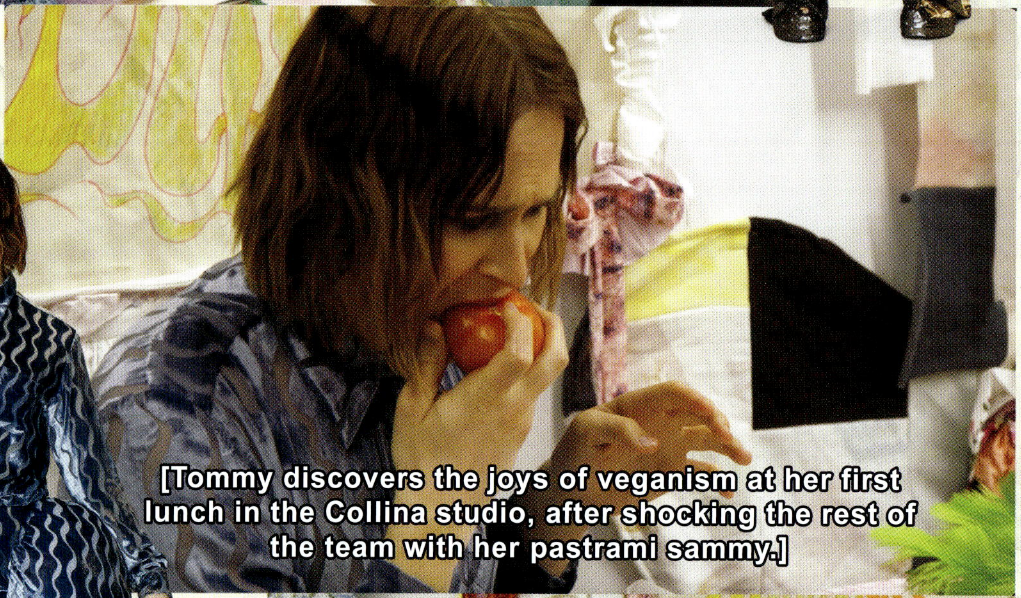

[Tommy discovers the joys of veganism at her first lunch in the Collina studio, after shocking the rest of the team with her pastrami sammy.]

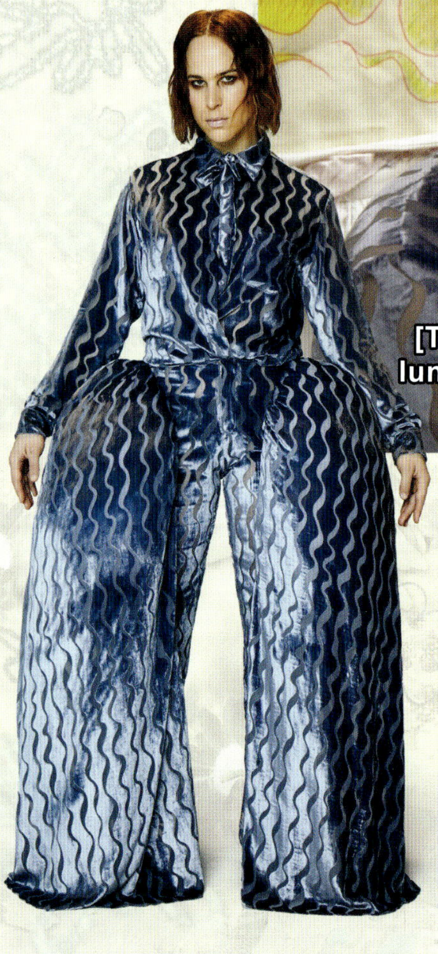

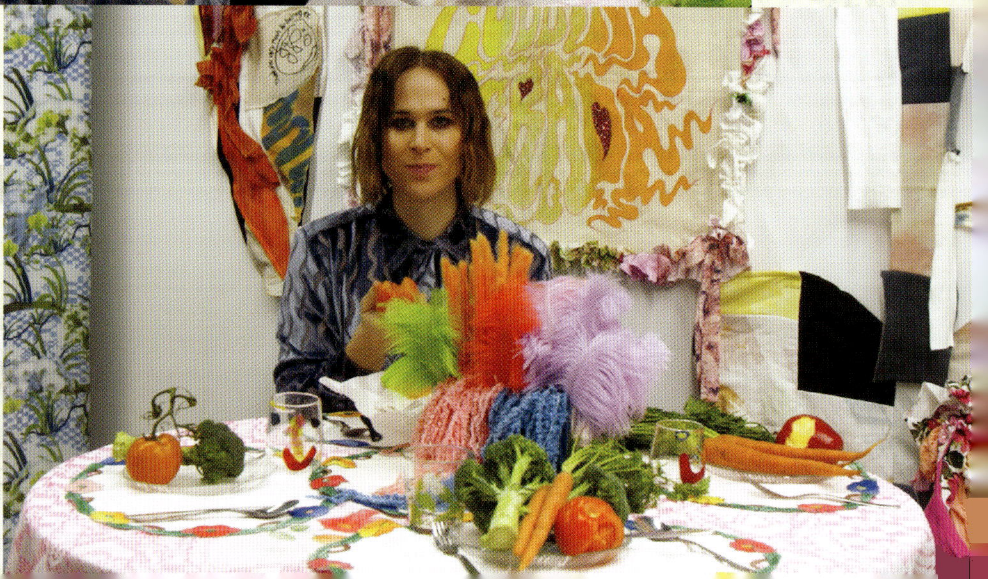

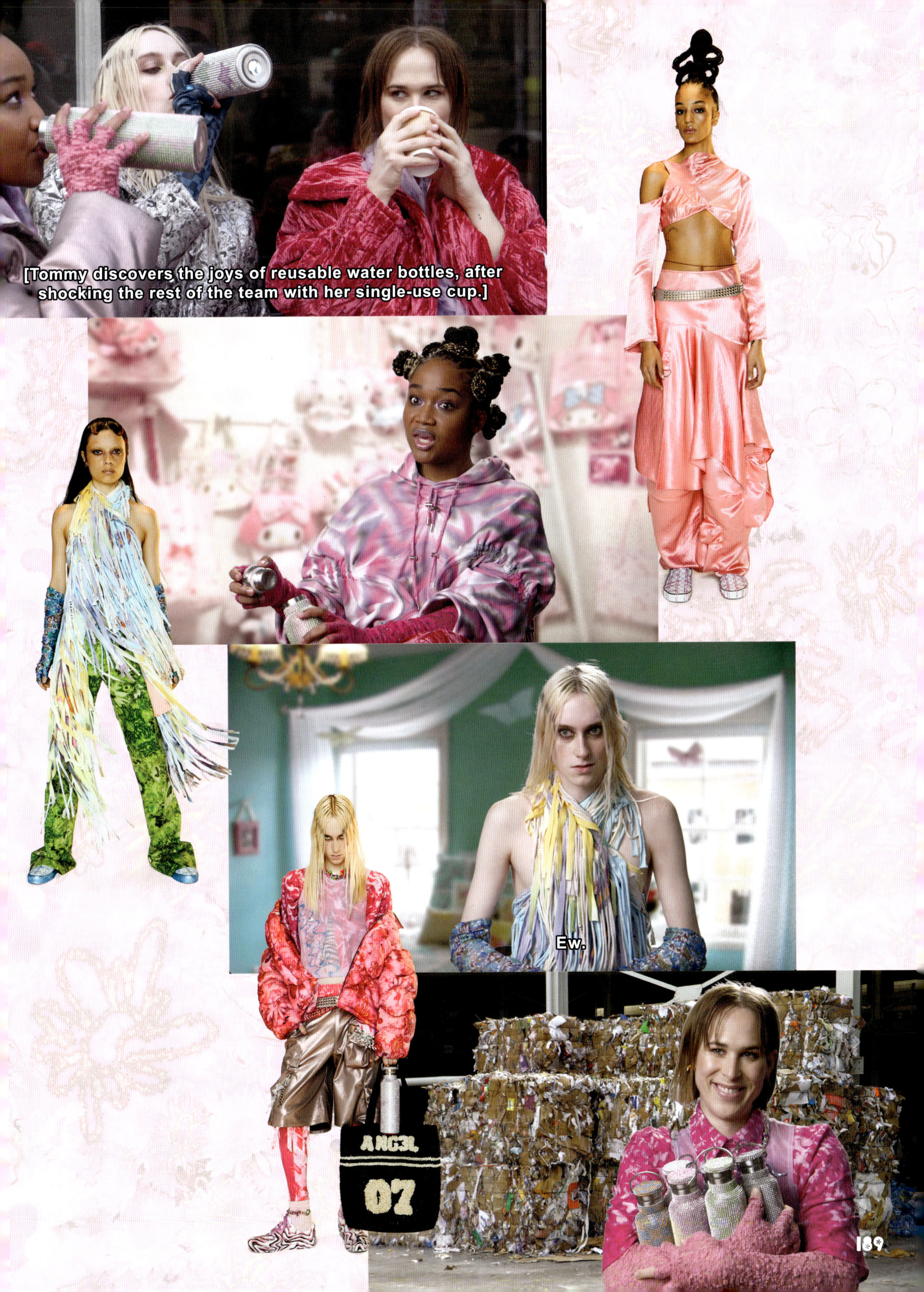
[Tommy discovers the joys of reusable water bottles, after
shocking the rest of the team with her single-use cup.]
Ew.
ANG3L
07

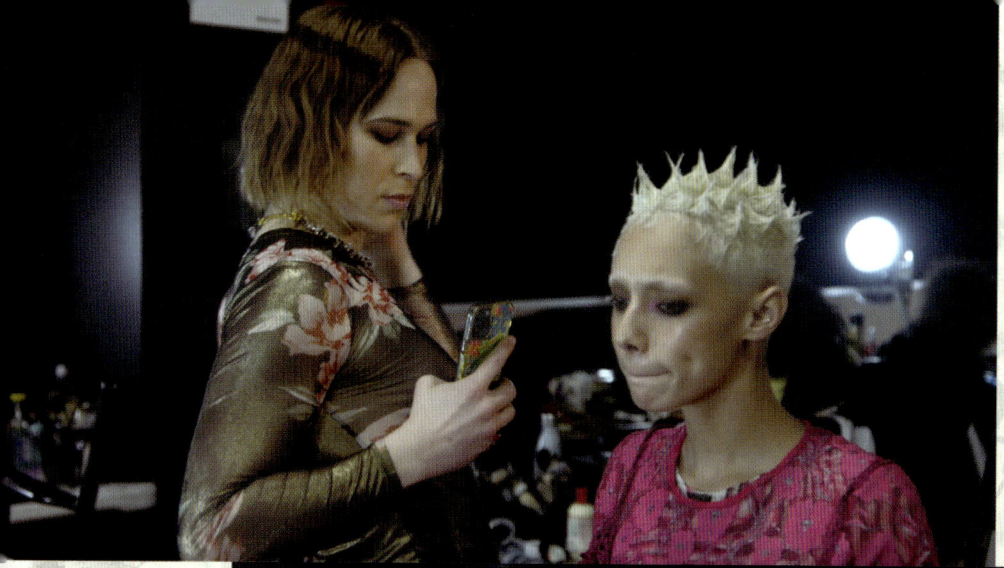

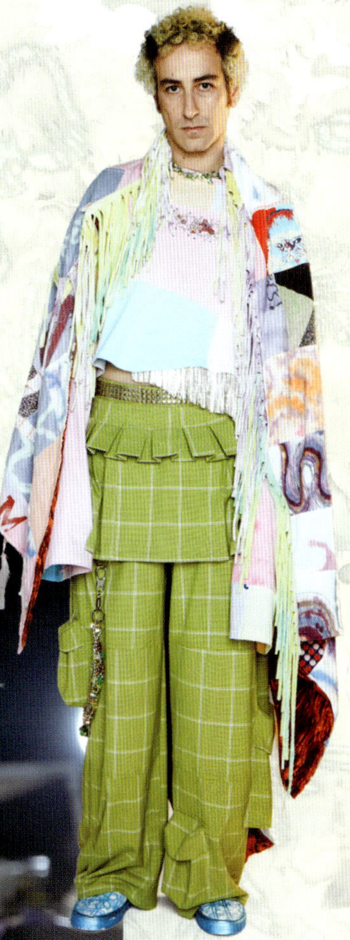

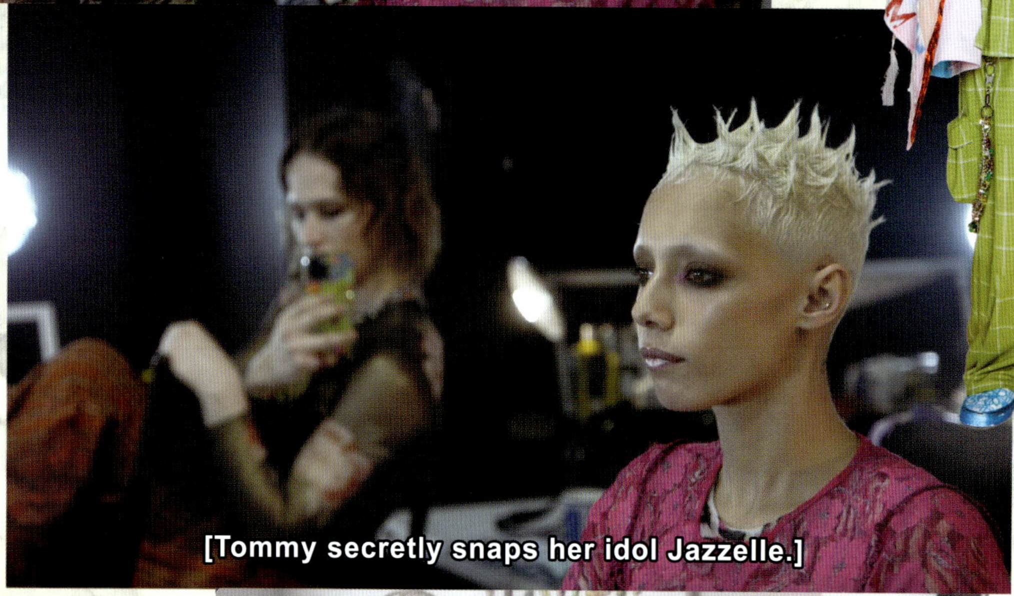
[Tommy secretly snaps her idol Jazzelle.]

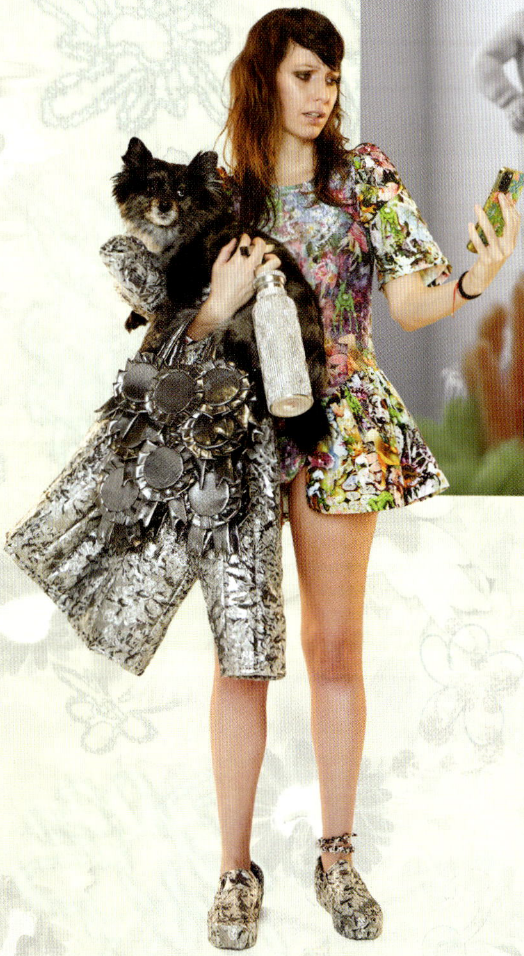

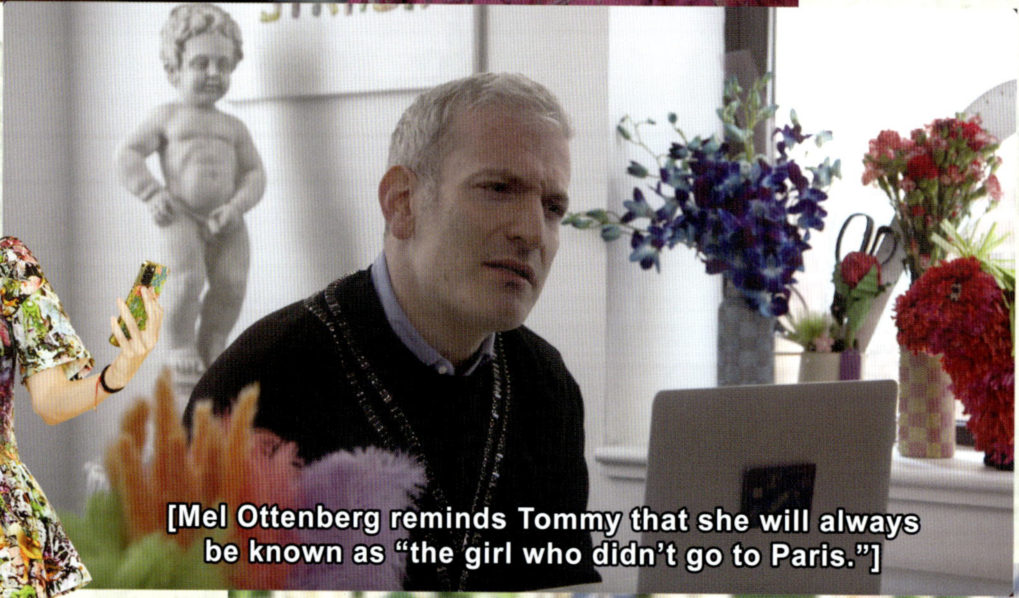
[Mel Ottenberg reminds Tommy that she will always be known as "the girl who didn't go to Paris."]

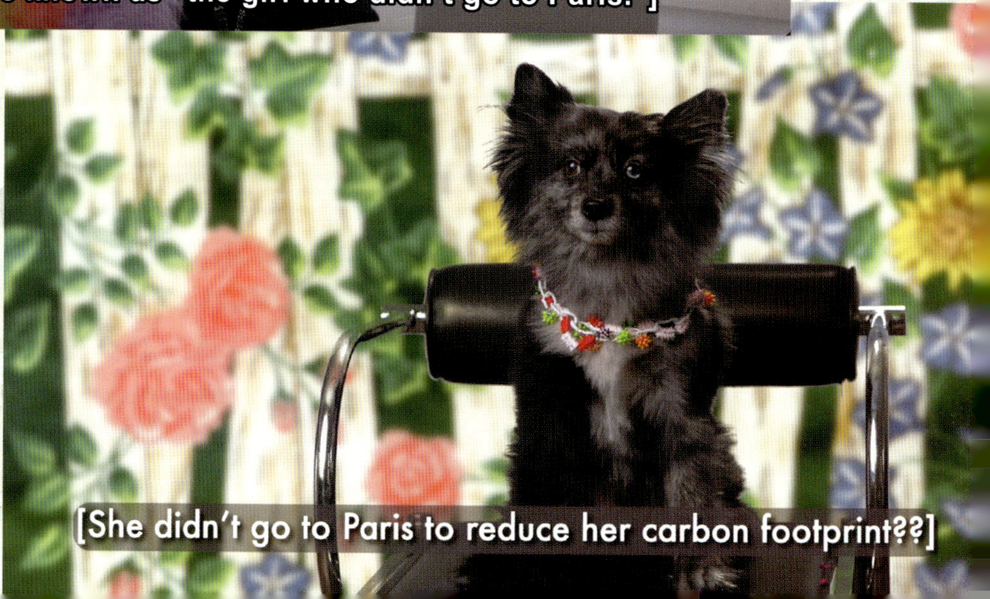
[She didn't go to Paris to reduce her carbon footprint??]

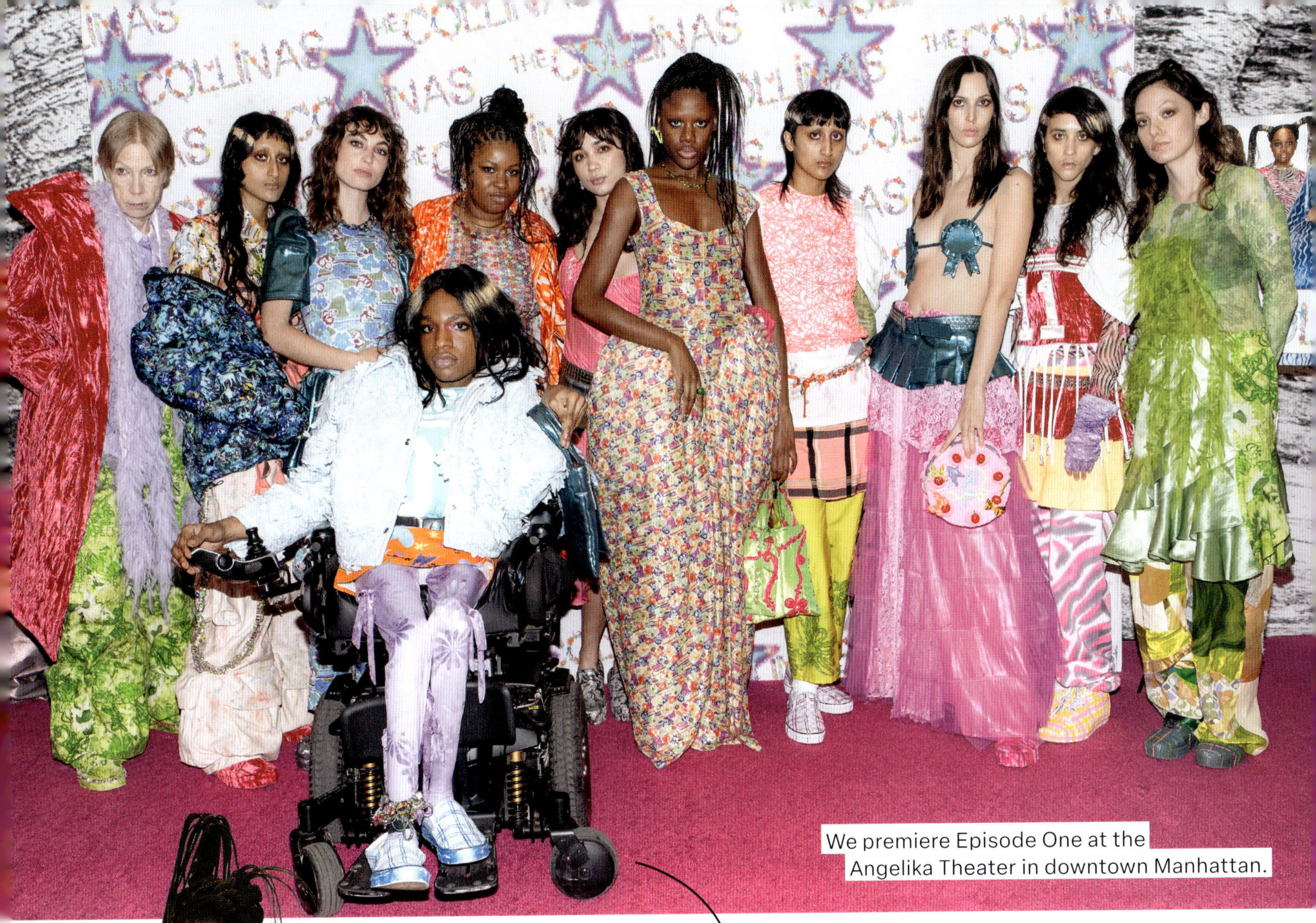

We premiere Episode One at the Angelika Theater in downtown Manhattan.

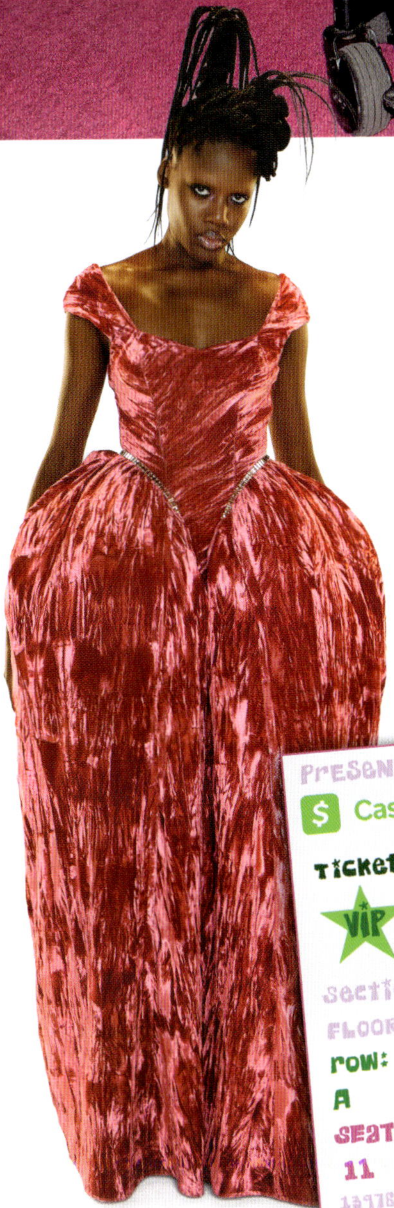

"Collina Strada is doing everything right and always has. The work that Hillary and Charlie have done in such a short time has gone so far and has made such an impact through the fashion industry. They bring it, and they bring something new to the table. They understand that it is indeed imaginative, beautiful & fashionable to include every type of body and person in their vision for each collection. Working with them has been some of the most lovely and powerful moments of my life."

-Aaron Rose Philip

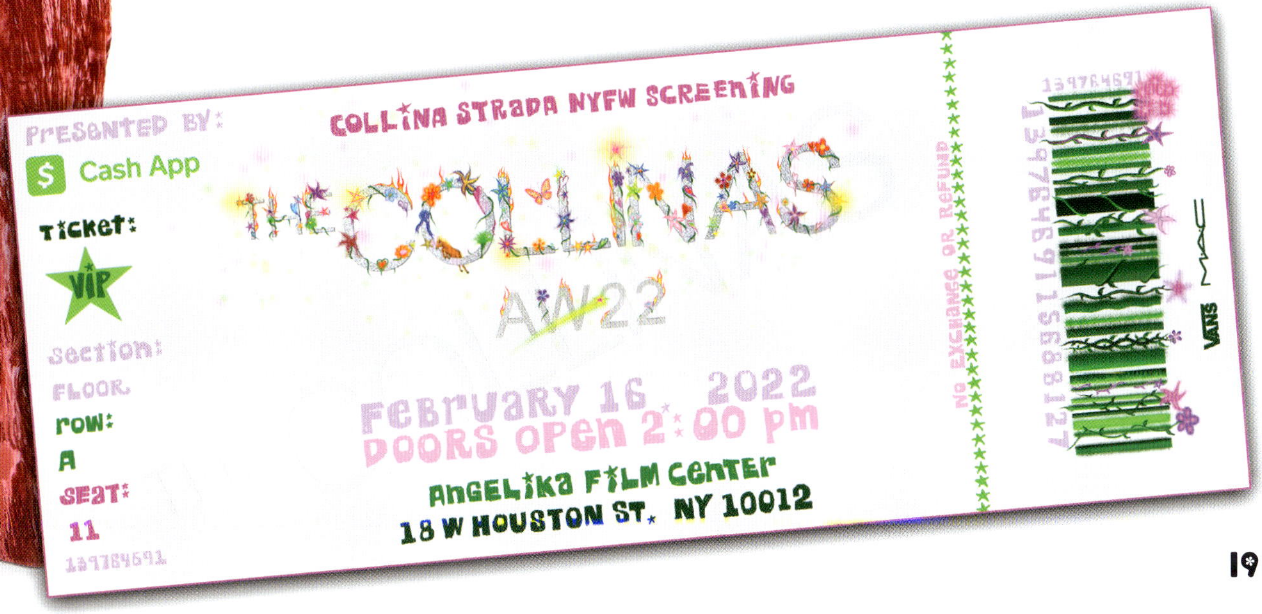

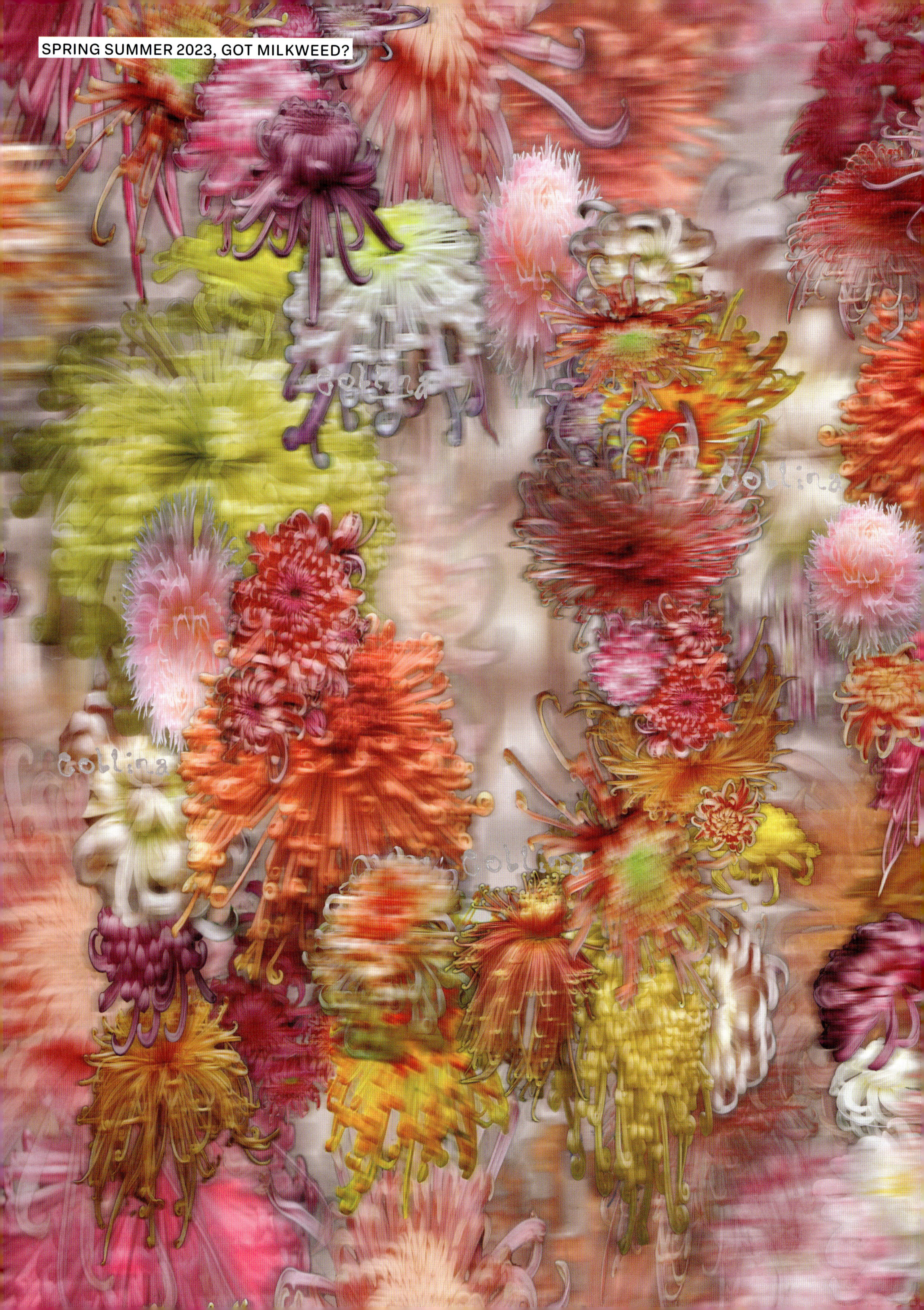

SPRING SUMMER 2023, GOT MILKWEED?

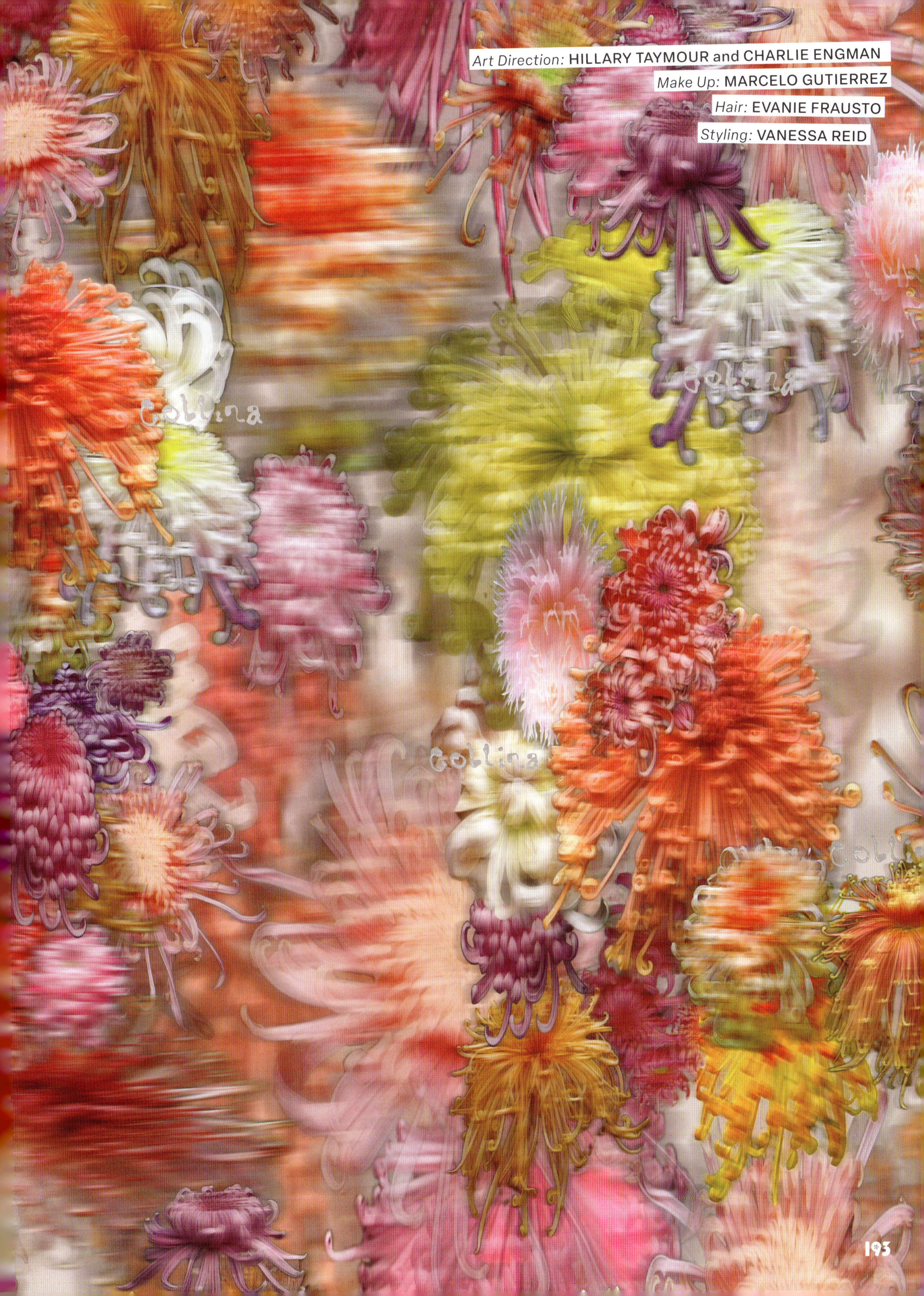

Art Direction: HILLARY TAYMOUR and CHARLIE ENGMAN
Make Up: MARCELO GUTIERREZ
Hair: EVANIE FRAUSTO
Styling: VANESSA REID

got milkweed?

Spring Summer 23

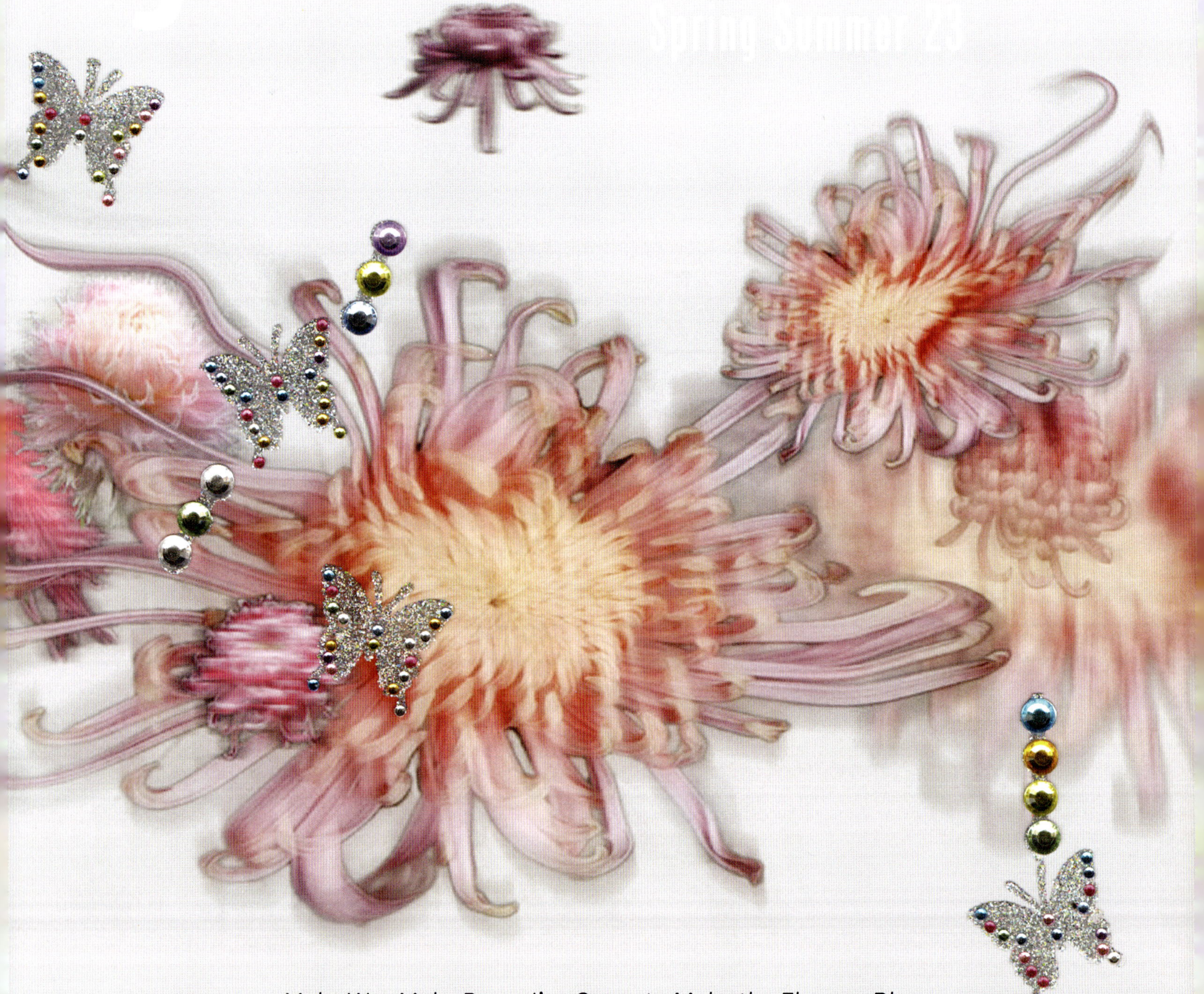

Make Way Make Room I've Come to Make the Flowers Bloom

We based this collection on the butterfly's symbolic cycle of life, death, and rebirth, and its role in fueling the world's plants, including those we turn into fabric. Our runway was the Naval Cemetery Landscape, a former cemetery-cum-butterfly-habitat and a part of the *Brooklyn Greenway,* overflowing with local, intentional flora—like milkweed, *the only plant monarch butterfly caterpillars will eat*—in an effort to bring pollinators back to NYC. The looks took us from kooky caterpillar era to full 'fly glow-up, as the collection embraced the fact that we are in that mysterious, gooey, in-between stage in our journey to do better by *Mommy Earth.*

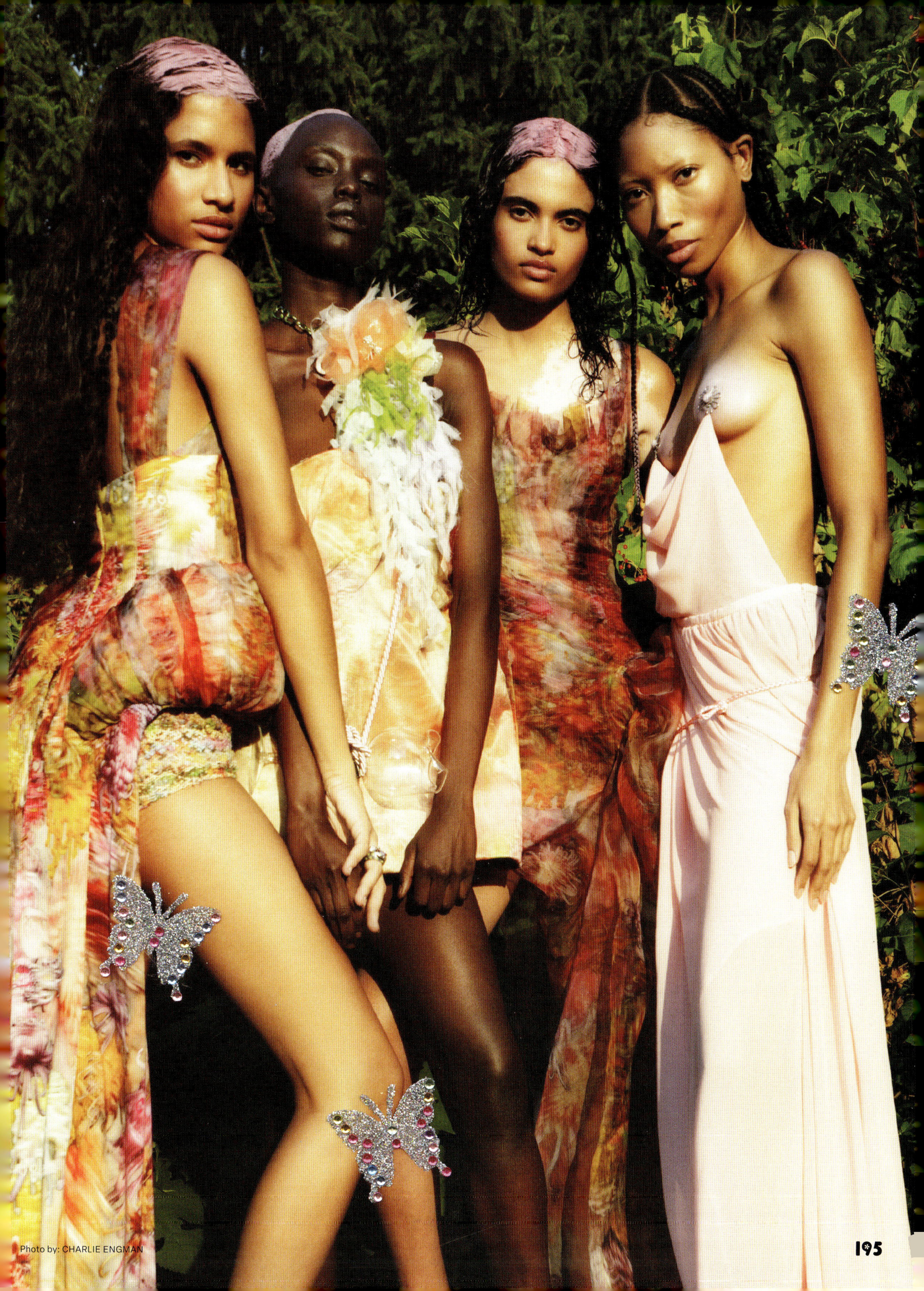

Photo by: CHARLIE ENGMAN

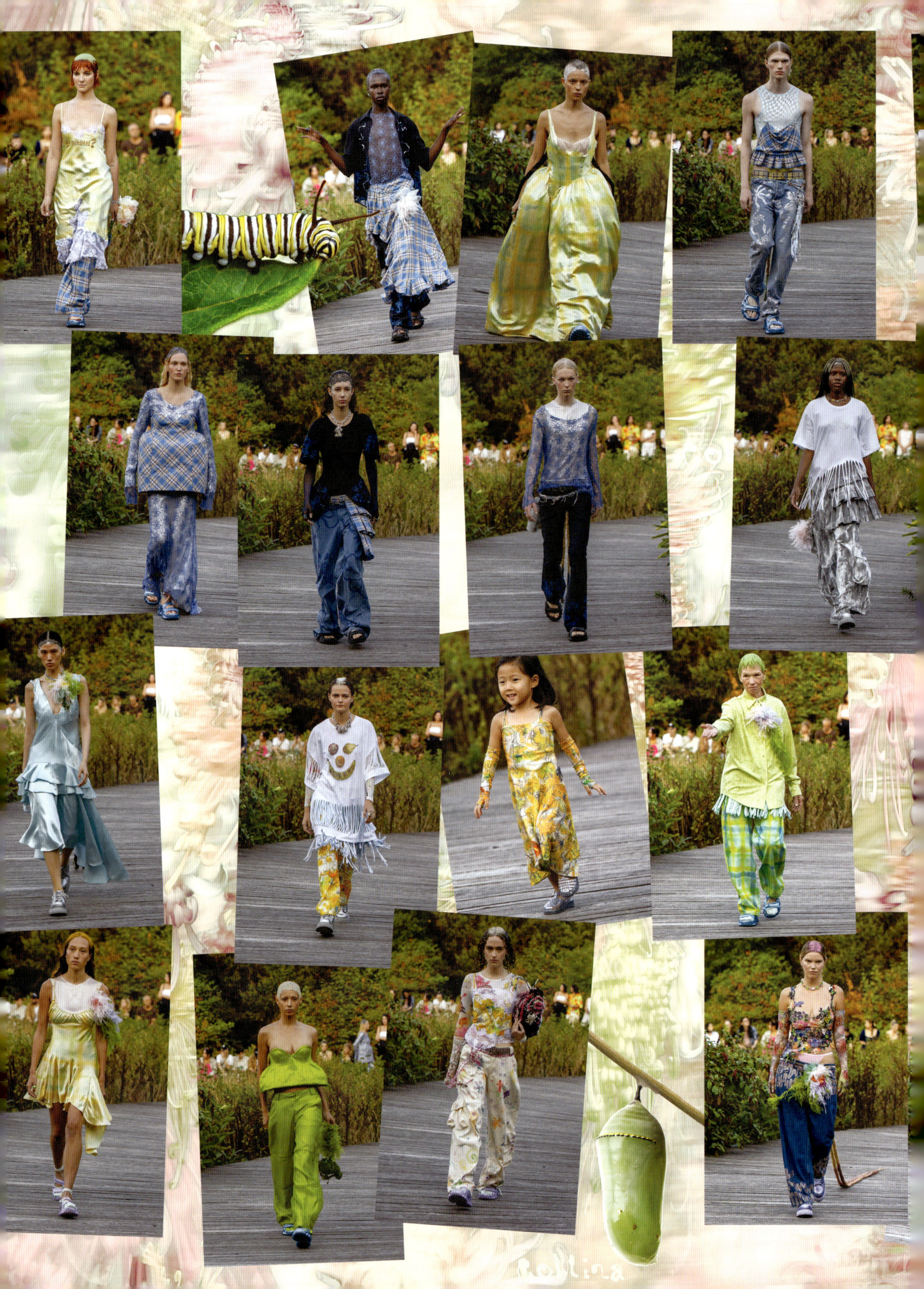

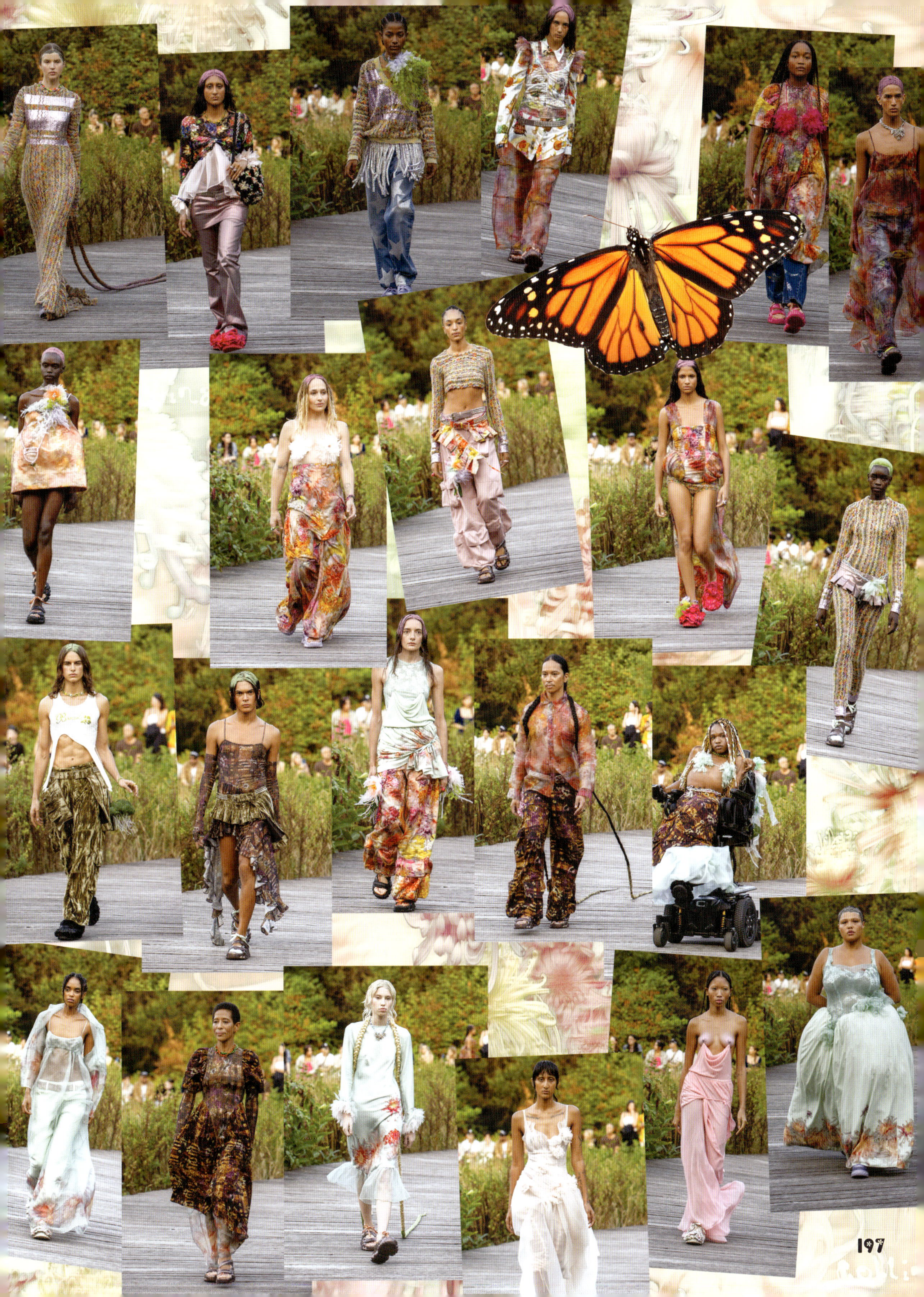

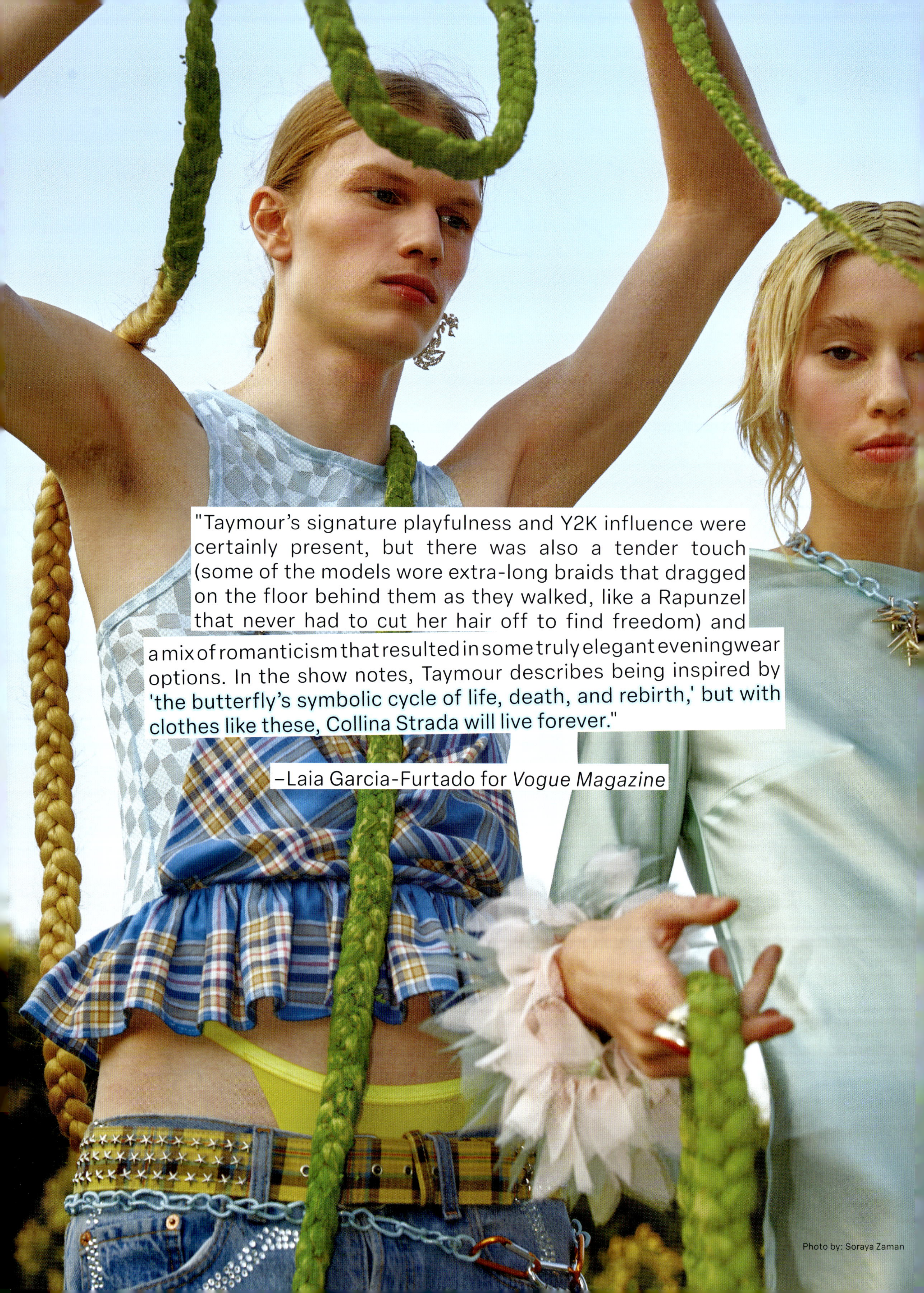

"Taymour's signature playfulness and Y2K influence were certainly present, but there was also a tender touch (some of the models wore extra-long braids that dragged on the floor behind them as they walked, like a Rapunzel that never had to cut her hair off to find freedom) and a mix of romanticism that resulted in some truly elegant eveningwear options. In the show notes, Taymour describes being inspired by 'the butterfly's symbolic cycle of life, death, and rebirth,' but with clothes like these, Collina Strada will live forever."

–Laia Garcia-Furtado for *Vogue Magazine*

Photo by: Soraya Zaman

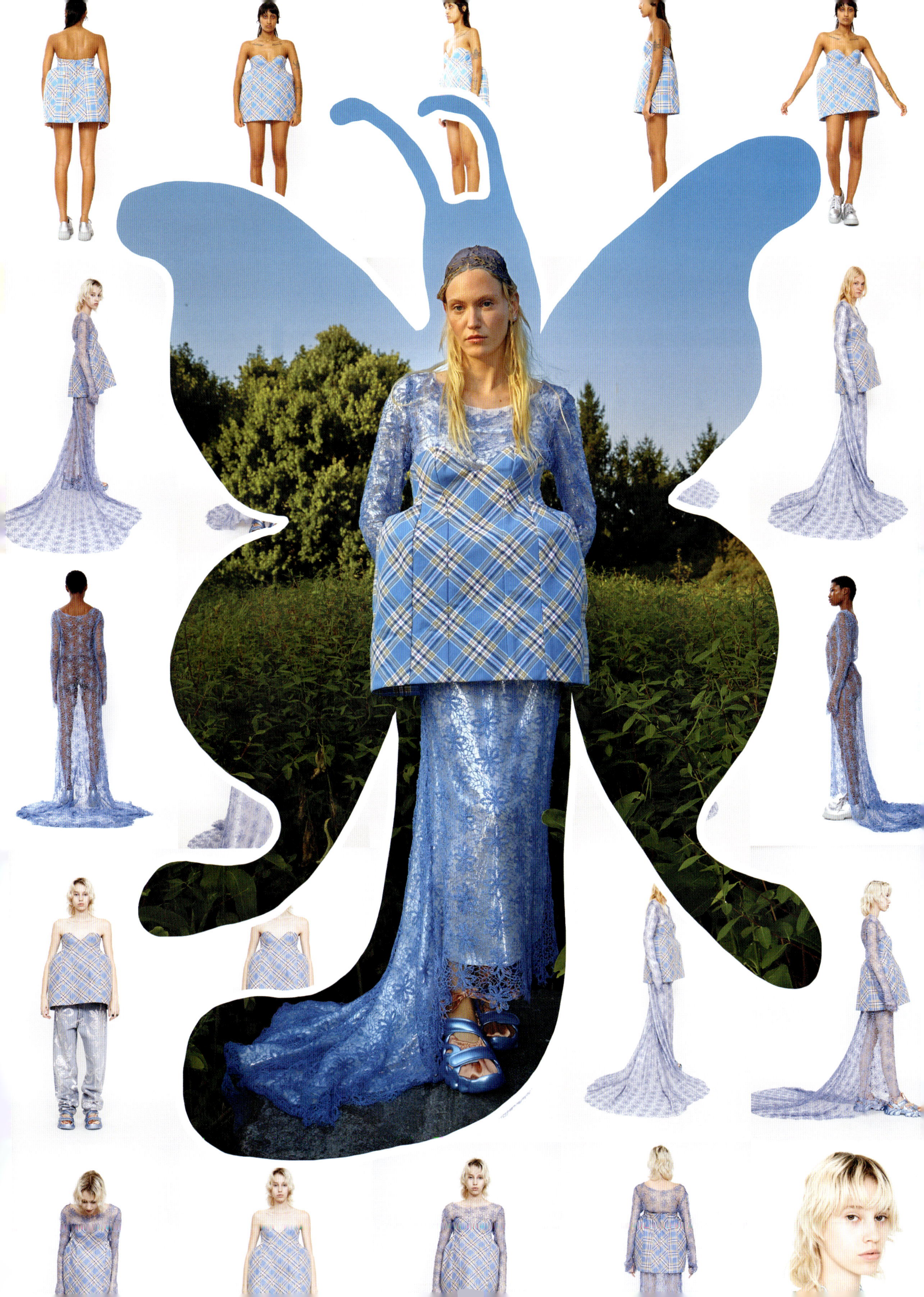

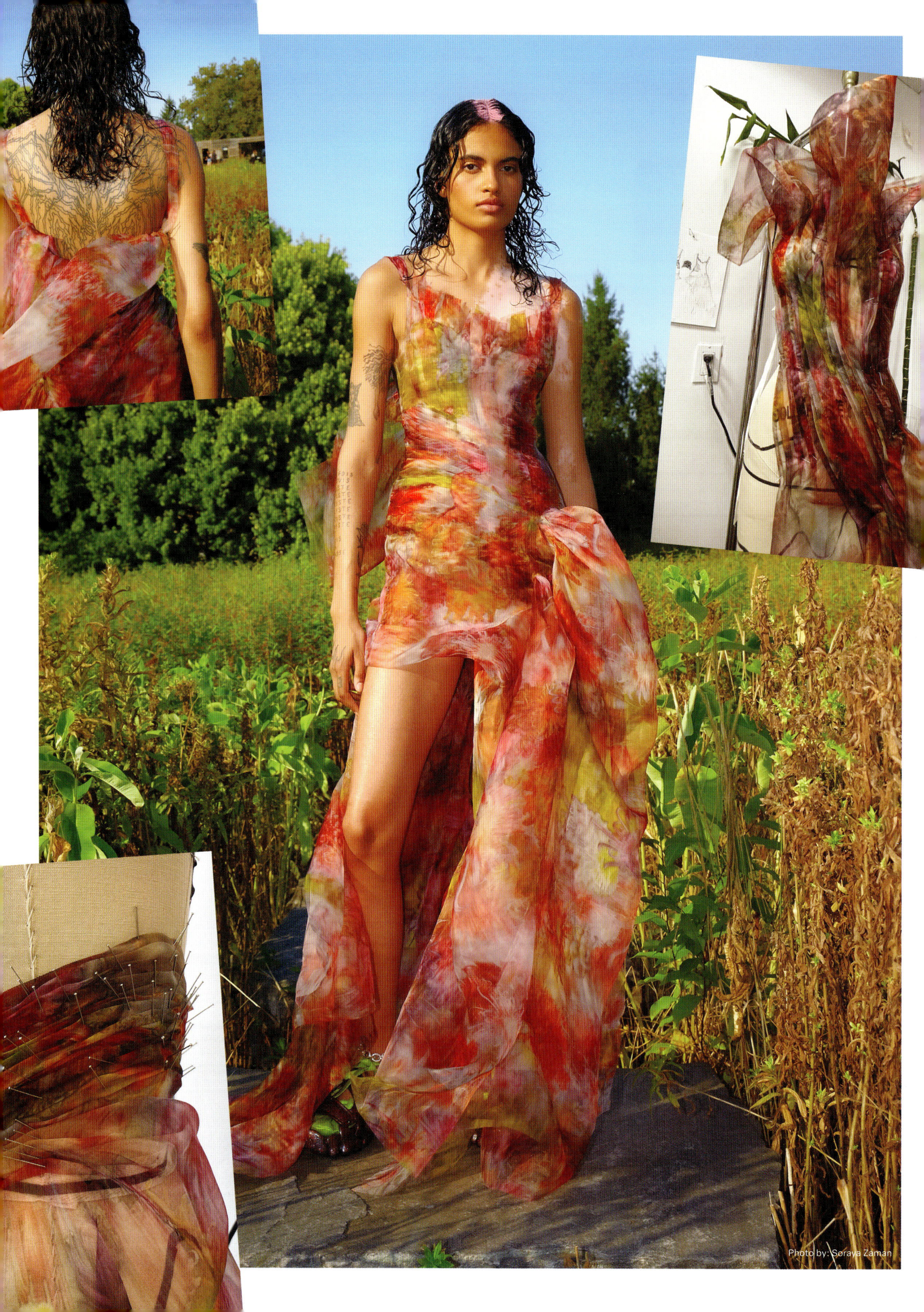

Photo by: Soraya Zaman

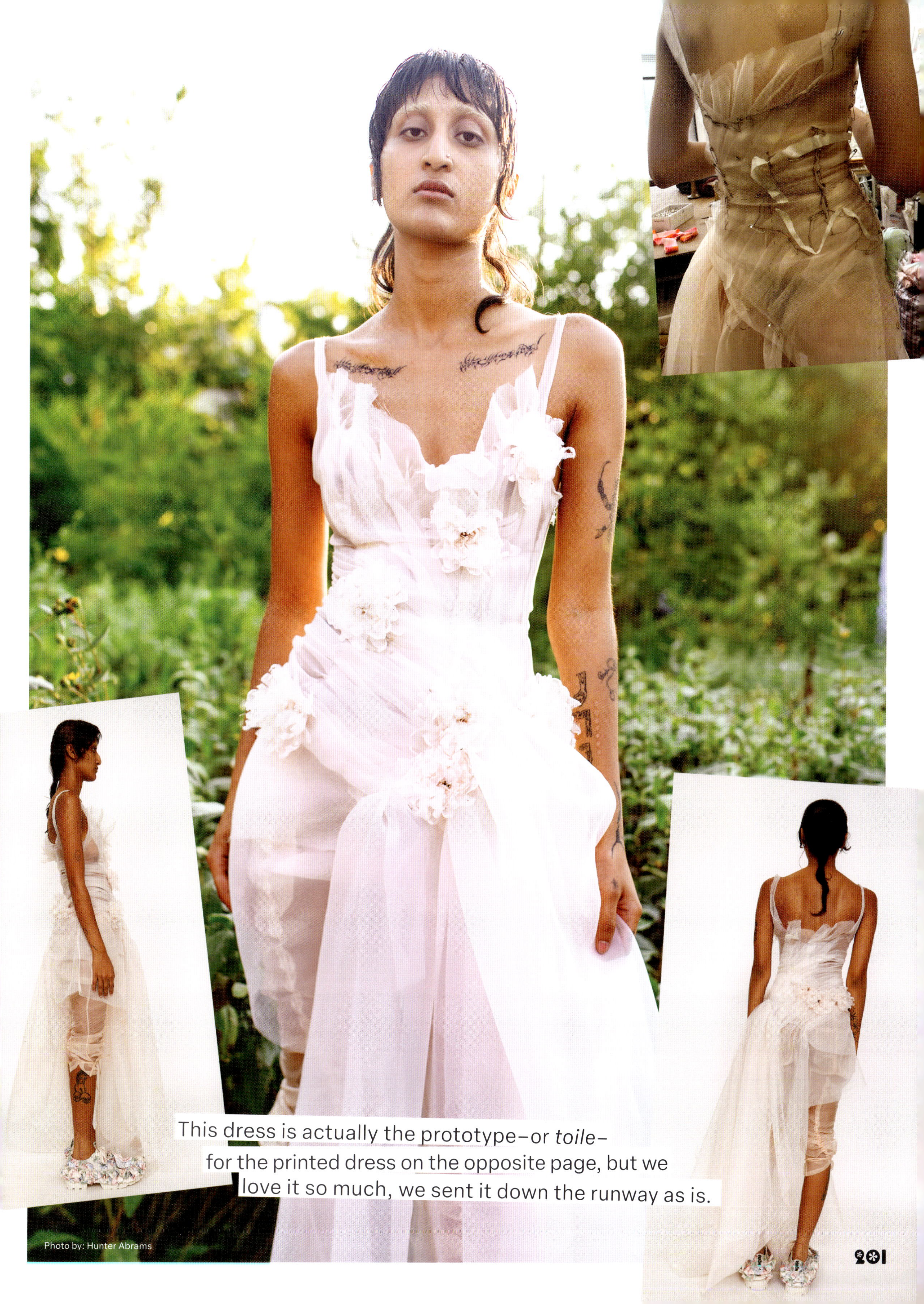

This dress is actually the prototype—or *toile*—
for the printed dress on the opposite page, but we
love it so much, we sent it down the runway as is.

Photo by: Hunter Abrams

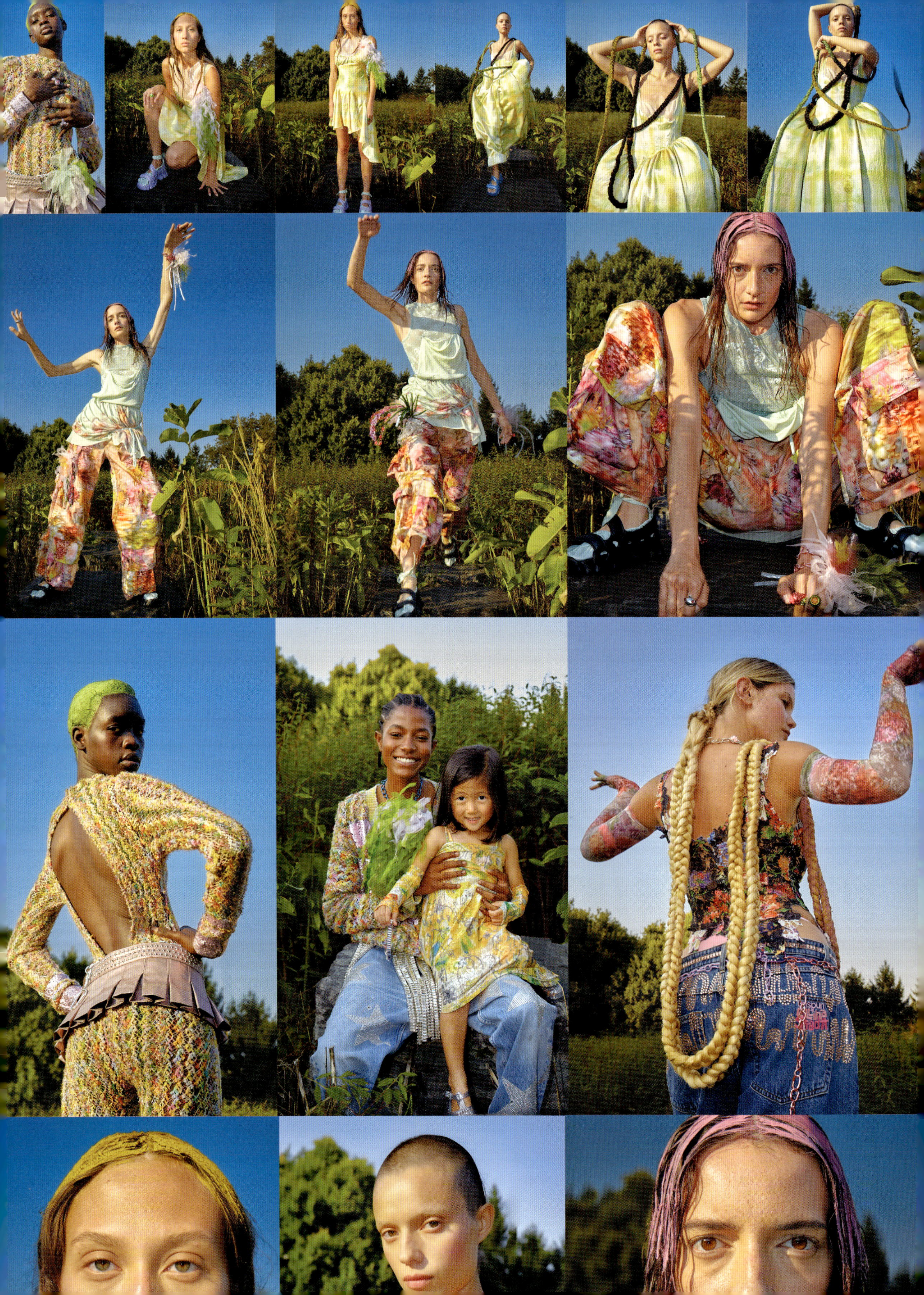

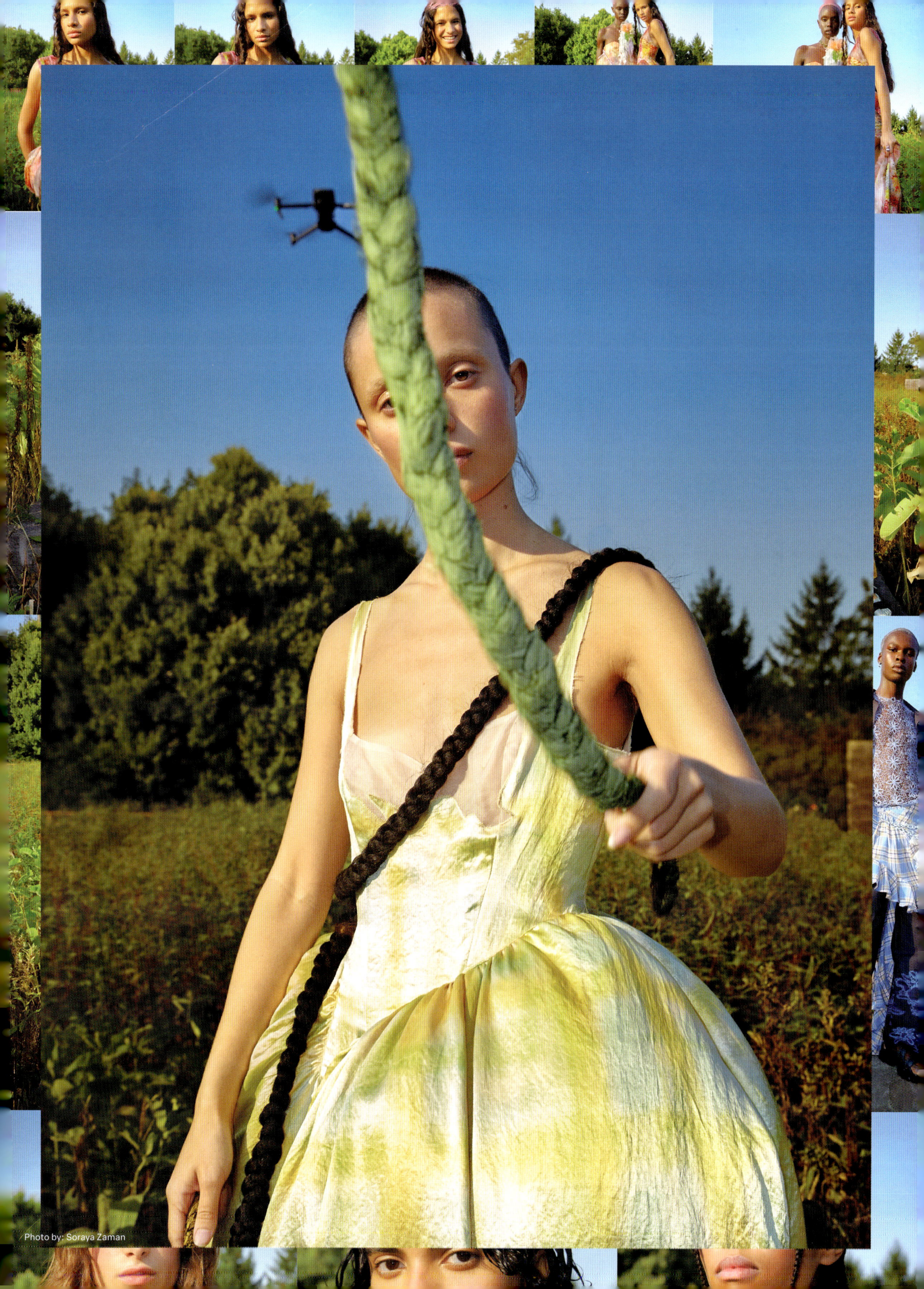

Photo by: Soraya Zaman

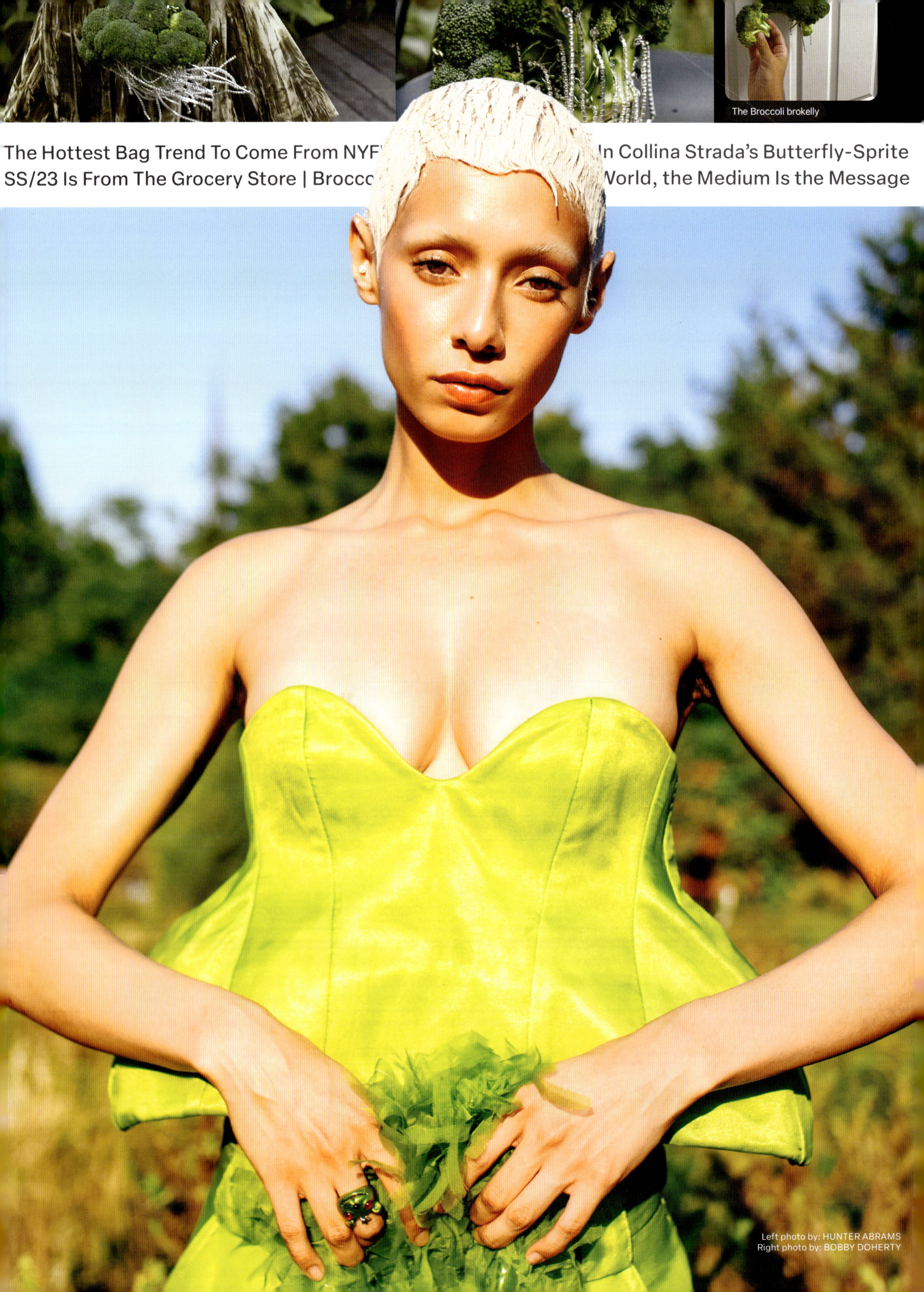

Left photo by: HUNTER ABRAMS
Right photo by: BOBBY DOHERTY

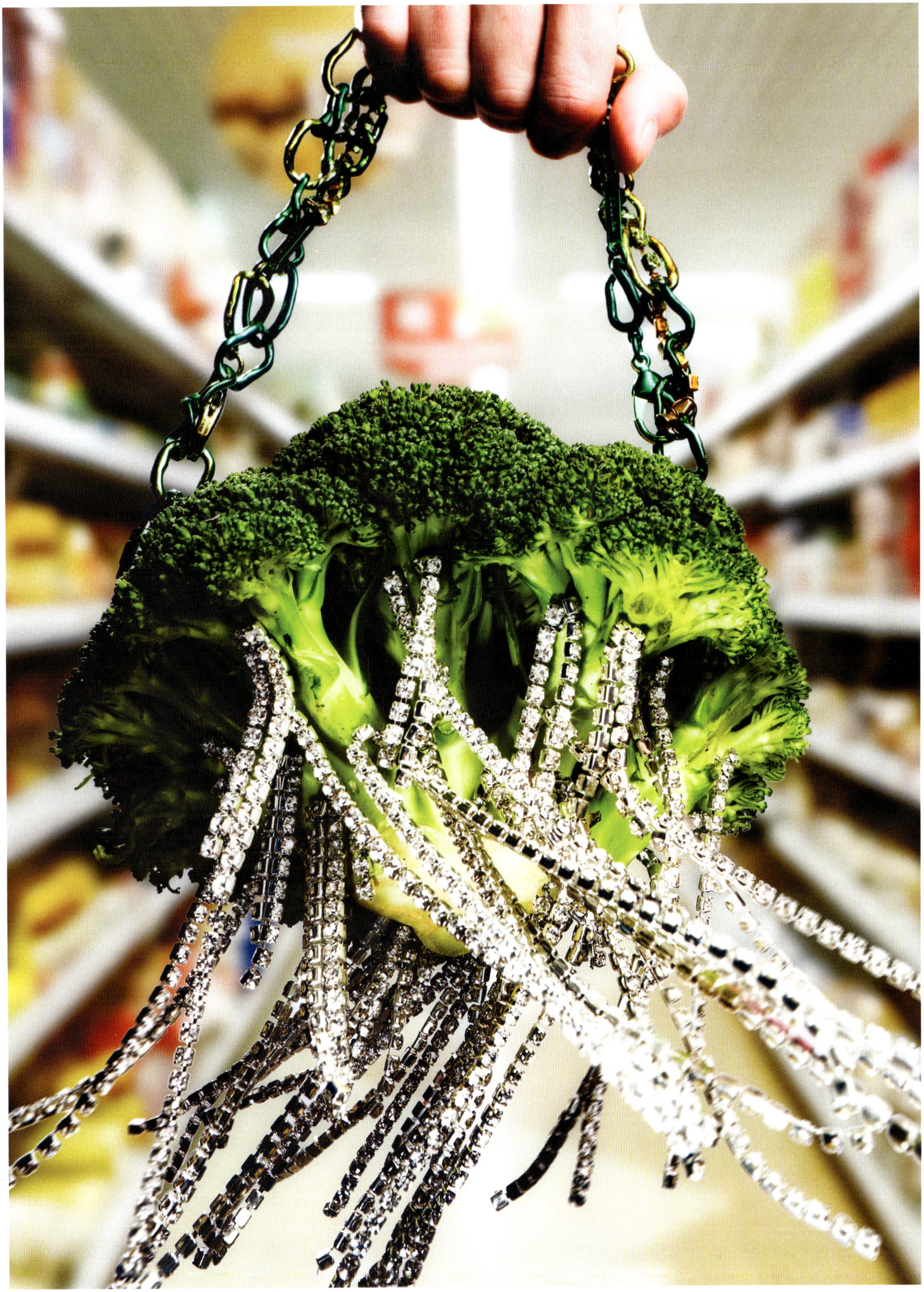

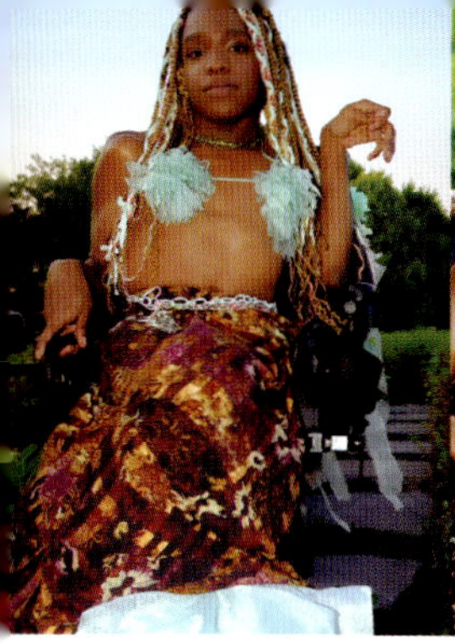
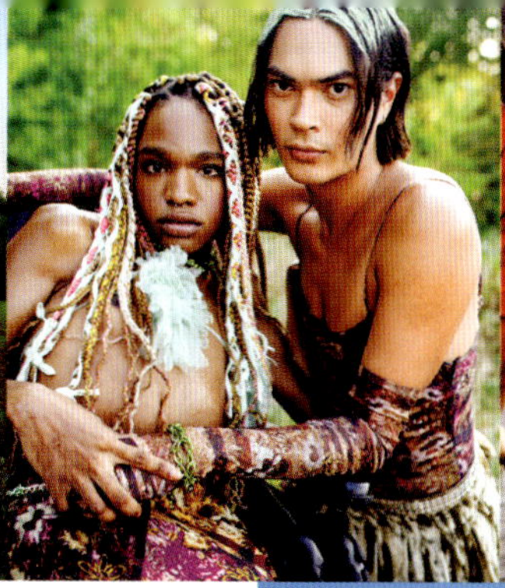
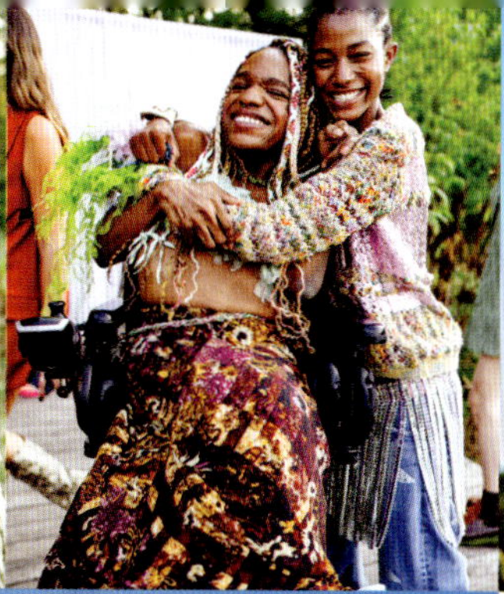
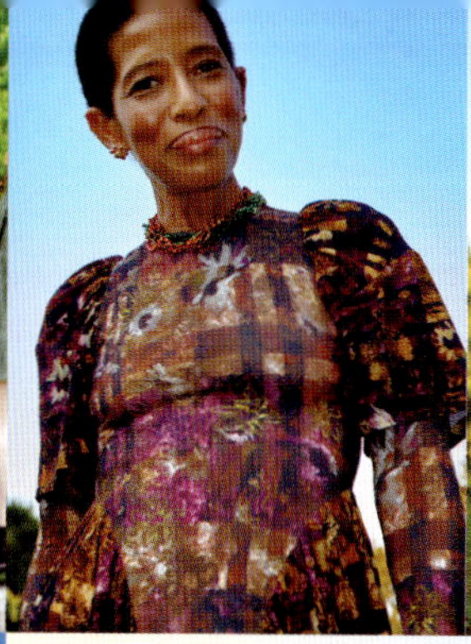
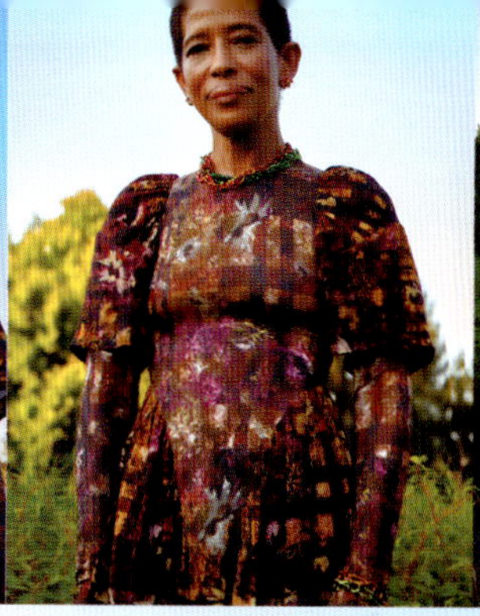
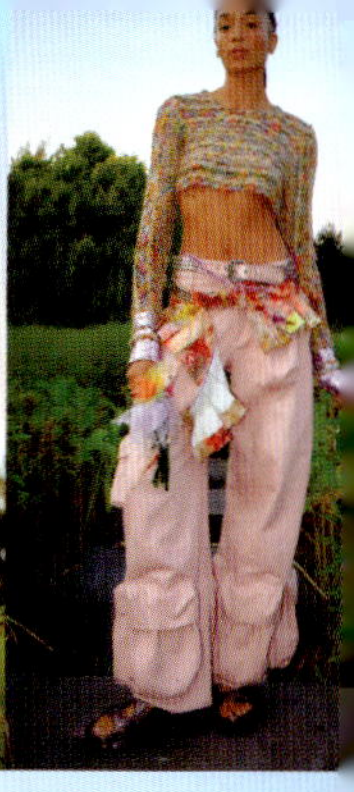
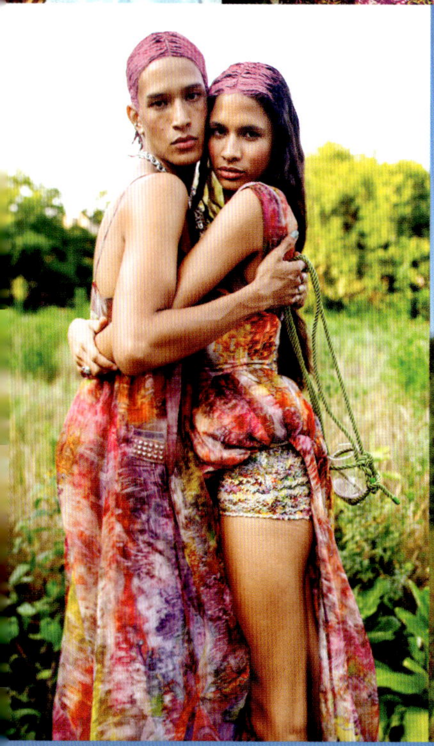
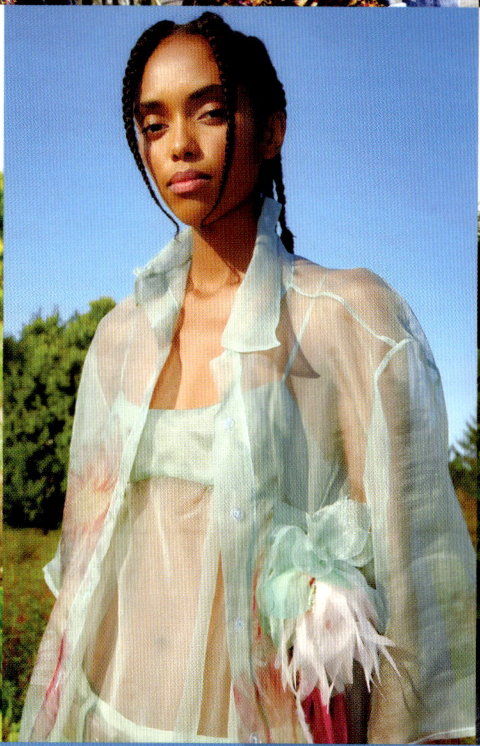
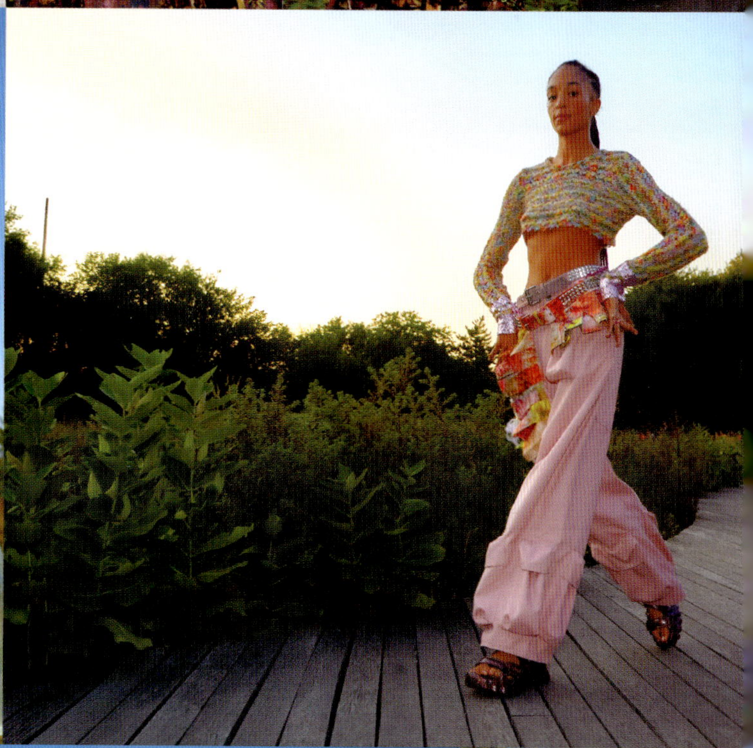
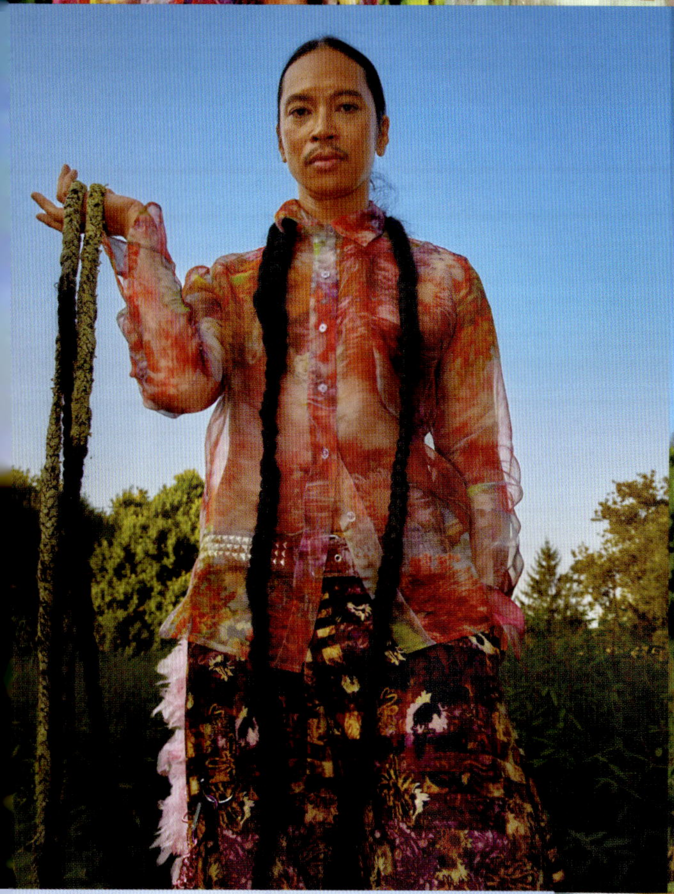
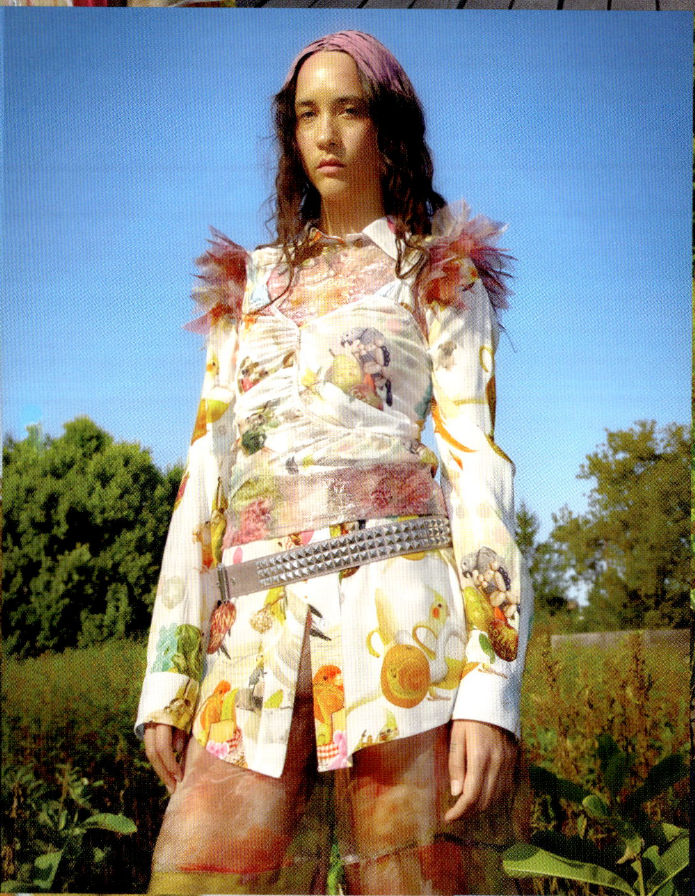
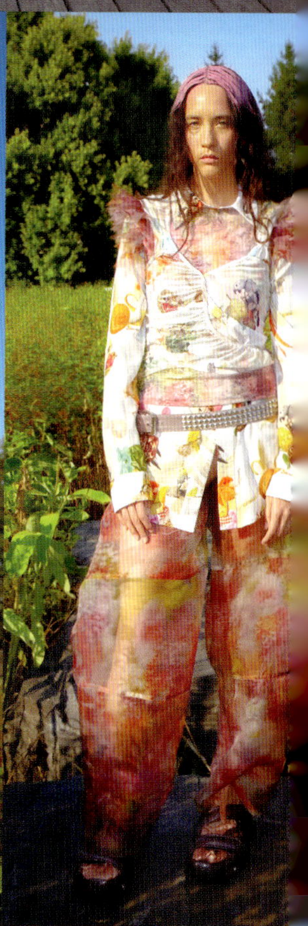
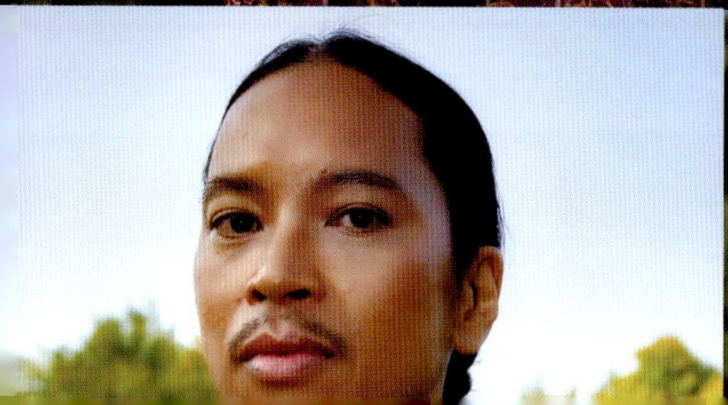
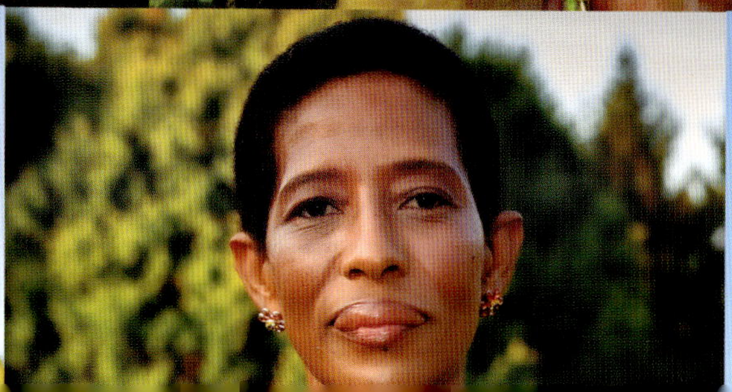
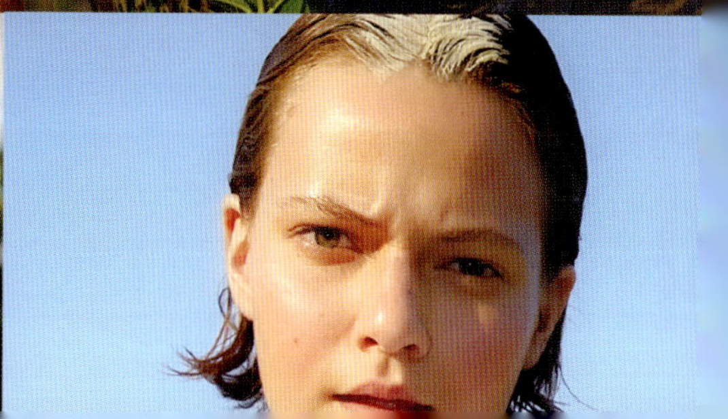

"In the work of designers like Hillary Taymour of Collina Strada, whose earth-first collection of ginormous flower-power cargo pants, shrunken T-shirts, and deconstructed court dress (panniers, corsets, trains) recycles and remixes not just materials but also historical moments and even vegetables (broccoli purse, anyone?) and seems increasingly prescient rather than fringe."

–Vanessa Friedman for *The New York Times*

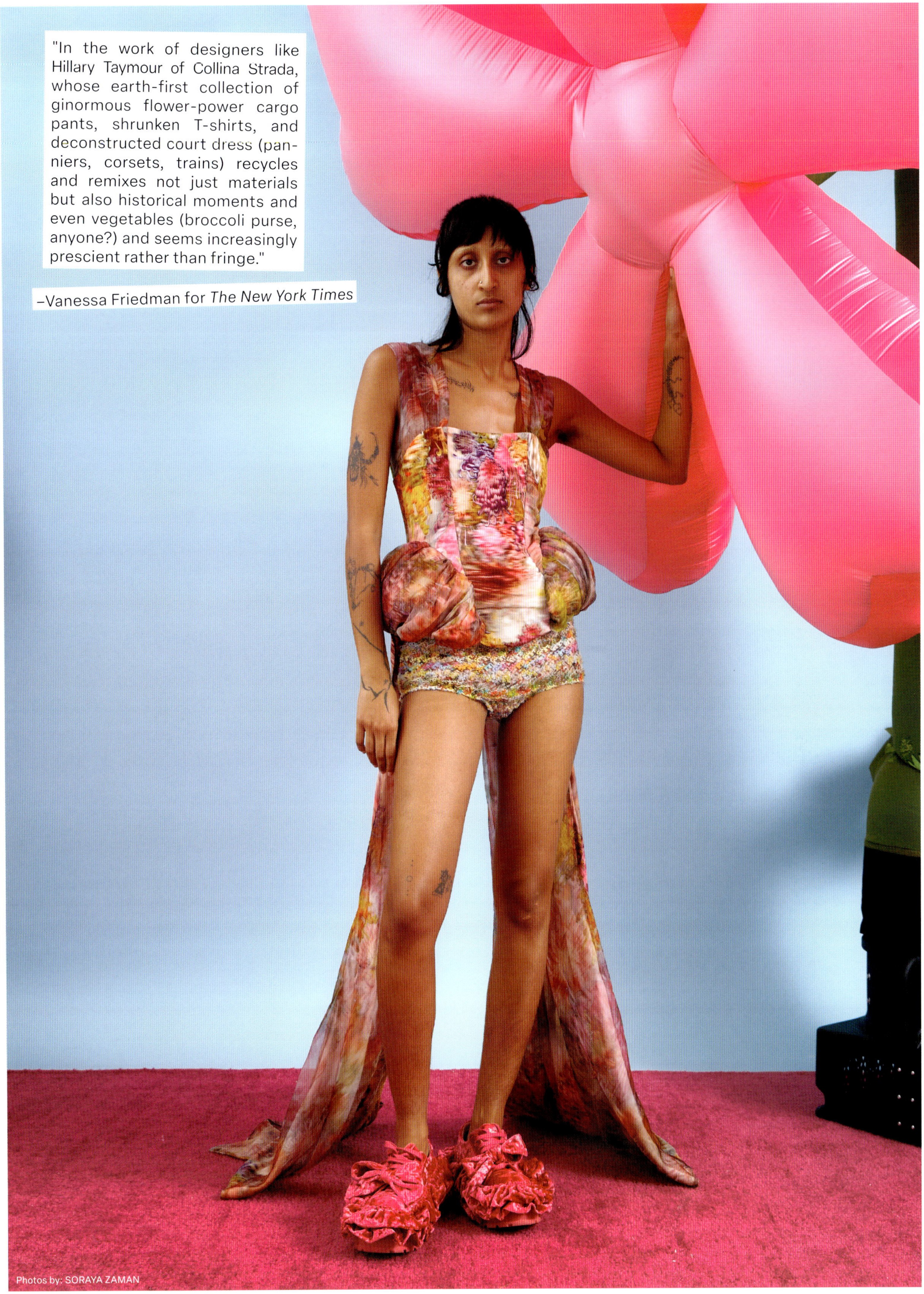

Photos by: SORAYA ZAMAN

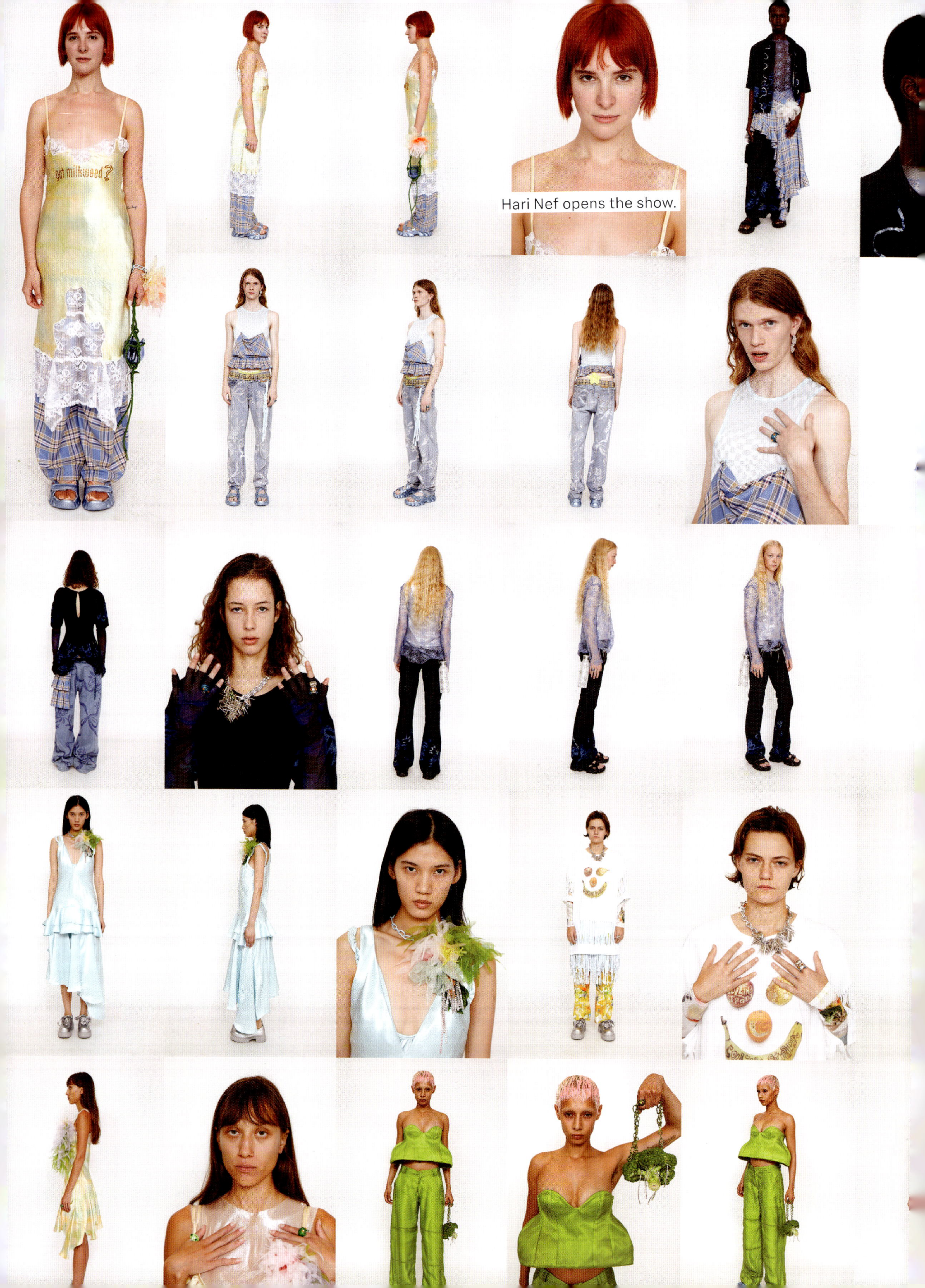

Hari Nef opens the show.

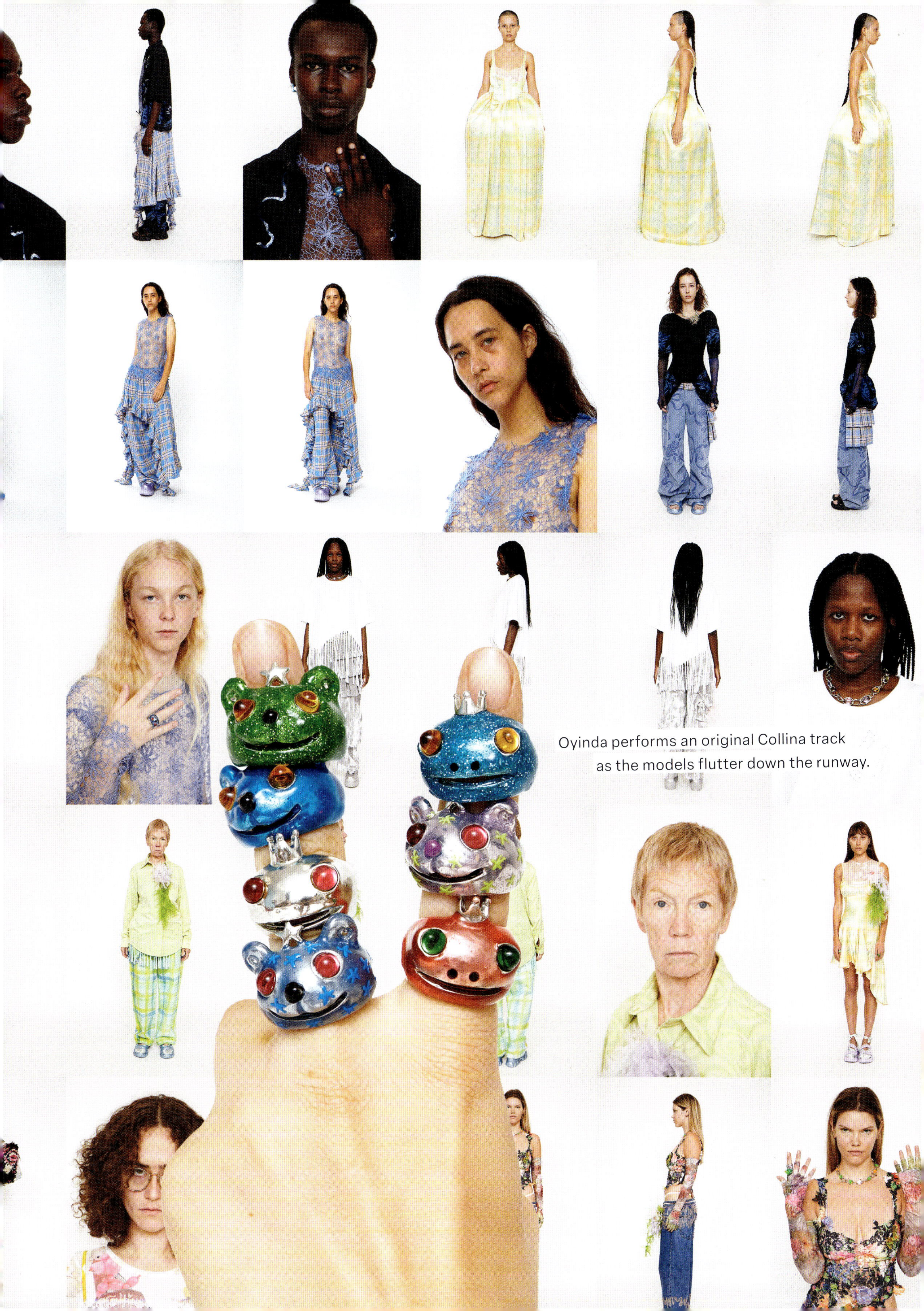

Oyinda performs an original Collina track as the models flutter down the runway.

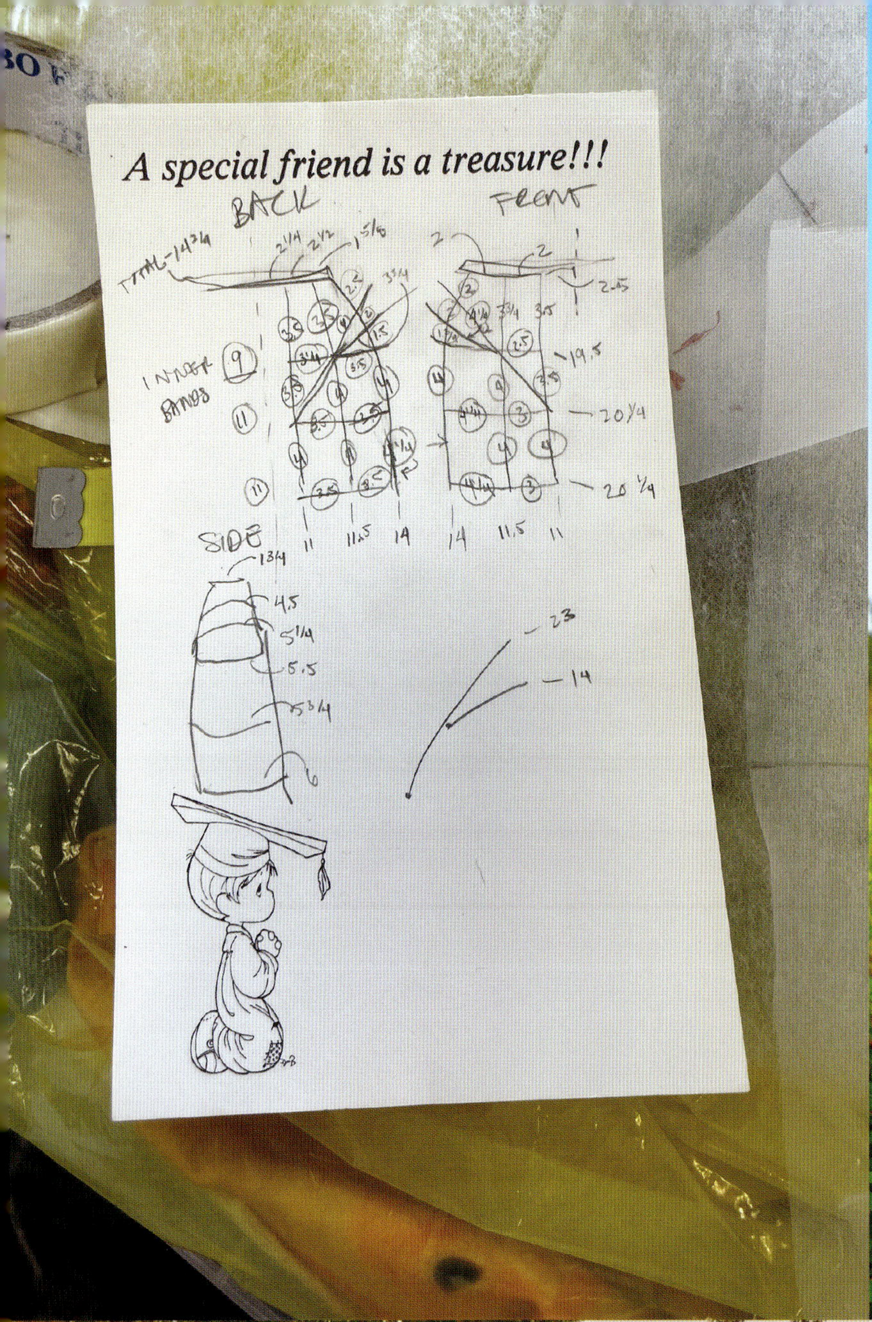

A special friend is a treasure!!!
BACK
FRONT
SIDE

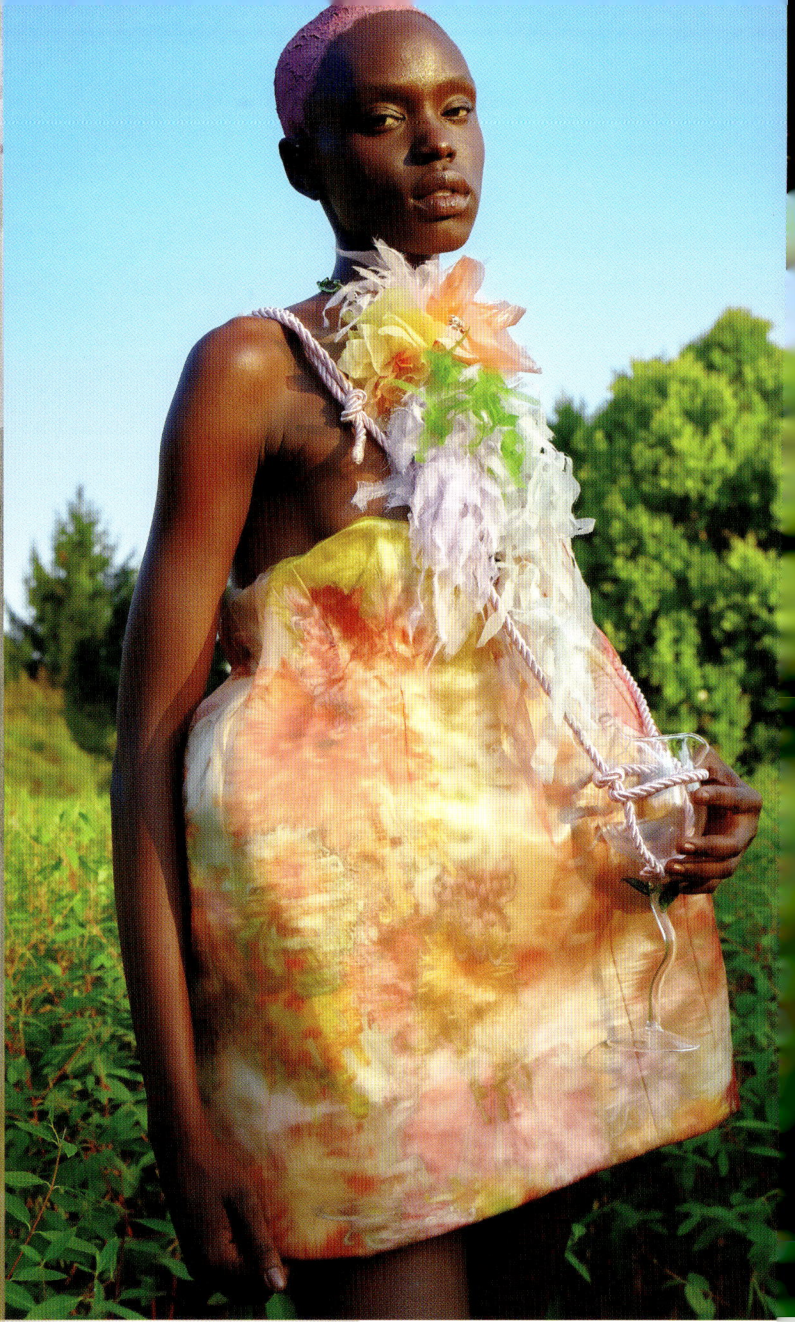

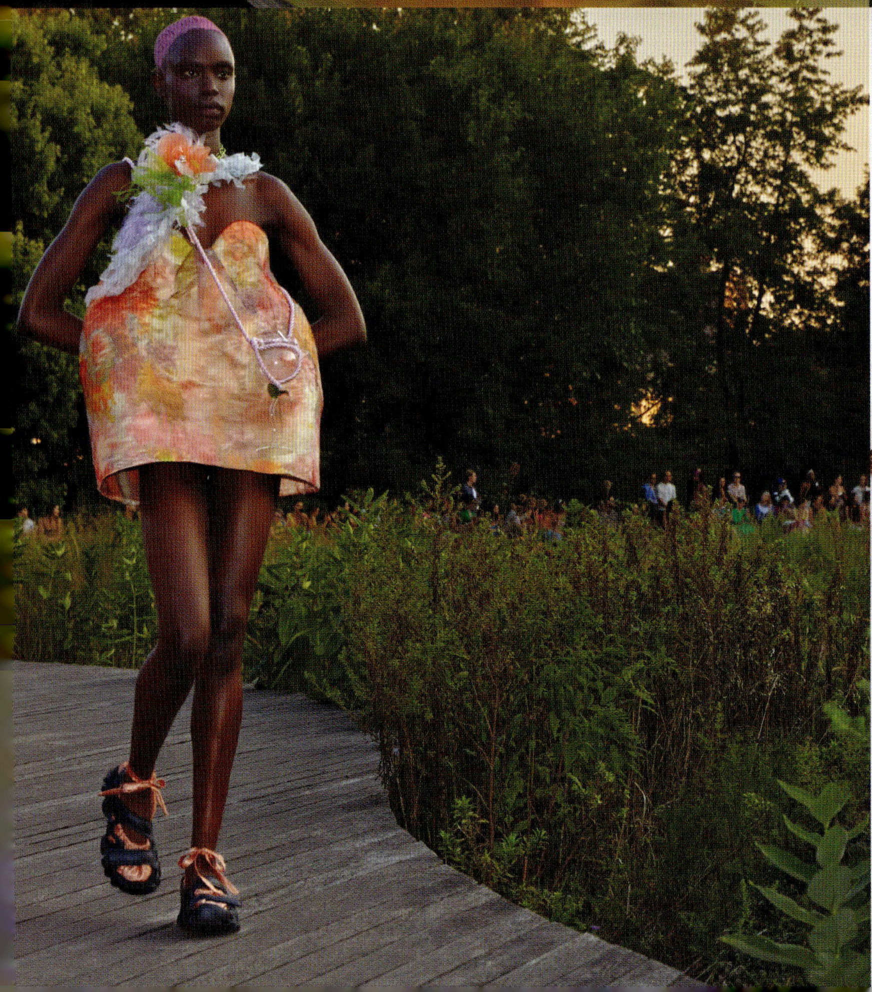

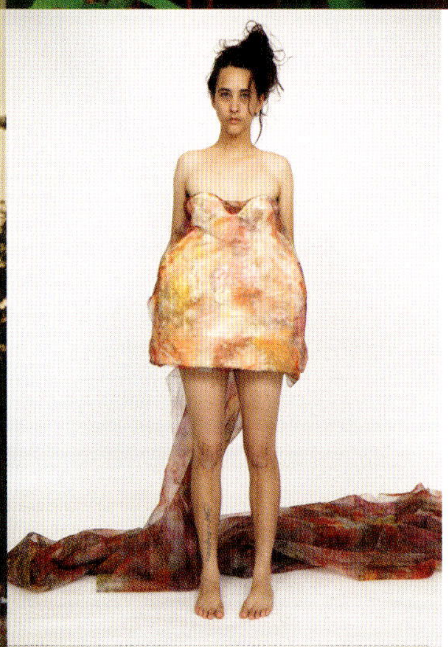

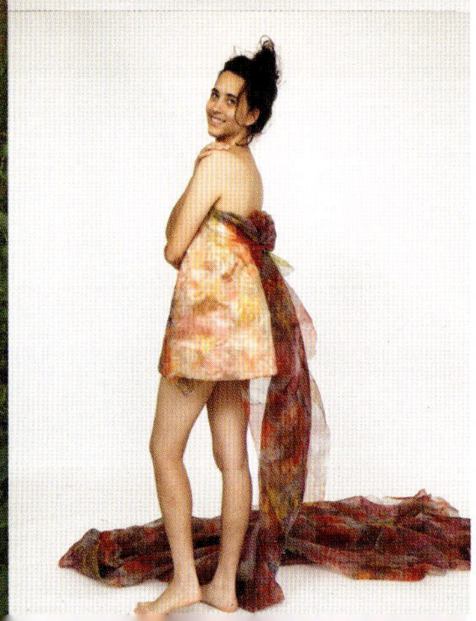

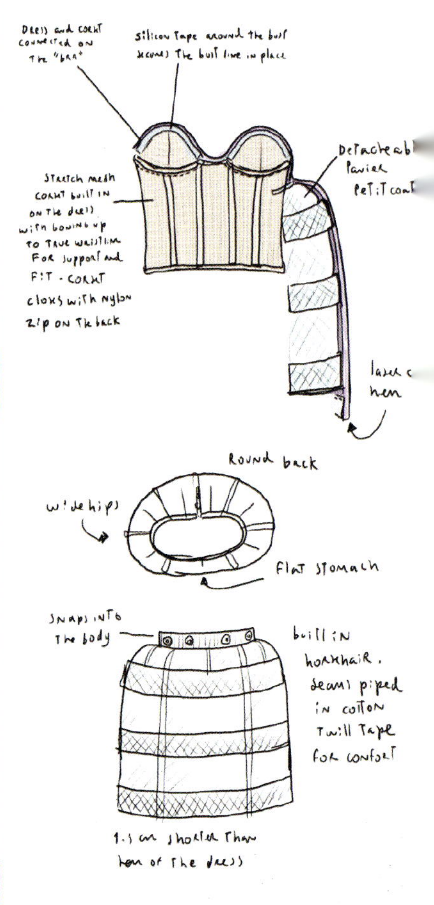

Dress and corset connected on the "bra"
Silicon tape around the bust secures the bust line in place
Stretch mesh corset built in on the dress with boning up to true waistline for support and fit - corset closes with nylon zip on the back
Detacheabl
Panier
Petit cont
laser c
hem
Round back
wide hips
Flat stomach
Snaps into the body
built in horsehair. Seams piped in cotton twill tape for confort
1.5 cm shorter than hem of the dress

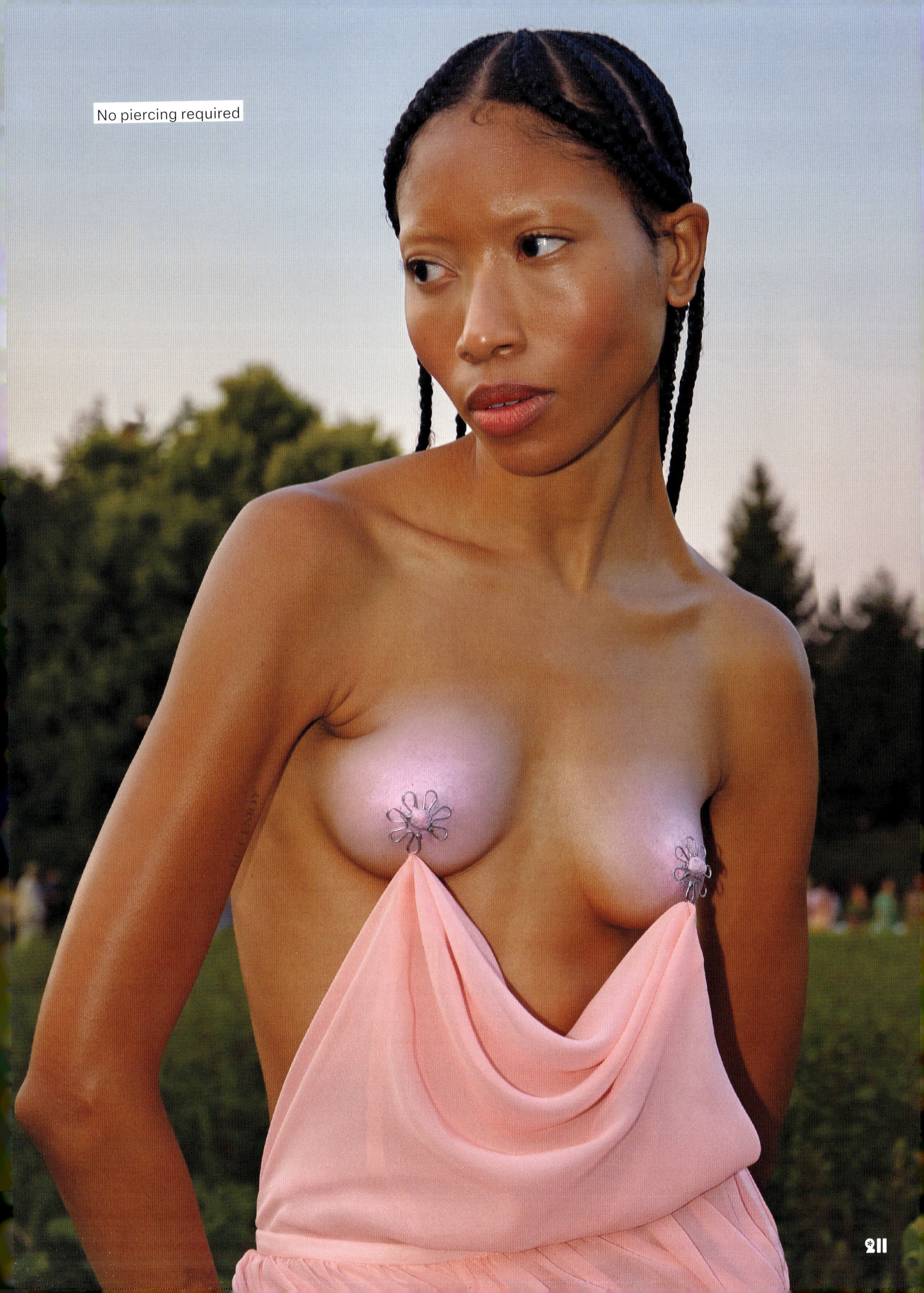

No piercing required

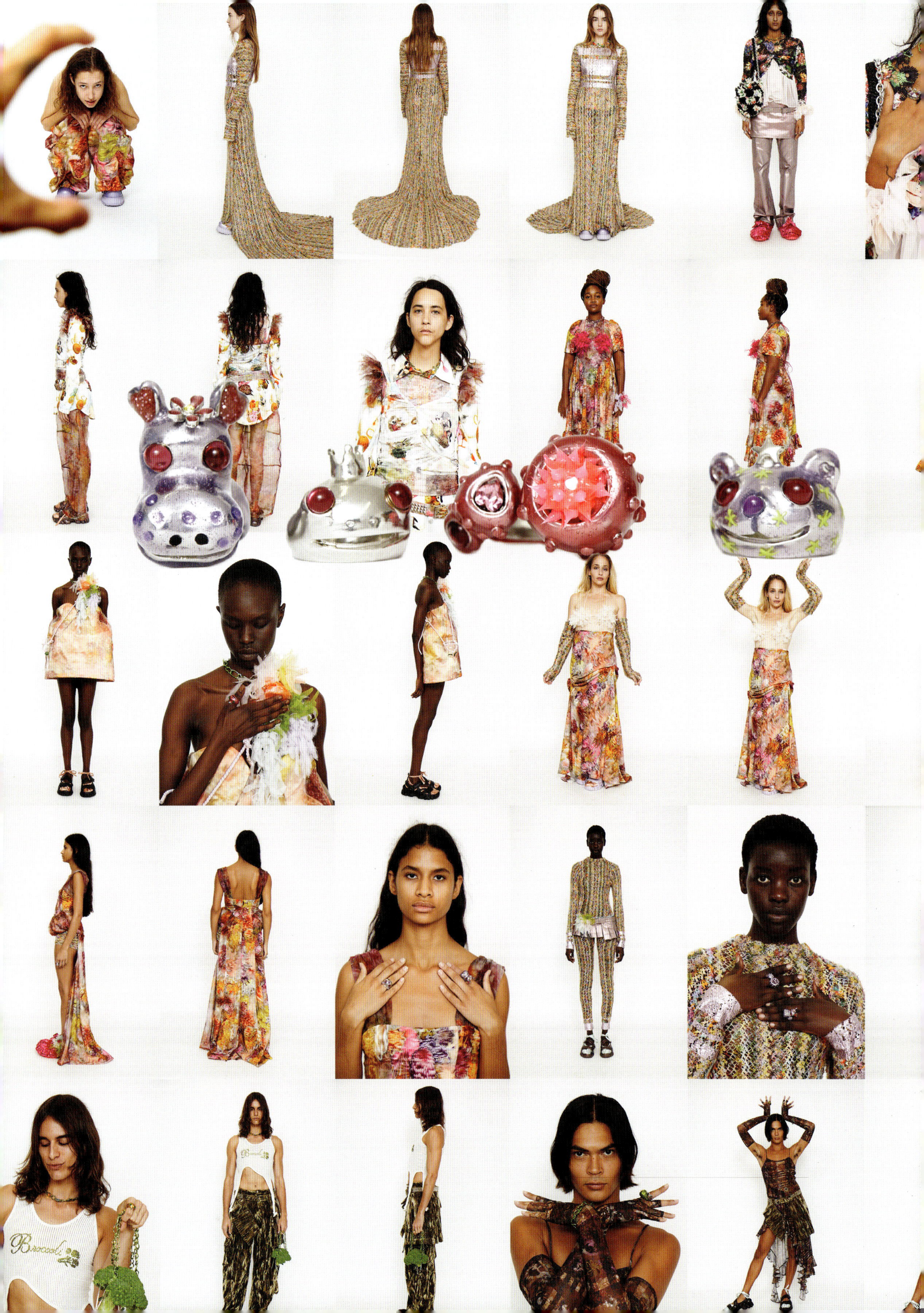
Broccoli

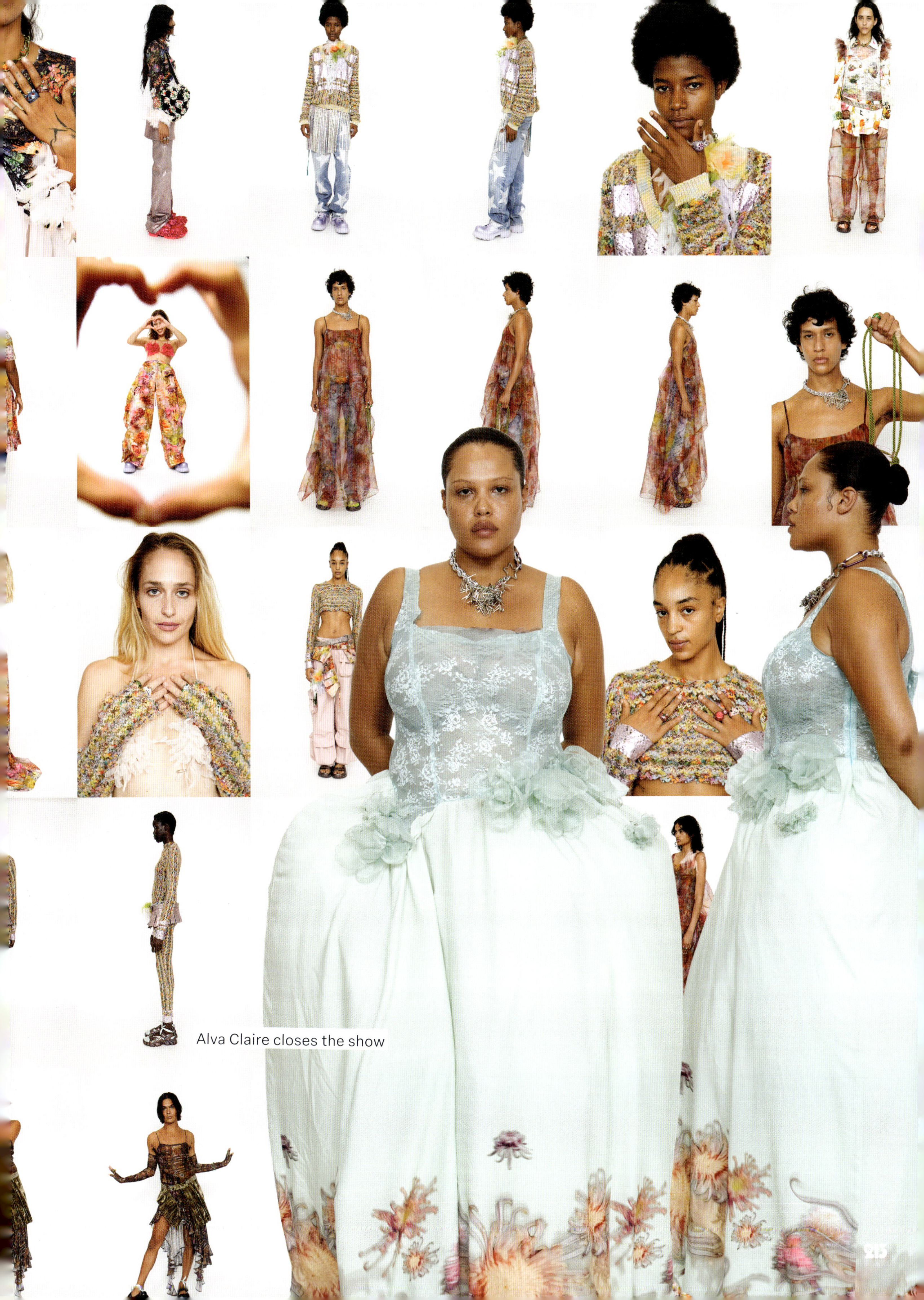

Alva Claire closes the show

A POEM BY KIMBERLY DREW

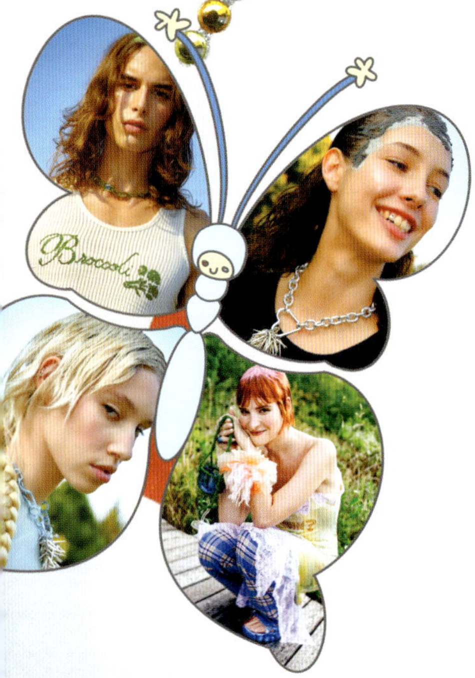

This morning I attempted to write about
what it meant to be a Collina, but kept dreaming
of a mouth full of stone and clay.

A tongue that can carry girl, bro, and sweetheart
with the same ease, now also wrapping itself around
the ingredients of brick and mortar.

Being a Collina is straddling the bridge of Lucille Clifton's
starshine and clay. It's remaining untamed in a world
hell-bent on our misery. A celebration of each divergence.

Collinas, like the spotted knapweed, the kudzu,
the purple loosestrife, and the Canada thistle are invasive.
We are in your gardens and embedded deeply into your lawns.
A seed, a tumbleweed.

A Collina is a genderless expanse.
Fat-assed, long-legged, paraplegic
and dreaming lucid.

A Collina is a warm heart. A whiff of lavender.
A ripe fruit swelling with the ripeness
of its own season.

Acidic, not parasitic.
Lactic and haptic.

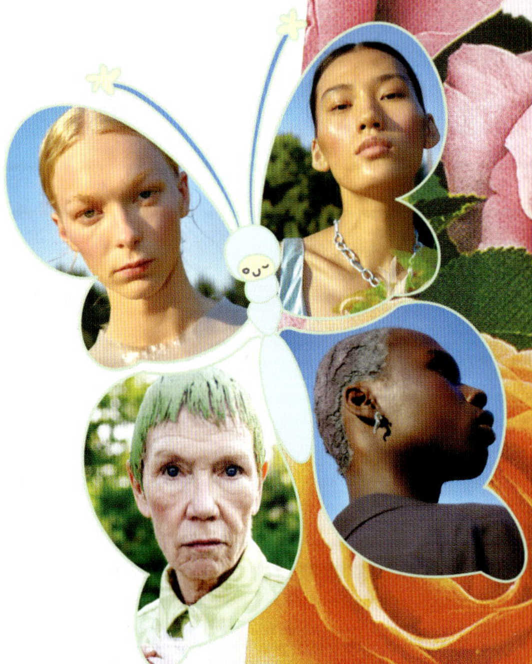

Collina is cloth and a dream. An invitation to our
tiniest selves to come play. A reminder that there is only
one planet. A reminder to love our mother.
To compost with care.

Everything we touch has a life cycle, and we can't unsee it.
Each chance encounter met with bravery.
Anything can be love at first sight or a lesson.

Collina is a romance.
It's tulle, rose sylk, deadstock fabrics, orange fibers.
Recycled denim. It's ethical sourcing. A dance in a sun shower.
A run to the farmers market.

Most of all, being one of the Collinas keeps me malleable
as wet clay. It keeps me luxuriated in the baking sun.
Ready for life's pulls and tugs, for the high heat of the kiln.

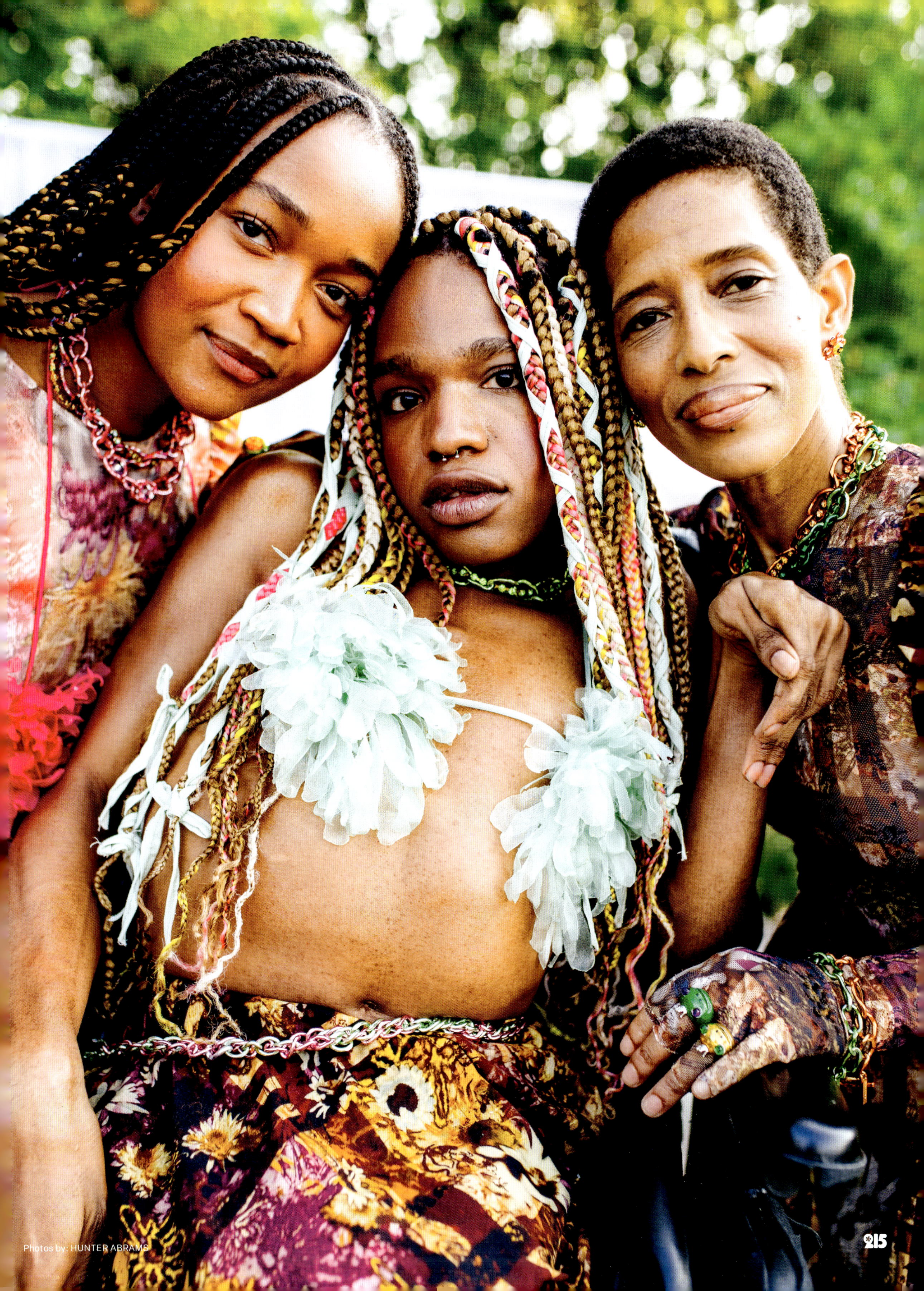

Photos by: HUNTER ABRAMS

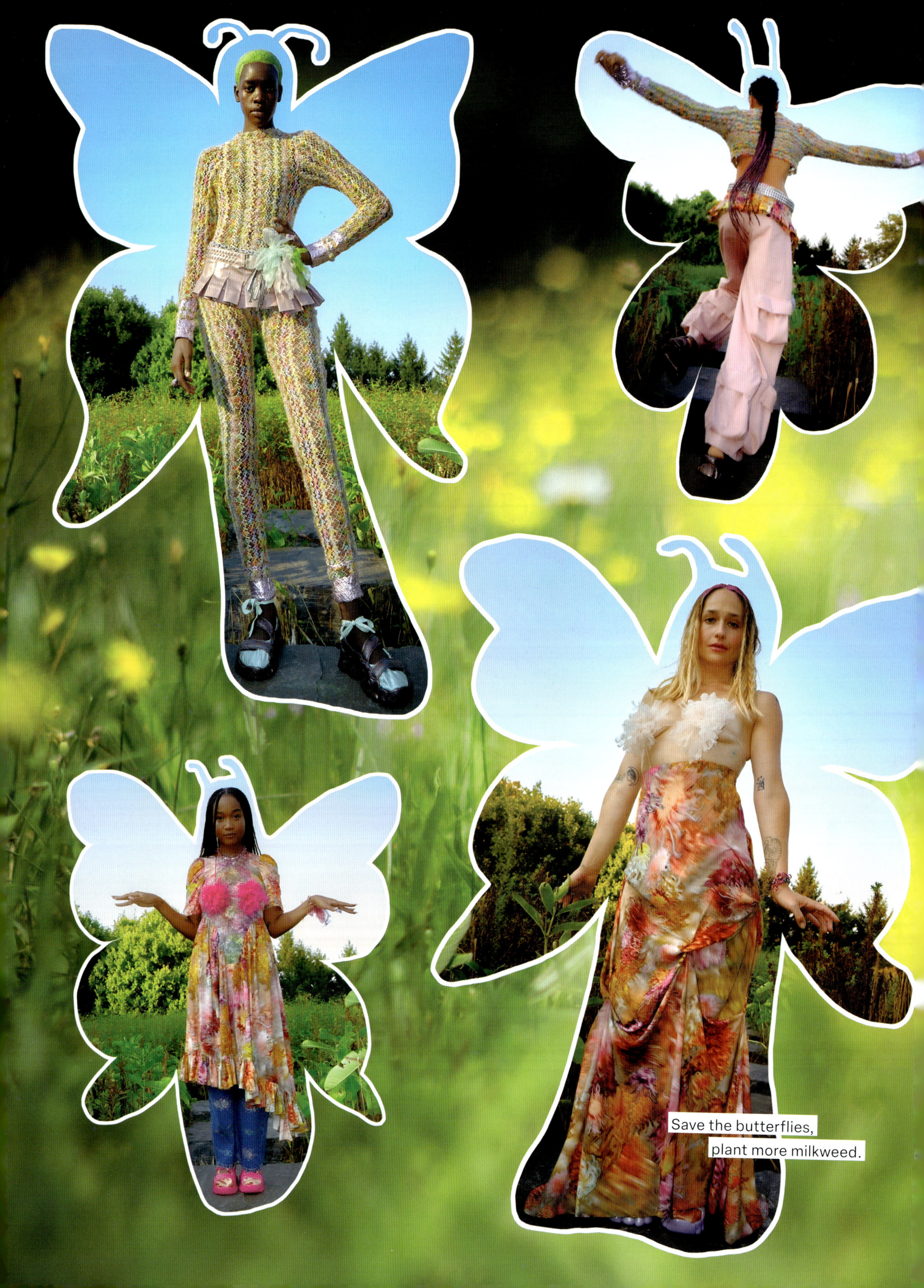
Save the butterflies,
plant more milkweed.

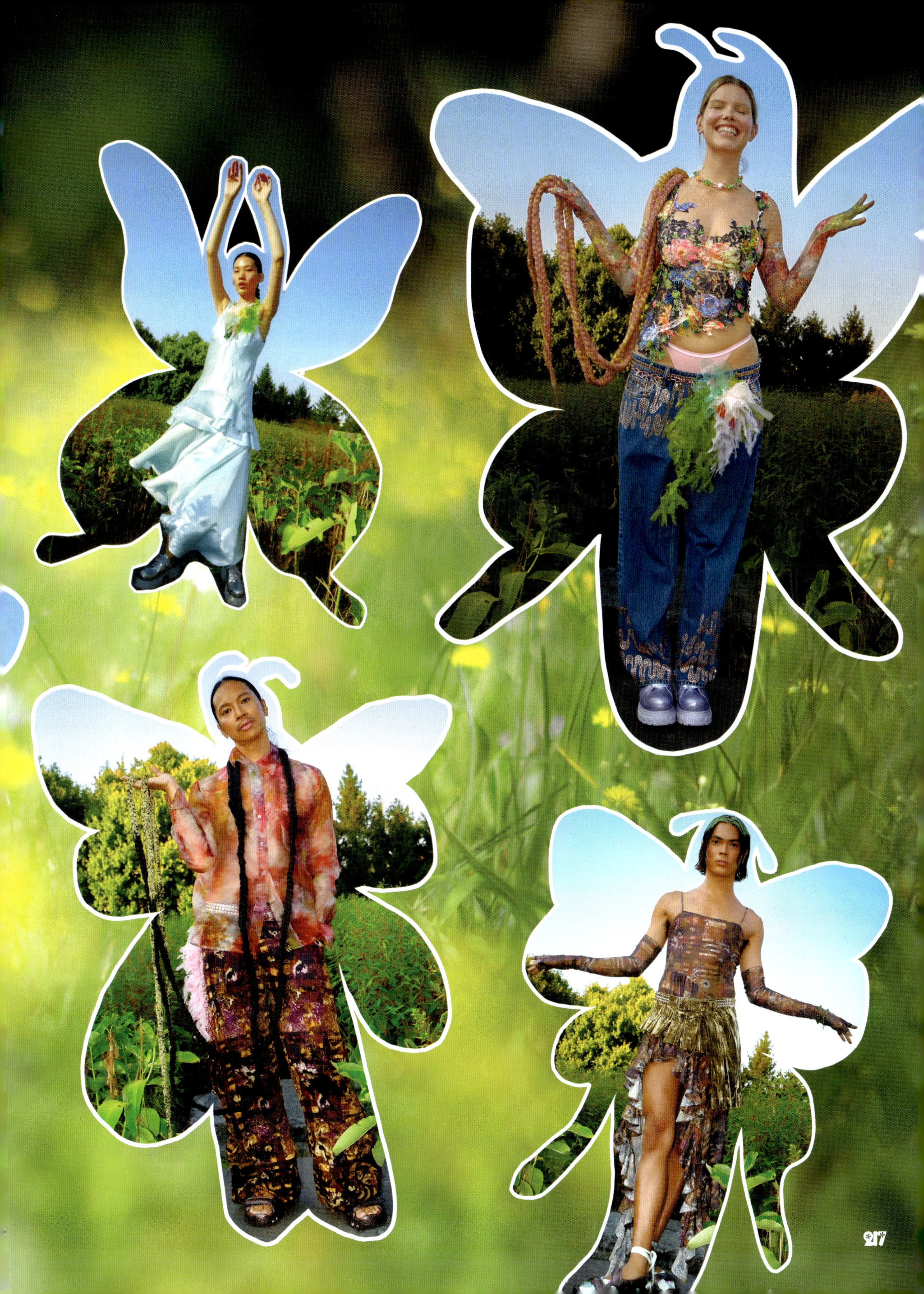

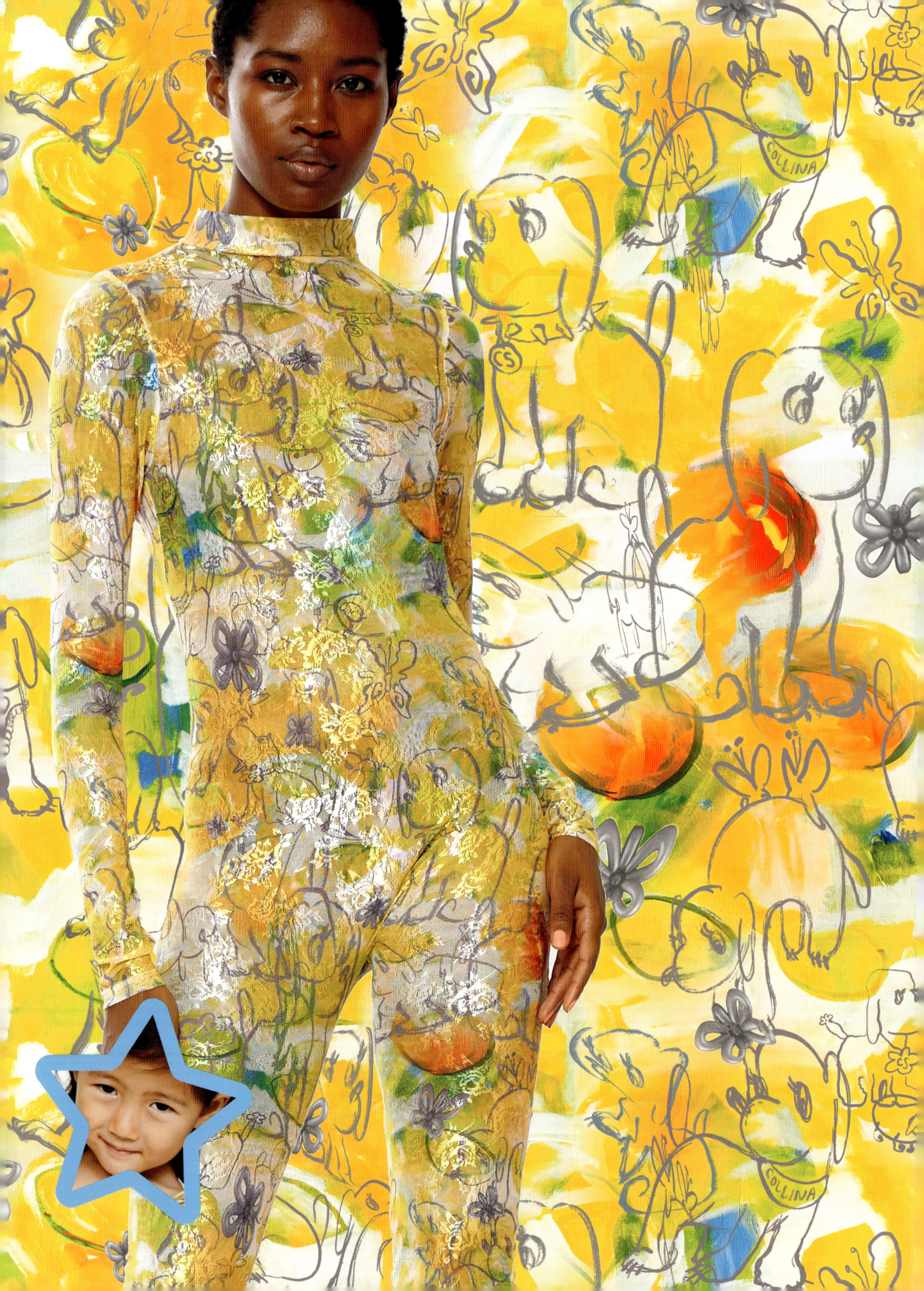
COLLINA
COLLINA

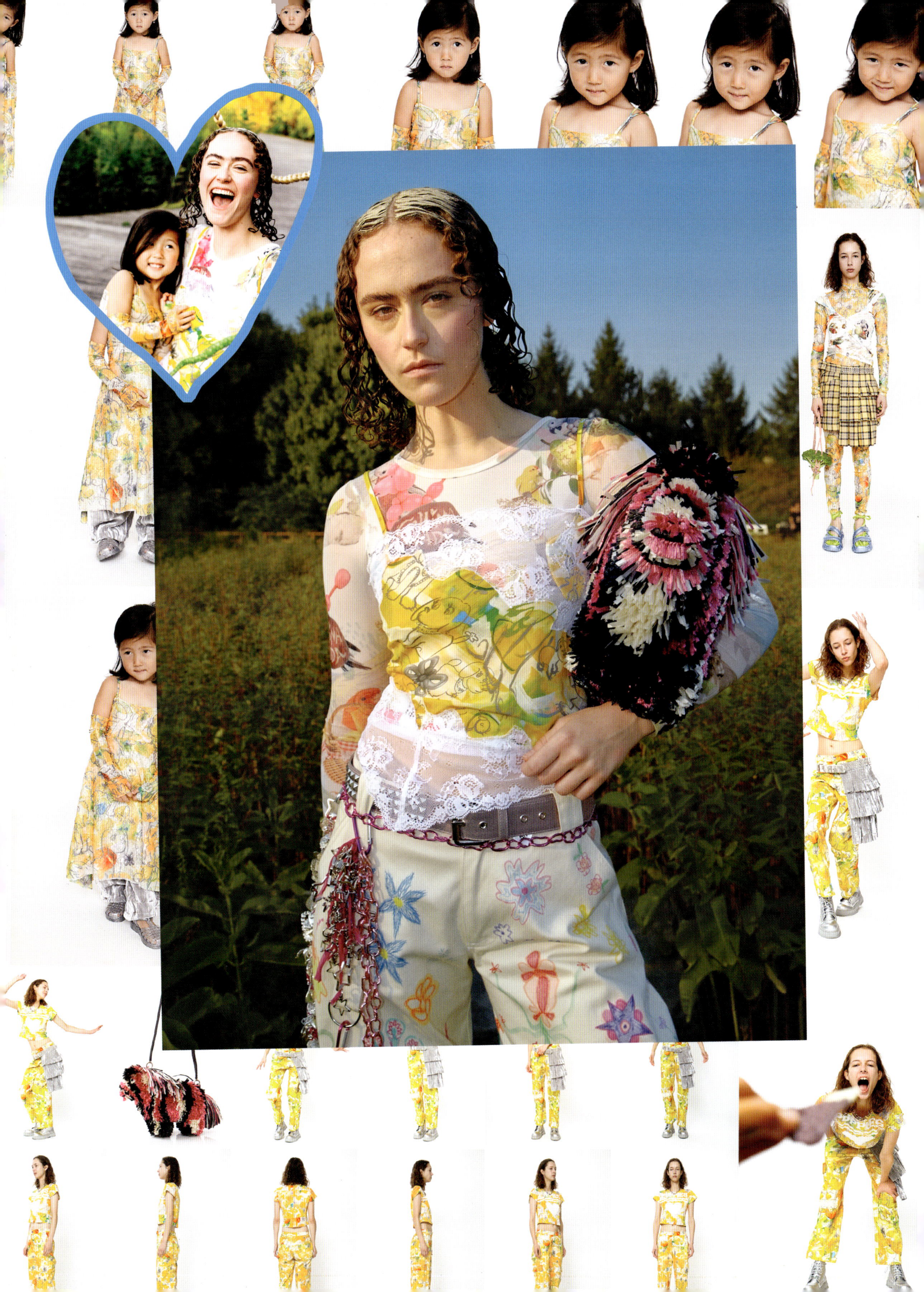

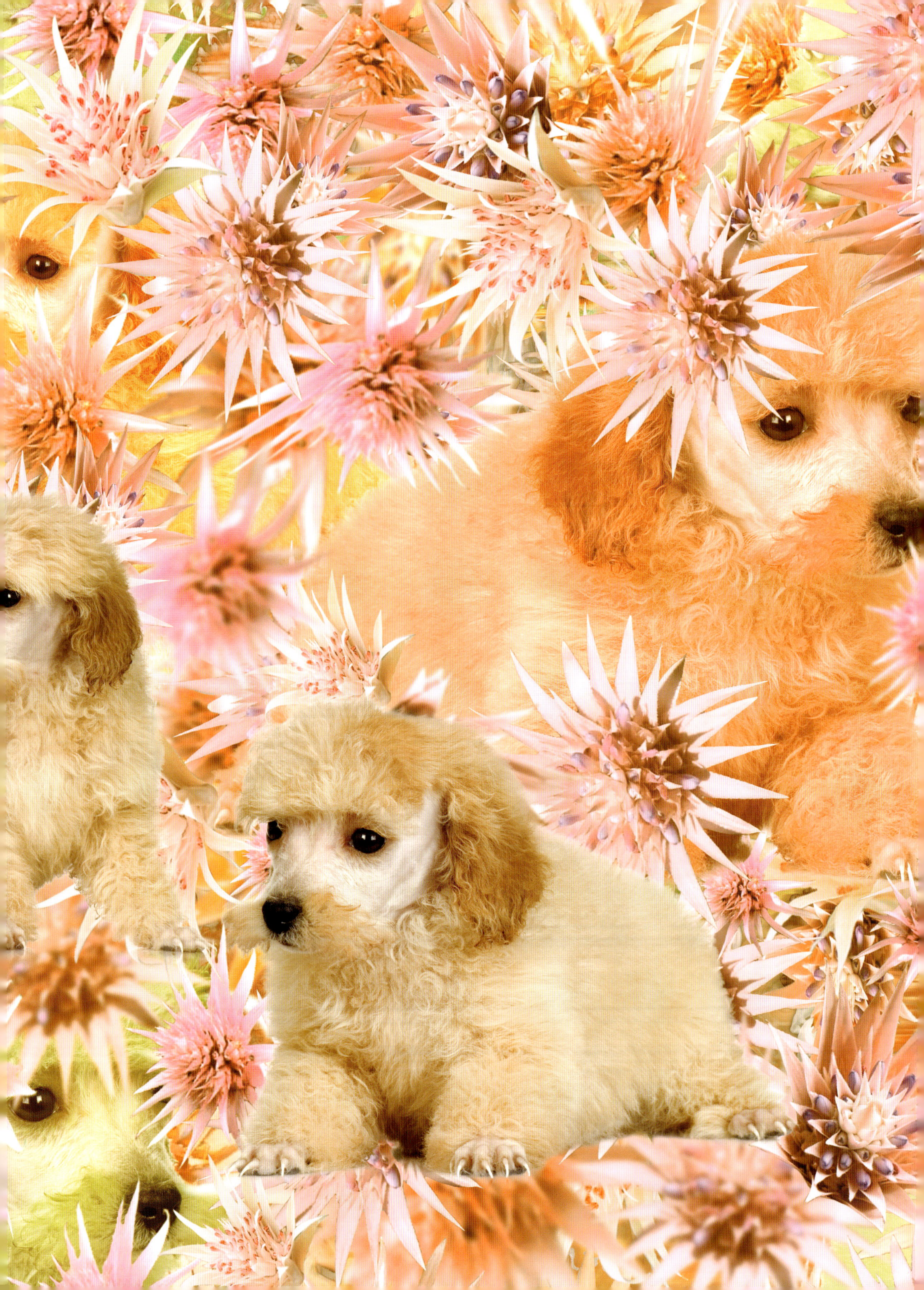

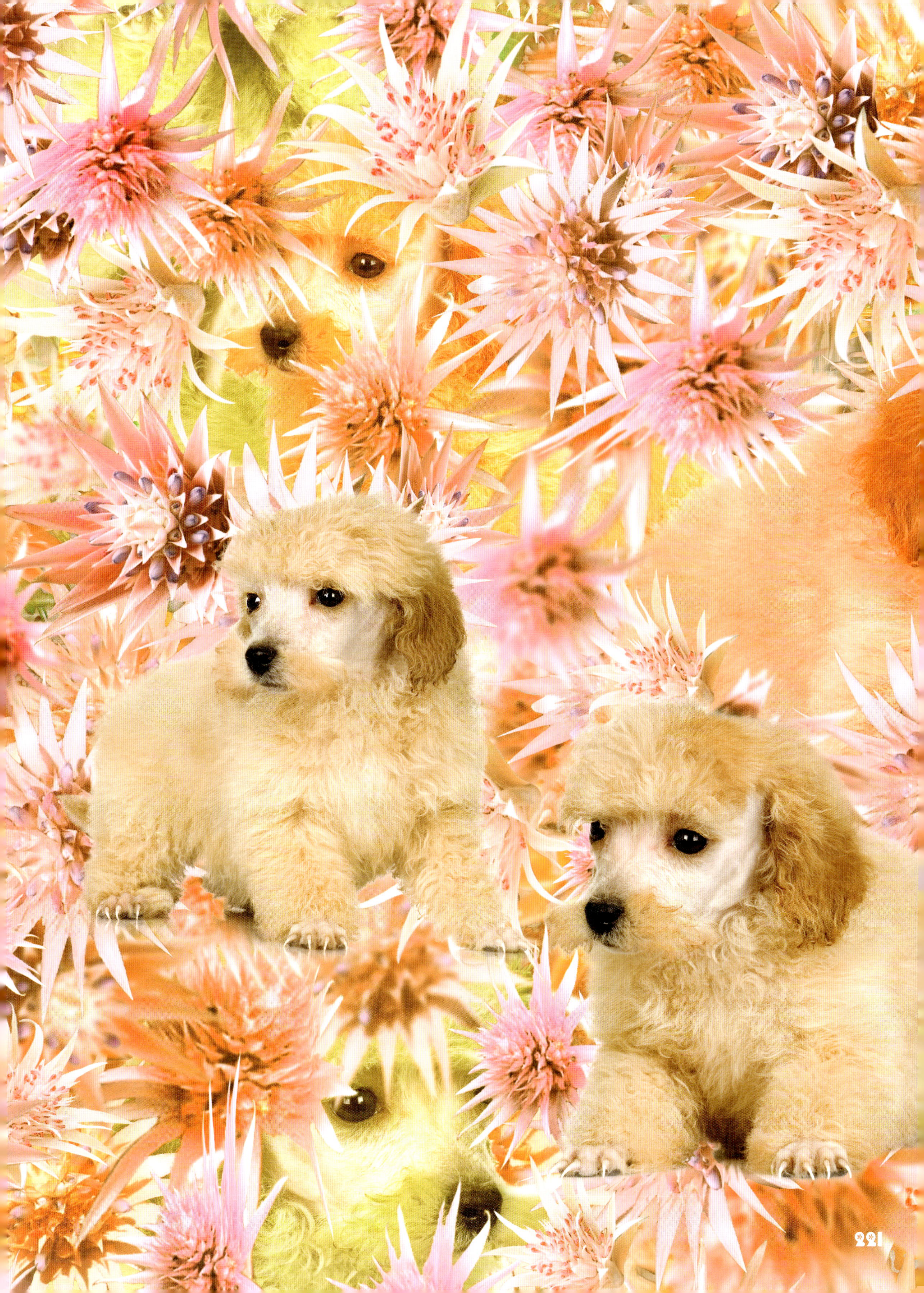

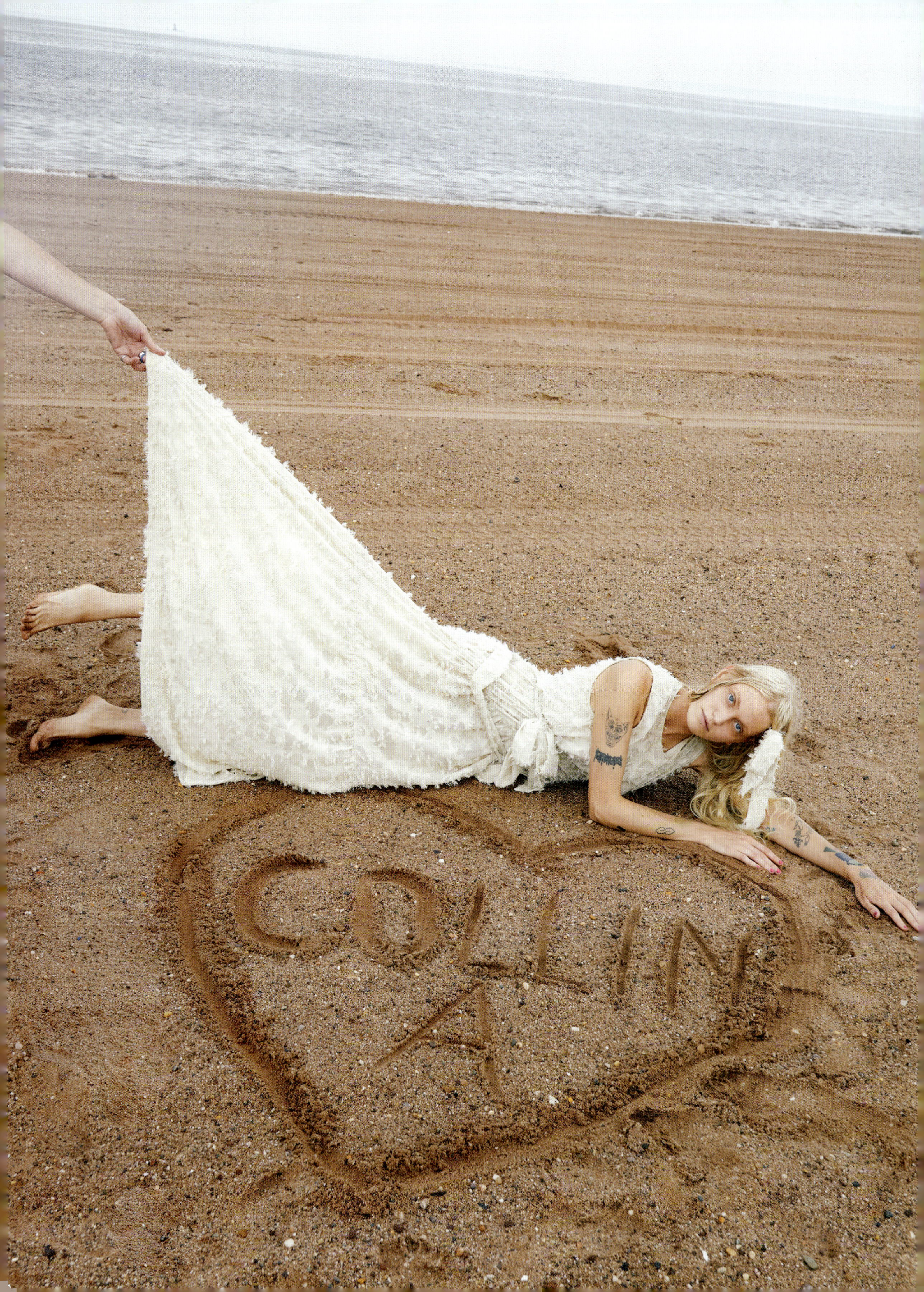
COLLIN
A

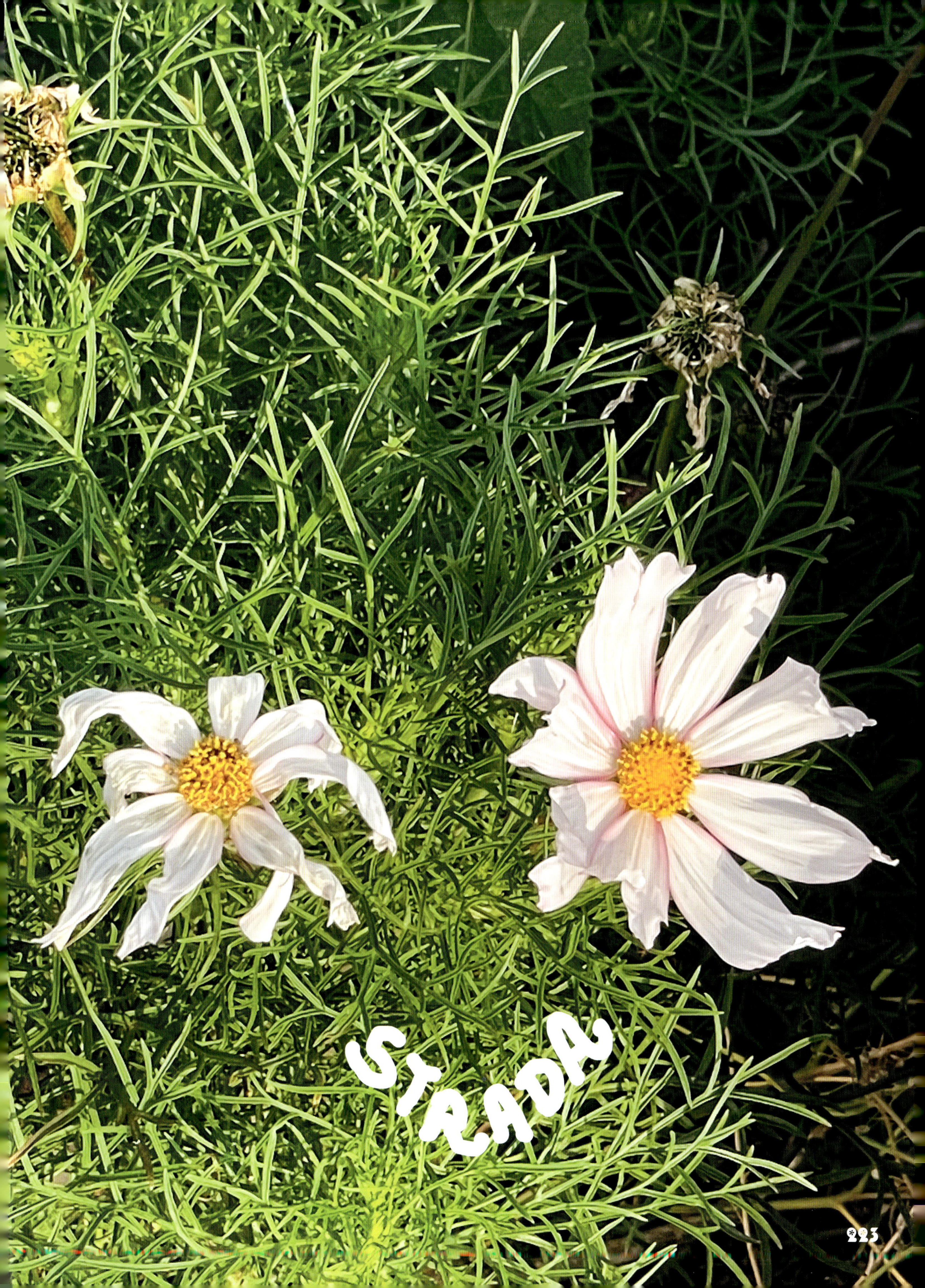
STRADA

A special thank you to:

Paige Gilligan
Regina Mun
Karolina Leiber
Eva Nelson
Mannat Kaur
David Aliperti
Ben Detrick
Lindsey Solomon
Krystle Kemp
Soraya Zaman
Hunter Abrams
Chloé Horseman
Cris Fragkou
Bobby Doherty
Freeka Tet
Jefferson Wenzel
Becky Akinyode
Sara Hiromi
Liz Ricketts & Branson Skinner
Rustee McCain Engman

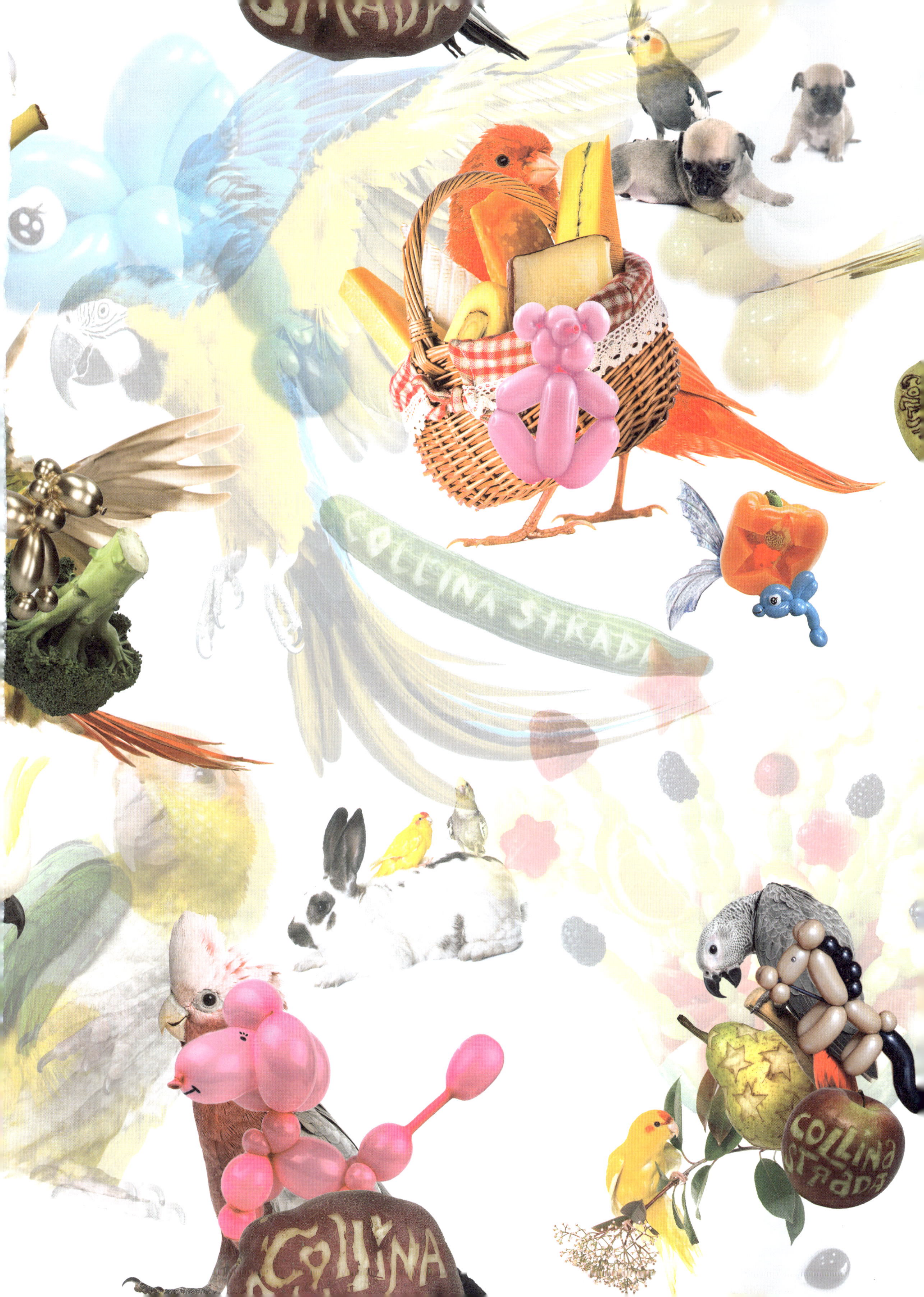
COLLINA STRADA
COLLINA STRADA
COLLINA

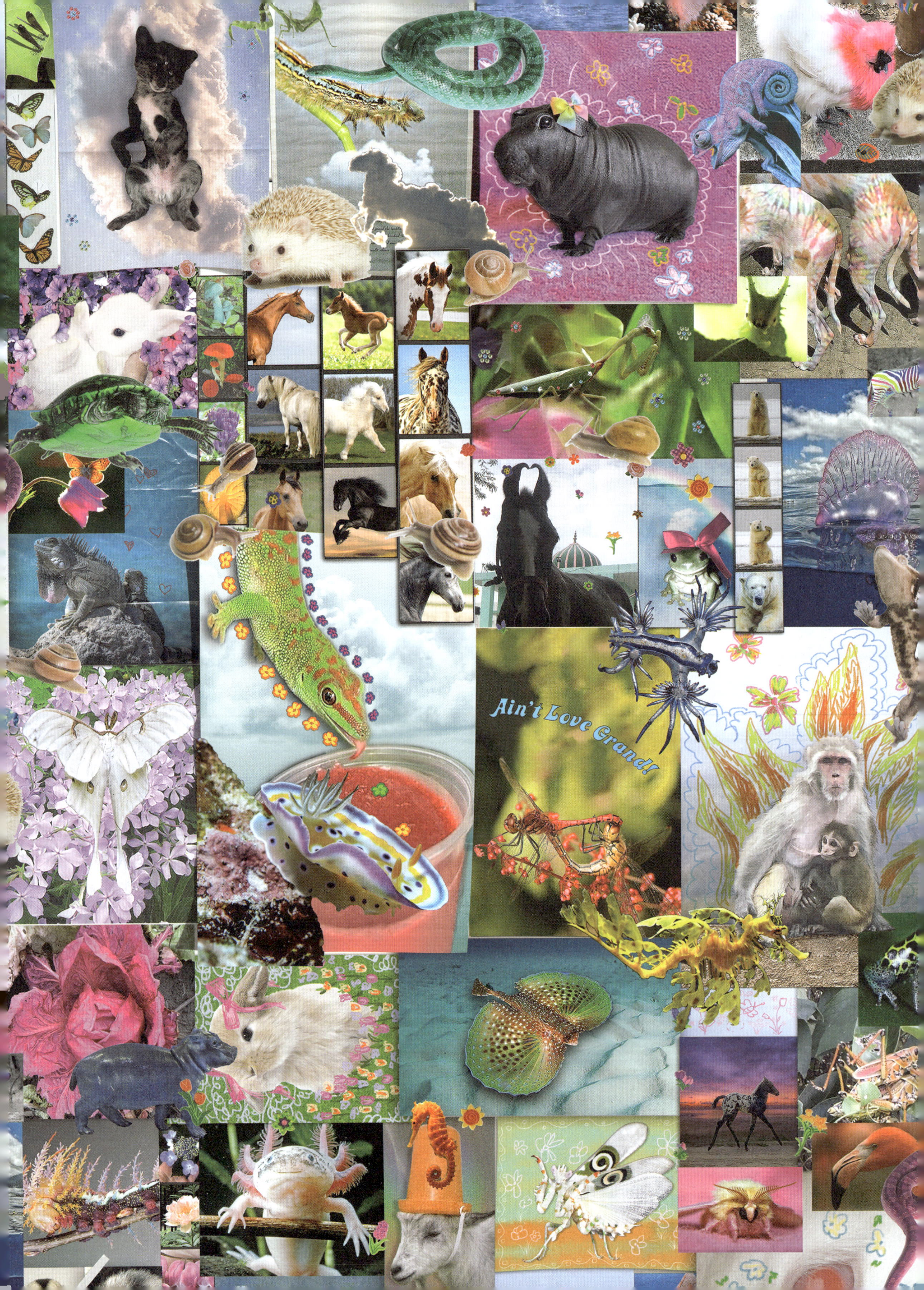
Ain't Love Grand!

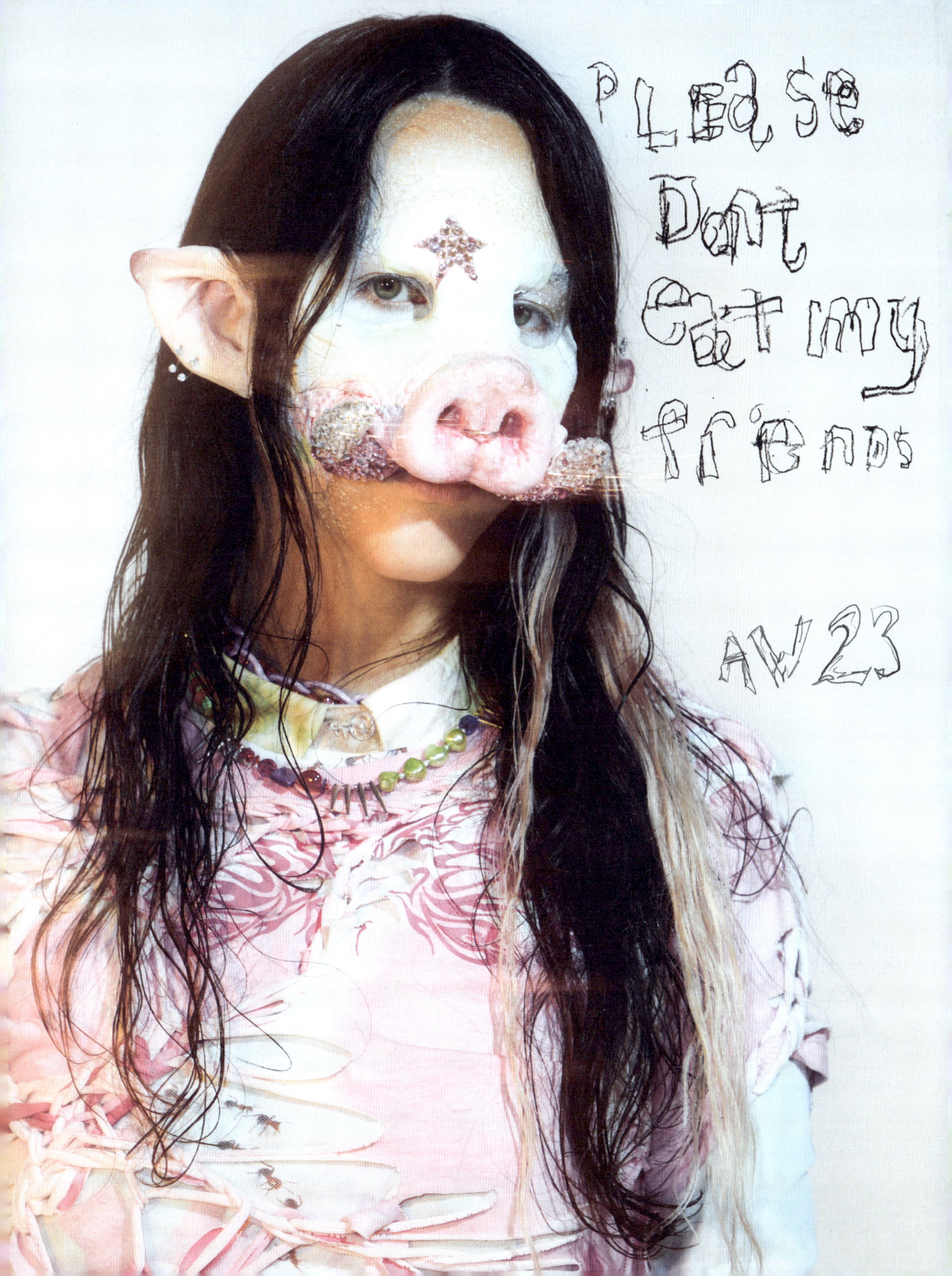
PLease
Dont
eat my
friends
AW23

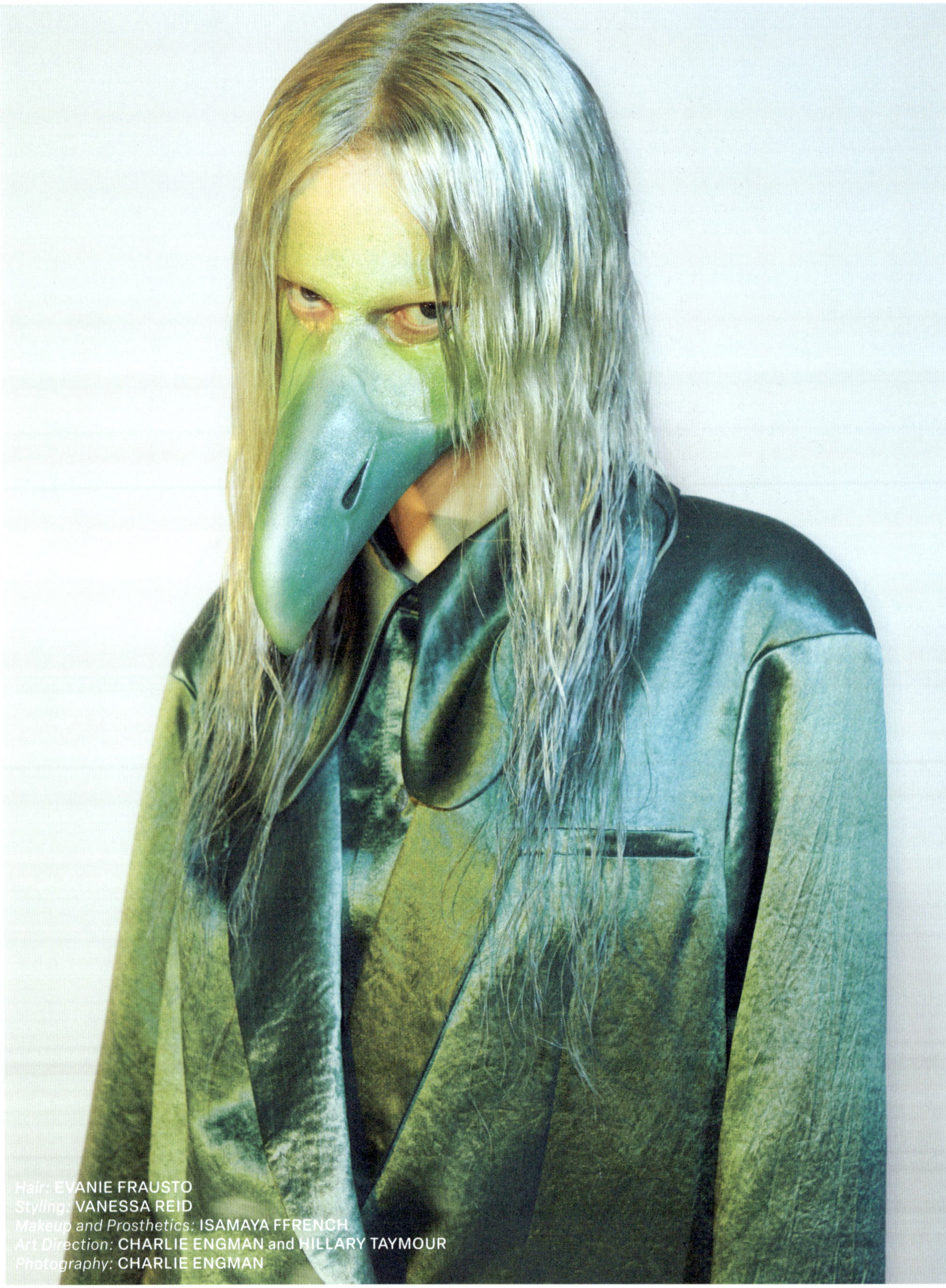
Hair: EVANIE FRAUSTO
Styling: VANESSA REID
Makeup and Prosthetics: ISAMAYA FFRENCH
Art Direction: CHARLIE ENGMAN and HILLARY TAYMOUR
Photography: CHARLIE ENGMAN

You know that fun fungus fact about how everything is connected by microscopic little filaments under our feet? How humans and worms share 70% of their DNA? How flora and fauna live together in an intricate, nonlinear, nonhierarchical, yet tenderly delicate and complicated balance of mutual benefit and connectivity? How we're all in this together, from the tiniest house mouse to the tallest supermodel?

This season was our celebration of these primal truths. This collection, like all Collina collections, strived to honor both our inner show pony, who is playful and likes to ruffle feathers, and our inner workhorse, who is reliable, durable, and strangely practical.

Our duck ducks were fully goosed in these head-to-hoof looks.

Woof.

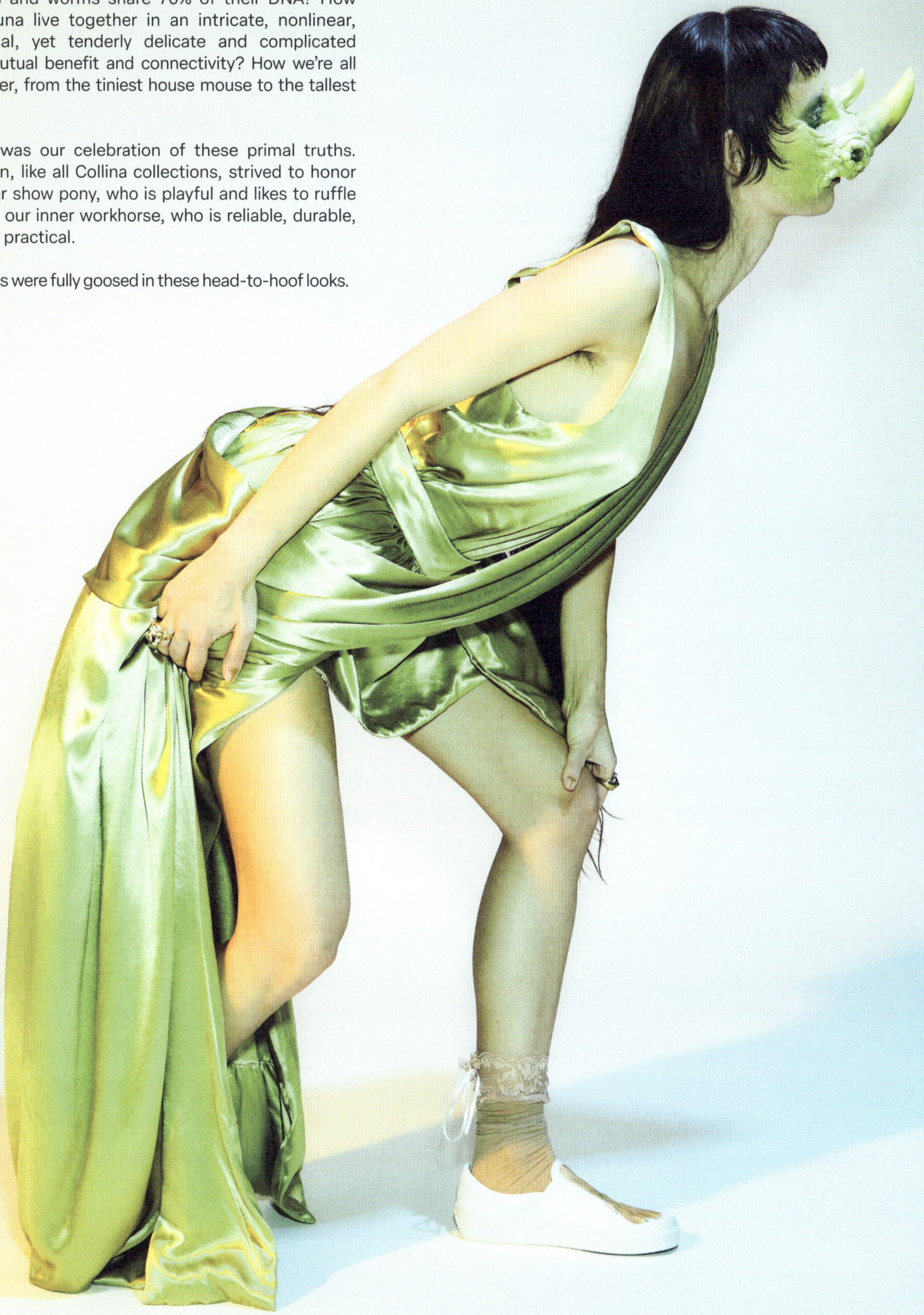

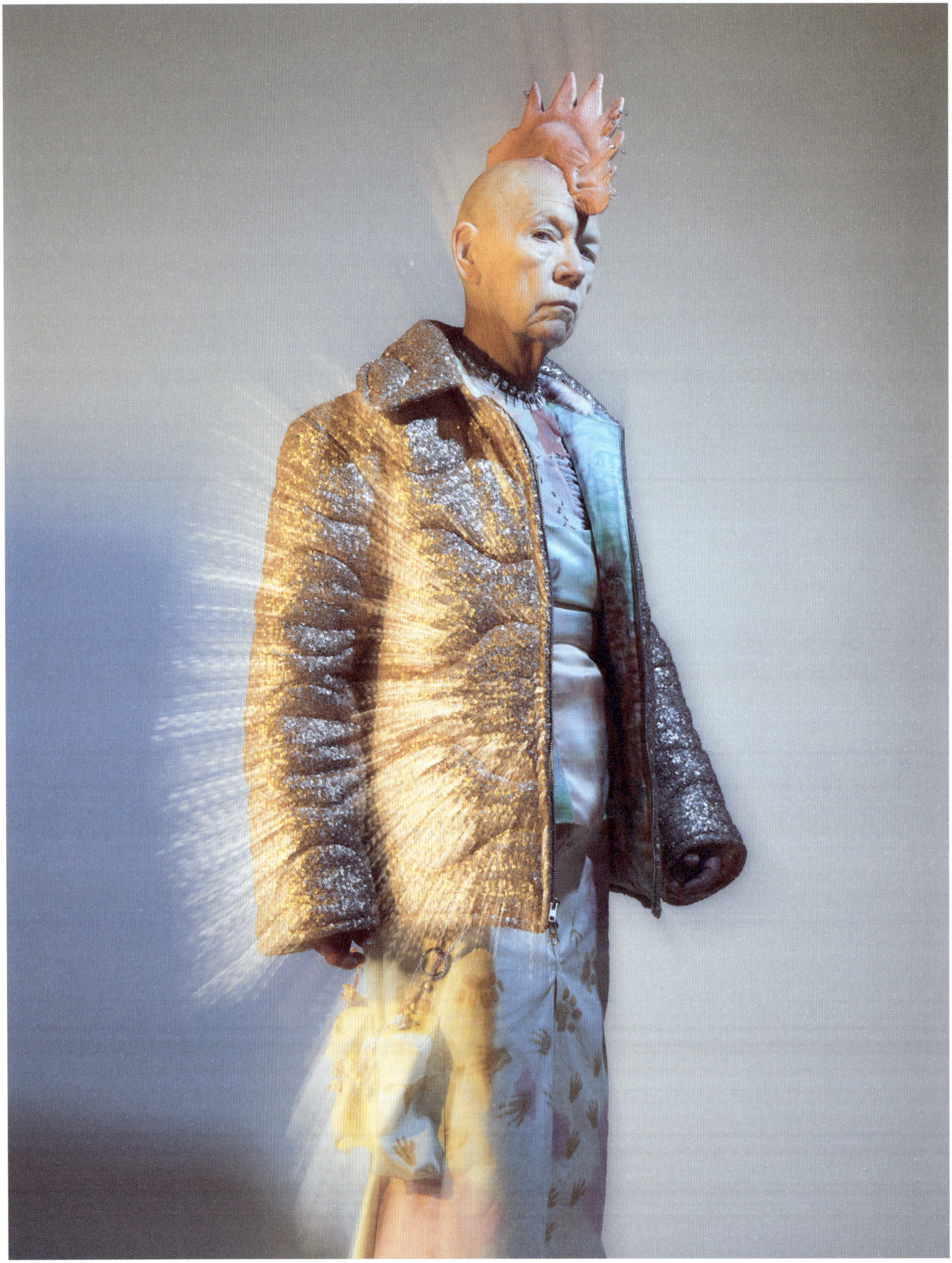

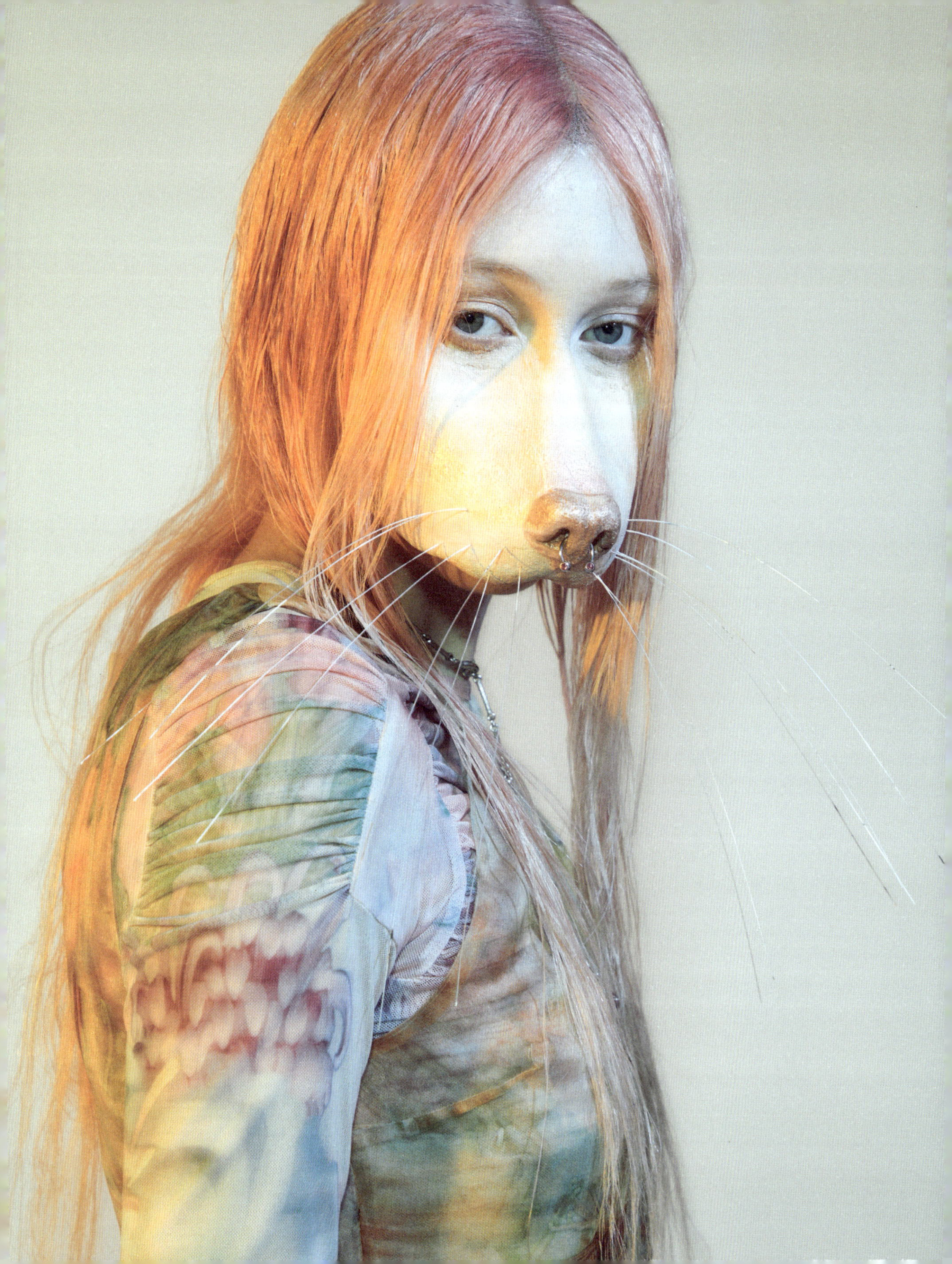

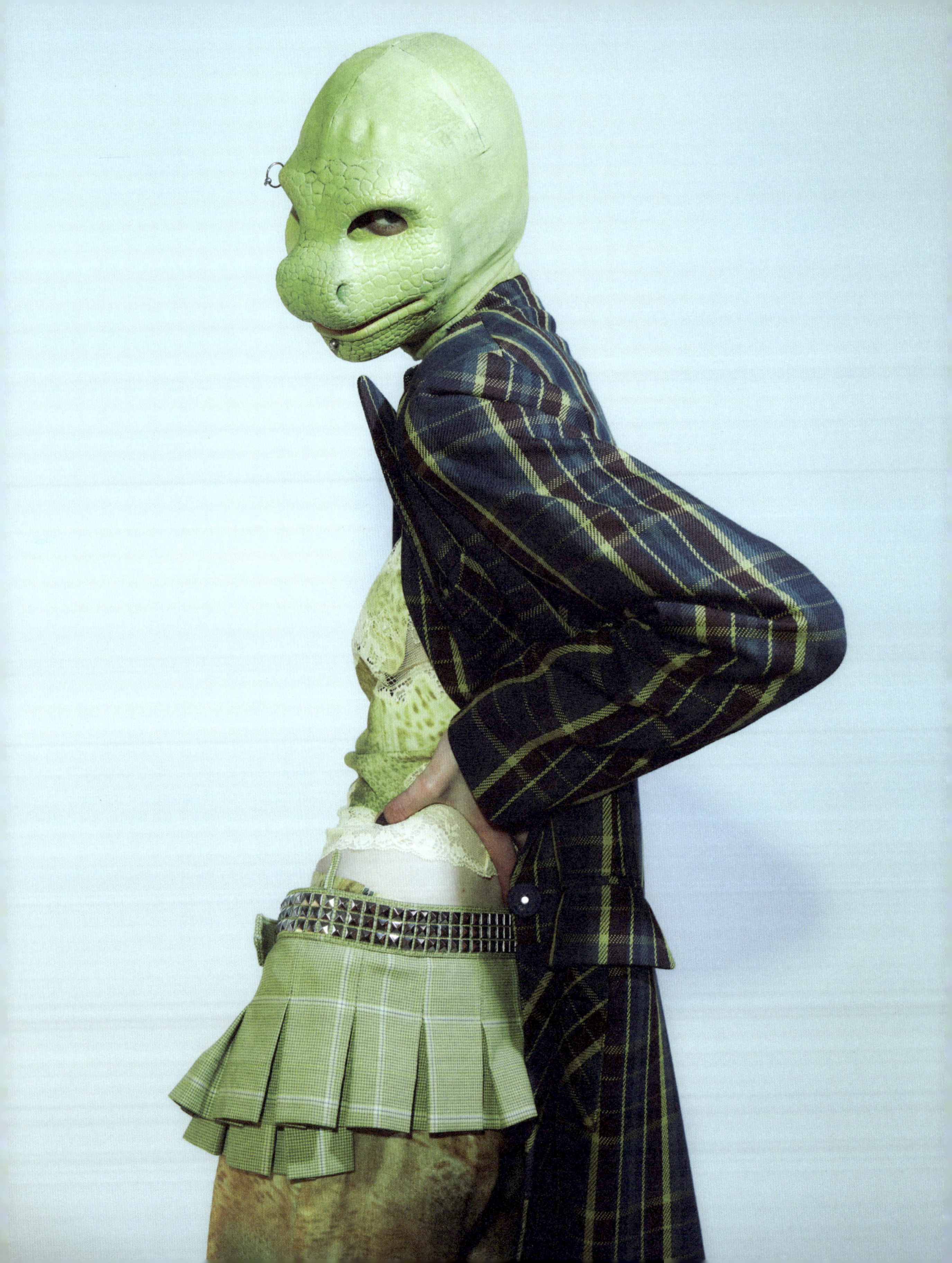

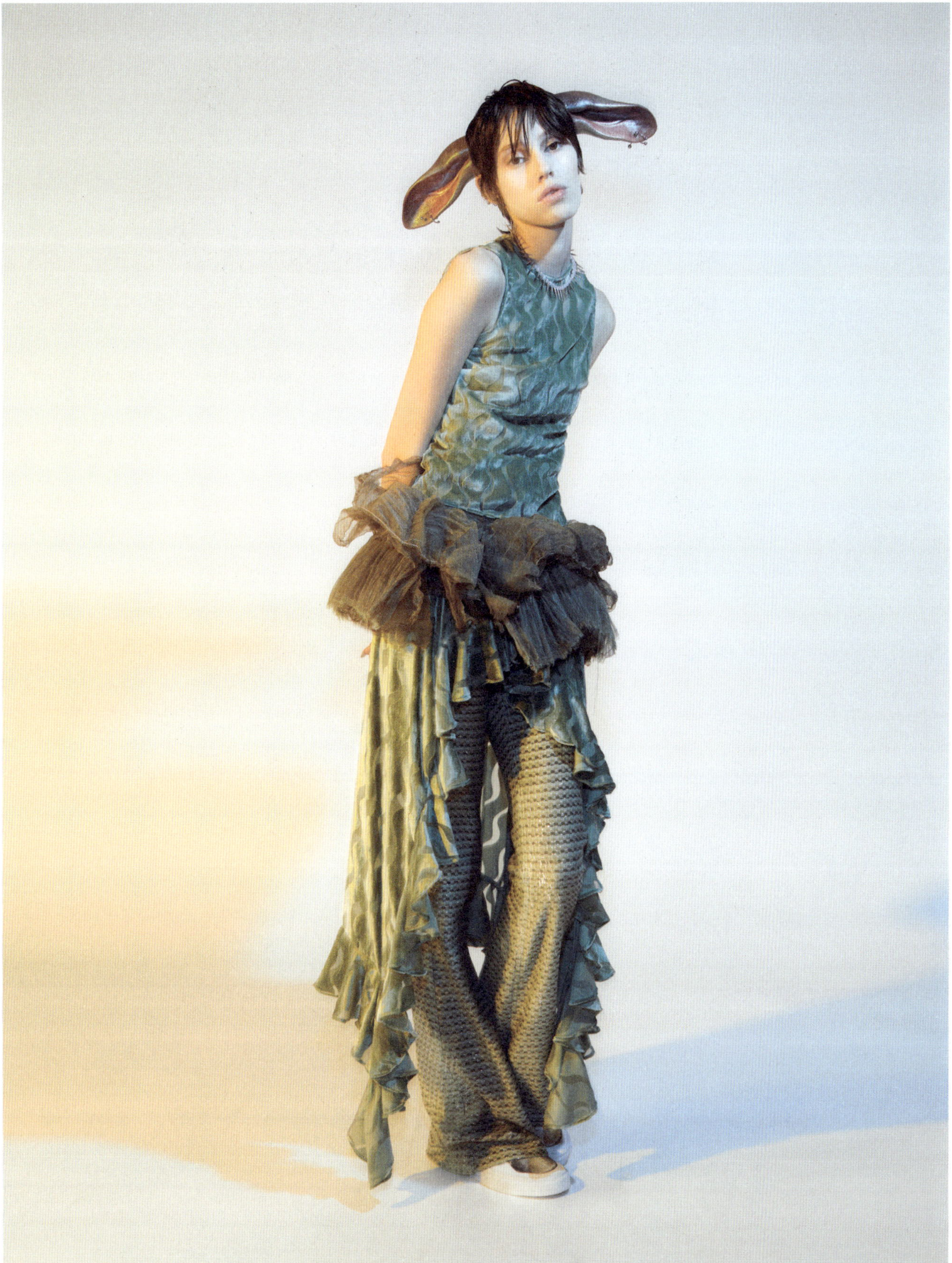

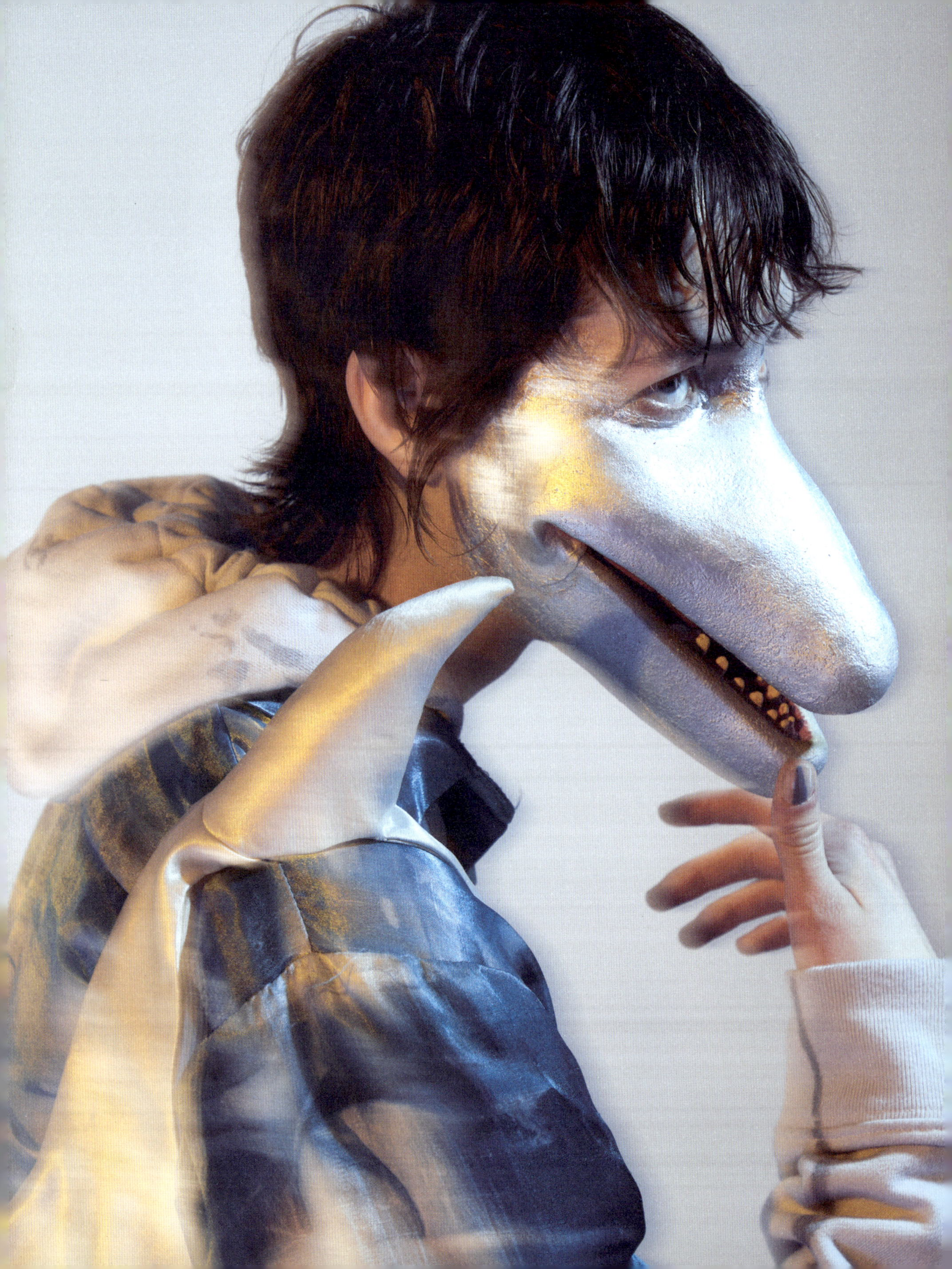